Christmas, 1980

To Cindy
    from Wendy, Bill & Jamie

Best wishes,
Marianne Moore Pitts
    for Mary Moore

THE MARY MOORE COOKBOOK

The MARY MOORE Cookbook

Lovingly dedicated to my sister, Sarah Pearl Clark

Published by
The Mary Moore Cookbook
Marianne Moore Pitts — Peter Moore
39 Spruce Street, Toronto, Ontario
M5A 2H8

Edited by
Peter Moore

Printed by
D. G. Seldon Printing Limited
Hamilton, Ontario

Cover Design by Robert Murray
Cover Photograph by Ronald B. Smith

First Printing	—	*April, 1978*
Second Printing	—	*June, 1978*
Third Printing	—	*July, 1978*
Fourth Printing	—	*August, 1978*
Fifth Printing	—	*September, 1978*
Sixth Printing	—	*October, 1978*

Foreword

The writer of a daily food column finds herself at many a table around the world where good friends and good food make for happy visiting. I include mementos from just such times, but the recipes offered here are, by far the greatest part, from my own table and the tables of my readers. From my readers, indeed, came the countless pushes and encouragements to which this book owes its birth, for without them it would not have been written.

I started writing about food as a bride. My background included training by my mother, Alfretta Kindree, daughter of a Southern Ontario farming family; courses in dietetics in Toronto; English and History at Missouri State Teachers' college; English courses at McMaster University in Hamilton. Not until my sisters Pearl and Doris and I started a canning company, Mary Miles Foods, did the business of serious experimenting with formulas become a regular way of life. During the second world war, with sugar rationed, I was asked to write a cookbook using corn syrup instead of sugar, and well I remember a chocolate cake for which the testing and retesting ran through sixteen soggy sponges before the right combination of ingredients was finally found! In those days, a single parent, with Marianne and Peter bustling in with their chums, I truly learned what a source of merriment and hospitality a kitchen can be, and over the years my kitchen, in various busy and aromatic states, has seen the invasion of many a food-fancier, and seen, as well, some of the early culinary creations of ten well-loved grandchildren.

Readers from Atlantic to Pacific send dozens of letters every day. Although answering them often means working nights and weekends, it is from the treasured recipes they have shared with me, and from my own recipes they most frequently demand, that the contents of this cookbook have been gathered. Scores of readers, never met but often corresponded with, are old friends. They, and many others for whom good eating is one of the ways to the heart, it has been my privilege to know and to help and be helped by through the medium of my column, a column which, I find it hard to believe, first made its appearance fifty years ago today.

March 17, 1978

Acknowledgements

To my elder sister, Pearl Clark, go loving thanks not only for the intervention that first led me into print, but, along with my younger sister, Doris Clark, for a lifetime of encouragement and interest in the arts of cooking and hospitality. My daughter and son, Marianne and Peter, and their families, have been constantly and devotedly involved with my work. Maureen MacDonald, eight years my secretary, has labored carefully and cheerfully over the ongoing work of the column while at the same time attending to a mountain of details in the preparation of the cookbook.

I am indebted to many others but special mention must go to:

Air Canada
B. C. Fisheries Association
Bailey, Cecile
Batcheller, Dorothy
Bradshaw, Lena
Brown, Barbara
Brunt, Margaret
Campogotti, Frank
Cappelli, Mary
Cayley, Ruthe
Chabanel, Sister
Clark, Dea
Clark, Doris
Clark, Pearl (Peady)
Clark, Winnifred
Cowley, Ethel
Duddy, Margaret
Durnin, Primrose
Fenemore, Dee
Fick, Pearl
Fill, Dr. Helen
Fisheries Council of Canada
Gilbert, Pearl
Gillespie, Iris
Gilmer, Nora
Glenhyrst Arts Council
Greenburg, Harvey
Gumbert, Mrs.
Gundersen, Sylvia

Hegler, Margaret
Hicks, Jessie
Higgins, Isabel
Himes, Dorothy
Hope, Marguerite
Illman, Mugsy
Illman, Wanda
Illman, Dr. Wm.
Janzen, Ina
Janzen, Shirley
Kincaid, Rose
Kool, Carol
Kyle, Charlotte
LeRiche, Dr. W. Harding
Lester B. Pearson,
   College of the Pacific
Levett, Jane
Lucas, Ed
Lundy, Joyce
MacDonald, Emmie
MacNichol, Rilla
McKay, Mrs.
McMillan, Cora
Miller, Eleanor
Ministry of
   Agriculture and Food
Munro, Ellen
Ontario Food Council

Parry, Barbara
Peter and Margaret Moore
   & Family
Marianne & Herbert Pitts
   & Family
Pitts, Swea
Pollock, Helen
Ralph, Joan
Reed, Garny
Roberts, Marg.
Robb, George
Ross, Betty
Rozanski, Marian
Schofield, Lou
Service, Jean
Shaw, Mabel
Shirriff, Robert
Smith, Dorothy
Solomon, Gwyn
Stanbridge, Elsie
Telfer, Pat
Thomas, Mary
Urfey, Donna
Welsh, Mrs.
Weatherly, Mrs.
Witter, Chuck
Witter, Doris
Wright, Laura

. . . the printer, Dave Seldon, without whom this cookbook would not have become a reality; Don and Jean McCrimmon for their proof reading; the cover designer Robert Murray and the cover photographer, Ronald B. Smith.

Table of Contents

METRIC COOKING CONVERSION GUIDE

Imperial versus Metric

COOKS SHOULD BUY
>
> two pieces of metric measuring equipment:
>
> - one pyrex measuring cup with metric measuring marks on one side AND Imperial measuring marks on the other side.
>
> - A 5-spoon set of metric measures: 1 ml, 2 ml, 5 ml, 15 ml, and 25 ml (millilitres)

LIQUID MEASURES:
>
> 1 ounce equals 28 millilitres (ml)
>
> 1 cup (8 ounces) equals 225 ml.
>
> 2½ cups (1 pint) equals 550 ml.
>
> 2 pints (1 quart) equals 1.12 litres
>
> 4 quarts (1 gallon) equals 4.5 litres (L.)

DRY MEASURES:
>
> 1 teaspoon equals 5 millilitres (ml.)
>
> 1 tablespoon equals 15 ml.
>
> ¼ cup equals 60 ml.
>
> 1 cup (16 tablespoons) equals 250 ml.
>
> 2 cups equals 500 ml.

COMPARISONS (approximate):
>
> 5 ml. equals 1 teaspoon
>
> 15 ml. equals 1 tablespoon
>
> 30 ml. equals 1 ounce
>
> 60 ml. equals ¼ cup
>
> 250 ml. almost equals 1 generous cup
>
> 500 grams equals 1 generous pound
>
> 1 ounce equals a generous 28 grams
>
> 3½ ounces equals 100 grams
>
> 1 pound equals 0.45 kilograms
>
> 2.2 pounds equals 1 kilogram (kg)
>
> 35.196 Imperial ounces equals 1 litre
>
> 33.814 American ounces equals 1 litre

Appetizers

Mushroom Butter Spread

1 lb fresh firm mushrooms
¼ C butter
1 Tbsp minced onion (raw or bottled)
1 Tbsp chopped parsley (fresh or bottled)
1 beef bouillon cube
1 C boiling water
¼ tsp curry powder
1 Tbsp gravy browner
4 Tbsp flour
5 Tbsp cold water

Scrub mushrooms, drain and put through medium knife of grinder. Melt butter in large frying pan, add mushrooms and onion and parsley and gently sauté until soaked with butter but not brown at all. Remove from heat. Dissolve beef bouillon cube in boiling water. Mix together to a smooth paste the curry powder, gravy browner, flour and cold water. Add bouillon cube liquid to mushrooms in pan and return to heat and stir in the flour paste until thick. Remove from heat. Cool. If desired, this may be stored in covered jar in refrigerator for as long as a week.

Notes: 1. To make into toasted rolled sandwiches, spread Mushroom Butter not too generously on crustless slices of bread and roll them up like little logs and place on broiler pan and toast under hot broiler until golden. Serve straight from the oven. 2. Spread thinly on broiled steaks or beef liver one minute before they are done.

Sausage Balls With Peach Dip

MEATBALL MIXTURE
1 lb sausage meat
1½ Tbsp onion, chopped
2 C soft bread crumbs (not packed)
1 egg
½ tsp salt
½ to 1 tsp poultry seasoning
⅛ tsp pepper

PEACH SAUCE
One 28-oz can peaches, chopped finely
    (reserve 1¼ C syrup, see below)
2 Tbsp brown sugar
1 tsp butter
1 tsp lemon juice
1 Tbsp cornstarch

To make meatballs, in large bowl combine well all meatball ingredients. Shape into ¾" balls. In large frying pan heat 2 Tbsp cooking oil. Brown meatballs on all sides, reduce heat, cover and cook 15 minutes.

To make Peach Sauce, in pot combine peaches, 1 C peach syrup, brown sugar, butter and lemon juice. Make a paste of the cornstarch and remaining ¼ C syrup (or water if not enough syrup) and stir in until thickened and clear, then cook 10 minutes longer. Force through sieve. Discard residue in sieve. Re-heat sauce to boiling.

Serve meatballs in chafing dish with hot peach sauce poured over or put a toothpick in each meatball, arrange on platter with dish of hot sauce in centre.

Salmon or Tuna Puff Tartlettes
(twenty 2-inch diameter)

PASTRY
1 C sifted all-purpose flour
⅓ C shortening
1 Tbsp butter
½ tsp salt
2 Tbsp cold water

FILLING
⅓ C canned red salmon (or tuna) drained
    and mashed
1 tsp chopped green onion or chives (or bottled)
3 Tbsp dairy sour cream
1 Tbsp drained green relish (or finely chopped
    sweet pickle)
½ tsp salt
1 stiffly beaten egg white
Grated Romano or Parmesan or Cheddar cheese

Make Pastry by cutting shortening and butter into flour and salt with pastry blender until size of peas. Drizzle in water, tossing with a fork until flour is dampened. Between palms press into a ball and roll out on lightly floured board very thinly, ⅛" thick. Cut out with 2¼" cutter and line twenty-two 2" tart tins. Bake these tart shells at 425° for about 8 minutes, or until barely baked.

To make Filling, mash the drained salmon or tuna and add all remaining ingredients except egg white and grated cheese. Near serving time beat egg white until stiff and fold into filling. Fill each baked 2" tart shell with a rounded teaspoonful of filling. Do not overfill. Top each with a level ¼ tsp of grated cheese. Pat it down gently with tip of fork. Bake at 375° about 12 to 15 minutes or until tartlettes are puffy and tinged with gold. With great care remove from pans onto napkin-lined serving tray and serve hot.

Cold Cheese Balls

½ lb mild Cheddar cheese grated
    (room temperature)
½ lb process cheese, shredded
One 3-oz pkg white cream cheese
1 Tbsp Worcestershire sauce
¼ tsp Tabasco sauce
1 small clove garlic crushed to a pulp
1½ tsp chili powder
1½ tsp paprika

Cream the 3 cheeses together until perfectly smooth. Add the Worcestershire and Tabasco sauces and crushed garlic, mix well and chill thoroughly. Sprinkle a long sheet of heavy wax paper with the chili powder and paprika mixed. Turn chilled cheese mixture out on them and form into a 1" roll under your palms. Cut into ¾" pieces and roll these into balls, coating them all over with the spices as you shape them. Arrange, not touching, on flat serving plate and chill before serving. Serve with fancy crackers.

Hot Cheese Balls

2 C fine Holland rusk or Zwieback crumbs
4 eggs, yolks and whites separated
½ tsp Worcestershire sauce
½ tsp salt
½ lb sharp process Canadian Cheddar cheese,
　shredded

Beat the egg yolks and add 1½ C of the crumbs to them. Mix in the seasonings and cheese. Beat the egg whites until stiff and fold them in until smoothly incorporated. Using a tablespoon as a measure shape mixture into balls and drop onto remaining crumbs on wax paper, carefully rolling them over to coat all sides. Have ready deep hot fat at 350° and fry balls in it until delicately browned on all sides. Drain on paper towels and serve hot. Makes 36.

Trayful of Dippables

Use tiny snow-white cauliflowerets, Spanish onion rings, green pepper rings, tomato wedges or cherry tomatoes, radish roses, tiny broccoli tops, carrot curls, celery sticks. Make a Creamy Dip: 1 pkg dry onion soup mix, 2 C dairy sour cream, 2 Tbsp capers (optional), 2 tsp chopped chives or green onion or green onion flakes, few drops Tabasco. Gently combine all ingredients. Chill. Makes about 2 cups.

Tuna Holiday Dip

One 6½-oz can chunk light tuna, drained
1 C fresh dairy sour cream
2½ tsp (½ pkg) dry salad dressing mix
　(Canadian or old-fashioned French)
½ tsp horseradish
1½ tsp lemon juice
2 tsp chives
1/16 tsp salt
4 drops Angostura Bitters or Tabasco sauce

In medium-sized bowl break up drained tuna, but do not beat in beater. Add and stir in with a fork the remaining ingredients until blended and consistency is soft enough to pick up on potato chips or melba toast or ritz crackers but not so soft that it will drip. Pile into attractive serving dish and chill. Serve surrounded with raw cauliflowerets, squares of green pepper, carrot curls, tiny scrubbed raw button mushrooms, crackers and chips. Supply decent-sized serviettes, not little scrappy ones that are good only as a gesture.

Broiled Bacon-Wrapped Chicken Livers

To serve four, cut 6 chicken livers into halves. Cut 6 strips side bacon in halves. Wrap livers in bacon and fasten with toothpicks. Marinate in small deep vessel in soy sauce all day, turning over once. At the cocktail hour broil under preheated broiler on glass pie plate, supporting livers on sides with toothpicks up. Turn over when top is frizzled and finish other side. Serve at once.

Hot Cheese Canapés

½ C butter, less 1 Tbsp
1 C sifted all-purpose flour
2 C scalded milk
2 egg yolks
½ C grated Parmesan cheese
1 C shredded old Cheddar cheese
　(packed down a little)
1½ Tbsp dry white or red wine (optional)
1 whole egg
2 Tbsp cold water
About 1½ to 2 C fine dry breadcrumbs

In a large heavy saucepan barely melt the butter and stir in the flour. Slowly add, while stirring, the scalded milk until smoothly blended and stir for at least 2 minutes over medium heat. Beat egg yolks and stir a little of the hot mixture into them and return to saucepan, stirring to mix. Add cheeses and stir until they are melted and blended. Remove from heat and add wine, if used. Turn into buttered 9 × 9 pan, smooth top and chill overnight.

Cut into 1″ squares. Dredge these with flour. Beat egg and add water. Dip floured squares in egg, drain a moment, then dip in crumbs and transfer to large platter to dry. At serving time heat ¾″ of oil to bubbling hot in shallow medium fry pan. Carefully slip in about 4 of the crumbed canapés and fry until golden on bottom then turn over with slotted spoon and brown other side. Transfer to paper-lined kitchen platter and keep hot while you fry all remaining canapés. Serve at once. Makes 50 or 60.

Cheese Christmas Wreath

One Dutch Edam cheese ball
Twenty-four ¾″ cubes cheddar or
　other firm cheese
Red and green glacé or maraschino
　cherries
Crystallized ginger
Whole pecans
Stuffed olives
Mandarin orange sections

On a round plate center the Edam cheese. Leave the red wax coating on but cut a 4″ slice from the top. Plunge a cheese knife or scoop in top for guests to help themselves. For the traditional Christmas red and green, surround with a dense border of crisp parsley.

Select about 24 long colorful picks and impale ¾″ cubes of cheese on each. Make 6 variations: Above the cheese cubes press on a green cherry. Make four of these. Continue with another four using a red cherry. The next four top with a cube of crystallized ginger. The next four are topped with a jumbo pecan but be careful for pecans are brittle and will break easily. The next four are topped with a stuffed ripe or green olive, the next with mandarin orange sections. Press the bottom tip of each pick alternately into the base of the cheese ball on a gentle slant.

Canapé Spreads

CHICKEN LIVER PASTE: To ½ lb chicken livers add ¾ C hot water. Simmer covered 15 minutes. Gently sauté 1 Tbsp chopped onion in 2 Tbsp butter for 2 minutes. Add to drained and dried livers and force through finest knife of food chopper. Add ½ tsp salt, ⅛ tsp pepper and grind again to a smooth paste. Chill.

CHOPPED CLAM AND CHEESE SPREAD: Drain liquid from 1-lb can whole or minced clams. Chop clams very finely and add ¼ C white cream cheese, 2 Tbsp sour cream, ½ tsp salt and ⅛ tsp pepper. Chill.

ROQUEFORT AND CREAM CHEESE SPREAD: Mix to a smooth paste ½ C each of Roquefort and white cream cheese with 1 tsp each of Worcestershire sauce and dry mustard. Add 2 Tbsp mayonnaise or soft butter. Good for canapés but even better for stuffing celery. Pipe it attractively into short stalks of celery or use a slender knife. Perfect as a dip for tiny white cauliflowerets, but add extra mayonnaise for this purpose.

SALMON SPREAD FOR SHRIMP CANAPÉS: Mash finely or put through finest knife of grinder one 4-oz can drained red salmon. Work into it 1½ Tbsp mayonnaise and 1 tsp lemon juice. Spread on round canapé bases. Top each with one whole large shrimp.

TOAST BASES FOR CANAPÉS

Trim the crusts from fine-textured white bread which is sliced very thinly. Cut into fancy shapes: oblongs, stars, rounds, triangles. Gently sauté on one side in a little butter; they must not be butter-soaked. Dry and cool on wax paper. When serving time approaches spread untoasted side with one of the above spreads. Garnish the canapés daintily with sprigs of parsley, slices of stuffed olive, strips of pimiento, finely chopped ripe olives or hard-cooked egg yolk sieved.

Fondue Bruxelloise

3 Tbsp butter
6 Tbsp flour
¼ tsp salt
Pepper
1 C milk
1½ C grated Cheddar cheese
1 egg, beaten
Flour
Fine sifted breadcrumbs

Melt butter, remove from heat. Add flour, pepper and salt; blend until smooth. Add milk, slowly, stirring constantly to avoid lumps. Cook, stirring, until smooth and thickened over low heat. Add cheese, cook stirring until cheese melts. Pour into buttered 9 × 5 pan so that fondue is ½" thick. Chill in refrigerator. Cut into fingers 2 × 1 × ½". Roll in flour, then beaten egg, then breadcrumbs. Fry in deep fat at 375° about 3 minutes or until golden brown. Drain. Serve hot. Makes 16.

Golden Chicken Nuggets

4 chicken breasts
¼ C grated Parmesan cheese
¼ C finely grated Cheddar cheese
½ C fine dry breadcrumbs
1 tsp thyme
1 tsp basil
½ tsp salt
⅛ tsp pepper
½ C melted butter or margarine

Skin and bone chicken breasts. Cut meat into 1½" squares.

In a bowl mix dry together Paremsan cheese, Cheddar cheese, breadcrumbs, thyme, basil, salt and pepper. In a medium-sized pot melt butter or margarine. Dip chicken pieces in it, then roll in the dry crumb mixture to completely coat. Arrange chicken pieces in a single layer on a foil-lined baking sheet. Bake at 400° for 10 or 12 minutes. Serve hot or cold.

Chicken Bouchées

Make Bouchées from CHOUX PASTE recipe (see Index: Pastries).

With sharp knife cut slice from top of each Bouchée. At serving time fill with CHICKEN SALAD: 1½ C diced cooked chicken, ⅓ C chopped stuffed olives, ¾ C finely chopped inner celery, ½ tsp salt, shake of pepper, ½ C best-quality genuine mayonnaise. If desired, add ½ C grated Cheddar cheese. Mix lightly. When bouchées are filled, decorate each with slice of stuffed olive.

Soups

Bean and Bacon Soup

1 lb dried white navy beans
10 C cold water
¼ to ½ lb end smoked side bacon
1 medium onion
2 slices lemon
1 bay leaf
½ tsp salt
2 chicken bouillon cubes

Wash beans under running water in a large sieve. Soak them in a soup kettle overnight in cold water. In the morning put them on to cook. Put through grinder the smoked bacon end, onion and lemon slices and add to soup pot. Also add the bay leaf, salt and chicken bouillon cubes, cover and simmer about 3½ hours. To purée this soup, if desired, cool it to room temperature and beat in the beater bowl at slow speed to break up most of the beans. Serves eight to ten.

Senate Bean Soup

1 lb white navy beans
10 C cold water
1 medium onion chopped
6 oz raw smoked ham chopped
1¼ tsp salt
¼ tsp pepper
⅛ tsp garlic salt
2 tsp sugar

Wash the beans and soak overnight or all morning in the cold water. Add onion and chopped ham and bring to the boil, then simmer covered 4 hours. Add all remaining ingredients and simmer half an hour longer. Taste to see if salt needs adding.

Variations: 1. If you can order and buy smoked ham hocks in your area they would be more economical but would have to be removed from the soup when they are tender, bone discarded and meat cut up and returned to soup. 2. If you have a leftover ham bone from a roast smoked ham, leave some meat on it and use it instead of the smoked ham in the recipe. 3. One large potato, chopped, could be added. 4. Add 1 C diced celery and 2 minced garlic cloves.

Chunky Beef and Vegetable Soup

9 C water
3 C (1¼ lb) diced or cubed stewing beef
1 beef bouillon cube
1 Tbsp salt
¼ tsp black pepper
¼ C raw rice
1 C broken up noodles
1 C diced (¼") carrots
1 medium onion chopped
1 medium parsnip diced (¼")
1½ C chopped celery
1 C shredded cabbage

In the soup pot heat the water and meat and add all remaining ingredients as you get them ready. Bring to boil, reduce heat, cover and simmer 4 hours. Serves ten.

Beef and Barley Soup

2 C chopped (not ground) roast or cooked
    beef (or raw)
9 C cold water
1 C tomato juice
1 C barley
½ C finely chopped onion
½ C carrots, cut in thin 1 × ⅛" strips
3 beef bouillon cubes
1 tsp salt
⅓ C finely chopped celery

Combine all above ingredients in large soup pot and simmer, covered, for 3 hours or until barley is tender. Taste for salt.

Potage Basque

The greatest satisfaction of this soup is that you can use up leftover broth. This could be chicken, beef, veal, ham, heart, tongue.

2 Tbsp barley
2 C meat broth
2 Tbsp butter (or ham fat) (first amount)
½ medium-small onion, chopped
1 C finely chopped green cabbage
2 Tbsp butter or margarine (second amount)
2 Tbsp flour
2 C milk
2 chicken bouillon cubes
½ tsp celery salt (optional)
5 slices side bacon, chopped, or ½ C finely
    chopped cooked ham

Soak barley in broth one hour. Simmer, covered, for 2 hours. Sauté the chopped onion and cabbage in the first amount of butter (or ham fat) but do not brown. Melt second amount of butter, stir in the flour and bouillon cubes and celery salt (if used) to blend, then stir in milk until thick. Add to barley and broth. Stir in sautéed cabbage and onion. Taste for salt. Chop and fry the bacon until dry and crisp but not brown. Drain on paper toweling. Serve the soup in preheated bowls sprinkled with crumbled bacon or ham. Six servings.

Homemade Chicken Noodle Soup

4 C chicken broth (see note #1 below)
1 C ¼" broad noodles
2 Tbsp raw rice
1 chicken bouillon cube
½ C finely chopped celery
½ C finely diced carrot
½ to 1 C tomatoes, fresh peeled or canned

Simmer all above ingredients except tomatoes together until rice is soft and tender. Add tomatoes. Bring to boil. Taste to see if soup is salty enough. *Notes:* 1. To the water in which a chicken is boiled, add half a bay leaf, 1 Tbsp minced onion, 1 tsp salt. When chicken is cooked, chill broth overnight then skim off the fat. 2. To extend this soup, add a can of condensed vegetable soup and a can of hot water. 3. You might add 1 C diced chicken.

Cabbage Soup

1 lb ground chuck beef
1 medium onion, chopped
½ C diced celery
½ green pepper, chopped, or 2 Tbsp green
    pepper flakes
2 Tbsp oil
2 tsp salt
2 Tbsp sugar
¼ tsp pepper
½ tsp paprika
One 28-oz can tomatoes
Two 5½-oz cans tomato paste
4 C hot water (see below)
2 beef bouillon cubes
2 to 4 chili peppers (optional)
3 Tbsp chopped parsley or parsley flakes
2 C raw potatoes, diced
1 C raw carrot, diced
6 to 7 C coarsely chopped cabbage, packed
    (about 1 small head)

In very large soup pot sauté ground beef, onion, celery and green pepper in the oil until redness is gone from the meat. Chop the meat all the time it is sautéing. Add remaining ingredients except cabbage and combine thoroughly. Simmer uncovered for 1 hour, stirring occasionally. Fish out chili peppers if used. Add cabbage, combine and simmer covered 1 hour longer. *Note:* If soup is too thick for your taste add 1 or 2 cups hot water. Serve generous amounts in large soup bowls with rye bread. Eight to ten servings.

Jumbo Gumbo

One 3-lb chicken
4 C water (first amount)
1 bay leaf
¼ C barley
1 C chopped celery
⅔ C chopped onion
1 C diced (¼") carrot
¼ C raw long grain rice
¼ C catsup
4 C water (second amount)
¼ tsp basil
¼ tsp pepper
2 tsp salt

Put the chicken on to cook in a large soup pot with the bay leaf in the first 4 C water. Add giblets: heart and gizzard but not the liver (see below). Simmer covered until meat begins to fall from bones. Remove chicken to utility tray. Slip off and discard skin and bones. Cut meat and giblets coarsely. Carefully skim most of the fat from the broth. Fish out bay leaf. Now add the barley to the broth and simmer until nearly tender, about 1 hour, then add celery, onion, carrot, rice, catsup, 4 C water (second amount), basil, pepper and salt and simmer until rice is soft. Now add chicken meat and bring to boil. Serves eight.

Note: Add the liver to the soup pot about 3 minutes before serving time to barely cook it. Then fish it out. Use it mashed with mayonnaise and finely chopped celery leaves for lunch sandwiches next day.

Cream of Chicken Noodle Soup

4 C strained chicken broth (fat skimmed off:
    see below)
½ C ¼" diced carrots
½ C ¼" diced potatoes
1 Tbsp raw rice
1 Tbsp chopped onion
¾ C broken fine noodles
1 chicken bouillon cube
1 Tbsp cornstarch
1 C milk

Use chicken broth from boiling a chicken, strain and chill it, then skim off the hardened fat to use for some other purpose.

Measure the broth into the soup pot and add the carrots, potatoes, rice, onion, noodles and the bouillon cube. Cover and cook gently until carrots are tender. Stir the cornstarch into the milk until smooth then stir this paste into the soup until thickened a little. Cook 1 minute longer, stirring. This is a thick, nourishing soup.

Note: If desired, dice some leftover chicken meat and add as much as 1 cup.

Oyster and Spinach Soup

2½ C whole milk
½ pint raw oysters and liquid or one 8-oz can
    whole oysters
¼ C spinach purée or one 6-oz jar creamed
    spinach purée baby food
½ tsp salt
Small shake pepper
Small shake garlic salt
½ tsp Worcestershire sauce
2 Tbsp butter
2 Tbsp cornstarch
About ¼ pint whipping cream

Gently cook oysters in top of double boiler until firm. Drain off liquid and reserve it. Grind or blender-buzz oysters to a pulp. Push through sieve to make them into a smooth purée.

In top of double boiler add oyster liquid to oyster purée, mix well, then add milk, spinach purée, salt, pepper, garlic salt, Worcestershire sauce. Heat over boiling water until very hot. Melt the butter and stir in the cornstarch. Stir this paste into the soup until thick. Beat with rotary beater to be sure you have a smooth blend. Cook 5 minutes longer, stirring occasionally. Turn into 4 ovenproof individual casseroles. Top each with a large puff of whipped cream. Slide under hot broiler to tinge the whipped cream a golden brown, watching it every second. Serve at once.

Cream of Lentil Soup

One 14-oz pkg lentils
4 C cold water (first amount)
2 C broth from boiling spareribs or hambone
    or pork shoulder
2 C water (second amount)
½ C diced carrots
½ C chopped celery
½ C chopped onion
1 small bay leaf
2 tsp salt
1 chicken bouillon cube
About 4 C milk

Soak the lentils overnight in the 4 C cold water in a cool place. About 2 hours before serving time add broth, water (second amount), vegetables, bay leaf, salt and bouillon cube, and simmer 2 hours. Press through strong strainer, rubbing until only the little skins of the lentils are left in strainer. Return to heat and add half as much milk as there is purée, about 4 cups. Mix and heat through and serve. If desired sprinkle with a few croutons or a lot of finely chopped parsley. Yield: about 3 quarts.

Cream of Shrimp Soup

¼ C margarine
2 tsp finely chopped onion
¼ C flour
1 chicken bouillon cube
1 C 10% cream
2 C milk
One 4¼-oz can small shrimp and liquid
2 Tbsp sherry

Into the top of a double boiler measure the margarine and onion and *over direct heat* blend and stir for a minute or two then blend in flour. Now stir in chicken bouillon cube, cream and milk until thick. Add the shrimps and their liquid. Place top of double boiler over bottom and cook covered for 5 or 10 minutes. Add sherry. Ladle into cream soup cups and sprinkle with little mounds of finely chopped parsley at center.

Oxtail Soup

1 oxtail (about 1½ lb)
6 C cold water (first amount)
½ C finely chopped celery
1 large carrot finely diced
1 medium onion chopped
¼ C macaroni alphabets
¼ C raw rice
2 beef bouillon cubes
2 tsp salt
¼ tsp pepper
3 C water (second amount)

In a soup pot simmer the disjointed oxtail in the 6 C water for 4 hours, covered. Remove from heat and lift out meaty oxtail bones. Cover broth and let chill overnight. Skim all fat from broth and discard it . Trim and discard all fat from oxtail bones and chop and return meat to broth.

Now add all remaining ingredients, being careful to chop the vegetables finely. Simmer until vegetables are tender, about half an hour. Now taste. If necessary, add more salt and 1 to 2 C water. Yield: two quarts.

Pea Soup

1 lb dry green (or yellow) split peas
1 ham bone with a little meat attached from roast
    ham or ¼ lb fat salt pork with rind removed
    and finely chopped
12 C cold water
¼ C chopped onion
1 medium stalk celery, chopped
1½ tsp salt (add only 1 tsp if fat salt
    pork is used)
¼ tsp pepper
¼ of a bay leaf

Tip peas into a large sieve and wash under running cold water. Turn into large soup pot with lid and add the cold water, cover and let stand in cool place overnight. Three hours before mealtime add all remaining ingredients and simmer covered for 3 hours, stirring frequently. At serving time fish out the ham bone and bay leaf and discard. With a slotted spoon lift out any pieces of ham which have fallen from bone and chop them and return to soup. Serve in preheated soup bowls, with crusty French bread. Twelve servings.

Mulligatawny

One 3-lb chicken
10 C water
2 chicken bouillon cubes
1 tsp salt
¼ tsp garlic salt
½ C raw long grain rice
1 C chopped onion (preferably Spanish)
1 C chopped or shredded carrot
1 C chopped unpared apple
½ to 1 tsp curry powder
⅛ tsp pepper

Simmer chicken in water 1½ hours until meat will fall from bones. Transfer chicken to utility tray. Chill broth and skim off fat and use for some other purpose. When chicken is cool enough to handle carefully separate both breasts from breast bone and wrap and freeze for another purpose. Slip all remaining meat from bones and discard bones and skin. Chop meat, about 2¾ C (minus breasts). To the skimmed broth add all ingredients except meat and simmer one hour. Then add chopped chicken meat and bring to boil. Serves eight.

French Onion Soup

1 large Spanish onion (4 C when sliced)
Boiling water for blanching (see below)
¼ C butter
6 C hot water
6 beef bouillon cubes
1 tsp salt
⅛ tsp white pepper
⅛ tsp garlic salt
3 slices stale bread halved diagonally
½ C Parmesan cheese

Cut the Spanish onion in half horizontally and slice it wafer thin. Blanch by pouring boiling water over, to cover. Let stand 5 minutes and drain well.

In a large dish (preferably flameproof so it can be transferred to oven) melt the butter and add onions and sauté, stirring, until limp but not browned. Add the 6 C hot water, beef bouillon cubes, salt, pepper, garlic salt and cook stirring until cubes dissolve, then stir frequently but gently until onions are limp and tender, about 25 minutes in all. If bread is not stale enough to be crisp cut each slice into 2 triangles and place on pie plate in hot oven to crispen. If soup is in frying pan or pot turn it into a large baking dish or 6 large individual baking dishes. Cover with bread triangles. Sprinkle with Parmesan cheese and bake under preheated broiler until bubbling and golden, about 8 or 10 minutes. Serves six.

Minestrone

2 C dried navy beans
1 C chopped celery with leaves
1 C finely chopped onion
1 minced garlic clove
½ C olive oil (or salad oil)
2½ C canned tomatoes
¼ C chopped parsley
2 C shredded cabbage
1 small zucchini squash thinly sliced
2 C cut macaroni or elbows or shells
1 Tbsp salt
4 peppercorns
Grated Parmesan cheese

Soak beans in 10 C water overnight. Bring to boil in the same water, reduce heat, add salt and peppercorns, cover and simmer 1 hour. Sauté celery, onion and garlic in olive oil for 10 minutes or until lightly browned. Add to beans with tomatoes and parsley. Bring to boil, reduce heat, cover and simmer for 1 hour. Add cabbage, zucchini and macaroni and simmer uncovered for 15 minutes, stirring occasionally. Serve sprinkled with grated Parmesan cheese.

Crabmeat and Corn Chowder

½ C butter
1¾ C finely chopped Spanish onion
1 C finely chopped celery
1 green pepper chopped
2½ C fresh corn cut from the cob or drained kernel corn.
⅓ C chopped pimiento
1 Tbsp salt
1 chicken bouillon cube
8 C milk
Three 6-oz cans crabmeat including brine
¾ C flour

In a very large pot (do not use enamel) melt the butter and in it gently sauté the onion, celery, green pepper and pimiento for 5 minutes, stirring. Add the corn and cook over medium-low heat stirring for 5 minutes. (Incidentally, at this stage, the above combination would be good for a summertime vegetable medley). Now stir in the flour, salt and chicken soup cube until blended. Add the milk and stir constantly until thick. Cut up crabmeat and add and heat through and serve in preheated soup bowls. Ten servings.

Scotch Broth

One little lamb shank weighing 5 oz
5 C water
¼ C barley
1 medium onion chopped
½ C chopped carrot
½ C chopped celery (including tops)
½ C chopped cabbage
1½ tsp salt
½ bay leaf

In soup pot put shank, water and barley on to simmer, covered for 1½ hours. Add all remaining ingredients and cook 1 hour longer. Remove shank. Discard bone and gristle. Chop meat and return to pot and heat through. Taste. If you prefer richer soup you might add a chicken bouillon cube. Serves four.

Vichyssoise

One 2½-lb chicken (see below)
6 C water
2 C diced potatoes
3 leeks or ¼ large Spanish onion, chopped
⅛ tsp mace or nutmeg
½ tsp salt
1 chicken bouillon cube
1 C milk
½ C 18% cream
Chopped chives (for garnish)

Simmer the chicken in the water, covered, until it will fall from bones. Let it stand in broth until cool enough to handle. Remove chicken to utility tray and strip meat from bones and use the cooked chicken meat for another purpose such as Chicken Divan, à la King, sandwiches or salad. Discard skin and bones.

Strain broth and boil it down rapidly until it measures 3 cups. Add potatoes and leeks or onion and boil, covered, until vegetables are tender, about 15 to 20 minutes. Force through fine sieve. To this purée add the mace, salt, chicken bouillon cube, milk and cream and reheat, but do not boil. Serve at once garnished with finely chopped chives. If this soup is served cold it is thicker due to the jellied chicken broth and it may require more salt. Four to six servings.

Vegetarian Vegetable Soup

¼ C pot barley
½ C dry lima beans
8 C water
1 C raw macaroni alphabets or broken noodles
1 C finely chopped celery (1 large outside stalk)
1 C ¼" diced carrots
1 C chopped and peeled tomatoes (or canned)
1 medium onion chopped fine
½ C chopped parsley (packed, including stems)
2½ tsp salt
⅛ to ¼ tsp pepper
1 C milk
3 Tbsp cornstarch

Two hours before mealtime put on to cook in the water the barley and limas and let cook 1 hour then add all remaining ingredients except milk and cornstarch and cook 1 hour longer. At mealtime stir the cornstarch into the milk to a smooth paste. Stir into soup until thick and boiling again. It is now ready to serve.

Gazpacho

Two 4" pieces of green onion tops
2" chunk of peeled cucumber
Four 2" ripe tomatoes peeled
½ C water
2 chicken bouillon cubes
Dash of Tabasco

Put all Gazpacho ingredients into blender. Buzz 30 seconds. Put into two large soup bowls or large stemmed glasses. Chill before serving.

Note: If desired substitute ½ C undiluted canned consommé for the water and the chicken bouillon cubes.

Turkey Soup

Bones from one 12-lb turkey (preferably with a little meat attached)
8 C cold water
¼ C tomato paste or 1 C canned tomatoes
½ can undiluted mushroom soup (optional)
One 1½" onion chopped
1 C chopped outer celery
2 Tbsp rice
1 C noodles (pressed down and broken to measure)
1 C ¼" diced carrots
1 C chopped turkey meat
1 tsp salt
½ C fresh frozen peas

Add cold water to turkey carcass and simmer 3 hours covered. Strain through colander. Cut any meat from bones, chop and add to broth. Chill, preferably overnight, and skim off fat. To skimmed broth add all remaining ingredients—you may substitute other vegetables for those listed—and simmer until carrots are tender, about half an hour. Taste for salt. Serve as a main course soup accompanied by a hot bread or toast and a generous dish of cut-up Cheddar cheese. Eight servings.

Cream of Asparagus or Broccoli

2 C (packed) cut up asparagus (or broccoli) including trimmed stalks
2 C hot water
¼ bay leaf
2 Tbsp chopped onion
2 chicken bouillon cubes
4 Tbsp butter
4 Tbsp flour
½ C 10% cream
½ C milk (see below)

Combine the prepared asparagus (or broccoli) in a pot with the hot water, bay leaf, onion and chicken bouillon cubes. Bring to boil and simmer, covered, until vegetables are tender, about 15 minutes.

Meanwhile in a large pot make a Thick White Sauce by melting the butter, stirring in flour until blended, then cream and milk until very thick. If desired use 1 C homo instead of ½ C each cream and milk.

When vegetables are tender drain off and reserve ½ C of their liquid. Stir remaining vegetable liquid into thick white sauce. Cool the vegetables and the reserved liquid a little (so they do not crack your blender) and tip into blender and buzz until reduced to a smooth purée. Add purée to white sauce and stir to blend. Reheat in top of double boiler or, if over direct heat, stir constantly until boiling. Serve with sprinkling of Croutons made by toasting ¼" cubes of bread in oven at 325° until golden, stirring frequently to brown evenly. Four servings.

Kamloops Clam Chowder

4 strips bacon chopped
1 small onion chopped
2 stalks celery chopped
½ green pepper chopped
1 clove garlic minced
¼ bay leaf
Two 10-oz cans whole baby clams plus liquid
½ C water
2 C diced potatoes, raw
1 tsp HP Sauce
¼ tsp salt
⅛ tsp pepper
¼ C oil
¼ C flour
½ C 18% cream
2 C milk

To large pot add bacon, onion, celery, green pepper and garlic and sauté gently for 5 minutes, stirring often. Now add the bay leaf, the liquid from the canned clams, the water, diced potatoes, HP sauce, salt and pepper and simmer until potatoes are barely tender. Combine oil and flour and stir into chowder until thick. Add clams, cream and milk, bring to boil. Remove bay leaf. Serves six.

Cream of Corn Soup

1 C diced cooked potato
2 slices side bacon chopped
1 medium onion chopped
2 C milk
One 14-oz can cream style corn
½ tsp salt
Shake of pepper

Cook about 2 medium potatoes in their skins first to get 1 cup when peeled and diced. In large pot sauté the chopped bacon and onion very gently, stirring constantly, until onions are limp. Neither bacon nor onion should be browned or they will spoil the colour of the finished soup. Now add the milk, corn, salt, pepper and prepared potatoes and bring to simmering point and serve topped with croutons or a sprinkling of finely chopped parsley. Four servings.

Cream of Carrot Soup

1½ C chopped raw carrots
1 medium onion chopped
1 C water
½ tsp salt
2 Tbsp bacon fat or margarine
2 Tbsp flour
1 chicken bouillon cube
2½ C milk
Finely chopped parsley (for garnish)

Cook together the carrots, onion, water and salt 30 minutes until tender. Cool enough to turn into your blender. Blend until you have a smooth purée.

Make a White Sauce: Melt bacon fat or margarine, stir in flour until blended, then chicken bouillon cube. Stir in milk until thick. Add carrot purée and reheat in double boiler. Serve topped with finely chopped parsley. Four servings.

Cream of Celery Soup

2 C cut up celery
1 C water
2 Tbsp butter
2 Tbsp flour
½ tsp salt
2 C milk
1 chicken bouillon cube

Simmer the celery in the water, covered, until very tender, about 30 minutes. Cool enough to tip into blender then blend until puréed to a mush.

Make a Thin White Sauce by blending the butter, flour and salt then stirring in the milk until thick. Add the chicken bouillon cube. Add the puréed celery to the white sauce and heat in top of double boiler. Serves four.

Cream of Mushroom Soup

2 C halved white mushrooms
1 C water
2 Tbsp butter
2 Tbsp flour
½ tsp salt
2 C milk
1 chicken bouillon cube

Simmer mushrooms in water, covered, for 5 minutes. Reserve 2 or 3 pieces of mushrooms to slice for topping soup when served. Cool enough to tip into blender then blend until puréed.

Make a Thin White Sauce by blending butter, flour and salt then stirring in milk until thick. Add the chicken bouillon cube. Add the puréed mushrooms to the white sauce and reheat in top of double boiler. When served top each bowl with 2 or 3 thin slices of the reserved mushrooms.

Bright Green Cream of Spinach Soup

One 10-oz package spinach
3 C milk
1 chicken bouillon cube
4½ Tbsp butter
3 Tbsp flour
¼ tsp salt

Heat milk in double boiler with chicken bouillon cube. Wash and cook spinach, covered, 3 minutes, in only the water that clings to its leaves. Turn it once during this 3-minute period. Cool a little then turn all into blender goblet, pushing mass down against blades and buzz until puréed. You must have liquid down in well of goblet to start puréeing action. Add purée to hot milk in double boiler. Rinse out blender goblet with some of the milk. Melt the butter and blend in flour and salt. Stir into hot milk and spinach mixture in double boiler until slightly thickened and serve. This is very bright green and delicate and could be garnished with a little whipped cream if desired. Serves six.

Tomato Soup

1 C leftover sliced tomatoes, or canned
⅛ tsp baking soda
⅛ tsp oregano
1 Tbsp flour
2 Tbsp soft butter
½ slice fresh bread broken up
2½ C hot (not boiling) water
¼ C skim milk powder

Into blender goblet put all but skim milk powder and blend at high speed for 30 seconds. Add skim milk powder and blend 15 more seconds. Tip into pot and heat and serve.

Hearty Meatball Soup

SOUP
1 C dry white pea beans
9 C water (divided, see below)
1 tsp salt
1 clove garlic, finely chopped
½ C diced celery
½ C grated cabbage
½ C diced turnip
½ C diced carrot
2 medium-sized onions, thinly sliced
2 beef bouillon cubes
One 28-oz can tomatoes
1 bay leaf
1 C spaghetti, broken
MEATBALLS
1½ lb ground chuck beef
2 Tbsp onion flakes (soak in warm water 10
    minutes, then drain)
¼ C fine breadcrumbs (1 slice)
1 medium egg
¼ C tomato juice
¼ tsp black pepper
¼ tsp sweet basil
¼ tsp garlic powder

To cook Beans, in large soup pot combine beans and 5 C of the water. Cover, bring to boil and boil 2 minutes. Remove from heat and let stand, covered, for 1 hour. Add salt, Return to heat and when boiling reduce heat to simmer. Simmer covered for 30 minutes.

To make Meatballs, combine all meatball ingredients blending well. Using a teaspoon, spoon out a small amount of the mixture and shape into bite-size balls, about 60. In frypan lightly brown on all sides (no fat required). Drain surplus fat from pan reserving 2 Tbsp. Transfer meatballs to large plate.

To make Soup, stir-fry vegetables and garlic in the reserved 2 Tbsp fat in the frying pan for 5 to 10 minutes or until golden. To the undrained beans add the vegetables, garlic, remaining 4 C water, beef bouillon cubes, tomatoes and bay leaf. Cover and simmer 1 hour, stirring occasionally. Add meatballs and raw spaghetti to the soup and simmer 30 minutes more. To thicken, make a smooth paste of 6 Tbsp flour and ¾ C cold water and stir into soup until thick. Taste for more salt. Serves ten.

Cream of Cauliflower Soup

1 C cooked cauliflower (packed)
½ chicken bouillon cube crushed
1 Tbsp flour
¾ tsp salt
Shake of pepper
2½ C hot (not boiling) water
¼ C skim milk powder
⅓ C grated old Cheddar cheese
1 tsp chopped fresh or dried chives

Press cauliflower down onto blades of blender and add the chicken bouillon cube, flour, salt, pepper and hot water. Blend at high speed for 30 seconds. Add skim milk powder and blend for another 15 seconds. Tip into heavy pot and heat to just below boiling, then stir in cheese. Heat through but do not boil. Add chives and serve at once. Four servings.

Hearty Hungarian Soup

2 medium onions, chopped
3 Tbsp butter or margarine or oil
2 lb stewing beef cut into 1″ cubes
½ lb beef liver, cubed
2½ tsp salt
1½ tsp paprika
2 green peppers, cored and coarsely chopped
One 19-oz can tomatoes (or 2 large fresh chopped)
2 long carrots scrubbed and diced
3 medium potatoes, pared and diced
1 Tbsp parsley flakes (or fresh chopped)
2 tsp Worcestershire sauce
6 C water

In a very large heavy frying pan or soup kettle sauté onions and green peppers in butter (or margarine or oil) until limp but not brown. Add beef and liver cubes and stir to brown them on all sides. Add all remaining ingredients and combine thoroughly. Cover, bring to boil, reduce heat and simmer 1½ to 2½ hours or until tender. Serves six.

Main Course Chicken Soup

In advance, cook a 5-lb chicken in 5 C water with 1 bay leaf until meat falls from bones, about 2½ hours. Lift to utility tray, remove meat. Discard skin and bones. Strain broth and chill. Skim off fat. Refrigerate meat, covered.

4 C chicken broth
4 C water
1 C diced (¼″) carrots
1 C finely chopped celery
1 large cored and pared tomato (or 1 C canned)
1 medium onion chopped
1 medium potato diced (¼″)
3 Tbsp barley
3 Tbsp rice
¼ C tiny macaroni shells or elbows
3 chicken bouillon cubes
1 tsp (or more) salt
2 C lean diced (½″) cooked chicken (see above)

Combine all soup ingredients above and cook until barley is tender. Serve as a main course.

Kentucky Burgoo

2 lb stewing beef cut into 1½″ cubes
One 3-lb chicken
1 tsp Tabasco sauce
3 tsp salt (divided, see below)
11 C water
2 C pared, diced potatoes
2 C chopped onions
1 clove garlic, minced
2 C pared, sliced carrots
One 28-oz can tomatoes (or equivalent in
    fresh chopped)
One 8-oz can tomato sauce
5 beef bouillon cubes
One 10-oz pkg fresh frozen cut green beans
    (or a 19-oz can plus liquid)
Two 10-oz pkgs frozen whole kernel corn
    (or equivalent cut from cob)
Two 10-oz pkgs frozen okra (or peas)
1 C chopped parsley (or ¼ C parsley flakes)

In a large preserving kettle combine beef cubes, whole chicken, Tabasco sauce, 1 tsp salt and water. Cover, bring to boil, reduce heat and simmer, covered, 1½ hours. Remove chicken from pot and set aside to cool. Add the 2 tsp salt and all other remaining ingredients to pot. Cover and simmer 1 to 1½ hours or until beef is tender.

Meanwhile, remove skin from chicken and pull meat from bones. Cut into bite-sized pieces. Add chicken to beef mixture and heat through. Discard skin and bones. Serves twelve.

Shrimp Chowder

4 strips bacon chopped
1 C chopped onion
2 large potatoes diced (¼″)
1 C boiling water
2 tsp salt
⅛ tsp white pepper
¼ tsp basil or thyme
4 C milk (divided, see below)
1 lb small fresh frozen shrimp almost thawed
¼ C flour
2 Tbsp tomato paste
1 chicken bouillon cube

In bottom of soup pot sauté bacon and onion together until onions are limp. Bacon should not be browned. Add diced potatoes and water and simmer until potatoes are nearly tender. Add salt, pepper, basil or thyme and 3½ C of the milk. Stir flour into remaining ½ C milk until smooth and stir it into soup until thick.

During last 8 to 10 minutes stir in shrimp and chicken bouillon cube. During last 30 seconds add tomato paste to give chowder a pinker tinge. Six servings.

Cream of Cucumber Soup

3 cucumbers (or one 10″ English cucumber,
    see below)
4 Tbsp butter (divided, see below)
3 Tbsp flour
3 C chicken broth (or water and bouillon,
    see below)
1 C milk
1 C 18% cream
2 tsp Angostura bitters

Pare and remove seeds from cucumbers and slice thinly. *Note:* If you use an English cucumber it is not necessary to remove seeds. Melt 2 Tbsp of the butter in a frying pan, add the sliced cucumbers and cook gently until they are soft and transparent, about 15 minutes. Do not brown. Set aside.

Melt remaining butter, blend in flour, then stir in milk and broth until thick. If you do not have broth substitute 3 C hot water to which you have added 3 chicken bouillon cubes.

Now add cooked cucumbers and cook gently about 10 minutes. Cool somewhat then turn into blender and beat until perfectly smooth. Taste for salt and pepper. Add cream and bitters. Serve cold or hot. Eight servings.

Borsch

2 medium onions shredded or finely chopped
2 medium carrots shredded
2 C shredded peeled beets (or one 20-oz can
    drained beets)
1 C shredded cabbage
6 C hot water (divided, see below)
3 beef bouillon cubes
1 Tbsp butter
2 tsp vinegar
1 tsp salt
1 tsp sugar
¼ tsp flavored salt

To the prepared vegetables add 2 C of the hot water and simmer covered 20 minutes. Add remaining ingredients and simmer half an hour longer. Serve in large soup bowls with a spoonful of fresh dairy sour cream on top.

Meats

Beef

Hamburg

Veal, Pork & Lamb

Organ Meats

Beef

Oxtail or Beef Ragout

2 Tbsp oil
2 medium onions chopped
¼ tsp oregano
⅓ C flour
1½ tsp salt
¼ tsp pepper
1¾ lb oxtails or stewing beef cut up
2 C hot water

In a heavy pot or frying pan with lid, or pressure cooker, heat oil and sauté onions until limp. Into a paper bag measure the oregano, flour, salt and pepper. Add the separated oxtails or cut up beef and shake to coat meat. Tip all into pot or pan and stir constantly over medium-high heat to remove whiteness from flour. Do not burn the onions. Add hot water, cover and simmer 3¼ hours, or, if you cook this in your pressure cooker, cook at 10 pounds pressure for 1 hour. If you use oxtails, lift out bare bones. Serves five.

Roast Prime Ribs of Beef

The proper way to roast beef is by the low-slow method as follows:

One 9-lb standing prime rib roast (3 ribs,
    preferably red brand)
Salt
Pepper
Paprika

Wash and dry roast. Sprinkle all cut sides fairly generously with salt, pepper and paprika. Stand rib side down on rack in pan. Roast at 225° for 5 hours, uncovered without any water. This gives well cooked outer slices and pink slices for those who want it medium rare. For those who want it rare reduce time to 4 hours, but put a meat thermometer in thick part of roast and do not allow the meat thermometer to rise above 140°.

Swiss Steak

2-lb slice of round steak
⅓ C flour
½ tsp salt
¼ C margarine
¼ C chopped onion or chives
1 beef bouillon cube
1 C boiling water

On a heavy board sprinkle half of flour and half of salt on one side of round steak and pound all into the meat with steak pounder or edge of strong saucer. Turn over and pound remaining flour and salt into other side. This extends the area of the meat and breaks up tough fibers. With sharp knife slit fat edges to prevent curling.

In large heavy casserole (or frying pan) melt margarine and sear meat on both sides until deep gold. Add onion or chives and beef bouillon cube, pour boiling water over. If you have used a frying pan transfer to a baking dish large enough to accommodate it flat out. Cover with lid or foil and bake at 300° for 1 hour then reduce heat to 225° for 2 more hours. Swiss Steak should have at least 3 hours cooking to be fork tender. Cut into serving pieces and spoon a little of the rich pan gravy over each. Serves four to six.

Beef Stroganoff

1 Tbsp butter or margarine
½ medium onion chopped
One 2½-lb sirloin steak, trimmed and cut
    (see below)
½ to 1 lb fresh mushrooms quartered
One 10-oz can undiluted consommé or
    beef bouillon
1 tsp Worcestershire sauce
½ tsp salt
¾ C dairy sour cream
3 Tbsp flour
¼ C water (or red wine)
Noodles

Patiently prepare sirloin steak by cutting it into strips 3 × 1 × ¼″, trimming away all fat, gristle and bone. In large frying pan sauté onion in butter or margarine until limp, not brown. Add meat strips and sear, turning constantly (not more than 5 minutes). Remove pan from burner. Scrub and quarter mushrooms and add to pan along with consommé, Worcestershire sauce and salt.

Meanwhile cook ½ to ¾ pound noodles in large amount of boiling salted water until almost tender.

About 5 minutes before serving time, heat contents of pan to boiling, then stir in sour cream until just below boiling. Make a smooth paste of the flour and water (or wine) and stir in until thickened. Drain noodles and serve Beef Stroganoff over them.

Swiss-Barbecued Blade Steaks

Two 1½-lb blade or chuck steaks
Flour
¼ C bacon drippings
½ lemon, thinly sliced
1 large onion, sliced
2 Tbsp brown sugar
¾ tsp salt
¼ tsp freshly ground black pepper
½ tsp barbecue seasoning
1 Tbsp parsley flakes
1¼ C tomato juice
2 Tbsp Worcestershire sauce

Sprinkle the blade steaks on both sides with flour. Now brown them in hot bacon drippings on both sides. Transfer steaks and fat to roasting pan large enough to fit them in one layer. Arrange lemon slices, then onion slices over steaks. Sprinkle with brown sugar. Then sprinkle over the salt, pepper, barbecue seasoning and parsley flakes. Carefully pour tomato juice and Worcestershire sauce evenly over all. Cover and bake at 250° for 3½ hours.

Old Time Double-Crust Meat Pie

This recipe calls for leftover roast beef and leftover gravy.

PASTRY
⅔ C shortening
2 Tbsp butter
2¼ C sifted all-purpose flour
1 tsp salt
2½ Tbsp ice cold water

FILLING
4 C leftover roast beef
1 C leftover gravy
2 medium potatoes
1 small onion
¼ chopped green pepper
1 beef bouillon cube
½ tsp salt

Make rich plain pastry by cutting shortening and butter into flour and salt, until size of peas. Drizzle in, while you toss with a fork, the ice cold water until all flour is dampened. Press into ball between palms. Roll out half to fit deep 9″ pie plate, and line pie plate. Roll out and gash other half.

Scrub potatoes until clean. Put on to cook in 1 C water and boil until three-quarters tender. Do not cook until soft.

While potatoes are boiling grind enough leftover beef to make 4 C. As you put the meat through the grinder add the onion so that it is mixed through the meat. To the ground meat add leftover gravy and green pepper. When the potatoes have cooked enough (save their liquid) peel and chop them into ¼″ cubes and add. Add potato water and beef bouillon cube and salt. Mix well and stir over medium heat until mixture just begins to boil. If it is too thick add a little more water. It should be just wet enough to pour.

Pour hot meat filling into lined pie plate. Seal on gashed top crust, crimping edges carefully. To glaze, brush top with beaten egg yolk (or white). Bake at 450° for 15 minutes then reduce heat to 325° for another 20 minutes or until filling begins to bubble through gashes and crust is golden. Serve cut into wedges.

Beef Bourguignon

3 lb tender beef sirloin, cut into 1″ cubes
2 C red wine
½ C butter
2 C quartered mushroom caps
¼ C chopped shallots or green onions
1 Tbsp flour
½ C chopped back bacon (optional)

Melt 6 Tbsp of the butter in a deep casserole. Add beef cubes (if desired back bacon may be added at this stage). Cover and braise (bake) in a hot oven at 400° for 20 minutes. Meanwhile sauté mushroom caps and shallots or green onions in remaining 2 Tbsp butter. Stir in flour. Add red wine and mix well. Pour over beef, cover and return to oven for 30 minutes. Serves six.

How to Broil a Steak

One 2-lb sirloin steak (about 1″ thick)
Paprika
Garlic (optional)

Warm steak to room temperature. Preheat broiler oven 10 minutes in advance. Trim half of the fat from the edge of the steak. Slit remaining fat around edge to prevent curling up. Grease the bars of the rack on the broiler pan with a piece of the steak fat. Place steak at center of greased rack. Sprinkle fairly liberally with paprika. Do not salt or pepper. If you like garlic rub steak surface with cut clove of garlic.

If broiler burner is electric, insert broiler rack so top surface of steak is 3″ below burner. If broiler burner is gas, top surface of steak should be 4″ below burner. Take note of time. Broil 4 minutes on top side or until deep gold and edges are turning brown. Turn steak over and broil other side 4 to 5 minutes. To test remove steak from broiler oven and with pointed knife make a deep slit at thickest part. Steak will be pale pink inside. If you want your steak rarer cook it a shorter time, if well done, 2 or 3 minutes longer. Sprinkle with salt and pepper, transfer to preheated platter and serve at once. Never keep the steak waiting for people to come to the table.

Notes: 1. Steak may be pan broiled by inverting a small rack in a frying pan and placing steak on it to keep it from touching the fat which accumulates in bottom of pan. Heat should be moderate, not high. Never cover a pan broiled steak. 2. Thicker 1½ to 2″ steaks could require as long as 30 to 35 minutes to broil to medium doneness.

Sunday Pot Roast

4 lb boneless rolled cross rib or blade roast
    or brisket point
1 tsp salt
¼ tsp pepper
½ C water

Grease the bottom of a heavy pot and brown the meat on both sides. Browning steams up the kitchen but is a necessary step in pot roasting. Sprinkle with salt and pepper. Add water, cover and simmer 3½ hours covered, turning each hour. If desired, meat may be transferred to small roasting pan and roasted in the oven at 325° for same period of time, turning every hour.

Transfer meat to preheated platter. To make gravy stir together 5 Tbsp flour in ½ C cold water to make a smooth paste. Stir in to pan juices over medium heat until thickened. If there are any lumps strain and reheat gravy.

Corned Beef Hash Topped with Eggs For Two

2 Tbsp butter
One 15-oz can corned beef hash
4 medium-sized eggs
1 Tbsp water

Melt butter in frying pan. Open both ends of hash can and push contents out onto plate. Cut crosswise into 4 even rounds. Carefully transfer to bubbling butter in pan and make depression with tablespoon in each big enough to accommodate a small egg. If edges split coax them together again with knife and spoon. Quickly fill each depression with an egg, add 1 Tbsp water and put on lid and cook on *medium high* until film forms over yolk (not more than 5 minutes). Serve at once.

Beef and Kidney Pies

Makes five individual pies

FILLING
1 beef kidney (¾ to 1 lb)
½ lb stewing beef
2 C water
2 Tbsp margarine
1 chopped onion
1 beef bouillon cube
2 Tbsp flour
½ tsp salt
Half of a 12-oz pkg fresh frozen green peas

ENGLISH PASTRY
1½ C stirred but not sifted cake and pastry flour
1½ tsp baking powder
¾ tsp salt
¾ C shortening (divided, see below)
⅜ C boiling water
1½ tsp lemon juice
1 large egg yolk (divided, see below)

Slice kidney lengthwise into 4 strips and trim out all fat. Cut into ¾" pieces. Soak in cold water 1 hour. Drain. Rinse again in cold water and drain. Add 2 C water to the kidney and the cut up beef, bring to boil, cover and simmer 3 hours (or pressure cook 1 hour at 5 pounds pressure).

To make English Pastry cut half of the shortening into the flour, baking powder and salt until size of peas. In another bowl add the boiling water to the remaining half of shortening and stir until melted. Stir into flour mixture along with the lemon juice and half of the egg yolk. (Reserve remaining half yolk for glazing pies later. Save leftover white for another purpose.) Mix thoroughly and chill 30 minutes.

In a large frying pan or pot melt margarine, add onion and sauté until soaked, then add bouillon cube, flour and salt and blend. Stir in cooked meat and all its broth until boiling and thickened. Spoon into five 4½" diameter individual baking dishes. Sprinkle the peas over top.

Roll out 5 pastry rounds ¼" thick to fit tops, gashed at center before fitting on. To the leftover half egg yolk add 1½ Tbsp cold water and brush tops with this to glaze. Bake at 375° about 1 hour or until gravy bubbles a little through gashes. Serve piping hot.

Roast Tenderloin of Beef

Properly, beef tenderloin should be *larded* with pork lard, using a larding needle. Since so few kitchens have this tool we will ignore it.

A beef tenderloin usually weighs between 3 to 5 lb, and one end tapers. Fold tapered end under to equalize the thickness. Cover with strips of bacon lengthwise (or spread generously with butter) and tie with string. Place on rack in roasting pan. Do not cover or baste. Roast at 500° 2 minutes and immediately reduce heat to 350° and roast for 20 to 30 minutes in all. Difference in time depends on weight of tenderloin. It will be cooked rare at center. If you want your tenderloin medium, roast it 10 to 15 minutes longer. Season on the outside when transferred to preheated platter.

Beef Wellington

Buy a fillet of beef. About 7 pounds is the average size. Try to get one that has been hung in the carcass for 21 days.

Sprinkle it with salt and pepper, and for an extra gourmet touch, spread it with *Pâté de Fois Gras*. Now sear it over high heat in large pan until brown all over and cooked for about ¼" on the outer surfaces. This is smoky work but necessary.

Roll out a very large oblong of rich plain pastry or puff pastry, more than twice as large as you would need for a 9" pie. Brush it with beaten egg. Place the slightly cooled fillet of beef in center and wrap it snugly in the pastry with the overlap on top. Brush with dilute egg wash (diluted with water to prevent it browning too soon and too much). Place on large cookie sheet and bake at 400° for 40 minutes. This gives you well done meat at both ends and rare cuts at center.

Top-of-Stove Barbecued Braising Ribs

2 lbs braising ribs
2 Tbsp oil

SAUCE
One 1½-oz pkg onion soup mix
¼ C vinegar
2 Tbsp brown sugar
1 C catsup
½ C water
1 Tbsp prepared mustard
½ C celery, diced
1 Tbsp salt

Ask the butcher to cut each strip of ribs into 3 with his cleaver. Separate them into bite-sized pieces and brown in oil in Dutch oven or a heavy frying pan with lid.

In a small bowl combine all Sauce ingredients. Pour over meat and mix. Cover and simmer 1¾ hours, stirring occasionally to make sure all meat is well coated with sauce. Serves four.

Cornish Pasties

PASTRY

2¼ C stirred but not sifted all-purpose flour
1 tsp salt
⅔ C lard
½ C cold water

FILLING

1 lb best quality lean sirloin steak cut in ¾" cubes
½ C diced yellow turnip
½ C diced carrots
½ C diced potatoes
¾ C chopped onion
1 Tbsp chopped parsley or bottled flakes
⅛ tsp pepper
1 tomato, sliced

To make pastry, cut the lard into the flour and salt until size of peas, then drizzle water over, tossing with a fork until pastry easily presses into a ball. Chill 1 hour. Divide evenly into 3 parts and roll each out in an oval shape about 10 × 8".

Mix together all filling ingredients except tomato. Place filling on center of each pastry oval, lengthening it into a long mound. Top with sliced tomato. Dampen edges of pastry, fold ends over filling, bringing sides up and pinch together in a long seam across entire top. Leave a ½" hole at center. (Into this later you pour a little hot water). Be sure all seams are sealed for the Pastie must not leak when baked. Place on ungreased baking sheet. Brush with 1 egg yolk mixed with 1 Tbsp cold water. Bake at 425° for 15 minutes then reduce heat to 350° for 1 hour. After 30 minutes add about 1½ Tbsp hot water through vent in top of each Pastie. Makes three.

Beef (or Chicken) Chow Mein

You will have to purchase some of these ingredients at a Chinese grocery store: 1 C each celery cut in narrow 3" diagonal strips, Chinese greens (Bok Toy) cut in narrow 3" strips, Chinese pea pods cut in two, ½ C each Chinese water chestnuts cut thin, and button mushrooms sliced thick, 2 C fresh bean sprouts, ⅓ C hot peanut oil, 2 C raw beef or chicken cut in 3" very flat narrow strips ¼" wide.

Heat oil in large frying pan, add beef or chicken and sauté gently, stirring, for 5 minutes, then cover and cook over low heat 7 minutes. Add all other ingredients and cook uncovered 5 minutes, mixing gently. Now sprinkle with 2 tsp salt, 1 tsp soy sauce, ¼ tsp garlic salt. Cook for 2 minutes gently lifting with forks to mix. Add ½ C beef or chicken stock, cover and steam 5 to 7 minutes.

Stir 2 Tbsp cornstarch into ½ C cold beef or chicken stock and carefully stir this in, then turn ingredients gently until covered with glaze. Cover and cook 3 to 5 minutes longer, with vegetables still crisp. Serve over crisp Chinese Fried Noodles. Garnish top with slivered toasted almonds and finely chopped fresh green onions and stems. Serves six.

Deluxe Shepherd's Pie

PASTRY

1¼ C stirred but unsifted cake and pastry flour
½ tsp salt
⅓ C shortening
2 Tbsp butter
1 Tbsp cold water

FILLING

2 C (packed) ground or finely chopped lean leftover roast beef
1 small onion ground or chopped
One 10½-oz can undiluted vegetable soup
1¾ C (packed) unseasoned mashed potatoes (cook 3 medium-large)

First cook potatoes in boiling salted water, covered until tender.

Meanwhile make the Pastry by cutting the shortening and butter into the flour and salt until size of peas. Drizzle in the water, tossing with fork, until all flour is damp. Press into ball between palms, roll out on well-floured board to fit deep 9" pie plate.

Combine the ground or chopped beef and onion with the undiluted soup. Drain and mash potatoes until perfectly smooth. Turn meat mixture into pastry-lined pie plate. Smooth top. Carefully cover with spoonfuls of mashed potatoes and with a fork spread all over top. Brush top with melted butter. Bake at 400° for 25 minutes then reduce heat to 350° for 10 minutes longer.

If desired this pie may be made in advance, then cooled and stored in refrigerator. When mealtime approaches, to reheat, sprinkle top with ⅔ C shredded Cheddar cheese and bake at 350° for 20 minutes or until cheese is tinged with gold and pie is heated through. Serves six.

Sweet and Sour Suey

1 lb ground chuck beef
One 19-oz can pineapple chunks
One 19-oz can chop suey vegetables, drained
3 Tbsp soy sauce
1 Tbsp cornstarch
1 tsp salt
⅛ tsp ginger

Into an ungreased frying pan put the ground chuck, turn on heat and chop until it is all broken up and the red color has disappeared.

In a small bowl stir together the soy sauce, cornstarch, salt, ginger, and juice drained from pineapple. Tip this into the frying pan with meat and stir until thick and boiling. Add the pineapple chunks and mix. At the last minute add the drained chop suey vegetables and gently stir until heated through but still crisp.

Serve on bed of rice on large platter: Bring to boil 3¾ C water with 1 Tbsp butter and 1½ tsp salt. Add 1½ C raw long grain rice, cover, bring to boil. Turn off heat for 5 minutes. Turn heat on as low as possible and cook 25 minutes longer. *Variations:* Add ¼ C blanched almonds or ¼ lb sliced mushrooms or ¼ C sliced ripe olives, during cooking period. Serves six.

Chinese Green Pepper Steak

2 lb lean round steak
¾ C soy sauce (divided, see below)
2 Tbsp honey
1 tsp ground ginger
½ C cooking oil (divided, see below)
2 large onions, thinly sliced
2 large green peppers cut in long fine strips
1 C water
2 tsp cornstarch

With sharp knife trim bone and fat from round steak and cut it into very thin strips about 3″ long and ⅛″ thick. In a medium bowl mix together ¼ C of the soy sauce and the honey and ginger. Add the meat and mix it around to coat. Marinate in refrigerator 1 hour.

About 15 minutes before serving time heat ¼ C oil in pot. Add onions and green peppers and stir over medium heat for 3 or 4 minutes.

In a large frying pan heat remaining ¼ C oil. Drain the meat and reserve any leftover marinade. Brown meat in hot oil on high heat for 2 or 3 minutes. Reduce heat and add water, onions and green peppers and stir. In a cup mix together until smooth the remaining ½ C soy sauce, any reserved marinade and cornstarch. Stir into meat mixture until thickened and cook 2 minutes longer. Do not overcook for the onions and green peppers should retain some of their crispness. Serve on fluffy boiled rice. Six servings.

Easy Beef Fondue Sauces

Note: Cook 1″ cubes of steak in hot oil in Fondue pot and dip in any of the following sauces.

BEEF SAUCE: Combine ¼ C thick horseradish with either 1 C sour cream or 1 C bottled barbecue sauce.

ORIENTAL SAUCE: Blend 3 Tbsp butter with 1 Tbsp cornstarch and stir in 1 C hot water until thick. Add 3 Tbsp soy sauce and 2 tsp lemon juice and heat through.

SOUR CREAM HOLLANDAISE: Combine in a small saucepan 1 C sour cream, 3 egg yolks, 1 Tbsp lemon juice, ½ tsp dry mustard, ½ tsp Worcestershire sauce and ¼ tsp salt. Cook stirring until hot but not boiling and serve warm.

Braised Shank Beef or Oxtails

3 lb shank beef or oxtails cut into 2″ pieces
3 Tbsp margarine or butter or cooking oil
Two 10-oz cans consommé undiluted
1 medium onion sliced
1 green pepper chopped
2 C peeled and chopped tomatoes or
   canned tomatoes
3 long slim carrots sliced as thinly as possible
1 tsp salt
⅛ tsp pepper
½ tsp thyme or basil
Grated rind of ½ lemon
1 tsp lemon juice
1 garlic clove chopped

Brown either shank beef pieces or cut up oxtail in the margarine on both sides. Transfer to very large baking dish. In fat remaining in pan sauté the onion and garlic for 2 or 3 minutes. Add all remaining ingredients to frying pan, give a good stir, and tip over meat in casserole. Cover and bake at 300° for 4 hours. Serves five or six.

Carbonnade de Boeuf

2-lb slice boneless round steak
1 can Brown ale (or 1 bottle of beer)
2 Tbsp oil
1½ Tbsp chopped raw onion
1 tsp garlic powder
1 Tbsp flour
1 bay leaf
1 Tbsp parsley flakes
½ tsp thyme
½ tsp salt
1 tsp brown sugar
A few gratings of nutmeg

Put the steak in a shallow dish, pour ale over to cover and marinate in refrigerator overnight.

Drain and dry meat on paper towels. Reserve marinade. Cut meat into 4 or 5 pieces and sauté in oil in frying pan over high heat until brown on both sides. Transfer meat to shallow baking dish.

Into frying pan measure onion, garlic and flour and over low heat mix well. Add ale and stir until thick then add bay leaf, parsley, thyme, salt, sugar and nutmeg and mix. Pour over meat. Cover and bake at 225° for 3½ hours.

Serve with baked or mashed potatoes, noodles or corn pancakes.

Spiced Beef

Note: This requires 2 weeks' preparation.

7½ to 8 lb totally lean round of beef
1 oz saltpeter (buy at drugstore)
2 Tbsp brown sugar
2 tsp ground cloves
2 tsp grated nutmeg
2 tsp allspice
1 C non-iodized (pickling) salt
2 Tbsp finely crushed bay leaves
1 C water

In a bowl combine the saltpeter, sugar, spices, salt and bay leaves. Place beef on soft absorbent cloth large enough to wrap around beef generously. Sprinkle dry ingredients over beef rubbing them in on all surfaces. Wrap beef in the cloth and place in stone crock or crockery bowl and store in refrigerator. No water is required. Every day for 2 weeks turn beef and knead spices into it without removing cloth. During the marinating period the spices draw out quantities of juice. The liquid wetting the cloth keeps the whole beef marinating.

To cook, remove cloth, wash beef under tap water, removing most of the bay leaves. Place in round pan or dish, with 1 C water. Cover snugly with foil. Roast slowly, 3 to 3½ hours at 300°. Remove foil. While still hot pack beef into tight-fitting bowl or crock, cover with a heavy plate that fits within rim and weight down with clean rock until cool. Store in refrigerator and as needed cut very thin slices with razor sharp knife for luncheon plates or sandwiches.

Clay Baker Goulash

2 lb round steak (1½" cubes) or stewing beef
2 large onions, chopped
2 Tbsp butter or oil
1 green pepper, chopped
1 C warm water
1 beef bouillon cube
One 28-oz can tomatoes or 4 C peeled tomatoes, packed
One 5½-oz can tomato purée or paste
1 tsp salt
1 Tbsp paprika
1 or 2 Tbsp caraway seed
One 28-oz can sauerkraut, drained

To prepare clay baker—you can also use a covered baking dish—let soak in cold water while you prepare the ingredients.

In a very large frying pan heat the butter or oil and add the meat cubes and chopped onion. Sauté until meat is browned on all sides. Remove from heat and add all remaining ingredients. Mix well. Turn into the clay baker or large baking dish, cover snugly and set in cold oven. Turn heat to 325° and bake for 1½ hours then reduce heat to 300° and continue baking 1½ hours longer.

Serve with hashed brown potatoes, rye bread and a chef's salad. Eight servings.

Beef Hash

2 C ground cooked beef, packed
⅓ to ½ C leftover gravy
1 onion ground
2 C ground raw potatoes
½ tsp celery seed
¼ to ½ tsp salt
⅛ tsp pepper
2 Tbsp butter or margarine
¼ C cream (optional)

Note: Every good cook has a food grinder.

Grind cut up leftover cooked beef along with the onion and potatoes and mix well at once. Stir in gravy, celery seed, salt and pepper. Melt butter or margarine in large heavy frying pan and when bubbly turn in hash mixture and spread it out evenly. When it is golden on bottom stir and turn it over. If desired, pour over ¼ C cream. Cook slowly until a rich gold crust forms on bottom and potatoes have a waxy texture, not mushy. Divide into quarters and transfer, bottom side up, to preheated dinner plates. Serve with warm catsup. Four servings.

Bachelor Oven Pot Roast

Over a shallow baking dish about the size of a layer cake tin, spread a 2-foot length of foil. Stand a 2½-lb roast on it. In a cup mix together 1 tsp beef or chicken soup base, 1 tsp paprika and ¼ tsp garlic salt. Rub this into surfaces and into crevices of both cut sides of roast. Now bring ends of foil together and fold carefully on top and at sides. Put in cold oven. Turn heat to 225° and roast 4 hours.

To make Gravy, carefully tip juices under meat into a little pot. Mix together 1½ Tbsp flour and ¼ C water to a smooth paste. Stir into meat juices until thick, using wire whip to stir out any lumps.

Beef Stroganoff For Forty

17 lb of sirloin steaks
7 Tbsp butter
3 C chopped onions
4½ lb mushrooms
6 cans consommé, undiluted
3 Tbsp Worcestershire sauce
3½ tsp salt
1⅔ C flour
2 C red wine
5 C dairy sour cream
5½ lb noodles

Cut all fat, bones and gristle from steaks and cut into 3 × 1 × ¼" pieces of perfectly lean meat.

In large roasting pan sauté onions in butter until limp then add meat and cook at medium-high, stirring until all redness disappears, about half an hour constantly stirring. Add scrubbed, halved mushrooms, consommé, Worcestershire sauce and salt. Stir the flour into the wine with wire whip to a smooth paste and stir in until thickened. At this stage hold hot in oven at 275°. As serving time nears cook noodles in preserving kettle in very large amount of salted water, about 12 minutes. Stir sour cream into beef and return to oven to heat it through. Drain noodles. Serve Stroganoff from chafing dishes and noodles from outsize bowls or platters.

Marinated Flank Steak

2 lb flank steak
3 Tbsp vinegar
2 Tbsp water
¼ C salad oil
1 bay leaf
⅛ tsp garlic salt
⅛ tsp pepper
¼ tsp rosemary
½ tsp salt
6 juniper berries (optional)

Notes: 1. This is similar to the marinade used to tenderize and flavor venison. 2. Juniper berries are a delicious herb; if there are any juniper bushes on or near your property pick off some of the drier berries then dry them thoroughly at home and use in your meat cookery, especially with stewed lamb. 3. Change herbs given according to your family's taste.

Mix together the vinegar, oil and seasonings. Pour this marinade over the flank steaks and cover and refrigerate. Turn the steaks frequently leaving them for 1 to 3 days. When ready to serve drain and pat dry. Broil under hot broiler, turning once, until done according to your family's likes. Serves four.

Marinated Sirloin Steaks on a Bun

To serve ten, buy 2 extra thick and juicy large sirloins weighing nearly 3 lb each. When they are boned and some of the excess fat is trimmed you will have a little over 5 lb. With a rolling pin, pound these on a heavy workboard until flattened to nearly double their original area.

Then make Marinade: ¼ C oil, 2 Tbsp lemon juice, 2 Tbsp vinegar, 2 tsp Worcestershire sauce, 2 cloves garlic thinly sliced, 1 tsp rosemary, 1 tsp salt, ½ tsp dry mustard, ⅛ tsp white pepper. Mix together and pour half of it on a broiler pan and lay the steaks in it, then pour the remainder over, rubbing it into the surface with your fingertips. Let the steaks soak in this marinade for 5 hours, turning 3 or 4 times.

Cut pieces of steak to hamburg bun size and— fry both sides briefly. Serve in buns.

Belgian Beef Stew With Noodles

2 lb boneless chuck beef or round steak
¼ lb diced lean side bacon (about 4 slices)
Boiling water
2 Tbsp butter (divided, see below)
5 medium onions peeled and quartered
1 clove garlic chopped (or ¼ tsp bottled minced garlic)
3 Tbsp flour
2 tsp salt
¼ tsp pepper
One 12-oz bottle of beer
1 Tbsp lemon juice
Finely chopped parsley (optional)

In a small bowl pour boiling water over diced bacon to cover and let stand 1 minute. Drain. Discard liquid.

In frying pan melt 1 Tbsp of the butter. Add drained diced bacon, quartered onions and minced garlic. Cook, stirring frequently, until onions are golden and bacon limp and transparent. Transfer to heavy kettle.

Cut the meat into 1½" pieces. In frying pan melt the remaining 1 Tbsp butter over a high heat and add a few pieces of the meat at a time leaving them in only long enough to brown them. As pieces of meat are browned transfer to kettle. Stir in the flour, salt and pepper. Add the beer. Bring to boiling then reduce heat and simmer covered, 1½ hours. (Stir occasionally and if it becomes too thick add a little more beer.) Remove from heat and stir in the lemon juice.

Serve over noodles: a 12-oz pkg in large amount boiling salted water cooked until almost tender, about 12 minutes. Garnish with finely chopped parsley. Serves five or six.

Round Steak Roll

2-lb slice boneless round steak ½" thick
2 slices bacon chopped and sautéed
¼ C chopped green onion, including stems
1 small tomato finely chopped (about ⅔ C)
3 Tbsp prepared mustard (divided, see below)
2 Tbsp butter, melted
¼ C fine dry breadcrumbs

Cut steak in half lengthwise, trim fat and pound both sides with meat pounder or rolling pin to flatten and enlarge.

Meanwhile sauté bacon until nearly crisp. Add onions and stir-fry 1 minute longer. Remove from heat and skim bacon and onions out of fat. In a small bowl combine sautéed bacon and onion mixture, tomatoes and 2 Tbsp of the mustard. Spread this filling mixture over 1 slice of the steak. Top with second slice of steak, rolling up like a short jelly roll and tucking in any protruding ends. Tie securely with string at ½" intervals so that when cutting, each slice is held together with string. Place in shallow baking pan. Combine melted butter, breadcrumbs and remaining 1 Tbsp mustard. Spread over top of steak roll. Bake at 325° for 45 to 60 minutes until done to your liking. Slice between then remove strings, and serve on preheated platter.

Beef Stew Teriyaki Style

Note: This requires marinating 24 hours in advance.

1¼ lb stewing beef, preferably shank meat
¼ tsp powdered ginger
½ tsp garlic salt
1½ tsp sugar
2 Tbsp soy sauce
2 Tbsp sherry (or pineapple juice)
1½ C water (first amount)
½ tsp salt
1 C cubed (¾") carrots
1 C chopped celery
3 Tbsp flour
½ C water (second amount)

Before mealtime mix together in a deep pie plate the ginger, garlic salt, sugar, soy sauce and sherry. Tip the stewing beef into it and let stand half an hour. Turn all pieces of meat over, cover and refrigerate until next afternoon.

Three and a half hours before mealtime, tip into heavy pot with lid and mix well. Add water and salt and simmer covered 3½ hours, but half an hour before it is finished add the carrots and celery. Just before serving stir the 3 Tbsp flour into the ½ C cold water to make a smooth paste and stir in until thick. Serve over rice. Five servings.

Full Flavored Beef Stew

4 Tbsp margarine
1½ lb stewing beef (preferably shin)
½ C flour
1 tsp salt
⅛ tsp pepper
3 or 4 C hot water
1 beef bouillon cube
2 medium tomatoes peeled and quartered
    (or 1 C canned, drained)
4 medium onions, whole
4 medium carrots, quartered
4 medium potatoes, quartered
1 C chopped celery including some leaves

Melt margarine in frying pan. Dredge the cut-up beef in a mixture of the flour, salt and pepper and add the meat and all of the flour mixture to the pan and sear it, stirring, until golden on all sides. Add 2 C of the water, cover and simmer 2 hours, stirring occasionally. Add another cup of water, bouillon cube, tomatoes and whole onions and simmer, covered, ¾ hour more. Then add the potatoes, carrots and celery and 1 more cup water and simmer another ¾ hour. Serve with hot crusty rolls and a shredded cabbage salad. Serves three or four.

Oven Beef Stew

2 lb stewing beef cut into 1″ cubes
¼ C flour
¼ tsp thyme
¼ tsp marjoram or basil
¼ tsp celery seed
⅛ tsp sage
1¼ tsp salt
1/16 tsp pepper
4 medium onions, sliced
6 medium potatoes thinly sliced
2 medium carrots thinly sliced
1½ C hot water
2 beef bouillon cubes
1 tsp Worcestershire sauce
¼ C dry white wine or cooking sherry (optional)
Butter or margarine (see below)

Mix together flour and seasonings and dredge meat pieces in them. In a large casserole with tight-fitting cover arrange in layers half of the meat, half of the onions, half the potatoes and carrots. Then repeat. Add beef bouillon cubes to hot water and add Worcestershire sauce and wine if used. Pour evenly over casserole contents. Dot top with butter or margarine. Cover and bake at 325° for 3 hours. Serves six.

Hamburg

Blender Meat Loaf

2 broken up slices of bread
1 egg
½ C water
1 small onion quartered
1 cut up stalk celery
2 tsp salt
¼ tsp pepper
2 tsp Worcestershire sauce
2 lb ground beef

Blend all ingredients but the ground beef in your blender until finely chopped. Turn into bowl and mix with ground beef. Pack into ungreased loaf pan and bake at 350° for 75 minutes.

Peachy Meat Loaf

1 lb hamburg meat
½ lb sausage meat or chopped bologna
½ C fresh bread crumbs
½ C milk
1 small onion, finely chopped
1 egg
1¼ tsp salt
¼ tsp thyme
3 canned peach halves, drained
3 tsp crabapple jelly (or other red jelly)

Combine all ingredients except peach halves and crabapple jelly. Press into 1½-qt loaf pan. Arrange peach halves, depression side up, in a row, on top. Spoon jelly into depressions. Bake at 350° for 30 minutes, then carefully tip off all excess fat and bake 20 minutes longer. Serves four to six.

Sweet and Sour Meat Loaf

1 small onion, minced
1 C canned tomatoes
¼ C brown sugar
¼ C vinegar
¼ C crushed crackers
1 tsp prepared mustard
1 egg
2 lb hamburg meat
1 tsp salt
¼ tsp pepper

In small bowl mix onion, tomatoes, sugar and vinegar enough to break up tomatoes.

In larger bowl mix together crackers, mustard, egg, meat, salt and pepper. Add half of tomato sauce mix. Press into 1½-qt casserole or loaf pan. Pour over remaining tomato sauce. Bake at 400° for 45 minutes. Serves six.

Barbecued Beef Loaves

This makes eight individual loaves.

BARBECUE SAUCE
½ C butter or margarine
½ C chopped onion
½ C catsup
¼ C light brown sugar firmly packed
1½ tsp chili powder
3 Tbsp Worcestershire sauce
1 tsp salt
⅛ tsp pepper
⅛ tsp Tabasco sauce (optional)

MEAT MIXTURE
2 lb ground chuck
2 eggs
½ C cracker crumbs
⅓ C chopped green pepper
¼ C milk
¼ C catsup
1½ tsp salt
¼ tsp pepper
8 slices onion

Make Barbecue Sauce first: In a saucepan melt the butter or margarine, add onion and cook until limp and soaked in butter, about 3 minutes. Stir in all remaining sauce ingredients and simmer 5 minutes stirring occasionally.

To make Meat Mixture, in large bowl combine ground chuck, eggs, cracker crumbs, green pepper, milk, catsup, salt and pepper. Divide meat mixture into 8 equal portions. Place each on an 8 × 8 square of double foil. Shape each into a small meat loaf. Spoon 2 or 3 Tbsp Barbecue Sauce over each meat loaf and top each with a slice of onion. Bring up sides of foil and securely wrap and pinch them so juice cannot escape. Place foil packages on 2 large cookie sheets. Bake at 350° for about 35 or 45 minutes. (Shorter or longer period of baking depends on how well done you like your meat). Open one package and test for doneness. To serve remove foil. Top each with a slice of tomato and serve at once.

Hot or Cold Meat Loaf

2 lb sausage meat
1 lb ground chuck
1 C onion chopped
4 C fine fresh bread crumbs
¾ tsp poultry seasoning
1 egg

In a large bowl combine all meat loaf ingredients thoroughly. Pack meat mixture into a standard loaf pan and bake at 350° for 1¾ to 2 hours.

Notes: 1. Place loaf pan on foil or cookie sheet to prevent fat from spilling in your oven. 2. Check meat loaf after 1 hour to see if the surface is as brown as you would like it, cover loosely with a sheet of foil for remaining baking time. 3. Pour off accumulated fat once or twice during baking time, and when meat loaf is finished.

When cooked, carefully turn over and out on serving platter to cut hot at the table, or onto a large plate to cool thoroughly before wrapping and storing in refrigerator for a cold supper or hearty sandwiches.

Mixture For Meat Cakes or Meat Loaf

3 lb ground chuck
2 slices bread
1 C milk
2 eggs
¼ C catsup
1 tsp salt
2 tsp green onion flakes or chopped cooking
       or green onion
¼ tsp dry mustard
¼ tsp garlic salt

Into a big bowl put the slices of bread and pour the milk over them to soak while you add all remaining ingredients. Mix thoroughly to break up and mash the bread and mix it through the mass of meat evenly. For the current meal serve one of the following, freeze the other.

BROILED MEAT CAKES: For a family of four shape 4 large thick meat cakes using nearly half of the meat mixture. Wrap a long strip of side bacon around the edge of each and fasten in place with toothpicks. Broil 4″ from preheated broiler, turning when top is golden brown. Broil and brown other side. Do not overdo these, they should be pink inside when served.

MEAT LOAF: At the same time pack the remaining meat mixture into a medium baking dish or casserole. Cover with foil and freeze (or store in refrigerator if to be used within 2 days). When you wish to serve it, thaw and turn out on the center of a small roasting pan. You might parboil 10 small potatoes until they are nearly tender and arrange them around the meat loaf and bake all 1½ hours at 375°. At half time turn the potatoes over and sprinkle with salt and paprika. With Meat Loaf, serve Tomato Sauce.

TOMATO SAUCE: In a medium frying pan melt 4 Tbsp butter or margarine and add 1 finely chopped cooking onion and gently sauté without browning until tender and translucent. Stir in 3½ Tbsp cornstarch, then gently stir in one 20-oz can of tomatoes until thickened. Add 1 tsp salt and 1 tsp sugar. Serve generous amounts over or beside each serving of meat loaf.

Slumgullion

2 lb ground chuck
1 medium onion, chopped
1 green pepper, chopped
¼ lb mushrooms washed, drained, sliced
       (or one 4-oz can mushroom pieces, drained)
½ lb cheese, cubed
One 10-oz can tomato soup (undiluted)
One 19-oz can tomatoes
One 12-oz pkg ¼″ noodles
¼ C butter or margarine
2 C small buttered bread cubes (4 slices bread)

In large frying pan gently break up meat with fingers. Sauté onion and green pepper with meat until all redness disappears. (No fat is needed). Add sliced mushrooms, cheese, tomato soup and canned tomatoes and mix well. Simmer 5 minutes.

Meanwhile in large pot cook noodles in several cups of boiling, salted water 10 minutes. Drain through colander, return noodles to pot and add butter or margarine, tossing gently with fork until butter melts and evenly coats the noodles. Butter one large 3-qt casserole or 2 medium 1½-qt casseroles and spoon in alternate layers of noodles and meat mixture until all is used, beginning and ending with a noodle layer. Top with buttered bread cubes. (Butter each slice of bread first, then cut the bread into ¼″ cubes). Bake at 350° uncovered for 1 hour making sure bread cubes are golden and crisp.

Homemade Hamburgers

1 lb ground chuck
1 tsp salt
⅛ tsp pepper
1 tsp Worcestershire sauce
2 Tbsp finely chopped onion
½ C undiluted evaporated milk
1 Tbsp butter or margarine
4 or 6 buns
Onion rings and sliced tomatoes

Lightly mix beef, seasonings, onion and milk and shape into 4 or 6 patties. The mixture will be quite moist to handle. Have butter or margarine hot in frying pan, add patties and brown on each side, but do not overcook. Serve on buttered toasted buns with rings of onions and sliced tomatoes.

Spaghetti Sauce

This makes fourteen cups. The color is rosy and the flavor exceptionally good. Surplus may be frozen.

2 lb ground chuck
2 cooking onions, chopped
One 7½-oz can tomato sauce
One 10-oz can tomato soup, undiluted
One 13-oz can tomato paste
One 28-oz can tomatoes
3 C water
3 Tbsp sugar
2 Tbsp Worcestershire sauce
1 tsp Tabasco
3 tsp salt
1½ tsp oregano
1 tsp garlic salt
1 tsp basil
1 tsp celery seed
½ tsp pepper

In large pot without any fat sauté meat and onions until all redness disappears from meat, and onions are soft but not brown. Constantly chop to break it up as it cooks. Add all remaining ingredients and combine thoroughly. Simmer uncovered about 2½ to 3 hours, stirring often. Serve over fine almost tender noodles topped generously with Parmesan.

Baked Stuffed Green Peppers

6 medium small green peppers
1 lb hamburg or ground chuck
1 tsp minced onion
1 egg
½ tsp sugar
1 tsp salt
⅓ C rice
1⅔ C boiling water (divided)
1 C tomatoes (canned or fresh or
    canned tomato sauce)

Wash the green peppers, cut in halves lengthwise, remove seeds and ribs. Pour over them 1 C boiling water, cover and let stand over low heat 5 minutes. Pour ⅔ C boiling water over the rice and let stand covered until it soaks up the water. Mix all ingredients well. Drain peppers but save the liquid. Fill peppers with meat stuffing. Place on shallow baking dish. Pour reserved liquid around and bake 40 minutes at 375°.

Large Quantity Spaghetti Meat Sauce

2 lb ground chuck
3 bay leaves, crushed
1 lb fresh mushrooms, washed and chopped finely
2 cloves garlic, chopped finely
2 large green peppers, chopped finely
2½ C onions, chopped finely
Two 13-oz cans tomato paste
One 28-oz can tomato sauce plus one 7½-oz can
    tomato sauce
2 Tbsp Italian seasoning
2½ Tbsp salt
½ C granulated sugar
1 tsp pepper
5 (or more) chili peppers
9 C water

In very large preserving kettle brown and break up constantly the ground chuck until redness disappears. Add bay leaves, mushrooms, garlic, green peppers, cooking onions and 2 C of the tomato sauce and combine. Add all remaining ingredients including remaining tomato sauce and simmer steadily, uncovered, for 2 hours, stirring frequently. Make sure you fish out all the chili peppers at the end of the cooking time. If you wish the sauce to have a darker color, add about 1½ tsp red food coloring. Serve over almost tender spaghetti or noodles topped with Parmesan. Surplus may be frozen.

Beef Porcupines

2½ lb ground round steak or chuck
1 C soft whole wheat breadcrumbs
2 eggs
1½ tsp salt (first amount)
½ tsp paprika
1 beef bouillon cube
1 C raw long grain rice
One 28-oz can tomatoes
1 C water
1 tsp chili powder (optional)
1 tsp salt (second amount)

In a large bowl mix together the meat, crumbs, eggs, salt, paprika and melted beef bouillon cube. Measure 1 C raw long grain rice onto a large plate. Shape the meat mixture into twelve 2½" balls. Roll each in raw rice to coat completely.

In a very large frying pan combine the tomatoes, water, chili powder and second amount salt and bring to boil. Place rice-coated meat balls in the tomato sauce carefully in one layer. Do not crowd. Simmer 1 hour. Rice on bottom of balls is softer than top but do not be tempted to turn them or you will misplace the top rice. The rice on top swells and cooks and is tender and sticks out like porcupine quills. Carefully transfer to preheated serving platter and pour sauce around.

Sweet and Sour Meat Balls

This recipe makes 64 meat balls, serves 16. Half could be frozen.

MEAT BALLS

2 lb sausage meat
1½ lb ground chuck
2 C rolled oats
2 eggs
½ C evaporated milk
1½ tsp Worcestershire sauce
2 tsp onion powder
1 tsp celery seed
½ tsp salt
¼ tsp pepper
⅛ tsp garlic powder

SWEET AND SOUR SAUCE

⅞ C vinegar
¼ C lemon juice
5 Tbsp cornstarch
Two 10-oz cans consommé undiluted
1¼ C brown sugar, packed
½ C corn syrup
⅛ tsp garlic powder

Prepare meat balls by thoroughly combining all meat mixture ingredients in large bowl. Roll tightly into 1″ balls between your floured palms. Roll in flour to lightly coat. Place as many as possible in cold frying pan (no fat), turn heat to medium-high and brown on all sides. Remove to paper towelling to drain. Fat now in pan rendered from sausage in balls is sufficient to prevent sticking. Continue until all meat balls are browned and drained, then place in very large pot or small roasting pan.

Prepare Sweet and Sour Sauce mixture by combining in a medium bowl the vinegar, lemon juice and cornstarch to a smooth paste. Stir in consommé, brown sugar, garlic powder and corn syrup. Pour over meat balls. Return to heat, bring to boil, then reduce heat and simmer, uncovered, half an hour spooning sauce over meat balls several times. Serve from preheated bowl or chafing dish with mashed potatoes, fluffy rice or noodles.

Meat Balls Stroganoff

1 lb lean minced beef (not hamburg)
1 tsp salt
¼ tsp pepper
¼ C milk
1 egg, beaten
½ C fine dry breadcrumbs
2 Tbsp salad or cooking oil
½ C chopped onions
One 10-oz can whole mushrooms, drained
2 Tbsp flour
¼ tsp paprika
One 10-oz can condensed cream of
   mushroom soup
1 C dairy sour cream
8 oz noodles

Combine minced beef, salt, pepper, milk, egg and crumbs. Mix thoroughly. Shape into 1½″ balls. In heated oil in frying pan, brown meat balls on all sides. Remove meat balls to a warm platter.

Add onion and mushrooms to frying pan and sauté until onion is transparent, about 5 minutes. Stir in flour and seasonings. Add undiluted soup and simmer over low heat for 5 minutes, until sauce thickens. Stir in dairy sour cream. Add meat balls. Cover and keep over very low heat until meat balls are cooked through, at least 15 minutes. Serve over cooked noodles.

To cook noodles, have 3 qts water boiling with 1 Tbsp salt. Add noodles, stir until water returns to boiling, then cook until almost tender, about 10 minutes. Drain through colander and turn onto preheated serving platter. Serves six.

Hawaiian Meat Balls

This recipe serves eight. Double it if you are having 16 people to a party, or halve it if there are only 4 to serve for a family meal.

MEAT BALLS

2 lb ground chuck
2 eggs
¼ C green onion flakes
½ tsp garlic salt
½ tsp salt
2 Tbsp Shortening
Flour

SWEET AND SOUR SAUCE

6 Tbsp brown sugar
¼ tsp ginger
½ tsp garlic salt
¼ tsp dry mustard
½ tsp salt
½ tsp onion powder
2 Tbsp cornstarch
¼ C vinegar
1 C water
6 Tbsp catsup
2 Tbsp soy sauce
One 10-oz can crushed pineapple and juice

To make Meat Balls, mix together ground beef, eggs, green onion flakes, garlic salt and salt, and shape into thirty-five 1″ balls. Dredge with flour and, in large frying pan, brown on all sides in shortening. Remove meat balls from pan.

To make Sweet and Sour Sauce, mix dry sauce ingredients well. Stir in wet sauce ingredients. Turn into fat in pan and stir until thick and boiling. Return meat balls to pan, cover and simmer 10 minutes. Serve over or with fluffy boiled rice.

Devilled Meat Balls

2 lb best quality lean ground beef
One 4½-oz can devilled ham
½ tsp salt
½ tsp garlic powder
¼ tsp pepper
½ C catsup
½ C fine dry breadcrumbs
2 Tbsp prepared mustard (preferably Dijon)
4 tsp horseradish
2 eggs

Variation 1: WINE SAUCE
Two 8-oz cans tomato sauce
½ C dry red wine
2 Tbsp sugar

Variation 2: BUTTERMILK SAUCE
1¾ C buttermilk
½ lb diced process Swiss cheese
2 tsp cornstarch
⅛ tsp pepper
¾ tsp dry mustard
6 drops Tabasco

To make meat balls, in a large bowl combine all meat ball ingredients. Shape into 40 balls and place on 2 greased baking sheets about 1½″ apart. Bake at 475° for 15 to 20 minutes. Transfer to chafing dish or preheated deep platter and pour sauce over.

To make Wine Sauce, simply combine all ingredients and heat, stirring until barely boiling. Pour over meat balls and serve.

To make Buttermilk Sauce, combine all ingredients in top of double boiler and cook, stirring until somewhat thickened.

Chili Con Carne, Mild and Mexican

1 lb dry red kidney beans (or two 20-oz cans)
1¾ lb ground chuck
1 bay leaf
1 onion chopped
3½ C peeled and chopped tomatoes
    (or one 28-oz can)
3 tsp salt
3 tsp (or more) chili powder
2 tsp paprika
⅛ to ¼ tsp cayenne pepper (optional, see below)
¼ tsp garlic powder (optional)

In large pot soak the beans in 6 C cold water six hours or overnight. Add enough water to cover 1″ above beans, bring to boil, reduce heat to simmer, and cook covered 1 hour.

In very large frying pan or heavy kettle sauté meat, bay leaf and onions, stirring and chopping constantly until fat is rendered out of chuck and meat is seared. No other fat is required. Add tomatoes, salt, chili powder and paprika and stir until boiling. Simmer at least half an hour, preferably longer. Drain beans and measure the drained liquid. Make it up to 2½ C. Add beans and liquid to pan or pot and gently stir until boiling, and simmer a few minutes longer. If canned beans are used add as you would cooked beans, including liquid in cans, plus one additional cup of water. Taste to see if seasonings should be increased.

Serve in large soup bowls with toast, preferably rye.

For Mexican Chili Con Carne, add the optional cayenne pepper and garlic powder and taste. Add more cayenne if you wish it hotter. Serves eight.

Modest Meat Pies

FILLING
4 lb ground beef
1 C chopped onion
4 Tbsp flour
4 C water
4 Tbsp liquid bovril
Two 10-oz cans mixed peas and carrots undrained
1 tsp salt

PASTRY
5½ C unsifted all-purpose flour
1 tsp salt
1 lb lard
1 egg
2 Tbsp vinegar
Water (see below)

This makes six 7″ freezable meat pies. Make the Filling first by browning the meat in Dutch oven or large pot on high heat, stirring frequently to prevent sticking, for 20 minutes. Add chopped onion and flour and stir in. Add water and bovril and cover and simmer 1 hour. Add salt and cool. Add peas and carrots and liquid from cans.

To make Pastry, in large bowl cut lard into flour and salt with pastry blender until size of peas. Beat egg in 8-oz measuring cup, add vinegar, then fill cup with cold water. Add to flour mixture, tossing with fork until mixture holds together. Roll dough out and line six 7″ foil pie plates and fill each with meat filling. Roll, cut out and gash 6 top crusts and seal on filled pies, crimping edges.

Bake number of pies for current meal at 425° for 10 minutes, then 375° for 20 minutes longer. Wrap and freeze remaining pies.

Individual Meat Pies

Line individual pie plates or muffin tins with best quality pastry. Then make Meat Pie Filling.

MEAT PIE FILLING
⅔ C undiluted evaporated milk
1½ lb ground beef
½ C fine cracker crumbs
1 egg
1½ tsp salt
¼ tsp pepper
1 tsp dry mustard
¼ C finely chopped onion
½ C finely chopped green pepper (optional)

Mix all ingredients together and fill individual pies ⅔ full. Cut out gashed pastry tops to fit top and seal edges. Bake at 450° for 10 minutes then reduce heat to 350° until delicate brown on bottom, about 10 minutes longer. Exact time depends on the size of your individual pie tins.

Salisbury Steaks with Onion Gravy or Celery Sauce

1 lb ground beef
½ lb bulk sausage meat
1½ C cooked rice (see below)
1 tsp salt
½ tsp pepper
2 eggs

Variation 1: ONION GRAVY
3 C water (divided, see below)
1 pkg onion soup mix
2 Tbsp flour

Variation 2: CELERY SAUCE
1 can of cream of celery soup
1 C hot milk
½ C buttered crumbs
1 tsp paprika

For 1½ C cooked rice, cook ½ C raw long grain rice in 1¼ C boiling water, covered, until tender and all water is absorbed, starting it on high heat and when boiling, reducing heat as low as possible.

Combine beef, sausage meat, cooked rice, salt, pepper and eggs. Shape into 6 slightly flattened footballs. Place in greased baking dish and bake at 450° for 40 minutes. Serve with either Gravy or Sauce, below.

ONION GRAVY: Heat 2½ C of the water, add onion soup mix and cook, covered, 10 minutes. Mix flour with remaining ½ C water until smooth and gradually stir into soup. Cook, stirring, until thickened. Serve in separate sauceboat.

CELERY SAUCE: Pour off excess fat from pan (after first 20 minutes' baking period) and pour over the Salisbury steaks the celery soup mixed with hot milk. Sprinkle top with ½ C buttered crumbs mixed with 1 tsp paprika and bake 20 minutes longer at 350°. Serves six.

Pork, Veal, & Lamb

Roast Loin of Pork

4½ lb pork loin

Notes: 1. Be sure the butcher has chopped through the backbone at regular intervals to make carving easy. 2. If you have a meat thermometer insert it at the center top of the roast.

Rub the top fat surface of the pork loin with a mixture of ½ tsp each of salt, paprika, rosemary and ¼ tsp black pepper. Place on rack in roasting pan. Roast at 325° for 40 to 45 minutes per lb or until internal temperature registers 185°, (well done). You may choose to roast at 200° for 5 hours or until internal temperature registers 185°, (well done). This latter temperature is preferable. Pork should always be well done.

GRAVY: Transfer roast to preheated serving platter and tip 6 Tbsp fat from pan into saucepan including the sediment. Discard surplus fat. Stir 5½ Tbsp flour into it and add 1 beef bouillon cube, otherwise this gravy is pale in color. Stir in 3 C hot water until thick. (Liquid from cooking mild-flavored vegetables such as potatoes or carrots or beans may be used as some of the liquid.) Taste the gravy and add salt and pepper as desired.

PAN ROASTED POTATOES: These are ideal with roast pork, if you are roasting at 325°. Cut potatoes in halves crosswise and parboil in salted water for 10 minutes. Drain. Add to roasting pan 1¼ hours before roast is due to be done, turning them over once and sprinkling with salt and a little paprika.

Marinated Roast of Pork

One 4- or 5-lb roast of pork: loin or shoulder cut
2 large onions sliced
2 carrots sliced
2 stalks celery sliced
5 bay leaves
8 whole peppercorns
Medium dry red wine

Carefully trim excess fat from roast. Lower roast into a deep glass or enamel or crockery bowl. Add vegetables, bay leaves and peppercorns, tucking them under, around and on top of roast. Pour over enough wine to almost cover the meat. Cover bowl and refrigerate for 24 hours, turning roast a couple of times during this period. As mealtime approaches, drain and dry roast and strain and reserve marinade. Discard solids.

Place marinated roast on rack in open pan. Sprinkle with salt and pepper. Roast at 325°. A 4-lb loin roast requires 2½ hours, a 5-lb roast 3¼ hours. A 4-lb shoulder roast requires 3 hours, a 5-lb shoulder roast 3½ hours. Baste frequently with a little of the reserved strained marinade.

To make gravy carefully skim fat from pan drippings. Add remaining marinade to pan drippings. Measure. For each cup combine 1 Tbsp flour with ¼ C cream or evaporated milk until smooth and stir in until thick. To be sure there are no lumps, beat with wire whisk or strain.

Honey Garlic Spareribs

3 lbs short meaty spareribs cut into 1-rib pieces
MARINADE
Grated rind from 1 orange
½ C soy sauce
⅓ C honey
½ tsp garlic salt
¼ tsp pepper

Arrange the ribs on your broiler pan in one layer. Mix together the grated orange rind, soy sauce, honey, garlic salt and pepper. Pour evenly over ribs and let stand 1 hour at room temperature, turning all ribs over at halftime. Bake at 325° for 1 hour, turning ribs over when half baked. Serves four.

Ham and Pork Roll

1 lb ground or finely chopped cooked ham
1 lb sausage meat
½ tsp minced garlic
1 small onion, finely chopped
2 tsp salt (divided, see below)
½ tsp pepper
½ to 1½ tsp curry powder
¾ tsp sage
1 egg white
¼ C white or rosé wine
¼ C evaporated milk
8 or 9 slices bacon
2 qts boiling water
¼ C vinegar

In large bowl combine thoroughly the cooked ham and sausage meat, garlic, onion, 1 tsp salt, pepper, curry powder, sage, egg white, wine and evaporated milk. With your hands make sure everything is evenly mixed.

Rinse a cheesecloth in cold water and wring out. Place 8 or 9 strips of bacon side by side touching, down the length of the cloth so you have a 12″ wide area of bacon. Pile meat onto bacon and shape meat into a long roll measuring 12″ long and 4″ wide. Fold bacon strips around loaf. Roll loaf up in the cloth and tie both ends very tightly with string—like a Christmas cracker. Also tie a loose string around the middle. Holding surplus cloth at each end of roll, transfer to a rack in a large kettle. Add boiling water, remaining 1 tsp salt and vinegar. Cover and simmer 2½ hours. Tip off liquid. Lift out roll and let stand 10-15 minutes on paper towelling. Unwrap while still warm. Delicious hot or cold. Serves eight.

Note: Do not let meat roll stand longer than 10-15 minutes without unwrapping it or bacon will stick to cloth and pull away from meat.

Baked Ham with Mustard Glaze

One 5- to 7-lb bone-in smoked ham or
　　smoked picnic shoulder
1 C brown sugar
2 tsp dry mustard
3 Tbsp flour
3 Tbsp vinegar
Whole cloves

With sharp pointed knife remove all rind from ham. Trim fat to an even thinness. Bake on rack in an open pan at 325° for 25 minutes to the pound: total time about 2½ to 3 hours. Then cut gashes diagonally in fat to form diamonds. Place in clean baking dish.

To make Glaze, combine brown sugar, mustard, flour and vinegar. Spread over meat and insert cloves in design. Bake uncovered about 15 minutes at 425°, basting occasionally. Let stand 5 minutes. Spoon glaze over top when ham is on serving platter.

Roast Ham with Orange Glaze

One 10- to 12-lb whole ham
One 6-oz can frozen orange juice concentrate,
　　thawed, undiluted
¼ C molasses
¼ C prepared mustard
3 Tbsp grated orange rind
⅛ tsp Tabasco
Whole cloves

Place ham on rack in a shallow baking pan. Bake at 325° for 3 hours. Remove ham from oven and neatly remove rind and half of the fat. Carefully score fat surface and stud with whole cloves. For glaze, blend together undiluted orange juice concentrate, molasses, mustard, orange rind and Tabasco. Brush part of mixture over ham without disturbing cloves. Bake 45 minutes longer, brushing with remaining glaze at 15 minute intervals.

Baked Stuffed Pork Tenderloins

2 whole pork tenderloins, about ¾ lb each
6 strips bacon

STUFFING
2 Tbsp butter
¼ C finely chopped celery
2 Tbsp finely chopped onion
2 Tbsp finely chopped green pepper
2 C soft bread crumbs (not packed)
½ C chopped apple
2 Tbsp raisins
¾ tsp salt
⅛ tsp pepper
¼ tsp poultry seasoning or thyme
1 Tbsp red currant jelly
Shake of nutmeg

On a board split tenderloins almost through lengthwise. Open them up and pound a little with rolling pin to make them flat and thinner.

Melt the butter in a large frying pan and add celery, onion and green pepper and sauté gently, stirring. Add bread crumbs and combine and cook slightly until crumbs are soaked. Remove from heat and add apple, raisins, seasonings, red currant jelly and nutmeg and mix well.

Cover one flattened tenderloin with stuffing. Place second tenderloin on top. Arrange strips of bacon touching side by side on counter and lift prepared tenderloins on to them. Draw ends of bacon up and over and wrap. Fasten securely with toothpicks. Transfer to small roasting pan and roast at 325° about 1½ hours until tender. Do not overbake. Serves six.

Melton Mowbray Pie

Notes: 1. If you make this into individual pies you will require more pastry, about 1½ times as much. 2. The following amount of gelatin results in a very firm filling. If desired reduce gelatin to 2 Tbsp.

ENGLISH PASTRY
3 C unsifted flour
1 Tbsp baking powder
1½ tsp salt
1½ C best-quality shortening
¾ C boiling water
1 Tbsp lemon juice
1 egg yolk.

Sift together the flour, baking powder and salt and cut in ¾ C of the shortening with a pastry blender. To remaining shortening add the boiling water and stir until shortening is melted. Add lemon juice, then the egg yolk and stir. Stir this into the flour mixture then knead for 3 minutes. Chill for 1 hour so it may be handled easily. Divide pastry into 2 portions. One portion should be about ⅔ of the dough, with which line sides and bottom of medium-large baking dish. Reserve remaining pastry for top.

FILLING
1 lb pork shoulder
1 lb veal or beef shoulder
1 lb ham (uncooked)
2 small onions
2 Tbsp Worcestershire sauce
1 tsp sage
1 tsp thyme
¼ tsp pepper
¾ tsp salt
4 hard-cooked eggs
3 Tbsp gelatin
1 can consommé, undiluted.

Cut eggs in half lengthwise and place 4 halves in bottom of pastry-lined pan. Cut meat into small cubes and mix with chopped onions and seasonings. Arrange half of meat mixture over eggs. Repeat layers. Seal top pastry to edges. Cut 2 small holes in top. Bake at 425° until light brown, about 15 minutes. Reduce heat to 250° and bake 2½ hours longer, or until meat is tender. When pie is baked and still hot, soften gelatin in ¼ C cold water. Dissolve in the 1 can hot undiluted consommé. Pour through holes in top of hot pie slowly. Refrigerate overnight. Slice and serve cold.

Baked Ham Steak with Orange Topping

One center cut ham steak 1¼″ thick (or two 4¼″ diameter slices from ready-to-eat ham —see below)

TOPPING
Grated rind from 1 orange
¼ C raisins
1 Tbsp orange juice
1 Tbsp melted butter or margarine
Segments from 1 orange each cut in half
2 Tbsp brown sugar

Place ham slice on baking dish. Cover and bake at 325° for 1 hour. Combine all Topping ingredients and spread over cooked ham slice but not too close to edges. Return to oven for 20 to 25 minutes.

If you are using two ready-to-eat ham slices the 1 hour roasting time is not necessary. Simply spread Topping on the two slices and bake uncovered about 25 minutes at 325°.

Shoulder Pork Roast with Herb Fruit Stuffing

One 3-lb boneless pork shoulder roast
STUFFING
2 C fine bread crumbs, not packed
½ C finely chopped celery or 1½ tsp celery seed
1 small cooking onion finely chopped
½ finely chopped cored and seeded green pepper
¼ C melted butter or margarine
1 tsp poultry seasoning
1 tsp salt
⅛ tsp pepper
1 Tbsp parsley flakes or finely chopped
      fresh parsley
½ C finely chopped apple (skin included)
¼ C finely chopped dried apricots
      (optional but recommended)
2 Tbsp apple juice or water

To prepare Stuffing, in frying pan sauté celery (or celery seed), onion and green pepper in butter or margarine until limp but not brown. Meanwhile in large bowl combine thoroughly the bread crumbs, poultry seasoning, salt, pepper, parsley flakes (or fresh parsley), apple, apricots (if used) and apple juice (or water). Add sautéed vegetables and their butter and mix to completely coat crumbs with butter.

Split open pork roast and pack all of the stuffing tightly on bottom half. Stuffing layer is quite thick. Place top half of pork roast on stuffing, press together, bind and tie securely with string at 8 evenly spaced intervals around the roast. Place roast on rack in small roasting pan and roast, uncovered, at 225° for 4 hours with meat thermometer at center of bottom layer of pork. It should register 175° when done. This low-slow roasting of the pork assures tenderness and retains moisture. Remove from oven and let rest a few minutes before carving, but do not cut off strings until meat is sliced. Slice with very sharp knife. Applesauce is a good accompaniment. Serves eight.

Homemade Headcheese

2 lb pork hocks
4 C hot water
1 bay leaf
1 slice onion
1 stalk celery chopped
8 pepper berries
2 pkgs plain gelatin (about 1¾ Tbsp)
½ tsp basil
1 tsp salt

Wash pork hocks and add hot water, bay leaf, onion, celery and pepper berries and simmer covered 4 hours. Drain through colander catching all broth, about 2 ½ C. Chill then skim off all fat. Remove meat and discard bones. Put meat through coarse knife of grinder. You may include some of the gelatinous cartilage for it is good protein.

To the fat-free broth add the gelatin, salt and basil and heat, stirring, to dissolve gelatin. Immediately remove from heat. Add ground meat and mix. Pour into a 4-cup mold of any shape and chill. This jellied meat mold is full of rich flavor and slices excellently.

Savory Baked Pork Chops

½ C raw long grain rice
1 C boiling water
¼ tsp salt
Twelve ¾″ thick pork chops
½ small onion chopped
One 10-oz can cream of celery soup
1 tsp salt (second amount)
1 tsp Worcestershire sauce
½ tsp savory
2 Tbsp catsup
1 soup can full of hot water

Cook the rice first in the boiling water with the ¼ tsp salt, covered, 25 minutes.

Trim the excess fat from the pork chops and arrange in one layer, overlapping, in large shallow baking dish.

As soon as the rice is cooked gently stir all remaining ingredients into it and blend. Using a big spoon, ladle the sauce evenly over the top, covering all of the pork chops. Now cover snugly with foil. If you prepare this in advance, store it in the refrigerator until baking time. Bake at 350° for 1 hour, covered with foil throughout entire baking period. Serves six.

Deluxe Sausage Rolls

This recipe makes a large quantity of flaky pastry. Use what you need and freeze remainder for future.

PASTRY

5 C unsifted cake and pastry flour
1 lb shortening
2 tsp baking powder
2 tsp icing or granulated sugar
1 tsp salt
1 egg, beaten
2 tsp vinegar
Water (see below)

MEAT FILLING

1 lb sausage meat (in bulk or chub)
1 small onion, finely chopped
¼ green pepper, finely chopped
½ C water
½ C fine breadcrumbs
1 egg, beaten
1 beef bouillon cube
¾ tsp summer savory
½ tsp salt
¼ tsp sage
¼ tsp garlic salt
⅛ tsp pepper

To make Pastry, in bowl combine flour, baking powder, icing sugar and salt. Cut in shortening with pastry blender until size of peas. In a one-cup measure combine egg and vinegar and stir to blend. Add water to bring liquid up to ¾ cup mark. Pour into flour mixture and stir until thoroughly combined and dough will pack into a ball between your palms. Wrap in wax paper or plastic bag and chill in refrigerator while you prepare filling.

To make Meat Filling, in large frying pan sauté sausage meat with onion and green pepper until meat is browned. Mash constantly with potato masher to break up meat finely. Remove from heat. Tip frying pan and drain off all fat. Stir in all remaining ingredients, return to low heat and cook, stirring for 5 minutes. Let cool completely before assembling rolls.

To assemble, roll out about one-half of the chilled pastry to ⅛″ thickness. Cut into eighteen 4″ squares. Wrap and freeze remainder. You will have to pick up scrap ends and roll them several times before you have 18 pastry squares. Take 3 heaping teaspoonfuls of filling and with your hands shape it like a 4″ link sausage. Place at center of square of pastry and lap sides. These are open-ended. Place fold side down on baking sheet. Continue until all filling is used up. Brush each roll with a mixture of 1 Tbsp sugar dissolved in 1 Tbsp milk. Bake at 400° for 15 minutes then reduce heat to 350° and bake 20 to 25 minutes longer. Serve hot.

Party Pork, Chinese Style

1 lb pork shoulder or pork chops trimmed
    and cut in ¾" cubes
¼ C flour
1½ tsp salt
⅛ tsp pepper
2 Tbsp butter or oil
1 C celery, diced
1 green pepper, slivered
1 small onion, sliced thinly
One 19-oz can pineapple tidbits, undrained
¾ C catsup
½ C brown sugar, packed
1 Tbsp prepared mustard
1 Tbsp Worcestershire sauce

Trim off fat and cut pork into ¾" cubes. In a small bowl combine flour, salt and pepper and dredge pieces of meat in it to completely coat. Heat the oil in a large frying pan and brown the meat pieces. Reserve any leftover flour for later.

Meanwhile in large bowl mix thoroughly the celery, green pepper, onion, pineapple and juice, catsup, brown sugar, mustard, Worcestershire sauce and flour left from dredging. Pour over browned meat and mix. Cover and simmer 30 minutes.

Serve over fluffy boiled rice cooked by adding 1 C raw long grain rice to 2½ C boiling water and ½ tsp salt and simmer, covered, 30 minutes. Serves four.

Baked Spareribs

2 lb pork side spareribs

SAUCE
One 10-oz can condensed tomato soup
½ C chopped celery
½ C chopped onion
2 Tbsp vinegar
2 tsp prepared mustard
2 tsp Worcestershire sauce
⅛ tsp Angostura Bitters or Tabasco Sauce

Trim excess fat from spareribs. Cut strips into pieces of 2 ribs each and layer in large baking dish with cover. Combine all sauce ingredients and carefully pour over top, easing some into crevices between ribs. Cover and bake at 350° for 2 hours, turning ribs over once at halftime during baking period. Serves four.

Egg and Bacon Pie

Pastry for 2-crust pie
1 lb side bacon cut into bite-sized pieces
4 eggs
¼ C milk
1 Tbsp bottled onion flakes or ¼ C chopped onion
½ tsp salt
⅛ tsp pepper

Into large frying pan put bacon and sauté until transparent. Tip off excess fat. Finish sautéeing until crisp. Remove from heat. Beat eggs until mixed. Reserve 1 Tbsp beaten egg for brushing top of pie. Add milk, onion and seasonings and add to bacon in pan and stir over low heat until barely set. Cool. Pour into deep 9" pastry-lined pie plate. Cover with gashed top crust and seal edges. Brush top crust with reserved beaten egg. Bake at 450° for 10 minutes then reduce heat to 350° for 20 to 30 minutes longer or until crust is evenly golden.

French Canadian Tourtière

PASTRY
4 C stirred but unsifted all-purpose flour
2 tsp salt
¼ tsp turmeric (optional)
1⅓ C shortening
⅓ C butter
4 Tbsp ice cold water

FILLING
2¼ lb ground lean fresh pork
2 C raw shredded potatoes (packed)
1 C chopped onion
2½ tsp salt
1 tsp savory
¼ tsp ground cloves
1 clove garlic finely chopped
½ tsp sage (optional)
½ C hot water
½ C soft breadcrumbs
1 small egg (for glaze)
1 Tbsp water (for glaze)

Make Filling first: Combine all filling ingredients except breadcrumbs, egg and water, and cook stirring in large pot until meat is grey and hot then cover and simmer 30 minutes. Cool, then stir in crumbs.

To make Pastry: Cut the shortening and butter into the flour, salt and turmeric until size of large peas. Drizzle in water, 1 Tbsp at a time, tossing with fork. Pack into ball between palms. Roll three-fifths of this pastry to line bottom and sides of a deep 10" baking dish. Roll out remaining pastry for top. Transfer to plate and chill all pastry in refrigerator while filling is cooling.

Pour cooled filling into pastry-lined baking dish and cover with well-gashed top crust and seal and crimp edges. Glaze top by brushing with the one small egg beaten with the 1 Tbsp water. Bake at 400° for 40 minutes or until rich gold and filling is bubbling through gashes. Serves ten.

Quiche Lorraine

PASTRY

1 C all-purpose flour
⅓ C shortening
½ tsp salt
2 Tbsp cold water

FILLING

2 C well-packed ground cooked ham
2 eggs
1½ C milk (or ¾ C each milk and cream)
½ tsp prepared mustard
1 tsp minced onion
1 C grated old Cheddar cheese

To make Pastry, cut shortening into flour and salt and add water gradually, mixing lightly with fork until dough may be pressed into a ball. Roll out to fit 9″ pie plate and bake 5 minutes at 450°.

In a bowl combine ground cooked ham, eggs, milk (or milk and cream), mustard and onion. Beat to mix well and pour into partially baked crust. Reduce heat to 250° and bake 45 minutes. Ten minutes before baking time is up sprinkle top with 1 C grated old Cheddar cheese. Raise pie to upper shelf of oven and raise heat to 375° to brown top.

Pork Parmegiano

1 lb ⅛″-thick sliced fresh lean pork (or veal)
2 small eggs, beaten
1 Tbsp water
1¼ C fine dry breadcrumbs
½ C salad or olive oil

TOMATO SAUCE

2 Tbsp salad or olive oil
½ C minced onion
1 garlic clove chopped
2 C canned tomatoes (preferably Italian)
1 Tbsp sugar
½ to 1 tsp salt
½ tsp oregano
¼ tsp basil
⅛ tsp pepper
½ lb sliced Mozzarella cheese
Grated Parmesan cheese

If you are on friendly terms with your butcher ask him to slice boned fresh pork loin as thinly as possible and to trim off all fat and weigh out 1 lb. If you cannot get this service buy about 1½ lb pork loin and bone it out, cut off fat and with razor-sharp knife slice it ⅛″ thick.

Make Tomato Sauce by sautéing onion and garlic in oil until limp, about 3 minutes. Add tomatoes, sugar and seasonings and bring to boil, stirring, then simmer covered 10 minutes. Remove from heat.

Beat eggs with water and dip slices of pork in it then into crumbs and fry in oil until golden on both sides, adding more oil as needed. Have ready a large shallow baking dish. Cover bottom with 1 layer of fried pork. Pour half the tomato sauce over. Cover with half the Mozzarella. Repeat these 3 layers. Sprinkle top with Parmesan and bake at 375° until golden and boiling at edges, about 25 minutes.

Skewered Wieners

1 lb wieners
About 24 medium mushrooms (about ½ lb)
2 green peppers
One 19-oz can chunk pineapple

Scrub mushrooms, cut wieners into 3 even pieces each, cut green peppers into 1¼″ squares. Drain the pineapple. Put all ingredients on separate plates. Start skewering with a green pepper square, then a piece of wiener, then a pineapple cube, then mushroom, carefully impaling whole mushroom including stem. Repeat, nearly filling skewers. Place on grill 6 or 8″ above glowing embers and turning as soon as bottoms are cooked.

Barbecued or Broiled Pork Chops

8 thick loin pork chops

BEER BARBECUE SAUCE

1 C bottled barbecue sauce
1 C beer
1 tsp Worcestershire sauce
2 tsp salt

TOMATO BARBECUE SAUCE

1 C tomato juice
¼ C vinegar
2 tsp sugar
1 tsp salt
¼ tsp pepper
⅛ tsp garlic salt

Mix together either Beer or Tomato Barbecue Sauce ingredients (or simply use bottled barbecue sauce).

To serve eight, select rib, loin or shoulder chops cut 1¼″ thick. Place on grill 5″ from coals or preheated broiler. Broil for 10 or 15 minutes on each side, brushing with Barbecue Sauce of your choice on both sides. Serve hot from the grill.

Barbecued Spareribs

3½ to 4 lb spareribs (about 3 lean strips)

SAUCE

½ C catsup
2 Tbsp HP sauce
2 Tbsp cider vinegar
¼ C water
¼ tsp Worcestershire sauce
½ clove garlic chopped
½ tsp salt

Combine all barbecue sauce ingredients about 1 hour before needed.

Spread spareribs in shallow baking pan and roast for 1 hour at 350° then drain off all fat. Re-arrange ribs in pan and brush liberally on top with prepared barbecue sauce. Return to oven for 15 minutes. Remove from oven, turn, brush other side liberally. Return to oven for 15 to 20 minutes until attractively browned. Cut ribs into serving pieces of 2 ribs each. Four servings.

Sauerkraut and Wieners

12 medium potatoes
Two 28-oz cans sauerkraut, drained
¼ C hard butter or margarine
2 beef bouillon cubes
2 to 2½ C hot water (divided, see below)
1 lb best quality wieners, cut up

Wash, pare and quarter potatoes. Into very large baking dish or roasting pan put potatoes and drained sauerkraut. Toss with 2 forks to mix. Cut the butter or margarine into pieces and dot it over top. Combine the beef bouillon cubes with 2 C of the hot water and pour evenly over top. Bake at 300° uncovered for 2 hours, but every 20 minutes remove from oven and toss with forks to combine potatoes, sauerkraut and juice. Cut each wiener into 8 pieces and add, tossing, to combine. Continue to bake uncovered 1 hour longer, still tossing every 20 minutes, adding the remaining ½ C hot water if mixture becomes too dry. Serves six to eight.

Pork Hocks with Beans

1 lb white navy beans
7 C cold water (divided, see below)
4 lb pork hocks
1¾ tsp salt
½ tsp flavor salt
¼ tsp pepper
¼ C chopped onion
½ C chopped celery and leaves

Wash beans and soak overnight in a soup kettle in 4 C of the cold water in a cool place.

Four hours before mealtime put them on to cook adding the remaining 3 C water, washed hocks, salts, pepper, onion and celery. Bring to boil and simmer covered until beans are tender and meat is falling from bones. Allow most of 4 hours and turn hocks over at halftime. Serves six.

Baked Cottage Roll

3½-lb cottage roll
¼ C brown sugar
Whole cloves

RAISIN SAUCE
1 Tbsp flour
1 Tbsp butter or margarine
1 C apple juice or apple cider
½ C raisins

Scrape off the cornmeal from the cottage roll and place in shallow baking dish. Score fat, then spread evenly with the brown sugar and dot with whole cloves. Bake at 325° for 2 hours.

Serve with Raisin Sauce: In pot blend together flour and butter. Stir in the apple juice or cider and raisins until thick.

Holiday Veal and Ham Pie

ENGLISH PASTRY
3 C unsifted all-purpose flour
1 Tbsp single-acting baking powder
1½ tsp salt
1½ C good quality shortening (divided)
¾ C hot water
1 Tbsp lemon juice
1 egg yolk

FILLING
2 lb lean shank veal cut into 1″ pieces
½ lb smoked lean cottage roll or ham
3 hard-cooked eggs, sliced
One 10-oz pouch-pack fresh frozen peas in butter sauce, barely thawed
One 8-oz can whole oysters or ½ pint raw (optional, see below)
One 10-oz can mushroom pieces and stems
1 slim carrot cut into thin round slices
1 slice lemon chopped
1 chicken bouillon cube
1 C boiling water
½ tsp salt
¼ tsp pepper
¼ tsp mace
¼ tsp rosemary
1 C rich gravy (or 1 more cup boiling water and 1 more chicken bouillon cube)

Make Pastry by sifting together the flour, baking powder and salt. Cut in half of the shortening until size of peas. Melt remaining shortening in hot water. Stir into flour mixture, then stir in egg yolk and lemon juice until blended. Chill covered until firm.

Select a large baking dish. Use about ⅔ of pastry to line sides. Now add filling: put in half of raw cut-up veal, half of ham, all of the hard-cooked egg slices to make one complete layer. Add mushrooms and liquid, oysters and liquid if used. Add peas and carrots in a single layer then chopped lemon. Sprinkle with salt, pepper, mace and rosemary. Add remaining veal with ham on top. Pour over hot water in which chicken bouillon cube is dissolved. Roll remaining dough to ¼″ thickness making 1″ larger all round than your baking dish. Gash top. Place over filling and seal and crimp edges. Brush top all over with 1 egg yolk beaten with 2 tsp cold water. Bake at 450° for 10 minutes. Cover loosely with foil and bake at 300° for 3 hours. If crust is browning too much pinch foil closer to top edge and reduce heat to 250° for last 1½ hours. Serves six.

Breaded Pork Chops

To make four ¾″ thick breaded chops, dip each in 1 beaten egg, then in CRUMB COATING (see Index). Render out fat trimmed from chops and sauté chops until golden. Then turn and brown other side. Serve with spiced crabapples.

Veal Marengo

1¼ lbs stewing veal cut into bite-sized pieces
¼ C flour
1 tsp salt
⅛ tsp pepper
¼ tsp basil
¼ tsp thyme
2 Tbsp oil
½ small garlic clove finely chopped
½ C chopped cooking onions
⅔ C white wine
1 C canned (or fresh peeled) tomatoes
Rind from half an orange cut into 1 × ¼" strips
Noodles (see below)

Into a strong paper bag measure the flour, salt, pepper, basil and thyme. Add about half of the cut-up veal and shake to dredge meat. Have ready a large frying pan with heated oil in it and transfer dredged meat from bag into oil. Dredge remaining veal in flour mixture in bag and tip all into pan. Brown meat until gold, turning often. Add garlic and onion and gently sauté until they are limp but not brown. Add wine, tomato and orange rind and simmer covered, 1½ hours or until veal is tender.

About 20 minutes before serving time cook half of a 12-oz package of broad noodles in large amount of boiling water with 1 tsp salt until almost tender. Drain through colander. Turn out on large preheated platter and pour Veal Marengo over all. Serves four.

Veal Cordon Bleu

1½ lb veal cutlet, pounded
4 narrow slices Swiss or Gouda cheese
4 narrow slices ham (or chipped beef)
2 eggs
½ tsp salt
About 2 C fine soft breadcrumbs
¼ C butter

The veal cutlet must be pounded until it is twice the size and not more than ¼" thick. Cut it into 4 oblongs 6½ × 4½". Cover half of each oblong with slice of cheese. Top with ham (or chipped beef) and fold over uncovered half to make a turnover. Press down hard.

Beat eggs with salt in shallow bowl. Spread crumbs on plate. Dip veal turnovers in egg, then in crumbs. Repeat. Let rest on crumb plate for an hour to set and firm up. (This step helps to keep turnovers from splitting at open side when cooked.)

At mealtime melt butter in large frying pan and sauté turnovers until golden on bottom then carefully turn and brown other side. Reduce heat, cover and cook 5 minutes. Veal is very tender and does not require long cooking. The cheese inside melts in the process. Serve at once. Four servings.

Economical Veal Parmesan

1¼ lbs stewing veal
1 large egg
2 Tbsp cold water
⅓ C Newfoundland Fried Chicken Spice coating
    (See Index, Newfoundland Fried Chicken)
⅓ C grated Parmesan cheese
2 Tbsp margarine

First step takes patience. Place pieces of veal on board and trim off all gristle and fat. Then pound each piece with rolling pin or meat pounder until ¼" thick. (These pounded pieces will be a little ragged at the edges but this does not take away from their finished appearance.)

Beat the egg with the cold water. Mix the Newfoundland Fried Chicken Coating with the cheese very well. Dip the pieces of pounded veal in the egg then in Coating on both sides. Let rest in single layers on 2 large plates 1 hour to dry and firm up. At mealtime quickly sauté in margarine on both sides. Store remaining Chicken Coating for future use.

Veal Ragout with Noodles

2½ lb boneless veal shoulder
⅔ C flour
¼ tsp pepper
4 Tbsp cooking or salad oil
2 medium onions, sliced
⅛ tsp garlic powder or 1 clove garlic,
    finely chopped
⅛ tsp rosemary
1 tsp salt
½ C canned tomato sauce
1 C water
1 chicken bouillon cube
½ C white cooking wine (optional)
⅓ C finely chopped parsley
¾ C sliced green or ripe olives or salad olives
Buttered noodles with poppy seeds (see below)

Cut the boneless veal into 1" cubes. Put the flour and pepper in a strong paper bag and shake the veal cubes in them to dredge. In very large frying pan heat the oil and brown the floured veal until golden. Add the garlic and onions and sauté until onions are limp but not brown. Add all remaining ingredients except olives and parsley. Cover and simmer about 2 hours, or until veal is tender. (Note: If you do not wish to add the wine you will have to add a little more water to the ragout as it cooks, for it should be fairly moist when finished.) Ten minutes before serving time add the sliced olives. Two minutes before serving time add the parsley.

To prepare noodles, cook about half of a 12-oz package of noodles in 2 qts boiling water to which you have added 1 tsp salt, until almost tender, about 10 minutes. Drain through colander. Return to saucepan and add at least ¼ C butter and 2 to 4 Tbsp poppy seeds. Mix gently to coat all noodles with butter and seeds, but be gentle to avoid breaking them.

Turn into center of large preheated platter and surround with the rosy pink border of boiling hot Veal Ragout. Serves six.

Super Veal Stew

2½ lb boneless lean shoulder veal, cut into
    1½" cubes
½ C flour
1½ tsp salt
¼ to ½ tsp pepper
½ C margarine
1½ C chopped celery
1½ C chopped onion
¼ tsp thyme
2 C hot water

Be sure the veal is lean and well trimmed. Dredge the veal cubes in the flour mixed with the salt and pepper. Mix together well. Melt margarine in heavy pot until bubbling then add dredged meat and all of the flour and brown it, turning, until golden. Add the celery, onion and thyme. Add water, stirring until thick, then cover and simmer 50 to 60 minutes. Serve on unbuttered noodles. Six servings.

Veal Scallopini

2½ lb veal cutlets sliced thinly and pounded
    (see below)
1¼ C fine dry cracker crumbs
1 large egg
3 Tbsp milk
½ tsp salt
½ C oil or butter
1 clove garlic, finely chopped
1 medium onion, finely chopped
1 medium green pepper, finely chopped
1 C dry white wine or cooking sherry
½ tsp salt

The veal should be pounded to ¼" thickness. Your butcher may be willing to do this with his cleaver for you, but if not pound it with your rolling pin. Cut it into serving-size pieces. Beat the egg with the milk and ½ tsp salt. Dip each piece of meat into the egg, then into the crumbs to coat them evenly. Spread them out on a platter and let them rest for half an hour.

Meanwhile gently sauté the garlic, onion and green pepper in the oil or butter until they are soaked with fat, but not brown. Skim them out of the pan and reserve. Now sauté the crumbed meat pieces in the fat in pan, adding more fat if needed, until they are gold on both sides. As each piece of meat is done transfer it to a large shallow baking dish. When meat pieces are all done spoon sautéed vegetables evenly over all, pour wine over all, and sprinkle with remaining ½ tsp salt. Bake at 300° for ¾ hour, basting and turning meat pieces once during this period. You may also simmer this dish on top of the stove, covered, for 1 hour.

This is usually served with spaghetti. Boil thin spaghetti from a 14-oz package in 3 quarts salted boiling water 10 minutes and drain it through a colander. Coat it with a tomato sauce made of 1¼ C V8 juice, 3 oz tomato paste (half of a 6-oz can), 1 Tbsp sugar, ½ tsp each salt and garlic salt. The bowl of tomato-sauced spaghetti should be liberally sprinkled with Parmesan cheese. More Parmesan could be passed at the table. Serves eight.

Wiener Schnitzel

1 lb sliced veal (see below)
Twenty-four 2" crackers rolled finely
½ tsp salt
2 eggs
2 Tbsp water
¼ C butter

Ask the butcher to slice the veal ⅛" thick or buy a cutlet and pound it with steak pounder or rolling pin until very thin, about 18 × 8" when pounded. Cut into 8 serving-size pieces. Beat eggs with water in a shallow bowl. Mix crumbs with salt and spread out on large plate. Dip pieces of meat in crumbs then in egg, then in crumbs again. Place on large plate to dry half an hour. Heat butter in large frying pan until pale gold. Sauté breaded veal over medium-high heat until golden on bottom. Turn over and brown other side, only about 5 or 6 minutes. Serve at once. Four servings.

Broiled Lamb Chops with Green Goddess Rice

Eight 1" thick loin lamb chops
1 C raw long grain rice
2 C boiling water
1 chicken bouillon cube
1 tsp salt
1 Tbsp chopped chives
1 Tbsp chopped parsley
⅛ tsp garlic salt
½ C fresh dairy sour cream (room temperature)

MINT SAUCE
1 C finely chopped fresh mint leaves, packed
¼ C boiling water
1 tsp sugar
¼ tsp salt
¼ C vinegar

Combine mint sauce ingredients in order given.

In heavy saucepan add the 2 C boiling water, chicken bouillon cube and 1 tsp salt to rice and bring to boil, covered. Turn off heat for 5 minutes then turn on heat as low as possible and cook 25 minutes longer or until all water is absorbed and rice is tender.

Meanwhile heat broiler burner 10 minutes in advance. Arrange lamb chops on broiler pan and broil 5" from burner until first side is golden brown. Turn chops over, sprinkle with salt and broil other side until golden brown and cooked through, about 18 to 20 minutes in all for 1" thick chops. Arrange in 2 rows on long sides of preheated platter. Arrange cooked rice in a row between them. Stir chopped chives and parsley and garlic salt into sour cream and spread over surface of rice. Sprinkle top with additional chives and parsley and serve at once. Serves four.

Roast Leg of Lamb

The average leg weighs a little over 5 pounds. If frozen thaw it and trim off excess fat. Wipe meat all over with a damp cloth. Sprinkle all over with salt, pepper and rosemary. Place on rack in roasting pan and roast uncovered at 325°. For medium done, roast 2 hours; well done, 2½ hours.

Moussaka

2 lb lean ground lamb (no fat)
Two 8" eggplants sliced (see below)
Oil
1 C chopped onion
1 tsp salt
⅛ tsp allspice
⅛ tsp pepper
½ C tomato paste
1 large chopped tomato
½ C chopped parsley
1 chicken bouillon cube

MOCK BECHAMEL SAUCE
3 Tbsp butter
4 Tbsp flour
½ tsp salt
2 C milk
2 egg yolks

Wash and slice eggplants ¼" thick unpeeled. Fry until all are browned in oil. You will have to add more oil to pan before you are finished.

In another large frying pan sauté onions and meat in a little more oil until red color disappears, then add salt, allspice, pepper, tomato paste, tomato, parsley and chicken bouillon cube and mix well.

Have ready a very large baking dish, about 13 × 9". As you fry the eggplant slices place a layer in the baking dish. Cover with a layer of meat mixture, then a layer of fried eggplant slices, then another layer of meat. Finish with layer of eggplant slices.

To make Mock Bechamel Sauce, blend butter, flour and salt. Stir in milk until thick. Beat egg yolks, stir a little sauce into them, then stir into sauce for a minute. Pour all over top of Moussaka. Bake at 300° for 2 hours. Serves eight.

Lamb Curry

2½ lb stewing lamb
1 or 2 tsp curry powder
2 C hot water
1½ tsp salt
1 bay leaf
1 medium onion chopped
2 Tbsp chopped parsley
¼ C flour
3 Tbsp cold water

Cut lamb into 2" pieces. Trim off excess fat. Turn meat into large hot frying pan and when some of the meat fat has melted add curry powder and stir until meat is seared. Add hot water, salt, bay leaf, parsley and onion. Simmer covered about 1½ hours or until tender.

Mix together to a smooth paste the flour and cold water and stir in until thick. Serve with fluffy boiled rice prepared by boiling together covered, 1 C long grain rice, 2 C boiling water and ½ tsp salt, until all water is absorbed.

Accompaniments: Chutney, flaked or unsweetened desiccated coconut, peanuts, chopped banana (dipped in lemon juice to prevent discoloration), canned, drained mandarin orange sections. Serves six.

Lamb Stew

2 lb lamb stew meat
6 Tbsp flour
1½ tsp salt
1 tsp curry powder
1 tsp paprika
2 C hot water
6 medium-small onions
3 medium carrots cut up
1 C fresh frozen peas

Trim off surplus fat and cut meat into 2" pieces, cutting between and including the ribs. Discard all but a 3" piece of fat and render it out in a heavy pan. Measure the flour, salt, curry and paprika into a strong paper bag and dredge the meat in it. Tip all (including flour mixture leftover in bag) into hot pan and sear over high heat until golden brown, turning frequently. Fish out the piece of fat and discard. Add the water, cover and simmer until tender, about 2 hours. Chill thoroughly and skim off fat. Reheat, add onions and carrots and cook until vegetables are tender, about 40 minutes. Add peas, bring to boil and cook until peas are barely tender, about 2 or 3 minutes. Serve with crusty rolls or French bread. Three servings.

Organ Meats

Beef Kidneys Burgundy

2 beef kidneys (about 11 oz each before trimming,
    2 C when diced)
3 Tbsp margarine
One 28-oz can tomatoes
1 Tbsp sugar
2 cloves garlic finely chopped
2 C chopped onion
¼ tsp marjoram
¼ tsp basil or thyme
½ bay leaf
2 whole cloves
1 C red wine
½ tsp salt

Cut the kidneys in quarters lengthwise and trim off all center fat. Then cut in ¾″ pieces and soak in cold water half an hour. Drain. In large frying pan melt margarine and add drained kidneys and sauté until all traces of raw meat disappear, about 5 minutes. Add tomatoes, sugar, garlic, onion, marjoram, basil or thyme, bay leaf and cloves. Cover and simmer gently 1 hour. Just before supper add wine and salt and bring to boil and serve over rice or noodles. Serves six.

Liver Pâté

1 lb frozen then slightly thawed chicken
    or baby beef livers
¼ lb side bacon
1 Tbsp minced onion
1 tsp garlic salt (or clove of garlic)
½ tsp thyme
½ tsp salt
¼ tsp cinnamon
¼ tsp nutmeg
¼ tsp black pepper
2 slices stale bread
2 eggs

Force slightly thawed chicken livers—freezing them gives the necessary firmness to force through grinder—through the fine knife of meat grinder along with the bacon and all seasonings. Put bread through machine last to clean it out and to extend pâté and give it body. If you do not have a blender put purée through fine knife of grinder again to make it smoother. If you have a blender buzz half of the liver mixture in it at a time to make it perfectly smooth. Remember that the professional finish in making liver pâté is its velvety texture. Beat eggs and stir into mixture thoroughly. Turn into small loaf pan (or 3 or 4 individual baking dishes) filling ⅔ full. Cover tightly with lid or foil. Stand in shallow pan of hot water and bake at 275° for 2 hours. This is a good imitation of *pâté de fois gras*.

Herbed, Sliced Beef Tongue with Mushrooms

One 3-lb beef tongue
1 bay leaf
1 Tbsp chopped onion
1 tsp salt
SAUCE
¼ C butter or margarine
½ lb mushrooms, chopped
2 Tbsp flour
½ tsp salt
½ tsp basil
½ C chopped green pepper
1 C liquid from cooking tongue (see below)

Cook tongue in water to not quite cover, add the bay leaf, onion and 1 tsp salt. Simmer, covered, for 4 hours, turning once at halftime.

About 15 minutes before mealtime make the Sauce by melting the butter or margarine and gently sautéing scrubbed and chopped mushrooms in it for about 3 minutes. Stir in flour, salt and basil and green pepper for 1 minute then stir in the 1 C broth in which tongue was cooked, until thickened.

Now transfer tongue from broth to board, peel off skin and trim off glandular portion and little bones from underside. Slice neatly with sharp knife and place slices overlapping on preheated platter. Immediately pour boiling hot sauce over and serve at once. Six servings.

Spaghetti Caruso

¼ lb spaghetti
½ lb fresh chicken livers quartered
½ tsp salt
2 Tbsp butter or margarine
One 10-oz can mushroom stems and pieces
    (or ½ lb fresh sliced mushrooms)
¼ C finely chopped onion
One 7½-oz can tomato sauce
¼ to ½ tsp Italian seasoning or oregano

First cook the spaghetti until almost tender in a large saucepan in plenty of salted water.

Meanwhile in a frypan sauté the quartered chicken livers gently in the butter or margarine, sprinkling them with the salt. Sauté only until barely set. Add the onion, mushrooms, tomato sauce and seasoning and simmer gently 5 minutes.

Drain spaghetti through sieve or colander. Divide onto 2 or 3 dinner plates, pour sauce over and serve.

Sweet and Sour Sliced Beef Heart

One 3½-lb beef heart
1 small onion chopped (first)
1 bay leaf
1½ tsp salt
2 Tbsp margarine
½ green pepper chopped
1 small onion chopped (second)
2 Tbsp cornstarch
2 C broth from cooking heart (see below)
2 Tbsp lemon juice
3 Tbsp sugar
½ tsp salt
½ tsp curry powder

Be sure to trim all fat and connective membranes from top of heart and put heart on to cook in large pot with the first onion, bay leaf and 1½ tsp salt in water to ¾ cover. Bring to boil, reduce heat to simmer, cover and simmer 5½ hours, turning heart over once at halftime.

Near mealtime make the Sweet and Sour Sauce by melting the margarine in a medium-sized frying pan. Add the green pepper and onion and sauté gently 5 minutes. Stir in the cornstarch and then add 2 C of the broth in which heart was simmered, lemon juice, sugar, ½ tsp salt and curry powder until thick. Simmer gently 5 minutes.

At mealtime put the cooked heart on a cutting board and with sharp knife cut neatly into ¼″ slices and arrange these overlapping on preheated large platter. Pour the hot sauce over. Garnish with parsley.

Crumbed Sweetbreads

1 lb sweetbreads, parboiled, chilled and sliced
1 egg
1 Tbsp water
1 Tbsp lemon juice
⅔ C fine dry bread or cracker crumbs
Salt and pepper
¼ C butter or margarine
Parsley

Beat egg, stir in water and lemon juice. Dip sliced sweetbread in the egg mixture, then into crumbs to coat. Sprinkle with salt and pepper. Heat butter or margarine in frying pan until hot, lay in the crumbed sweetbreads and brown to a light golden brown on both sides. Remove to hot platter and serve at once.

Sautéed Calves' Liver

Allow one full size ⅜″ thick slice calves' liver and 3 or 4 strips side bacon per person. Broil the bacon in advance and drain on paper towels and keep hot in warming oven. Melt 1 or 2 Tbsp butter in heavy frypan. Dredge slices of liver sparingly in flour, sprinkle lightly with salt and gently sauté in hot butter until under side is set and pale gold. Turn over and quickly cook other side. This all takes less than 5 minutes. If you cook it longer you are drying out the meat and giving it the leathery texture so deplored by liver lovers. Serve at once on preheated plates with broiled bacon.

Curried Chicken Giblets

1⅓ lb chicken giblets (gizzards and hearts)
4 C cold water
1 tsp salt (first amount)
1 bay leaf
3 Tbsp margarine
1 tsp curry powder
1 apple unpeeled, chopped
1 onion chopped
2 stalks celery chopped
3 Tbsp flour
1¼ tsp salt (second amount)
1 C long grain raw rice
2⅓ C boiling water
1 tsp salt (third amount)

Cut gizzards in halves. Add hearts and the 4 C cold water, first amount salt and bay leaf and simmer gently, covered, 4 hours.

Near mealtime melt margarine in large frying pan and add curry powder, apple, onions and celery and sauté gently for 15 minutes. Stir in flour and second amount salt to blend then add cooked giblets and their broth and stir until thickened. Serve over rice: Into heavy pot measure rice. Add boiling water and third amount salt. Cover. Bring to boil. Turn on heat very low for 25 minutes longer. Spoon rice onto large platter and pour curried giblets over. Serves seven.

Pâté Pierre

One thick (½ lb) pork chop, fat on and bone off
½ lb lean veal shoulder meat
1 lb frozen slightly thawed chicken livers
1 medium onion
1 garlic clove
1 slice whole wheat bread
2 large eggs
¼ C sherry
1 tsp allspice
1 finely crumbled bay leaf
1 tsp salt
½ tsp pepper
Pinch of thyme
¾ lb slice ham cut in 4″ narrow strips
1 green pepper cut in fine strips
About 10 slices bacon
3 slices crustless whole wheat bread, toasted

Put through grinder twice the boned pork chop, veal, slightly thawed chicken livers, onion and garlic. After second grinding follow with one slice whole wheat bread to clean out machine.

In a large bowl to the ground mixture add the eggs, sherry, allspice, crumbled bay leaf, salt, pepper and thyme. Mix well. Line a standard loaf pan with the bacon crosswise, letting ends hang over edges. Spoon a third of meat mixture into pan smoothly. Cover with a layer of the ham strips alternately with green pepper strips. Spread over another third of ground mixture. Again cover with a layer of ham strips alternately with green pepper strips. Spread on remaining ground mixture. Top with the 3 slices crustless whole wheat toast. Lap overhanging bacon over toast. Now wrap in double layer of foil pinching edges securely. Have about 1″ hot water in a larger pan. Lower loaf pan into it and bake at 350° for 2 hours. Cool at room temperature but do not unwrap. Cover with weight, possibly a clean brick. Refrigerate 48 hours then turn out and slice thinly.

Sherried Veal Kidneys

2 or 3 veal kidneys (order from butcher)
About ½ C flour
½ tsp salt
About ¼ C butter
2 Tbsp chopped onion
½ C sherry
2 beef bouillon cubes
6 Tbsp water
¼ C finely chopped parsley

Slit the fat side of the kidneys and with sharp pointed knife trim out fat and venous portion and discard. Slice kidneys and measure. You should have about 3 C. Soak in cold water 2 hours. Drain and pat dry with paper towels. Dredge in the flour and salt to coat.

In large frying pan melt butter and when bubbling add the floured kidneys and sauté on high heat for 1 or 2 minutes turning constantly. Reduce heat and add all remaining ingredients and stir constantly until boiling gently then reduce heat again to simmer and stir for 4 or 5 minutes. Serves six.

Liver Creole

1½ lb thinly sliced beef liver or
    halved chicken livers
¾ C flour
½ tsp salt
⅛ tsp pepper
SAUCE
2 C tomato juice
1 medium onion, chopped
1 green pepper, chopped
¼ tsp salt
⅛ tsp pepper
1 tsp Worcestershire sauce
1⁄16 tsp garlic powder (or ¼ tsp garlic salt)
½ tsp celery seed
1 Tbsp chopped parsley
¼ lb mushrooms, washed and chopped

To make Sauce, in pot combine all sauce ingredients except mushrooms. Bring to boil, reduce heat and simmer, uncovered, about 25 minutes, stirring occasionally. Some liquid will boil down and sauce will thicken. Add mushrooms and simmer 2 or 3 minutes longer.

Meanwhile prepare liver. Combine flour, salt and pepper in a shallow bowl. Dredge pieces of liver in it to coat. Place liver on holding plate until sauce is almost finished. Heat 4 Tbsp oil or butter in frying pan, add floured liver and quickly brown on both sides, about 2 minutes per side. Do not overcook or liver will become tough. Serve at once with sauce. Six servings.

Baked Stuffed Heart

One 2-lb beef heart (see note below)
2 Tbsp margarine
1 small onion chopped
¼ C chopped celery
¼ tsp oregano
¼ tsp celery seed
½ tsp salt
2 or 3 slices cubed bread

Wash heart thoroughly. Trim off all fat and trim off arteries and veins. Melt the margarine in a frying pan, add the onion, celery, oregano, celery seed and salt and gently sauté until vegetables are soaked.

Remove from heat and stir in bread cubes. Fill heart cavity with stuffing. Tie snugly with string. Bake covered on rack in roasting pan at 300° for 2½ hours. *Note:* If beef heart is average-size, about 3 lb, it will require about 3½ hours' baking.

To Boil a Beef Tongue

Wash a 4-lb beef tongue. Put in pot with snug lid. Add 1 sliced onion, 2 bay leaves and 1 Tbsp salt. Bring to boil. Lower heat to simmer and cook 4 hours. To serve hot lift from broth and peel off skin and trim off rough tissues and bones at base of tongue. Slice, hot or cold, starting at side of tongue.

Curried Tongue

3½ C diced cooked beef tongue (well packed)
¼ C butter or margarine
1½ tsp curry powder
2⅔ Tbsp flour
½ tsp salt
⅛ tsp garlic powder
2 chicken bouillon cubes
2 C boiling water

For economy's sake buy a large beef tongue. Cover it with water, bring to boil and simmer covered until tender, 3 to 4 hours. While warm, lift from broth and peel off skin and trim off fat from base of tongue. Cut into dice and measure 3½ C. (Any leftover is good sliced cold or for sandwiches.) Melt butter, stir in curry powder until it is hot and soaked with butter, (called "cracking the curry"). Blend in the flour, salt, garlic powder and bouillon cubes, then stir in the boiling water until thick. Add diced tongue and heat through. Serve on fluffy boiled rice.

Poultry

Newfoundland Fried Chicken

4 cut up frying chickens
SPICE COATING
4 C flour
1 tsp dry mustard
1 tsp onion salt
1 tsp turmeric
2½ Tbsp salt
2 Tbsp meat tenderizer
1 tsp garlic powder
1 tsp curry powder
1 tsp ground cloves
1½ tsp finely crumbled sage
1 Tbsp pepper

DIP
2 beaten eggs
2 C milk

Mix spice coating ingredients thoroughly. Wash then cut frying chickens into serving pieces. Shake off water. Dip chicken pieces in egg-milk mixture and dip in spice coating.

In a heavy pot heat ½" oil until bubbling and fry 4 pieces at a time on both sides until golden, about 5 minutes. Drain on paper towels. Transfer to large baking dish. Continue until all required pieces are golden and in baking dish. Bake at 300° for 45 to 60 minutes.

Breast of Chicken Mornay

6 chicken breasts
4 Tbsp butter
2 Tbsp finely chopped onion
4 Tbsp flour
¼ tsp poultry seasoning
¼ tsp salt
⅛ tsp pepper
2 C milk
1 egg
¼ C light cream
6 thin slices cooked ham
6 slices processed Swiss cheese
½ C fine dry breadcrumbs
3 Tbsp butter, melted

Simmer chicken breasts, covered, in small amount of water until tender, about 30 minutes. Remove skin and bones and cut each breast in 3 even slices. Melt butter in heavy saucepan. Sauté onion until golden. Blend in flour, poultry seasoning, salt and pepper. Gradually stir in milk and cook over medium heat, stirring constantly, until smoothly thickened. Remove from heat. Beat egg with cream and stir into hot sauce and cook, stirring constantly, a few moments longer. In broad shallow buttered baking dish, layer, alternately, slices of chicken, ham and cheese. Cover with sauce. Combine breadcrumbs and melted butter and sprinkle over top of casserole. Bake at 350° for 20 to 25 minutes.

Roast Stuffed Chicken

One 4½-lb roasting chicken
STUFFING
4 C soft bread crumbs
2½ Tbsp butter
¼ C mild onion chopped
8 tiny rosemary leaves
½ tsp salt

Dry chicken on inside and outside with paper towels. Put gizzard and heart on to simmer in small saucepan, in 2 C water, covered, for 2½ hours. Add liver during last 5 minutes.

Make stuffing by melting butter in large frying pan, adding onion and rosemary, and sautéing until onion is soaked with butter but not brown. Add soft bread crumbs and stir over low heat until crumbs are just slightly crispened but not browned. Fill bird with stuffing and fasten with 2 or 3 skewers. Tie wings and legs to body with string. With your fingers, spread butter all over skin. Roast chicken on rack in shallow roasting pan at 325° for 1 hour, then reduce heat to 300° for 1½ hours longer. Remove strings and skewers before transferring to preheated platter. Be sure the carving knife is sharpened to make the carver's job an expert one.

Gravy: tip most of the fat from roasting pan and discard. With spatula scrape pan sediment and about 4 Tbsp of remaining fat into saucepan. Stir in ¼ C flour. Now stir in giblet liquid made up to 2 cups by adding hot water (or vegetable liquid), the chopped giblets and 1 chicken bouillon cube. Stir until thick and pour into preheated gravy boat. Serves five.

Oven Fried Chicken

3 whole chicken legs
6 wings
3 breasts
3 backs
3 each livers, hearts, gizzards, necks
¾ C margarine
COATING
1½ C flour
1½ tsp salt
1½ tsp paprika
1 tsp celery seed

Put hearts and gizzards and necks on to cook, covered until tender, in 1 cup water. Reserve livers to add for the last 5 minutes. Chop and use these parts for sandwich fillings.

Melt margarine on broiler pan in preheated oven at 325°. Mix all coating ingredients in large strong paper bag. Pat all chicken pieces fairly dry. Add legs and wings to bag and shake to coat. Arrange on broiler pan in margarine. Coat breasts and backs. Arrange in one layer on broiler pan. Turn all pieces over to butter both sides. Bake at 325° for 1 hour, turning each piece over at half-time. Of course this is at its best hot fresh from the oven but it is also good cold at a picnic. Serves eight.

Chicken and Dumplings

STEW

One 5½- to 6-lb dressed boiling fowl
8 C water
5 or 6 medium-large carrots, chunked
12 whole medium cooking onions
1 tsp salt
⅛ tsp pepper

DUMPLINGS

2 C sifted cake and pastry flour
4 tsp baking powder
½ tsp salt
2 Tbsp shortening
⅔ C milk

In a large soup kettle simmer the whole fowl with the water, covered, until tender, about 4 hours. Be sure it is beginning to fall apart. Lift bird to utility tray and cut it into serving pieces discarding what skin and bones you readily can. Arrange in large baking dish, pour 2 C of the broth over the chicken, cover with foil and keep hot in oven at 225° until final serving time. Skim off as much surplus fat as you can from remaining broth. Add carrots, onions, salt and pepper and cook until tender.

To make Dumplings, sift together the flour, baking powder and salt. Cut in shortening until size of peas with pastry blender. Quickly stir in milk just until all flour is moistened.

Have stew boiling hard. Dip a serving spoon in the broth then use it to spoon 6 dumplings onto vegetables in boiling hot broth. Cover at once and cook on medium heat for 15 minutes. Serves six.

Chicken Florentine

Note: to serve 2 meals to a working couple make this up in 2 medium-sized or 4 individual casseroles.

2 C fine raw noodles (packed)
1 tsp salt
4 C boiling water
One 10-oz pkg fresh frozen chopped spinach
    or broccoli, thawed
Most of the meat from a 5-lb cooked chicken

CREAM SAUCE

¼ C butter or margarine
3 Tbsp flour
½ tsp salt
1¾ C milk
Parmesan cheese

Cook noodles with salt in boiling water for 10 minutes. Drain through colander. Turn into 1 average shallow casserole or 2 medium-small or 4 individual ones. Cover with thawed spinach or broccoli. Cover generously with pieces of cooked chicken meat. Any surplus chicken could be used for sandwiches.

Make Cream Sauce by melting the butter or margarine. Stir in flour and salt then stir in milk until thick. If desired, a little Parmesan may be added to sauce. Pour sauce over chicken, being sure it flows between crevices. Sprinkle generously with Parmesan cheese. Bake at 375° for 30 minutes. Serves four.

Chicken with Pineapple

3 Tbsp flour
½ tsp salt
¼ tsp pepper
3 Tbsp water
2 C 1″ cubes raw chicken
Oil for deep-fat frying
3 tsp soy sauce
2 rings pineapple, cut in quarters
8 pieces green peppers, cut in same size
    as pineapple
2 carrots sliced wafer thin, diagonally
1½ C water
½ C vinegar
3 Tbsp brown sugar
1 Tbsp molasses
2 Tbsp cornstarch
¼ C canned pineapple juice (from
    canned pineapple above)

Mix flour, salt, pepper and water to a smooth batter. Pour over the chicken. Stir until the chicken is well coated, then place the chicken, one piece at a time until you have a single layer, in deep hot oil. Fry until golden brown. Skim out, drain on paper towelling and continue until all pieces are fried. Mix the soy sauce, pineapple, green pepper, carrots, water, vinegar, sugar and molasses and cook slowly, stirring well. Let boil for 3 minutes. Mix the cornstarch and pineapple juice. Stir into the mixture and cook until thickened. Add the fried chicken, mix and serve with hot fluffy boiled rice. Serves four.

Crusty Chicken Pie

¼ C butter or margarine
¼ C flour
1 C milk
1 C chicken broth
2 C diced chicken
½ C drained cooked diced celery
1 C drained peas
½ C canned broiled sliced mushrooms
¾ tsp salt
1 tsp lemon juice

Melt butter or margarine, blend in flour, stir in milk and broth. Cook until thick, stirring constantly. Add remaining ingredients and heat. Place in casserole. Top hot filling with cheese biscuits.

BISCUITS

2 C sifted pastry flour
4 tsp baking powder
½ tsp salt
⅓ C cold butter or shortening
⅔ C milk
Grated cheese

Sift dry ingredients into bowl and cut in butter or shortening with pastry blender until the size of large peas. Pour milk into center of flour mixture. Stir until mixture leaves the sides of the bowl. Knead gently on lightly floured surface for 1 minute, then spread out to ¼″ thickness. Sprinkle with 1 C grated cheese. Roll as a jelly roll and then cut into ½″ slices.

Bake pie at 425° about 20 minutes. Serves six.

Chicken Broccoli Delight

Two 3½ lb chickens
½ bay leaf
½ onion, sliced
1 tsp salt
1 qt water
1 lb broccoli heads or 2 pkgs fresh frozen
    chopped broccoli
2 C soft bread crumbs mixed with
2 Tbsp melted butter
½ C grated Parmesan cheese

SAUCE
6 Tbsp chicken fat (skimmed from broth,
    see below)
6 Tbsp flour
3½ C broth (from cooking chickens)
2 chicken bouillon cubes
½ lb sliced mushrooms

Simmer chickens in water with bay leaf, onion and salt until tender, beginning to fall from bones. While quite warm strip meat from bones. Cut into chunks. Discard bones and skin. Strain and chill broth. Cook broccoli until half tender.

To make the Sauce, skim fat from chilled chicken broth and melt it and blend it with the flour. Stir in broth and chicken bouillon cube until thick. Add sliced mushrooms while sauce is boiling, then remove from heat.

To assemble, use one large 13 × 9″ casserole (or two 8 × 8″) and put a close layer of chicken in bottom. Cover with cooked broccoli. Cover with half the mushroom sauce. Repeat these 3 layers. Cover with buttered crumbs and top with Parmesan cheese. (If desired refrigerate at this stage overnight or until mealtime.) Bake at 350° for 35 to 40 minutes or until bubbly and golden. Serves twelve.

Note: If desired serve with a rich egg sauce made by melting 6 Tbsp butter or margarine and blending in 5 Tbsp flour and 1 tsp salt. Stir in 1½ C each milk and chicken broth (or water and 2 chicken bouillon cubes) until thick. Stir in 2 beaten egg yolks. Serve in preheated sauce boat.

Chinese Chicken Fried Rice

½ C butter or peanut oil
3 eggs slightly beaten
1½ C chopped cooked chicken (or pork)
1 to 1½ Tbsp soy sauce
3 C cooked rice (1 C raw long grain,
    see note below)
½ C onion sliced thinly
1½ tsp salt
Shake of pepper
1 can Chinese bean sprouts, drained
⅓ C fresh green onion tops (optional)
2 Tbsp pimiento squares (optional)

To cook rice, bring to boil 2½ C water with 1 tsp salt. Add 1 C raw long grain rice. Immediately cover and bring to boil. Without removing lid turn off heat for 5 minutes then turn heat on low for 25 minutes longer. This produces fluffy separate grains of rice.

Melt butter or peanut oil in frying pan. Add slightly beaten eggs and fry for a minute but do not allow to become at all firm. Break up with fork

while cooking. Add the chicken, rice, onion, salt and pepper and last, the bean sprouts. Pour over a little of the soy sauce to suit your taste. Cook together only until hot, covering pan for a few minutes. Use 2 forks for mixing. The onion and pimiento squares may be added for color and flavor.

Chinese Sweet and Sour Chicken

8 chicken legs
8 chicken thighs
¾ C flour
1 tsp salt
¼ tsp pepper
½ C butter
1 C hot water

SAUCE
¼ C cornstarch
¼ C sugar
6 Tbsp vinegar
4 C hot water
6 Tbsp catsup
3 Tbsp soy sauce

To prepare chicken, mix flour, salt and pepper in strong paper bag and shake dried chicken pieces in them to coat. Melt butter in large shallow baking dish (or 2 medium pans), add chicken pieces, turn each over to coat with butter, add hot water and bake at 350° for 45 to 50 minutes, turning once.

To make Sauce, mix sauce ingredients together in order given in large saucepan and cook stirring until slightly thickened. Serve chicken on a platter with hot sauce poured over. Six to eight servings.

Chicken Cacciatore

One 3-lb chicken, cooked (see below)
3 Tbsp oil
2 small onions, finely chopped
1 green pepper, finely chopped
¼ C chopped celery
⅛ tsp garlic salt
1¼ tsp salt
⅛ tsp pepper
½ tsp oregano
2 Tbsp chopped parsley
2 small bay leaves, crushed
One 19-oz can tomatoes
One 8-oz can tomato sauce
One 10-oz can tomato soup (undiluted)

In large pot cook chicken in enough water to ¾ cover. Bring to boil, reduce heat and simmer covered about 1 hour or until meat is tender. Remove meat to utility tray and when sufficiently cool strip meat from bones. Discard skin and bones. Chop or pull meat apart in rather large, irregular-shaped pieces.

In large frying pan sauté onion, green pepper, celery and garlic salt in oil until vegetables are limp but not browned. Add cooked chicken pieces, seasonings, tomatoes, tomato sauce and tomato soup and mix well. Bring to boil, reduce heat and simmer uncovered 1 hour, stirring frequently. Serve with generous portions of cooked spaghetti. Serves six to eight.

Large Quantity
Balled Chicken and Pineapple

3½ lb turkey or chicken breasts

BATTER
6 eggs
1 C flour
2 tsp salt
½ tsp white pepper
Oil to ½" depth in frying pan

SAUCE
¾ C sugar
¾ C vinegar
¾ C cornstarch or arrowroot flour
5 C pineapple juice (get 2 C from canned
   pineapple below)
Two 19-oz cans pineapple tidbits
4 or 5 drops yellow food coloring

Put breasts in shallow roasting pan, skin side up and bake at 325° for 1¼ hours. Remove breasts to utility tray and when sufficiently cool strip meat from bones and cut into ¾" pieces.

To make Batter, in beater bowl beat eggs until well mixed, then beat in flour, salt and pepper until very smooth.

Heat oil to bubbling hot. Dip pieces of chicken into batter to coat then place in oil. Fry until golden brown on both sides, turning once. Do only about 10 pieces at a time to prevent the temperature of the oil from dropping. Remove and drain on paper towels then place in serving dish. Keep hot. When all chicken is fried, make Sauce. In large pot combine sugar, vinegar and cornstarch and stir until completely mixed. Slowly stir in pineapple juice, cook until thickened then add yellow food colouring and cook 2 minutes longer stirring. Add pineapple chunks. Pour over chicken pieces gently lifting them to make sure all are well coated. Serve with fluffy boiled rice. Twelve to sixteen servings.

Chicken Cordon Bleu

6 chicken breasts
Six 4" square slices cooked ham
Six 4 × 1 × ¼" fingers of genuine Swiss cheese
Salt
White pepper
¼ C butter
¼ C cream
½ C boiling water

Cut the meat from the bones and skin on each chicken breast, keeping the meat in one fillet. Roll the slices of ham around the fingers of Swiss cheese. Place at center of chicken fillet and wrap sides and end around it and place, smooth side up, in large shallow buttered baking dish. Sprinkle generously with salt and white pepper.

Pour the boiling water over the butter and stir until melted. Add cream. Pour a third of this basting liquid over the chicken evenly. Cover and bake at 325° for about 1½ hours, basting with remaining liquid at 15-minute intervals. During last 15 minutes remove cover to brown top. When serving this, spoon pan gravy over each chicken roll. Serve with buttered noodles. Six servings.

Battered Chicken

15 chicken pieces
1 bay leaf
1 slice onion
1 tsp salt (first amount)

BATTER (sufficient for 15 pieces)
1⅓ C unsifted all-purpose flour
2 tsp baking powder
½ tsp salt (second amount)
1 egg
1⅓ C milk

Note: If you do not need all of this batter for your current meal, cover leftover amount and refrigerate, but use within 4 or 5 days.

Cook chicken pieces in minimum of water with the bay leaf, onion and salt until barely tender, not falling apart. Lift out chicken pieces and cool on tray or platter.

To make Batter, beat together the flour, baking powder, salt, egg and milk until perfectly smooth. Have ready a large frying pan with ½" hot oil in it at 350°. Working near the stove, dip each piece of dried cool chicken in batter, allowing excess batter to drip off, then placing in hot oil. Proceed until pan is full. Turn over each piece when it is rich gold on bottom and brown other side. Skim out with slotted spoon and drain on paper towelling. Keep warm. Continue until all pieces for present meal are fried.

Oven Fried Chicken Wings

4 lb chicken wings
½ C margarine

CRUMB COATING (double amount: store
   remainder for future use)
1 C very fine dry breadcrumbs
¼ C flour
½ tsp salt
¼ tsp icing sugar
¼ tsp flavor salt
¼ tsp paprika
¼ tsp curry powder
⅛ tsp garlic salt

With a heavy knife cut off and discard wing tips. Wash and dry wings. Mix all Coating ingredients in a large bowl. Using only half the mixture, drop all chicken wings in and coat them.

In a large 9 × 13" baking dish melt margarine and put chicken wings in and turn each piece over to coat with margarine. They will be crowded. Bake at 350° for 45 minutes, turning each wing at halftime. Serves six.

Chicken Hollandaise with Tea Biscuits Supreme

6 Tbsp butter or margarine
1 Tbsp finely chopped onion (or bottled flakes)
½ C cornstarch
4 C chicken broth (see below)
2 tsp lemon juice
1⅓ C inner celery chopped finely
1 tsp salt
¼ tsp paprika
4 C chopped cooked chicken
1 C fresh frozen green peas, thawed
4 egg yolks

Buy a chicken weighing about 4 lb and cook it covered, in 4 C water until tender. This will yield the chicken meat and broth the recipe requires.

In a large saucepan or frying pan melt the butter gently and add the onion. Blend in cornstarch then stir in chicken broth until thick. Add lemon juice, celery, salt and paprika. Cook, stirring, 1 minute. Beat yolks slightly. Stir a little of the hot mixture into them and then stir these yolks into the hot mixture and cook gently, stirring for 1 minute. Stir in chicken and peas and cook, stirring 1 minute longer.

It is now ready to serve over TEA BISCUITS SUPREME (see Index).

Baked Chicken

2 whole chicken breasts cut into 4 pieces
2 chicken wings
¼ C flour
1 tsp paprika
1 tsp salt
¼ C butter
½ C boiling water
¾ C milk

In a bag mix together the flour, paprika and salt and shake chicken pieces in them to coat. Reserve leftover flour for making gravy later. Arrange chicken in buttered shallow pan skin side up. Melt the butter in the boiling water and pour half of this liquid evenly over chicken pieces. Bake at 325° for ¾ hour until skin is golden brown. Turn chicken pieces over and pour over them the remaining butter-water mixture. Bake half an hour longer at 300°.

To make Gravy, remove chicken pieces from pan to platter and keep warm. To reserved flour mixture add milk and stir until smooth. If baking dish can be used on top of the stove, stir milk mixture into liquid in pan until thick, or, if necessary, transfer pan juices to a pot to make gravy. Pour gravy over chicken, garnish with parsley and serve.

Chicken Rolls Supreme

6 single chicken breasts (about 3 lb)
2½ C soft breadcrumbs (7 slices in blender)
½ C grated Parmesan cheese
1 tsp salt
¼ C parsley flakes
¾ C melted butter
¼ tsp garlic powder
½ tsp dry mustard
¾ tsp Worcestershire sauce

In a large bowl mix breadcrumbs, Parmesan cheese, salt and parsley flakes. Set aside. Gently melt butter in medium pot and add garlic powder, mustard and Worcestershire sauce. Set aside but do not allow it to congeal.

Either buy boned breasts or bone out chicken with very sharp pointed knife. (Put bones on to cook in 2 C water for soup for a later meal.) Dip breasts in butter mixture to thoroughly coat, then coat with the crumb mixture on both sides. Roll breasts up tightly and place open side down in buttered large shallow baking dish. Continue until all are coated and rolled. Pour any leftover butter mixture over rolls. Cover and bake at 325° about 1¼ hours, basting with any surplus butter in bottom of dish once or twice. Six servings.

Individual Chicken Pies

PASTRY
1 C unsifted cake and pastry flour
½ tsp salt
⅓ C shortening
2 Tbsp butter
2 Tbsp cold water

FILLING
2 C cut up cooked chicken meat packed
  (or pork, beef, turkey)
1 large carrot diced (¼")
¾ C diced potatoes
½ green pepper in strips
  (or ½ C peas or green beans)
2 C boiling water
2 chicken bouillon cubes

Cook the vegetables in the boiling water, covered, until tender, not more than 15 minutes. Drain and reserve liquid. You must have 1½ C. Dissolve the chicken bouillon cubes in the liquid.

Apportion the vegetables evenly into four 4" individual baking dishes. Cover each with ½ C of the chicken and pour some of the reserved cooking liquid over each, using it all.

To make Pastry, cut shortening and butter into flour and salt until size of peas. Add water, tossing with fork, until you can press pastry into a ball between your palms. Roll out in a long 4½" strip thinly. Cut out rounds to cover tops of pies. Slash at center. Glaze tops by brushing with 1 beaten egg yolk diluted with 1 Tbsp water. Bake at 400° for 25 minutes or until bubbly and golden.

Chicken Marengo

6 single chicken breasts (about 2½ lb)
½ tsp salt
¼ tsp pepper
¼ C cooking oil
2½ C chopped Spanish onion
½ bay leaf
¼ tsp oregano
¼ tsp thyme
¼ tsp marjoram
1½ C hot water
2 chicken bouillon cubes
One 10-oz can mushrooms and liquid
⅓ C tomato paste
One 12-oz pkg fresh frozen lima beans
3 Tbsp flour

Sprinkle the chicken breasts with salt and pepper and brown them in the hot oil on both sides in a large frying pan until golden. This takes about 10 to 15 minutes. Add onion, bay leaf, oregano, thyme, marjoram, hot water and chicken bouillon. Simmer covered 1 hour. Dip out ½ C of the liquid and reserve it. To pan add mushrooms and their liquid, tomato paste and frozen limas and simmer covered until limas are thawed and tender, about 20 minutes.

Into the reserved and cooled liquid stir the flour to a smooth paste. Lift out the chicken pieces onto a hot platter. Stir flour paste into contents of pan until thick. Pour all over chicken pieces and serve. Six servings.

Coq Au Vin Blanc

4 single chicken breasts (about 2¼ lb)
5 Tbsp flour
¼ tsp salt
¼ tsp paprika
⅛ tsp pepper
¼ C butter
½ C white wine
1 C boiling water
2 chicken bouillon cubes
¼ tsp thyme
¼ tsp garlic salt
½ bay leaf

Into a strong paper bag measure the flour, salt, paprika and pepper. Shake chicken breasts to coat.

Melt butter in frying pan and brown chicken breasts in it until golden. Transfer chicken to holding plate. To pan add all of the flour mixture leftover in the bag and stir into the butter in pan. Mix together the wine, water, bouillon cubes, thyme, garlic salt and bay leaf. Stir into pan until gently boiling. Lower heat. Return chicken breasts to pan and simmer covered one to 1¼ hours. Serve over fluffy rice. Four servings.

Island Chicken

One 3½-lb frying chicken cut up (or 4 to 6 breasts
    or legs and thighs)
2 Tbsp lemon juice (1 lemon)
⅓ C soy sauce
1 tsp sage
1 tsp salt
½ tsp pepper
1 tsp ginger
Flour for dredging
¼ C oil
1 large cooking onion cut in chunks
1 C boiling water

In a small bowl mix together the soy sauce, lemon juice, sage, salt, pepper and ginger. Put chicken pieces in a large shallow bowl and pour sauce over, being sure each piece of chicken is coated. Allow to marinate for half and hour or longer in refrigerator.

Lift the chicken pieces out (reserving any remaining liquid) and roll in plain flour to dredge. Brown in oil in large frying pan until deep gold. Transfer to large shallow casserole, skin side up. preferably not overlapping. Pour water in at side. Sprinkle onion over evenly. Pour the reserved marinade sauce over all then cover with lid or foil and bake at 350° for 1 hour. Serve with or on fluffy boiled rice.

Chicken Pilaf

½ C butter or margarine
2 C cooked chicken, cut up
2 Tbsp bottled onion flakes
2 tsp salt
⅛ tsp pepper
½ tsp oregano
1 C raw long grain rice
2½ C chicken broth (from cooking chicken)
1 C canned tomatoes
½ C cashews or blanched almonds

In frying pan melt butter or margarine and add cut up chicken and onion flakes and sauté to soak onions with butter. Do not burn. Add salt, pepper, oregano and rice. Stir well. Then add chicken broth and tomatoes and stir. Cover, reduce heat and cook 20 minutes, then add nuts, heating through and serve.

Almond Soo Guy

Cut 4 single raw chicken breasts into 1″ pieces, discarding bones. Dip in BATTER: 1 C sifted flour, 2 tsp baking powder ½ tsp salt, 1 egg, ⅔ C water. Mix all ingredients until smooth. Fry batter-covered chicken pieces in about ⅓ C hot oil, turning until brown on all sides, about 4 to 7 minutes. Remove from pan to baking dish.

Tip off all but 2 Tbsp oil. Stir in 2 Tbsp cornstarch and when blended stir in 1 C pineapple juice, ¼ C soy sauce and ¼ C hot water in which 1 chicken bouillon cube is dissolved. Stir until thick. Taste for salt and pepper, also more soy sauce if desired. Pour over chicken pieces and bake, covered, at 300° for 30 minutes. Sprinkle with shredded almonds and serve.

Curried Chicken Wings In Double Boiler

2½ lb chicken wings (allow 4 wings per serving)
1½ C hot water
½ C finely chopped celery
¼ tsp celery salt
⅛ tsp garlic salt
3 Tbsp arrowroot flour or cornstarch
1 tsp (or more) curry powder
½ tsp salt

With a sharp heavy knife cut off and discard the chicken wing tips. Put clipped wings into top of large double boiler and add the hot water, celery and celery salt and garlic salt. Place over boiling water, cover, and reduce heat to simmer for 4 hours, gently turning wings at halftime.

Tip off broth containing celery and measure 2 C. Let cool and skim off fat. Mix together arrowroot flour (or cornstarch), curry powder and salt and stir into broth until smooth, then cook stirring until thickened. Pour over chicken wings in double boiler and reheat to serve.

Chicken (or Turkey or Ham) Croquettes

2 C ground chicken (or turkey or ham)
      well packed
1 Tbsp green celery, including some tops
1 Tbsp green onion
3 Tbsp butter
2 Tbsp flour
¾ tsp salt
¼ tsp curry powder (optional)
¾ C hot milk
¼ C hot cereal cream
1 egg yolk
1 to 1½ C fine breadcrumbs
1 large egg
1 Tbsp water
¼ C butter

Put chicken (or turkey or ham) through food grinder and follow it through with the celery and onion. Heat milk and cream. In large saucepan melt the 3 Tbsp butter and stir in flour, salt and curry powder (if used) until blended. Stir in hot milk and cream until thick. Remove from heat and stir in egg yolk and ground chicken and vegetables. Chill in refrigerator.

When thoroughly cold this croquette mixture is easy to handle. Have ready in a shallow dish the egg beaten with the water and on a large shallow dish the crumbs. Also have ready a large shallow baking dish with the ¼ C butter melted in bottom. With moistened palms shape croquette mixture into 12 logs 3½″ long by 1½″ in diameter. Dip each in egg, drain a little, then roll in crumbs. Transfer each to butter in baking dish, roll them over to coat with melted butter on all sides. They should not touch. Chill again to retain shape.

Bake at 375° for 25 to 30 minutes until golden. If these do not brown well enough on top, turn on broiler for a few minutes only—watching carefully—to brown them to your liking. Serves four.

Chicken Loaf

½ Tbsp butter or margarine
½ Tbsp flour
½ C milk
½ C breadcrumbs
2 egg yolks
1 C cooked macaroni or rice
1 C cold cooked chicken (from 3 backs)
½ C mushrooms cut in strips
1 Tbsp canned pimiento, finely cut
½ C heavy cream
1½ tsp salt
1 tsp parsley, finely chopped
Whites of 2 eggs

Melt butter, add flour, and stir until well blended. Pour milk over gradually while stirring constantly. Bring to a boil and add breadcrumbs, well beaten egg yolks, macaroni cut into ½″ pieces (or rice), chicken, then mushrooms and pimiento. Add cream, beaten until stiff, salt and parsley. Stir until thoroughly mixed and fold in egg whites, beaten until stiff.

Turn into a mold lined with buttered paper, cover with foil and bake at 350° for 30 to 40 minutes. Remove from mold to hot serving dish and garnish with parsley. Serve with tomato or white sauce.

Chicken Breasts Birchwood

8 chicken breasts (3½ lb) deboned (see below)
4 Tbsp butter (divided, see below)
½ lb scrubbed, sliced mushrooms (or ½ C
      sliced olives)
⅓ C flour
¼ tsp salt
1 C chicken broth (from boiling bones)
¼ C sour cream or table cream or milk
3 Tbsp sherry (optional)

Ask butcher to debone chicken breasts, or do it yourself with a very sharp knife. Cook bones in 4 C water until any meat falls from them. Strain. Measure 1 C broth.

In large frying pan melt 2 Tbsp butter and sauté chicken breasts until golden on both sides. Remove from pan and keep warm. Add 2 Tbsp more butter to pan. If mushrooms are used add them to pan and sauté until limp. Remove and reserve. Add flour and salt to pan and stir to blend. Stir in the 1 C chicken broth until thick. Stir in cream or milk. Return chicken breasts to pan, cover and simmer 45 minutes, turning breasts once. Transfer breasts to large shallow baking dish. Pour gravy over. Cover with sautéed mushrooms or sliced ripe olives.

Cover all with HOLLANDAISE SAUCE (see Index) and when Hollandaise is spread over, sprinkle with sherry if used. Place about 6″ from hot broiler until heated through and bubbly and golden.

Fried Chicken

4 whole chicken legs including thighs
    (½ lb each)
3 Tbsp butter
½ C flour
½ tsp salt
½ tsp paprika
2¼ C milk

Dry the chicken legs. In strong paper bag mix together flour, salt and paprika. Shake chicken legs, one at a time, in flour mixture, firmly grasping top of bag and shaking to coat. (Reserve flour in bag for making gravy later.)

In large frying pan that has a lid to fit it, melt the butter until golden, add chicken and cook until crisp on both sides, about 10 minutes. At arm's length add 1 Tbsp hot water to center of pan, cover, reduce heat to simmer and cook 30 to 35 minutes longer, turning over once, until tender. Remove to preheated platter.

To make Gravy, add leftover flour mixture to pan drippings and stir well to mix. Now stir in milk until thick, beating out lumps if necessary. Serve over chicken or in preheated gravy boat. Four servings.

Party Chicken Fricassee

15 lbs of dressed boiling chickens
5 oz flour
1½ Tbsp salt
1½ tsp pepper
9½ oz melted fat
3 qt boiling water
5½ oz flour (second amount)
1 pint hot milk
1½ Tbsp salt (second amount)

Cut chicken into portions for serving. Dredge with 5 oz flour. Heat fat in roasting pans. Add floured meat and brown lightly in oven. Transfer chicken to stock pot. Add boiling water, salt and pepper. Cover and simmer until tender (2 to 3½ hours). Remove from heat, drain off stock, retaining 1½ qt. (Reserve remaining stock for later use in soups or sauces.) Measure fat from roasting pans, about ¾ C. If there is less add necessary quantity of some kind of fat to make up to this amount. Add flour (second amount) to fat and blend until smooth. Add chicken stock and hot milk gradually, stirring constantly. Add salt (second amount). Cook slowly until no flavor of raw starch remains. Pour over meat. Reheat before serving. Serves 25.

Paella

One 3-lb chicken
4 C water
2 tsp salt
1 small onion sliced
¼ tsp pepper
1 C long grain rice
1½ Tbsp butter or olive oil
2 cloves garlic, chopped
¼ tsp saffron (optional)
1 lb fresh frozen de-veined shrimp
One 12-oz pkg fresh frozen green peas
12 clams in shell (or one 10-oz can clams)

Simmer the whole chicken in the water with the salt, onion and pepper until tender and meat will easily fall from bones. Remove from broth to large tray until cool enough to handle. Strain and reserve all broth. Strip chicken meat from bones discarding skin and bones. Cut meat into large bite-sized pieces.

In large frying pan sauté together in the oil or butter the rice and garlic until rice has soaked up the fat. Add 1½ C of the reserved broth and simmer 15 minutes to nearly cook the rice. Add saffron, if used. Add cut-up chicken, defrosted shrimp, and the fresh frozen peas and simmer and stir gently until rice is barely tender, adding the remainder to the broth as Paella moisture evaporates and more liquid is needed. Turn Paella out onto preheated large platter, garnish top center with hot clams and garnish border plentifully with parsley or baked or fried bananas or grilled crumbed tomatoes. *Note:* If clams in shell are used place on top of Paella during last few minutes of cooking, cover and steam until shells open.

Brunswick Stew

By one old tradition, a skinned and cleaned black squirrel—if you can catch one—is added to this stew.

One 4-lb boiling fowl
2 tsp salt
4 potatoes, pared and cubed
1 C fresh or canned kernel corn
2 diced onions
1 C lima beans, fresh or dried
2 tomatoes, canned or fresh
2 C or 1 pkg or 1 can of sliced okra (if available)
¼ lb diced salt pork or side bacon
1 Tbsp flour
1 Tbsp butter
½ tsp pepper

Disjoint chicken. Put 8 C water and the 2 tsp salt on to boil. Add chicken pieces, potatoes, corn, onion, beans, tomatoes, salt pork or bacon and okra (if used). Cover and simmer for 3 hours, stirring gently every half hour. Mix butter and flour to a smooth paste and stir in a little of the hot broth, then add to simmering pot, stirring. Cover and cook 15 minutes longer. Taste for salt and add if desired.

Turkey and Egg Bake

2 C diced turkey (or chicken) packed
1½ C soft bread cubes packed
½ tsp poultry seasoning
¼ tsp salt
1 C shredded cheese (packed, divided)
2 Tbsp chopped onion
3 Tbsp milk
4 eggs

In a bowl gently combine the turkey (or chicken), bread cubes, poultry seasoning, salt, half of the cheese, chopped onion and milk. Put an equal amount into each of 4 buttered individual casseroles—this is about 1 cup each—or all into 1 medium casserole. Bake at 350° for 10 minutes. Remove from oven. Make a depression in center of each dish with back of serving spoon or if using 1 medium casserole make 4 depressions. Drop a raw egg in each depression. Sprinkle tops evenly with remaining cheese. Return to oven and bake 10 minutes longer or until eggs are barely set. Serves four.

Turkey Tetrazzini

1 lb spaghetti
¼ C butter or margarine
1 C finely chopped celery (including a few tender leaves)
1 medium Spanish onion chopped
1 green pepper chopped
½ lb mushrooms scrubbed and sliced
¼ C flour
2 tsp salt
2 C milk
½ lb (2 C) shredded old Cheddar cheese
2 C (packed) coarsely cut cooked turkey (or chicken)
¼ C sherry
2 or 3 Tbsp chopped canned pimiento

In a large pan melt the butter or margarine and add the celery, onion and green pepper and gently sauté covered for 15 minutes. Add the prepared mushrooms and cook slowly 5 minutes longer. Sprinkle flour and salt over and stir in. Stir in milk until thick. Stir in cheese then turkey, sherry and pimiento. Carefully continue heating.

Serve over generous amount of spaghetti cooked in several cups of boiling salted water about 12-15 minutes. Drain through colander.

Note: If this Turkey Tetrazzini is frozen you may want to add 1 C milk when reheating as it thickens on standing and this addition would stretch it a little.

Turkey Tonnato

This is a cold meat course calling for 2 lb sliced cold cooked turkey breast. Veal could be substituted.

TUNA SAUCE
¾ C oil
1 egg yolk
⅓ C canned tuna (drained, packed)
2 Tbsp lemon juice
¼ C whipping cream
¼ C boiling water
1 chicken bouillon cube
2 Tbsp capers, drained, washed and dried
Finely chopped parsley

Arrange the turkey slices neatly overlapping on a long narrow platter.

The Sauce is the important part of this dish and is easy to make. Dissolve the chicken bouillon cube in the boiling water. Cool. Into your blender pour oil, yolk, tuna and lemon juice. Buzz about 15 seconds. Remove this purée to a small bowl. Slowly add the cream, beating all the time with a wire whip. As soon as ¼ C broth is cool, slowly add it. Add drained and dried capers. Pour over turkey slices leaving a few ends of the slices uncoated. Carefully sprinkle a 1″ band of chopped parsley down full length at center. Chill. Serves six or seven.

Turkey-Mushroom Individual Pies

PASTRY
2 C stirred but unsifted cake and pastry flour
1 tsp salt
⅔ C shortening
3 Tbsp butter
4 Tbsp cold water

FILLING
4 C cooked turkey meat cut in bite-size pieces
2 medium potatoes diced
½ C chopped onion
2 C water
Two 10-oz cans sliced mushrooms (or ½ lb sliced raw mushrooms plus 1½ C water)
3 chicken bouillon cubes
1 tsp salt

To make the Pastry, cut the butter and shortening into the flour and salt with pastry blender until size of peas, then drizzle in cold water, tossing with fork until all flour is dampened. Roll out on floured board and cut into rounds to fit tops of 6 individual earthen baking dishes. Roll pastry thicker than usual and use all of this amount.

Cook together in pot the potatoes, onion and water for about 8 minutes until nearly tender. Add the mushrooms. Now into baking dishes apportion the turkey evenly. Cover with the mixture of vegetables and broth. Stand baking dishes on a cookie sheet and put in 425° oven to heat up. Lift pastry rounds and place on top of hot filling and bake at same temperature for 10 minutes longer, then reduce heat to 350° until fillings bubble and top is golden. Serves six.

Roast Stuffed Turkey

14.25 lb took 20 min/lb

20.5 lb took 5.25 hrs.

12 to 15-lb oven-ready bird *unstuffed*
450 down to 325, door opendance 15 min/lb

STUFFING

1 loaf bread pulled into crumbs
1 C sliced mushrooms
1 C sliced celery
½ C chopped apple
½ C chopped onion
¼ C chopped parsley or flakes
½ C butter or margarine
1 tsp salt
⅛ tsp pepper
½ to 1 tsp sage or rosemary or
thyme

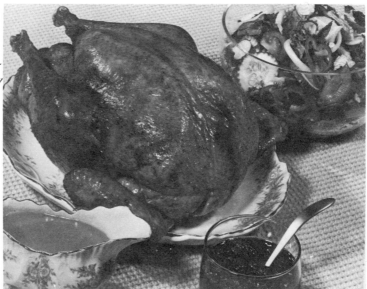

In large frying pan melt butter and sauté all vegetables and apple until wilted. Add to breadcrumbs in large bowl and add seasonings and mix. Stuff prepared bird and truss snugly. *Note:* Do not stuff bird in advance.

To roast, dry outside of stuffed bird and spread all over with soft butter. Put in oven at 325° for 4½ to 6 hours, without water or cover, basting occasionally when drippings collect in pan. If desired, cover with tent of foil for first 4 hours, then remove to allow skin to brown and crispen.

To make Gravy (4 cups), transfer turkey to hot platter. Pour excess fat from pan but leave ½ C fat and all sediment in pan. Place over low heat and blend in ½ C flour. Now add 4 C hot water and stir until thick. Add salt to taste. Strain if necessary.

Super Turkey Hash

2 C well packed turkey meat (cooked)
4 medium potatoes
1 medium onion
½ green pepper, seeded
2 Tbsp chopped canned pimiento
¾ tsp salt
3 Tbsp butter
¼ C heavy cream (optional)

Put through the grinder the turkey meat, raw potato (scrubbed and trimmed, unpared and quartered), onion peeled and quartered, and green pepper. Mix in the chopped pimiento and salt. Melt butter in frying pan and spread hash mixture over entire surface and cook on low heat, covered, until potatoes are tender and bottom is crusty and gold. If you add the cream, do so at halftime, pouring it evenly over top. Cream makes the hash richer and moist. Uncover, turn off heat and let hash stand for a minute or so to stop steaming. Loosen edges and fold over and slip onto preheated platter. Serves four.

Convener's Party Turkey For Fifty

One 13-or 14-lb turkey (to make 14 C packed
when cooked and cut up)
7 C water
2 lb fresh mushrooms scrubbed and sliced
3 medium green peppers chopped
1 Tbsp chopped onion
Three 4-oz jars pimientoes chopped coarsely
One 8-oz jar stuffed olives sliced

SAUCE

1 lb butter
4 C unsifted cake and pastry flour
2 Tbsp salt
⅓ C chicken bouillon cordial
10 C (2 Imperial qts) 2% milk scalded
8 C turkey broth (see below)

Buy a frozen turkey and if possible have the butcher cut it into quarters. Partially thaw overnight then put the quarters in a large roasting pan, add 7 C water, cover and simmer 5 hours turning quarters over once. Lift to utility tray and when cool slip out all bones, peel off skin and discard both. Cut meat into 1″ pieces and chill. Strain and chill broth overnight. Skim off and discard fat.

Measure 8 C broth and simmer in it the mushrooms, peppers and onions 5 minutes. Remove from heat.

Make basic White Sauce by melting butter in large preserving kettle and stirring in flour and salt until blended. Now stir in chicken bouillon cordial, scalded milk and hot broth containing vegetables until thick. Stirring constantly, add cut up turkey, pimientoes and olives and stir until it returns to boil. It is now ready to serve.

After The Ball Turkey

4 C cut up cooked turkey
6 Tbsp butter or margarine
1½ C diagonally cut celery
1 medium onion chopped
6 Tbsp flour
1 tsp salt
⅛ tsp pepper
3 C milk
One 10-oz can cream of mushroom soup undiluted
2 Tbsp chopped canned pimiento
¼ tsp basil
¼ C sherry
½ to 1 C grated cheese
½ to 1 C buttered crumbs

In a very large pan gently sauté the celery and onion in the butter until soaked, not browned at all. Stir in flour, salt and pepper. Stir in milk until thick. Add the turkey, soup, pimiento, basil and sherry. Turn into one very large casserole or 2 medium, and, if desired, freeze one. Sprinkle evenly with cheese and crumbs. Bake at 350° about 30 minutes or until bubbly and golden. Serve over fluffy rice. Ten servings.

Rock Cornish Game Hens With Wild Rice Stuffing

6 Cornish Game Hens
1 tsp salt
6 slices side bacon
2 Tbsp butter
STUFFING
1 C raw wild rice
½ C chopped onion
½ lb mushrooms, sliced
1 C shaved filberts (or orange sections)
6 Tbsp butter
½ tsp marjoram
½ tsp thyme

Wash rice and simmer in 2½ C boiling water, covered, with 1 tsp salt for 50 minutes. Drain. Sauté onions, mushrooms, filberts in the butter until limp but not brown. Add orange if used instead of filberts. Add to rice and seasonings. This yields 3½ C stuffing, ample for 6 hens. Sprinkle cavities of hens with salt and stuff and truss them. Place 2 half slices bacon over each bird and roast, uncovered, at 350° for 1 to 1½ hours until tender. Baste with pan drippings to which you have added the 2 Tbsp butter. Do not overbake these tender little birds.

Stuffed Roast Goose

1 fresh or fresh frozen goose, 10½ lb
STUFFING
7 C soft white breadcrumbs
½ C butter
1 apple or 4 soaked and stoned prunes
½ C finely chopped onion
½ C finely chopped celery
1 tsp salt
¼ tsp sage
¼ tsp basil
¼ tsp marjoram
¼ tsp rosemary
¼ tsp pepper

If goose is frozen thaw at least 48 hours in refrigerator. Make Stuffing one day in advance: In large frying pan melt butter and gently sauté until limp the onion, celery and apple or prunes, then add all seasonings and bread and stir over medium heat until breadcrumbs begin to crispen. Cool. Turn into plastic bag and chill in refrigerator overnight.

Seven hours before serving time, insert bagful of stuffing, open end down, into cavity of goose and slowly withdraw bag, shaking it to coax stuffing out. Skewer opening shut. Tie wings and legs to body. Prick skin all over with skewer to let fat flow freely. Place a rack in roaster and put in oven at 250° for 7 hours cautiously tipping off fat as it accumulates about every hour.

Roast Duck à l'Orange

One 5-lb dressed duck
2 apples, pared, cored and chopped
Grated rind and slices from 1 large orange
½ tsp salt
½ tsp curry powder
1½ Tbsp flour
1 C orange juice
¼ C white wine (or cognac)

Wash and dry the duck. In a bowl mix together the apple, grated orange rind, salt and curry powder and spoon into dried duck cavity. Place on rack in roasting pan. Tie legs and wings to body. Sprinkle skin sparingly with salt. Cover top surface with thin slices of orange including white rind left on after grating. If necessary fix these orange slices with toothpicks. Cover bird with a tent of foil and roast at 350° for 3½ hours, removing foil for last half hour. Do not undercook: hip joint should move freely.

Transfer duck to preheated platter. Carefully cut string and slip it off without disturbing orange slices. Remove toothpicks if used. Pour off all excess fat from pan and into brown sediment stir flour to blend. Stir in orange juice and wine (or cognac if used) until thickened. Pour into preheated sauce boat and serve sauce, stuffing and slice of orange with each portion of duck. Serves four.

Storable Top-of-Stove Stuffing

One loaf 4-day-old bread (20 slices)
1⅓ C dried bottled onion flakes
½ C dried bottled celery flakes
¼ C dried bottled parsley flakes
2 tsp salt
1 tsp turmeric

Cut or tear bread into ¼" cubes. Spread out evenly on 2 cookie sheets and put in oven at 200° to thoroughly dry. After half an hour switch pans on shelves and carefully stir the crumbs. After 1½ hours turn off oven and leave them in until oven is cold. Then divide bread cubes into 4 even lots and tip each into a small plastic bag.

Mix together well the onion, celery and parsley flakes, salt and turmeric. Divide seasonings into 4 even lots and tip these into small plastic sandwich bags and fasten tops. Store 4 large and 4 small bags well sealed.

To prepare Stuffing: Into a pot measure 1½ C hot water and add ¼ C margarine and 1 pkg Stored Seasonings. Bring to boil, cover, reduce heat and simmer 5 minutes. Add 1 pkg Stored Bread Cubes and gently stir in with fork over low heat for 1 minute. Remove from heat and let stand covered 5 minutes. Serve to 4 or 5 people instead of potatoes.

Coat-and-Roast

12 slices bread
Butter (see below)
¼ C dried red and green sweet pepper flakes
¼ C parsley flakes
2 tsp cornmeal
½ tsp onion salt
½ tsp celery seed
½ tsp paprika
½ tsp salt
⅛ tsp garlic powder
¼ tsp pepper
1 tsp sugar
1 Tbsp whole wheat flour (optional)
2 tsp flavor salt
1 Tbsp grated Parmesan cheese

Butter bread on one side. Arrange, buttered side up, on large cookie sheets and toast at 250° until golden and crisp, about 1 hour. Buzz toasted bread slices, pepper flakes and parsley flakes in blender until as fine as possible. In bowl combine crumbs with all remaining ingredients. It is now ready to use, about enough for 11 lbs of chicken pieces. *Note:* Leftover coating should be stored in plastic bag in refrigerator.

Rice Stuffing For Duck or Goose

¼ C chopped onion
4 Tbsp butter or margarine or bacon drippings
1 C raw long grain rice
1½ C hot water
½ to 1 tsp salt
¼ tsp sage or rosemary
¼ tsp thyme
1½ tsp grated orange rind

Gently sauté the onion in the fat until limp, then add raw rice and sauté until rice is straw-coloured. Add the salt and water and cover tightly and simmer 20 minutes (barely tender). Add remaining seasonings. This amount is sufficient for 1 duck; double the quantities for a goose. If desired, ½ C white raisins may be added.

Celery and Nut Stuffing

A standard loaf of bread will stuff a 15-to 16-lb bird generously. Adjust this stuffing which calls for 1 loaf of bread to the size of your bird. *Note:* Turkey should be stuffed the day it is roasted, not before.

2 medium onions, chopped
¼ C butter or margarine
1 loaf day-old bread
½ C chopped pecans, almonds or walnuts
1 tsp rosemary or poultry seasoning or sage
¾ C chopped celery
2 tsp salt
¼ tsp pepper
¼ C hot water
1 chicken bouillon cube

Sauté the onion in the butter or margarine gently until transparent. Pull the loaf of bread into ¼" pieces and toast lightly on broiler pan. Add sautéed onions. Dissolve bouillon cube in boiling water and add in addition to all remaining ingredients. Toss lightly and stuff, not too tightly packed, into oven-ready bird.

Crumb Coating

2 C dry sifted toasted breadcrumbs
Oil for brushing (see below)
½ C flour
1 tsp salt
½ tsp fruit sugar
¼ to ½ tsp garlic salt
½ tsp flavor salt

To make Crumb Coating brush sparingly with oil (or melted butter) the slices from half a standard loaf of bread. Arrange overlapping a little on broiler pan and dry out until crisp in oven at 200°. Buzz in blender (or force through grinder) until extremely fine. To the 2 C add all remaining crumb coating ingredients and mix well.

Sage
marjoram
thyme
parsley

Fish

Three Batters For Fish

FIRST

1⅓ C unsifted flour
2 tsp baking powder
¼ tsp salt
⅔ C milk
1 egg

Mix and sift dry ingredients, add milk gradually and well beaten egg, and beat until smooth.

SECOND

1 C unsifted flour
1 tsp baking powder
½ tsp salt
1 egg
⅓ C milk
1 Tbsp melted shortening

Beat all until smooth.

For both the above batters, dry pieces of fish cut in serving portions. Fresh haddock and halibut are used commonly. Dip each piece in batter, drain, lower into deep bubbling fat. Do not fry more than 3 or 4 pieces at a time as temperature of fat must not drop. Turn over with slotted spoon when underside is golden brown, then brown other side. Drain on paper towel before serving.

THIRD

This batter is sufficient for 2 lb fresh haddock, halibut or sole, or fresh frozen, thawed fish of your choice.

1½ C lukewarm water (divided, see below)
1 tsp sugar
1 tsp granular yeast (one-half foil package)
1 Tbsp oil
1½ C unsifted all-purpose flour
1 tsp salt
⅛ tsp pepper

In a one-cup measure dissolve the sugar in ½ C of the lukewarm water. Sprinkle yeast over, give one stir, and let stand 10 minutes. Stir down, then stir in oil.

In a bowl combine flour, salt and pepper. Pour in yeast mixture and remaining 1 C lukewarm water and beat well for 2 minutes until perfectly smooth. Cover and let stand under light bulb 30 minutes, then give several stirs.

Each piece of fish should be about 4 × 2½" and half an inch thick. Heat oil to depth of 3" in an 8" deep pot to 370°. You must have a thermometer. Working on counter as close as possible to hot pot of oil on burner, dip each piece of fish in batter, turning several times to be sure it is well coated then slide into hot oil. Fry only 2 or 3 pieces at a time depending on the size of your pot. Keep oil at 375°. Fry to a medium-gold color on one side then turn and fry other side. This takes about 5 minutes in all depending on thickness of fish. Drain on paper towels then place on cookie sheet in warm oven while you fry remaining fish.

If you have some batter left, peel and slice a cooking onion and separate the concentric circles. Dip them in batter and fry. They take only a few seconds to turn gold on the bottom then are turned. Drain and serve hot with your fish.

Sole Fillets Florentine

One 10-oz pkg spinach
1½ lb sole fillets
2 Sauces (below)

FIRST SAUCE

1½ Tbsp butter
1 tsp chopped onion
1 Tbsp flour
½ tsp salt
½ C milk (or cream)

SECOND SAUCE

2 Tbsp butter
2 Tbsp flour
1 tsp salt
1 C milk
½ C Parmesan cheese

Wash well and drain spinach. Cook covered 4 or 5 minutes in no water until wilted down, turning over at half time. Drain well through sieve. Chop.

To make First Sauce, sauté onion in butter until soaked but not brown, then blend in flour and salt. Stir in milk (or cream) until thick. Add drained and chopped spinach. Spread all over bottom of 13 × 9" shallow pan.

The sole fillets must be prepoached 1 minute. To a large shallow pan add 1 C hot water. Arrange sole fillets overlapping in it. Cover and just bring to boil one minute. Remove at once. Lift carefully to cover spinach.

To make Second Sauce, in pot blend butter, flour and salt then stir in milk until thick. Spread all over top of sole fillets. Sprinkle generously with Parmesan. Put in oven at 425° until it bubbles—10 to 12 minutes—then pass under preheated broiler until cheese is gold and bubbly. Serves five.

Sole Parmesan

1½ lb sole fillets
Mayonnaise
Parmesan cheese

Spread a shallow pan with butter. Place sole fillets cut side up on it in one layer. Brush with mayonnaise. Sprinkle all over lightly with Parmesan cheese. Put in oven preheated to 450°. Turn off bottom burner. Broiler burner should be on high. Place sole on shelf about 6" below broiler. It takes about 5 minutes to cook and bubble if oven and broiler are hot enough. Garnish with wedge of lime or lemon. Serves four.

Shrimp Cocktail

Use clean (de-veined) cooked shrimps (or drained canned shrimps) that have been chilled. Serve in stemmed glasses lined with delicate lettuce leaves.

Top with chilled COCKTAIL SAUCE (for 30 shrimps): 2 tsp prepared horseradish, 3 Tbsp tomato catsup, 1 tsp salt, 2 Tbsp vinegar, 4 Tbsp lemon juice, ¼ tsp Tabasco. Mix together and pour over shrimp and chill.

Tuna Cakes

4 medium potatoes (about 2 C when cooked
    and mashed)
3 Tbsp green pepper, chopped finely
3 Tbsp onion, chopped finely
1 Tbsp oil
One 13-oz can tuna, well drained
2 eggs, beaten
1 Tbsp chopped parsley or bottled flakes
1 chicken bouillon cube
1 tsp salt
¼ tsp pepper
3 Tbsp butter or margarine
¾ C grated process cheese
2 Tbsp finely chopped pickle

Scrub and cook 4 medium potatoes in their skins. When they are tender, peel and put in the beater bowl and beat, then measure. You should have about 2 C.

In frying pan sauté onion and green pepper in oil until limp but not brown. Into a large bowl measure all of the above ingredients including the sautéed onion and green pepper and mix thoroughly. Shape into 8 or 10 uniform balls and roll each in flour. Pat each ball flat making a cake about 3″ in diameter and ½″ thick. Transfer cakes to a cookie sheet sprinkled liberally with flour. Turn cakes over once to make sure both sides have a good coating. Refrigerate about 1 hour on same flour-sprinkled cookie sheet before frying, to let cakes set.

In large frying pan melt 3 Tbsp butter or margarine until bubbling. Transfer tuna cakes directly from refrigerator to frying pan and fry until bottom has a golden brown crust. Turn and brown other side. Ten servings.

Maritimer's Cod Divan

One 10-oz package fresh frozen fiddlehead greens
One 14-oz package fresh frozen cod fillets

SAUCE
¼ C butter or margarine
6 Tbsp flour
¾ tsp salt
¾ tsp lemon pepper
2 C milk
Paprika

Make the sauce first by melting the butter and stirring in the flour, salt and lemon pepper until blended. Stir in the milk until thick. (This is thicker than a medium white sauce because the 2 frozen items thin it as it bakes).

Tip the fiddleheads into bottom of greased medium baking dish and gently separate them. Pour half the sauce all over them. Cover with the frozen cod fillets cut into serving-size pieces and cover with remaining hot sauce. Sprinkle with paprika. Bake 55 to 60 minutes at 350°. Serves four.

Stuffed Rainbow Trout

One 5-lb rainbow trout or lake trout, cleaned
3 C cubed fresh bread
¼ C butter or margarine (room temperature)
1½ C chopped mushrooms
1 C grated carrots
½ C chopped green onions including tops
¼ C chopped parsley
2 tsp salt
¼ tsp pepper
⅓ tsp marjoram
1/16 tsp garlic powder
1½ Tbsp lemon juice
1 egg

If frozen, thaw fish. Remove head from fish, then wash and dry. Sprinkle inside of fish with salt and pepper. With string and large darning needle start from tail end of fish and sew up cavity half way, leaving string loose so stuffing can be pushed in.

Prepare stuffing by thoroughly combining all stuffing ingredients in large bowl. Pack stuffing into cavity and sew remainder of cavity firmly, expecting it to gape somewhat. Place fish on a rack on a baking dish. Brush both sides with oil and bake at 325° for 50 to 60 minutes. Test for doneness at backbone. As fish bakes, brush every 15 minutes with a mixture of ¼ C melted butter or margarine and 1½ tsp lemon juice. *Note:* Do not try to turn fish over, because skin sticks to rack. Place fish on rack on large platter and make a long gash down spine. Server can then lift portions neatly away from bone. Serve a spoonful of stuffing and a wedge of lemon with each portion.

Swedish Creamed Cod Supper

1 lb dried salt cod, or fresh frozen cod fillets
4 Tbsp margarine
4 Tbsp flour
2 C 2% milk
Salt, if fresh cod used
Pinch of pepper

Soak salt cod in cold water 24 hours, changing the water at least 4 or 5 times during that period.

Barely cover soaked cod with cold water, bring to boil and simmer 5 minutes. (*Note:* If fresh or fresh frozen cod is used do not soak but parboil it in the same way.) Drain and with a fork break up fish into bite-size pieces.

To make sauce, blend margarine and flour then stir in milk until thick. Pour over cooked cod. Taste sauce to see if you should add salt. Add a pinch of pepper.

Traditionally this is served over quartered hot boiled potatoes with canned green peas. Corn is good too. If you do not fancy it served over potatoes, serve the sauce over the fish with parsleyed potatoes at the side. Four servings.

Tartar Fish Sticks

Separate and arrange 1 lb frozen fish sticks on cookie sheet. Brush lightly with melted butter and bake at 400° for 15 minutes. Remove from oven.

You are going to make sandwiches, so sparingly spread half of fish sticks with half of Tartar Sauce (below). Cover same half with strips of cheese (mild Cheddar or Colby or Mozzarella) slightly narrower and shorter than fish sticks. Top with remaining fish sticks. Spread with remaining half of Tartar Sauce. Return to oven and bake 3 to 5 minutes longer at 400° or until cheese begins to melt and is heated through. You may want to turn on top burner for last few minutes. Serves four.

TARTAR SAUCE
½ C mayonnaise
½ tsp prepared mustard
1 tsp parsley flakes
½ tsp chopped green onion or chives
1½ tsp drained chopped sweet pickle or green relish
1½ tsp finely chopped olives (optional)
Half a chopped hard-cooked egg (optional)
1 tsp lemon juice

Mix ingredients together in order given.

Coquilles Saint-Jacques

1 lb fresh or fresh frozen scallops
½ C water
Juice of half a lemon
½ medium onion
2 peppercorns or shake of pepper
½ tsp salt
¼ bay leaf
2 Tbsp butter
¼ lb mushrooms
1 large seeded tomato
2 Tbsp butter (second amount)
2 Tbsp flour
1 Tbsp cream or evaporated milk
2 Tbsp sherry (optional)
Shake of garlic powder
½ C fine cracker crumbs mixed with
2 Tbsp melted butter (third amount)
Sprinkle of Parmesan cheese (optional)

Simmer scallops in ½ C water for 6 minutes with lemon juice, onion, peppercorns, salt and bay leaf. Drain but reserve liquor. Cut each scallop into about 4 pieces and turn into bowl. Gently sauté washed and sliced mushrooms in 2 Tbsp butter (first amount) until saturated but not brown. Skim from pan. Add to scallops leaving butter in pan. Gently sauté chopped tomato in remaining butter in pan until saturated with butter, but not soft. Add to scallops. Put 2 Tbsp butter (second amount) in pan, blend in flour, then stir in ½ C scallop liquor until thick. Add cream and sherry, if used, and stir into scallop mixture. Add a shake of garlic powder. Fill scallop shells or individual baking dishes or 1 shallow baking dish with mixture. Sprinkle with buttered crumbs and a little Parmesan cheese if desired. Bake at 375° about 15 or 20 minutes.

Shrimp Avocado Lunch Plate

4 ripe avocados
2 lb fresh frozen cocktail shrimp
1 C mayonnaise
2 tsp dill weed or pickle (see below)
Bibb or Boston lettuce

Well in advance thaw shrimps and dry them by patting between 4 paper towels.

Be sure the avocados are slightly soft. Cut in halves vertically. Remove pit. Peel. Line breakfast or dinner-sized plates with Bibb or Boston lettuce. Slice each half avocado in 6 long crescents and arrange in a fan on center of plate, broad ends out.

Add mayonnaise to thawed and dried shrimp. Mix well then pour off all excess liquid. They should not look smeared with dressing. Over center of fan of avocados place a generous mound of shrimp. Neatly sprinkle top of shrimp with dill weed. Serve with homemade whole wheat rolls or sliced party rye bread.

Note: If you cannot find dill weed, chop enough well drained dill pickles to make ⅔ C and mix with the shrimp. Serves eight.

Shrimp Newburg

One 5-lb carton fresh frozen large shrimp
1 bay leaf
1 sliced onion
1 Tbsp salt

SAUCE
⅔ C butter
½ C flour
½ tsp salt
5 C homogenized milk
2 egg yolks
¼ C dry sherry
½ C well drained mashed canned tomatoes
1 tsp paprika

Almost thaw the shrimp, tip into very large pot, cover with boiling water, add the bay leaf, onion and salt and bring to boil. Boil 3 minutes only. Immediately remove from heat and drain through large colander to cool.

The next step is the hardest. Shell and de-vein the shrimp: it takes 2 hours with help.

To make Sauce, blend butter, flour and salt, then stir in milk until thick. Set aside until 10 minutes before serving time. Combine yolks, sherry, paprika and mashed tomatoes. Ten minutes before mealtime add yolks-sherry mixture to white sauce and heat through, stirring all the time. When it is just below boiling point, add cooked cleaned shrimp and gently stir constantly until heated through. Serve over wild rice.

WILD RICE: Soak in 6 C water overnight one 6-oz pkg wild rice with 1 C raw long grain white rice. One and a half hours before mealtime bring to boil with 1 tsp salt. Cover, reduce to a simmer and cook until tender. Serves twelve.

Lobster Thermidor

One 12-oz can frozen shelled lobster including
   liquid (see below)
3 Tbsp butter
3 Tbsp flour
½ C liquid from lobster
½ C table cream (18%)
1 C milk
½ C fine breadcrumbs
1 C grated cheddar cheese (divided, see below)

Thaw lobster and neatly remove flat pieces of
bone that may be buried in the claws. Be careful to
reserve intact eight 2 or 3″ tail or claw tips to garnish top later. Reserve liquid in can. Cut the
lobster into ¾″ pieces.

Melt the butter and blend in the flour.
Measure lobster liquid into a 2-cup measure. You
should have about ½ C. Fill cup to 1-cup mark
with cream. Fill to 2-cup mark with milk. Now you
have 2 C of combined lobster liquid, milk and
cream. Stir into blended butter and flour until
thick. Add crumbs and half cup of the cheese and
mix to blend and melt. Remove from heat. Add
lobster pieces. Apportion into 8 ungreased shells
and place one claw tip on top of each. If necessary,
use a shallow baking dish. Sprinkle remaining
cheese sparingly over. Place filled shells on broiler
pan and bake on center shelf of oven at 400° about
10 to 12 minutes or until bubbly. Eight servings.

Variations: 1. To extend thermidor to serve
10, add 1 C chopped mushrooms to mixture when
adding lobster. 2. Substitute ½ C sherry for ½ C
milk.

Salmon Steaks with Egg Sauce

Six ¾″ thick red salmon steaks thawed
¼ C melted butter
1 tsp salt

SAUCE
⅓ C mayonnaise
3 Tbsp flour
1 tsp salt
1¾ C milk
1½ tsp grated lemon rind
2 Tbsp lemon juice
1 hard-cooked egg, separated

Place thawed steaks on greased broiler pan.
Combine butter and salt. Brush steaks with half
the mixture. Place fish 3″ away from preheated
broiler burner. Broil 4 or 5 minutes. Turn, brush
with remaining sauce and broil 3 or 4 minutes
longer or until fish is just opaque at bone, no
longer. Do not overcook. Remove to a heated platter and keep warm.

To make Sauce, combine mayonnaise, flour
and salt in a saucepan. Gradually stir in milk.
Cook over medium heat stirring constantly until
smoothly thickened and mixture comes to the boil.
Add lemon rind and juice. Sliver egg white and
fold into sauce. Sieve egg yolk. Pour sauce over
fish and sprinkle with sieved egg yolk. Serve at
once.

Salmon Mousse

One 1-lb can best quality red salmon
1¼ Tbsp plain gelatin
¾ C cold water
1 tsp grated onion
¾ tsp salt
⅛ tsp pepper
1 C mayonnaise
3 Tbsp lemon juice
½ tsp curry powder (optional)
½ tsp Worcestershire sauce
1 Tbsp chopped parsley

Turn the salmon out into a bowl and mash it coarsely, including bones (mashed) and liquid on salmon. Soak gelatin in ¼ C of the cold water for 5 minutes in a little bowl. To the mashed salmon add the remaining water, onion, salt, pepper, mayonnaise, lemon juice, curry powder (if used), Worcestershire sauce and parsley. Stand the soaked gelatin in bowl or cup in very hot water and stir until dissolved. Stir into the salmon mixture thoroughly. Pour into a one-quart mold and chill until firm. If this is carefully covered while refrigerated it may be made 1 or 2 days in advance.

To turn out, dip mold in hot water for 10 seconds then invert on large plate. Garnish with inner lettuce leaves, devilled eggs and sweet pickles.

Salmon Quiche

Begin with one unbaked deep 9 or 10″ pie shell.
PASTRY
1¼ C stirred but unsifted all-purpose flour
½ tsp salt
⅓ C shortening or margarine
3 Tbsp butter
2½ to 3 Tbsp cold water

FILLING
1 C chopped or shredded cheese (Swiss or Cheddar or process)
2 Tbsp chopped onion
Two 7¾-oz cans salmon or shrimp drained (reserve liquid)
3 eggs
1 C milk
¼ tsp basil or tarragon or oregano

To make Pastry, cut the shortening or margarine and butter into flour and salt with pastry blender until size of peas. Drizzle in cold water tossing with fork. Pack into a ball between your palms and roll out on lightly floured board to 10″ diameter. Line large deep pie plate, making a high strong fluted rim.

Strew cheese over bottom of crust; cover it with the onion. Drain and flake the salmon and arrange it over onion to cover.

In a bowl mix together eggs, salmon liquid and milk. Pour evenly over all. Sprinkle with basil or tarragon or oregano. Bake at 375° about 55 minutes or until set and flecked with gold. Serve hot cut into 6 wedges with a green vegetable such as broccoli.

Supper Salmon Loaf

Two 7¾-oz cans salmon
1 C dry cracker or breadcrumbs
¼ C milk
¼ C margarine
3 large eggs, yolks and whites separated
1 Tbsp lemon juice
1 Tbsp grated onion
2 Tbsp chopped parsley
½ tsp Worcestershire or HP sauce
¼ tsp salt
⅛ tsp pepper

Open cans of salmon and drain off and reserve juice, about ⅓ C. Pour it over the crumbs in a large bowl. Heat milk and margarine together to barely melt margarine. Add to crumbs in bowl and let soak. Flake and add salmon, mashing bones and adding them too. Stir in egg yolks, lemon juice, onion, parsley, Worcestershire or HP sauce, salt and pepper. Beat whites until stiff and fold in. Butter an 8 × 5 loaf pan and line bottom with one layer of buttered wax paper. Turn in salmon mixture. Stand loaf in shallow pan of boiling water to 1″ depth. Bake at 350° for 40 minutes until firm. To turn out loosen sides with narrow knife then invert. Peel off wax paper. This loaf serves six, but to stretch it, serve with the sauce at right.

HARD-COOKED EGG SAUCE
(could be used for vegetables too)

3 Tbsp butter or margarine
3 Tbsp flour
½ tsp salt
⅛ tsp pepper
1 chicken bouillon cube
1½ C milk
1 hard-cooked egg, chopped

Melt margarine or butter in a small pot and stir in flour, salt, pepper and chicken bouillon cube. Stir in milk and cook stirring until thick. Stir in chopped, hard-cooked egg. This is a basic medium white sauce that is all-purpose. You can omit egg and add chopped chives or parsley or olives or pimiento or whatever your imagination contrives.

Hell's Kitchen Salmon Chowder

½ C (¼ lb) melted butter
1 C chopped celery
1 C chopped Spanish onion
2 C diced (½″) raw potatoes
½ C flour
¼ tsp pepper
¼ to ½ tsp salt
1 qt (5 C) milk
One 6-oz can evaporated milk
2 C salmon or 1 lb cooked or two 7¾-oz
   cans (see below)

In a large heavy pot melt the butter and add the prepared celery, onion and potatoes. Gently sauté for 20 minutes, stirring often. Do not brown, just soak the vegetables with butter and half cook them. Stir together the flour, pepper and salt and stir into the half-cooked vegetables. Slowly add the milk and evaporated milk stirring until thick. Flake the salmon and add it too. If canned is used be sure to add the can liquid. Bring just to below boiling point and serve at once in preheated bowls.

Note: This chowder is thick and of course should be served as a main course with a hot bread such as cheese tea biscuits or biscuits supreme or garlic bread or wheat germ or bran muffins. Serves ten.

Party Glazed Salmon

One 6 to 8 pound fresh salmon, dressed
POACHING LIQUID
3 qt water
1 C white vinegar
2 onions, sliced
2 carrots, sliced
3 stalks celery, sliced
½ C chopped celery leaves
¼ C parsley sprigs
3 bay leaves
1 tsp thyme
2 tsp white peppercorns
1 Tbsp salt
3 or 4 thin slices lemon

Combine all poaching ingredients. Simmer 40 to 50 minutes. Cool and strain. Use for cooking the fish.

To cook salmon, measure the thickness of the fish. Rinse and dry. Wrap in double thickness of cheesecloth. Place on rack in fish kettle or roasting pan. Pour cooled and strained Poaching Liquid (above) over the fish to half cover. Bring slowly to a boil. Reduce heat, cover, and simmer about 10 minutes per inch of fish (20 minutes per inch if frozen). Cook until fish flakes easily. Cool in liquid. Drain, reserving 5 C of the cooking liquid for Glaze. Remove cheesecloth and chill fish on a rack over a tray.

GLAZE
4 tsp plain gelatin
5 C cold cooking liquid, reserved, above

Mix gelatin and cold cooking liquid. Boil uncovered until reduced to 3½ C. Strain. Chill in refrigerator until thick and syrupy.

To glaze salmon, once it is chilled remove skin, leaving a collar at neck and a little at the tail. Scrape away fat deposits and any grey meat. Spoon cold syrupy glaze over the fish. Chill. When first glaze has set, repeat. Garnish on top with thin slices of lemon, strips of pimiento and green pepper and capers, dipping each item in glaze first. Chill. Spoon more glaze over entire fish. Chill. Arrange on platter, garnishing platter with watercress, lemon and cucumber slices, lemon baskets filled with cherry tomatoes and tomato chutney. Serve with Tartar Sauce. Twelve to fifteen servings.

Party Glazed Salmon

French Fried Scallops with Tartar Sauce

Dry one pound of scallops. Defrost and dry if frozen. Dip each in one beaten egg and then in fine crumbs. Fry about 8 scallops at a time in ½″ deep bubbling hot oil for about 4 minutes, turning once. Drain on paper towel and serve with Tartar Sauce.

TARTAR SAUCE (simplified)

To serve 3 people add to ¼ C stiff mayonnaise, 1½ tsp each of finely chopped chives, finely chopped stuffed olives and bottled green relish, and 1 tsp lemon juice. Mix well. Serve with fried scallops (or many other fried fishes).

Baked Perch Fillets Velouté

2 lb fresh frozen ocean perch fillets

SAUCE
3 Tbsp margarine
2 Tbsp flour
¾ tsp salt
1¼ C water
Grated rind half lemon
¼ C lemon juice
2 tsp sugar
½ tsp dry mustard

Barely thaw fillets. Arrange evenly in buttered 13 × 9″ baking dish.

To make Sauce, melt margarine, stir in flour and salt to blend then stir in water, lemon rind and juice, sugar and dry mustard until thick. Pour hot over fish fillets. Sprinkle top with paprika and basil.

Bake at 400° until bubbly and tinged with gold. Do not overbake. Remove from oven when you can flake the fish with tines of fork and flesh is opaque. Serves six.

Holiday Seafood Chowder

3 lb fish fillets such as cod, haddock, halibut
3 strips bacon
1 large onion chopped
4 medium potatoes, diced
Two 19-oz cans tomatoes
1 Tbsp salt
⅛ tsp pepper
¼ tsp thyme
¼ tsp mace
4 Tbsp butter
One 5-oz tin lobster
1 qt milk

Cut fillets into 1″ pieces. Fry bacon till crisp, remove from drippings, crumble and set aside. Cook onion in bacon drippings till tender. Combine cooked onion, potatoes, tomatoes and seasonings. Cover and simmer for 10 minutes. Add fish and simmer 10 minutes longer. Drain lobster and break into pieces. Add lobster, butter and heated milk to fish mixture. Bring to simmering temperature but do not let boil. Garnish with crumbled bacon sprinkled over top. Serves twelve.

Crumbed Seafood Bake

One 14-oz can fresh frozen lobster
1 lb fresh frozen scallops
1 tsp whole pickling spices
½ onion, sliced
1¼ C fine breadcrumbs
2 eggs
2 Tbsp water
5 Tbsp butter

Defrost the lobster. Over the scallops pour boiling water to cover, add the pickling spices and onion and bring to boil, covered. Remove from heat and let stand 5 minutes. Drain well and dry. Carefully break the lobster into bite-size chunks and remove any cartilage. Have the crumbs in a shallow bowl. Roll all the fish pieces in them. Beat the eggs with the water well, and pour over fish pieces and roll all around in this crumby-eggy coating. Transfer to shallow baking dish in which 4 Tbsp of the butter have been melted, but be sure to place the lobster pieces at regular intervals, so the server is fair in apportioning them to the diners. Put the scallops in the empty spaces. Sprinkle with more crumbs, sparingly. Dot with remaining 1 Tbsp butter. Bake at 350° for 20 minutes, until pale golden, but at half time carefully turn each fish piece over.

Oysters Casino

1 qt raw oysters
About ⅓ lb side bacon
Parmesan cheese

SAUCE
⅔ C catsup
2 tsp Worcestershire sauce
8 drops Tabasco
½ C very finely chopped green onion
 (including tops)
1½ C very finely chopped celery
2 Tbsp lemon juice

Note: You will need individual shells.

Make the Sauce in advance by chopping the onion and celery and combining with catsup, Worcestershire, Tabasco and lemon juice.

Drain the oysters well. Reserve the oyster liquor and include in a cream soup at a future meal. Divide the well drained oysters into all of the shells you have but do not crowd them. Put 1 Tbsp sauce over each shell. Carefully and neatly sprinkle Parmesan around perimeter of shell. Top each with ⅓ slice bacon. Arrange prepared shells on 2 broiler pans. Insert under preheated broiler 6″ from heat, and broil until bacon sputters. Turn off heat and wait 2 minutes and turn it on again until bacon is cooked. You must not leave the oven: watch it all the time. When one broiler pan is done switch pans and broil second panful keeping first pan hot below. Serve 3 shells per person.

Oyster Stew

1 cut up peeled clove of garlic
1 slice onion
4 Tbsp butter
1 tsp Worcestershire sauce
1 pint oysters, drained
4 C milk (or 2 C evaporated milk and 2 C water)
1½ tsp salt
⅛ tsp pepper
Dash of paprika
Crackers

Rub the inside of the saucepan well with the garlic and onion and then discard them. Melt butter in saucepan over low heat. Add Worcestershire sauce and oysters (make sure there are no bits of shell) and heat until the edges of the oysters begin to curl. Add milk, oyster liquid, salt, pepper and paprika. Heat to just below boiling point and serve piping hot with crackers.

Shrimps Florenceville

2 lb shelled de-veined shrimp almost thawed
One 10-oz pkg fresh frozen fiddleheads
    (or asparagus tips) almost thawed
4 Tbsp butter
½ C chopped green pepper
½ C chopped green onion
1 chicken bouillon cube
4 Tbsp cornstarch
2 C boiling water
¼ tsp salt (optional)
¼ tsp celery pepper (optional)

In a large pot or frying pan melt the butter and in it gently sauté the green pepper and onion until limp, about 5 minutes. Stir in cornstarch until blended, then stir in the boiling water and bouillon cube until thick. Drain any water from the thawed shrimp. Add the shrimp and fiddleheads or asparagus tips and stir very gently over medium heat and bring to boil. Taste for salt. Add celery pepper if used. Serves six.

Scalloped Oysters

Drain 1 pint raw oysters. Combine 6 Tbsp table cream with the drained oyster liquor. Mix together ½ C dry breadcrumbs and 1 C fine cracker crumbs with ½ C melted butter. In a buttered small baking dish put a third of the buttered crumbs, next half the oysters, then another third of the crumbs, and another layer of oysters. Pour liquid over evenly. Add remaining crumbs. If desired dot top with 2 Tbsp butter. Bake 20 minutes at 400° and serve with tossed salad and crusty hot bread. Serves four.

Crab and Shrimp Supreme

½ C coarsely chopped green pepper
½ C chopped green or mild onion
⅓ C butter or margarine
½ lb sliced fresh mushrooms
⅓ C flour
¾ tsp dry mustard
1 C milk
1 C shredded old Cheddar cheese
1 C drained canned tomatoes
1 tsp Worcestershire sauce
½ tsp salt
One 7-oz pkg fresh frozen shrimp
    (shelled and de-veined)
One 6-oz can crabmeat

Gently sauté in the butter the green pepper, onion and mushrooms until they are wilted but not brown. Add the flour, mustard and when blended stir in the milk until thick. Add the cheese, tomatoes, Worcestershire sauce and salt. Stir to melt cheese. Then add shrimp and crab and stir just enough to mix then cook over low heat a short time to thaw and cook shrimp. Do not overstir. Serve over rice.

Crab Bisque

One can of crab meat
1 can of spinach soup
1 can of cream of tomato soup
2 soup cans of milk or cream

Heat the combined soups with milk or cream, stirring until smooth and hot. Add crab meat. Heat through. Serve in heated bowls. Sprinkle with croutons.

Smoked Haddock

1¼ lb piece smoked haddock
    (buy a thick chunky piece)
4 medium large potatoes
4 medium large carrots
SAUCE
3 Tbsp margarine
2½ Tbsp flour
¼ to ½ tsp salt
1½ C milk

Scrub, pare, cut in halves crosswise and boil potatoes and carrots in separate saucepans in salted water until tender. Simmer smoked haddock in hot water to nearly cover, in covered saucepan for 30 minutes.

Make a simple white sauce by melting the margarine, stirring in flour and salt, and when blended stir in milk until thickened.

Serve one quarter of haddock on center of each plate. Arrange 2 potato halves and 2 carrot halves alternately around haddock. Spoon hot white sauce generously over fish and partially over vegetables. Sprinkle top with finely chopped parsley. This is a delicious, economical old-fashioned family meal.

Note: Fresh frozen cod could be used instead of smoked haddock.

English Fish and Chips

2 lb haddock fillets
6 baking-size potatoes (quite large)

BATTER

⅞ C unsifted all-purpose flour (1 C less 2 Tbsp)
1 tsp baking powder
½ tsp salt
1 egg
¾ C water
2 Tbsp lemon juice

Prepare the potatoes first by washing and paring and cutting into strips the size of your little finger. Soak in cold water 10 minutes. Drain. Dry and refrigerate 15 minutes.

Now make the Batter by beating all batter ingredients together until smooth.

Fill to 1½″ depth a large deep pan or pot with good quality shortening or oil. Use a large pot as it may tend to foam up when potatoes are added. Heat until bubbling. Cook dried potatoes, a large handful at a time, until soft but not colored. Skim out, drain on paper towelling and set aside. Continue until all potatoes are partially done.

Increase temperature of fat. Cut pieces of fish into 6 even pieces and dry them. Dip in batter, drain on edge of bowl and lower 3 pieces into fat and cook until gold. Test a piece to see if it is done at center. Continue until all fish is fried. Keep hot.

Now increase temperature again and fry chips a second time until deep gold. This double frying makes chips crisply tender. Drain well on absorbent paper and serve fish and chips at once. Six servings.

Stuffed Baked Whitefish

One 3-lb whitefish (weighed when cleaned)

STUFFING

2 C soft breadcrumbs
2 Tbsp finely chopped onion
¼ C margarine
3 Tbsp chopped sweet pickle
½ tsp salt

In a medium frying pan melt the margarine and sauté the onion in it until soaked but not brown. Remove from heat and add cubed bread, pickle and salt and gently combine.

Carefully remove spine bone from fish deftly loosening it with your pointer finger. Fill cavity with stuffing. Close fish and fasten with 3 small skewers.

Place on a long strip of buttered foil on broiler pan. Brush top with butter. Bake at 450° for 20 minutes. *Note:* Allow 10 minutes' cooking time per inch of stuffed thickness measured at the thickest part. You will know the fish is cooked when the flesh down to the backbone has lost its watery look, turning a milk-white color, and when it flakes easily on testing with a fork. Remove skewers and transfer fish to a preheated platter. Garnish generously with big sprigs of parsley and wedges of lemon and serve with tartar sauce. Five to six servings.

Baked Fish Fillets with Cheese Sauce

1 lb fish fillets, fresh or frozen
¼ tsp salt
1 Tbsp butter
1 Tbsp chopped green onion
1 Tbsp lemon juice
One 10-oz can cheese soup
¼ C milk
½ tsp curry powder
2 C cooked rice (see below)
⅛ tsp paprika

If fillets are frozen thaw them. Sprinkle with salt. In frying pan melt butter or margarine and add onion and gently sauté until limp, not brown. (If onion flakes are used watch closely for they burn readily). Add lemon juice, soup, milk and curry powder. Barely heat through. Butter a shallow baking dish and spread rice evenly over bottom. (Cook ⅔ C raw long-grain rice in 1½ C boiling water with ½ tsp salt for ½ hour, covered, to get required 2 cups). Arrange fish fillets uniformly on top. Pour hot cheese sauce evenly over fillets. Sprinkle with paprika. Bake at 400° for 30 to 35 minutes. Four servings.

Oven Method For Fish Fillets or Steaks

Cut fish in individual portions and soak for 3 minutes in milk to which 2 tsp salt have been added. Drain and roll in fine breadcrumbs. Place on greased baking dish, dot with butter. Bake at 500° (extremely hot) allowing 10 minutes per inch thickness of fish. Heat may be reduced for larger fish towards end of cooking time.

Newfoundland Fish Chowder

½ C finely chopped bacon
1 C finely chopped onion
2 C diced raw potatoes
3 C hot water
1 tsp salt
⅛ tsp pepper
1 lb fresh frozen fish fillets cut small
  (cod, haddock, perch)
⅔ C (one 6-oz can) evaporated milk

In a large pot gently sauté together the bacon and onion until limp but not brown. Add diced potatoes, water, salt and pepper. Bring to boil, cover and simmer 10 to 15 minutes until potatoes are tender but not mushy.

Cut the fish fillets into 1″ pieces and add. Bring to boil for 2 minutes. Add milk. Bring to boil. Serve in preheated soup bowls or soup tureen along with rye bread. Four servings.

Tuna Fish Pie

FILLING
6 Tbsp butter
½ C chopped green pepper (or celery)
Two ⅛" thick slices medium onion
3 Tbsp flour
½ tsp salt
3 C milk
1¾ C flaked tuna, drained
2 Tbsp lemon juice

CHEESE ROLLS
1½ C sifted all-purpose flour
3 tsp baking powder
½ tsp salt
3 Tbsp shortening
½ C milk
¾ C grated medium old Cheddar cheese
2 Tbsp chopped canned pimiento or fresh
    sweet red pepper

To make Filling, in a large saucepan melt butter, add green pepper (or celery) and onion and cook gently until limp but not brown. Stir in flour and salt until blended then stir in milk until thick. Add flaked tuna and lemon juice and turn into large baking dish and cover with Cheese Rolls.

For the Cheese Rolls, sift together flour, baking powder and salt. Cut in shortening with pastry blender until size of large peas. Stir in milk to make a soft dough. Turn out on floured board and turn over then knead 10 times. Roll out to oblong 8 × 12". Sprinkle uniformly with cheese and chopped pimiento. Roll up like a jelly roll starting at narrow end. With sharp knife cut into 8 even slices, flatten slightly and place on top of tuna mixture. Bake at 450° about 30 minutes or until bubbly and rolls are baked through. Serves six.

Poached Salmon with Tarragon White Sauce

2-lb piece fresh (or frozen) salmon
Boiling water

SAUCE
3 Tbsp butter
2½ Tbsp flour
¾ tsp salt
¾ tsp leaf tarragon
1½ C milk
1 hard-cooked egg, chopped

To poach the salmon wrap it in a sheet of parchment paper or 2 jay cloths. Place it in a broad pan and add boiling water to half cover. Put on lid, bring to boil, reduce heat to simmer. After 10 minutes carefully turn salmon over and simmer 15 minutes more. Do not overcook. This method produces soft moist flesh that has no rival for flavor and texture. Skin will cling to wrapping when unrolled.

To serve, make a slit through natural center line of salmon and lift serving sections away from the bone. Serve with Tarragon White Sauce made by blending the butter, flour, salt and tarragon, then stirring in the milk until thick over medium heat. Five or six servings.

Sole Fillets Boulogne

2 lb sole fillets
One 4-oz can cocktail shrimp, drained
2 hard-cooked eggs

SAUCE
¼ C butter
¼ C flour
½ tsp salt
1 chicken bouillon cube
½ C 10% cream
1½ C milk
2 Tbsp lemon juice

Make the Sauce first by blending butter, flour, salt and then stirring in cream and milk and bouillon cube until thick. Remove from heat. Stir in lemon juice.

On a large sheet of foil on broiler pan arrange all sole fillets side by side, slightly overlapping to be sure all are in a single row to make serving easy. Spread all sauce over. Bake at 450° for 7 minutes. Do not overcook. Remove from oven and dot with the drained shrimp. Pass under very hot broiler until bubbly and tinged with rich gold.

Have ready the hard-cooked egg yolks and whites, separated. Finely chop the whites. When fish is ready, with care and the aid of a helper, transfer it to a platter, still on the foil. Trim off excess foil. Carefully push egg yolks through fine sieve to form a 3" wide stripe over entire length down center. Make a border at both sides with the chopped whites. Add a few tiny sprigs of parsley to the white border. Serves six.

Broiled Halibut Steaks

1½ lb halibut steaks or other fish fillets
About 2 lemons (see below)
½ tsp salt
⅛ tsp pepper
2 Tbsp melted butter
¼ tsp paprika

Cover the rack on your broiler pan with foil and turn up the edges slightly. Butter it and place fish steaks or fillets on it. Peel one of the lemons removing rind and white pith, and slice pulp into lemon wheels. Cover fish fillets with these. Squeeze the juice from second lemon and mix it with the salt, pepper, melted butter and paprika and pour over fish.

Preheat oven to 400°. Place broiler pan 5" from burner and broil fish until done: a ¾" steak requires about 20 minutes. Broil until fish and lemon are flecked with deep gold. Test thickest part of one to see if the fish will flake. Carefully transfer to preheated platter. Lift foil carefully and pour excess juice from it over fish. Garnish with parsley and lemon twists and serve. Four servings.

Cod Cakes

½ lb cod (1 C when thawed, cut up, packed)
1 C cut up raw potato, packed
½ C warm water
1 small egg
¼ C flour
¾ tsp salt
⅛ tsp garlic salt
2 Tbsp butter

In a saucepan measure the cod, potatoes and water. Bring to boil then reduce heat, stirring 2 or 3 times, cooking 15 minutes when potatoes will be tender. Stir in egg, flour and seasonings then remove mixture to large plate. In heavy frypan melt butter until bubbly and spoon 6 even mounds of mixture into butter in pan. Flatten slightly with pancake turner and brown. Turn over and brown other side. Serve at once. Three servings.

Vegetables

French Artichokes Vinaigrette

To serve four, buy 2 large fresh French artichokes. Cut off excess portion of bottom stem, flush with base. Pull off 3 or 4 bottom leaves if they are brown. With scissors snip off ¼″ tips of all of the larger outside leaves. Wash in running water. Cook in boiling water to cover, adding 1 Tbsp salt, and ¼ tsp garlic salt (if desired). They will be tender in 45 minutes. If a bottom leaf pulls out easily the artichoke is done. Drain and chill. When cold carefully cut in half vertically. At the center attached to the base is the bearded "choke," which is bristly and inedible. You should remove this. A sharp pointed spoon is a good dissection instrument. Place each prepared artichoke half on a small plate. Fill hollow with cold Sour Cream Mayonnaise: 3 Tbsp dairy sour cream, 3 Tbsp genuine mayonnaise, ½ tsp chives or chopped fresh green onion, ⅛ tsp salt, 1 tsp lemon juice or vinegar. Serve as first course.

How to Cook Fresh Asparagus

Wash asparagus thoroughly, cut off tough ends, be sure no sand lurks under the scales. Trim 1″ off the bottom. Stand in a tall pot, add ¾″ boiling water, cover and cook 7 to 10 minutes or until barely tender. The tips cook in the steam and color remains bright green. Drain carefully without breaking tips and serve at once with Hollandaise or Drawn Butter Sauce.

Old-Fashioned Creamed Asparagus

Make 2 C rich white sauce by melting 4 Tbsp butter, stirring in 4 Tbsp flour until blended. Stir in ½ C cream and 1 C milk (or use all milk), and stir until thick. Add about ½ tsp salt and shake of pepper. Stir in the sieved yolk of one hard-cooked egg if desired, or sieve a hard-cooked egg yolk over the top of the finished dish. Cut tough outer skin and ends from about 1½ lb fresh asparagus and cut all but the tips into 1″ lengths. Leave the tips about 2″ long. Cook in ½ C boiling water until barely tender then add them, water and all, to prepared hot cream sauce, which is thick enough to allow this dilution.

Crumbed French Fried Green Beans

Allow about 8 whole green beans per person. Wash and remove stem end. Leave bottom tip on. Dry beans. Shake in paper bag with ½ C flour and ½ tsp salt. Then dip beans into 1 egg beaten with 2 Tbsp water. Drain and coat with fine cracker or corn flake crumbs. Drop about 10 raw crumbed beans into 1″ of hot oil at 375° and fry for about 4 minutes in all, carefully turning with slotted spoon at halftime. Drain on paper towelling and keep hot until whole batch is fried.

Yellow Beans with Crumb Butter

Cook 1 qt cut up yellow beans in a minimum of salted, boiling water until barely tender. Drain. Melt ¼ C butter until it is lightly tinged with gold. Add 2 or 3 Tbsp soft white breadcrumbs and stir until they are soaked and slightly crispened. Spoon over hot yellow beans and serve.

Baked Beans

Wash 1 lb dried white beans and soak in cold water to cover overnight. Add a little more water to barely cover and simmer, covered, until tender, from half to one hour. Place 2 whole peeled medium onions in the bottom of the bean pot or baking dish with lid and pour cooked beans and whatever liquid is on them over the onions in alternate layers with ½ lb of smoked pork squares cut into 1″ dice (or ½ lb bacon ends or bacon chopped). Mix together in a small bowl 1½ tsp salt, ¾ tsp dry mustard, ⅛ tsp pepper, 3 Tbsp brown sugar, ⅓ C molasses, 2 Tbsp catsup. Mix well together and add 1 C boiling water. Pour over beans and pork and coax it to flow down. Add just enough hot water to cover beans. Cover and bake at 300° for 6 hours, carefully stirring once or twice.

Large Quantity Baked Beans

Cook 40 slices (2 lb) bacon until crisp. Drain, reserving 1¼ C of drippings. Crumble the bacon. Cook 5 C of chopped onions in bacon drippings until tender. Add onions and bacon drippings to:

Seven 48-oz cans pork and beans
1¼ C liquid honey (or 1¼ C brown sugar)
1¼ C Worcestershire sauce
3½ or 4 Tbsp prepared mustard

Mix well and bake uncovered in a large Dutch oven or in six 3-qt casseroles at 325° for 1½ hours. Serves seventy-five.

Savory Lima Beans

1 lb dried lima beans
4 C cold water
½ tsp salt
3 Tbsp margarine or butter
½ lb (3 C) washed and sliced mushrooms
2 Tbsp chopped onion (or bottled flakes)
½ green pepper chopped
2 Tbsp flour
2 tsp paprika
1 tsp salt (second amount)
1 C reserved bean liquid (see below)
1 C dairy sour cream
2 Tbsp chopped parsley (or bottled flakes)

Rinse beans in cold water then soak in the 4 C cold water overnight in the pot in which they are to be cooked. Add ½ tsp salt and simmer covered 2 hours until tender. Drain. Measure liquid and reserve 1 C.

In large saucepan or very large frypan melt butter or margarine and in it gently sauté until limp but not brown the mushrooms, onion and green pepper, about 3 to 4 minutes. Then stir in flour, paprika and second amount of salt until blended, then add reserved 1 C bean liquid and sour cream, stirring until slightly thickened. Add drained cooked beans and parsley and heat, stirring gently 3 or 4 times. Serve in preheated vegetable dish. Eight servings.

Zesty Beet Casserole

One 10-oz can rosebud beets
1 Tbsp cornstarch
2 or 3 Tbsp sugar
½ tsp salt
2 Tbsp lemon juice or vinegar
1 Tbsp margarine or butter
2 Tbsp prepared horseradish

Drain beets through sieve and reserve the can liquid. Tip beets into small casserole. In a saucepan mix the cornstarch, sugar and salt, and when blended stir in the reserved can liquid and vinegar or lemon juice and cook stirring until thick. Stir in margarine and horseradish and pour over beets in casserole. Cover and bake 30 minutes at 375°. Serves five.

Harvard Beets

One 10-oz can diced or shoestring beets
    including liquid
Grated rind of 1 large orange
⅓ C orange juice
¼ tsp tarragon (optional)
5 tsp cornstarch
1 tsp salt
2 tsp sugar

Tip can of beets into top of double boiler. Add orange rind and juice. Heat over boiling water. Mix together remaining ingredients and stir in until thick. Cover and cook 5 minutes longer, stirring once or twice.

Herbed Shoestring Beets

Drain one 20-oz can shoestring beets. Turn into saucepan. Add 1 Tbsp each vinegar and lemon juice, 1 sucaryl tablet (or 2), a pinch each of thyme, basil and rosemary (or any one of these) and ¼ tsp salt. Heat through, watching carefully and serve. *Note:* Using sliced beets this is good when served cold.

Cheese and Asparagus Puff

4 large or 5 medium eggs
2 C milk
½ tsp salt
Pinch of pepper
1 C fine cracker crumbs
1 pimiento chopped (optional)
1 lb fresh asparagus (or canned or
    or frozen ½" pieces)
10 oz (2 C packed) Edam or Gouda cheese
    cut into ¼" cubes
2 Tbsp melted butter

First prepare the crumbs and dice the cheese. Then cut 4" spears from asparagus stalks. Trim and cut into ½" pieces the tender bottom ends of stalks.

Into large casserole break eggs and beat with rotary beater. Add all remaining ingredients except asparagus tips and melted butter. Stir until thoroughly blended. Wipe sides clean with paper towel. Arrange asparagus tips on top like spokes of a wheel. Drizzle melted butter all over top and bake at 350° for 50 to 60 minutes uncovered. Serves six.

Note: This casserole may be assembled in advance but butter should be poured over just before baking.

Baked Beets Julienne

3½ C shredded cooked beets or two 15-oz
    cans shoestring beets
¼ C beet liquid or hot water
2 Tbsp lemon juice
2 Tbsp grated mild onion
½ C dairy sour cream
½ tsp salt
Pepper to taste
½ C fine dry bread crumbs
3 Tbsp melted butter or margarine

If canned beets are used drain them, reserving ¼ C liquid. Mix beets, sour cream, the ¼ C beet liquid or hot water, lemon juice, onion, salt and pepper. Turn into greased casserole. Mix crumbs and melted butter; sprinkle over beets. Bake at 375° about 25 minutes, or until bubbling hot and golden. Serves 6 to 8.

Broccoli Soufflé

1 can undiluted cream of celery
     (or mushroom) soup
3 eggs, separated
1 C finely chopped, drained, cooked, fresh or
     fresh frozen broccoli (or
     spinach or asparagus)
¼ C grated onion
Pinch of rosemary (optional)
⅛ tsp nutmeg
½ C grated Parmesan or old Cheddar cheese

Heat the undiluted soup to just below boiling. Remove from heat and stir in the beaten egg yolks and finely chopped broccoli and green onion and seasonings. Beat the egg whites until very stiff. Fold into soup mixture evenly. Turn into buttered casserole. Sprinkle top with cheese. Set dish in pan of warm water and bake at 350° for 50 minutes or until set and golden-crusted.

Broccoli and Cauliflower with Mushrooms

Combine equal amounts of broccoli and cauliflower cut into 1½" pieces. For 8 people you will need about 6 C. Cook in minimum amount of boiling water until tender. (Do not overcook or the bright green of the broccoli will fade to olive.) Drain. Gently sauté ½ to ¾ lb scrubbed sliced mushrooms in about ¼ to ⅓ C butter until limp and soaked. Add to drained broccoli and cauliflower. If desired add ¼ tsp rosemary, and salt and pepper to taste.

Chinese Stirred Broccoli

About 2½ C coarsely cut broccoli tops
     with some stems
1 Tbsp oil
1 clove garlic minced
¼ tsp ginger
1 chicken bouillon cube
1 Tbsp soy sauce
¼ C boiling water
10 water chestnuts, thinly sliced

Soak the broccoli in 2 C cold water with 1 tsp salt for 5 minutes. Drain well. Heat the oil in a frying pan and sauté the garlic and ginger in it until golden. Add drained broccoli and stir and toss. Melt chicken bouillon cube in ¼ C boiling water, stir into broccoli along with soy sauce and water chestnuts. Cover and steam gently for about 6 minutes, until broccoli is barely tender and still bright green. Serve with beef and rice.

Herbed Broccoli

Trim the heavy coarse outer skin and ends from about 2 or 3 lb of broccoli. Stand upright in a deep narrow pot, add boiling water to half cover, and cook, steaming, for about 15 minutes or until barely tender. Drain and remove to hot serving dish. Heat together ½ C butter, 3 Tbsp lemon juice, 1 finely chopped clove of garlic, ¼ tsp oregano, ¼ tsp salt and shake of pepper. When this bubbles pour it hot over the broccoli and serve at once.

Crunchy Broccoli Casserole

3 C fresh broccoli flowerets (or two 10-oz
     pkg fresh frozen chopped)
2 Tbsp margarine (first amount)
1 Tbsp grated onion
2 Tbsp flour
½ tsp salt
½ tsp sugar
¼ tsp pepper
1 C sour cream
¾ C stale bread crumbs
1 Tbsp margarine (second amount)
¼ C Parmesan or grated Swiss or
     Cheddar cheese

Precook the broccoli flowerets (or chopped broccoli) for about 4 minutes. Do not overcook. Drain and turn into medium casserole.

Make a sauce by melting the margarine (first amount) and sautéing the grated onion in it for 1 minute, then blend in the flour, salt, sugar and pepper. Stir in the sour cream until thick. Pour all over broccoli.

Melt the 1 Tbsp margarine, remove from heat and stir in the stale bread crumbs. Sprinkle over top. Sprinkle cheese over all. Bake at 350° for 20 to 25 minutes until bubbly and broccoli is tender. Serves six.

Marinated Brussels Sprouts

1 lb small firm Brussels sprouts
1 C Italian French Dressing (see below)
½ tsp dill weed
½ C thinly sliced small green onions
     including some green tops

Select small firm sprouts if possible. Wash and trim off bottoms and loose side leaves. Cook in boiling water with 1 tsp salt until only ¾ tender, about 8 to 10 minutes. Drain in colander and chill quickly under running cold water. Drain and pat dry. Turn into flat dish in one layer, add dill weed and onion and marinate overnight in Italian French Dressing.

ITALIAN FRENCH DRESSING

¼ C lemon juice (or vinegar)
¼ C water
¾ C corn oil
1 Tbsp catsup or canned tomato paste
1 tsp paprika
1 tsp salt
¼ tsp garlic salt
¼ tsp black pepper
¼ tsp dry mustard
Shake of cayenne

Mix all ingredients in jar with cover, shake well. Pour over sprouts, store covered overnight, turning them once. Serve marinated sprouts, well drained, with a toothpick.

Brussels Sprouts with Hungarian Sauce

1 C hot water
2 chicken bouillon cubes
¼ C dry white wine or vin rosé (optional)
1½ lb fresh Brussels sprouts, washed
    and trimmed
2 Tbsp butter or margarine
2 Tbsp flour
1 tsp salt
½ tsp caraway seeds
¼ tsp cayenne pepper
1¼ C milk
1½ C dairy sour cream

In a large saucepan heat the water with the bouillon cubes until dissolved, add wine (if used) and Brussels sprouts. Cover and cook 10 minutes or until just tender but still bright green. Drain well.

Make Hungarian Sauce: Melt butter or margarine in saucepan, blend in flour, salt, caraway seeds and cayenne pepper. Slowly stir in milk until thick. Add sour cream and heat through.

Turn hot drained Brussels sprouts into preheated serving dish, pour sauce over and serve. Six servings.

Sweet and Sour Stuffed Cabbage

MEAT MIXTURE
1 large green cabbage
2 tsp salt, divided
1 lb ground chuck
½ C onion, chopped
1 clove garlic, chopped finely
½ tsp pepper
1 egg, beaten

SAUCE
One 28-oz can tomatoes
1 small onion diced
2 stalks celery, diced
3 Tbsp chili sauce
1 Tbsp brown sugar
1 Tbsp vinegar

Wash cabbage thoroughly under cold water removing damaged leaves. Using a sharp paring knife, cut a circle in top of cabbage and scoop out as much of the center as possible, leaving a firm shell of cabbage about ¾" thick. Reserve insides for a future salad. Sprinkle 1 tsp of the salt over the cabbage shell and place in a large pot. Add 1½" boiling water and boil gently 10 minutes, uncovered. Remove and drain. Tie cabbage with string around circumference at this stage.

Brown meat, onion and garlic in frying pan. No fat is needed. Stir in pepper and the remaining 1 tsp salt and mix. Remove meat from stove and mix in beaten egg. Stuff this meat mixture into the hollowed cabbage. Place cabbage in a large pot and pour canned tomatoes around. Cover and simmer 30 to 40 minutes until tender. Transfer cabbage to platter, remove string. Add remaining ingredients to tomatoes in pot and simmer 10 minutes. Cut cabbage into wedges and pour tomato sauce mixture over. Serves five.

Quick-Cooked Shredded Cabbage

4 C finely shredded (not grated) cabbage
2 Tbsp milk
2 Tbsp water
1½ Tbsp butter

Shred cabbage thread-thin. Add all remaining ingredients and mix. Cook, covered, over fairly low heat, until cabbage is nearly tender. Do not let this burn. When liquid has evaporated it will be ready to serve. Four servings.

Red Cabbage with Apple

1 medium-small finely shredded red cabbage
    (4 C packed)
3 Tbsp butter or margarine
2 cooking apples pared and sliced
1 small onion thinly sliced
¼ C water
Shake of ground cloves
2 tsp vinegar
2 tsp sugar

In a large frying pan melt the butter or margarine and add the shredded cabbage and cook stirring for 5 minutes. Stir in apple, onion, water, cloves, vinegar and sugar and when well mixed, cover, reduce heat and cook gently about 25 minutes, stirring every 5 minutes.

Steam-Fried Cabbage

4 C shredded cabbage
3 or 4 Tbsp butter
1 medium onion chopped
¼ to ½ tsp salt

In large frying pan gently sauté together the butter and onion until just limp. Add cabbage. Cover and reduce heat to simmer for 15 to 20 minutes, turning 2 or 3 times, until cabbage is crisply tender. Sprinkle with salt. Serves four.

Glazed Carrots

For 6 large barely cooked carrots cut into strips or chunks, mix together ¾ C light brown sugar, ¾ C hot liquid in which carrots were cooked, 2 Tbsp butter, ½ tsp salt. Pour over carrots and simmer or bake covered, turning once or twice until nicely glazed, about one hour.

Carrots in Parsley Sauce

To serve six, scrub 6 large carrots, cut off tops and tips and boil whole in 1 C boiling water with ½ tsp salt, covered, until tender. Drain but reserve liquid. To liquid add enough milk to make 1½ C. Chop carrots coarsely. Add to liquid along with ½ C chopped parsley. Heat. Stir 3 Tbsp flour into ¼ C cold water until smooth, and stir this paste into the carrots until thick. Stir over low heat for another couple of minutes.

Carrot and Spinach Casserole

VEGETABLES
4 C (packed) wafer thin carrot slices
1 C sliced onion
4 C hard packed fresh chopped spinach
    (or thawed fresh frozen)

SAUCE
¼ C butter or margarine
¼ C flour
1 tsp salt
2 C milk
2 C grated medium or old Cheddar cheese
1 C dry breadcrumbs

Combine sliced carrots and onion and put on to cook in minimum of water (or steamer) and cook until tender. Chop the spinach and put half of it in a large shallow baking dish. Cover evenly with half the cooked, drained carrots and onions.

To make Sauce, blend butter or margarine with flour and salt over medium heat then stir in milk until thick. Remove from heat and stir in cheese. Pour half of the sauce over carrots. Repeat these 3 layers, pressing them down as well as you can and finishing with sauce. Sprinkle top with crumbs. Bake at 350° for 35 minutes. This may be made in advance and refrigerated, in which case bake about 5 minutes longer.

Carrot Creation

4 C carrot chunks
1 C potato chunks
¼ C melted butter (first amount)
1 chicken bouillon cube chopped fine
½ tsp salt
2 slices bread crumbed in blender (1 C)
2 Tbsp melted butter (second amount)

Scrub and cut the carrots in 1″ chunks. Scrub and pare and cut potato in 1″ chunks. If you have a steamer steam until tender, otherwise cook until tender in a minimum of water. Reserve ½ C of the cooking liquid. Put half of the cooked potato and carrots in blender with ½ C of their liquid. Blend until perfectly puréed. Add remaining carrots and potatoes and continue until all are puréed, about 3 minutes at high speed. Now remove goblet from machine and add the butter, chicken bouillon cube and salt. Turn into shallow medium casserole. Gently mix crumbs with 2 Tbsp melted butter and sprinkle over top. Bake at 350° about 25 to 30 minutes.

Cauliflower

Stop overcooking cauliflower. Undercook it. To save its flavor and nutrients and color cook in boiling water until still a little crisp. Lovely with cheese sauce.

Crumbed Cauliflower

Separate cauliflower into flowerets and cook until barely tender in boiling salted water. Do not overcook. Drain and turn into shallow baking dish. Cover with a mixture of ½ C fine bread crumbs and ½ C shredded old Cheddar cheese. Pass under preheated broiler until golden brown.

Glazed Carrots with Brussels Sprouts

3 long narrow carrots
1 lb pkg Brussels sprouts
2 Tbsp butter
2 Tbsp sugar
½ tsp salt

Scrub carrots and cut into 1″ chunks. Trim Brussels sprouts and cut a shallow cross in the root end of each to hasten cooking. Cook carrots and Brussels sprouts in minimum of water 10 minutes or until not quite tender, or steam them. Be sure to remove from heat before the green of the sprouts fades. Drain. Combine butter, sugar and salt in frying pan and heat and stir to melt. Add vegetables and shake and turn gently for about 5 minutes to glaze. Serves four to six.

Creamed Cauliflower

One medium (6″) cauliflower broken
    into small flowerets
2½ Tbsp butter or margarine
1½ Tbsp flour
½ tsp salt
1½ C milk
¼ C chopped chives (optional)
2 Tbsp parsley seeds (optional)
¼ C chopped green pepper (optional)

Cook cauliflower in as little water as possible until crisply tender, or better still steam it. Drain. Turn into preheated vegetable dish and keep hot. Meanwhile make sauce by melting butter or margarine and stirring in flour and salt to blend. Stir in milk until thick. Add herbs if used. Pour over cauliflower and stir in a little. Serves six.

Cauliflower Polonaise

One 6 or 7″ cauliflower
1 hard-cooked egg
¼ C finely chopped parsley

SAUCE
3 Tbsp margarine
4 Tbsp flour
½ tsp salt
¼ tsp celery seed
2 C hot water

Leave cauliflower whole but ream out some of the core at bottom to hasten cooking. If you have a collapsible vegetable steamer cook the cauliflower over steam. If you cook it in water use as little as possible and cook until barely tender. Cauliflower should be partly crisp. Drain. Turn into preheated vegetable dish and keep hot in warm oven.

Make the Sauce by melting margarine, stirring in flour, salt and celery seed until blended then stir in water until thick. Pour hot over cauliflower. Then carefully peel hard-cooked egg. Cut in half and lift out yolk. Chop the white as finely as you can and mix with the chopped parsley. Hold a sieve over the center of the cauliflower and push the egg yolk through. Do not touch it, simply let it pile up. Carefully spoon the chopped white and parsley in a neat narrow border all around edge. Serves six.

Marinated Cauliflowerets

½ cauliflower broken or cut into small
　　flowerets (2 C)
FRENCH DRESSING
(for salads or for marinade)
1 C salad oil
¼ C lemon juice (or vinegar)
1½ to 2 tsp salt
1 tsp paprika
2 tsp sugar
½ tsp dry mustard
½ tsp garlic salt
1 tsp Worcestershire sauce
1 tsp basil
6 drops Tabasco (optional)

　　Cook cauliflowerets in lightly salted water 5
minutes, no more. Drain and chill in cold water.
Drain again and turn into shallow bowl.
　　Mix together all French Dressing ingredients
and shake well. Pour over chilled drained
cauliflowerets. Store covered in refrigerator 6
hours (or longer). Drain well, reserving all French
Dressing for later salads. Serve as a relish with
cold meats or as a garnish for tomato and lettuce
salads.

Cauliflower Au Gratin

One 7″ cauliflower
1½ Tbsp butter (first amount)
3 Tbsp butter (second amount)
3 Tbsp flour
½ tsp salt
Shake of white pepper
1¾ C milk
⅓ C grated Cheddar cheese (dried out)

　　Break or cut cauliflower into medium-sized
flowerets. Cook in boiling salted (½ tsp) water to
cover, with lid on for about 12 minutes or until
nearly tender. Drain through colander. In bottom
of shallow baking dish melt the 1½ Tbsp butter,
turn cooked cauliflower into it, then turn each
floweret over to coat with butter.
　　Melt the 3 Tbsp butter, blend in flour, salt and
pepper, then stir in milk until thick. Pour this hot
sauce evenly over the cauliflower in baking dish.
Sprinkle evenly with cheese. Bake at 350° about 30
minutes. Serves six.
　　Note: This *au gratin* treatment may be used
for same quantities of either Brussels sprouts or
broccoli. Remember that these vegetables should
still be bright green when cooked.

Braised Celery

　　Wash well under running water a heavy head
of celery. Cut into 3″ lengths right through head including leaves. To serve four adequately, cut off
about ¾ of the whole head leaving on a 4″ stump to
use for raw hearts later. Put into pot with 1 tsp
sugar, 1 melted chicken bouillon cube, 1 Tbsp butter, ⅓ C hot water. Cook, covered, until tender,
about 12 to 15 minutes.

Cauliflower Casserole

One 5″ cauliflower
½ sweet red pepper
½ sweet green pepper
1 C sliced celery
1 green onion chopped
3 Tbsp butter
3 Tbsp flour
1 tsp salt
1½ C milk
⅔ C bread crumbs
½ C grated or shredded cheese

　　Break cauliflower into flowerets and cook in
boiling salted water about 7 minutes. Meanwhile
prepare peppers by cutting into strips. Chop celery
and onion. When cauliflower has cooked 7 minutes
add remaining vegetables and cook about 3
minutes. Drain.
　　Make Medium White Sauce by melting butter
or margarine, stirring in flour and salt to blend,
then stir in milk until thick. Add drained
vegetables to sauce and turn into shallow medium
casserole. Sprinkle top with bread crumbs,
sprinkle cheese over and bake at 350° about 20
minutes until bubbly and cheese is melted. Serves
five.

Sunday Celery Dish

2½ C celery including some tops, cut into
　　½″ pieces
1 C boiling water
½ tsp salt
1½ C coarsely broken crackers
1 C milk
2 Tbsp butter
¼ lb mushrooms scrubbed and cut in halves
¾ C coarsely shredded Cheddar cheese

　　Cook celery in boiling salted water 15
minutes. Do not drain. To it add crackers and
milk. Gently sauté mushrooms in butter until limp
but not brown. Tip celery-cracker mixture into
medium baking dish, cover with mushrooms.
Cover mushrooms with cheese. (If desired
refrigerate until mealtime). Bake at 400° for 30
minutes. Serves four.

Celery and
Mushrooms Normandy

3 C celery, sliced ¼″
1 C chicken broth or 1 C hot water and
　　1 chicken bouillon cube
¼ lb mushrooms or one 3-oz can sliced mushrooms
¼ C butter
¼ tsp pepper
1 tsp soy sauce
½ C toasted slivered almonds

　　Simmer the celery in the chicken broth until
just tender, then drain. Sauté the mushrooms in
butter, season with pepper and soy sauce and add
to celery. Toss with almonds and serve hot.

Crumbed Eggplant

1 large eggplant (or 2 medium)
1 egg
¼ tsp salt
1 Tbsp water
About 1 C soft bread crumbs

Cut large eggplant in ¾" slices and pare it. Cut each slice in half crosswise. Parboil for 5 minutes, covered. Drain. In shallow bowl beat egg with salt and water to mix. Dip eggplant slices in egg then in crumbs on a plate. Let set a little before frying. Melt 3 Tbsp margarine in large frying pan and fry crumbed eggplant over medium heat until golden on bottom, then turn and fry other side. Serves six.

Quick Eggplant

4 C pared diced (½") eggplant
⅔ C chopped onion
2 Tbsp margarine
¼ tsp salt

Melt the margarine in a frying pan with a lid. Add eggplant, onion and salt. Stir once or twice. Cover. Cook over low heat 20 minutes, stirring once or twice. Heat must be low for it is the steam from the vegetables that cooks them and prevents them frying.

Eggplant Casserole

One 1¼ lb eggplant (6 C when pared and cut
   into ¾" cubes)
2 medium-large white onions chopped
2 Tbsp margarine
½ C grated Parmesan cheese (divided, see below)
1 C dry breadcrumbs (divided, see below)
1 tsp salt
1 egg

Cook the cubed eggplant and chopped onion in a minimum amount of water 15 minutes, then drain through colander and return to pot. Add the margarine, half of the cheese, half the crumbs and the salt. Mix gently then stir in egg. Turn into medium-sized casserole. Mix together remaining crumbs and cheese and sprinkle evenly over top. Bake at 350° for 30 minutes till crumbs are tinged with gold. Serves four.

Eggplant Parmegiano

Wash, slice thinly, but do not pare long narrow eggplant. To one unbeaten large egg add ¾ tsp salt and ⅛ tsp pepper and 1 Tbsp water and dip eggplant slices in it, then fry them in ½" oil in a large frying pan until gold on both sides. Drain on paper towels.

Have ready 2 C canned tomatoes or peeled sliced raw tomatoes and ½ lb thinly sliced Mozzarella cheese and ¼ C grated Parmesan cheese. Arrange these ingredients between the sautéed eggplant slices, sprinkling them with a little salt and pepper, in a buttered baking dish. Sprinkle top with more Parmesan and pour any leftover egg into crevices. Bake at 350° for about 30 minutes.

Corn

1. Corn on the Cob: To cook it on the cob requires only the length of time needed to bring it to the boil. Then it is done. Longer cooking starts a toughening process. Never boil corn more than one minute.

2. Corn off the Cob: Cut corn from cob and measure. Add a quarter of this amount of chopped fresh green pepper. Sauté gently in butter until peppers are limp but not brown. Serve sprinkled with salt and pepper.

Creole Corn

2 Tbsp butter or margarine
⅔ C chopped green pepper
¼ C chopped Spanish onion
1 C chopped tomato, fresh or chunks from canned
1 C cream style corn
½ tsp salt

Measure into the top of the double boiler the butter or margarine, green pepper and onion, and gently sauté for 5 minutes, stirring. Then add the tomato, corn and salt. Put top of double boiler over bottom containing boiling water, cover and cook 10 minutes. It is now ready to serve.

Corn Pudding

2 C fresh corn kernels (or canned kernel corn)
2 C scalded milk
2 eggs, slightly beaten
1 tsp sugar
1½ Tbsp melted butter or margarine
1 tsp salt
¼ tsp pepper

Add corn to scalded milk then add to all remaining ingredients. Pour into buttered casserole or baking dish. Bake in a pan of warm water at 325° for 1 hour, or until firm. If desired, ½ C minced cooked ham or grated cheese and 2 Tbsp minced onion may be added to pudding mixture before baking, to make this into a more nutritious casserole for a meal that is short on protein.

Corn with Green Pepper and Onion

3 Tbsp minced onion
½ C diced green pepper
3 Tbsp butter or margarine
3 C raw corn kernels (or fresh frozen)
6 Tbsp light cream or milk
½ tsp salt

Cook the onion and green pepper in the butter in a saucepan over low heat until just tender. Add the remaining ingredients and cook 2 or 3 minutes longer, or until corn is barely tender.

Summer Succotash

6 ears fresh corn
2 C fresh lima beans or chopped yellow beans
¾ C cream or rich milk
1 Tbsp butter
½ tsp salt
⅛ tsp white pepper

With sharp knife cut the corn kernels from the cobs. Cook the beans in salted water to barely cover for 8 minutes. Add corn and cook 5 minutes longer. Drain well. Add cream or milk, butter, salt and pepper and heat to nearly boiling. Serve at once.

Corn and Mushroom Medley

One 12-oz can kernel corn (not drained)
¼ lb scrubbed and cut up mushrooms
¼ C coarsely chopped bottled or canned pimientos
2 Tbsp butter
2 Tbsp flour
¼ tsp salt

In shallow pan blend butter, flour and salt. Add corn including liquid, mushrooms and pimientos and stir until thickened a little and heated through. Serves four.

Fiddlehead Greens

Buy a 10-oz pkg of frozen Fiddlehead Greens. Bring ¾ C water to boil with ½ tsp salt and ½ tsp sugar. Tip in unthawed fiddleheads. Cover. Bring to boil, reduce heat to simmer and cook until thawed and barely tender. Do not overcook. Drain, add butter.

Sautéed Mushrooms

Under running water scrub mushrooms until clean, then drain well. In large frying pan melt ¼ C butter. Add a clove of garlic to the pan. When hot and fragrant add drained mushrooms and cook, stirring, over medium high heat until mushrooms absorb fat and are very hot and tender-crisp, not more than 3 to 5 minutes. They are now ready to serve. Discard garlic. If desired, cut mushrooms into 4 pieces, then they require only 3 minutes sautéing.

Creamed Mushrooms

½ lb small whole mushrooms, well washed
1½ C hot milk
3 Tbsp butter
2½ Tbsp flour
½ tsp salt

Over direct heat in top of double boiler blend butter, flour and salt then stir in hot milk until thick. Add washed mushrooms, place over boiling water in double boiler, cover and cook about 10 to 15 minutes. Serves four.

Lenten Mushrooms

1 lb mushrooms
2 Tbsp butter (first amount)
9 Tbsp (½ C plus 1 Tbsp) flour
9 Tbsp (½ C plus 1 Tbsp) butter (second amount)
3 C milk
2 tsp Worcestershire Sauce
1½ tsp salt
¼ tsp pepper
½ lb grated cheese (2 C fairly well packed)
4 hard-cooked eggs, sliced
½ green pepper diced
¼ C chopped pimiento

Scrub and slice mushrooms. Sauté in the 2 Tbsp butter until soaked but not brown. In another pot melt second amount of butter and blend in flour. Now stir in milk until thick and smooth. Stir in Worcestershire sauce, salt, pepper and cheese. Add sautéed mushrooms, sliced hard-cooked eggs, green pepper and pimiento. Turn into buttered baking dish and bake at 350° for 30 minutes until lightly browned and bubbly. Serve over Fluffy Rice made by adding 1¼ C raw long grain rice to 3 C boiling water and 1 tsp salt. Bring to boil covered. Turn off heat for 5 minutes. Turn heat on as low as possible and cook 25 minutes longer. Serves six.

Mushrooms Béchamel

12 to 16-oz whole mushrooms, scrubbed
1½ Tbsp margarine
2 Tbsp flour
1 C hot water
1 chicken bouillon cube
¼ C chopped parsley

In top of double boiler over direct heat blend margarine and flour, then stir in water and chicken bouillon cube until quite thick. Add scrubbed whole mushrooms—which will thin the sauce—and place over boiling water in bottom of double boiler. Cover and cook 15 minutes. Add parsley.

Spinach with Mushrooms

2 pkg spinach
One 10-oz can mushrooms, stems and pieces
1½ Tbsp butter
1½ Tbsp cornstarch
¼ to ½ tsp salt

Wash spinach thoroughly. Drain well. In large kettle cook covered in the water that clings to its leaves, turning over as soon as bottom leaves wilt. Cook until barely tender. Drain in colander and chop coarsely. Return to pot. In a saucepan stir and heat together to blend the butter, cornstarch, salt. Stir in mushrooms and liquid until thickened. Stir into spinach and heat through.

Barley and Mushroom Casserole

3 Tbsp butter or margarine
½ Spanish onion chopped
½ lb raw mushrooms quartered
1 C raw barley
3 C hot water
½ tsp salt
1 chicken bouillon cube

Sauté together gently the onion and barley in the butter or margarine until they are soaked with it, but not brown. Add salt, bouillon cube and 2 C of the hot water and simmer until water is absorbed. Add remaining 1 C hot water and turn into casserole dish. Cover and bake at 325° for 1 hour. Remove from oven, add washed and quartered mushrooms, stirring in gently. Replace cover and bake ½ hour longer.

Marinated Mushrooms and Green Peppers

¾ lb medium-small raw mushrooms
1 large green pepper
Onion French Dressing (see below)

Under running water scrub mushrooms, then cut them in halves down through the stems. Drain and dry. Wash the green pepper and cut in half and remove seeds and ribs. Cut into pieces about 1 × ½″. Combine with mushrooms.

ONION FRENCH DRESSING: ½ C salad oil, 2 Tbsp vinegar, ½ tsp salt, ½ tsp sugar, ½ tsp paprika, ¼ tsp dry mustard, 1 tsp onion salt, ½ tsp Worcestershire sauce, ½ clove garlic, sliced. Combine all ingredients. Shake well and pour over mushrooms and green pepper in bowl, cover and refrigerate for 24 hours, stirring 3 or 4 times. Drain at serving time and serve cold with hot or cold beef or any cold meats or fish.

Stuffed Green Peppers

4 medium-sized green peppers
1 lb ground hamburg
¾ C soft bread cubes
½ tsp salt
1 egg, slightly beaten
2 Tbsp onion, finely chopped
1 can condensed cream of cheese soup

Remove tops and seeds from peppers. Steam shells about 5 minutes. Combine remaining ingredients, using only ½ can of the soup. Mix well. Fill peppers with stuffing. Place in shallow baking pan. Bake 30 minutes at 375°. Remove from oven and pour remaining half of soup over peppers, then return to oven and continue baking an additional 15 minutes. Serves four.

Steam-Fried Green Peppers and Cucumbers

To serve eight, use 2 large cucumbers and 3 large green peppers. Wash and pare cucumbers. Cut into quarters lengthwise and trim out seed portion, saving it for a future salad. Wash green peppers and cut each into 8 strips lengthwise, removing seeds and inner ribs. Have ready in large frying pan about 3 Tbsp melted butter. About 12 to 15 minutes before serving time add the prepared cucumbers and green peppers, turn heat medium-low, cover, and steam-fry until they are wilted and heated through but still crisp.

Baked Rice-Stuffed Green Peppers with Cheese Sauce

4 medium green peppers
STUFFING
6 slices bacon
2 Tbsp bacon drippings
2 C cooked rice (see below)
½ C chopped green onion
½ tsp salt
¼ tsp pepper
¼ tsp thyme

SAUCE
2 Tbsp butter or margarine
2½ Tbsp flour
1½ C milk
½ tsp salt
⅛ tsp pepper
⅛ tsp paprika
½ C grated old Cheddar cheese

Wash peppers, cut off tops and remove ribs and seeds. Fill peppers with rice stuffing (below) and bake in pan containing ¼″ of water at 375° for 40 minutes. Serve with cheese sauce (below).

To prepare Stuffing, fry bacon until crisp; drain and crumble. Cook rice and onion in bacon drippings until drippings are absorbed. Add salt, pepper and thyme. Add bacon and mix well.

To prepare Sauce, melt butter and blend in flour. Gradually stir in milk and cook, stirring constantly, until sauce is thickened and smooth. Add seasonings and cheese. Cook until cheese is melted.

Easy Stuffed Peppers

6 medium-sized peppers
2 C ground leftover cooked ham, chicken
   or other meat
2 Tbsp grated onion
½ tsp salt
Dash of pepper
1 C soft bread cubes
1 egg, slightly beaten
1 can condensed tomato soup

Cut off tops of peppers, remove stems and seeds. Wash and drain upside down. Combine meat, onion, salt, pepper, bread, egg and half the can of soup. Mix well. Stuff peppers with this mixture and cover and boil gently in 1" of salted water for 30 minutes, or until peppers are tender. Drain carefully. Heat remaining soup and pour over peppers when serving. Serves six.

French Fried Onion Rings

3 medium-large onions
1 egg white
½ Tbsp flour
2 tsp milk
½ tsp salt

Slice onions across in ½" slices and soak in ice cold water for 1 hour then drain and dry. Separate rings. Make a batter of remaining ingredients. Coat dried onion rings with mixture and fry in deep fat at 375° until golden brown and crisp.

Onions Au Gratin

8 cooking onions sliced ½" thick
½ tsp salt
1 C boiling water

SAUCE
2 Tbsp butter or margarine
2 Tbsp flour
½ tsp salt
Shake of pepper
1 C milk
¼ C onion liquid (from cooking onions)
½ to ¾ C grated Cheddar cheese
3 slices buttered bread (diced)

Cook the sliced onions in the salted boiling water 10 minutes. Drain, reserving ¼ C liquid for sauce. Turn onions into buttered baking dish.

Make the Sauce by blending melted butter, flour, salt and pepper, then stirring in milk and onion liquid until thick. Remove from heat and stir in cheese until melted. Pour over onions in baking dish. With a fork help sauce to flow down through onions. Butter 3 slices of bread and cut into ¼" dice. Sprinkle over sauce in baking dish. Bake at 375° for 25 to 30 minutes or until bubbly. Serves six.

White Onions with Green Pea Sauce

To serve six, boil 12 medium-small white onions in large amount boiling salted water until tender, about 30 minutes. Drain. Turn into medium-large baking dish.

Make a white sauce: heat 2 C milk. Melt ⅓ C butter, stir in ¼ C flour, ½ tsp salt until blended, then stir in hot milk until thick. Remove from heat. Add one 12-oz pkg fresh frozen green peas and stir to thaw. Pour over onions in baking dish being sure sauce flows between. Mix together ½ C each soft breadcrumbs and grated old Cheddar cheese and sprinkle over top. Bake at 350° until bubbly and golden, about 30 minutes.

Stuffed Onions

Select 6 large (at least 3") onions. Peel and cook until nearly tender in boiling salted water (about 25 minutes). Drain. Cool enough to handle. With sharp pointed knife remove 1" core from each. Chop half of the cores, reserving others for soup. To chopped cores add 5 Tbsp shredded cheese, 1½ Tbsp melted butter, 1 Tbsp catsup and ½ tsp salt. Stuff into cavities in onions. Stand in well-buttered baking dish, touching, and bake about 30 minutes. Do not bake too long or they droop. If desired, top with buttered crumbs and return onions to oven for 5 or 10 minutes.

Parsnip Puffs

2 C puréed cooked parsnips (strainer or blender)
2 Tbsp melted butter
1 egg, yolk and white separated
Salt and pepper to taste
¼ C milk or cream

To the puréed cooked parsnips add the melted butter, seasonings and milk or cream. Beat the egg yolk and add it. Beat the egg white until very stiff and fold in. Spread on platter and chill. With buttered palms shape into rolls 1 × 3". Roll in buttered very fine cracker crumbs. Place on buttered baking dish and bake at 375° until puffy and golden brown.

Crumbed Parsnips

Scrub and pare about 6 medium parsnips. Cut into ½" slices, cutting wide slices in half crosswise. In saucepan barely cover with boiling salted water and cook not more than 10 minutes. Drain and discard liquid. Let dry and then dredge with flour, about ¼ C. Beat an egg with 1 Tbsp water and ½ tsp salt. Have ready about 1½ C very fine dry breadcrumbs. Dip parsnip pieces in egg then in crumbs. Transfer to large frying pan with generous amount of butter and fry until golden on both sides. Serves six to eight.

Glazed Parsnips and Carrots

Scrub 3 medium parsnips and 3 medium carrots. The parsnips should be pared but not the carrots. Cut all into 1″ chunks. Cook in small amount of boiling salted water until nearly tender, about 12 minutes. Drain.

Over medium-high heat melt ¼ C butter or margarine with 2 Tbsp light brown sugar and 1 Tbsp finely chopped parsley. Carefully add drained parsnip and carrot chunks and turn them almost constantly in this glaze for about 5 minutes until they become an even golden brown.

Savory New Green Peas

Steam 3 C fresh new peas on a rack or in a sieve or in a cheesecloth bag in tightly covered pan for 15 minutes. For perfection do not allow them to touch the boiling water. Gently sauté ¼ C minced chives or small green onions in ¼ C butter until limp and soaked with butter, then add ½ C fine strips of cooked ham, 2 tsp sugar, ½ tsp salt, ⅛ tsp freshly ground black pepper. Heat stirring for about 2 or 3 minutes. Remove from heat, add hot peas and 1 Tbsp finely chopped mint leaves and serve at once in preheated vegetable dish.

Potatoes Berney

4 very large potatoes
⅓ C milk
1 egg
2 Tbsp butter
½ tsp salt
Flour
1 egg (second)
2 Tbsp water
2 C shredded and finely chopped almonds
    or sesame seeds
3 Tbsp butter (second amount)

Boil potatoes in salted water until soft. Drain and mash until very smooth. Add milk, 1 egg, 2 Tbsp butter and ½ tsp salt and beat until smooth. Spread on shallow pan or plate and chill. Then with buttered palms shape into rolls or balls. Have ready 3 shallow bowls, flour, second egg beaten with water, almonds or sesame seeds. Roll potato in flour then in egg, then in almonds. Chill on plate to set and dry. Half an hour before mealtime melt the 3 Tbsp butter in a shallow pan, carefully add chilled potato rolls and roll each over in the butter to coat. Bake at 375° about 25 to 30 minutes or until crusty.

Crisp Potato Pancakes

Scrub 3 medium potatoes eating-clean and grate them finely directly into a bowl containing 1 beaten egg (this prevents browning). Add 1 small onion grated and 2 Tbsp flour, ½ tsp salt, ½ tsp baking powder, ⅛ tsp pepper and mix all well. Heat a little shortening in frying pan and using a rubber spatula slide a little of the pancake mixture from a tablespoon into the hot fat. Fry only a few pancakes at a time, spreading and flattening with back of spoon. When bottom is crisp and brown turn and brown other side. Keep pancakes hot in low oven as you fry them. Serves four.

Dauphine Potatoes

6 medium large potatoes
2 tsp salt
½ tsp white pepper
½ tsp nutmeg
3¾ C milk
2 eggs
1 C shredded Gruyere or old Cheddar cheese

Carefully cut potatoes into ¹⁄₁₆″ slices. Heat the milk and shred the cheese.

In a large bowl stir the salt, pepper and nutmeg into potatoes. Beat the eggs, stir the cheese and hot milk into them and pour over the potatoes and mix well. Then turn into a large casserole, cover and bake at 350° for 30 minutes, then remove lid and bake 1 hour longer until nearly set and a gold film forms on top. Serves six.

Lyonnaise Potatoes

6 medium potatoes
2 Tbsp butter (first amount)
2 Tbsp oil
½ C finely sliced onions
2 Tbsp butter (second amount)
About ½ tsp salt
¼ tsp pepper
Chopped parsley

The potatoes should be cooked in their skins only until partly tender. Peel and slice thinly. In a heavy frying pan heat the butter (first amount) and oil, and sauté potatoes until pale gold. In another pan sauté onions in second amount of butter until soft but not brown. Add them to the potatoes in heavy pan and mix together carefully to avoid breaking potatoes. Sprinkle with salt and pepper and parsley and serve.

Swedish Potatoes

6 large potatoes, pared
¾ C dairy sour cream
One 4-oz pkg white cream cheese
    (room temperature)
1½ tsp onion salt
½ tsp salt
¼ tsp white pepper
2 Tbsp butter

CRUMB TOPPING
1½ Tbsp melted butter
¾ C soft fine breadcrumbs

Cook pared potatoes in salted boiling water until tender. Drain and mash until smooth. Add sour cream, cream cheese, onion salt, salt, pepper and 2 Tbsp butter and beat until light and fluffy and there are no lumps. Turn mixture into a well-buttered medium-large casserole.

To make a crumb topping, in a pot melt the 1½ Tbsp butter. Remove from heat and add breadcrumbs. Toss gently with fork. Pat crumbs on top of potato mixture to completely cover. Bake at 350° for 30 minutes until heated through. Remove from oven and let stand 10 minutes before serving. Eight servings.

Crisp Broiled Potato Slices

6 medium-large potatoes pared and
    sliced thinly (⅛")
Cooking oil
Salt
Sesame seeds

Scrub, pare and slice potatoes ⅛" thick. Soak in cold water 15 minutes. Drain and dry. Arrange in single layer on greased broiler rack. Brush top with oil and sprinkle with salt. Put 5" under preheated broiler and broil until pale gold. Remove and turn each slice. Now sprinkle liberally with sesame seeds and a little more salt. Return to oven and broil again until golden. Serve at once to retain crispness.

Potato Cheese Puff

1¾ C hot mashed potatoes (3 large)
1 C grated Cheddar cheese (packed)
2 Tbsp butter or margarine
1 tsp salt
2 large eggs, yolks and whites separated
½ C milk
¼ tsp pepper
⅛ tsp dry mustard
¼ C grated cheese (second amount, for topping)

Scrub, pare and quarter potatoes and cook in large pot in small amount of lightly salted boiling water until tender. Drain and mash until perfectly smooth. Add grated cheese, butter and salt and beat until cheese and butter are melted.

While potatoes are cooking pour ½ C milk into measuring cup, add egg yolks and pepper and mustard. Beat these into the potato mixture until thoroughly blended. Beat egg whites until they will stand in soft peaks. Fold into potato mixture with rubber spatula until smoothly blended. Butter a 1-qt baking dish and turn mixture into it. Sprinkle grated cheese over top and bake at 350° for 45 minutes. Serve at once. Four servings.

Scalloped Potatoes

2 Tbsp butter (first amount)
2 Tbsp flour
1½ tsp salt (or less)
2 C milk
6 C sliced potatoes (not packed)
1 Tbsp melted butter

Melt butter (first amount) in large saucepan, stir in flour and salt, then add milk slowly, stirring until sauce thickens. Add potatoes and heat, stirring, until the sauce boils again. Turn into a greased casserole being sure all potatoes are coated with sauce. Drizzle melted butter over. Bake covered at 350° for 1 hour or until potatoes are tender. *Note:* After melted butter has been added this can be refrigerated, covered, until baking time. Serves four to six.

Baked Potatoes with Seasoned Butters

Scrub potatoes until skin is eating clean. Dry and prick with a sharp-tined fork. Bake at 425° for 60 to 70 minutes, time depending on size.

Crosscut top ½" deep and spread with one of these Seasoned Butters: 1. Onion Butter: Cream ⅓ C soft butter or margarine with 1½ tsp grated onion; 2. Horseradish Butter: Cream ⅓ C butter with 1 Tbsp drained horseradish; 3. Herb butter: Cream ⅓ C butter with ¼ tsp each basil, tarragon and thyme.

Baked Herbed Rice

1 C raw long grain rice
2½ C boiling water
1 chicken bouillon cube
¾ tsp salt
2 tsp chopped chives
2 tsp chopped parsley

Dissolve salt and bouillon cube in boiling water. Add chives and parsley. Measure rice into buttered medium-large casserole with snug fitting cover. Pour liquid over rice and stir. Cover and bake 1 hour at 350° without removing lid.

Rice in Chicken Broth

Into heavy pot measure 1 C raw long grain rice, 1 tsp salt, 2 chicken bouillon cubes and 2 C boiling water. Stir to dissolve bouillon cubes. Bring to boil covered then turn off heat for 5 minutes. Turn heat on simmer for 25 minutes.

Rice in Tomato Juice

Into heavy pot measure 1 C raw long grain rice, 1 tsp salt. Add 2 C tomato juice, bring to boil, cover, turn off heat for 5 minutes. Turn heat to simmer for 25 minutes.

Wild Rice

Soak in 6 C water overnight one 6-oz pkg wild rice with 1 C raw long grain white rice. One and one half hours before mealtime bring to boil with 1 tsp salt. Cover, reduce heat to simmer and cook until very tender.

Risotto

2 C strained fatless chicken broth
2 Tbsp butter or margarine
⅞ C (1 C less 2 Tbsp) raw long grain rice
½ tsp curry powder
1 tsp salt
¼ C currants
¼ C grated Parmesan cheese

Note: If you do not have any chicken broth add 2 or 3 chicken bouillon cubes to 2 C hot water and use that for your broth.

In heavy pot melt butter or margarine and add rice and curry powder and over medium heat stir until rice is parched: opaque and slightly scorched.

Now add chicken broth, salt and currants. Bring to boil covered. Turn off heat for 5 minutes. Turn heat on as low as possible for 25 minutes longer, when rice will have absorbed broth and each grain will be separate and tender. Gently stir in Parmesan and serve.

Spinach Soufflé

One 15-oz pkg fresh spinach
SAUCE
2 Tbsp margarine
3 Tbsp flour
1 C milk
2 eggs, yolks and whites separated
2 Tbsp finely chopped onion
1 tsp salt
Shake of pepper
8 rosemary leaves or ¼ tsp nutmeg
Grated cheese

Wash the spinach and drain well. Press into large pot and cook covered, without adding any water, turning it over when it is boiling. Cook until tender enough to chop finely. Drain well.

Make the Sauce by blending together in a pot the margarine and flour. Stir in the milk until thick. Stir in the egg yolks, onion, salt, pepper, rosemary or nutmeg and chopped spinach. Beat egg whites until stiff in large bowl and fold spinach sauce into them until all puffs of egg white are blended in. Turn into straight-sided ungreased 6-C soufflé dish. Sprinkle with grated cheese. Stand in pan of hot water and bake at 325° for 50 minutes. Serves four.

Baked Spinach

Wash 2 lb spinach and chop it roughly into ½″ strips. Cut 6 slices of bacon into 1″ strips and sauté gently with ½ C chopped green onion until light brown. Remove from heat, add ½ tsp cinnamon or ¼ tsp nutmeg, 2 Tbsp cider vinegar, 1 tsp salt and a little freshly ground black pepper. Stir this into the chopped spinach and press it all into a large baking dish. Cover and bake at 350° for 30 minutes.

Savory Spinach Squares

⅓ C raw rice
⅔ C hot water
One 10-oz pkg fresh spinach
2 eggs
⅓ C milk
2 Tbsp melted butter
2 or 3 Tbsp chopped onion
1 or 2 Tbsp chopped parsley
½ tsp Worcestershire sauce
¾ tsp salt
¼ tsp thyme
¼ tsp nutmeg
1 C shredded cheese (process or Cheddar)

Cook rice in hot water, covered, until tender. Cook spinach in water which clings to leaves after washing, turning over when steam forms. Cook until slightly tender and drain well through sieve. Chop.

Beat eggs. Add milk, melted butter, onion, parsley, Worcestershire sauce, salt, thyme, nutmeg and cheese. Stir in rice and spinach. Turn into greased shallow 1-qt baking dish and bake at 350° for 25 to 30 minutes or until set and bubbly and golden. Cut into squares to serve.

Spinach Supreme

Two 10-oz pkgs spinach
1 small onion chopped
2 Tbsp butter or margarine
2 Tbsp flour
1⅓ C hot milk
½ tsp salt
Shake of pepper
Shake of nutmeg
One hard-cooked egg sliced or chopped
½ C breadcrumbs
½ C shredded or grated Cheddar cheese

Wash spinach and drain. Cook, covered, in water clinging to leaves until limp and barely soft enough to chop. Drain well through colander. Chop coarsely.

In a medium-large frying pan melt butter or margarine and in it sauté onion gently for 3 or 4 minutes. Do not brown. Stir in flour to blend then stir in milk until thick. Add chopped spinach, salt, pepper, nutmeg and sliced or chopped egg and stir to blend. Turn into a greased medium casserole. Mix crumbs and cheese and sprinkle over top. Bake at 375° for 25 minutes until crumbs are golden brown.

Hubbard Squash

Scrub a large Hubbard squash. Dry it and place on a foil-lined pan and bake at 375° for 2½ to 3 hours.

Cut squash open, remove seeds and scoop out flesh. In flat-bottomed saucepan mash 4 C until perfectly smooth. Add 3 Tbsp butter or margarine, 1 tsp salt, ¼ tsp pepper, ⅛ tsp nutmeg and ¼ C hot cream. Beat while reheating until nearly boiling. Serve garnished with parsley.

Baked Acorn Squash with Pineapple

3 small acorn or pepper squashes, halved
½ C canned crushed pineapple, drained
2 Tbsp pineapple juice (from above)
2 Tbsp brown sugar
6 Tbsp butter or margarine
¼ tsp ground nutmeg
1 tsp salt

Scoop out seeds and rough fibers from halved squashes. Place, cut side up, in greased baking dish, fill centers with 1 tsp each pineapple juice, brown sugar and butter or margarine. Cover and bake at 400° for about 30 minutes or until tender. Scoop out cooked squash, leaving ¼" thick wall. Mash and combine with remaining 4 Tbsp butter and other remaining ingredients, beating all well together. Spoon back into shells and return to oven at 425° for about 15 minutes.

Stuffed Squash

One pepper squash (7 × 5")

STUFFING

2 Tbsp butter or margarine
2 Tbsp chopped onion
¼ C chopped celery
1½ C soft breadcrumbs
½ tsp salt
¼ tsp savory
⅛ tsp pepper
½ C chopped or canned tomatoes
    or tomato juice

MEAT MIXTURE

1 lb ground chuck
2 Tbsp chopped onion
1 tsp salt
1 tsp Worcestershire sauce
½ C fresh or canned tomatoes
    or tomato juice
¼ tsp oregano

Wash and cut squash in half vertically. Scrape out seed portion. Parboil, cut side down, in large shallow pan, covered, for 10 minutes. Drain. Sprinkle hollows with salt.

To make Stuffing, in large frying pan gently melt butter, add onion, celery and breadcrumbs and sauté until crumbs soak up butter. Meanwhile add salt, savory, pepper and tomatoes. Remove from heat. Divide into 2 portions.

Combine all Meat Mixture ingredients in large bowl. Divide into 4 portions. Put one portion in hollow of each salted squash half. Cover with half of the stuffing. Cover each with remaining meat mixture, mounding it up, but pressing hard to edges to seal in stuffing. You need all of both. Place on large shallow baking dish, add about ¾" hot water, cover snugly with foil and bake 2 hours at 350°. To serve, cut in wedges. Serves six.

Baked Pepper Squash

Wash and cut squash into the number of wedges you need. Use large squash for six, medium squash for four. Scrape out seed portion. Puncture flesh with sharp 2-tined fork in about 5 places. Fill each section with 2 tsp each brown sugar and butter. Sprinkle with salt and nutmeg. Arrange on shallow pan, add ½ C water, cover with foil and bake at 350° for 1½ hours. Add more butter to squash sections just before serving.

Baked Stuffed Sweet Potatoes

6 medium sweet potatoes
2 or 3 Tbsp butter
¼ tsp salt
⅛ tsp nutmeg
Pinch of pepper

You are going to use the skins later as shells, so to prevent them crisping too much wrap scrubbed sweet potatoes in foil and bake at 400° about 40 to 45 minutes. (Test for tenderness by piercing fork through foil.) Cut potatoes in half lengthwise and scoop out centers into a bowl. Add butter and spices and beat well. Refill shells and sprinkle tops with a little brown sugar and grated rind of orange. Return to oven for a few minutes to reheat. Serves six.

Sweet Potato Casserole with Orange

8 medium sweet potatoes
½ tsp nutmeg
½ tsp cinnamon
2 oranges, sliced wafer thin
¼ C light brown sugar
¼ C white sugar
6 Tbsp butter
1 Tbsp cornstarch

Scrub and cook the sweet potatoes in boiling salted water until tender. Drain and save the water. Peel and slice thinly, then arrange a layer in a greased casserole, sprinkle with nutmeg and cinnamon and add half of the orange slices. Repeat in layers until sweet potatoes and orange slices are used up.

Meanwhile make a sauce of the sugars, ¼ C butter and 1 C potato water. Mix the cornstarch with 2 Tbsp more of the cold potato water and add to the sugar mixture. Cook until thick and smooth, stirring constantly. Pour over potatoes, dot with remaining 2 Tbsp butter and bake at 350° for 45 minutes. Serves eight.

Pan Glazed Sweet Potatoes

Cook 6 small or 3 large sweet potatoes in boiling water until barely tender. When cool enough to handle, remove skins, cut in halves or quarters crosswise. In large frypan put ⅓ C brown sugar, ⅓ C hot water and 3 Tbsp butter and bring to boiling. Place potatoes in this syrup and cook uncovered gently until they absorb glaze, basting and turning several times. Serve hot.

Baked Crumbed Tomatoes

6 firm tomatoes, medium-sized
½ C stale breadcrumbs (blender)
3 tsp sugar (divided, see below)
Salt
About 1 Tbsp melted butter

Wash tomatoes and cut in halves horizontally without removing cores. Sprinkle each sparingly with salt and ¼ tsp sugar. Lightly mix crumbs with melted butter. Cover each with 1 Tbsp buttered crumbs and gently pat them down. Bake at 400° about 8 minutes, watching carefully, until top is golden.

Green Tomato and Onion Casserole

To serve four, select 4 medium-large green tomatoes. Wash and remove core. Slice ¼" thick into buttered casserole. Between layers arrange 1 thinly sliced large mild Spanish onion. Sprinkle layers generously with salt and a little pepper. Dot top with 2 Tbsp butter or margarine. Cover and bake at 375° for 1 to 1¼ hours or until onions are very tender. Serve with beef.

Favorite Tomato Casserole

One 28-oz can tomatoes
4 slices bread
3 Tbsp butter
½ tsp salt
¼ tsp onion, minced or chopped

Generously butter the bread and arrange on broiler pan. Put in oven, turn on heat to 250° and leave it to dry for 30 to 35 minutes. Remove from oven and cut into quarters. Tip tomatoes into medium casserole and gently stir in salt and onion. Press dried bread quarters with points up, into tomatoes, standing them up like a forest of pickets. Bake at 350° for 30 minutes.

Crumbed Tomato and Small Onion Casserole

One 15-oz can whole small Italian or
    Bulgarian tomatoes
One 14-oz can small canned onions
1½ C soft bread crumbs
3 Tbsp water
⅛ tsp onion powder (or onion salt)
¼ tsp salt

In medium casserole arrange the drained canned onions in 2 rows on the outside edges. Arrange whole tomatoes in rows in center between them. Spinkle with the onion powder and salt. Melt butter, stir in breadcrumbs and spoon on top of vegetables in rows, allowing the vegetables to peek through. Bake at 375° for 20 to 25 minutes or until heated through and crumbs are deep gold.

Baked Root Vegetables

2 medium parsnips
2 large carrots
2 large potatoes
3 Tbsp butter or margarine
1 tsp salt
¼ tsp pepper

Pare parsnips and cut into 1¼" chunks. Scrub but do not pare carrots and cut into 1¼" chunks. Scrub but do not pare potatoes and cut into quarters. Turn into casserole with cover. Dot with the butter or margarine and sprinkle with the salt and pepper. Cover tightly and bake at 400° for 1 hour. Mix well after 30 minutes to coat with butter or margarine. Serves six.

Chef Rego's Turnips

Wash, pare, slice and cut a medium yellow turnip into ¾" cubes. Cook in salted water until tender. Drain. Add ½ C thick pulp from canned tomatoes or 1 medium tomato chopped finely, and 2 Tbsp butter and ½ tsp salt. Heat through, gently stirring. A colorful vegetable and a good way to lift turnips from ordinary to special.

Creamed Diced Turnip

4 C diced (½") turnip
4 Tbsp butter or margarine
3 Tbsp plus 1 tsp flour
½ tsp salt
⅛ tsp pepper
⅛ tsp nutmeg
2 tsp sugar
2 C hot milk

Cook turnip dice in boiling water till tender. Drain. Make sauce by blending flour, butter, salt, pepper, nutmeg and sugar and stirring in hot milk until thick. Add drained diced turnip and heat through. Serves six.

Turnip and Vegetables Au Gratin

1¼ C boiling water
1 tsp salt
1 small turnip (1 to 1½ lb)
1 large onion quartered
1 C celery stalks and leaves
½ green pepper cut in lengthwise strips
2 Tbsp cornstarch
¼ C cold water
1 Tbsp butter or margarine
½ C grated Cheddar cheese

Cut off 1 slice from side of turnip then turn on flat side to make working easier. Slice and pare and cut into finger strips. Bring the water and salt to boil in a pot and add the turnip and onion and cook gently, covered, for 15 minutes. Then add the celery and green pepper and cook till all are crisply tender. Drain off and reserve 1 C liquid. Keep drained vegetables hot. Stir cornstarch and cold water together to make a paste and stir into cooking liquid until thick. Add butter or margarine and cheese and stir to melt. Add drained vegetables and carefully reheat and serve. Four servings.

Turnip and Apple Casserole

1 medium-large turnip
1 tsp salt (first amount)
1 Tbsp butter (first amount)
1½ C pared, sliced apple
¼ C brown sugar (first amount)
⅛ tsp cinnamon
2 Tbsp butter (second amount,
    room temperature)
⅓ C brown sugar (second amount)
⅓ C flour
½ tsp salt (second amount)

Wash, slice, pare and cook turnip with first amount of salt in boiling water to barely cover, covered, until tender. Drain and mash well with 1 Tbsp butter. Spread half in bottom of shallow casserole. Mix together apples, brown sugar (first amount) and cinnamon and spread half over turnip. Repeat. Mix together to make a crumbly mixture the 2 Tbsp butter, ⅓ C brown sugar, flour and second amount of salt. Sprinkle all over top. Bake at 400° for 35 minutes. Serves six.

Turnip and Potato Casserole

One Spanish onion
4 C cut up turnip
1 C cubed potatoes
1 tsp salt
¼ tsp pepper
1 chicken bouillon cube
½ C boiling water
2 Tbsp butter

Slice the onion thinly into a medium casserole. Pour over it enough boiling water to cover and let stand 5 minutes. Drain off this blanching water. Pare and cut the turnip into ¾" slices and cut these into little strips about 2 × ½". Add to onions in casserole. Add pared and cubed potatoes (½") and mix through. Sprinkle with the salt and pepper. Dissolve the chicken bouillon cube in the boiling water and pour all over vegetables. Dot with butter. Cover tightly, bake at 400° for 1¼ hours. Serves six.

Chinese Spring Vegetables

1 lb fresh asparagus cut into ½"
    diagonal slices
½ C sliced green onions (include 2"
    of green stems)
2 Tbsp butter or margarine
½ lb washed and quartered mushrooms
1 chicken bouillon cube
1 Tbsp brown sugar
1 Tbsp vinegar
1 Tbsp soy sauce
¼ C cold water
2 tsp cornstarch

Before you start cooking have everything prepared and measured. Combine the chicken bouillon cube, brown sugar, vinegar, soy sauce, water and cornstarch in a small bowl and stir until smooth.

In a frying pan melt the butter or margarine and add the asparagus and onion and cook on medium heat for 3 or 5 minutes. (Asparagus should retain its bright green color and most of its crispness.) Add quartered mushrooms and cook stirring gently until coated with butter, about 1 minute. Stir in combined wet ingredients and cook just until thickened a little and boiling. Serve at once. *Note:* If desired thinly sliced celery and green pepper may be added or substituted for the asparagus.

Breaded Vegetable Marrow

1 medium vegetable marrow
1 large beaten egg
2 Tbsp water
½ tsp salt
About 1½ C buttered breadcrumbs (see below)
Butter or margarine for frying

Wash the vegetable marrow, cut into quarters lengthwise, remove seeds and cut the quarters into sticks or bars 4 × 1". Pare off skin. Steam until nearly tender, sprinkled with a little salt. Cool.

To make breadcrumbs, beforehand spread 5 slices bread with margarine, place on pan and put in oven at 200° until dry and crisp. Buzz in blender to reduce to crumbs. (If you do not have a blender mix dry breadcrumbs with 2 Tbsp melted margarine in frying pan.) Beat the water into the egg. Dip pieces of marrow in egg then coat with crumbs and fry in margarine or butter until golden on both sides.

Cheese-Stuffed Zucchini

6 small zucchini (6")
1 tsp salt
¼ tsp pepper
½ C grated cheese
½ C soft breadcrumbs
Paprika

Wash the zucchini and slice in half lengthwise. Parboil in boiling salted water, covered, until barely tender. Scoop out seedy portion in center and season shells with salt and pepper. Fill with cheese and crumbs, sprinkle with paprika, broil till cheese melts.

Savory Zucchini

About five 6″ zucchini
⅓ lb sliced side bacon
3 medium onions, peeled and sliced
1½ tsp salt
¼ tsp pepper
½ tsp basil or rosemary
2 Tbsp catsup

Wash but do not peel zucchini. Cut into slices. Cut bacon into 1½″ pieces and fry over medium heat until it begins to sizzle then add onion and cook 5 minutes, stirring frequently but do not brown. Put a layer of zucchini into a casserole, sprinkle with a little salt, pepper and basil, dot with catsup. Cover with a layer of onions and bacon, and repeat until casserole is filled, ending with bacon and onion. Dot top with catsup. Bake at 350° until zucchini is almost tender, about 30 minutes.

Ratatouille

¼ C oil (divided, see below)
1 C sliced onion
1 sliced clove of garlic
Three 6″ zucchini sliced
1 medium eggplant cubed (¾″)
2 green peppers sliced
One 28-oz can tomatoes (drained, see below)
⅓ C flour
1½ tsp salt

Measure 2 Tbsp oil into large casserole. Layer half of all vegetables (except tomatoes) over it. Combine salt and flour and sprinkle over. Repeat with remaining vegetables. Arrange drained tomatoes over top and drizzle remaining oil over. Reserve tomato juice for another purpose. Bake at 375° uncovered about 1 hour. This is a moist dish so serve it with cold sliced meat and a vegetable such as mashed squash, potatoes or turnip.

Eggs & Cheese

How To Poach An Egg

Eggs for poaching must be fresh. The whites of week-old eggs spread all through the boiling water when first dropped into it. The white of a fresh egg clings closely to the yolk.

In a shallow pan have boiling water to 1" depth and add 1 tsp vinegar. Break a fresh egg into a saucer and slip into boiling water. Water must be deep enough to cover top of yolk. Turn heat to very low and cook until yolk is consistency that you desire, about 4 minutes. Meanwhile make and butter toast. With slotted spoon carefully transfer poached egg to buttered toast and serve.

Boiling Eggs in The Shell

Measure 1 C water for each egg to be cooked. (If only one is to be cooked use narrow pot and measure in enough water to cover egg.) Bring water to hard boil. Add room temperature eggs (not cold from refrigerator). Cover pan and remove from burner. For soft eggs let stand 6 to 8 minutes. For hard-cooked eggs, let stand 25 minutes.

Omelette

Allow 1½ eggs per person. For six, separate 9 eggs into 2 bowls, putting yolks in the smaller one. To the yolks add 9 Tbsp warm water and ¾ tsp salt.

Beat the whites until stiff. Transfer beater to yolks without washing and beat yolks until thick. Fold the beaten whites into the yolks as lightly as possible. Have heated and ready a large heavy frying pan with 3 Tbsp butter melted to a rich gold. Immediately turn in omelette, leaving heat on high for 1 minute, then reduce heat to very low and cook until bottom is set and golden. Do not stir, just lift carefully at side and peek to see if bottom is firm. Have broiler burner preheated. Transfer omelette to shelf in oven about 7" below broiler to slightly dry off top and tinge with gold. Crease center, carefully fold over with spatula, cut into 6 wedges and serve on preheated plates at once.

Eggs Benedict

6 large eggs
6 round slices bread or English muffins, toasted
6 round slices ham or tongue
Hollandaise Sauce

First make HOLLANDAISE SAUCE (see index), and hold at room temperature.

Butter the toast or toasted muffins. Poach the eggs until medium done. Arrange buttered toast or muffins on preheated plates and cover with tongue or ham. Top with poached egg. Top each egg with a heaping tablespoon of Hollandaise Sauce. Serve at once.

Eggs Florentine For Two

1½ C fine noodles (packed)
½ tsp salt
4 C boiling water
One 10-oz pkg spinach
1 tsp lemon juice
3 hard-cooked eggs

MOCK HOLLANDAISE
2 Tbsp butter
1½ Tbsp flour
¼ tsp salt
1 C milk
1 beaten egg
1 tsp lemon juice

Cook the noodles in the salted water until nearly tender, about 15 minutes. Drain. Tip into buttered shallow medium-size oblong or oval casserole.

Wash spinach, drain and cook in covered pot with only the water clinging to leaves for 6 minutes, turning over once. Chop. Drain well. Spread over noodles and sprinkle with 1 tsp lemon juice.

Cut peeled hard-cooked eggs in halves lengthwise. Place in double row over center of spinach end to end.

Make Mock Hollandaise by blending together butter, flour and salt, then stir in milk, cooking until thick. Add lemon juice to beaten egg. Add 1 heaping tablespoon hot sauce to it and stir quickly, then stir into hot sauce using wire whip until thicker and smooth. While hot pour all of it over eggs allowing part of spinach and eggs to show. Bake at 350° for 20 to 25 minutes until bubbly and tinged with gold. Before serving decorate sides with rings of green pepper or strips of pimiento or tomato wedges.

Buttered Eggs

In top of double boiler over boiling water melt 6 Tbsp butter. Beat 6 eggs with ¾ C milk and ½ tsp salt, only until mixed and foamy. Turn into top of double boiler and cook, stirring constantly, until softly set. This takes at least 10 minutes constant attentive stirring. Serve at once on hot toast or toasted English muffins.or with hot buttered raisin bread.

Devilled Eggs

8 large eggs (room temperature)
2 Tbsp finely chopped chives
    (or young green onions)
6 Tbsp real mayonnaise
1 tsp prepared mustard
¼ tsp curry powder (optional)

Bring eggs to boil in warm tapwater, then remove from heat and let stand covered for 20 minutes. Flood with cold water. Peel chilled eggs and cut in halves lengthwise. Scoop yolks into bowl and add the chives, mayonnaise, mustard and curry powder (if used) and mix with fork until smoothly blended. Refill white halves, piling filling high. Garnish with paprika or tiny sprig of parsley.

Devilish Crab Eggs

8 hard-cooked eggs
¾ C thawed, boned crabmeat or
    one 7-oz can drained
3 Tbsp finely chopped celery
5 level Tbsp mayonnaise
1 tsp dry mustard
¼ tsp salt
4 drops Tabasco
⅛ tsp oregano
⅛ tsp curry powder
¹⁄₁₆ tsp garlic powder

Cover eggs with cold water, put on lid, bring to boil. Remove from heat and let stand half an hour. Chill with running cold water and peel. Cut in halves lengthwise. Carefully remove yolks into a bowl working neatly to keep whites unbroken.

To yolks add crabmeat, celery, mayonnaise, mustard, salt, Tabasco, oregano, curry and garlic powders. Mix until thoroughly blended and smooth. Fill egg whites with this filling, piling it high, gently packing. Top with tiny sprig of parsley. Serves eight.

Scotch Omelette

1 C fresh white breadcrumbs (softly packed)
1 C hot milk
½ tsp salt
4 large eggs, yolks and whites separated
2 Tbsp butter
1 tsp bottled onion flakes or grated onion
2 Tbsp quick-cooking rolled oats (optional)
1 C shredded cheese (sofly packed)

Soak breadcrumbs in hot milk with the salt. Beat egg whites until stiff. Without washing beaters beat egg yolks in another bowl until thick. Add soaked crumbs to yolks and fold them into beaten whites.

In large frying pan melt butter. Sprinkle the little bit of onion all over bottom of pan. When pan is hot turn in omelette. If used, sprinkle rolled oats all over top. Now sprinkle cheese over all and cook covered until bottom is rich gold. Do not burn. Remove from heat and dry off top under preheated broiler for about 3 minutes or until tinged with gold. Loosen edges and using 2 lifters fold over. Cut into 3 or 4 sections and serve on preheated plates with small boiled parsleyed potatoes and frenched green beans or buttered spinach. Serves 3 or 4.

Egg Rolls

FILLING
1 C diced onion
1 C thinly sliced celery
1 tsp cooking oil
1 Tbsp soy sauce
2 C diced cooked or canned chicken

PANCAKES (similar to Crêpes)
4 eggs
1½ C water
1½ C sifted all-purpose flour
1 tsp salt
Oil for frying

To make Filling, combine onion, celery and oil in a small saucepan. Cover. Cook over low heat 10 minutes or until just soft. Stir in soy sauce. Pour over chicken in a bowl and mix. Let rest while making pancakes.

To make Pancakes, beat eggs, add water and beat until foamy. Beat in flour and salt until smooth. (Batter is thin.) Heat an 8″ frypan. Add about 1 tsp oil, tilting pan to coat bottom completely. Pour batter into pan, ¼ C at a time. Cook 1 to 2 minutes or until top appears dry and underside is golden. Lift out onto paper towelling to cool. (Only one side is cooked.) Repeat with remaining batter, adding a little oil before each baking, to make 12 pancakes. Cool each separately on plate.

Spoon ¼ C chicken filling slightly off center on baked side of each pancake. Fold short end over filling, then fold both sides toward center and roll up, jelly-roll fashion, starting at open end, to completely enclose filling. Fasten with 1 or 2 toothpicks. Place in shallow dish. Cover and chill overnight: very important for crispness.

Heat 1½″ oil to 400° in electric or deep heavy frying pan. Drop in rolls, 2 or 3 at a time. Fry, turning once, 5 to 8 minutes or until golden and crisp. Drain on paper towelling. Keep rolls hot in warm oven until all are cooked. Remove picks and serve.

Mexican One-Eyes

Cut a hole from the center of each slice of bread with a 2″ cookie cutter or an egg cup. Add butter to large frying pan, about 3 Tbsp, and melt until bubbling. Put 4 slices of bread (with hole cut out) in pan. Drop a small egg in each hole. (The white will overflow a little.) Cook until egg is nearly set then turn each over for a brief moment. Lift out and serve. *Note:* The little circular cutouts should be fried too.

Spanish Omelette

1 medium potato, pared and sliced thinly
½ Spanish onion sliced thinly
4 eggs
½ to ¾ tsp salt
¼ tsp pepper
2 tsp olive oil
3 tsp cold water

In a medium pan, preferably with sloping sides, heat oil. Over low heat add potato slices in 3 layers, cover with sliced onions, cover with lid and cook slowly until potato is tender but not browned.

Beat eggs in a bowl, adding salt and pepper. When vegetables are soft turn heat up to medium and pour eggs over. As egg mixture cooks, lift edges with spatula and let liquid egg run underneath. When egg is nearly cooked but still a little runny on top, lift edges with spatula and pour 1 tsp cold water under omelette in 3 separate places (3 tsp cold water in all). Cover pan tightly and cook 2 or 3 minutes longer. Omelette should rise and should be served immediately, folded over. If to be served cold transfer to plate to cool.

Bachelor Omelette Fines Herbes

2 large eggs
1½ tsp chopped fresh parsley
1½ tsp chopped fresh chives
2½ Tbsp water
¼ tsp salt
1 small shake garlic salt
1 Tbsp butter

Note: An omelette pan is a useful acquisition: heavy aluminum 8½" diameter at the top, sloping in a curve to a flat bottom 5½" diameter, and 2" deep.

Break the eggs into a small bowl and add the parsley, chives, water, salt and garlic salt. Beat until slightly foamy. Melt the butter in the omelette pan until it is pale gold and bubbly, tipping pan to coat sides. At once on high heat add omelette mixture and with metal or rubber spatula start loosening edge at handle side and fold it a little and tip to make surplus liquid flow to uncovered side. Keep tipping and gently folding until all surplus liquid is softly set and then coax the total mass to roll to far edge and out of pan onto preheated plate.

Venetian Eggs

Select 4 large firm tomatoes. Cut a thick slice from the top of each. Scoop out enough of the center to accommodate a small egg. To prepare pan melt about 2 Tbsp butter in it and place tomatoes in pan. Sprinkle hollow with salt. Drop 1 small egg into each. Sprinkle with salt and paprika. Add 2 Tbsp water to pan. Cover. Cook about 5 minutes until top of egg is filmed over.

Creamed Hard-Cooked Eggs On Rice

8 hard-cooked eggs, sliced
6 Tbsp butter or margarine
½ C finely chopped green onions
¼ C flour
1 to 3 tsp curry powder (optional)
1½ tsp salt
⅛ tsp pepper (preferably white)
3 C hot milk

Gently sauté onion in butter until wilted but not brown. Remove from heat and stir in flour, curry powder (if used), salt and pepper. Return to heat and stir until bubbling then stir in milk until thick. Add sliced hard-cooked eggs and stir gently to heat through. This is at its best served over hot, fluffy boiled rice. Serves four.

Supper Egg Cups

2 Tbsp butter or margarine
2 Tbsp flour
½ tsp salt
1¼ C milk
½ C grated old Cheddar cheese (packed)
1 tsp Worcestershire sauce
6 large eggs
6 Tbsp fine soft breadcrumbs
Parmesan cheese

Make a Cheese Sauce by melting the butter or margarine and stirring in the flour and salt. Stir in milk until thick. Stir in cheese until melted. Add Worcestershire sauce.

Spoon half of the hot sauce into bottoms of 6 individual custard cups. Break an egg into each. Top each with remaining sauce. Sprinkle tops with 1 Tbsp each fine crumbs. Sprinkle sparingly with Parmesan cheese. Place cups in a shallow pan, filling the pan to 1" depth with hot water. Bake at 350° for 20 minutes.

Eggs Divan

6 large eggs
¼ C butter or margarine
¼ C flour
1 tsp salt
2⅓ C hot milk
2 C fresh frozen peas (or broccoli,
    spinach, asparagus)
½ lb (about 2 C) shredded mild or
    medium Cheddar cheese
Paprika

Put the eggs in cold water, cover, bring to boil, stand off heat for 20 minutes. Flood with cold water and peel and cut in halves lenghtwise. While they cool make a sauce by blending the butter or margarine with the flour and salt and stirring in hot milk until boiling. Remove from heat.

Arrange peas (or other green fresh frozen vegetables) in shallow medium-large baking dish. Over them place the halved hard-cooked eggs in a single layer. Pour hot sauce over all. Cover with generous layer of shredded cheese. Sprinkle with paprika. Bake at 350° for 20 minutes. If desired, this dish may be made in advance and refrigerated until near mealtime. Serves four.

Curried Eggs

8 hard-cooked eggs, sliced
½ C chopped onion
6 Tbsp butter
¼ C flour
1 tsp curry powder
3½ C milk
2 tsp salt
⅛ tsp pepper

Sauté the onion in the butter. Remove from heat and blend in the flour and curry. Return to heat, stir until smooth, and gradually add the milk, stirring until thickened. Add the eggs and season with salt and pepper and heat through, carefully stirring. Good served over rice. Makes 4 servings.

Scrambled Eggs

9 large eggs
¾ C warm water
2 tsp Worcestershire sauce
¼ tsp Tabasco
1 tsp salt
⅛ tsp pepper
⅛ tsp garlic salt
⅓ C butter

Beat eggs to mix them until barely foamy. Stir in remaining ingredients except butter with fork. Have butter heating in a large frypan until it begins to turn gold. Immediately turn egg mixture in. Stand ready to push back the underneath cooked portion, as soon at it sets, over medium high heat. Continue pushing back the set portion, allowing liquid part to run forward until all is set and the mass is in golden layered folds. It should be barely set and streaked with gold. Fold over like an omelette and serve at once on preheated platter. Serves six.

Egg Burgers: Four Varieties

For each serving break 1 extra large egg into a moderately hot, lightly buttered small frying pan. Immediately stir with a spoon to break up yolk and mix streakily with white until softly set. Remove from heat at once and spread on bottom of toasted hamburger bun. Sprinkle with salt.

Variations: 1. Top with thin slice processed cheese or grated Cheddar, a slice of tomato and remaining half of bun. 2. Top egg with chopped crumbled bacon. 3. Top egg with chopped mushrooms which have been gently fried in a little butter. 4. Top salted egg with a little finely chopped green onion and green relish.

Eggs Veriton

6 hard-cooked eggs, quartered lengthwise
3 bags spinach (10-oz each)
5 Tbsp butter
6 Tbsp flour
1 tsp dry mustard
1 Tbsp sugar
1 tsp salt
3½ C hot milk
Juice of 1 lemon (almost ¼ C)
2 Tbsp green onion flakes or
    1 small onion, minced
6 to 12 oz (1 or 2 C) ground or
    chopped cooked or uncooked ham
One 4-oz can grated Parmesan cheese
½ to 1 C breadcrumbs
Paprika

Cover eggs in saucepan with cold water, cover, bring to boil and simmer 5 minutes. Drain and chill in cold water. Cut into quarters lengthwise.

Clean spinach under running water. Drain. Cook, covered, with only the water that clings to the leaves, in very large pot until barely limp but still bright green. Drain and chop coarsely. Turn into large buttered casserole.

Make Sauce by melting butter, stirring in flour, mustard, sugar and salt until blended, then hot milk until thick. Stir in lemon juice and onion flakes and ham and half of the Parmesan cheese. Bring just to boil, stirring. Pour half of the sauce over the spinach, persuading it to flow between crevices. Line up the hard-cooked egg quarters in 3 even lengthwise rows. Pour remaining sauce over, being sure each egg quarter is covered. Mix remaining Parmesan cheese with breadcrumbs, sprinkle evenly over top and sprinkle delicately with paprika. Bake at 350° for 30 to 35 minutes. Serve hot with generous tossed salad and fresh French or rye bread. Six to eight servings.

Salmon Soufflé

1½ Tbsp butter or margarine
2 Tbsp flour
½ tsp curry powder
½ tsp nutmeg
½ tsp salt
⅛ tsp pepper
1 C milk
One 8-oz can salmon
5 medium eggs, yolks and whites separated

In a large heavy saucepan melt the butter and stir in the flour, curry powder, nutmeg, salt and pepper. Stir in the milk until thick. Remove from heat. Beat egg yolks, stir in a little of the hot sauce, then stir them into the hot sauce until smoothly blended. Mash the salmon, including liquid, with a fork and add it to the sauce. Beat egg whites until stiff but not dry. Fold them into the hot mixture until smoothly incorporated but do not beat. Turn into straight-sided ungreased soufflé dish or casserole. Stand this in large shallow pan containing 1″ boiling water. Bake at 350° for 1 hour. Serve at once. Four servings.

Cheese Strata

12 slices crusts-on 60% whole wheat bread
½ lb sliced process cheese (6 to 8 slices)
4 large eggs
2½ C milk
1 tsp prepared mustard
2 Tbsp minced onion (or 2 green onions chopped)
1 tsp salt
¼ tsp pepper

Butter 6 of the slices of bread and fit them, buttered side down, in a buttered 13 × 9″ pan. Cover with cheese slices. Cover with remaining unbuttered bread slices. In bowl beat the eggs, then add the milk, mustard, onion, salt and pepper and mix. Pour evenly all over bread and let stand 1 hour or all day in refrigerator.

Fifty minutes before mealtime bake in oven at 325° until puffy and golden. Serve at once. If desired, 1 C ground ham or drained kernel corn or grated cheese could be added to the milk mixture before pouring it over the bread slices. Serves six.

Welsh Rarebit

1 lb mild Cheddar cheese (do not
    use old Cheddar)
1 Tbsp butter
1 C beer
1 large egg beaten
1 tsp Worcestershire sauce
1 tsp salt
¼ tsp dry mustard
Bacon (optional)

Shred cheese, about 6 C not packed. In top of double boiler melt butter and add beer and when it is warm stir in cheese with a fork until melted. Stir in beaten egg and seasonings until blended. Serve on toast and if desired garnish top with chopped crisp cooked bacon bits or curls. Serves six.

Pyrohy

1 tsp sugar (first amount)
¼ C lukewarm water
1 pkg granular yeast
1 C scalded milk
¼ C shortening or butter
2 eggs, beaten
1½ tsp salt
1 Tbsp sugar (second amount)
4½ to 5 C sifted flour
Filling (see below)

Dissolve the 1 tsp sugar in the lukewarm water, sprinkle the yeast over and let stand 10 minutes. To the hot scalded milk add the butter or shortening and cool to lukewarm. Add the eggs, salt, 1 Tbsp sugar and yeast liquid. Mix enough flour to make a medium soft dough as for bread, about 4½ C. Knead on floured board until smooth and satiny. Return to bowl, cover, and let rise until double in bulk. Punch down, knead a few times in the bowl and let rise again. Cut off small egg-sized pieces of dough and roll ¼″ thick. Place a generous portion of the Cottage Cheese Filling (below) in the center, bring the edges together and press to seal securely.

COTTAGE CHEESE FILLING: 1 lb dry cottage cheese, 1 Tbsp thick sour cream, 2 eggs beaten, ½ tsp salt, 1 Tbsp chopped dill pickle, if desired. Press the cottage cheese through a sieve or mash it well. Add the remaining ingredients and mix thoroughly.

Shape Pyrohy into an oblong with a plump center and tapering ends. Dip them after they are filled and shaped into melted butter. Place, sealed side down, on a greased baking sheet, spacing them 1½″ apart. Cover and let them rise in a warm place until light and doubled. Bake at 375° for 30 to 35 minutes, depending on their size.

Eggs Foo Yung

4 eggs
1½ tsp salt
¼ tsp pepper
¾ C chopped onions
1 Tbsp soy sauce
1 C chopped cooked pork or chicken
    or shrimp
1 C bean sprouts, fresh or drained canned
4 Tbsp chopped green onion, including tops

Lightly beat the eggs, salt and pepper. Stir in the onion, soy sauce, meat or fish, sprouts and green onions. Heat a small amount of oil in frying pan. Using ¼-cup measure, drop measured amount of mixture into hot oil, cooking only 4 mounds at a time, turning each over when browned on bottom. Reduce heat and cook and brown other side. Repeat until egg mixture is cooked.

Serve with Sauce: Mix 1 Tbsp soy sauce with 1 Tbsp cornstarch, 1½ C chicken broth and 2 tsp molasses. Cook stirring, until thick. Pour over omelettes and serve. *Note:* If you do not have chicken broth on hand, add 1 chicken bouillon cube to 1½ C hot water as a substitute.

Yorkshire Pudding

¾ C unsifted all-purpose flour
½ tsp salt
2 large eggs
1½ C milk
3 Tbsp beef fat or margarine

Two hours before mealtime measure flour, salt and eggs into beater bowl and beat 1 minute. Add milk slowly, while beaters are on low and beat until batter is smooth. Cover and let stand at room temperature 2 hours.

Fifteen minutes before mealtime have oven heated to 450°. In an 8 × 8" baking dish melt the beef fat or margarine until it is bubbling and golden, very hot indeed. With care remove it from oven and add the Yorkshire pudding batter. It should sizzle and start to cook at sides. Immediately return to oven and bake 10 to 12 minutes until puffed to top of dish and rich gold. Cut into 4 or 6 squares and serve at once.

Cheese and Tuna Roll

BISCUIT DOUGH
2 C stirred but unsifted all-purpose flour
4 tsp baking powder
½ tsp salt
3 Tbsp shortening
⅔ C milk

FILLING
1 C shredded Edam cheese lightly packed
One 7-oz can tuna, drained
One 4-oz can salmon
2 Tbsp chopped onion
1 beaten egg (reserve 1 Tbsp)
½ tsp salt
¼ tsp pepper
One 10-oz can cut green beans, drained

SAUCE
4 Tbsp margarine
4 Tbsp flour
¼ tsp nutmeg
2 C milk
2 C shredded Edam cheese lightly packed

Make the Biscuit Dough first by sifting together the flour, baking powder and salt. Cut in shortening with pastry blender until size of peas. Add milk to form a soft dough, with as little mixing as possible. Spread large double sheet of wax paper on counter, sprinkle generously with flour and pat and roll dough out to 18 × 12" oblong.

Combine all Filling ingredients (except 1 Tbsp egg) in a bowl and spread over dough to within 1½" of back long edge. Using the front edge of the wax paper to help you, transfer all to large greased cookie sheet. Still using the wax paper to help you, roll up like a jelly roll. If desired shape into a ring and press ends together. Carefully slip out wax paper.

To remaining 1 Tbsp egg add 1 tsp water and brush top of roll with it. Bake at 350° for 40 minutes.

Meanwhile make Cheese Sauce by blending margarine, flour and nutmeg, then stirring in milk until thick. Remove from heat and stir in cheese until melted.

Transfer Roll to platter. Cut into wedges with hot cheese sauce spooned over each serving.

Cheese Omelette

4 large eggs
⅓ C milk
½ tsp salt
2 Tbsp butter
1 C shredded Cheddar cheese

In a mixing bowl combine eggs, milk, salt and cheese with beater until mixed and frothy. In a 9" slope-sided frypan over medium-high heat melt butter until it is bubbly and gold. Immediately pour in egg mixture. As soon as it sets at edges, reduce heat a little and run spatula around edge tilting pan to allow uncooked part to flow underneath. Repeat. Tilt pan yet again and using spatula, carefully fold over half the omelette. Have preheated platter at hand and slant pan to a sharp angle and coax omelette to roll into a second fold. Slide out of pan onto platter. Sprinkle with chopped chives or parsley and serve at once with hot crisp buttered whole wheat toast or a baked potato in its jacket. Serves two or three.

Fail-proof Yogurt

This recipe makes five 16-oz jars. You need a thermometer.

6 C warm water, divided
2 C skim milk powder
¼ C plain commercial yogurt
One 16-oz can evaporated milk

Into your blender measure 2 C of the warm water and the skim milk powder and blend. Add yogurt and blend. In a large bowl mix the evaporated milk with the remaining 4 C warm water. Stir in milk-yogurt mixture.

Have ready at hand 5 clean straight-sided 16-oz glass jars. Have on a low burner your roasting pan with rack in, containing 3" warm water at 120 to 125°.

Pour prepared yogurt mixture into jars to fill within ¾" of tops. Stand in pan of warm water. Prop thermometer against side of pan. Cover roasting pan. Turn off burner. Inspect every half hour to see if temperature is steady. If temperature has dropped turn burner on low for 5 minutes then turn if off but keep your eye on the temperature. It should hold around 120°.

In 2 hours you have set but mild-tasting yogurt. In 4 hours you have set yogurt with a characteristic sour taste.

Cool, then refrigerate. It mixes excellently with any good jam.

Cocktail Cheese Mousse

¾ C milk
2 egg yolks
4 tsp gelatin
½ C diced process cheese
Two 4-oz pkg pimiento white cream cheese
1 C cottage cheese
⅓ C sweet pickle relish
1 tsp vinegar
1 tsp dry mustard

In a small saucepan mix together the milk, yolks, gelatin and diced process cheese. Cook stirring until smooth. Do not boil. Set aside.

In beater bowl beat cream cheese, cottage cheese, relish, vinegar and mustard until blended. Beat in milk mixture until smooth. Turn into oiled 4-cup mold. Chill until firm. To turn out, lower into hot water for 5 seconds and turn over and out onto serving plate. Garnish with bread and butter pickle slices overlapping around border and shape a 3-leaf clover with them on top, or shape scalloped poinsettia leaves from canned pimientos and garnish edge and top with them. Serve with fancy crackers and wafers to spread them on.

French Toast

Note: You need an unsliced loaf of bread for French Toast since it should be sliced thicker than the regular ½" slices that the bakeries cut.

Eight ¾" slices bread
4 eggs
2 C milk
2 tsp sugar
¼ tsp salt
¼ tsp cinnamon (optional)
Bacon drippings or butter for frying

Cut the slices of bread in halves to make them easy to turn in frying pan. Beat the eggs until foamy in a shallow bowl then beat in the milk, sugar, salt and cinnamon (if used). Soak the half slices of bread in the egg-milk mixture about 5 minutes or until they are saturated. Drain over bowl for a moment then transfer to frying pan in which you have 2 Tbsp melted bacon fat or butter and brown it. Turn over with narrow spatula when bottom is golden and brown other side. Fry about 4 halves at a time keeping the slices that are cooked in warming oven until all are done. Serve hot with bacon or chicken livers or sausages. Four servings.

Pickled Eggs

3 C white vinegar
1½ C water
1½ tsp salt
1 tsp whole cloves
1 tsp pepper berries
2 Tbsp sliced ginger root
    (or ½ tsp celery seed)

Tie spices in bag and put into vinegar with salt and water and boil 10 minutes. Remove spice bag and let solution cool. Hard-cook a dozen eggs, dash into cold water to cool, remove shells. Pack in quart jars, pour vinegar over to cover, seal. Let stand 2 days.

Top-of-Stove Cheese Soufflé

1½ Tbsp butter or margarine
2 Tbsp flour
½ tsp dry mustard
½ tsp salt
⅛ tsp pepper
1 C milk
1 C grated old Cheddar cheese
4 eggs (yolks and whites separated)

In top of double boiler over direct heat melt butter or margarine and stir in flour, mustard, salt and pepper. Stir in milk until thick. Remove from heat and stir in cheese until melted. Separate egg yolks from whites. In a large bowl beat yolks until thick and stir sauce into them slowly. In another bowl beat egg whites until they form soft peaks, not stiff. Gently fold into cheese sauce. Pour into ungreased top of 8-cup double boiler that has a tight fitting lid. Cook, covered, over gently boiling water for 1 hour. (Knife inserted in center will come out clean.) Soufflé will puff up high and light if you do not peek during cooking. Serve at once.

Swiss Fondue

½ clove garlic
¾ lb shredded Swiss cheese
    (2½ C lightly packed)
1 C white wine (divided, see below)
⅓ C Kirsch (optional)
2¼ tsp cornstarch
¼ tsp baking soda
Generous shakes of white pepper,
    nutmeg and paprika

Rub the inside of the fondue pot with the garlic then discard garlic.

In a small custard cup mix cornstarch with the Kirsch (if used) or ¼ C of the wine. Set aside. Put wine (or remainder of it) into fondue pot and heat until bubbles start to rise to surface. Start adding shredded cheese, a third at a time, stirring until it melts and is blended. When it starts to boil stir in cornstarch mixture until it thickens a little more. Reduce heat and sprinkle in baking soda and spices and mix.

Have ready in a bun basket 1½" chunks of fresh French bread. Impale bread on fondue forks and dunk into cheese mixture until coated on all sides. Let cool a moment before eating. Four people can easily be grouped around the hot pot.

Cheese Soufflé

¼ C margarine
¼ C flour
½ tsp salt
1½ C hot milk
½ lb grated or shredded Cheddar cheese
4 eggs

In a large saucepan blend the margarine, flour and salt then stir in the hot milk until thick. Remove from heat and stir in cheese. Divide the yolks from the whites of eggs. Put the whites in the beater bowl and beat until stiff. Meanwhile add a little of the cheese mixture to the yolks and return them to the pot and stir in to blend well. Fold in stiffly beaten whites.

Turn into unbuttered baking dish and bake at 375° about 35 minutes. Serve at once. Four servings.

Pasta

Macaroni and Cheese see page 103

Lasagna

SAUCE
2 Tbsp oil
1½ lb ground round or chuck beef
1 medium onion chopped
¼ tsp garlic salt
1 tsp salt
½ tsp pepper
1 tsp rosemary
One 14-oz can tomato sauce
One 10-oz can mushrooms
1 chopped green pepper
2 C hot water

OTHER INGREDIENTS
8 lasagna noodles
2 tsp salt
1 C cottage cheese
8 large slices Mozzarella cheese (2 pkg)

In a large frying pan sauté the meat and onion in the oil and brown lightly, stirring all of the time to break up the meat. Add the garlic salt, salt, pepper, rosemary, tomato sauce, green pepper, mushrooms and hot water and simmer uncovered for 30 minutes.

Meanwhile cook the 8 lasagna noodles in a large pot in 2 or 3 qt of boiling water with the 2 tsp salt for 20 minutes. Drain and rinse in cold water to prevent clinging together.

Into a very large pan measure 2 C of the sauce. Arrange layers as follows: 4 lasagna noodles, cottage cheese, 4 slices Mozzarella, half of remaining sauce, 4 lasagna noodles, all of remaining sauce and finally 4 slices Mozzarella. Cover snugly with buttered doubled foil. Bake at 350° for 30 to 40 minutes. Let rest 15 minutes before serving for cutting into squares. Serves eight to ten.

Fettucine Al Burro

½ lb fresh mushrooms
2 Tbsp butter (first amount)
½ C (¼ lb) butter, softened (second amount)
¼ C whipping cream
½ C grated Parmesan cheese
1 lb fettucine (¼" Italian noodles)
6 to 8 qt water
1 Tbsp salt

In a large frying pan melt the 2 Tbsp butter. Wash, pat dry and slice the mushrooms. Sauté mushrooms in butter until limp but not brown. Set aside.

To make Sauce for fettucine, in a small bowl cream the ½ C butter until light and fluffy. Beat in the cream a little at a time then mix in the grated cheese until thoroughly blended and set aside until fettucine is cooked.

Cook the fettucine in a large pot in the salted boiling water about 10 minutes. Drain in colander and transfer to hot serving bowl. Add the butter-cheese mixture and toss it with the fettucine until every strand is well coated. Stir in the mushrooms. Serve at once and pass extra Parmesan cheese. Serves six.

Ravioli

PASTE
1½ tsp melted shortening
½ tsp salt
1 egg, yolk and white separated
½ C lukewarm water
About 2 C sifted bread flour

FILLING
½ lb freshly ground beef, veal, lamb, pork,
    or leftover roasted meat, chicken, etc.
¼ C cooked spinach finely chopped
¼ C chopped parsley or ⅛ C parsley flakes
½ tsp salt
⅛ tsp nutmeg
⅛ tsp pepper
1 small clove garlic, finely chopped
1 small onion, finely chopped
1 Tbsp Parmesan cheese
1 small egg

If using cooked meat, put through food chopper. Add finely chopped spinach to meat and other ingredients, except egg. Cook mixture over low heat for several minutes until thoroughly blended. Remove from heat and add egg and beat. Cool. This makes the Filling.

To make Paste, melt shortening and combine with salt, beaten egg yolk and lukewarm water. Beat in about 2 C sifted bread flour, a little at a time, to form medium dough. Turn onto well-floured board, knead until smooth. Cover and let stand 30 minutes.

Now roll into a rectangle 16 × 18". Brush half of dough with well beaten egg white. Arrange filling evenly by teaspoonfuls over dough, leaving about 1" space between each measure. Cover with other half of dough, press down between each section, starting in center, to exclude air. Seal. Cut into squares with ravioli wheel (or knife) and with fingers pinch around any edges that are still not completely sealed. Let stand about 1 hour, turning over once.

Lower into rapidly boiling salted water, cover and cook gently about 20 minutes. Remove with perforated ladle and drain. Arrange on large platter, sprinkle with grated Parmesan cheese and cover with tomato sauce.

Cannelloni with Vegetable and Meat Filling

One 8-oz pkg Cannelloni noodles

FILLING

1½ lb ground chuck beef
½ pkg dry onion soup mix (see Sauce below for second ½ pkg)
½ tsp salt
½ tsp celery seed
¼ tsp pepper
¼ tsp garlic powder
1 tsp Worcestershire sauce
¼ C catsup
¼ C milk
2 C frozen mixed vegetables, thawed
2 eggs, beaten

SAUCE

One 13-oz can tomato paste
3 C water
½ pkg dry onion soup mix
    (leftover from Filling above)
3 Tbsp sugar
1 tsp oregano or Italian seasoning
1 tsp onion salt
¾ tsp salt

Prepare Filling in frying pan by sautéing ground chuck beef and onion soup mix until redness disappears from meat. Add salt, celery seed, pepper and garlic powder, Worcestershire sauce, catsup, milk and mixed vegetables. Remove from heat and quickly stir in beaten eggs. Return to heat and cook, stirring for 2 or 3 minutes. Set aside while preparing sauce.

To prepare Sauce, combine all sauce ingredients in a pot and bring to boil. Reduce heat and simmer, uncovered, 10 minutes. Keep hot.

Cook Cannelloni noodles in very large amount of salted boiling water only 4 minutes. Drain and rinse thoroughly with cold water. Cover bottom of 9 × 13″ baking dish with part of sauce. Use a small spoon to fill each noodle with meat filling and arrange in tightly packed rows. Add remaining sauce. Cover and bake at 375° for 30 minutes. Serves six to eight.

Noodles Romanoff

3 C broad dry egg noodles, well packed,
    about half a 12-oz pkg
1 tsp salt
4 C chicken broth (or 4 C boiling water plus
    4 chicken bouillon cubes)
¾ C dairy sour cream
¾ C cottage cheese
½ tsp salt
⅛ tsp garlic salt
½ tsp Worcestershire sauce
½ C Cheddar or Parmesan cheese, grated

Add the 1 tsp salt to the chicken broth and bring to boiling. Add dry noodles and cook 20 minutes, stirring frequently. Drain. Save chicken broth for adding to soup for another meal. Gently stir in all remaining ingredients except grated cheese. Turn into buttered casserole, sprinkle top with grated Cheddar or Parmesan cheese and bake at 350° for 30 to 40 minutes. Serves four or five.

Manicotti

One 8-oz pkg manicotti (these are tubes: hoselike sections of outsized macaroni, 1″ diameter, 4″ length)
Boiling water
1 Tbsp salt
1 Tbsp oil

FILLING

2 eggs
3 C cottage cheese
1 C grated Mozzarella cheese
½ C grated Parmesan
¼ C chopped chives or parsley
½ tsp salt
⅛ tsp pepper
⅛ tsp nutmeg

SAUCE

One 28-oz can spaghetti sauce

In a large pot bring water to boil with the salt and oil. Add only 8 of the manicotti at a time and boil vigorously 6 minutes. Drain and cool, separated, on plate. Handle carefully or they may break. Repeat with remaining manicotti

Combine all filling ingredients. Pour half of the sauce in bottom of 13 × 9″ baking dish. With small teaspoon carefully fill each manicotti making it stretch to fill all sixteen. Arrange, touching, side by side in sauce in baking dish. The last 4 will have to be fitted in at side. Pour remaining sauce all over top. Sprinkle with extra Parmesan cheese. Cover snugly with foil and bake at 350° for 30 to 40 minutes. Allow 2 manicotti for each serving.

Rotini Roma

16 oz rotini (nearly 5 C: spiral
    or corkscrew pasta)
2 tsp salt (first amount)
16 C boiling water
¼ C oil
½ C coarsely chopped green pepper
½ C chopped onion
½ C chopped celery
½ C shredded carrot
½ tsp salt (second amount)
¼ tsp oregano
¼ tsp garlic powder
1½ lb lean ground beef
1¾ C canned spaghetti sauce or
    equivalent in homemade
½ C Parmesan cheese

Bring water to boil in large pot. Add salt and rotini and boil 15 minutes uncovered. Drain through colander.

Meanwhile heat oil in frying pan and add green pepper, onion, celery, carrot, ½ tsp salt, oregano and garlic powder and sauté about 1 minute then add ground beef and mash with potato masher to break it up, then cook stirring until redness goes out of meat. Do not brown. Add spaghetti sauce, mix well, cover and simmer 15 minutes.

As soon as rotini is drained turn out on large preheated serving dish, cover all but edges with sauce and sprinkle Parmesan at center. Serve at once. Italian bread sticks and more Parmesan could be passed at the table. Serves six or eight.

Meatballs with Almond Mushroom Fusilli

One 10-oz can condensed tomato soup
1 C sour cream
1¼ lb ground chuck beef
1 tsp salt
⅛ tsp pepper
1 egg
⅓ C breadcrumbs
3 Tbsp margarine
1 C chopped onion
½ bay leaf
1 tsp lemon juice
1 tsp paprika
½ lb fusilli (spring noodles)
    or ¼" noodles
2 oz sliced blanched almonds
¼ lb scrubbed and sliced mushrooms
Chopped parsley

Combine soup and sour cream in small bowl. In a large bowl mix well meat, salt, pepper, egg, crumbs and ¼ C of the sour cream mixture. Shape meat into 18 balls. Melt margarine in large frying pan and lightly brown meat balls. Tip off excess fat and reserve. Add onions, remaining sour-cream-and-soup mixture, bay leaf, lemon juice and paprika. Gently mix, cover and simmer 20 minutes.

Meanwhile put fusilli on to cook in a large pot in plenty of salted water and cook until almost tender.

Add reserved fat from meat pan to small frying pan and add the almonds and mushrooms stirring constantly until soaked but not brown at all. Drain fusilli through colander, return to pot, stir in sautéed almonds and mushrooms. Now turn meat balls and sauce into center of large preheated platter. Arrange fusilli mixture around in neat border. Sprinkle border generously with finely chopped parsley and serve. Six servings.

Cufondly

1¼ C uncooked elbow macaroni or
    1" pieces spaghetti
4 C boiling water
1 tsp salt
1½ C milk
⅜ C (6 Tbsp) butter or margarine
1 tsp minced onion (fresh or bottled)
½ green pepper, chopped
1½ Tbsp chopped parsley
1 tsp salt (second amount)
1½ C soft breadcrumbs
1½ C shredded old Cheddar cheese
4 large eggs, yolks and whites separated
1 or 2 Tbsp chopped pimiento (optional)
3 or 4 Tbsp chopped olives (optional)

Cook the macaroni or spaghetti in the boiling salted water until almost tender, about 10 minutes. Drain and rinse in cold water to separate pieces.

Heat together to scalding point the milk, butter or margarine, onion, green pepper, parsley and salt. Remove from heat and add crumbs and cheese and mix gently. Stir a little of the mixture into the beaten egg yolks then stir this back into the hot cheese mixture. Add macaroni or spaghetti, and pimiento and olives (if used). Fold in gently the stiffly beaten egg whites, being careful not to break them down. Butter bottom of large soufflé dish and turn soufflé mixture in, filling ⅔ full. Stand this on a larger shallow pan containing warm water. Bake at 375° for 35 minutes. Serve at once.

Shrimp-Stuffed Pasta Shells

4 oz large macaroni shells
    (lumaconi, see below)
2 qt boiling water
1 tsp salt

FILLING
2 Tbsp chopped onion
½ C finely chopped celery
1 Tbsp oil
One 12-oz pkg spinach
1 C cottage cheese
One 7-oz can small shrimp
    (drained weight 4½ oz)
1 egg
½ tsp salt
⅛ tsp oregano
1 tsp lemon juice

SAUCE
2 Tbsp chopped onion
3 Tbsp oil
3 Tbsp flour
¼ tsp salt
1 chicken bouillon cube
1½ C milk
¾ C water

TOPPING
1 C shredded old Cheddar cheese

Note: Since some of the shells tend to break, cook a surplus, about 6 oz in the salted water until almost tender but not soft. Drain. Add any broken leftovers to your soup pot. You need 40 perfect shells.

Cook spinach, turning 2 or 3 times until some liquid forms, until tender. Drain well and chop.

To make Filling, sauté onion and celery in oil 5 minutes. Do not brown. Combine with drained chopped spinach, cottage cheese, shrimps (drained), egg, salt, oregano and lemon juice. Arrange shells on a large plate and fill each with 1 heaping silver teaspoonful of filling.

Make Sauce by sautéing the onion in the oil until soft, but not brown, then stir in flour, salt and bouillon to blend. Stir in milk and water until thick. Pour half of the sauce into bottom of large shallow baking dish. Arrange stuffed shells in 3 neat parallel rows on it. Bake covered with foil at 375° for 15 minutes. Pour remaining sauce all over top, sprinkle with cheese and bake uncovered until bubbly and tinged all over with gold. Serves six.

Note: If made in advance, this dish should be reheated covered at 300° until hot, about 25 to 30 minutes.

Noodles Florentine

6 oz ¼" noodles (4 C packed)
One 10-oz pkg raw spinach
2 C (1 lb) cottage cheese
½ C dairy sour cream
½ C grated Parmesan
½ tsp salt
¼ tsp Tabasco
¼ tsp basil
¼ tsp thyme
¾ C fine dry bread crumbs
1 Tbsp melted butter or margarine

SAUCE
1 chicken bouillon cube
1 Tbsp flour
1 Tbsp margarine
1 C boiling water

Cook noodles in large potful of boiling water with ½ tsp salt, 15 minutes. Drain through colander.

Wash spinach. Drain well. Cook in pot in only the water clinging to its leaves, turning over once or twice, until almost tender. Drain and chop. Turn into large bowl. Add cottage and Parmesan cheeses, sour cream, salt, Tabasco, basil and thyme. Gently stir in noodles. Turn into 1½-qt casserole.

To make Sauce, blend flour and margarine, then stir with bouillon cube in boiling water until thick. Pour all over casserole ingredients. Cover with crumbs made by melting the butter or margarine and stirring in crumbs. Bake at 350° for 40 to 45 minutes. Serves six.

Macaroni and Cheese

2 C elbow macaroni
8 C boiling water
1 Tbsp salt
½ lb shredded mild Cheddar cheese
    (2 C lightly packed)
2 Tbsp margarine
2 Tbsp flour
¾ C milk
1 C dairy sour cream
½ C finely chopped onion
½ C finely chopped celery

Into a very large pot measure the water and salt, bring to boil, add macaroni elbows, stirring, and boil uncovered 15 minutes. Drain through colander and return macaroni to pot.

Meanwhile make Sauce by melting margarine. Blend in flour, then stir in milk and sour cream until thick. Reserve ½ C of the shredded cheese for the top. Add all remaining cheese to sauce and stir in. Add onion and celery. Mix with drained macaroni and turn into medium casserole. Sprinkle reserved cheese all over top and bake at 350° for 45 minutes.

Spaghetti and Meat Balls Casserole

¼ lb spaghetti
¾ C grated mild Cheddar cheese

MEAT MIXTURE
One slice whole wheat bread
½ C hot water
1 lb hamburg
1 egg
⅛ tsp garlic salt
1 Tbsp catsup
¼ tsp oregano
½ tsp salt
2 Tbsp oil

TOMATO SAUCE
One 19-oz can tomatoes
2 bay leaves
1 onion chopped
1 Tbsp sugar
1 tsp salt
½ tsp oregano
¼ C catsup

Cook spaghetti in 2 qt salted water 20 minutes. Drain through colander.

To make meat balls, in a large bowl soak bread in hot water 5 minutes. Add all meat ball ingredients except oil and mix thoroughly. Shape into 12 balls. Brown on all sides in oil. Set aside.

To make Tomato Sauce, cook gently together all sauce ingredients for 15 minutes.

To assemble casserole, turn cooked spaghetti into 9 × 9" baking dish, cover with browned meat balls. Pour sauce over all. Cover with cheese. Bake at 325° for 45 minutes. Serves six.

Casseroles

Potluck Meatballs Creole

MEATBALLS
1 lb ground chuck beef
¼ C water
1 egg
½ C rolled oats
1 tsp salt
½ tsp onion powder

INGREDIENTS FOR BASE
One 28-oz can tomatoes
1 envelope spaghetti sauce mix
½ C green pepper, finely chopped
2½ C water
1½ C minute rice

To make Meatballs, in large bowl thoroughly combine all meatball ingredients. Shape into 16 or 18 meatballs 1″ in diameter. Put in cold frying pan, turn heat to medium, turning to brown on all sides. Drain on paper towelling and set aside.

In large shallow baking dish combine tomatoes, spaghetti sauce mix, green pepper, water and minute rice. Top with meatballs. Bake uncovered, at 350° for 1 hour. Serves four to six.

Casserole For Ten

2 C raw tiny shell or elbow macaroni
2 lbs ground chuck beef
1 large onion, chopped
One 10-oz can tomato soup, undiluted
One 10-oz can mushroom soup, undiluted
One 10-oz can cream of chicken soup, undiluted
One 10-oz can cheddar cheese soup, undiluted
One 10-oz can water
1 tsp salt
½ tsp pepper
¼ C melted margarine
1 C fine soft breadcrumbs
Paprika
Parsley flakes

In large pot of boiling, salted water cook macaroni shells or elbows until tender, about 10 minutes. Drain. Meanwhile in large pot sauté meat and onion until redness disappears from meat and onion is tender. Add soups, water, salt, pepper and cooked drained macaroni and blend thoroughly. Pour into very large casserole.

Combine melted butter and breadcrumbs and sprinkle evenly over top. Sprinkle liberally with paprika and parsley flakes. Bake uncovered at 350° until bubbly, about 45 minutes.

Old-Fashioned Cheese Fondue

2 C stale bread cubes (½″)
1½ C grated cheese packed
2 eggs
2 C milk
¾ tsp salt
⅔ C bread crumbs
2 Tbsp melted butter

Arrange bread cubes and cheese in layers in buttered baking dish. Beat eggs and stir in salt and milk and pour over bread and cheese and let stand 20 minutes to soak. Stir melted butter into bread crumbs and sprinkle over top. Stand baking dish in larger shallow pan containing 1″ hot water. Bake at 400° about 25 minutes or until firm and golden.

Pork Chop Casserole with Fruited Rice

Six ¾″ pork chops
½ C chopped onion
1½ C minute rice or ⅞ C raw long grain rice
2 C hot water
1 C chopped apple
1 C chopped pitted prunes (dried or drained stewed)
1½ tsp salt
⅛ tsp pepper
¼ tsp basil or rosemary

Trim excess fat from chops and render it out in the frying pan then add and brown chops. Transfer to holding plate. Discard fat scraps. Add onion and gently cook 5 minutes, stirring. Tip onions into medium-large casserole. Rinse out pan with 1 C of the hot water and add to casserole. Add rice and 1 more cup hot water. Now stir in the apple, prunes, salt, pepper and basil or rosemary. Cover with chops. Put on lid and bake at 350°. If minute rice is used it requires 45 minutes. If raw rice is used, cook 60 to 70 minutes. Serves six.

Chicken Noodle Casserole

2 C ¼″ egg noodles
3 C chicken broth
2 long slender carrots cut in ¼″ slices
2 C cut-up fresh green beans
Sliced cooked chicken equivalent of 2 breasts and 1 whole leg
2 Tbsp margarine (first amount)
2 Tbsp flour
1 tsp salt
1½ C fine whole wheat breadcrumbs
2 Tbsp melted margarine (second amount)

Cook noodles until tender in 3 C unsalted chicken broth. Drain and reserve broth. Cook carrots and beans in minimum of water until nearly tender and reserve liquid. Add vegetable liquid to reserved chicken broth and measure. You need 2 C. (Add water if necessary).

Tip the noodles into a medium-large shallow casserole. Cover with the cooked vegetables, then with a generous overlapping layer of sliced cooked chicken.

Make a Sauce by blending the margarine (first amount) with flour and salt and stirring in the 2 C measured broth until thick. Pour all over chicken, easing it between the cracks to flow to bottom.

Melt the second amount of margarine and stir in crumbs with a fork. Sprinkle these all over top. Bake at 325° for 1 hour. Serves five.

Bologna Casserole with Cheese Sauce

¾ lb bologna cut into ¾" cubes (about 2 C)
6 C raw cabbage coarsely shredded (packed)
½ C raw long grain rice
1½ C boiling water
½ tsp salt

CHEESE SAUCE
4 Tbsp margarine
4 Tbsp flour
½ tsp salt
⅛ tsp pepper
1 tsp celery seed
About 2 C milk (see below)
½ lb cut up process cheese

In heavy pot bring 1½ C water to boil with the salt. Add rice. Bring to boil again, cover, turn off heat for 5 minutes. Turn on heat to simmer for 25 minutes until all water is absorbed. Remove from heat.

Meanwhile cook shredded cabbage in ¾ C water with ½ tsp salt, covered, until crisply tender, about 10 minutes. Drain and reserve liquid.

To make Cheese Sauce, melt the margarine and stir in flour, salt, pepper and celery seed and stir until blended. Remove from heat. Measure reserved cabbage liquid in 2-cup measure. Add milk to bring level up to 2-cup mark. Stir in margarine-flour mixture with wire whip until thickened. Stir in cheese until melted.

In a 2-quart casserole combine bologna, cabbage and rice. Pour Cheese Sauce over, sprinkle with paprika. Bake uncovered at 325° about 30 minutes until bubbly and gold.

Potato and Sausage Scallop

3 large potatoes (1½ lb)
2 Tbsp margarine
½ C chopped onion
¼ C chopped green pepper
1 lb link beef sausage (or ½ lb thinly sliced Polish sausage)
⅔ C grated Parmesan cheese
3 eggs
½ tsp salt
½ tsp basil
⅛ tsp Tabasco sauce
1½ C milk

Scrub potatoes and cook in salted water until barely tender, not soft. Drain and peel. Meanwhile melt the margarine and in it gently sauté the onion and green pepper 5 minutes. Do not brown.

Slice the peeled potatoes into a medium-large casserole. Cover with sausages. Sprinkle grated cheese evenly over. Spoon onion-green pepper mixture over evenly. Beat eggs with the salt, basil and Tabasco and add milk and beat in. Pour evenly over casserole contents. Bake at 350° for 30 minutes or until custard is set. Serves six.

Super Sausage Casserole

1¼ C tiny macaroni shells (or elbows)
1 tsp salt
4 C boiling water
1 lb pork sausage meat
½ C chopped onion
½ C chopped celery
½ green pepper, chopped
⅛ tsp oregano
¼ tsp pepper
1 tsp salt
One 7½-oz can tomato sauce
One 19-oz can tomatoes
⅔ C grated Cheddar cheese
⅔ C soft bread crumbs

Cook macaroni shells or elbows in the boiling water with salt 15 minutes until nearly tender. Drain through colander.

In large frying pan sauté together the sausage meat, onion, celery and green pepper, stirring and chopping constantly until all sausage meat is broken up and vegetables are soaked with fat. Add seasonings and tomato sauce and tomatoes and mix. Add drained macaroni shells.

Turn into large casserole. Mix together the cheese and crumbs and sprinkle over top. Bake at 350° for 40 to 45 minutes. Serves six.

Seven Layer Dinner

1 lb sausages
1 C diced turnip
1 C diced carrot
1 C diced potato
1 C chopped celery
1 C shredded cabbage
One 10-oz can kernel corn (drain and reserve liquid)
1 can cream of asparagus soup
1 Tbsp chopped onion
Salt
Paprika

In large shallow buttered baking dish arrange the 6 vegetables in layers in order given but sprinkle each sparingly with salt as you layer them. Sprinkle onion over top. Top all with a single close layer of sausages. Stir corn liquid into asparagus soup and pour over all. Sprinkle with paprika. Bake covered with lid or foil at 350° for 1 hour then remove lid and bake 30 minutes longer.

Wiener and Noodle Casserole

1 medium onion, chopped (½ C)
½ C chopped celery
3 Tbsp butter or margarine
.3 C garden vegetable juice (canned)
6 wieners cut in ¼" slices
4 oz broad or narrow noodles
½ tsp salt
¾ C grated cheese

Cook onion and celery in butter in frying pan about 5 minutes. Stir in all remaining ingredients except cheese. Cover tightly, cook over medium heat, stirring often, for about 20 minutes or until noodles are tender. Sprinkle cheese over top and cook just until melted. Makes 4 servings.

Curried Tuna Casserole

2 C fine spaghetti, broken into 2" pieces
¼ C melted butter or oil
1 large onion, chopped
1 green pepper, chopped
1 large carrot, grated
1 to 2 tsp curry powder
Two 10-oz cans cream of chicken soup, undiluted
½ C milk
Two 6½-oz cans tuna, drained
1 C potato chips, coarsely crushed

In large pot cook spaghetti in boiling salted water until barely tender, about 8 minutes. Drain through colander.

Meanwhile in large frying pan sauté onion, green pepper and carrot in butter or oil until crisply tender but not browned. Remove from heat. Stir in curry powder, soup, milk and tuna until thoroughly blended. Add cooked spaghetti and combine. Transfer to large casserole. Sprinkle crushed potato chips over top. Bake at 350° for 20 to 25 minutes until bubbly. Serves six.

Sole Fillet and Noodle Casserole

1 C broken egg noodles packed
1 lb fresh frozen sole (or other fish) fillets
1 large tomato, sliced
About 7 slices Swiss or Gouda cheese
3 Tbsp chopped parsley
½ C slivered almonds

SAUCE
2 Tbsp butter
¼ lb scrubbed and sliced mushrooms
⅓ C chopped onions
4 tsp flour
½ tsp salt
1⅓ C milk
1 chicken bouillon cube
⅓ C boiling water

Thaw fish fillets. Cook noodles in boiling salted water until almost tender, about 10 minutes, and drain through sieve.

Make Sauce in medium frypan by melting butter and gently sautéing mushrooms and onions in it until just limp. Add flour and salt and when blended stir in milk and boiling water, in which bouillon cube has been softened, until thick. Pour half of the sauce into a broad shallow baking dish. Sprinkle with half the parsley and stir in drained noodles. Cover with tomato slices.

Place thawed fillets on board and sprinkle each sparingly with salt, pepper, a little lemon juice and remaining parsley. Roll up like little jelly rolls and place, open side down, on tomato slices in dish. Top each roll with a slice of cheese. Pour remaining sauce evenly over. Sprinkle with almonds and bake, covered, 20 minutes at 375°, then uncover and bake 10 minutes longer or until bubbly and tinged with gold. Garnish with tomato wedges and parsley. Serves five.

Split Wiener Casserole

1 lb wieners (10 or 12)
9 to 12 medium-small potatoes
    (3 C when cooked and mashed)
1 tsp salt
3 Tbsp butter or margarine
One 7½-oz can tomato sauce
4 slices process cheese, sliced
Parsley flakes

Pare potatoes and cook in boiling water with the 1 tsp salt until tender. Drain, add butter and mash until all lumps disappear. You should have about 3 C.

Meanwhile slit each wiener lengthwise and arrange side by side along each side of a greased 13 × 9" baking dish leaving a bare strip along center. Spoon 1 tsp tomato sauce into each wiener slit. Spoon mashed potatoes into bare center of baking dish, piling high. Sprinkle with parsley flakes. Cut each slice of process cheese into 3 strips and arrange evenly over top of all. Bake at 375° for 30 minutes uncovered then pour remaining tomato sauce evenly over all, return to oven and bake 5 minutes longer. Cut into sections and remove with lifter to dinner plates. Serves 4 or 5.

Two Chicken Casseroles

Use one casserole for current meal and one to freeze. Each casserole serves five.

One 3½-lb chicken
Water
1 Tbsp chopped onion or bottled onion flakes
½ bay leaf
1 lb ¼" noodles
Two 11-oz pkgs fresh frozen mixed vegetables
Two 10-oz cans cream of vegetable soup
1½ C fine fresh breadcrumbs
¼ C melted margarine

Simmer the chicken and gizzard and heart and onion and bay leaf in water to ¾ cover, covered for 2 hours until meat will fall from bones. Drop liver in just before removing from heat. Lift chicken from broth onto utility tray and strip meat from skin and bones. Discard skin and bones. (Strain broth and chill.)

Cook noodles in plenty of salted water 15 minutes. Drain. Tip into 2 medium-large casseroles. Cover each with a package of fresh frozen mixed vegetables. Cover each with chicken, having sliced the breasts, using all of the chicken. Cover each with 1 can cream of vegetable soup diluted with 1 can water. Cover each with ¾ C crumbs which have been mixed with the melted margarine. Bake at 375° for 45 minutes.

Serve one for the current meal. Wrap and freeze second casserole. When frozen casserole is needed thaw and reheat at 300° for 30 minutes or until bubbly.

Steak Bake

1½ lb sirloin steak cut in narrow strips
⅓ C flour
1 tsp salt
¼ tsp pepper
1 small onion, sliced
1 green pepper slivered
One 19-oz can tomatoes
One 10-oz can mushrooms, drained
One 10-oz pkg fresh frozen frenched green
    beans thawed and drained
3 Tbsp light molasses
3 Tbsp soy sauce

Cut meat into narrow strips and place in a 2½ quart casserole. Sprinkle with flour, salt and pepper. Toss to coat meat, leaving excess flour in bottom of casserole. Bake this dry mixture uncovered at 400° for 20 minutes. Remove from oven and mix in onion, green pepper, tomatoes, mushrooms, beans, molasses and soy sauce. Cover and return to 400° oven and bake another 30 minutes. Serves four or five.

Quick Turkey and Vegetable Casserole

2 C bite-size pieces cooked turkey
One 10-oz pkg frozen French fries
2 Tbsp chopped onion
One 10-oz pkg frozen carrots and peas
One 10-oz can cream of mushroom soup
1 C boiling water
½ tsp Worcestershire sauce
⅓ C grated Parmesan cheese

Line bottom of buttered large casserole with half of the frozen French fries. Cover with chopped onion and then with a thick layer of cooked turkey, then frozen carrots and peas. Top with remaining French fries. Combine soup, Worcestershire sauce and water and pour evenly over all. Sprinkle with grated Parmesan cheese. Bake uncovered at 350° for 1 hour. Serves five or six.

Tampa Tuna Casserole

Two 6-oz cans flaked tuna
2 hard-cooked eggs, sliced
1½ C cooked carrots, diced
½ C cooked peas
2 Tbsp chopped onion
2 Tbsp butter
2 Tbsp flour
⅔ C milk
1 can cream of celery soup, undiluted
Shake of cayenne
½ tsp curry powder
½ C mayonnaise
½ tsp paprika

Drain tuna and arrange in layers with the sliced hard-cooked eggs, carrots and peas in a shallow medium casserole.

In frypan, sauté the onion in butter for 2 or 3 minutes, then stir in the flour then the milk, until thick and smooth. Add remaining ingredients and taste for seasoning. Pour sauce evenly over tuna. Sprinkle with additional paprika and bake at 400° until bubbly, about 20 minutes. Serves four to six.

Seafood Casserole

1 C butter or margarine
2 small onions chopped
3 Tbsp flour
2 tsp salt
3 C milk
1 Tbsp chopped parsley
1 lb raw shrimp in shells or 1 lb fresh
    frozen or canned shelled shrimp
2 lb sole (or cod) fillets
½ lb mushrooms
6 large potatoes

Note: If shrimp are raw in shells barely cover with cold water, add 1 sliced onion, 1 bay leaf and bring to boil covered. Immediately remove from heat and let stand 15 minutes. Drain and remove shells. Set aside.

In large frying pan melt butter or margarine. Add onion and gently sauté 5 minutes. Blend in flour and salt, then stir in milk until thick. Remove from heat and stir in parsley.

Scrub and pare potatoes. Slice ⅛" thick and carefully, neatly, closely line sides and bottom of one very large shallow casserole (or two medium) with potato slices. Cut fish fillets into bite-sized pieces, and cover potatoes with them; cover with washed and quartered mushrooms then cover with shrimp. Pour sauce all over top being sure it filters through contents. Brush protruding edges of potatoes with some of the sauce. Bake at 375° for 40 minutes. Serves ten.

Turkish Lamb Pilaf Casserole

3½ to 4 C cooked lamb
1 C raw long grain rice
2⅔ C skimmed lamb broth (or water and
    1 chicken bouillon cube)
1 tsp salt
2 onions, chopped
6 large soft prunes (not soaked) stoned
    and chopped coarsely
½ C light raisins
¼ C chopped canned pimiento
½ C tomato paste
1 C water
⅛ tsp ginger
¼ tsp cinnamon
¼ tsp pepper
1 tsp salt
½ C shredded blanched almonds

Bring broth to boil, add raw rice and the first tsp salt and simmer covered for half an hour, adding onion during last 10 minutes. Combine prepared lamb, prunes, raisins and pimiento. Combine tomato paste, water and seasonings. Stir the tomato paste mixture into meat mixture. Divide rice-onion mixture in half. Add half to meat mixture.

Have ready and buttered two 4-C casseroles. Divide mixture evenly into both. Cover both with remaining rice-onion mixture. Top each with almonds. Cover with plastic bags. Freeze. If one casserole is needed for current meal bake uncovered at 350° for 30 minutes. If frozen solid put in oven at 375° for 1¾ hours, covered, removing cover during last 10 minutes, to brown almonds.

Veal and Vegetable Casserole with Biscuit Topping

2½ to 3 lbs stewing veal
1 onion, chopped
¼ C oil
2 Tbsp flour
2½ C hot water
2 C diced (¼") carrots
1½ C chopped celery
4 C diced (½") potatoes
2 tsp salt
1½ tsp Worcestershire sauce

BISCUITS
2 C all-purpose flour
1 Tbsp baking powder
½ tsp cream of tartar
¾ tsp salt
½ C margarine
¾ C milk

In very large frying pan sauté cubed (1") veal with onions in oil until lightly browned. Turn all into large casserole. Rinse out frying pan with the 2½ C hot water and add to veal in casserole. Add all remaining ingredients except biscuits. Bake covered at 325° for 2½ hours.

During last half hour make Biscuits by sifting together flour, baking powder, cream of tartar and salt. Cut in margarine or shortening with pastry blender until size of peas. Quickly stir in milk. Turn out on lightly floured counter. Pat to ¾" thickness. Cut out with 2¼" cutter, about 14. Fifteen minutes before mealtime raise temperature of oven to 425°. Remove casserole and place biscuits on top of boiling hot contents. Do not recover. Return to oven to bake biscuits about 12 minutes. Serves 7 or 8.

Salmon Casserole

4 C ¼" noodles (packed)
Boiling water
2 Tbsp margarine
2 Tbsp flour
3 C milk
2 C flaked smoked salmon
    (or one 1-lb can salmon including liquid)
1 C chopped celery
¾ C chopped parsley
½ C breadcrumbs
¼ to ½ C grated cheese

Do not add salt to the water in which you cook the noodles if using smoked salmon. Cook noodles in large amount of unsalted boiling water about 12 minutes. Drain through colander. Turn half into 13 × 9" baking dish. Meanwhile make a thin white sauce by melting margarine, blending in flour and stirring in milk until slightly thickened. Cover noodles with flaked salmon (if canned is used pour its liquid over too). Cover salmon with celery and parsley. Cover with remaining noodles. Now pour all white sauce over, gently coaxing it through the contents with a fork. Combine crumbs and cheese and sprinkle over top. Bake at 375° about 40 or 45 minutes until bubbly and golden.

Hard-Cooked Egg and Shrimp Casserole

8 hard-cooked eggs cut in halves lengthwise
3 C scrubbed sliced small mushrooms
Two 10-oz cans fresh frozen shrimp soup, thawed
Two 8-oz cans shrimp (4½ oz dried weight)
1½ C fresh breadcrumbs

Arrange the hard-cooked egg halves, cut side up, in bottom of large shallow baking dish. Cover with layer of mushrooms. Pour canned shrimps including their liquid evenly over the mushrooms. Spoon the thawed shrimp soup over all and smooth the top. Sprinkle evenly with crumbs and bake at 325° for 20 minutes. If when baking time is up crumbs are not brown, pass under preheated broiler for about a minute to tinge with gold. Serves six.

Party Tuna Casserole

Four 6-oz cans flaked tuna, drained
    (or equivalent in chopped chicken)
4 hard-cooked eggs, sliced
4 C frozen mixed vegetables, cooked (see below)
1 medium onion, chopped
4 Tbsp butter or margarine (first amount)
4 Tbsp flour
2 C milk
Two 10-oz cans cream of chicken soup, undiluted
Shake of cayenne
1 tsp curry powder
½ C mayonnaise
1 tsp paprika
½ tsp celery seed
2 C fine breadcrumbs (about 3 slices)
¼ C melted butter

In medium pot cook the mixed vegetables in ¾ C boiling water with 1 tsp salt until tender, about 8 minutes. Drain.

In large mixing bowl combine thoroughly the drained tuna, sliced eggs and cooked vegetables.

In another pot sauté onion in the 4 Tbsp butter or margarine until limp but not browned. Remove from heat and stir in flour. Stir in milk until thick and smooth over heat. Stir in soup, cayenne, curry powder, mayonnaise, paprika and celery seed. Pour this sauce over tuna mixture and stir to thoroughly combine. Turn this into a 13 × 9" buttered casserole. Sprinkle over the bread crumbs which have been tossed in the melted butter. Sprinkle with additional paprika and bake at 400° until bubbly, about 20 minutes. Serves twelve to sixteen.

Turkey Élégante

One 8½ to 9-lb turkey
3 qt (15 C) boiling water
1 tsp salt (first amount)
1 bay leaf
1 Tbsp chopped onion or bottled flakes
1¼ C raw long grain rice
3 C turkey broth (from boiling turkey,
    first amount)
1 tsp salt (second amount)
6 Tbsp butter
6 Tbsp flour
1 tsp salt (third amount)
2 C turkey broth (second amount)
1½ C milk
½ C chopped Swiss cheese packed
1¼ C buttered soft breadcrumbs
24 medium-small mushrooms (garnish)
24 ripe olives (garnish)

Place turkey in large kettle or roasting pan with lid, add boiling water, 1 tsp salt, bay leaf and onion, cover and boil gently 4 hours, turning over carefully at half time. By this time meat is loosening from bones. Remove from heat and lift to big utility tray. Slip meat from bones and skin. Strain and reserve broth. Chill meat and broth.

When time comes to assemble this casserole, cook the rice in 3 C of the reserved broth with 1 tsp salt, covered, until tender and broth is absorbed, about 30 minutes. Spread rice in bottom of very large baking dish or 2 medium-large casseroles. Cut chilled turkey meat into thick slices. Arrange on top uniformly. Pour over all a Sauce: Melt butter, blend in flour and salt, then stir in 2 C turkey broth, milk and cheese until thick. Pour hot over turkey, sprinkle with buttered crumbs. Bake at 375° for 35 minutes. Scrub mushrooms and steam 5 minutes. Heat olives in their liquid. Arrange mushrooms and olives around edge, decoratively. Ten to twelve servings.

Beef and Vegetable Dinner

3¼ lb blade steaks (see below)
1 C warm water
2 C cut up green beans
3 Tbsp flour
2 tsp salt
1 packet dry chicken soup base
4 medium onions thickly sliced
2 C carrots thickly sliced
2 C small potatoes thickly sliced

Cut all fat and bone from blade steaks. Cut lean meat into serving size pieces.

Into a large casserole pour the 1 C water and then add the cut meat in one crowded layer. Cover with all of the green beans. Mix well together the flour, salt and chicken soup base and sprinkle evenly over beans. Now add a layer of onions, then a layer of carrots and finish with the potatoes. Cover and bake at 325° for 3 hours. Serves six.

Noodles Parmegiano

Sliced white meat from one 3½-lb
    boiled chicken
½ lb egg noodles
½ tsp salt
¼ C butter or margarine
2 Tbsp flour
1 tsp salt
1½ C chicken broth (from boiling the chicken)
½ C grated Parmesan cheese

Cook the chicken in 3 C water, covered, until tender. Lift from broth to tray or platter and when cool enough, slice all of the white meat to use for this dish. Meanwhile cook noodles in 7 C boiling water with the ½ tsp salt about 12 minutes. Drain.

Make the Sauce by melting the butter, stirring in the flour and 1 tsp salt until blended, then chicken broth until thick. Add ¼ C Parmesan cheese. Into a large casserole turn half of the noodles. Cover with half of the sliced chicken. Pour over half of the sauce. Repeat these layers. Sprinkle remaining Parmesan cheese over top. Bake at 400° for 20 minutes turning top burner on during last 2 or 3 minutes until top is bubbly and golden. Serves four.

Chicken or Turkey or Tuna Casserole

¾ C long grain rice
1¼ C chicken broth or water
½ tsp salt
2 Tbsp finely chopped mild onion
1 C fresh frozen green peas
2 C cooked chicken or turkey cut into
    large pieces (or one 16-oz can tuna)
1 C soft breadcrumbs
3 Tbsp flour
3 Tbsp butter
½ tsp salt (second amount: omit if tuna used)
¾ C chopped process or grated Cheddar cheese
1½ C milk

Cook rice in broth covered, with ½ tsp salt and onion until rice is tender and all liquid is absorbed.

Make Cheese Sauce: Heat milk and cheese together to simmering point. Remove from heat. Melt butter, blend in flour and salt (second amount) then stir in hot milk-cheese liquid until thick. Remove from heat.

Into large casserole turn the cooked rice and cover with the fresh frozen peas. Cover with chicken or turkey or tuna meat. Pour hot sauce over all. Cover with soft breadcrumbs. Bake at 350° for 35 minutes or until a little bubbly and crumbs are pale gold. Serves six.

Sausage Meat Dinner Casserole

2 C cooked macaroni (use half a 7-oz pkg)
1 Tbsp bacon fat or butter
1 lb sausage meat
1 medium onion, chopped
One 14-oz can kernel corn, drained
One 20-oz can tomatoes
½ large green pepper, chopped
1 tsp salt
¼ tsp pepper
3 slices bread, cut into ½" cubes
2 Tbsp butter
¼ C grated cheese, preferably Parmesan

Cook macaroni in boiling salted water until tender and drain. Melt bacon fat or butter, add sausage meat and break up with fork and stir until golden. Add onion and sauté a few moments longer. Turn into large casserole, add all remaining ingredients except bread cubes, butter and cheese, and mix well. Smooth top, sprinkle bread cubes over, dot with butter, sprinkle with cheese. Bake at 325° for 1½ hours.

Turkey and Vegetable Casserole

½ lb noodles or spaghetti
2 C thinly sliced (⅛") carrots, packed
2 C thinly sliced Spanish onion, packed
2 C chopped fresh (or fresh frozen) broccoli
1 C hot water
½ tsp salt
About 1½ lb sliced leftover white and
    dark turkey meat

SAUCE
¼ C margarine
2½ Tbsp flour
3 C liquid from cooking vegetables
    (see below) plus milk
1 tsp salt
½ C grated cheese (optional)
1 C fine soft breadcrumbs

Put noodles or spaghetti on to cook in a large amount of boiling salted water and cook until almost tender, about 15 minutes. Drain through colander. Tip into very large casserole.

Cook the sliced carrots and onions in the 1 C water with ½ tsp salt and cook 10 minutes then add the broccoli and cook 5 minutes longer. Drain, but reserve liquid. Distribute vegetables evenly over noodles or spaghetti. Arrange sliced turkey overlapping over vegetables.

Make the Sauce by melting margarine and blending in flour and salt. To the vegetable liquid add enough milk to make 3 C. Stir into margarine-flour mixture until thick. Stir in cheese if used. Pour over turkey, easing it through all contents with a fork. Sprinkle top with fine soft breadcrumbs. Bake at 350° for 30 minutes or until bubbly and golden. Serves eight.

Gala Chicken Casserole

2 C cooked rice (see below)
One 12-oz can asparagus pieces
¼ C chopped pimiento or salad olives
2½ C cooked chicken pieces
One can condensed cream of mushroom soup
⅓ C milk
½ tsp salt
¼ tsp pepper
⅔ C grated sharp or process cheese

Simmer a 3-lb chicken in water not quite to cover with one small onion sliced and ½ tsp salt, until meat will fall from bones. Carefully remove to tray or platter and as soon as it cools sufficiently remove meat from bones and cut up. Strain broth and measure 2 C. Cook 1 C rice in this broth half an hour.

Butter a 13 × 9" casserole and turn in rice and smooth it to cover bottom. Add layer of asparagus and pimiento or salad olives. Cover with the chicken pieces. Mix together soup, milk, salt and pepper and pour over chicken. Sprinkle grated or shredded cheese over top. (If prepared in advance chill in refrigerator until 30 or 40 minutes before mealtime.) Bake at 375° about 30 minutes or until cheese bubbles and is golden and casserole is heated through. Serves four to six.

Hard-Cooked Egg and Noodle Casserole

8 eggs
2 C broken noodles, packed
2 qt water
1 tsp salt (first amount)
3 Tbsp margarine
2 Tbsp chopped green pepper
2 Tbsp chopped onion
1 tsp salt (second amount)
2 Tbsp flour
1½ C milk
1 C shredded cheese
1 C fresh breadcrumbs (preferably whole wheat)

Hard-cook the eggs by covering with cold water, bringing quickly to boil. Reduce heat at once to simmer, cover and cook over lowest possible heat 15 minutes. At once flood with cold water to chill, then crack shells and peel.

Meanwhile cook the noodles in the salted water (1 tsp) for 15 minutes until almost tender. Drain through colander and tip into large shallow casserole. Cut eggs in halves crosswise and stand them, cut side up, in noodles, pressing them down a little to make them steady.

In a frying pan melt the margarine and gently sauté the green pepper and onion until soaked but not brown. Stir in flour and salt (second amount) and when mixed stir in milk until thick. Stir in cheese. Pour hot sauce all over eggs and sprinkle crumbs on top. Bake at 350° for 20 minutes until bubbly and brown. Serves four.

Deluxe Egg and Rice Casserole

¾ C raw long grain rice
2 C boiling water
¾ tsp salt (first amount)
8 hard-cooked eggs (see below)
3 Tbsp margarine or butter
⅓ C green pepper coarsely chopped
⅓ C chopped mild onion
2 Tbsp flour
½ tsp salt (second amount)
1 chicken bouillon cube
½ tsp curry powder
1½ C water which includes liquid from
    canned shrimp
One can small shrimp (4¼ oz drained weight)

Cook eggs by putting in cold water to cover, bringing to boil. Reduce heat to simmer, cover and let cook 15 minutes. Immediately flood with cold water to chill.

Cook the rice in boiling water with salt (first amount). Bring to boil covered. Turn off heat for 5 minutes, then cook at simmer for 25 minutes.

Drain shrimp and reserve and measure brine and make it up to 1½ C by adding water. Make a sauce by melting the margarine or butter. Add green pepper and onion and sauté gently for 2 or 3 minutes. Stir in the flour, salt (second amount), chicken bouillon cube and curry powder, then add the water and shrimp liquid and stir until thick.

To assemble, tip the cooked rice into large shallow casserole. Carefully shell chilled hard-cooked eggs. Cut them in halves crosswise and arrange cut side up in a circle around edge of casserole, pushing them down a little into the bed of rice. Tip shrimp into center of casserole. Pour sauce over all. Bake at 350° about 25 minutes or until bubbly. Serves five.

Wiener and Vegetable Casserole

MEAT AND VEGETABLES
Eight 2″ potatoes quartered (or 4 medium-size cut in eighths)
One 3″ Spanish onion sliced thinly
½ to ¾ lb fresh green beans cut in thirds
1 lb (12) wieners

SAUCE
¼ C margarine
6 Tbsp flour
1 tsp salt
½ tsp dry mustard
⅛ tsp pepper
2 C skim milk

Scrub and scour the potatoes but do not pare. Cut into quarters (or eighths) and place in bottom of well-buttered large casserole. Cover with sliced bacon, then with the cut beans, then with the wieners.

To make Sauce, in a medium pot blend the margarine, flour, salt, mustard and pepper. When smooth stir in the milk until thick. Pour hot sauce over wieners and any exposed vegetables. Cover. Bake at 375° for one hour, which will leave a slight crispness in the onions and beans. Serves four.

All-Purpose Macaroni Casserole

2 C macaroni shells or elbows
1 tsp salt (first amount)
6 C boiling water
1 lb ground chuck beef
2 chopped onions
4 C lightly packed shredded mild cheese
One 19-oz can tomato juice
1 C water
1 tsp salt (second amount)
2 C breadcrumbs
3 Tbsp butter

Put the macaroni shells or elbows on to cook first in the salted water. Cook 12 minutes. Drain through colander. Return to pot.

Put meat in dry frying pan with onion and stir and chop until meat turns grey, about 5 minutes. No fat is needed. Add to drained macaroni along with cheese, tomato juice, water and second amount of salt. Mix and turn into large casserole. Gently heat crumbs and butter until blended. Sprinkle over top of casserole. Bake at 350° about 40 minutes. Serves six.

Crabmeat Casserole

4 hard-cooked eggs, sliced
½ C margarine (first amount)
1 large stalk celery chopped (¾ C)
⅓ green pepper chopped (½ C)
⅔ C sifted all-purpose flour
1 tsp salt
2⅔ C milk
1 can pimiento chopped (optional)
Two 7-oz cans crabmeat (or lobster)
One 4¼-oz can small shrimp
¾ C breadcrumbs
2 Tbsp melted margarine (second amount)
Parmesan cheese
⅓ C blanched almonds

Hard-cook the eggs in water to cover, bring to boil, then turn off heat and leave on burner for ½ hour. Flood with cold water, remove shells.

In a large frying pan melt margarine and in it gently sauté the green pepper and celery for 5 minutes. Blend in flour and salt then stir in milk until thick. Add undrained crabmeat and shrimps, sliced hard-cooked eggs, and pimiento if used. Turn into very large casserole. Cover with crumbs which have been mixed with melted margarine. Sprinkle top with Parmesan. Sprinkle almonds all over. Cover and bake at 350° for 20 minutes then remove cover and bake 15 to 20 minutes longer until bubbly and golden. Serves eight.

Macaroni Mackerel Casserole

1½ C cooked elbow macaroni
Two 7-oz cans mackerel
½ C chopped green onion tops
2 medium carrots shredded (¼")
⅓ C sliced celery
2 hard-cooked eggs sliced

SAUCE

1½ Tbsp bacon fat or beef drippings or
    margarine
1½ Tbsp flour
½ tsp salt
2 C milk
¼ C old cheese grated
Ten 2" crackers

In a bowl empty the mackerel, liquid, bone and skin and mash the bones with a fork. Add cooked macaroni, onions, carrots and celery. Mix well. Gently stir in sliced eggs. Turn into a medium-large casserole.

To make Sauce, blend fat, flour and salt. Stir in milk until thick. Stir in cheese. Pour over casserole ingredients making sure the sauce flows through. Crush the crackers with a rolling pin and sprinkle all over top. Bake at 375° until bubbly and golden, 30 to 35 minutes.

Double Hawaiian Casserole

1 C raw rice
2 C boiling water
1 tsp salt
¼ C butter or margarine
2 large green peppers, slivered
2½ C celery, chopped
One 1½-lb can of ham cut into ½" cubes,
    about 3 C packed (reserve jelly from ham:
    see below)
One 19-oz can pineapple tidbits, drained
    (reserve liquid)
One 10-oz can mushroom stems and pieces,
    drained (reserve liquid)
1 tsp honey
1 tsp prepared mustard
3 Tbsp soy sauce
¼ tsp powdered ginger

In saucepan, combine raw rice, boiling water and salt. Bring to boil, cover, reduce heat and simmer 15 minutes. Remove from heat and let stand 5 minutes covered.

Meanwhile in very large frying pan melt butter or margarine. Sauté peppers and celery until crisply tender, about 8 minutes. Stir in cubed ham, pineapple tidbits and mushrooms. Add cooked rice and blend thoroughly. Divide mixture evenly into two 2-qt casseroles.

In saucepan combine jelly from ham, pineapple juice and mushroom liquid. Heat to dissolve jelly then measure amount of liquid. You should have 2 C. If not, add water. Stir in honey, mustard, soy sauce and ginger and bring to boil. Pour 1 C liquid over ham-rice mixture in each casserole. Gently, using fork, coax liquid down. Cover and bake at 375° about half an hour, just enough to heat through. Serves eight to ten.

Corned Beef Casserole

4 hard-cooked eggs (see below)
3 large potatoes (at least 1 lb)
2 Tbsp margarine or bacon drippings
1 medium onion chopped
One 12-oz can corned beef (room temperature)
⅔ C milk
2 Tbsp mayonnaise
¼ tsp prepared mustard
1 Tbsp chopped parsley or chives

Hard-cook eggs by covering with cold water, bringing to boil covered. Remove from heat and let stand half an hour. Flood with water to chill. Wash and pare potatoes and cut into eighths and cook in minimum of boiling salted water until tender. Drain.

In a large frying pan melt margarine (or bacon drippings) and in it sauté onion until limp, not brown. Add drained potatoes and gently sauté chopping until they brown a little. Flake and add corned beef stirring and mixing for 2 or 3 minutes. Turn into greased 8½" casserole. Pour over evenly the milk.

To prepare eggs, cut into halves crosswise. Working carefully scoop out yolks into small bowl and mix with the mayonnaise, mustard, parsley or chives until smooth. Then fill the eight whites with the yolks, mounding a little.

With the back of a spoon make a 1" depression in the corned beef hash at eight even intervals. Lower stuffed eggs into them. Cover with foil and bake at 350° until heated through, about 20 to 30 minutes. Serves four to six.

Shrimp Casserole

2 lb fresh frozen shrimp
1 Tbsp lemon juice
3 Tbsp salad oil
¾ C raw long grain rice
2 Tbsp butter
¼ C minced green pepper
¼ C minced onion
1 tsp salt
⅛ tsp pepper
⅛ tsp mace
Generous shake of cayenne (optional)
1 can undiluted tomato soup
1 C whipping cream
½ C cooking sherry
½ C whole blanched almonds

In the morning put fresh frozen shrimp in a saucepan, pour boiling water over to barely cover, add 1 tsp salt and bring to boil. Reduce heat, cover and simmer 5 minutes. Drain. Turn into large casserole, sprinkle with the lemon juice and oil and refrigerate. Cook the rice in 1½ C boiling water and ½ tsp salt, covered, for half an hour. Cool and refrigerate.

One and a half hours before mealtime, gently sauté green pepper and onion in butter 5 minutes. Add to shrimp in casserole. With fork spread rice over evenly, sprinkle with the salt and all remaining ingredients except ¼ C of the almonds, which are halved and strewn over top at last. Bake uncovered at 350° for 55 to 60 minutes. Serves six.

Large Quantity Salmon Casserole

Note: This recipe serves eight. For 48 servings see bracketed figures.

One 1-lb can salmon (6 lb)
2 small eggs, beaten (9 large)
2 C milk (2½ Imperial qts)
1½ C not packed ¼" noodles (12-oz pkg)
1 Tbsp lemon juice (⅓ C)
½ tsp salt (1 Tbsp)
⅓ C chopped celery (2 C)
2½ Tbsp finely chopped onion (1 C)
½ to ⅔ C fine cracker or breadcrumbs (3 to 4 C)
⅛ tsp pepper (1 tsp)

Boil noodles in salted water until almost tender, about 8 minutes, and drain. Skin and bone salmon and break up coarsely and combine all remaining ingredients except crumbs. The mixture is very wet at this stage. Turn into large buttered casserole. (Turn 48-serving amounts into six large buttered casseroles.) Sprinkle evenly with crumbs. Bake uncovered at 350° for one hour.

Hamburg Yum Yum

½ C raw long grain rice
1 C boiling water (first amount)
½ tsp salt
1 lb ground chuck
1 medium onion, chopped
1 C celery, chopped
1 can cream of mushroom soup undiluted
1 can cream of chicken soup undiluted
½ C water (second amount)
¼ C soy sauce
Chinese noodles

In a heavy pot add the rice to the 1 C boiling water with the salt. Cook covered over low heat for 20 minutes or until all water is absorbed by rice.

In large frying pan brown ground chuck with onion and celery. (No fat needed). Add the cooked rice, soups, ½ C water and soy sauce to the meat mixture. Blend, then turn into a well-buttered 7 or 8-cup casserole. Sprinkle with Chinese noodles. Bake at 350° for 20 to 30 minutes or until bubbling throughout. *Note:* If desired a mixture of ½ C each grated cheese and cracker crumbs may be sprinkled over top instead of noodles. Serves four.

Oyster and Ham Casserole

1 pint oysters
2 C diced cooked ham
2 Tbsp butter
2 Tbsp flour
½ C milk
2 C peas
Pepper
12 unbaked baking powder biscuits

Drain oysters and keep the liquor. Melt the butter and stir in flour. Add ½ C oyster liquor and milk. Cook until thickened, stirring constantly. Add oysters, ham, peas, and pepper to taste. Pour into casserole, arrange biscuits on top. Bake at 425° for 15 minutes. Serves six.

Casserole Cabbage Rolls

1 lb ground chuck beef
1 Tbsp cooking oil
1 chopped onion
1 tsp salt
⅛ tsp pepper
3 Tbsp raw long grain rice
One 10-oz can tomato soup
1 soupcan water
3 C coarsely shredded cabbage

In large frying pan sear the ground chuck beef in oil for a minute or two then add onion, salt, pepper and rice. Mix well while gently sautéing for 2 or 3 minutes, then add soup and water and mix well. Turn cabbage into greased baking dish or casserole. Pour meat mixture evenly over the raw cabbage. Do not stir. Bake covered 1½ hours at 325°.

Ham Strata

9 slices bread, crusts off
¾ lb Cheddar cheese
Two 10-oz pkgs fresh frozen broccoli
    (or 4 C chopped cooked green beans)
One 1-lb canned ham sliced or chopped
    (or equivalent in cold cooked ham)
6 eggs
4 C milk
1 chopped green onion
½ tsp salt
2 tsp French mustard
7 sandwich-size slices process cheese

Line bottom of 9 × 13" pan with the crusts from the bread. Cover with sliced Cheddar cheese. Cover with thawed, uncooked broccoli or cooked green beans. Cover with sliced ham. Cover with crustless bread slices. Beat eggs, then add milk, onion, salt and mustard and mix. Pour all over ingredients in pan. Cover with process cheese slices. Sprinkle with paprika. Refrigerate 6 hours to soak. Bake at 325° for 1 hour. Serves ten.

Fish Casserole Supreme

1 Tbsp margarine
¼ C chopped onion
1 can (10-oz) condensed cheese soup
1 can (10-oz) condensed cream of mushroom soup
One 4½-oz can small shrimp (drained)
One 7-oz can flaked tuna
⅛ tsp pepper
2 lb fresh frozen boneless, skinless thawed
    cod (or other fish) fillets
About ¾ C fine dry breadcrumbs

In a large pot or frying pan melt the margarine and gently sauté the onion for 2 or 3 minutes. Add the soups, shrimp, tuna and pepper. (Salt is not necessary as the condensed soups provide it.) Stir to blend. Pour about a third of this rich sauce into a shallow 3-qt baking dish. Arrange cod (or other fish fillets) over sauce in a single layer. Cover with all of remaining sauce. Cover completely with crumbs. Bake at 350° about 25 to 30 minutes.

Salads

Chef's Tossed Salad see page 119

Caesar Salad

Note: This salad should be assembled at the last minute.

2 C ¼" bread cubes (see below)
⅓ C crisp bacon bits
½ C good quality oil
1 finely chopped clove of garlic
    (or ½ tsp garlic salt)
5 C torn romaine or Bibb lettuce
    (fairly well packed)
1 egg, soft-cooked in shell 1 minute
1 tsp Worcestershire or HP Sauce
¼ C lemon juice
½ tsp salt
⅛ tsp pepper
¼ C grated Parmesan cheese
¼ C crumbled blue cheese (optional)
6 anchovy fillets, cut up (optional)

Toast bread cubes in oven at 200° until dried out but not brown. Fry about 3 slices side bacon until just crisp. Chop and drain on paper towel. Add garlic to oil and pour half of it over the dry bread cubes. Wash and dry greens, tear into bits and put in large salad bowl. Mix together 1-minute egg, shelled, Worcestershire or HP Sauce, lemon juice, salt, pepper and remaining half of oil-garlic mixture.

Just before mealtime sprinkle Parmesan over greens and toss all together and serve. If blue cheese and anchovies are included add them along with the Parmesan. Serves six.

Deluxe Chicken Salad

3 C diced cooked chicken
    (see cooking note below)
¼ C finely chopped chives (or green onions)
2 Tbsp finely chopped green pepper
½ C finely chopped celery
7 or 8 chopped pimiento-stuffed
    olives (optional)
⅛ tsp celery salt
½ C mayonnaise
Salt (second amount if needed)
Pepper

In a large bowl combine chicken, chives or green onions, green pepper, celery, olives (if used) and celery salt. Toss with the mayonnaise to thoroughly blend. Taste a spoonful and add salt and pepper if needed. This salad is lovely if you chill it several hours before serving then scoop it into cupped lettuce leaves. It also makes a good filling for large stuffed tomatoes.

Note: To cook a frozen chicken thaw it and put in a large pot and cover two-thirds with water. Sprinkle with 1½ tsp salt. Add 1 medium onion, chopped, and 1 bay leaf. Cover, bring to boil, reduce heat to simmer and cook 2 hours or until meat is tender and falls from bones. Cool enough to handle chicken then lift it to a utility tray and strip meat from skin and bones. (Put broth in refrigerator for soup, skimming off fat before using. Use surplus chicken for sandwiches or à la king.) Serves six.

Twelve-Day Coleslaw

DRESSING
1½ C vinegar
½ water
1¼ C granulated sugar
1 tsp celery seeds
1½ tsp mustard seeds
½ tsp turmeric
1½ tsp salt

SALAD INGREDIENTS
1 medium-large hard green cabbage,
    finely shredded
1 medium-large carrot, finely shredded
½ Spanish onion or one whole white
    onion, grated
1 or 2 green peppers, shredded
½ C salad olives including pimiento,
    chopped (optional)

In a saucepan stir together the dressing ingredients and bring to boil, being sure sugar is dissolved. Cool.

Combine all salad ingredients in a large bowl, shredding cabbage, carrot and peppers finely and grating onion and chopping olives (if used). Pour cooled dressing over and mix well. Store in covered glass jars in refrigerator 12 hours or twelve days before using. Serves twelve.

Bridge Party Fruit Salad

LETTUCE CUPS; Allow 3 well-cupped leaves for each individual salad plate, carefully drying them. Have ready: 1. Drained canned grapefruit sections; 2. Drained canned pineapple rings; 3. Bananas cut in halves crosswise, spread with mayonnaise and rolled in chopped blanched almonds; 4. Plump stoned prunes filled with white cream cheese; 5. Choice dessert figs filled with cubes of Gouda or Swiss cheese; 6. Small bunches of choice grapes. To assemble, put 1 ring of pineapple on lettuce leaves to form base. On both sides put 2 large sections of canned grapefruit. At front of salad put a nut-coated banana half. In center of pineapple ring put a stuffed prune. Then place a small bunch of grapes and a stuffed fig attractively where you think. Serve with Fruit Cream Dressing.

FRUIT CREAM DRESSING: 3 Tbsp sugar, 2 Tbsp flour, 2 eggs, 2 Tbsp vinegar, 1 lemon, juice and grated rind, 1 C juice from canned pineapple, 1 C cream, whipped. Mix sugar and flour in upper part of double boiler. Add beaten eggs, vinegar, fruit juice and grated rind. Cook over gently boiling water, stirring constantly, until thick. Chill. Just before serving fold in 1 C cream, whipped.

Crisp Shredded Cabbage Salad

½ medium new cabbage shredded
    (about 4 C not packed)
½ C mayonnaise
¼ tsp celery seed
1 tsp chopped green onion or chives
Tomato wedges (for garnish)

Just before mealtime shred the cabbage on the ¼" shredder and in a bowl mix it with the mayonnaise and seasonings. If you want to add a little salt do so just before serving. Turn into salad bowl and garnish with a border of small tomato wedges. Serves five.

Four Bean Salad

One 19-oz can cut green beans
One 19-oz can cut yellow wax beans
One 19-oz can red kidney beans
One 19-oz can lima beans
One Spanish onion, thinly sliced
One green pepper, thinly sliced

Drain and combine above ingredients and marinate several hours or overnight. Stir several times in the following dressing.

½ C sugar
½ C vinegar (could be wine vinegar)
½ C salad oil
1 tsp salt
Pepper to taste
½ tsp dry mustard
½ to 1 tsp tarragon
½ to 1 tsp basil
2 Tbsp parsley

Drain before serving. Reserve marinade. Return any leftovers to it, cover and refrigerate. Serves sixteen to twenty.

Chef's Tossed Salad

½ medium head iceberg lettuce
8 romaine leaves (or more)
4" piece English cucumber
½ green pepper
2 tomatoes
1 stalk celery
4 medium mushrooms
½ C French Dressing

Wash and dry all ingredients. Tear the lettuce and romaine into bite-size pieces. Slice the cucumber wafer thin, cut the green pepper in fine shreds, cut tomato into eighths, chop the celery very small and slice the mushrooms wafer thin. If desired rub your bowl with a cut clove of garlic. Add all prepared vegetables, pour salad dressing over and toss with salad servers.

Note: All of this salad preparation should be done at the last moment to conserve vitamin content and to avoid limp greens.

Antipasto Salad

SALAD
⅔ head leaf lettuce, torn
⅓ head Chinese cabbage, chopped
½ C celery, diagonally sliced thinly
½ C chopped cucumber, skin scored and included
4 or 5 green onions, chopped, including stems
4 oz mozzarella cheese cut in narrow strips
⅓ lb pepperoni, thinly sliced
2 medium tomatoes, cut in eighths
¼ C fresh parsley, coarsely chopped
1 C croutons (see note below)
½ C grated parmesan cheese

DRESSING
⅓ C wine vinegar
⅔ C oil
1 Tbsp lemon juice
½ tsp dry mustard
1 tsp salt
1 Tbsp fresh parsley, chopped
¼ tsp pepper
2 tsp minced garlic
2 tsp basil
1 tsp oregano
5 large or 10 small fresh mushrooms,
    washed and sliced

To make Dressing, 4 hours in advance combine all above dressing ingredients in large jar and shake well and let stand at room temperature or store overnight in refrigerator.

To make Salad, toss all salad ingredients except croutons and parmesan cheese. Just before serving pour all of the dressing over and toss again. Toss croutons in lightly then sprinkle parmesan cheese over all and serve.

Note: Make croutons by cutting 2 slices bread into ½" cubes and toasting them in the oven at 250° until dry and golden.

Main Course Summer Salmon Salad

Two 7¾-oz cans red salmon, drained
One 5" head iceberg lettuce
    (or 4 C shredded romaine packed)
15 spinach leaves shredded
1 medium cucumber, scored and
    sliced paper thin
5 or 6 radishes sliced thin
¼ lb fresh small mushrooms sliced thin
2 stalks celery sliced thin
½ green pepper cut in thin strips
3 green spring onions finely chopped
1 tsp lemon juice
Mayonnaise or French dressing or
    dressing of your choice

Wash and dry lettuce or romaine and spinach and cut or chop or shred as above. (The iceberg lettuce should be cut into 1" cubes.) Scrub and slice mushrooms. Combine them with cucumber, radishes, celery, pepper and onion and stuff into a large plastic bag and refrigerate.

When serving time nears tip salad ingredients into large bowl and add drained flaked salmon, lemon juice and ⅓ C mayonnaise or French dressing. Add dressing sparingly for you do not want a puddle in the bottom of your salad bowl. Serves six.

Best Beet Salad

4 C diced (⅜") cooked beets
    (if canned drain well)
1 C finely chopped inner celery
¼ C finely chopped chives or green
    onions including tops
1 Tbsp (or more) chopped parsley
1 Tbsp lemon juice
⅓ C genuine mayonnaise
¼ to ½ tsp salt (see below)
2 hard-cooked eggs, chopped

Note: If you cook your own beets more salt is needed. If you use canned beets drain them well and use less salt.

In a large bowl mix together the mayonnaise, lemon juice and salt. Add diced (drained) beets, celery, chives and parsley and chopped hard-cooked eggs and mix well. Taste. You may want to add more salt and lemon juice or make it a little moister by adding more mayonnaise. Made in advance this salad improves. Serves eight.

Cucumbers in Sour Cream

2 unpared average-sized cucumbers
1 tsp salt
¼ C sour cream
2 Tbsp lemon juice
½ tsp sugar
½ tsp dill seeds (optional)

Wash the cucumbers and slice, unpared, wafer thin. They should be so thin you can see through them. In a bowl sprinkle salt over and mix in. Refrigerate covered 1 hour. Drain and press out excess liquid. Cover with ice cubes until near serving time. Drain thoroughly, discarding any unmelted ice. Press out excess liquid again. Stir in sour cream, lemon juice, sugar and dill seeds (if used). They are now ready to serve in place of a salad or as a relish accompaniment to a cold meat platter.

Best Potato Salad

4 C diced (½") cooked new potatoes
2 hard-cooked eggs chopped
1 C finely chopped inner celery
2 Tbsp finely chopped sweet Spanish
    or green onion or chives
½ tsp salt
6 to 8 Tbsp genuine mayonnaise

Scrub potatoes and cook without peeling in boiling water, covered, until nearly tender. Drain, cool and peel. Cut in ½" dice. Mix in all remaining ingredients and chill for 1 hour before serving.

Variations: 1. Substitute chopped cucumber for the celery; 2. Add ⅔ C cooked fresh green peas; 3. Add ½ C shredded raw carrot; 4. Add ¼ C chopped salad olives. Serves six to eight.

Sylvia Salad

3 medium large cooked potatoes diced
½ C cooked green peas
¼ C chopped green onion or chives
¼ C genuine mayonnaise
8 lettuce leaves
2 C flaked tuna
2 C cut green beans cooked and chilled
4 or 5 flat anchovies cut up
2 sliced hard-cooked eggs
½ cucumber scored, sliced but unpared
2 tomatoes cut into thin wedges
16 ripe olives

Make a Potato Salad by combining first 4 ingredients. Then brush lettuce leaves with French Dressing and with them line a huge salad bowl. Make a bottom layer of all of the potato salad. Next layer is the flaked tuna. Cover that with the cooked green beans and sprinkle anchovies over. For the top garnish, make 2 border circles of hard-cooked egg slices, tomato wedges and cucumber slices alternating them. Pile ripe olives in center. Serves eight.

Sweet and Sour Salad

DRESSING
¼ C vinegar
½ C oil
¼ C liquid honey
2 Tbsp chili sauce or catsup
¼ C finely chopped green onion
¼ tsp Tabasco
½ tsp salt

SALAD INGREDIENTS
1 medium head iceberg lettuce cut or
    torn into bite-sized pieces
12 thinly sliced radishes
½ C chopped parsley
1 chopped green pepper
2 chopped green onions
½ C raisins (light if possible)

Into a jar with tight-fitting lid measure all dressing ingredients and shake well. Combine all salad ingredients in large wooden salad bowl rubbed with half a clove of garlic. At the last moment before serving shake the dressing and pour over sparingly. Toss. Serves eight.

Tossed Green Salad Parmesan

Use 3 different types of lettuce such as iceberg, leaf, Bibb, romaine, endive, about 6 cups. Rub your salad bowl with a cut clove of garlic. Now mince this clove of garlic and heat it in a frying pan with 2 Tbsp salad oil and ½ C bread cubes (½"), stirring until delicately browned. Remove and drain on paper towel. Add to the greens. Sprinkle with freshly ground black pepper, ½ tsp salt, ½ C thin strips of salami. Now comes the funny part. Next put an egg into boiling water for 1 minute. Remove egg from water, break over salad and stir in, to coat the greens. Add sufficient Parmesan French Dressing to moisten, about ⅓ cup, and toss. Chill, covered, for 1 hour.

Bacon and Tomato Salad

8 strips bacon fried until crisp
1 medium head iceberg lettuce torn or chopped
1 dill-size cucumber peeled and sliced
4 medium tomatoes chopped
5 sliced radishes
French or Italian French Dressing

Fry the bacon until crisp, tipping off excess fat as it collects. Drain and cool on paper towel. Chop into ¼' pieces and reserve half for garnishing later. Mix remaining bacon with lettuce, cucumber, tomatoes and radishes. At serving time toss with minimum amount of French dressing and sprinkle top with remaining bacon. Serves six.

Selfridge's Shrimp Salad

Generous amount Bibb lettuce washed and dried
6 hard-cooked eggs
1 large long cucumber scored with fork
    and sliced
4 small tomatoes sliced
About 2 C fresh cooked or canned shrimp
1 tsp curry powder
About ½ C mayonnaise

Cover 4 large lunch plates with Bibb lettuce, having round tips form a scalloped edge around border. Cut hard-cooked eggs into quarters lengthwise. Arrange 5 quarters around border of plate. Place cucumber slices between eggs. Make an inner ring of overlapping small tomato slices. At center place a pile of shrimp, about ½ C to each plate. Into mayonnaise stir the curry powder and with 1 Tbsp of it top each pile of shrimp. Now it is ready to serve.

Spinach Salad

One 10-oz pkg spinach (see below)
5 slices side bacon (see below)
1 C small mushrooms measured after slicing
⅓ C whole salted cashews

DRESSING
⅔ C cottage cheese
1 egg
⅓ C oil
⅓ C red wine or wine vinegar
¼ tsp dry mustard
¼ tsp salt
¼ tsp salad herbs
¼ tsp nutmeg
⅛ tsp black pepper
½ tsp Worcestershire sauce

In a small bowl beat all of the dressing ingredients. Beat with rotary beater until blended, about ½ minute.

Into a very large bowl put well washed spinach, stems removed, dried, and torn-up coarsely. Add bacon which has been fried until just crisp and drained well on paper towel and crumbled. Add washed, dried, sliced, small mushrooms. Pour blended dressing over and mix very well to be sure spinach is coated with dressing. Sprinkle cashews on top.

Meat-Eater Salad

SALAD DRESSING INGREDIENTS
¾ C salad oil
⅓ C tarragon vinegar (see below)
1 tsp salt
1 tsp dry mustard
1 tsp dry parsley
1 tsp lemon juice
½ tsp Worcestershire sauce
¼ tsp pepper
¼ tsp thyme

SALAD INGREDIENTS
1½ C leftover meat: ham, tongue, chicken,
    beef, salami, etc.
¼ lb small fresh mushrooms, left whole
2 potatoes, boiled, peeled, quartered and cubed
1 green pepper cut in ½" squares
½ Spanish onion, thinly sliced
1 stalk celery, cut diagonally
6 radishes thinly sliced
1 dill pickle, sliced
Garnish: 2 hard-cooked eggs and parsley

To make Tarragon Vinegar heat 1 C white vinegar with 4 tsp dried tarragon and simmer 1 minute. Bottle. Refrigerate. Strain as needed.

Combine all Salad Dressing ingredients in a jar and shake. Put Salad ingredients in a large bowl. Pour salad dressing over and mix gently. Cover. Chill in refrigerator 6 hours to marinate.

Serve in individual salad bowls lined with leaf or Bibb or iceberg lettuce and garnish top with hard-cooked egg slices and parsley. If you serve soup before and a substantial dessert after, this salad makes an adequate main course with hot biscuits or rolls or muffins.

Tossed Salad for Twenty-Two

2 large heads iceberg lettuce
One 5" compact white cauliflower
½ bag washed and dried spinach (2 C packed)
1 scored, sliced unpeeled cucumber
1 finely sliced green pepper
½ C chopped chives
One flat 2-oz can drained, chopped anchovies
4 strips bacon, fried and drained and crumbled
½ C sliced stuffed olives
3 Tbsp drained capers (optional)
1 C shredded Swiss cheese
½ to ¾ C Vinaigrette French dressing

Break up lettuce and spinach by hand. Shred the cauliflower on ½" shredder. In a large bowl add all other ingredients except dressing and mix. Add dressing and mix.

Almond and Sour Cream Salad

In a bowl toss together 2 C torn lettuce leaves, 2 C torn, washed and dried spinach leaves, 1 spring onion including green tops finely chopped, 1 C finely chopped raw cauliflower, ¼ C sliced radishes, ¼ C chopped toasted almonds, shake of salt, ¼ C fresh dairy sour cream and 1 Tbsp lemon juice. Toss all ingredients lightly and serve at once.

August Garden Salad

¼ large unpared cucumber, sliced paper-thin
1 medium tomato, cut in bite-sized pieces
½ green pepper, cut in shreds
½ pared, medium-size raw beet,
　　shredded on ¼" shredder
½ C tiny cauliflowerets or cauliflower
　　sliced wafer-thin
½ C new green cabbage, sliced as thinly
　　as possible
Shake of garlic salt
¼ to ⅓ C mayonnaise
Cupped lettuce leaves

Lightly toss together all ingredients except lettuce leaves. With them line salad bowl and turn into it the tossed salad.

Zesty Vegetable Salad

SALAD INGREDIENTS
2 C turnip pared and sliced ⅛" thick
　　then cut into 1½" pieces
1½ C small carrots, pared and thinly coined,
　　1⁄16" thick
2 C one-inch cauliflowerets
1 green pepper, seeded and slivered
2 C boiling water
1 tsp salt

MARINADE
½ C white vinegar
⅓ C granulated sugar
¼ C salad oil
¼ tsp curry powder
1 tsp salt
¼ tsp pepper

Prepare vegetables and drop into the salted, boiling water. Do not cover. Boil for 5 minutes only, mixing vegetables gently with a fork until tender-crisp. Drain and cool.

Meanwhile prepare Marinade by combining all marinade ingredients in a screw-top jar. Cover and shake vigorously. Pour marinade over cooled vegetables and toss lightly. Refrigerate covered at least 4 hours or overnight, stirring vegetable mixture occasionally and carefully.

Large Quantity Pineapple Cole Slaw

4½ lb shredded cabbage
1¼ oz finely chopped onions
1 Tbsp salt
2 C French dressing
One 19-oz tin drained pineapple chunks

Shred cabbage finely and soak one hour in ice cold salted water. Drain well and dry. Add chopped onion. Sprinkle evenly with salt. Add drained pineapple chunks and French dressing and mix lightly. Chill. Serves 25.

Potato Cheese Salad

4 large potatoes cooked in skins
2 hard-cooked eggs
½ C chopped green onions including tops
　　or chopped chives
6 radishes thinly sliced
⅔ C cubed Swiss or Cheddar cheese
½ tsp tarragon
1 tsp salt
Shake of pepper
Bibb or iceberg lettuce

DRESSING
½ C dairy sour cream
1 tsp dill weed
1 Tbsp white vinegar
¼ tsp garlic salt
1 Tbsp oil
Small shake of cayenne

Cook the potatoes in their skins until barely tender. Drain, rinse with cold water, peel and carefully cut into ½" cubes. Slice hard-cooked eggs and cut slices in half. In a large bowl combine potatoes, eggs, onions, radishes, cheese, tarragon, salt and pepper. Mix together dressing ingredients and pour over salad and gently toss. Chill thoroughly. Line a wooden salad bowl with washed and dried lettuce leaves and turn salad into it. Serves five or six.

Crabmeat Salad

One 7-oz can crabmeat
½ C chopped inner celery
3 or 4 Tbsp mayonnaise
¼ tsp Tabasco sauce
1 tsp lemon juice

Drain crabmeat and flake it with a fork, removing any bones. Add celery, mayonnaise, Tabasco and lemon juice, and mix. Serve on 4 small cupped lettuce leaves granished with "petals" made of ripe or green olives. *Note:* Shrimp or lobster may be used instead of crabmeat. Serves four.

Avocado, Grapefruit and Tomato Salad

1 large or 2 medium ripe avocados
One 19-oz can grapefruit sections, drained
2 large ripe tomatoes
Genuine mayonnaise
5 cupped iceberg lettuce leaves

Peel and cut the avocado into 15 crescent-shaped wedges. Drain the grapefruit. Wash and cut the tomatoes into 15 wedges. Arrange these wedges alternately and overlapping on the lettuce leaves snugly enough that when they are transferred to plates they keep their shape. Arrange all 5 salad-filled lettuce cups on large platter and top each at center with about 1½ Tbsp genuine thick mayonnaise. Serves five.

Salad Filled Tomatoes

¼ C elbow macaroni (see below)
2 C water
¼ tsp salt
½ C diced cooked ham (or chicken or
   turkey or broken up canned salmon or tuna)
1 Tbsp finely chopped chives or green onion
2 Tbsp finely chopped cucumber
2 Tbsp mayonnaise
5 medium-large tomatoes, washed but not peeled
20 serrated slices cucumber (for garnish)

Cook elbow macaroni in water and salt 15 minutes until nearly tender. Drain and chill in cold water, then drain and dry. In a bowl add macaroni to diced ham with the chives or green onion and chopped cucumber. Add sufficient mayonnaise to moisten well.

Wash and dry tomatoes and carefully remove the core. Now cut through to within ½" of bottom to make 8 sections, place in individual salad bowls and gently open up to look like flower petals. Fill opened tomatoes with filling and garnish sides with cucumber slices. Chill. Serves five.

Deluxe Shrimp Salad

One 12-oz pkg fresh frozen de-veined shelled
   raw shrimp
1½ tsp salt (first amount)
3 C boiling water (first amount)
½ C tiny macaroni shells
4 C boiling water (second amount)
½ tsp salt (second amount)
½ C finely chopped inner celery
½ C thawed uncooked fresh frozen green peas
3 Tbsp finely chopped blanched almonds
About ⅓ C genuine mayonnaise

To the raw shrimp add the 1½ tsp salt and 3 C boiling water and bring to boil. Stand off heat for 3 minutes then drain in sieve. Cool. Cook macaroni shells in the 4 C boiling water with the ½ tsp salt until tender. Drain. Add to cooled shrimp.

Add all remaining ingredients and chill. Serve on well-cupped lettuce leaves. Four servings.

Variations: 1. Instead of macaroni use cooked rice prepared by cooking ½ C raw rice with ½ tsp salt in 1½ C boiling water 30 minutes. Rinse in sieve under running cold water and drain. 2. Substitute cashews or shelled sunflower seeds for the almonds. 3. Add 1 unpared cored chopped dessert apple.

Waldorf Salad

2 red dessert apples diced ¼" (2½ C packed)
2 C finely chopped inner celery
½ C broken walnuts or pecans or blanched almonds
¼ C mayonnaise

Wash, core but do not pare apples. Cut into ¼" dice. Use only choicest inner celery. Add nuts and mayonnaise and mix.

Grapes

Reception Chicken Salad

This recipe makes about forty-five ¾-cup or sixty ½-cup servings.

10 C cubed (½") cooked chicken
10 C diced inner celery
16 hard-cooked eggs, chopped
3 to 4 C mayonnaise
2 C drained canned cubed pineapple
1 Tbsp salt
6 C pared diced cucumber
3 C toasted blanched almonds,
   coarsely chopped
6 heads lettuce, washed and dried,
   separated into cups

Combine all ingredients except lettuce. Chill. Serve in lettuce cups. *Note:* This must be made on the day it is to be served.

Bridge Salad Luncheon Plate

One 8-oz can red salmon or tuna well drained
About ⅓ C genuine mayonnaise (first amount)
8 long inner stalks celery
2 ripe avocados
8 large tomatoes
Two 14-oz tins canned grapefruit sections
32 Bibb or small romaine lettuce leaves
32 large cooked shelled shrimp
About ¾ C mayonnaise (second amount)
About ½ C catsup

Drain and mash the salmon to a purée and mix in the ⅓ C mayonnaise. Cut the celery into 32 even pieces and stuff with the salmon mixture.

On 8 tea plates arrange 4 Bibb or romaine lettuce leaves on each like a 4-pointed star and put the stuffed celery on center rib of each leaf. Between the 4 spaces arrange, overlapping, 1 wedge avocado, 1 wedge tomato and 1 drained grapefruit section. At center put about 2 Tbsp of a mixture of the ¾ C mayonnaise and catsup and on top of it place in a circle 4 large shrimp. Serves eight.

Macaroni Shell Salad

One 7-oz pkg tiny macaroni shells
   (2 C raw; 4 C cooked)
1 tsp salt
¼ C chopped fresh chives
½ C coarsely chopped blanched almonds
2 C finely shredded cabbage
1 medium carrot shredded finely
½ green pepper chopped
1 medium stalk celery
1 Tbsp grated Parmesan cheese
½ C best quality mayonnaise

. Cook the macaroni shells in 2 qt boiling water with 1 tsp salt until almost tender, about 15 minutes. Drain and cool.

In a large bowl gently combine cooled macaroni shells with the chives, almonds, cabbage, carrot, pepper, celery, Parmesan and mayonnaise. Cover with saran and chill. At serving time line sides of salad bowl with a few leaves of Bibb or iceberg lettuce or watercress and turn salad into it. Serves eight.

Tangy Vegetable Salad

This salad marinates overnight.

1 medium-large new potato
1 medium long slender carrot
1 medium onion
2 C unpared sliced (⅛") cucumber, packed
2 firm slightly underripe tomatoes
One 14-oz can cut green beans, drained

MARINADE
¼ C oil
¼ C lemon juice
¼ C corn syrup
1 Tbsp chopped parsley (or bottled flakes)
1 tsp salt
¼ tsp curry powder
⅛ tsp garlic powder

Scrub and scrape potato and carrot. Peel onion. Steam or cook together whole, in minimum of water until still slightly crisp and barely tender, not soft. Drain, chill and cut into ⅛" slices. Cut unpared cucumber into ⅛" slices and tomatoes into ½" wedges. Drain beans.

Into holding bowl or jar with lid turn all 6 prepared vegetables. Mix all marinade ingredients and pour over. Gently mix, cover, refrigerate overnight, and gently stir once or twice during the marinating period. Serves six to eight.

Salad Dressings

Emem's Mayonnaise

3 large egg yolks
1 Tbsp dry mustard
1 Tbsp sugar
1 Tbsp salt
4 Tbsp cold lemon juice
2½ C cold salad oil

In your beater bowl combine egg yolks, mustard, sugar and salt. Beat together until very thick. Then begin to add cold oil: slowly add about 2 Tbsp in a thin ⅛" stream while still beating at high speed. Then slowly add 1 Tbsp lemon juice while still beating at high speed. At this stage emulsion begins to take place. Slowly add ¼ C cold oil in a very thin stream while beating on high. Turn off beaters and with rubber scraper scrape down sides. Repeat this alternate slow addition of oil and lemon juice until all of both are added. Again turn off beaters and with rubber scraper scrape down sides. You may increase size of oil stream a little once emulsion is firmly established. Do not hurry or emulsion may separate. Turn into jar, cover and keep refrigerated. Makes 3 cups.

Green Mayonnaise

3 large (or 4 small) cold egg yolks
1 Tbsp dry mustard
2 tsp salt
2 Tbsp sugar
2 C cold salad oil
6 or 7 Tbsp cold lemon juice
½ C finely chopped fresh chives
½ C finely chopped fresh parsley
⅛ tsp green food coloring

Into beater bowl measure egg yolks, mustard, salt and sugar and beat at high speed until very light. Now patiently and carefully start adding cold oil in the thinnest possible stream, no wider than 1/16" or it will fail to emulsify. As soon as oil starts to collect on top, stop flow of oil and add 1 tsp lemon juice while beating. Continue in this slow steady way until you are sure emulsification is established. Then you can increase diameter of oil stream to ⅛", but never hurry it. Continue adding alternately, until all oil and lemon juice are added and beaten in. Remove beaters and stir in chives, parsley and green food colouring until blended. Store in refrigerator in tightly covered jars.

Blender Mayonnaise

1 egg
¾ tsp salt
½ tsp dry mustard
1 Tbsp vinegar
1 Tbsp lemon juice
1 C cold salad oil

Put egg, salt, dry mustard, vinegar, lemon juice and ¼ C of the oil in blender. Cover and process at high speed for 2 minutes. Remove feeder cap and add remaining oil through small opening in a slow, steady, small stream with speed on high. You may have to stop blender and scrape down sides with rubber scraper to keep ingredients flowing to blades. Store in covered jar in refrigerator. Makes 1¼ cups.

Thousand-Island Dressing

1 C genuine mayonnaise
1 medium stalk celery finely chopped
½ green pepper finely chopped
1½ Tbsp white onion finely chopped
2 hard-cooked eggs, shredded or sieved
2 tsp paprika
⅛ tsp cayenne pepper
½ tsp salt
1 Tbsp thick tomato paste
½ C finely chopped drained stuffed olives
2 Tbsp chopped walnuts (optional)

Pat dry the celery, pepper, onions and olives. Into bowl measure mayonnaise and add all remaining ingredients and mix well. Store in covered jars in refrigerator.

Fruit Cream Dressing

3 Tbsp sugar
2 Tbsp flour
2 eggs
2 Tbsp vinegar
1 C canned pineapple juice
Juice and grated rind 1 lemon
1 cup whipping cream, whipped

Mix all but cream, in order given, in top of double boiler, mixing as you measure. Stir over boiling water until thick. Chill. Just before serving fold in whipped cream.

Reducers' Salad Dressing

⅔ C buttermilk
1 tsp freshly grated orange rind
1 tsp paprika
1 tsp salt
1 tsp fresh frozen chopped chives
1 tsp celery seed (optional)
1 tsp fresh lemon juice

Shake together in small covered jar and store in refrigerator.

Italian French Dressing

¼ C white vinegar
3 Tbsp water
⅔ C oil
1 tsp sugar
¾ tsp salt
¾ tsp garlic salt
½ tsp oregano
½ tsp dry mustard
¼ tsp black pepper
¼ tsp celery seeds

Shake in tightly covered bottle or jar always before using. Store in refrigerator.

Low-Calorie Boiled Dressing

1 Tbsp cornstarch
2 tsp flour
½ tsp salt
5 tsp sugar
¼ tsp mustard
⅛ tsp onion salt
⅛ tsp garlic salt
⅛ tsp celery salt
1/16 tsp white pepper
1 Tbsp cooking oil
¼ C vinegar
4 tsp lemon juice
1 C boiling water

In a small heavy saucepan mix well together the first nine ingredients. Then stir in the oil. Then stir in the vinegar and lemon juice. Stir in boiling water and cook over high heat, stirring until thick. Cook, stirring, one minute longer. Cool and chill. When chilled through, beat for 2 minutes before storing in refrigerator in covered jar or bottle.

Emulsified French Dressing

¼ C lemon juice or white vinegar
1 Tbsp paprika
1½ tsp salt
½ tsp garlic salt
½ tsp dry mustard
3 Tbsp sugar
1 whole cold medium egg
1 cold egg yolk
1 C cold oil

Into beater bowl measure lemon juice or vinegar, paprika, salt, garlic salt, mustard and sugar. Beat at high speed for 2 minutes. Add the whole egg and yolk and beat 5 minutes more. Now slowly add the oil, one measuring teaspoon at a time, beating at high speed all the while until all cold oil is added. Store in covered bottle.

San Francisco Roquefort Dressing

½ C cottage cheese
⅓ C genuine mayonnaise (not salad dressing)
2 Tbsp Roquefort or Danish blue cheese
¼ tsp salt
1 tsp lemon juice

Measure all ingredients in above order into blender goblet and beat until satin smooth.

Pink Salad Dressing

1 C salad oil
½ C vinegar
½ C water
½ C catsup
1½ tsp salt
3 Tbsp sugar
2 tsp horseradish
2½ tsp prepared mustard
1 tsp paprika
1 tsp Worcestershire (or Soy) sauce

Shake well and store covered in refrigerator.

Green Goddess Dressing

One 10-oz carton (½ pt) dairy sour cream
½ C genuine mayonnaise (not salad dressing)
⅓ C well dried spinach or top romaine
   leaves, packed
¼ C well dried parsley including stems, packed
¼ tsp garlic powder (or ½ tsp garlic salt)
8 drops Tabasco

Into blender goblet put half the sour cream. Now add the spinach or romaine leaves, parsley, garlic salt and Tabasco. Then add the mayonnaise and remaining sour cream and push them down into the greens. Cover and blend at high speed until you have a perfectly smooth jade green purée. Store in refrigerator in covered jar. *Note:* Because of the sour cream content this dressing will not keep as long as most salad dressings do.

Homemade Herb and Garlic Dressing

½ C oil
2 Tbsp white vinegar
2 tsp sugar
½ tsp salt
¼ tsp finely crumbled dried parsley
¼ tsp garlic salt (or very finely
   chopped clove of garlic)
¼ tsp basil
¼ tsp celery seed (optional)
¼ tsp marjoram
¼ tsp white pepper

Mix all ingredients together in a jar with a tight-fitting lid and shake well each time before using.

All-Purpose Salad Dressing

¼ C flour
2½ tsp dry mustard
¼ C sugar
2 tsp salt
¼ tsp paprika
2 Tbsp oil (first amount)
½ C white vinegar
1 C boiling water
2 or 3 large egg yolks (beaten)
1 C cold oil (second amount)

In top of double boiler mix together dry the flour, mustard, sugar, salt and paprika. Add the 2 Tbsp oil and vinegar and mix in. Stir in boiling water and cook stirring over boiling water until thick. Quickly stir in egg yolks. Cool by standing top of double boiler in cold water, stirring frequently. When cold transfer to electric beater bowl. At high speed start adding the cold oil, 1 tsp at a time, counting to ten between additions until you have added ½ C. After that you can add oil a little faster but be sure each amount is incorporated before you add more. Beat at high speed until all oil is added, spoon into a 3-cup jar with lid on and store in refrigerator.

Old-Fashioned Salad Dressing

⅔ C water
⅔ C white vinegar
½ C sugar
1 tsp salt
1 Tbsp flour
1 tsp dry mustard
¼ tsp turmeric (for color and flavor:
   do not omit)
2 eggs
One 6-oz can (¾ C) evaporated milk

In a heavy pot bring water and vinegar to a gentle boil. Meanwhile mix together dry in a bowl the sugar, salt, flour, mustard and turmeric. Stir in eggs and milk and add this to hot water-vinegar mixture and stir with wire whip or rotary beater until thick. Cool and pour into covered jar and refrigerate until needed for salads or sandwiches. Makes 2½ cups.

Jellied Molds

Molded Carrot & Meat Salad see page 128

Molded Carrot and Meat Salad

1 envelope (1 Tbsp) plain gelatin
¾ C cold water
½ C mayonnaise
¼ C sour cream
¼ C orange juice
1 Tbsp lemon juice
¼ tsp salt
½ tsp dry mustard
1½ C carrots shredded finely on ⅛" shredder
2 Tbsp finely chopped green onion
2 Tbsp chopped green pepper
1 Tbsp chopped canned or bottled
    pimiento (optional)
1 C diced (¼") ham or tongue or
    chicken or pork, cooked

In a measuring cup or little bowl soak the gelatin in the cold water 2 minutes then stand bowl in shallow boiling water and stir to dissolve. Remove from heat and let cool.

In a medium bowl mix together the mayonnaise, sour cream, orange and lemon juices, salt and dry mustard. Stir in the gelatin liquid and chill until softly set. Then stir in prepared carrots, onion, green pepper and pimiento (if used) and meat of your choice. Turn into a 4-cup mold or into 6 individual molds and chill until set. To serve, loosen sides with pointed knife and lower into hot water and count to five. Cover with serving plate and turn over and out. Garnish with curly endive. Serves four to six.

Empress Salad Ring

1 large hard-cooked egg, sliced
3 Tbsp (3 envelopes) plain gelatin
½ C sugar
2 tsp salt
½ C water (first amount)
2½ C water (second amount)
¼ C vinegar
¼ C lemon juice
2 Tbsp finely chopped green onion
¾ C pitted ripe olives
1 C finely chopped inner celery
1 C coarsely grated carrot
⅓ C thinly sliced radishes

Hard-cook the egg and chill it. In a large bowl mix together the gelatin, sugar, salt and ½ C water. Stand bowl in simmering water and stir until gelatin is dissolved. Remove from heat and add the 2½ C water, vinegar, lemon juice and onion. Cool until slightly thickened. Pour about ½ C gelatin liquid into a 5 or 6-cup ring mold. Peel and carefully slice hard-cooked egg in egg slicer and arrange in ring. Between slices place halves of some of the pitted ripe olives, rounded side down. Chill until egg slices and olives are set in jelly. Now to remaining jelly liquid add remaining olives, chopped, celery and carrots and radishes. Carefully spoon over firm layer. Chill until very firm.

When serving time arrives dip mold in hot water and count to ten. Invert large serving plate over jelly and turn over and out. Garnish with endive or watercress or delicate lettuce leaves and wedges of tomato and slices of cucumber.

Garden Vegetable Salad Mold

One 3-oz pkg lemon jello
1½ C boiling water
1 Tbsp prepared mustard
1½ C finely shredded cabbage
½ C finely shredded green pepper
¼ C sliced stuffed olives

Dissolve jello in boiling water. Cool until of consistency of liquid honey. Stir in mustard. Add and stir in vegetables and pour into a 3-cup mold to chill and set. Unmold onto lettuce-lined plate. Serve with mayonnaise.

Tomato Aspic Ring

3 C canned tomato juice
1½ Tbsp grated or finely chopped onion
½ bay leaf
¾ tsp salt
1½ tsp sugar
1½ Tbsp vinegar or lemon juice
5 tsp plain gelatin

Measure out ½ C of tomato juice, add the vinegar or lemon juice to it and soak the gelatin in them for 5 minutes. Heat together the remaining 2½ C tomato juice, onion, bay leaf, salt and sugar and simmer 10 minutes. Remove from heat. Stir in soaked gelatin until dissolved. Fish out bay leaf. Pour into a 6-cup ring mold and chill until firm. Turn out on fancy serving plate. Garnish with small cupped iceberg lettuce leaves filled with ripe olives. Serve with sour cream.

Spanish Tomato Aspic

One 14-oz can tomato sauce
1½ C water (divided)
2 envelopes plain gelatin
½ C corn syrup
1 Tbsp lemon juice
½ tsp Worcestershire sauce
1 C finely chopped celery
⅓ C finely chopped chives
⅓ C finely chopped green pepper

Measure the tomato sauce into a large bowl. Rinse out the can with 1 C of the water. In a small bowl soak the gelatin in the remaining ½ C water 5 minutes. Stand this small bowl in shallow pot of boiling water and stir until dissolved and clear. Add to tomato mixture along with the corn syrup, lemon juice and Worcestershire sauce. Chill until softly set. Then stir in the celery, chives and green pepper. Chill in a 4 or 5-cup mold until set. Stir it once or twice during the first half hour, for the vegetables may tend to rise to the top before it has a firm hold on them.

To unmold loosen sides with long narrow pointed knife. Lower mold into hot water and count to five. Cover with shallow serving bowl and turn over and out.

Red and White Holiday Salad

RED LAYERS

3 C tomato juice (divided)
⅓ C finely chopped onion (preferably green)
½ C finely chopped celery
1 bay leaf
1 Tbsp sugar
½ tsp salt
Shake of pepper
¼ C sweet pickle juice or mild vinegar
    mixed with 1 Tbsp sugar
2 pkgs plain gelatin (first amount)

WHITE LAYER

1 C water
2 Tbsp sweet pickle juice or vinegar mixed
    with 1 Tbsp sugar
1 pkg plain gelatin (second amount)
½ C mayonnaise
½ C dairy sour cream

This makes a red-white-red 3-layered mold. In a medium saucepan combine 2 cups tomato juice and the onion, celery, bay leaf, sugar, salt and pepper. Heat to boiling and reduce heat to simmer, covered, for 5 minutes, stirring once or twice.

Meanwhile combine remaining cup tomato juice, and the sweet pickle juice and two packages plain gelatin. Stir into hot tomato mixture until gelatin is dissolved. Strain half through sieve and pour into a 6-cup shallow mold. Let chill until sticky, but not firmly set, about 1 hour. Fish bay leaf out of remainder in sieve. Tip vegetables into bowl with remaining liquid and hold at room temperature but do not allow to set. Reserve for later.

About three-quarters of an hour later make the White Layer: Combine in a small pot the water, 2 Tbsp sweet pickle liquid and 1 pkg gelatin. Heat, stirring to dissolve gelatin. Remove from heat. Cool. When first layer is partially set mix mayonnaise and sour cream into clear white layer and pour over nearly set first red layer. Chill until it is nearly set then pour reserved portion of red layer with vegetables over and chill all until firm.

At serving time loosen top edges of mold with pointed knife then immerse mold to within 1″ of top in hot water for 5 seconds only. Turn over and out onto serving plate and garnish with curly endive or parsley or bread and butter pickles.

Holiday Ham Mold

2 hard-cooked eggs, sliced
2 envelopes plain gelatin
½ C cold water
2½ C boiling water
2 chicken bouillon cubes
¼ tsp salt
Dash pepper
1 tsp lemon juice
½ C finely chopped chives or green onion
½ C cooked diced (¼″) carrot (optional)
3 C diced (¼″) cooked ham
    (chicken could be substituted)

Hard-cook the eggs first by covering with cold water, bringing just to boil covered, turning off heat and letting stand 15 minutes.

Soak the gelatin in cold water 5 minutes. Add the chicken bouillon cubes and stir in boiling water to dissolve thoroughly. Add salt, pepper and lemon juice.

Pour a ½″ layer into a 6-cup mold and chill until nearly set. Arrange egg slices in attractive pattern over or in this jellied layer. (Hold remaining jelly mixture at room temperature.) Add about ¼ C of the reserved jelly liquid to fix egg slices and chill until set. Chill remaining jelly liquid until partially set then into it stir the chives or onion and carrots (if used) and ham. Slowly pour over egg-slice layer in bottom of mold and chill until firmly set.

To turn out, lower mold into hot water and count to five. Cover with serving plate and turn over and out.

Jellied Chicken Loaf

3 to 3½-lb chicken
¼ onion, chopped
1 bay leaf
2 tsp salt
4 tsp plain gelatin
¼ C cold water

Put the chicken in a pot, add the onion, bay leaf and salt and just enough water to cover three-quarters of it, about 3½ C. Simmer covered until meat falls from bones. Remove bird to utility tray. Remove and discard skin and bones. Strain broth. Chill until set (in freezer or overnight). Skim off all fat. Boil broth down until it measures 2 C. Soak gelatin in cold water. Stir into hot broth until dissolved.

Cut enough chicken meat (mostly white) into 1½″ pieces, about 3 C packed. Pour ¼″ of gelatin liquid into a 5 or 6-cup mold and arrange 1 layer of chicken pieces close together in it. Chill until set. Add remaining chicken pieces and pour all remaining gelatin liquid over. Pack down well with the bowl of a large spoon, to be sure liquid flows right through, and to smooth top. Chill until firmly set. This Jellied Chicken Loaf slices perfectly, especially if it is refrigerator cold. Serves six.

Gold and White Spring Salad

1 C canned crushed pineapple
Water (see below)
One 3-oz pkg lemon jelly powder
½ tsp salt
½ C finely grated carrot
1½ Tbsp plain gelatin
¼ C cold water
1 C mayonnaise
¼ C evaporated milk
½ tsp salt
1 Tbsp finely chopped green onion
½ C finely chopped celery
½ C finely shredded, partially pared cucumber
  (on ¼" shredder)

PINEAPPLE LAYER: Drain pineapple thoroughly. Measure juice. Make it up to 1½ C by adding water. Heat this to below boiling point, remove from heat, add jelly powder and stir until dissolved. Add salt and chill until partially set. Add drained pineapple and grated carrot. Pour into a 4-cup mold to half-fill. Chill until softly set. It should not be quite firm when you add the next layer.

CUCUMBER LAYER: Soak gelatin in water 5 minutes, then dissolve by stirring over hot water. To the mayonnaise add the salt, celery, onion, cucumber and evaporated milk. Mix. Now stir in gelatin liquid. When pineapple layer is softly set spoon this cucumber layer over evenly. Chill until firmly set. To turn out, have ready a large serving plate. Dip mold in hot water and count to ten. Invert serving plate over mold, now turn over quickly to turn jelly out on plate. Garnish with delicate green. Serves ten.

Crunchy Chicken Salad Mold

2 Tbsp plus 1 tsp plain gelatin
1 chicken bouillon cube
½ tsp salt
1½ C cold water
½ C skim milk powder
2 C sieved cottage cheese
1 C mayonnaise
½ C French or Italian Dressing
2 C coarsely chopped chicken
¼ C finely chopped celery
¼ C finely chopped green pepper
¼ C finely chopped green onion
2 Tbsp finely chopped parsley
2 Tbsp finely chopped pimiento

Soak gelatin, chicken cube and salt in cold water in pot 10 minutes then stir over low heat until dissolved. Turn into large bowl to cool to room temperature. Meanwhile sieve the cottage cheese. Stir together skim milk powder, sieved cottage cheese, mayonnaise and French or Italian dressing. Add to cooled gelatin liquid and using a wire whip fold in until smooth. Chill until mixture mounds on a spoon. At once fold in chicken, celery, pepper, onion, parsley and pimiento. Turn into 9 × 5" mold or 8 or 10 individual molds. Chill until firm. To unmold dip in hot water and count to five then invert plate over top and turn over and out. It does not slice neatly. Use a large spoon as your server.

Salmon Asparagus Mold

½ C boiling water
One 10-oz pkg fresh frozen asparagus
  or sixteen 6" fresh asparagus stalks
1 C cold water
3 envelopes plain gelatin
2⅔ C boiling water
2 chicken bouillon cubes
Juice of 1 lime or half a lemon
⅓ C chopped canned or bottled pimiento
Three 3¾-oz cans red salmon (1 C plus 2 Tbsp
  when drained and packed)

Into a pot measure the ½ C boiling water. Add the fresh frozen (or fresh) asparagus and cook, covered, until crisply tender. Drain and save liquid for later, about ½ C. Flood asparagus with cold water. Drain. Turn out on counter and cut off 1¼" tips. Reserve. Cut remaining stems into ½" pieces.

Into a pot measure the 1 C cold water, sprinkle gelatin over and stir quickly over heat until dissolved. Remove from heat.

To the ½ C asparagus liquid add the 2⅔ C boiling water, chicken cubes and lime juice and stir until dissolved. Stir in gelatin liquid. Chill, stirring frequently in pan of ice water until slightly thickened.

Pour 2 C of the jelly into a 6-cup mold and add at once all of the pieces of asparagus and chopped pimiento. Slide the asparagus tips, tip end down, all around sides at even intervals. Chill until nearly set. Immediately stir drained salmon into remaining jelly but keep at room temperature. To delay it setting stand in pan of lukewarn water. As soon as mold contents are softly set carefully spoon salmon mixture evenly over. Chill overnight.

When serving time arrives place curly endive or Boston lettuce leaves around sides of platter. Loosen edges of mold with pointed knife then lower for 5 seconds into hot water. Turn over and out on platter.

Perfection Salad

2 envelopes (2 Tbsp) unflavored gelatin
½ C sugar
1 tsp salt
1½ C boiling water
1½ C cold water
½ C vinegar
2 Tbsp lemon juice
2 C finely shredded cabbage
1 C chopped celery
¼ C chopped green pepper
¼ C canned pimiento coarsely chopped
⅓ C sliced stuffed olives

Mix gelatin, sugar and salt. Add boiling water and stir to dissolve gelatin. Then add the cold water, vinegar and lemon juice. Chill until partially set. Add cabbage, celery, green pepper, pimiento, and olives. Pour into an oiled loaf pan or mold which will turn out neatly. Chill until firm.

Waldorf Mayonnaise Mold

½ C cold water
2 pkgs (2 Tbsp) plain gelatin
One 19-oz can apple juice
2 Tbsp lemon juice
½ tsp salt
1½ C diced (¼") unpared red apple
1½ C finely chopped inner celery
½ C coarsely chopped pecans
6 whole pecans
½ C mayonnaise

Soak gelatin in a large bowl in the cold water 2 minutes then stand bowl in shallow boiling water and stir until gelatin is dissolved. Add apple and lemon juice and salt and stir to mix. Pour ¾ C into bottom of deep 4-cup mold and chill until set.

Meanwhile chop celery and nuts and apples. Immediately pour ½ C of the liquid jelly over apples to prevent browning. When jelly in bottom of mold is set arrange the 6 whole pecans in a circle on it and sprinkle some chopped apple around edge. Carefully pour ½ C liquid jelly over, not to disturb design and chill until set.

To remaining liquid jelly add the mayonnaise and with a wire whip beat to combine until smooth. Add all remaining apples, celery and pecans to mayonnaise-jelly mixture when second layer of jelly is set and add it to the mold and refrigerate until set and firm.

To turn out loosen sides with long slender pointed knife. Then stand mold in very hot water for 5 seconds. Invert plate over top and turn over and out. Serves six to eight.

Hard-Cooked Egg Ring

10 hard-cooked eggs, sliced
1 tsp salt
1 tsp sugar
⅛ tsp pepper
½ tsp dry mustard
¼ C mayonnaise
2 Tbsp (2 envelopes) gelatin
¾ C cold water
⅓ C vinegar
¼ C finely chopped parsley
¼ C finely chopped green onions including tops
1 C whipping cream
Watercress

Using top of double boiler soak the gelatin in the cold water for 5 minutes. Add the vinegar. Place over boiling water and heat until gelatin is dissolved. Remove from heat and cool to room temperature. Add mayonnaise, salt, sugar, pepper and mustard. Stir well. Add prepared hard-cooked eggs and parsley and onions. Whip cream and fold in.

Turn into oiled 6-cup ring mold. Chill until set. Warm bottom of mold in hot water for 10 seconds and turn out on large serving plate on which you have a generous bed of greens.

Chicken or Turkey Mousse

2 C ground cooked chicken or turkey
½ C salad dressing
2 Tbsp lemon juice
¾ tsp ground celery seed
¾ C heavy cream, whipped
Salt
Pepper
1½ Tbsp gelatin
½ C cold turkey or chicken stock
Lettuce
Cold cooked green peas or Brussels sprouts
Tomato
Parsley

Blend the chicken or turkey, salad dressing, lemon juice and celery seed. Fold in the whipped cream. Season to taste. Fold in the gelatin which has been softened in the cold turkey or chicken stock, then dissolved over hot water, and cooled.

Pour into a ring mold and chill until firm. Unmold on lettuce, fill the center with cold cooked fresh frozen green peas or Brussels sprouts and garnish with tomato wedges and parsley. Serves six to eight.

Tomato and Cottage Cheese Mold

4 C tomato juice (divided: see below)
2 Tbsp chopped onion
¼ C chopped celery stalks and leaves or
   1 tsp celery seeds
8 whole pepper berries
½ tsp salt
2 Tbsp lemon juice
¼ tsp Worcestershire sauce
2 Tbsp plain gelatin
1 C drained creamed cottage cheese

In a bowl soak the gelatin in ¼ C of the tomato juice.

Combine remaining tomato juice with onion, celery or celery seeds, pepper berries, salt, lemon juice and Worcestershire sauce and bring to boil and simmer 5 or 10 minutes. Place sieve over bowl in which gelatin is soaking and pour tomato mixture over to strain it. Remove sieve. Stir to dissolve gelatin. Pour 1½ C into five-cup mold and chill until set. Cover with even layer of drained cottage cheese. Press it down gently into jelly in bottom to form a bond. Pour ⅔ C of remaining tomato jelly over carefully, being sure some flows down between cheese curds. (Keep remaining tomato jelly at room temperature to prevent setting.) Chill contents of mold until set. Pour remaining tomato jelly mixture over and chill until firm.

To turn out, loosen sides with sharp-pointed knife. Dip mold in hot water for 5 seconds. Invert shallow serving bowl on top and turn over and out. Serves eight.

Orange Jelly Ring

One 6-oz can fresh frozen orange
    juice concentrate
1½ C water
2 envelopes plain gelatin
⅓ C water (second amount)
One 10-oz can Mandarin oranges
Grated rind of 1 large orange
1⅓ C unpared grated cucumber
    (see note below re draining)
2 Tbsp fresh lemon juice

In medium mixing bowl dilute the frozen orange juice concentrate with the 2 cans of water. Soak the gelatin in the ⅓ C water. Drain Mandarin orange sections and save and heat the syrup. Stir soaked gelatin into hot syrup until dissolved. Stir into orange juice along with the grated orange rind and lemon juice. Pour a little into ring mold to ½" depth. Arrange all of the Mandarin oranges in a neat ring in this shallow jelly and chill until nearly firm. Meanwhile grate the cucumber and press out all excess liquid and measure it. When bottom layer is nearly set cover with grated cucumber all around. Now slowly pour over all remaining jelly liquid, being sure it flows between cucumber. Chill until firm. To unmold loosen edges with a paring knife and lower into hot water and count to ten. Invert large serving plate over top and turn over and out. Fill center with cottage cheese.

Red and Yellow
Three-Layered Jelly

TOP LAYER

One 3-oz pkg strawberry jelly powder
1 C boiling water
¾ C cold water

MIDDLE LAYER

One 1-oz pkg (3⅔ Tbsp) custard powder
2 C milk (divided, see below)
2 Tbsp sugar
1 Tbsp plain gelatin

BOTTOM LAYER

4 C rhubarb cut into 1" pieces
½ C water
⅔ C sugar
2 Tbsp plain gelatin

To prepare Bottom Layer, cook rhubarb with water in a large pot over medium heat until rhubarb is tender. Add ⅔ C sugar and 2 Tbsp plain gelatin and stir to dissolve. Pour into bottom of an 8 × 8" pan and let cool in refrigerator until almost set.

To prepare Middle Layer, stir custard powder into ¼ C of the milk until smooth. Heat the remaining 1¾ C milk with the sugar and 1 Tbsp plain gelatin until dissolved. Pour the custard liquid into the hot milk mixture stirring constantly. Cook over medium heat until custard thickens. Cool then pour over partially set rhubarb layer and refrigerate until nearly set.

To prepare Top Layer, dissolve jelly powder in boiling water. Add cold water and stir. Cool in refrigerator until slightly syrupy. Pour over custard layer and chill until completely set. To serve cut into 2½ " squares.

Jellied Tuna Pâté Mold

1 hard-cooked egg
1 pkg plus ½ tsp plain gelatin
⅓ C cold water
2 Tbsp lemon juice
Two 6½-oz cans chunk tuna
1 green onion
½ C chopped celery including some tops
⅓ C mayonnaise
¼ C 1" strips canned or bottled pimiento
4 stuffed olives sliced

Soak the gelatin in the cold water 1 or 2 minutes then stand the cup containing it in shallow boiling water and stir until dissolved. Remove from heat and stir in the lemon juice. Remove 1½ tsp of this mixture to another cup and add 1½ Tbsp water. Pour this into bottom of small loaf pan and immediately place slices of stuffed olives in a long line at the center. Cover olive slices carefully and neatly with the sliced hard-cooked egg. Place strips of pimiento liberally along both sides. Chill until set.

Into blender put both cans of tuna and their liquid, cut-up onion, and celery, and press them down against blades and blend until all is perfectly puréed. Turn into bowl, stir in mayonnaise with wire whip, then stir in remaining gelatin liquid. When jelly on hard-cooked eggs is set, pour tuna mixture over and chill until firm.

To turn out, lower mold into hot water and count to five. Run knife around sides to loosen. Cover with oblong plate and turn over and out. Garnish with curly endive and cherry tomatoes.

Pear and Banana Lime Mold

One 6-oz pkg lime jelly powder
1¾ C boiling water
One 19-oz can pears (including syrup, see below)
2 Tbsp lemon juice
1 banana
⅞ C dairy sour cream

In a big bowl with pouring lip, thoroughly dissolve jelly powder in the boiling water. Drain pears well and stir pear syrup—about 1 C—and lemon juice into green jelly liquid. Pour ⅛" layer into bottom of 6 or 7-cup ring mold 8" in diameter. Slice the banana and arrange neatly in this thin layer of jelly liquid. Chill until softly set but be sure banana slices are anchored in it.

Into 1 C of the still liquid jelly stir the dairy sour cream. (Be sure no watery liquid from the sour cream is included.) Mix with wire whip. Carefully and slowly spoon over set bottom layer without disturbing bananas. Chill until softly set.

Arrange pear halves cut side down and narrow top ends pointing in toward tube of ring mold over set sour cream layer. Press down gently. Now slowly pour all remaining liquid green jelly over, aiming stream over hump of pears so it will flow gently into crevices. Chill until firm.

To serve, lower mold into hot water and count to five. Loosen sides with knife. Invert plate over top and turn over and out.

Bing Cherry Mold

One 15-oz can bing cherries
1 pkg plus 1 tsp plain gelatin
One 6-oz can fresh frozen orange or
    tangerine juice concentrate
¼ C sauterne (or sherry)
1 oz white cream cheese (refrigerator cold)

Drain cherries well. Measure juice. Remove pits. With sharp knife dipped in boiling water cut refrigerator-cold cheese into ¼" or ⅓" dice. Stuff all cherries with cheese dice. Soak gelatin in 1 C reserved cherry juice. Heat to boiling, stirring, to dissolve gelatin. Remove from heat and stir in concentrated fresh frozen orange or tangerine juice and sauterne or sherry. Cool to and keep at room temperature. In a 3-cup mold arrange in the bottom half the stuffed cherries. Spoon just enough of the gelatin liquid over to barely cover. Chill until set. Remove from refrigerator and add all remaining stuffed cherries in a layer and spoon just enough gelatin liquid over to cover. Chill until set solid. Pour on remaining gelatin liquid and chill until set.

Peach-Apricot Swirl

APRICOT MIXTURE
⅓ C granulated sugar
1 envelope plain gelatin
1½ C apricot nectar
½ C water
¼ tsp almond extract
1 lb fresh apricots pitted and diced or
    two 14-oz cans, drained and diced

PEACH MIXTURE
¼ C granulated sugar
1 envelope plain gelatin
½ C water
2 eggs, well beaten
One 6-oz frozen lemonade concentrate, thawed
1 C peach yogurt
3 medium peaches, peeled, pitted and diced or
    one 28-oz can peaches, drained and diced

To prepare Apricot Mixture, in saucepan combine the ⅓ C sugar and 1 envelope plain gelatin. Add apricot nectar and stir over low heat until gelatin is dissolved. Remove from heat. Stir in water and almond extract. Chill until partially set then fold in apricots.

Meanwhile prepare Peach Mixture by combining sugar and gelatin in saucepan. Add the water, beaten eggs and lemonade concentrate. Cook, stirring constantly over a low heat until thickened. Remove from heat. Beat in yogurt until thoroughly combined. Chill until partially set then fold in peaches.

When both mixtures are partially set pour half of the apricot layer into a 6½-cup mold. Spoon in half of the peach layer then swirl with spatula to marble it. Repeat a layer with remaining apricot mixture and then remaining peach mixture. Swirl a little again. Chill 6 to 8 hours or overnight. Unmold on serving plate. Garnish with a lemon twist. Serves ten to twelve.

Strawberry Cream Mold

One 3-oz pkg strawberry or
    mixed fruit jelly powder
1 C boiling water
½ C cold water (first amount)
1 envelope (1 Tbsp) plain gelatin
¼ C cold water (second amount)
1 qt strawberries
¾ C whipping cream
¾ C dairy sour cream
½ C fruit sugar
½ tsp vanilla

Dissolve jelly powder in boiling water, stirring long enough to dissolve all granules. Add the ½ C cold water and chill until softly set.

Soak the plain gelatin in the ¼ C cold water for 1 minute then dissolve by stirring over hot water until clear. Cool to room temperature.

Wash and stem strawberries. Slice enough to fill a 2-cup measure. Reserve remaining berries for decorating later. Fold sliced strawberries into softly set strawberry jelly.

Whip the cream until stiff. Beat in the sour cream, fruit sugar and vanilla. Blend in plain gelatin liquid. Working quickly spoon strawberry jelly and cream mixture alternately into a 6 or 7-cup ring mold. Draw your spoon through it in one complete circle of the mold to marble it. Chill until set.

To turn out, dip the bottom of the mold in hot water for 5 seconds. Loosen edges with pointed knife. Invert serving plate over top and turn over and out. Fill center of strawberry cream ring with reserved strawberries.

Lemon Cream Jelly Mold

JELLY MOLD MIXTURE
One 6-oz pkg lemon jelly powder
One 8-oz pkg white cream cheese,
    room temperature
3 C boiling water
3½ Tbsp vinegar
One 19-oz can crushed pineapple, drained
One 10-oz can mandarin orange sections,
    drained (first amount)

DECORATION
One 10-oz can mandarin orange sections,
    drained (second amount)
3 drained pineapple rings, halved

Into beater bowl cream together the jelly powder and cream cheese. Add the boiling water and beat on low until jelly powder is dissolved and mixture is perfectly smooth, scraping down sides once. Stir in the vinegar. Chill in refrigerator until syrupy. Fold in drained crushed pineapple and mandarin oranges. Pour into a 6 or 8-cup ring mold and chill until set in refrigerator. Unmold on serving plate.

To decorate cut the 3 pineapple rings in halves to make 6 crescents. Place upright at even intervals fitting narrow curve over rounded top of mold. Arrange drained mandarin oranges in a tight-fitting circle around base.

Cranberry Salad Mold

2 C raw cranberries
1 C boiling water
½ C sugar
¼ tsp salt
1 Tbsp plain gelatin
3 Tbsp cold water
⅔ C finely diced inner celery
½ C chopped blanched almonds or pecans
1 C canned drained, diced, pineapple

Add the boiling water to the raw cranberries in a saucepan and cook until cranberry skins break and cranberries are tender. Remove from heat. Soak gelatin in cold water 5 minutes. Stir into hot cranberries until dissolved, then add sugar and salt, stirring. Chill until it begins to set then add celery, nuts and pineapple. Turn into mold and chill until set. Serve on delicate cupped lettuce leaves garnished with sections of Mandarin oranges.

Cream Fruit Ring

RING

One 3-oz pkg lemon jelly powder
1 C boiling water
¾ C cold liquid (water and syrup from
    pineapple, see below)
15 marshmallows cut small
One 19-oz can crushed pineapple drained
¾ C (6-oz) pimiento cream cheese
    (room temperature)
½ pt whipping cream
4 red glacé cherries halved
4 green glacé cherries halved
8 large whole pecans

FRUITS

Clusters of Ribier grapes
Clusters of frosted Malaga grapes (see below)
Mounds of honey dew melon balls
Mounds of cantaloupe balls

To make Ring, dissolve thoroughly the lemon jelly powder in the boiling water. Add ¾ C of liquid made up of the juice drained from pineapple and water. Chill until half set.

Cut up the marshmallows with scissors dipped in hot water in about 6 pieces each. In a large bowl mix them with the cheese and pineapple and beat on high speed to blend. Wash beaters and whip the cream until stiff and fold it into the marshmallow-pineapple mixture. As soon as lemon jelly is half set fold it into the pineapple-cream mixture. Pour into one 4-cup ring mold (and one 2-cup mold for future meal). Chill.

To serve turn out at center of large round serving dish. Decorate top with halved green and red cherries and pecans.

To prepare frosted Malaga grapes dip small bunches in dilute egg white and then in granulated sugar. Make a border by arranging, alternately, clusters of Ribier grapes, honey dew melon balls, frosted Malaga grapes and cantaloupe balls. Carefully fill center with a cluster of frosted Malagas. Although this fruit ring takes time and patience to make, it makes a showy table center. Serves eight.

Ribbon Jelly

One 3-oz pkg lime jelly powder
One 3-oz pkg lemon jelly powder
One 3-oz pkg orange jelly powder
Boiling water (see below)
⅓ C plain yogurt or dairy sour cream
2 canned pear halves drained and
    sliced into four long petals

Set out 3 medium bowls and one 6 to 8-cup mold. Put one jelly powder in each bowl and thoroughly dissolve each in 1¾ C boiling water.

Reserve ½ C of the lime jelly liquid. In the bottom of your lightly oiled mold arrange the 4 canned pear petals like a flower. Pour in the 1¼ C lime jelly liquid. Chill until firm. Leave all remaining jelly liquid out to prevent jelling.

To the reserved ½ C lime jelly add about 1½ Tbsp yogurt or sour cream and thoroughly mix. Pour over congealed lime jelly. Chill until set.

Reserve ½ C lemon jelly liquid. Pour the 1¼ C lemon jelly over white lime layer and chill until set. To the reserved ½ C lemon jelly liquid add about 1½ Tbsp yogurt or sour cream. Blend thoroughly. Pour over set lemon jelly. Chill until set.

Reserve ½ C orange jelly liquid. Pour the 1¼ C orange jelly liquid over white lemon layer and chill until set. To the ½ C orange jelly liquid add 1½ Tbsp yogurt or sour cream and pour over set orange jelly. Chill until firm.

Note: 1. If jelly liquids on counter tend to softly congeal while they are waiting their turn, stand them in pans of warm water to arrest congealing. 2. Keep the completed mold in the refrigerator for 2 hours before turning out to make sure it is firm.

To unmold loosen sides with pointed knife, dip mold in hot water for 5 or 10 seconds and cover with plate and turn over and out. Serves eight.

Emerald Salad

One 6-oz pkg lime jelly powder
2 C boiling water
2 C cold water (divided, see below)
1 tsp plain gelatin
One 4-oz pkg white cream cheese
    (room temperature)
¼ C finely chopped walnuts or pecans
One 11-oz can Mandarin oranges, well drained
1 C thinly sliced inner celery

Soak the plain gelatin in ¼ C of the cold water 5 minutes. In a medium-large bowl dissolve jelly powder in boiling water. Stir in soaked gelatin until dissolved. Stir in remaining 1¾ C cold water. Chill in refrigerator until partially set. In a small bowl cream the cheese. Using a teaspoon as your measure, form cheese into balls rolling between your palms. Then roll in chopped walnuts. Gently fold cheese balls, drained Mandarin orange sections and celery into partially set jelly. Turn into 1½-quart mold and chill. Serves eight.

Rose Window Fruit Mold

One 6-oz pkg cherry jello
2 C boiling water
One 10-oz can pear halves
One 14-oz can sliced peaches
One 14-oz can pitted black cherries

Drain and reserve syrup from pears and peaches only. In a bowl dissolve the jelly powder in the boiling water. Add 1⅓ C fruit syrup.

To layer, pour 1 C of the liquid jelly into a deep 10″ pie plate or other round 10″ dish. Place a cherry in the hollow in a pear half and holding it firmly invert on bottom of pan in jelly liquid. Continue until you have a border of eight inverted cherry-filled pears arranged. Between each pear place a peach crescent (slice) using eight. Fill center with a layer of drained pitted black cherries. Chill until set. Keep remaining jelly at room temperature to prevent setting.

When chilled layer is firm lean the remaining peach crescents all around sides of dish where pears touch sides. Carefully pour about half of remaining liquid jelly over and chill again to fix peaches. Keep remainder at room temperature. When jelly is set the second time pour remainder of liquid jelly over. When set transfer to refrigerator and chill.

To unmold have ready a round serving dish at least 12″ in diameter. Dip bottom of mold in hot water and count to five. With narrow knife loosen sides. Invert serving dish over top and turn over and out. Serves eight to ten.

Sauces

Soft Custard Sauce

2 C hot milk
4 egg yolks (or 2 whole eggs)
¼ C sugar
¼ tsp salt
½ tsp vanilla

In top of double boiler mix well the egg yolks, sugar and salt. Place over gently boiling water in bottom of double boiler and slowly add hot milk, stirring constantly until it thickens a little. It will lightly coat a silver spoon. Remove from heat and add vanilla. Pour into serving pitcher and chill.

Note: This soft Custard may be made in advance and stored in refrigerator in covered jar. It is handy to have for serving over sliced bananas, or on new spring rhubarb, canned plums, stewed prunes, lemon snow or countless other desserts where a delicate sauce would take the place of pouring cream and give an otherwise plain dessert a good cook's finishing touch.

Black Cherry Sauce

One 14-oz can pitted sweet black cherries
1 Tbsp cornstarch (or preferably arrowroot flour)
1 Tbsp cold water

Buzz a can of cherries including juice in blender to reduce to purée. Stir the cornstarch (or arrowroot flour) into the cold water and stir this little paste into the puréed cherries over heat until boiling and a minuté longer, stirring. Cool and chill.

Hard Sauce

⅜ C (6 Tbsp) butter, no substitute
1½ C unsifted icing sugar
⅛ tsp salt
2 Tbsp sherry or brandy or rum
    (or orange or apple juice)
½ tsp almond extract
Nutmeg

Measure butter, icing sugar and salt into beater bowl and beat until very light. Beat in the 2 Tbsp of liquid of your choice and the almond extract until blended. Spoon into serving dish and peak up top surface with fork tips. Sprinkle sparingly with nutmeg. Refrigerate until hard.

Spicy Hard Sauce

2 C icing sugar (well packed)
½ C butter
¼ tsp salt
2 tsp vanilla
1 tsp cinnamon
¼ tsp cloves

Put all ingredients in beater bowl and beat until perfectly blended and creamy. Pile in a mound in a shallow bowl. Peak the top up with a fork. Sprinkle lightly with nutmeg. Chill until hard. Serve with hot steamed pudding. This sauce may be made 3 or 4 days in advance and covered and stored in refrigerator.

Hot Lemon-Nutmeg Sauce

1 Tbsp cornstarch
½ C light brown sugar
⅛ tsp salt
½ tsp nutmeg
¼ C lemon juice
¾ C boiling water
2 Tbsp butter

Mix well together dry in a small saucepan the cornstarch, brown sugar, salt and nutmeg. When thoroughly blended stir in the lemon juice and boiling water and cook, stirring until thick. Remove from heat and stir in butter. If to be stored, let cool and pour into glass jar with cover and refrigerate, then reheat when needed.

All-Purpose Hot Pudding Sauce

⅔ C dark brown sugar
2 Tbsp cornstarch
¼ tsp salt
2 C boiling water
¼ C butter
¼ C lemon juice

In a medium pot mix well together the sugar, cornstarch and salt. When thoroughly mixed stir in boiling water and cook stirring until thick. Remove from heat and add butter and lemon juice. If desired this pouring sauce may be made in advance and reheated at dessert time.

Raspberry Sauce

One 15-oz pkg fresh frozen raspberries
Water (see below)
1 Tbsp cornstarch (or preferably arrowroot
    flour for clarity)
2 Tbsp sugar

Thaw frozen raspberries and drain through a sieve and measure juice. Push raspberries through sieve to purée them until just seeds are left in sieve. Make up to 2 C by adding water to the juice and purée.

In saucepan mix dry together the cornstarch (or arrowroot), sugar and salt. Then stir in raspberry purée and syrup and cook stirring until thick and one minute longer. Cool. Pour into jar, cover and chill.

Orange Sauce

1 Tbsp cornstarch
½ C sugar
¼ tsp salt
1 C orange juice
2 tsp orange rind
Whole membraneless sections from 1 orange

In a small pot combine cornstarch, sugar, salt and orange rind, mixing well. Stir in orange juice and cook over high heat stirring until thick. Remove from heat and add orange sections. Serve over plain puddings to give them more life.

Large Quantity Fudge Sauce

¼ C butter or margarine
½ C cocoa
1⅓ C hot water
4 C granulated sugar
½ C corn syrup
½ tsp salt
2 tsp vanilla

In a large heavy pot combine butter or margarine, cocoa, hot water, sugar, corn syrup and salt. Stir over medium heat until dissolved, wiping down sugar on sides with damp cloth. Simmer 5 minutes, remove from heat, stir in vanilla. Serve hot or warm over ice cream, plain cottage pudding, blanc mange or junket.

Large Quantity Butterscotch Sauce

4 C light brown sugar
1 C milk
½ C corn syrup
¾ C butter or margarine

Combine all ingredients in large heavy saucepan. Bring to gentle boil and boil 2½ to 3 minutes. Remove from heat and pour into pitcher to serve warm or cold over ice cream. Stores well.

Vanilla Sauce

Combine in a saucepan ¼ C sugar, 1 Tbsp cornstarch, ⅛ tsp salt. Then stir in 1 C water or milk until thick. Remove from heat and add 1 Tbsp butter and 1 tsp vanilla. Serve hot.

All-Purpose Red Fruit Sauce

Mash fresh or fresh frozen strawberries or raspberries or bing cherries to measure 1 C well packed. In a saucepan mix together well ½ C sugar and 1 Tbsp cornstarch, then stir in the fruit and cook, stirring constantly, until boiling. Reduce heat and cook 5 minutes longer, stirring. Force through sieve. To the purée add 1 Tbsp lemon juice and ½ C sliced strawberries or fresh raspberries or pitted chopped bing cherries. If to be used at once this does not require further cooking. If to be kept in refrigerator for 3 or 4 days, heat in double boiler over boiling water for 15 minutes. Serve over sundaes or plain puddings.

Cocktail Sauce

Take ½ C chili sauce and mix thoroughly with ⅓ C each of catsup and prepared horseradish. To this add 1½ tsp Worcestershire sauce. Chill well before serving. For a sharper sauce add ¼ tsp salt, dash of pepper and 2 Tbsp lemon juice and a few drops of Tabasco.

Rum Sauce

½ C butter
1 C sugar
⅓ C water
1 egg, beaten
2 Tbsp lemon juice
½ tsp grated lemon rind
2 tsp rum flavoring
Dash of salt

Cream butter and sugar until fluffy in top of double boiler. Add water and egg and beat well. Place over boiling water for 15 minutes or until sugar is melted and sauce is slightly thickened, stirring constantly. Add lemon juice and rind, rum flavoring and salt. Cook 5 more minutes, stirring to blend. Serve warm.

Bechamel Sauce

1 small onion
2 Tbsp fat
¼ C chopped bacon
4 Tbsp flour
2 C milk
Salt and pepper

Slice the onion and slightly brown it in the fat with the bacon for 3 or 4 minutes. Add the flour and, when well mixed, stir in the milk until thick. Stir until it boils, then cook 1 minute longer. Add seasonings and strain if desired.

Mint Sauce

½ C very finely chopped fresh mint
¼ C vinegar
1 tsp sugar
¼ tsp salt
¼ C water

Heat together the vinegar, sugar and salt just to boiling. Add the finely chopped mint and the water. Serve with roast lamb or lamb chops.

Horseradish Cream

Into ½ pint whipping cream fold ½ C horseradish which has been well drained from bottled horseradish, and serve with roast beef.

Simplified Béarnaise Sauce

Stir together ½ C genuine mayonnaise, ⅛ tsp black pepper, ¼ tsp chervil, ¼ tsp chives, ¼ tsp tarragon and 1½ tsp wine vinegar or lemon juice.

Mushroom Sauce

Gently sauté ¼ lb washed sliced mushrooms in ¼ C butter until limp, not brown. Blend in 3 Tbsp flour, ½ tsp salt and 1 beef bouillon cube, then stir in 1¼ C boiling water until thick. If desired add shakes of garlic and celery salt and pepper.

Large Quantity All-Purpose Barbecue Sauce

This recipe makes twenty cups, and is freezable.

9 Tbsp oil
6 small cooking onions, finely chopped
3 green peppers, finely chopped
¾ C finely chopped celery
⅜ tsp garlic salt
1¼ tsp salt
⅜ tsp pepper
1 tsp oregano
6 Tbsp chopped parsley
4 small bay leaves, crushed
One 48-oz can tomato juice
One 28-oz can (or two 14-oz) tomato sauce
One 19-oz can tomatoes
One 13-oz can tomato paste
4 C water
Two 10-oz bottles chili sauce (optional)
6 Tbsp sugar
½ tsp cayenne pepper
3 whole chili peppers (optional)

In a very large soup pot or preserving kettle sauté onion, green pepper, celery and garlic salt in oil until vegetables are limp but not browned. Add all remaining ingredients. (*Note:* Tie the whole chili peppers, if used, on a string and attach string to pot handle for easy removal.) Bring to boil, reduce heat and simmer uncovered 2½ to 3 hours, stirring frequently. Remove chili peppers.

WAYS TO SERVE: 1. Brush on steaks when barbecuing or grilling; brush on roast of beef or pork or chicken in oven or on rotisserie; 2. Place cooked chicken or turkey in bottom of a baking dish. Pour sauce over to cover. Heat in oven at 325° until bubbly. Serve over hot buttered noodles or spaghetti; 3. Heat and use as a sauce over chicken-on-a-bun or hamburg patties or leftover reheated roast beef or pork; 4. Score edges of thick slices of bologna. Sauté in frypan to heat through and pour hot barbecue sauce over to serve.

Sweet and Sour Sauce

⅓ C soy sauce
½ C water
½ C canned consommé (undiluted)
2 Tbsp vinegar
¼ C sugar
2 Tbsp cornstarch
½ clove garlic crushed
¼ tsp finely chopped crystallized ginger

Combine the soy sauce, water, consommé and vinegar. Mix sugar and cornstarch and stir in. Add garlic and ginger. Cook very slowly, stirring constantly until thick and smooth. Delicious with all types of Chinese foods.

Sour Cream Sauce

Gently melt 2 Tbsp butter, blend in 2 Tbsp flour and ¼ tsp salt and stir in ½ C milk and 1 C sour cream until thick. Add 2 Tbsp finely chopped chives or green onion tops, and ½ tsp paprika.

Mustard Sauce

½ C brown sugar
2 tsp dry mustard
¼ tsp salt
⅛ tsp pepper
2 Tbsp cornstarch
1 C hot water
¼ C vinegar

In medium saucepan combine all dry sauce ingredients well. Then stir in hot water and vinegar over medium high heat until thick and boiling.

Raisin Sauce

1 Tbsp flour
1 Tbsp butter or margarine
1 C apple juice or apple cider
½ C seedless raisins

Blend together the flour and butter or margarine over heat. Stir in the apple juice or cider and raisins until thick. Serve hot with baked cottage roll or back bacon or baked ham.

Sweet and Sour Mustard Sauce

1 Tbsp butter or margarine
3 Tbsp brown sugar
2 Tbsp flour
1 Tbsp vinegar
1 C water
1 beef bouillon cube
3 Tbsp prepared mustard
1 Tbsp Worcestershire sauce

In saucepan combine butter and brown sugar until melted. Remove from heat and stir in flour until blended. Slowly stir in vinegar and water until there are no lumps. Return to heat, add beef cube and cook until thickened, stirring constantly, and beef cube is dissolved. Stir a little hot mixture into the prepared mustard then return all to saucepan, stirring to blend. Stir in Worcestershire sauce. Heat just to boiling and serve over meat.

Smoked Oyster Sauce

Heat the oil from one 4-oz can smoked oysters with 1 Tbsp butter and 1 chicken bouillon cube. Stir in 2 Tbsp flour and when blended, stir in 1¼ C milk until thick. Cut smoked oysters in half and add along with 1 Tbsp chopped fresh parsley. Heat through.

Tartar Sauce

½ C mayonnaise (not salad dressing)
½ tsp prepared mustard
1 tsp parsley flakes
½ tsp chopped green onion or chives
1½ tsp drained chopped sweet pickle
  or green relish
1½ tsp finely chopped olives (optional)
Half chopped hard-cooked egg (optional)
1 tsp lemon juice

Mix ingredients together in order given.

Savory Tomato Sauce

One 19-oz can tomatoes
1 tsp salt
2 tsp sugar
1 bay leaf
1 Tbsp chopped onion
1 Tbsp chopped celery with leaves
2 whole cloves
3 Tbsp cornstarch

Reserve ¼ C of the tomato juice to stir into the flour later. Simmer the tomatoes 15 minutes with all remaining ingredients except the cornstarch and reserved tomato juice. If you are not going to strain this, fish out the bay leaf and cloves. Strain if desired. Mix together cornstarch and reserved ¼ C tomato juice to a smooth paste and stir into tomato mixture until thick and smooth. Serve with omelettes, soufflés, fish or poached eggs.

Creole Tomato Sauce

To 3 Tbsp shortening melted in large fryer or Dutch oven add 1 C finely chopped celery, 2 Tbsp finely chopped parsley and 1 large chopped onion. Cook slowly until limp but not browned. Then add the following ingredients.

One 16-oz can whole tomatoes
1½ tsp salt
1 Tbsp Worcestershire sauce
Dash Tabasco
One 5½-oz can tomato paste
1 tsp sugar
½ tsp paprika (or chili powder)
½ C chopped sweet green pepper
¼ tsp garlic salt or 1 clove crushed
    fresh garlic
2 C cold water

Cook about 30 to 40 minutes, uncovered, to evaporate liquid somewhat, until thick. Then add 1 Tbsp cornstarch mixed with 1 Tbsp water, and stir until thick. Purée through sieve or blender.

Drawn Butter Sauce

4 Tbsp butter
2 Tbsp flour
¼ tsp salt
Shake of white pepper
1 C boiling water
1 or 2 tsp lemon juice

Melt butter, blend in flour, salt and pepper, then stir in boiling water until thick. Add lemon juice. Serve hot over green vegetable, or as a substitute for Hollandaise sauce.

Caper Sauce

3 Tbsp butter
3 Tbsp flour
½ tsp salt
1½ C milk
2 Tbsp capers including some liquid

Melt butter, stir in flour and salt until blended, then stir in milk until thick. Add capers and heat through.

Cheese Sauce

4 Tbsp butter or margarine
4 Tbsp flour
½ tsp salt
⅛ tsp pepper
2 C milk
¼ to ½ lb Cheddar cheese, shredded

Melt the butter or margarine in the top of a double boiler over hot water, or in heavy saucepan. Blend in the flour, salt and pepper. Add the milk and stir until the sauce is thickened and smooth. Add the cheese and stir until melted.

One-Cup White Sauce: Thin, Medium or Thick

THIN (used for soups): 1 Tbsp each butter and flour, ½ tsp salt, 1 C milk.

MEDIUM (to be served on vegetables): 2 Tbsp each butter and flour, ½ tsp salt, 1 C milk.

THICK (for croquettes): 4 Tbsp each butter and flour, ½ tsp salt, 1 C milk.

Method: Blend butter with flour and salt over low heat. Raise heat and stir in milk until thick.

Hard-Cooked Egg Sauce

3 Tbsp butter or margarine
3 Tbsp flour
½ tsp salt
⅛ tsp pepper
1 chicken bouillon cube
1½ C milk
1 hard-cooked egg, chopped

Melt margarine or butter in a small pot and stir in flour, salt, pepper and chicken bouillon cube. Stir in milk and cook stirring until thick. Stir in chopped hard-cooked egg.

This is a basic medium white sauce that is all-purpose. You can omit the egg and add chopped chives or parsley or olives or pimiento or whatever your imagination contrives.

Genuine Hollandaise

½ C butter
2 egg yolks
½ tsp salt
Speck of cayenne pepper
1 Tbsp lemon juice

Melt the butter in a saucepan gently. In a bowl beat the egg yolks until thick and lemon-colored. Add the salt, cayenne pepper, and 3 Tbsp melted butter, 2 or 3 drops at a time, beating. Then add remaining butter, slowly, alternately with the lemon juice, until all has been added. Store in the refrigerator until ready to use. This sauce melts readily when served on hot vegetables such as asparagus or broccoli or spinach.

Blender Hollandaise

3 egg yolks
1½ Tbsp lemon juice
1 Tbsp boiling water
¾ C butter melted until barely bubbling
⅓ tsp salt
Shake of cayenne pepper (optional)

Measure yolks and lemon juice into blender. Blend 10 seconds at high speed. Add boiling water and blend at medium speed 15 seconds. Add salt and then, in an ⅛" stream, add hot butter while blending at medium speed until all is in. Add cayenne pepper if used. You are finished. Pour into sauce boat and do not refrigerate.

Never Fail Hollandaise

1 C melted butter
4 egg yolks
½ tsp salt
Shake of cayenne
2 Tbsp lemon juice

Gently melt the butter and cool to room temperature. It should still be in a liquid state.

In beater bowl beat egg yolks until thick and pale. Add salt and cayenne. Beating at high speed, to well-beaten egg yolks add cooled melted butter slowly, 1 tsp at a time. Be sure each teaspoon of liquid butter is blended in before continuing with the next. After each 4 tsp add 1 tsp lemon juice and continue slowly until all of each is used. You may have to scrape mixture up from bottom with rubber spatula if the bottom of your beater bowl is broad.

This method for a cold Hollandaise eliminates the risk of curdling. Cover carefully and store in refrigerator. Use from it as a sauce on your dinner vegetables.

Brown Meat Gravy

Remove roast from roasting pan and tip off all fat, reserving ¼ C. Leave brown sediment in pan. Return ¼ C fat to pan and add 1⅔ C hot water (or potato water). Mix together in a small bowl 3 Tbsp cornstarch and ⅓ C cold water. Stirring constantly add cornstarch paste to pan gravy until thick, working all the time to loosen brown sediment sticking to pan. If desired this gravy may be strained. *Note:* If gravy is not brown enough add a beef bouillon cube when you add the hot water.

Brown Meatless Gravy

To make 1½ C, melt 3 Tbsp beef or chicken or pork drippings or butter or margarine and stir in 3 Tbsp flour or cornstarch. You could let this cook to brown a little, stirring. Stir in 1½ C boiling hot liquid—preferably broth or vegetable water—until thick. Now to flavor and color it add 1 or 2 or more beef bouillon cubes. When these are dissolved add salt and pepper to taste.

Giblet Gravy

Cook turkey neck, heart and gizzard in water to cover until tender. Reserve liver and add it only during last 5 minutes.

Near mealtime chop cooked giblets and neck meat and return to cooking liquid. Pour or skim excess fat from roasting pan and add rich sediment to giblet liquid. Make this up to 3 C by adding liquid from vegetables or hot water. Stir together 6 Tbsp flour with ½ C cold water with wire whip until smooth. Stir into giblet liquid until thick. Add 1 tsp salt and serve in preheated gravy boat.

Yeast Breads

Christmas Braid Bread see page 151

Sourdough Starter and Three Uses

In a large bowl mix 2 C all-purpose flour, 2 Tbsp sugar, 1 tsp salt, 2 C warm water. Let stand covered at room temperature 2 days. This becomes a spongy mass and developes a yeasty aroma. Refrigerate covered.

"Feed" at least once per week by stirring in 1 C flour, 1 C milk, ¼ C sugar to keep it active. Be prepared to use it often or if you are tired of it, cover and freeze then thaw and feed.

CHEESE BISCUITS (14)
1 C sourdough
4 Tbsp oil
2½ tsp baking powder
½ tsp baking soda
½ tsp salt
1 C flour
½ C Parmesan cheese

Mix all ingredients. Pat out on floured board and cut out with 2″ cutter. Bake at 425° for 8 to 10 minutes on ungreased pan.

HAMBURG BUNS (6 large)
1 C sourdough
¼ C oil
2½ tsp baking powder
½ tsp baking soda
½ tsp salt
1 C flour

Mix well all ingredients. Pat out and shape into 6 large buns on floured board. Bake at 425° for 8 to 10 minutes.

WHOLE WHEAT PANCAKES
1 C sourdough
¼ C oil
2½ tsp baking powder
½ tsp baking soda
½ tsp salt
¾ C whole wheat flour
¼ C wheat germ
¾ C water

Mix all ingredients thoroughly. Have ungreased griddle hot. Dip out ¼ C batter and bake on hot griddle until bottom is gold, then turn over and bake other side. Serve with butter or margarine and maple or table syrup.

Dilly Bread

1 pkg granular yeast
¼ C warm water
1 C creamed cottage cheese, heated to lukewarm (see note below)
2 Tbsp sugar
1 Tbsp minced onion
1 Tbsp butter or margarine
2 tsp dill seed
1 tsp salt
¼ tsp soda
1 unbeaten egg
2¼ C sifted all-purpose flour

Note: Be sure to heat the cottage cheese very slowly and just a little, because if you do not it will form into a tough rubbery ball.

Soften yeast in water 5 minutes. Combine softened yeast in mixing bowl with warmed cottage cheese, sugar, onion, butter, dill seed, salt, soda and egg. Add flour gradually to form a stiff dough, pausing to beat well after each addition. Cover and let rise for 2 or 2½ hours at room temperature until dough is light and doubled in size. Stir down dough. Turn into well-greased 8″ round casserole of 6-cup capacity. Let rise until light and risen 2 or 3″ higher than rim of baking dish. Bake at 350° for 50 minutes. Be sure not to underbake this loaf for a crisp brown crust is important. If desired, brush with butter and sprinkle with salt after baking but while still hot.

Five-Grain Health Bread
(2 loaves)

1 pkg granular yeast
3 C lukewarm water
½ C honey
⅓ C shortening (room temperature)
1½ C whole wheat flour
1½ C dark rye flour
½ C quick-cooking rolled oats
½ C corn meal
5 C unsifted all-purpose flour (divided)
1 Tbsp salt
¾ C skim milk powder

In a very large bowl soak the yeast, honey and shortening in the lukewarm water for 10 to 15 minutes while you measure all remaining ingredients. Then add remaining ingredients except 3 C of the white flour in order given and stir 50 times. Cover and let rise under light bulb until doubled in bulk, about 2 hours. This dough is moist and sticky.

Sprinkle kneading board with all of the remaining white flour, punch down and turn out dough on it and knead flour to make the dough firm enough to handle. Now knead it 250 times.

Shape into a 2-foot roll, cut in half, shape into 2 loaves and place in 2 standard buttered loaf pans and let rise about 1″ above rims of pans. Bake at 400° for 20 minutes, then reduce heat to 350° and bake about 40 minutes longer until crust is dark gold and crisp.

Note: Bread with a low white flour content (which contains the necessary gluten to make it rise) requires longer kneading and rising and higher temperatures than regular white bread.

Staff of Life
(5 loaves)

3 pkgs yeast (or 2 Tbsp)
1 C warm water (first amount)
⅓ C molasses
3 C rolled oats
1½ C boiling water
1 C cornmeal
1 C rye flour
5 C whole wheat flour
½ C bran
1 C sunflower seeds
½ C oil
6½ C warm water (second amount)
1 Tbsp salt
About 7 C all-purpose flour
    (divided, see below)

In a small bowl soak yeast in warm water and molasses 10 minutes. In a pot stir the oats into the 1½ C boiling water for 2 or 3 minutes. Remove from heat.

Into very large bowl measure cornmeal, rye flour, whole wheat flour, bran, seeds, oil, 6½ C warm water, salt and 4 C all-purpose flour. Mix well then add yeast liquid and oats mixture. Mix this very well. Scrape down sides and cover and let rise until doubled, about 1 hour.

Sprinkle kneading surface with 2 C flour. Turn dough out on it. Sprinkle top with one more cup flour and begin kneading. It will be sticky at first and you must persist and knead most of the flour in at least 200 kneads, or better still 10 minutes steady kneading. Shape into long roll. Cut into 5 even pieces. Roll each piece out with rolling pin and then roll up like a jelly roll and place in greased 8½ × 4½" loaf pans tucking in folded ends. Brush tops with melted margarine or oil, cover, let rise under light bulb until nearly 1" above rims. Do not allow them to overrise. Bake at 375° about 35 to 40 minutes. Cool on racks.

Lemon Bubble Loaf

1 pkg granular yeast
1 tsp sugar
½ C lukewarm water
1 C scalded milk
1 C sugar (divided)
1 tsp salt
¼ C butter
2 eggs
6 C sifted all-purpose flour
Finely grated rind 2 lemons
½ tsp mace
3 Tbsp melted butter

In large mixing bowl soak yeast with the 1 tsp sugar in the lukewarm water 10 minutes. Scald milk, remove from heat and add salt, butter and ½ C of the sugar, stir well and cool to lukewarm. Sift and measure flour. Add lukewarm milk mixture to risen yeast liquid along with 2 C of the flour and beat well, then add eggs and beat again. Add 3½ more C flour and beat as well as you can. (Reserve remaining ½ C flour for flouring board later.) Cover and let rise until very light.

Mix together in small bowl remaining ½ C sugar, grated rind and mace. Punch down dough, turn out on board floured with reserved flour and knead 100 times. Divide in half. Shape an 18" long roll and cut into 18 pieces. Generously butter a large angel food cake pan. Shape pieces of dough into round smooth balls and place in rings around bottom of pan. Brush generously with melted butter and sprinkle with half of the sugar-rind mixture. Roll remaining half of dough into 18" roll. Cut into 18 pieces, place on top of balls in pan, finishing with an attractive even arrangement on top, brush with remaining melted butter, sprinkle with remaining sugar-rind mixture. Let rise until above rim of pan. Bake at 350° for 35 to 40 minutes. If top becomes dark gold too soon, carefully cover it with foil to stop browning. Cool a little, loosen sides with long knife and lift out loaf. Serve on large round plate.

Pumpernickel
(3 loaves)

2 pkgs granular yeast
1 C lukewarm water (first amount)
2 tsp sugar
3¼ C lukewarm water (second amount)
2 squares unsweetened chocolate, melted
¼ C molasses
1 Tbsp margarine
2 C unseasoned hot mashed potatoes
¾ C cornmeal
2 Tbsp salt
2 Tbsp caraway seeds (optional)
3 C unsifted rye flour (usually dark)
1 C whole bran cereal or all bran
About 9¾ C unsifted all-purpose white flour

Scrub and trim blemishes from 4 medium potatoes; boil covered in water to cover until tender. Drain, peel and mash until there are no lumps. Measure 2 C.

In a very large mixing bowl soak the yeast and sugar in the 1 C lukewarm water for 10 minutes.

Meanwhile heat together in large pan until lukewarm the 3¼ C lukewarm water, melted chocolate, molasses and margarine. Remove from heat and mix in mashed potatoes, cornmeal, salt and caraway seeds. Mix well and stir into risen yeast liquid. Add the rye flour and bran and beat for 5 minutes. Add 3 C white flour and beat until you have a soft dough, at least 5 minutes. Now add 4 more cups white flour, mixing in well, scrape down sides of bowl, cover and let rise at least 1 hour. Sprinkle kneading board with 1 C of the leftover flour. Turn dough out on it. Sprinkle top with ½ C of remaining flour and begin kneading surplus flour into dough until it is not sticky. Flour your hands. As soon as it will hold its shape and is uniformly kneaded, shape into roll, cut in 3 pieces. Shape them into small footballs and place in buttered standard loaf pans. Let rise under light bulb 1 hour or until risen 1" above rims of pans. Bake at 350° about 55 to 60 minutes or until when rapped with knuckles it sounds hollow. Do not underbake. Switch and turn pans in oven at halftime. Carefully turn out on racks to cool.

Economy Bread

(6 loaves)

6 C lukewarm water
1 pkg granular yeast
3 Tbsp margarine
3 Tbsp salt
3 Tbsp sugar
1 C skim milk powder
18 C unsifted all-purpose flour
    (divided, see below)

Prepare the sponge the night before by beating together water, yeast, margarine, salt, sugar, skim milk powder and 6 C of the flour. Cover and let stand in cool kitchen over-night. Next morning add the 12 remaining cups of flour (this can be whole wheat or white flour or half and half). Knead at least 200 times. If amount of dough seems too unwieldy to knead in one batch, divide it into 2 parts and knead each separately. Divide into 6 equal parts and shape each into an oval and place in oiled standard loaf pans. Let dough rise, covered, at room temperature until risen about 1" above rims of pans, then bake at 375° about 50 minutes. Tap a loaf and listen for a hollow sound to test for doneness. Do not hesitate to overbake bread, especially whole wheat, to be sure it is thoroughly done.

Whole Wheat Bran Bread

(2 loaves)

2 C all-purpose flour
2 C whole wheat flour
2 C all bran cereal
2 Tbsp sugar
2 tsp salt
1 pkg (1 Tbsp) granular yeast
1½ C warm milk
2 Tbsp molasses
6 Tbsp margarine
2 eggs

In a bowl mix the white and whole wheat flours. Into a large bowl measure 1 C of these mixed flours. Add all bran, sugar, salt and yeast.

Heat together milk, molasses and margarine until warmer than lukewarm. Add to large bowl and beat at medium speed for 2 minutes, scraping down bowl occasionally. Now add the eggs and another ½ C of the mixed flours. Beat at high speed 2 minutes. Remove beaters and stir in all but ½ C of the remaining flours by hand. Cover and let rise at room temperature until doubled.

Turn dough out on board floured with remaining ½ C mixed flours and knead 5 minutes until all flour is kneaded in. Cut dough in half. Shape half into round loaf and place on greased 8" layer cake tin. Shape another for a small loaf pan. Let rise until well above rims of pans. Bake at 375° for 30 minutes or until firm to touch.

Whole Wheat Bread

(two loaves)

1 C scalded milk
1 C cold water
1 tsp sugar (first amount)
2 tsp granular yeast
2 Tbsp shortening
3 Tbsp sugar (second amount)
2 tsp salt
½ C wheat germ
3 C whole wheat flour (preferably stone ground)
1½ C all-purpose flour (divided)

In medium-sized pot scald milk. As soon as bubbles begin to form around edges remove from heat and add the cold water. Dip 1 C of this diluted milk into a bowl. Add 1 tsp sugar, stir to dissolve and then sprinkle yeast over top. To milk in pot stir in shortening, 3 Tbsp sugar and salt. Cover and let stand.

Into a very large bowl measure whole wheat flour, 1¼ C white flour and wheat germ and mix. Probably by this time yeast liquid is foamy. Add yeast liquid in bowl to milk mixture in pot and pour over the flours and with strong wooden spoon mix. Sprinkle kneading board with remaining ¼ C white flour. Turn dough out on it and knead 200 times, about 10 minutes. Return to bowl. Put in cold oven. On shelf below place a large shallow pan ¾ full of boiling water. Let rise 1½ hours.

Now punch down dough and cut in half. Roll each half out to ½" thickness. Roll up like jelly roll and place in oiled loaf pans 8½ × 4½" tucking in ends. Place in cold oven. On shelf below again place the large shallow pan replenished to ¾ full of boiling hot water. Close oven door. Let rise 1½ hours. Take from oven. Remove water-pan. Turn heat to 400° and bake 10 minutes then reduce heat to 375° about 20 minutes longer.

Wheat Germ Loaf

2 Tbsp (2pkgs) granular yeast
1 C wheat germ
2½ C unsifted all-purpose flour
    (divided, see below)
2 tsp salt
1½ C quite warm water
2 Tbsp molasses
2 Tbsp butter or margarine
    (room temperature)

Into a large beater bowl measure the yeast, wheat germ, 1 C of the flour and salt. Mix. Add quite warm water, molasses and butter or margarine and beat 3 minutes at medium speed, scraping down sides of bowl once or twice. Add ½ C more flour and beat 3 minutes, again scraping down sides of bowl.

Remove beaters. With strong spoon stir in 1 more cup flour to make a stiff batter. Scrape down sides of bowl, cover and let rise 1 hour until doubled. Then punch down dough and beat 1 minute. Turn into well greased 6-cup casserole and let rise until doubled. Bake at 375° about 40 minutes or until crusty and browned. It should sound hollow when you tap it.

Trinidadian Pita

1¼ C warm water
1 Tbsp oil
1 Tbsp sugar
1 tsp yeast
1½ C all-purpose flour
1½ C whole wheat flour
1 tsp salt
Corn meal (for sprinkling baking sheet)

Into a 2-cup measure put 1¼ C warm water. Add oil and sugar and stir. Sprinkle yeast over top, stir once and let stand 15 minutes.

Into a large bowl measure flours and salt. Add risen yeast liquid and mix well. This is a firm dough and must be kneaded for 5 minutes. Return to oiled bowl and let rise 3 hours. Then turn dough out on floured board and knead 25 times. Shape into long smooth 18" roll. Cut into 16 even pieces, shape each into a ball, then with rolling pin roll into ¼" thick rounds about 4" in diameter. Place onto cornmeal-sprinkled baking sheets. Let rise while you are heating the oven to 425° and bake about 8 to 10 minutes.

These, of course, are at their best when fresh. Make slits in sides and fill with a variety of fillings: 1. ground or chopped luncheon meat with chopped celery, green pepper and mayonnaise; 2. mashed tuna with chopped apple, lemon juice and mayonnaise; 3. chopped cucumber with chopped raw mushrooms, chopped green onions and sour cream, salt and pepper.

Homemade White Bread

(2 loaves)

1 pkg granular yeast
1 tsp sugar (first amount)
½ C lukewarm water
1¾ C scalded milk
½ C margarine
⅓ C sugar (second amount)
2 tsp salt
6½ C stirred but not sifted all-purpose
    flour (divided, see below)
2 eggs

In a large bowl soak the yeast with 1 tsp sugar in the lukewarm water 10 minutes. Remove the scalded milk from the heat and stir in the margarine, ⅓ C sugar and salt and stir until cooled to lukewarm. Add to risen yeast liquid along with 4 C of the flour and the eggs and beat for 5 minutes. Add 2 more cups of flour and beat and stir in with heavy spoon as well as you can until dough is smooth. Scrape down sides of bowl and cover and let rise at room temperature at least 2 hours or until more than doubled.

Sprinkle remaining ½ C flour on kneading board and turn dough out on it and knead at least 100 times or until all flour on board is kneaded in. Cut dough in halves, shape each into a small football and place in 2 well-greased loaf pans. Brush tops with mixture of 1 Tbsp each sugar and milk. Cover with damp towel and let rise until at least 1" above rims of pans, about 2 hours. Bake at 400° for 30 to 40 minutes or until well browned and hollow-sounding when tapped. Turn out and cool on rack.

Prune Bread

1 pkg granular yeast
1 tsp sugar (first amount)
½ C lukewarm water
1 C very hot tap water
2 Tbsp margarine
2 Tbsp sugar (second amount)
1 tsp salt
3⅞ C sifted all-purpose flour
1 egg
Grated rind 1 large orange
1 C chopped pitted uncooked prunes

In large mixing bowl soak yeast and sugar (first amount) in lukewarm water 10 minutes. To the hot tap water add the margarine, sugar (second amount) and salt and let stand until lukewarm. Add it to soaked yeast liquid along with 2 C of the flour and the egg and orange rind and beat for 5 minutes. Mix in 1¼ more cups of flour as well as you can, scrape down bowl sides, cover and let rise about 2 hours or until more than doubled in size. Punch down dough and turn out on board floured with some of remaining flour. Add the cut prunes and begin kneading until you have kneaded in and used up all remaining flour. Shape into loaf and put in large buttered loaf pan. (This is too much dough for a standard loaf pan so if you do not have an outsized pan break off enough dough to shape about 6 buns and bake them when risen on buttered pan at same temperature as bread but much shorter time.) Let bread rise at room temperature for about 1½ hours or until 1" above rim of pan and bake at 350° for 40 to 45 minutes until it is a deep rich gold. Cool on rack. Best toasted.

Oatmeal Honey Bread

2 tsp granular yeast
1 tsp sugar
½ C lukewarm water
1 C dairy sour cream
¼ tsp baking soda
4 Tbsp liquid honey (divided, see below)
1 tsp salt
1 C large flake or instant rolled oats
1¾ to 1⅞ C all-purpose flour
    (divided, see below)

In small bowl soak yeast with sugar in lukewarm water 10 minutes after giving it one stir.

Meanwhile heat until just warm the sour cream. Remove from heat. Pour into large mixing bowl and add the baking soda, 3 Tbsp liquid honey, salt, rolled oats, 1 C all-purpose flour and risen yeast liquid and stir hard for 5 minutes or mix in beater bowl which has dough hook or strong beaters. Stir in another ½ C flour until thoroughly blended. Sprinkle kneading board with about ⅓ C flour, turn dough out on it and knead well for 5 minutes or 200 kneads. Return to greased bowl and let rise about 30 minutes.

Turn out on lightly floured board and knead for 1 minute. Shape into round loaf and place in buttered 3" deep × 7" diameter round pan. Let rise about 1½ hours or until 1" above rim of pan. Bake at 400° for 8 minutes then reduce heat to 350° for about 30 to 35 minutes longer. Remove to rack and while warm brush all over top with remaining 1 Tbsp liquid honey.

High Protein Bread
(2 loaves)

½ C honey
⅓ C shortening or oil
4 C quite warm water
2 tsp granular yeast
2 C whole wheat flour
　　(preferably stone ground)
1½ C rye flour
½ C rolled oats
½ C soy flour
½ C wheat germ
½ C 100% bran or all bran
¾ C skim milk powder
1 Tbsp salt
About 4⅔ C all-purpose flour
　　(divided, see below)

Select your largest bowl and into it measure the honey, shortening and quite warm water. Stir to dissolve honey and shortening. Mixture is about lukewarm by now so sprinkle yeast all over top and give it one good stir and let it stand 15 minutes.

Meanwhile in another large container measure the whole wheat flour, rye flour, oats, soy flour, wheat germ, bran, skim milk powder and salt. Mix well and stir in 1¾ C all-purpose flour. Turn this all into the risen yeast liquid and stir at least 50 times, more if your arm holds out. Scrape down sides with rubber spatula and let rise until doubled, about 3 hours.

Sprinkle all remaining flour on your kneading board and turn dough out on it and knead it all in. Shape into 2 loaves and place into buttered pans. If desired brush tops with egg beaten with 1 Tbsp water to give it a shine. Let rise until 1″ above rims, nearly 2 hours, and bake at 400° for 15 minutes then reduce to 325° for 30 to 40 minutes longer or until crust is dark gold.

Note: I recommend that breadmakers use loaf pans that are 8½ × 4½ × 3″ for they produce a taller loaf than the standard loaf pan that is 9 × 5 × 2½″.

Nutty Crunch Bread
(4 loaves)

2½ C milk, scalded
1 C wheat germ
1 C oatmeal or rolled oats
1½ C lukewarm water
2 Tbsp brown sugar
2 pkgs granular yeast
½ C molasses (or honey)
½ C oil
¾ C sesame seeds
4 tsp salt
3 C whole wheat flour
5½ C unsifted all-purpose flour

Scald the milk in a large pot, remove from heat and stir wheat germ and oats into it and let cool. Into a large bowl measure the lukewarm water, brown sugar and yeast. Stir and let soak 10 minutes. To soaked cereal mixture add the molasses, oil, seeds, salt and yeast liquid. Mix well, then with wooden spoon stir in whole wheat flour. Now stir in 4 C of white flour to form a dough.

Flour your kneading board with ½ C of the remaining 1½ C flour, turn dough out on it, sprinkle top with ¼ C remaining flour and begin kneading. As you knead dough will become sticky so before you have finished kneading it 200 times knead in all remaining flour. Cut dough into 4 even pieces. Shape into loaves with oiled palms and drop into oiled loaf pans 8½ × 4½ or 9 × 5″. Cover and let rise 2 hours at room temperature or until just above rims of pans. Bake at 375° for 20 minutes then reduce heat to 350° for 20 minutes longer. Cool on racks.

Shirriff Bread
(3 loaves)

¼ C honey
1 C hot water (first amount)
2 Tbsp granular yeast
3½ C hot water (second amount)
¼ C molasses
2½ tsp salt
5 C stirred but unsifted all-purpose flour
5 C whole wheat flour
¾ C cracked wheat
1 C wheat germ
1 C bran
⅓ C flax seed
⅓ C sesame seed

Into a large basin measure the honey and 1 C hot water. Stir to mix until just above lukewarm. Sprinkle yeast over and let stand 15 minutes. Meanwhile in a bowl combine the 3½ C hot water, molasses and salt. Stir. When cooled down to just above lukewarm add to risen yeast liquid.

In a very large bowl mix together the whole wheat flour, white flour, cracked wheat, wheat germ, bran, flax and sesame seeds. Now scoop out and add 4 C of the flours to the liquids in basin. Stir for 5 minutes. Add 2 more cups and mix very well.

Tip all remaining flours out on kneading board and pat to about ¾″ thickness. Tip dough out on it. Pick up some loose flour from edges and sprinkle over top and begin kneading almost all of this flour in, about 10 minutes. Leave just a little flour on board for shaping loaves later.

Return dough to basin. Oil top. Cover with damp towel and let rise until doubled, about 1¼ hours. Turn dough out on kneading board again. Knead 25 times. Shape into roll. Cut into 3 pieces. Shape into loaves and put in well-oiled loaf pans. Oil tops. Cover again with damp cloth and let rise until above rims of pans, about 1 hour. Do not preheat oven. Put loaves in cold oven, turn on heat to 350° and bake 35 to 45 minutes. Test for doneness by tapping top. It will sound hollow if done. Cool on racks.

Golden Grain Bread

(4 loaves)

6 C warm water
1 C light brown sugar
⅓ C margarine
1 Tbsp granular yeast
4 C whole wheat flour
1 C Vita B cereal or cornmeal
½ C natural bran
1½ C cracked wheat
1 C quick-cooking rolled oats
4 C unsifted all-purpose flour (first amount)
5 tsp salt
1½ C skim milk powder
6 C unsifted all-purpose flour (second amount)

Into a large bowl measure the warm water, brown sugar and margarine. Stir a little, then sprinkle yeast over top and let stand 15 minutes.

Into an outsize bowl measure the whole wheat flour, Vita B or cornmeal, bran, cracked wheat, rolled oats and 4 C white flour, salt and skim milk powder. Mix well. Add the yeast mixture to the dry ingredients and with a heavy wooden spoon stir for 5 minutes. Cover and let rise at room temperature for 2 hours until it is more than doubled.

Pile the 6 C unsifted all-purpose flour on your kneading board. Turn dough out. Pick up some flour and sprinkle top with it and start kneading all the flour in, about 15 minutes. Shape into a long even roll and cut into 4 equal parts. Shape these into elongated footballs and put into greased standard loaf pans. Let rise 2 hours or until well above rims of pans. Bake at 400° for 20 minutes then reduce temperature to 375° for 30 to 35 minutes longer or until golden brown with a hard crust. Turn out on racks to cool.

Italian Bread Sticks

1 pkg granular yeast
1 tsp sugar
½ C lukewarm water
1 C scalded milk
2 tsp salt
2 Tbsp sugar (second amount)
2 Tbsp shortening
½ C warm water (second amount)
4½ C stirred but not sifted flour

In large mixing bowl soak yeast and the 1 tsp sugar in ½ C lukewarm water 10 minutes. To scalded milk add salt, 2 Tbsp sugar, shortening and second ½ C warm water and stir to dissolve sugar, then cool to lukewarm. Add to risen yeast liquid along with 1½ C flour and beat until smoothly blended. Stir in remaining flour and knead on floured board until perfectly smooth and squeaky. Return to scraped down bowl, cover and let rise in warmish place until more than doubled.

Punch down dough and knead on floured board for 2 or 3 minutes. Cut dough in half. Roll out half to less than ½″ thickness. Cut into ½″ wide strips. Cut strips in halves crosswise. Fold each strip over once and with floured fingers twist to 5″ long rope. Place 1″ apart on buttered baking sheets. This amount makes 40 sticks. (See note below.) To make 80 sticks repeat with second half of dough. Let rise until puffy and bake at 425°

about 20 minutes switching pans in oven. They must be baked until rich gold and crisp.

Variation: If you wish, make second half of dough into Mock Cheese Croissants by rolling it out to less than ½″ thickness and spreading with 3 Tbsp soft butter and sprinkling with ½ C packaged grated cheese. Roll up like jelly roll starting at long side, then with rolling pin roll out to 5 × 15″ oblong. Cut this slanting crosswise into 12 long triangles. Roll each up starting at base of triangle into a crescent and place on buttered baking sheet 2″ apart. Let rise until puffy, about 1¼ hours. Bake at 425° for 15 minutes then brush tops with milk and return to oven to finish baking until rich gold and baked through.

Freezer White Bread Dough

(2 loaves)

¼ C warm water (first amount)
1 tsp sugar (first amount)
1 Tbsp granular yeast
2 Tbsp sugar (second amount)
¾ C plus 1 Tbsp warm water (second amount)
1⅓ C all-purpose flour
¼ C skim milk powder
1 C warm water (third amount)
1⅔ tsp salt
3 Tbsp soft shortening
2⅔ C all-purpose flour for dough
About 1 C flour for board

Into a large bowl measure the ¼ C warm water and 1 tsp sugar. Sprinkle yeast evenly over top and let stand 10 minutes until bubbly. Then add the 2 Tbsp sugar, 1⅓ C flour, skim milk powder and the ¾ C plus 1 Tbsp warm water. Beat with beaters (or dough hook). This is a sponge. Cover and let rise until doubled and bubbly, about 40 minutes. Then add the 1 C warm water, salt, shortening, 2⅔ C flour and beat hard for 5 minutes. Sprinkle board with ⅔ C flour and knead dough for 5 minutes. Return to scraped down bowl, cover and let rise 2 hours. Punch down dough and knead in an additional ¼ to ⅓ C flour on board, turning dough over in flour before starting to knead 5 minutes.

Now cut dough in half. Flatten each half on a plate and chill in refrigerator ½ hour. (This completely checks rising when raw dough is put in freezer in next step.) Quickly shape chilled dough into 2 loaves and put in oiled loaf pans. Immediately slip pans into double plastic bags, sealing with twists and freeze. Early on the day you need the bread, take from freezer, unwrap and stand on counter to thaw and rise above rims of pans, about 6 hours. Bake at 425° for 15 minutes then reduce heat to 350° for 15 minutes longer.

Granary Bread

(2 loaves)

1 pkg granular yeast
3 C warm water
½ C honey
⅓ C shortening
1 C whole wheat flour
1½ C rye flour
⅓ C rolled oats
⅓ C cornmeal or farina
3⅓ C all-purpose flour (divided, see below)
1 Tbsp salt
¾ C skim milk powder
¾ C soy flour
3 Tbsp wheat germ

In a large bowl soak the yeast in the warm water with the honey 10 minutes. Add as you measure all remaining ingredients except 1⅓ C all-purpose flour. Mix well with strong spoon. Dough is stiff but you must give it at least 50 complete stirs. Scrape down sides of bowl, level top, cover and let rise 2 hours.

Punch down dough and turn out on counter floured with remaining 1⅓ C all-purpose flour. Turn dough over to flour top and knead 100 times. Knead in all flour. Shape into 2 loaves. Let rise in well buttered loaf pans about 1 hour. Do not allow to overrise. Bake at 400° for 10 minutes on center shelf of oven then reduce heat to 350° for about 25 minutes. Cool on rack.

Ezekiel Bread

Thanks to Ezekiel 4:9 and Dr. W. Harding leRiche for this idea.

½ C dry red lentils
½ C dry pearl barley
1 tsp dill seeds (optional but recommended)
2 C warm water (first amount)
2 C hot water
1 Tbsp granular yeast
½ C molasses or honey
½ C boiling water
4 Tbsp soy flour
4 Tbsp millet meal
2 C stone ground whole wheat flour
2 tsp salt
2 tsp oil
3 C all-purpose flour (first amount)
1 C warm water (second amount)
About 2½ C all-purpose flour (second amount)

Early in the morning soak the lentils, barley and dill seeds (if used) in the 2 C warm water. Let stand 5 hours. Add the 2 C hot water and simmer covered until very tender, about 1½ hours more. Cool to lukewarm.

Then make dough: Mix together the molasses or honey with the boiling water to blend and when just above finger temperature sprinkle yeast over top and let stand 20 minutes while you measure the remaining ingredients. Into a large bowl measure soy, millet, whole wheat flour, salt, oil, 3 C all-purpose flour and the cooked, cooled lentil and barley mixture. Add the second cup warm water and yeast liquid and beat hard for 5 minutes or mix with your hands if desired. Let rise covered until doubled, about 1¼ hours.

Sprinkle kneading board with remaining 2½ C all-purpose flour and turn this very wet dough out on it. Sprinkle some flour from board over top and begin kneading it all in. This dough is sticky.

Shape into 3 loaves and put into 3 buttered standard loaf pans and let rise 1½ hours until about ¾" above rims. Bake at 350° about 35 minutes until crusty, hollow-sounding and golden. If desired brush with melted butter while loaves are warm. Remove from pans and cool on racks.

Hovislike, Cool-Rise, Four-Grain Bread

(4 loaves)

6½ C lukewarm water
¼ C brown sugar
¼ C honey
¼ C shortening
2 tsp yeast
4 C all-purpose flour
  (see below for second amount)
3 C whole wheat flour
½ C yellow corn meal
½ C wheat germ
1 C rolled oats
1½ C skim milk powder
1 Tbsp salt
6 C all-purpose flour (second amount)

Into a big bowl measure the lukewarm water and add the sugar, honey, shortening. Give it a good stir and sprinkle yeast over top and let stand 10 minutes.

Meanwhile into a basin measure the 4 C all-purpose flour, whole wheat flour, corn meal, wheat germ, oats, milk powder and salt and mix well. (By this time yeast liquid has risen its required 10 minutes.) Add yeast liquid and stir for 5 minutes. Let rise 2 hours or until doubled.

Onto kneading board measure the 6 C all-purpose flour (second amount), spreading it out to cover a wide area. Turn risen dough out on it and pick up handfuls of flour and sprinkle all over top of this wet runny dough. Now knead it all in. This takes at least 10 minutes. Divide dough in half. Roll each half out to 1" thickness with rolling pin. Cut each in half again to give you 4 pieces. Roll each up like a jelly roll. Shape into 4 even loaves. Place in greased standard loaf pans and let rise at room temperature for ½ hour. Put into refrigerator overnight.

In the morning it will have risen above rims of pans. Remove and let stand at room temperature to warm up and rise a little more, about ½ to 1 hour. Bake at 400° for 15 minutes, then reduce temperature to 350° for 40 minutes longer, or until when tapped on top it sounds hollow. Turn out on racks to cool

Moore Bread

(3 loaves)

2 pkg granular yeast
2 Tbsp sugar
3 C lukewarm water
2 Tbsp soft margarine or butter or shortening
4 C sifted all-purpose flour
½ C skim milk powder
4 tsp salt
1 C quick-cooking rolled oats
3 C stirred but not sifted whole wheat flour
⅓ C soft, bright orange, rich cream cheese,
    cut-up (optional)

In large mixing bowl soak the yeast in the lukewarm water with the sugar for 5 minutes. Add the margarine or butter or shortening. Sift together the sifted all-purpose flour, skim milk powder and salt and beat into the yeast liquid, then beat in the quick-cooking rolled oats well. Now stir in 2 C of the whole wheat flour as well as you can. Turn out on board sprinkled with ½ C of the remaining flour and knead for 5 minutes or 200 times. Return to scraped-down bowl and let rise until doubled in warm place.

Turn out of bowl onto board sprinkled with remaining ½ C whole wheat flour and knead for 5 minutes or 200 times. Divide dough into 3 equal portions. If desired knead ⅓ C rich orange cream cheese into 1 portion until perfectly blended and smooth. (You may need to sprinkle board with a little more whole wheat flour as you knead the cheese into 1 loaf.) Shape the 3 portions into loaves and place in buttered loaf pans. Let rise in warm place until above rims of pans. Bake at 350° for 50 to 60 minutes until brown and hollow-sounding when tapped.

Christmas Braid Bread

DOUGH

2 pkgs granular yeast
1 tsp sugar (first amount)
½ C lukewarm water
1 C scalded milk
½ C sugar (second amount)
1 tsp salt
½ C shortening
2 eggs
4 C sifted all-purpose flour (divided)
1 C light Sultana raisins or chopped dates
½ tsp mace (or nutmeg)
1 tsp grated lemon rind

TOPPING

1 C unsifted icing sugar
5 tsp warm water
1 tsp lemon juice
8 red maraschino cherries halved
8 green maraschino cherries halved
About 24 whole medium pecans or
    equivalent in sliced almonds

To make dough, into large mixing bowl put yeast, sugar (first amount) and lukewarm water and let soak 10 minutes. To scalded milk add sugar (second amount), salt and shortening and cool to lukewarm. Add to risen yeast liquid along with eggs and 3½ C of the flour and beat 100 times.

Scrape down sides of bowl, cover and let rise in warm place until doubled, about 2 hours. Punch down dough and let rise a second time until doubled. Sprinkle kneading board with remaining flour, turn risen dough out on it, cover with raisins or dates, mace and lemon rind and knead until all are evenly distributed through dough. If you need more flour to prevent sticking sprinkle it on board.

To shape braid, cut dough into 2 pieces: one piece should be two-thirds of the dough the other one-third. Cut larger piece evenly into 3 and shape each into 18″ long strips rolling them under your palms. Place about 1″ apart on large buttered cookie sheet and braid loosely, broadening braid at center and pinching ends together. Repeat, making shorter braid about half the size of first with remaining dough shaped into 3 shorter smaller strips and place on center top of large braid, stretching and pinching its ends to the ends of the first braid. Glaze by brushing with mixture of 2 Tbsp each water and sugar. Let rise in warm place until doubled and puffy. Bake at 350° about 50 minutes until it has a deep gold crust.

While warm drizzle with icing made of mixture of icing sugar, water and lemon juice, then decorate with halved cherries and whole pecans or sliced almonds. This should be served warm and reheats satisfactorily at 275° wrapped in foil in about 20 to 25 minutes.

Sesame Cheese Bread

(2 loaves)

1 pkg (1Tbsp) granular yeast
1 tsp sugar
¾ C lukewarm water
1 C scalded milk
2 Tbsp sugar (second amount)
2 tsp salt
2 Tbsp butter
2 C shredded old Cheddar cheese
About 4¾ C sifted all-purpose flour
1 egg yolk (for top)
About 2 Tbsp sesame seeds (for top)

In your largest beater bowl soak the yeast with the 1 tsp sugar in the lukewarm water 10 minutes.

Meanwhile stir into the scalded milk the 2 Tbsp sugar, salt and butter and cool to lukewarm. Add milk mixture and cheese to risen yeast liquid. Add 3 C of the flour and beat until you have a smooth dough. Work in one more cup of flour. Cover with a towel and let rise until more than doubled.

Sprinkle kneading board with remaining ¾ C flour, punch down dough and turn out on floured board and knead 100 times. Cut into 4 pieces. Shape each piece into a long roll. Twine 2 together like a fat two-strand rope. Place each of the 2 loaves in buttered loaf pans, tucking ends under. Brush tops of loaves with undiluted egg yolk, using all of it. Now carefully sprinkle sesame seeds all over egg-yolk-brushed top and let rise for 2 hours. Bake at 375° about 30 minutes or until rich gold and slightly separated from sides of pans. Cool on racks.

Cracked Wheat Bread

(4 loaves)

1 C warm water
1 tsp sugar
2 pkg granular yeast
2 C scalded milk
2 C cold liquid (potato water or water)
2 C cracked wheat
¼ C shortening or margarine
¼ C sugar
1 Tbsp salt
9 to 10 C sifted all-purpose flour

Dissolve sugar in warm water and add yeast. Let stand about 10 minutes while doing the following: to hot milk add shortening, sugar, salt, cracked wheat and liquid. (The cold liquid will cool the hot milk to warm.) Stir risen yeast liquid and add milk mixture to it. Add about 4 C of the flour and give the mixture a quick beat. Mix in additional flour until dough leaves sides of bowl, about 5 more cups. Turn dough onto floured surface and knead. When dough is smooth and feels spongy, place in greased bowl, cover and leave until doubled. Punch down, cover and let rise again.

When doubled in bulk punch down dough again and turn out on lightly floured board. Cut into four. Round each piece, cover and let rest while greasing pans. Shape into 4 loaves. Place in pans. Cover, let rise until higher than edge of pans. Brush with melted butter and bake at 400° for 35 to 40 minutes. Remove from pans and cool on racks.

Chop Suey Loaf

¾ C Sultana raisins
¼ C chopped citron peel
¼ C chopped walnuts or pecans
⅓ C chopped glacé or well-drained
   maraschino cherries
1 C milk
¼ C lukewarm water
1 tsp sugar
1 pkg granular yeast
2 C sifted all-purpose or bread flour
   (first amount)
1½ tsp salt
1 or 2 tsp cinnamon
¼ tsp nutmeg
⅛ tsp cloves
¼ C butter or margarine
⅓ C lightly packed light brown sugar
1 egg
1¾ C sifted all-purpose flour (second amount)

Scald milk. Stir the 1 tsp sugar into the ¼ C lukewarm water in measuring cup. Sprinkle yeast over top, stir once and let stand 10 minutes or until it rises to top of cup. Sift together the flour, salt and spices. In large mixing bowl, cream the butter or margarine well with the light brown sugar until light and airy. Beat in the egg. Now stir in lukewarm milk and risen yeast liquid and sifted dry ingredients. Beat until smooth and elastic. Add prepared fruits and nuts and beat again. Now work in, while kneading on board, the 1¾ C sifted all-purpose flour (but do not work all of this amount of flour in if the mass of dough seems too stiff).

Shape into 2 loaves and place in greased loaf pans. Grease top of dough. Cover and let rise until doubled. Bake at 350° about 40 minutes or until done. Brush top with softened butter and cool on racks.

French Bread

(Two 16″ sticks)

1¼ C warm water
1 Tbsp sugar
1½ tsp salt
1 Tbsp margarine
1 pkg or 1 Tbsp granular yeast
About 3¼ C sifted all-purpose flour

Measure warm water into large mixing bowl. Stir in sugar, salt and margarine. Sprinkle yeast over top, give it one stir and let soak 10 minutes.

Meanwhile sift and measure flour. Add 2½ C to make a soft dough. Sprinkle kneading board with ½ C of the remaining flour and knead dough 200 times or about 10 minutes. Put back in greased bowl, turn over to grease both sides and let rise covered, until doubled, about 1½ hours. Punch down dough and knead 50 times. Return to bowl and let rise again until doubled.

Turn out on floured (with remaining ¼ C) board and cut in half. With rolling pin roll out to 8 × 10″ oblong. Starting at long side roll up tightly like a jelly roll. Pinch edges together. Holding each end stretch roll to 16″ length and taper ends. Repeat with second half. Place on separate buttered cookie sheets, diagonally, which have been sprinkled sparingly with cornmeal. Make diagonal slashes on top with sharp knife ¼″ deep at 2″ intervals. Brush loaves with Cornstarch Glaze (below). Let rise uncovered until doubled, about 1½ hours. Gently brush again with glaze. Bake at 400° for 12 to 15 minutes, brushing again with glaze after 10 minutes' baking.

CORNSTARCH GLAZE; In a very small pot blend 1 tsp each cornstarch and cold water. Stir in ½ C boiling water and cook stirring until thickened. Cool slightly before brushing on surface of loaves.

Spiced Raisin Loaf

1½ C raisins (plumped and dried, see below)
½ C lukewarm water
1 tsp sugar (first amount)
2 tsp granular yeast
½ C scalded milk
2 Tbsp sugar (second amount)
1½ tsp salt
1½ tsp nutmeg
2 Tbsp soft margarine
2 eggs
About 3½ C stirred but unsifted all-purpose
   flour (divided, see below)

Turn the raisins into a sieve. Place over boiling water and steam for 15 minutes to plump them. Pat dry.

Meanwhile in beater bowl add the sugar (first amount) and yeast to the lukewarm water and let soak 10 minutes.

Scald milk then remove from heat and to it add the sugar (second amount), salt, nutmeg and margarine and stir for about 1 minute to dissolve sugar. Cool to lukewarm. Add to risen yeast liquid. Also add 2 C of the flour and the eggs and beat for at least 5 minutes. Now stir in 1 more cup of flour and the raisins until thoroughly blended. Scrape down sides of bowl, cover and let rise 2 hours.

Sprinkle kneading board with remaining flour and turn dough out and knead 75 times. Shape into loaf and put in buttered standard loaf pan and let rise 1½ hours. Bake at 400° for 30 minutes. Turn out on rack to cool. If desired while warm brush all over with honey to glaze.

Homemade Rye Bread

(2 loaves)

½ C lukewarm water
1 tsp sugar (first amount)
1 pkg granular yeast
¾ C water
1 C milk
2 Tbsp honey
1 Tbsp margarine
2 tsp sugar (second amount)
1 Tbsp salt
1 Tbsp caraway seeds
2½ C unsifted dark rye flour
2½ C all-purpose flour (plus some for board)
2 Tbsp corn meal
1 egg white
2 Tbsp sugar (third amount)

Measure the ½ C lukewarm water into a large mixing bowl and stir in 1 tsp sugar and the yeast and let stand 10 minutes.

Into a pot measure the ¾ C water, milk, honey, margarine, 2 tsp sugar, salt and caraway seeds and heat, stirring, until sugar is dissolved and liquids are lukewarm. Add lukewarm liquids to risen yeast liquid. Combine flours and add 2 C to the liquids and beat hard until smooth. Add remaining flours and work in as well as you can, then turn out on floured board and knead 200 times. Return to scraped down bowl, cover and let rise at room temperature until doubled. Then punch down risen dough and knead 200 times on floured board. Shape into ball, cut in half, shape each half into longish roll about 3" in diameter at center with tapered ends.

Sprinkle corn meal on a very large cookie sheet and place loaves on it 4" apart. Brush tops with mixture of egg white and 2 Tbsp sugar. Let rise in warm place until nearly touching and tripled in size, about 2 hours. Bake at 400° for 15 minutes then reduce heat to 325° for half an hour longer or until when loaves are tapped they sound hollow. Transfer to racks to cool.

Herb Bread

(2 loaves)

4 tsp granular yeast
¼ C warm water
1 C scalded milk
¼ C shortening
¼ C brown sugar
2 tsp salt
1 tsp celery seed
½ tsp oregano
½ tsp basil
½ tsp curry powder
2 eggs
2 C whole wheat flour
2¾ C unsifted all-purpose flour (divided)

Soak yeast in warm water in large bowl or basin 10 minutes. (Use warm, not lukewarm, water because container immediately absorbs heat and reduces temperature.)

Scald milk and remove from heat and add shortening, sugar, salt, celery seed, oregano, basil, curry powder, eggs and whole wheat flour and beat hard for 5 minutes. Now add 2 C of the white flour and mix in. Sprinkle kneading board with ½ C of the remaining flour and knead 200 times. Return to bowl, cover and let rise in warm place 2 hours.

Punch down dough, turn out on board sprinkled with remaining ¼ C flour and knead 100 times. Divide in half. Shape into 2 loaves, put into 2 well greased loaf pans. Moisten tops with water and sprinkle generously with more celery seeds. Let rise in warm place 1 hour until ¾" above rims of pans. Bake at 375° for 35 to 40 minutes.

Hot Dog Rolls

2 tsp granular yeast
2 tsp sugar (first amount)
1 C lukewarm water
1 C scalded milk
¼ C shortening
½ C sugar (second amount)
2 tsp salt
2 eggs
About 6 C stirred all-purpose flour
    (divided, see below)

In a large bowl soak the yeast and the 2 tsp sugar in the lukewarm water 10 minutes. To the scalded milk add the shortening, sugar and salt and stir to melt and dissolve and cool to lukewarm. Add to risen yeast liquid along with 4 C of the flour and the 2 eggs and beat to mix well. Add another 1 C flour, mix in as well as you can, cover well and let rise overnight in refrigerator. Reserve remaining 1 C flour for kneading board.

In the morning stir down dough, turn out on floured (½ C) board and knead 100 times using remaining flour as you knead when necessary. Shape into two 16" long rolls, cut each into 12 pieces. Shape each into a smooth 5 × 2" roll. Place on greased baking sheets at least 4" apart. Brush top with 1 beaten egg diluted with 1 Tbsp water. If desired neatly sprinkle each with a variety of seeds: sesame, caraway, poppy. Let rise 2 hours or until size of hot dog rolls. Bake at 425° for 8 minutes, watching carefully, until golden.

Refrigerator Crescents and Caramel Rolls

1 pkg granular yeast
¼ C lukewarm water
¾ C scalded milk
¼ C butter
¼ C oil
1 tsp salt
¼ C sugar
3 C sifted all-purpose flour
1 egg

In beater bowl soak yeast in lukewarm water. To scalded milk add butter, oil, salt and sugar and stir to dissolve. Cool to lukewarm. Add to risen yeast liquid along with 1 C of the sifted flour and egg and beat at low speed for 5 minutes. Stir in remaining flour until blended. Scrape down sides of bowl, brush surface with oil and cover tightly and refrigerate. Use this dough for Crescents and Caramel Walnut Rolls.

CRESCENTS: Cut half of dough from bowl. Return remainder to refrigerator. On floured board roll out dough into an oblong ⅛" thick. Cut into six 7" squares. Cut each into 2 triangles. Brush with melted butter. Roll each up starting at wide end. Place well apart on greased cookie sheets. Let rise 3 hours. Bake at 400° for 10 to 12 minutes, watching carefully.

CARAMEL WALNUT ROLLS: Roll out half of refrigerator dough to ⅛" thickness on floured board into an oblong 16 × 12". Cut in half down the longer dimension. Brush with melted butter. Sprinkle with light brown sugar using 3 Tbsp in all. Sprinkle with about ½ to ⅔ C chopped walnuts. Roll up each half starting at long edge. Cut each into 6 even pieces. Butter muffin tins generously. Sprinkle bottom of each cup with ½ tsp brown sugar. Put in rolls cut side up. Let rise at room temperature 3 hours. Bake at 400° for 8 to 10 minutes. They bake quickly. Invert at once on cake rack before they cool and stick to muffin tins.

Jam Gems and Cinnamon Swirls

1 Tbsp (1 pkg) granular yeast
¼ C lukewarm water
1 tsp sugar (first amount)
1 C scalded milk
½ C sugar (second amount)
1 tsp salt
½ C shortening
2 eggs
About 4¼ C sifted all-purpose flour

In large bowl soak yeast and 1 tsp sugar in lukewarm water 10 minutes. To scalded milk add the ½ C sugar, salt and shortening and stir to dissolve and melt. When lukewarm add to yeast liquid along with the eggs and 2 C of the flour and beat 50 times. Stir in 2 more cups of flour as well as you can. Scrape down sides of bowl, cover and let rise at room temperature until doubled.

Punch down dough and turn out on kneading board. Sprinkle with about ¼ to ½ C flour and knead 100 times. Cut dough in half and shape each into 20" long rolls. Cut one of the rolls into 12 pieces and flatten each piece into a 4" round and line twelve 2¾" muffin tins with them. In each put 1 tsp jam. Now pinch the edges together to form a tight tulip-like top. Let rise in warm place until 1" above rims of pan.

Roll out remaining roll of dough to 15 × 9" oblong and brush with 2 Tbsp melted butter. Sprinkle with ⅓ C light brown sugar and 2 tsp cinnamon. Roll up lengthwise and stretch roll to measure 20". Cut into 16 pinwheels. Butter two 8" layer cake tins generously and place 8 pinwheels in each with 2 in center. Let rise until doubled and bake at 425° about 12 minutes or until rich gold. Cool on cake rack.

Crescent Rolls (Croissants)

¾ C scalded milk
1 pkg granular yeast
2 tsp sugar
½ C lukewarm water
6 Tbsp sugar (second amount)
5 Tbsp shortening
1 Tbsp salt
4 C sifted all-purpose flour
2 eggs (one for dough, one for brushing tops)

Scald milk on low heat. Into large mixing bowl tip yeast, add the 2 tsp sugar and lukewarm water, give them one stir and let soak 10 minutes. Remove scalded milk from heat and to it add the shortening and salt and stir and cool to lukewarm. Add to risen yeast liquid. Add 3 C of the sifted flour and one egg and stir and beat to mix as well as you can. Then add remaining 1 C sifted flour and stir in until all loose flour is incorporated. Scrape down sides of bowl, cover and let rise, perhaps 4 hours. *Note:* This is refrigerator dough and may be tightly covered and refrigerated as long as 2 or 3 days.

Punch down dough and knead on generously floured board 50 to 100 times. Divide into 3 equal portions. Shape each into ball and roll out each to 9" circle. Brush lightly with melted butter. Cut into 8 triangles. Roll up each triangle beginning at outside edge. Place on buttered cookie sheets points down. Curve ends in to make a crescent. At this stage brush with one egg mixed with 1 Tbsp cold water. Let rise until risen and puffy, about 1 to 1½ hours. Bake at 400° about 12 to 15 minutes. Serve warm if possible.

Homemade Crusty Rolls

1 pkg granular yeast
¼ C lukewarm water
1 tsp sugar (first amount)
1 Tbsp salt
1 Tbsp sugar (second amount)
2 Tbsp shortening (room temperature)
2 egg whites
¾ C lukewarm water
About 4 C sifted all-purpose flour
    (divided, see below)

In a large mixing bowl soak the yeast with the 1 tsp sugar in the ¼ C lukewarm water for 10 minutes. Then add the salt, sugar, shortening, egg whites and the ¾ C lukewarm water. Stir a little, then beat in 3 C of the sifted flour. Sprinkle board with half of the remaining flour. (Reserve remaining ½ C flour for second kneading later.) Knead 200 times, working the flour on board into dough. Dough should be smooth and elastic. Grease mixing bowl and return dough to it to rise, covered, at room temperature, until more than doubled, about 1½ to 2 hours. Punch down dough and knead 50 times on board sprinkled with remaining flour. Let rise again in bowl until doubled, about 1 to 1½ hours.

On lightly floured board punch down and knead 25 times. Shape into long roll under palms. Cut into 18 or 20 even pieces. Shape into round smooth balls about 2" or 2½" in diameter. Let rise 2" apart on greased baking sheets until doubled, about 1 to 1½ hours. Put large shallow waterpan in bottom of oven containing ½" boiling water. Bake rolls on center shelf of oven at 450° for 15 to 20 minutes. As soon as removed from oven drop into Hot Glaze Mixture: Mix 4 tsp cornstarch into 1½ cups cold water and stir until boiling and slightly thickened. Drain rolls a little, put back on baking sheets. Return to oven for about 5 minutes to dry glaze until shiny.

Bow Knot Rolls

1 C fresh smoothly mashed potatoes
2 pkg granular yeast
1 tsp sugar
½ C lukewarm water
1 C scalded milk
¾ C shortening
¼ C sugar
2 tsp salt
4½ C sifted all-purpose flour

Cook until tender 3 medium small potatoes to get 1 C mashed potatoes. Soak yeast in the lukewarm water with 1 tsp sugar for 10 minutes, giving it one stir at first. Add shortening, sugar and salt to the scalded milk and let cool to lukewarm. Add risen yeast liquid to the milk mixture and beat in 1 C of the sifted flour along with the mashed potatoes until smooth. Beat in 3 more cups sifted flour as well as you can, then turn dough out on board floured with ¼ C of the remaining flour and knead 100 times. Put in greased bowl, cover and let rise at room temperature until more than doubled.

Flour board with remaining ¼ C flour and punch down dough on it and knead 100 times until smooth and elastic. Divide dough in half. Break off pieces of dough the size of large walnuts and, to make bow knots, roll dough between palms into strips about 8" long and tie each into a single knot. Place on greased baking sheet. Proceed the same with remaining half of dough, placing bow knots at least 2" apart. Let rise at room temperature until light and nearly doubled. Bake at 400° about 15 to 20 minutes. Serve hot if possible.

Brioche

In this recipe the raw dough requires overnight refrigeration.

½ C scalded milk
½ C lukewarm water
1 tsp sugar
1 pkg granular yeast
½ C butter
⅓ C sugar
½ tsp salt
3 eggs
1 egg, separated
3½ C sifted all-purpose flour

Scald milk and cool to lukewarm. In big mixing bowl soak the yeast in the lukewarm water with the sugar for 10 minutes. Stir. Meanwhile cream the butter and shortening until light, gradually adding the sugar and salt.

Add the lukewarm milk to the soaked and stirred yeast liquid. Mix. Add creamed butter and sugar and mix and stir. (It will curdle but disregard.) Now add 1½ C of the sifted flour, 3 whole eggs and 1 yolk. (Reserve 1 egg white for glazing later.) Beat for 5 minutes. Beat in remaining 2 C sifted flour and, bravely, stir this stiff dough for 5 minutes. Scrape down from sides of bowl. Cover with damp cloth and let rise until doubled about 2 hours. Cover snugly with foil and put in refrigerator overnight.

Next day stir down and turn out soft dough on lighly floured board. Cut off about ¼ of the dough and set aside. Cut larger portion of dough into 18 equal pieces. Form into smooth balls. Place in well greased muffin pans. Cut smaller portion of dough into 18 equal pieces. Form these too into smooth balls, and, if desired, roll to coat in sesame seeds or finely chopped walnuts. Make a deep indentation in center of each large ball, dampen slightly with cold water, and press small balls into the indentations. Cover. Let rise in warm place free from drafts until more than doubled in bulk, about 1½ hours. Carefully brush with mixture of 1 egg white slightly beaten and 1 Tbsp sugar. Bake at 375° for 15 to 20 minutes.

Poppy or Sesame Seed Twists

1 pkg granular yeast
½ C lukewarm water
1 tsp sugar
2 Tbsp shortening
2 Tbsp sugar
2 tsp salt
⅔ C milk, scalded
1 egg
3½ C sifted all-purpose flour
Various seeds (see below)

Add the 1 tsp sugar to the lukewarm water and soften yeast in it for 10 minutes. Add shortening, sugar and salt to scalded milk in large bowl. Cool to lukewarm and add yeast liquid and beaten egg. Stir. Stir in flour until dough is smooth. Turn out on floured board and knead until satiny and smooth, about 300 times. Return to greased bowl, cover and let rise until doubled in bulk.

Punch down dough and roll out to ¼" thickness. Cut into strips ½" wide, and 6" long. Cross 3 strips in the middle and braid from center to each end. Press ends together and fold under. Brush tops with melted butter, then sprinkle generously some with poppy, some with sesame seeds. Place on greased baking sheet, and let rise until doubled in bulk. Bake at 425° for 12 or 15 minutes.

Cream and Sugar Twists

1 pkg granular yeast
¼ C lukewarm water
2 tsp sugar
4 C sifted all-purpose flour
1 tsp salt
1 C margarine or butter
1 tsp rum flavoring (or vanilla)
2 tsp lemon juice
2 tsp grated lemon rind
2 eggs
1 C dairy sour cream (room temperature)
¾ C light raisins or chopped candied pineapple
½ C sugar

In a large bowl soak yeast and 2 tsp sugar in lukewarm water 10 minutes. In another large bowl cut margarine or butter into flour and salt with pastry blender or 2 knives until size of peas.

To the risen yeast liquid add the flavoring, lemon juice, lemon rind, eggs, sour cream and raisins or pineapple and beat to blend. Now beat in flour mixture by hand for 5 minutes as well as you can. Cover and let rise for 4 hours or overnight in refrigerator. (This dough does not rise much.)

Now flour kneading board lightly. Sprinkle it with a little of the ¼ C sugar. Turn dough out and roll to a 14" square. Sprinkle dough with a little more sugar and fold dough over from each side to form 3 layers. Sprinkle with sugar and roll out again. Repeat folding, sugar sprinkling and rolling once more until all sugar is used up. Cut into strips 1 × 4". With floured fingers give each strip a couple of twists like a loose rope and place on unbuttered cookie sheets 2" apart. Bake at 350° about 15 to 20 minutes or until gold. Remove from pan with spatula. Serve warm. Makes forty.

Cheese Puffs

PASTE
⅓ C butter
1 C water
½ tsp salt
1 C sifted all-purpose flour
¼ tsp nutmeg
⅛ tsp pepper
1 C shredded Edam or Gouda cheese
4 eggs (room temperature)

TOPPING (optional)
1 egg
1 tsp water
Sesame seeds

Into a medium-large pot measure the butter, water and salt and bring to boil. Add flour, nutmeg and pepper all at once and stir as fast as possible with wooden spoon until mixture surrounds spoon and no longer sticks to sides. Remove from heat and stir in cheese then beat in eggs, one at a time, beating thoroughly between additions. Spoon up dessertspoonfuls of paste and with another spoon push off onto foil-covered greased baking sheet, at least 2" apart to allow for spreading. If topping is used beat egg with water and brush tops of unbaked puffs with it and sprinkle with sesame seeds. Bake at 450° at center of oven for 10 minutes then reduce heat to 350° and bake about 25 minutes longer. To test for doneness remove one puff from oven to see if it retains its full height. If it collapses at center bake remaining puffs longer until crust will retain its shape. *Note:* Do not spoon remaining dough onto baking sheets until just before first pan is baked.

Baked Crumpets

1 pkg granular yeast
½ C lukewarm water
1 tsp sugar
1½ C warm milk
2 Tbsp butter
2 tsp sugar (second amount)
½ tsp salt
Grated rind of 1 orange
2 eggs
3½ C sifted all-purpose flour
1 C barely thawed fresh frozen blueberries (optional)

In a large bowl soak yeast and 1 tsp sugar in lukewarm water 15 minutes.

To warm milk add the butter, 2 tsp sugar, salt and orange rind and stir to dissolve. Add to risen yeast liquid and beat in, then beat in eggs and flour until batter is perfectly smooth. Let rise 15 minutes. If desired add 1 C blueberries.

Now have ready greased muffin pans. (Genuine crumpet rings are hard to find but many a good crumpet has been made as follows.) Spoon batter in, filling ⅔ full and bake at 400° for 15 to 18 minutes, time depending on thickness of crumpet. Serve hot with butter or when cold split and toast and serve with marmalade or jam.

Sticky Pecan Buns

These quantities make 2 large pans of pecan rolls and one muffin pan full of clover leaf rolls.

2½ C milk (divided)
¾ C butter or margarine
1 pkg granular yeast
1 tsp sugar (first amount)
½ C lukewarm water
½ C sugar (second amount)
2 eggs
7 C unsifted all-purpose flour
2½ tsp salt
Cinnamon

GLAZE
1 C light brown sugar
¼ C soft butter
2½ Tbsp light corn syrup
6 oz whole pecans (1½ C)

Heat the milk to scalding. In a very large mixing bowl measure ½ C butter or margarine, ½ C sugar and the salt. Pour scalded milk over them and let cool to lukewarm. Add the 1 tsp sugar and ½ C lukewarm water to the yeast in a measuring cup and give it one stir and let stand 10 minutes. When milk mixture is cool add yeast liquid. Beat the eggs a little and add them and the flour. Mix with wooden spoon, then turn out on floured board and knead 100 times, adding more flour to board as needed. Shape into ball, return to greased bowl, turn dough to grease all sides, cover and let rise in warm place until doubled and light.

Punch down dough on floured board and knead 200 times. Cut off a piece of the dough that amounts to about one-fifth of it. Cut remaining dough in halves. With rolling pin roll out one of these large pieces into an oblong ¼" thick. Spread it with half of remaining ¼ C of melted butter and sprinkle liberally with cinnamon. roll up like jelly roll, starting at long side. Stretch this roll to lengthen it and slice it into 1¼" thick pinwheels. Place these close together in pans prepared with glaze.

GLAZE: Mix together over low heat, barely enough to blend, the brown sugar, soft butter and corn syrup. As soon as blended remove from heat. Cover bottoms of two 8" round pans with whole pecans. Drizzle glaze over nuts and arrange cut-out pinwheels, cut side down, on top of glaze. Repeat with second large piece of dough, the rolling out, spreading etc., and place in second pan. Cover and let rise about 1½ hours in warm place. Bake at 400° rather high in oven for 10 minutes, then reduce heat to 375° for another 15 minutes or until done.

The small piece of leftover dough may be made up into cloverleaf rolls (using a 12-cup muffin pan) or into 12 Parkerhouse or Poppy Seed Rolls.

Eveready Rolls

½ C lukewarm water
1 tsp sugar (first amount)
1 pkg yeast
¼ C shortening (room temperature)
⅓ C sugar (second amount)
1 egg
1½ C water
5 C unsifted all-purpose flour
1 tsp salt
1 tsp baking powder

In a one-cup measure dissolve the 1 tsp sugar in the ½ C lukewarm water. Sprinkle over yeast and let stand 10 minutes. Stir down with spoon.

In the meantime in large bowl combine the shortening, ⅓ C sugar and egg and mix as well as possible. Stir in yeast mixture, 1½ C water, flour, salt and baking powder to thoroughly combine. Turn dough out onto board floured with about ¼ C flour. Knead 8 to 10 minutes or 250 times. This dough is very sticky and will stick to board but do not add more flour. Put dough in medium sized, greased bowl and rotate to grease all surfaces. Cover top of dough and refrigerate.

When needed, grease a round or square 9" pan. Dough will rise a little so punch it down. Break off pieces and roll into balls about 2" in diameter between floured palms. Place 7 balls around outside of pan and one in center about ¾" apart. Let warm to room temperature and then rise until doubled and touching, about 2½ hours. Bake at 400° for 10 to 12 minutes. Remove from oven and immediately brush tops with melted butter.

Hamburg Buns

1 pkg (1 Tbsp) granular yeast
1 tsp sugar (first amount)
½ C lukewarm water
½ C scalded milk
2 Tbsp shortening
¼ C sugar (second amount)
1 tsp salt
1 egg
3 C sifted all-purpose flour
   (divided, see below)

In a large bowl soak the yeast and the 1 tsp sugar in the lukewarm water 10 minutes. To the scalded milk add the shortening, sugar and salt and stir to melt and dissolve and cool to lukewarm. Add to risen yeast liquid along with 2 C of the flour and the egg and beat to mix well. Add another ½ C flour, mix in as well as you can, cover and let rise 2 hours.

Stir down dough, turn out on board floured with remaining ½ cup and knead 100 times, using up any remaining flour as you knead. Shape into a 16" long roll, cut into 12 even pieces. Shape each into a smooth ball and place on 2 greased cookie sheets about 4" apart and flatten with your palm to make them about ¼" thick. Let rise until size of hamburg buns. Bake at 425° about 10 to 12 minutes or until golden. To keep the top surface soft brush sparingly with milk as soon as buns are removed from oven. Serve while warm.

Eveready Whole Wheat Buns

½ C lukewarm water
1 tsp sugar (first amount)
1 pkg granular yeast
¼ C shortening (room temperature)
2½ Tbsp granulated sugar
3½ Tbsp brown sugar
1 egg
1½ C water
2 C unsifted all-purpose flour
3 C whole wheat flour
1 tsp salt
1 tsp baking powder

In a one-cup measure dissolve the 1 tsp sugar in the ½ C lukewarm water. Sprinkle over yeast and let stand 10 minutes. Stir down with spoon.

Meanwhile in a large bowl combine the shortening, sugars and egg and mix as well as possible. Stir in yeast mixture, 1½ C water, flours, salt and baking powder to thoroughly combine. Turn dough out onto board floured with about ¼ C all-purpose flour. Knead 8 to 10 minutes or about 250 times. This dough is very sticky and will stick to counter or board and your hands but do not be tempted to add more flour. Put dough in medium sized, greased bowl and rotate to grease all surfaces. If to be refrigerated, cover top of dough snugly and refrigerate. When needed grease a round or square 9″ pan and use one-third of the dough, saving remainder for another day.

Break off pieces and roll into balls about 1¾ to 2″ diameter, between floured palms. Place 7 balls around inside edge of pan and one in center, all about ¾″ apart. Let warm to room temperature and then let rise until doubled and touching, about 2 to 2½ hours. Bake at 400° for 10 to 12 minutes. Remove from oven and immediately brush tops with melted butter and tip into napkin-lined basket and serve hot.

Hot Cross Buns

¾ C milk, scalded
½ C granulated sugar (first amount)
1 tsp salt
¼ C butter or margarine
1 tsp granulated sugar (second amount)
½ C lukewarm water
1 envelope or Tbsp granular yeast
2 large eggs, beaten (room temperature)
2½ tsp cinnamon
¾ tsp cloves
¼ tsp nutmeg
4½ to 4¾ C unsifted all-purpose flour
    (divided, see below)
1 C fresh raisins or currants
1 C mixed peel

Pour scalded milk into a large bowl, add the ½ C sugar, salt and butter or margarine and stir until dissolved and cooled to lukewarm.

In a one-cup measure dissolve the 1 tsp sugar in the lukewarm water. Sprinkle yeast over top and let stand for 10 to 12 minutes or until yeast has risen to top of cup, then stir it well with a fork. Add the softened yeast to the lukewarm milk mixture and stir to blend. Stir in the eggs, cinnamon, cloves and nutmeg. Beat in 2 C of the flour and

raisins or currants and mixed peel. Add another 2 C flour and work it into the dough. Turn out on floured surface and using the remaining ½ to ¾ C flour, knead 8 to 10 minutes or 200 to 250 times. Shape into a smooth ball and place in a large greased bowl. Rotate the dough around in the bowl so the complete surface of the dough is greased. Cover with a damp towel and top that with a plate and let rise until doubled in bulk, about 1½ hours. When dough has risen punch it down. Place dough on flat surface and shape into an 18″ roll. Cut off 18 even pieces and roll each into a ball between palms. Place on greased cookie sheets 2″ apart, 9 on each. Let rise again, uncovered, until doubled in size, about 2 hours. Preheat oven to 400°. Bake buns 10 minutes. When done, place on racks to cool and immediately brush them, top and sides, with a Glaze: In a saucepan combine 4 Tbsp icing sugar and ¾ C water. Bring to boil and simmer 3 minutes. This gives the buns a shiny finish. When cool, store in plastic bags.

Pineapple Danish

1 pkg granular yeast
1 tsp sugar
½ C lukewarm water
2½ C sifted all-purpose flour
1 tsp salt
2 Tbsp sugar
¼ lb hard butter
¼ lb hard margarine
1 egg

FILLING
¾ C pineapple jam
Red jam (see below)

In large bowl soak yeast and sugar in lukewarm water 10 minutes. In a mixing bowl combine flour, salt and sugar. Shred hard butter and margarine into them on ¼″ shredder. With 2 knives mix them in with a chopping motion. It should be lumpy. Add egg to risen yeast liquid and stir. Add flour mixture and stir as well as you can. Dough is stiff. Scrape down sides, cover, and chill 1 hour.

Now flour your board and roll out dough to 20 × 15″ rectangle. Cut into three 5″ wide strips. Spread ¼ C pineapple jam in a 1″ wide strip down full length of each at center. Moisten one edge. Cover pineapple filling with dry side. Overlap damp side to seal. Cut each strip into 6 pieces. Slash 3 times to within ½″ of edges. Spread-eagle on 3 buttered cookie sheets to look like four-pointed stars. Brush tops with 1 egg beaten with 1 Tbsp water. Let rise 1 hour. Bake at 425° about 10 minutes. Switch pans in oven at halftime.

Loosen from pans while hot as the pineapple filling tends to stick. Cool on racks. Fill centers with ¼ tsp strawberry or raspberry jam. Frost corners with plain icing made with 1 C icing sugar and 3½ tsp warm water. These should be served warm.

Prune Danish

1 pkg granular yeast
½ C lukewarm water
1 tsp sugar
2½ C sifted all-purpose flour
1 tsp salt
2 Tbsp sugar
½ lb hard butter shredded (see below)
1 egg
¾ C Prune Purée (see below)
Red jam

In large mixing bowl soak yeast with the 1 tsp sugar in the lukewarm water 10 minutes. Into another bowl measure the sifted flour and add the salt and 2 Tbsp sugar. Into this flour mixture shred the hard butter on ¼" shredder and mix it in evenly. It will be lumpy. To risen yeast liquid add the egg, beat a little then add flour-butter mixture and stir with strong spoon until evenly blended, scrape down sides of bowl, cover and chill dough 1 hour.

To make Prune Purée, stew 1½ C prunes in a little water covered until soft. Drain. Remove pits and force through sieve. Add ¼ C sugar, 1 tsp cinnamon. Stir over heat until thick and reduced to ¾ C. Cool.

Turn chilled dough out on well-floured board and roll out to 24 × 14" rectangle. Cut lengthwise into 3 even strips. Spread prune purée about 1" wide at center down entire length of each strip. Moisten one bare edge. Fold dry side over prune filling. Cover with moistened side. Cut each strip into 6 even pieces. With sharp knife slash each piece to within ½" of edges. Transfer to 3 buttered cookie sheets and spread-eagle each piece to look like a four-pointed star. Brush tops with one egg beaten with 1 Tbsp cold water. Let rise one hour at room temperature. Bake at 425° for 10 to 12 minutes. At this high heat these bake quickly and pans should be turned in oven and switched on shelves. Do not overbake. Dot center with red jam. Brush points with plain icing.

Pineapple or Raspberry Danish

1 pkg (Tbsp) granular yeast
1 tsp sugar
½ C lukewarm water
2¾ C sifted all-purpose flour (divided)
1 tsp salt
2 Tbsp sugar
½ lb hard butter
1 egg
¾ C pineapple or raspberry jam

In large mixing bowl soak the yeast and 1 tsp sugar in the lukewarm water 10 minutes. Meanwhile measure 2½ C of the sifted flour, salt and 2 Tbsp sugar into another mixing bowl. Into it shred the hard butter on ¼" shredder and mix it into the flour with a fork.

To risen yeast liquid add the egg and mix in. Then add the flour-butter mixture and with strong spoon combine as well as you can. Dough will be lumpy. Scrape down sides of bowl and chill 1 hour. Then sprinkle kneading board with remaining ¼ C flour and turn dough out. Flatten a little and turn over to flour other side. Now roll out to oblong 24 × 14". Cut into 3 even lengthwise strips. At center spread each with a 1" wide strip of pineapple or raspberry jam. (Be sparing or the jam will bubble out when baked.)

Moisten one bare edge. Cover jam with dry side. Cover that with moistened edge. Cut each folded strip into 6 even pieces, making 18 in all. Make 3 sharp slashes to within ½" of far side of each piece. Transfer to 3 buttered cookie sheets spread-eagling each pastry to look like a 4-pointed star. Brush tops neatly with 1 egg beaten with 1 Tbsp water. Let rise 1 hour at room temperature then bake at 425° for 10 minutes. Serve warm.

Butterfly Buns

1 pkg granular yeast
1 tsp sugar
¼ C lukewarm water
1 C scalded milk
¼ C shortening
¼ C sugar
¾ tsp salt
2 eggs
About 3½ C stirred but unsifted
    all-purpose flour

In beater bowl soak yeast and 1 tsp sugar in lukewarm water for 10 minutes. To scalded milk add shortening, sugar and salt and stir to melt and dissolve. Cool to lukewarm and add to risen yeast liquid. Beat in along with eggs. Add 2 C of the flour and beat 5 minutes. Add 1 more cup of the flour and mix in as well as you can with heavy spoon.

Sprinkle board with remaining ½ C flour and turn dough out on it and knead 50 times. (Leave leftover flour on board for kneading later.) Return to scraped down bowl, oil top, cover well and let rise at least 2 hours.

Turn out on floured board, knead 50 times again. Roll out into a ¼" thick sheet 18 × 14". Cut dough in half lengthwise. Brush both halves with melted butter. Roll each up like a jelly roll. Stretch them to about 10" lengths and cut each into 12 slices. Place on 2 greased baking sheets. Now to make the butterfly shape, make a deep indentation across center of each roll with the handle of a wooden spoon. Let rise about 1 hour. Bake at 375° for 20 to 25 minutes. Serve warm. Makes 2 dozen.

Chelsea Buns

TOPPING
¼ C butter or margarine
¾ C brown sugar, packed
3 Tbsp corn syrup
¾ C chopped nuts

DOUGH
½ C milk
½ C sugar (first amount)
¼ C shortening
2 tsp salt
½ C warm water
1 pkg granular yeast
2 tsp sugar (second amount)
3 C unsifted all-purpose flour
   (divided, see below)
1 egg

FILLING
2 Tbsp melted butter
½ C brown sugar
Cinnamon (see below)
¼ C chopped nuts
½ C chopped glacé cherries (optional)
½ C raisins

In a heavy pot combine all Topping ingredients and stir until butter is melted and ingredients are well combined. Spread evenly in bottom of an 8 × 12″ pan. Set aside.

To make Dough, in a small pot scald milk. Add the ½ C sugar, shortening or butter and salt and stir until sugar dissolves and butter melts. Cool to lukewarm. Measure warm water in a 1 C measure and stir in the 2 tsp sugar. Sprinkle yeast over, stir and let soak 10 minutes. In large bowl combine the lukewarm milk mixture with the yeast liquid. Add 2 C of the flour and the egg and stir until smooth. Stir in remaining 1 C flour thoroughly. (Dough will be slightly sticky.) Turn dough out onto well floured board and roll to a 12 × 18″ rectangle.

To prepare Filling, melt butter and brush over surface of dough. Sprinkle brown sugar over dough evenly and press down. Sprinkle entire surface lightly with cinnamon then sprinkle evenly over it the nuts, cherries (if used) and raisins. Start rolling dough up like a jelly roll, starting at longest side. Cut into 1″ slices and arrange cut side up on top of topping in pan. Space them, because they will join together as they rise. Let rise 2 hours at room temperature. Bake at 375° for 25 minutes. Let cool 2 or 3 minutes only. Then loosen with a lifter and turn over and out on rack to cool with caramel topping side up.

Quick Breads

Pumpkin Spice Loaf see page 163

Date and Nut Bread

1 tsp baking soda
1 C well-packed stoned chopped dates
1 C boiling water
3 Tbsp butter
1 C sugar
1 egg
1 tsp vanilla
1 C stirred but unsifted cake
    and pastry flour
1 C whole wheat flour
1 tsp baking powder
⅛ tsp salt
½ C chopped walnuts

Add baking soda to dates, pour boiling water over, mix and let stand. Cream the butter and sugar together well, then beat in egg and vanilla. Mix flours, baking powder and salt and add to creamed mixture alternately with the soaked dates. Add chopped walnuts and mix well. Bake in buttered, paper-lined loaf pan at 350° for 55 to 60 minutes. Slices and freezes well.

Glazed Pineapple Loaf

⅔ C canned diced pineapple, drained
    (save the syrup, see below)
¼ C butter
¾ C sugar
1 large egg, beaten
1⅔ C sifted all-purpose flour
3 tsp baking powder
1 tsp salt
¾ C milk
1 tsp grated lemon rind
1 tsp vanilla
2 Tbsp syrup (drained from canned pineapple)
1 Tbsp sugar

Prepare pineapple first by draining and drying on paper towels. Reserve 2 Tbsp of the syrup for the glaze and store remaining syrup for making a jelly or fruit cup at a future meal.

Into large bowl measure the butter and sugar and cream by hand until blended. Beat in egg. Sift together flour, baking powder and salt. In a measuring cup combine milk, lemon rind and vanilla. Add the flour mixture alternately with the milk mixture, to the butter-sugar mixture, stirring by hand until just blended. Do not overstir: batter should be slightly lumpy. Fold in pineapple, patted dry.

Turn into buttered loaf pan and bake at 350° for 45 to 50 minutes. Cool on cake rack in pan 10 minutes then turn out with top side up. Drizzle with mixture of 2 Tbsp pineapple syrup and 1 Tbsp sugar to give a shiny glaze. Cool completely on rack.

Raisin Loaf

2 C raisins
3 C boiling water
2 Tbsp butter or margarine
2 C granulated sugar
2 eggs, beaten
5½ C sifted all-purpose flour
1 tsp salt
4 tsp baking soda

In saucepan boil raisins in boiling water for 10 minutes and cool. While cooling mix butter or margarine, sugar and beaten eggs. Sift together flour, salt and baking soda. Add to butter mixture. Then add raisin mixture. Grease 2 standard loaf pans and divide batter evenly into them. Bake at 325° for 1 hour. If a soft crust is desired line pans with wax paper.

Cherry Loaf Cake

1 C butter (room temperature)
1 C white sugar
2 large eggs, unbeaten and cold
2 C unsifted all-purpose flour
    (divided, see below)
½ tsp salt
1 tsp baking powder
½ C cold milk
½ tsp pure vanilla extract
1 C red glacé cherries, chopped

Note: Do all mixing by hand and beat only enough to blend.

In large bowl cream together butter and sugar until well blended. Add eggs and mix just to blend. In medium-sized bowl combine 1¾ C of the flour, salt and baking powder and stir to combine them. Add half flour mixture to the creamed mixture and stir just enough to blend. Add all of the milk, mix in well then add the other half of the flour mixture, each time stirring only enough to have all ingredients well blended. Stir in vanilla. Dredge chopped cherries in the remaining ¼ C flour until as much flour as possible clings to them. Remove the cherries and discard the leftover flour. Line a standard loaf pan with 2 layers of foil, shiny side up, having foil overlapping pan at ends to ease removal. Spoon in ⅓ of the batter pushing it into corners and sprinkle with ⅓ of the cherries. Spoon in another third of the batter and cover it with another third of the cherries. Spoon the remaining batter in smoothing it and making sure it is pushed well into all corners. Sprinkle remaining cherries on top and press them down into the batter with the palm of your hand. Cover the top of the loaf pan with a layer of foil, shiny side up. Bake at 300° for 2 hours low in the oven. Also place an 8 × 8" cake tin, ¾ full of hot water, beside the loaf pan on the same shelf in the oven and leave it for the whole 2 hours of baking time. Remove covering foil 15 minutes before baking time is up. When cake is done, remove from oven and holding overlapping foil, lift it from loaf pan immediately. In about 5 minutes peel off foil from cake.

Apricot-Orange Loaf Cake

1 C butter (room temperature)
1 C white sugar
2 extra large eggs, unbeaten and cold
2 C unsifted all-purpose flour
    (divided, see below)
½ tsp salt
1 tsp baking powder
½ C orange juice
6 oz or 1 C soft dried apricots
    (chopped into quarters)

Note: Do all mixing by hand and beat only enough to blend.

In large bowl cream together butter and sugar until well blended. Add eggs and mix just to blend. In medium-sized bowl combine 1¾ C of the flour, salt and baking powder and stir to combine them. Add half flour mixture to the creamed mixture and stir just enough to blend. Add all of the orange juice, mix in well then add the other half of the flour mixture, each time stirring only enough to have all ingredients well blended. Cut the apricots into quarters and dredge in the remaining ¼ C flour until as much flour as possible clings to them. Remove the apricots and discard leftover flour. Stir in apricots. Line a standard loaf pan with 2 layers of foil, shiny side up, having foil overlapping pan at ends to ease removal. Spoon batter in, pushing it into corners. Cover the top of the loaf pan with a layer of foil, shiny side up. Bake at 300° for 2 hours low in the oven. Also place an 8 × 8″ cake tin, ¾ full of hot water, beside the loaf pan on the same shelf in the oven and leave it for the whole 2 hours of baking time. When cake is done, remove from oven and holding overlapping foil, lift it from loaf pan immediately. In about 5 minutes peel off foil from cake and cool loaf on wire cake rack.

Zucchini Zip Loaves

3 eggs
1 C oil
2 C sugar
1 tsp vanilla
2 C washed finely shredded, unpared zucchini,
    well packed
1½ C cake and pastry flour
1 C whole wheat flour
    (preferably stone ground)
½ C wheat germ
1 tsp salt
2 tsp nutmeg
1 tsp baking soda
½ tsp baking powder
½ C chopped nuts

In beater bowl beat together eggs, oil, sugar, vanilla and finely shredded zucchini. Now with beaters on low begin adding all remaining ingredients as you measure them. This batter is quite thin.

Double-wax-paper-line 2 loaf pans and butter the wax paper. Pour the batter in to about ⅔ full. Bake at 325° for 1 hour. Turn out on racks, peel off wax paper. Cool. Freeze one and use one for current meal.

Pumpkin Spice Loaf

3 C sifted all-purpose flour
2 tsp baking powder
2 tsp baking soda
1 tsp salt
2 tsp cinnamon
1½ tsp ginger
1 tsp nutmeg
1 tsp cloves
4 eggs
1½ C sugar
½ C corn syrup
1 C oil
2 C canned pumpkin or your own
    pumpkin purée
1 C raisins
1 C chopped nuts (divided, see below)

Sift together the sifted flour, baking powder, baking soda, salt and spices. In large beater bowl beat eggs until light, gradually adding sugar. Add corn syrup, oil and pumpkin and beat well. Remove beaters and fold in sifted flour mixture until batter is smooth. Add raisins and ¾ C nuts.

Line 2 standard loaf pans with buttered wax paper and turn batter into them. Sprinkle tops with remaining nuts. Bake at 325° about 65 minutes. Test for doneness by inserting toothpick at center. If it comes out dry loaf is done. The loaves crack a little on top but this does no harm. Turn out on cake racks to cool, peeling off wax paper. Cool completely. Freeze one and store for future use. Use sharp knife to slice cooled loaf.

Steamed Boston Brown Bread

1 C unsifted all-purpose flour
1 C unsifted whole wheat flour
1 C cornmeal
½ C sugar
1 tsp baking soda
1½ tsp salt
1 C seedless raisins
½ C molasses
1½ C buttermilk
2 Tbsp melted shortening

This requires only one mixing bowl. Mix together the flour, whole wheat flour, cornmeal, sugar, soda and salt. Stir in the raisins to flour them well. Add molasses and buttermilk and stir well. Add shortening and stir well.

Have ready three 20-oz empty tin cans (or four 15-oz) well-buttered, using your fingers to butter them carefully. Fill cans no more than ⅔ full. Cover amply with aluminum foil and tie with string securely. Steam 3 hours in covered steamer on rack in 2″ of water. Cool in cans, then untie and remove foil. With can opener remove bottom of can and gently push loaf out. Allow surfaces to dry off a little uncovered before wrapping and, if you wish, storing in the refrigerator.

Red River Pumpernickel

½ C molasses (or malt extract)
3 C hot water (just below boiling point)
3 C Red River Cereal
1 C whole wheat flour
2 tsp baking soda
1 tsp salt

In your 2-cup measure put the ½ C molasses then pour it into the beater bowl. Now in same measure (to rinse out the molasses) put the almost boiling water and add it. Mix together the Red River Cereal, whole wheat flour, baking soda and salt and add them and beat hard for 2 minutes. Cover very well and let stand 2 hours or overnight. Do not refrigerate.

Grease, paper-line and butter a standard loaf pan. Turn in batter and smooth top. Bake at 275° for 1 hour then reduce temperature to 250° for 1 hour longer.

Festive Fruit Bread

½ C butter or margarine (room temperature)
½ C light brown sugar (packed)
½ C corn syrup
2 eggs
1 C smooth applesauce
1 C raisins
1 C mixed fruit cake fruits
2¼ C unsifted all-purpose flour
3 tsp baking powder
½ tsp salt
1 tsp cinnamon
½ tsp nutmeg
¼ tsp ground cloves

Butter a standard 9 × 5″ loaf pan. Line with buttered wax paper. In bowl cream together butter and sugar. Stir in corn syrup. Add eggs, blending until fairly smooth. Stir in applesauce, raisins and mixed fruit cake fruits.

In another bowl stir together flour, baking powder, salt, cinnamon, nutmeg and cloves. Add to creamed mixture and mix until thoroughly combined and smooth. Turn into prepared pan, push into corners and smooth top. Bake at 350° for 1¼ hours or until done when tested with toothpick.

Rhubarb Loaf

2 C finely diced rhubarb (preferably red)
¼ C sugar (first amount)
3 C unsifted all-purpose flour
4½ tsp baking powder
1 tsp salt
1 C sugar (second amount)
1 Tbsp grated orange rind (optional)
½ C chopped nuts (optional)
1 egg
¼ C melted butter or margarine
½ C orange juice

Mix rhubarb and ¼ C sugar in bowl and let stand while preparing batter. In bowl combine flour, baking powder, salt, 1 C sugar, orange rind and nuts (if used).

Combine egg, butter and orange juice and stir into dry ingredients until blended. Fold in rhubarb. Turn into triple wax-paper-lined greased standard loaf pan. Bake at 350° for 1 hour. Cool on cake rack in pan 10 minutes. Turn out and peel off wax paper and cool to room temperature. If desired wrap and freeze.

Christmas Fruit Loaf

½ C butter or margarine
1 C granulated or icing sugar
     (first amount)
2 eggs
1½ C stirred but unsifted
     all-purpose flour
½ tsp baking powder
½ tsp salt
½ C milk
½ tsp almond extract
½ C mixed glacé fruits
½ C coarsely chopped almonds
2 Tbsp lemon juice
¼ C sugar (second amount)

Into beater bowl measure the butter or margarine and the sugar. Beat until light. Beat in eggs, scraping down sides of beater bowl with rubber spatula and continue beating in eggs for a minute. While beaters are on low add flour, baking powder, salt, milk and almond extract and beat until blended. Lift beaters and fold in fruits and nuts.

Double line loaf pan with wax paper, brushing top sheet with butter. Push batter well into corners. Bake on center shelf at 350° for 45 minutes. *Note:* If in pyrex pan, after 30 minutes' baking insert a cookie sheet under pan to protect bottom from overbaking.

The loaf cracks on top but this is part of its charm for you now brush it with a glaze: As soon as loaf is removed from oven slowly brush it all over with a mixture of the lemon juice and sugar (second amount). Use it all. Cool in pan. Remove from pan and chill before slicing. If desired wrap and freeze.

Banana Fruit Bread

⅓ C margarine or shortening
⅔ C granulated sugar
2 large eggs
4 medium bananas diced (1½ to 1¾ C)
1¾ C unsifted all-purpose flour
2¾ tsp baking powder
½ tsp cinnamon
⅛ tsp nutmeg
½ tsp salt
1 C chopped nuts
1 C candied mixed fruit cake fruits
¼ C raisins (optional)

In beater bowl cream together margarine or shortening and sugar until light. Add eggs and beat well. Mix in banana chunks and continue beating until almost all lumps of banana disappear.

In another bowl combine flour, baking powder, cinnamon, nutmeg and salt then add to creamed mixture and beat until thoroughly combined. Remove beaters. Stir in nuts, mixed fruits and raisins (if used). Spoon into a standard loaf pan, triple-lined with buttered wax paper. Bake at 350° for 1½ hours, placing a small pan of water in bottom of oven as you would for fruit cakes. Remove from oven and let rest in pan on cake rack about 30 minutes, then remove from pan, carefully peel off wax paper and let cool completely on rack. Store in plastic bag in refrigerator or wrap and freeze.

Date Orange Nut Loaf

1 large orange unpeeled cut up
2 C dates (packed before grinding)
2 C boiling water
2 tsp baking soda
2 Tbsp butter or margarine
2 tsp vanilla
2 C brown sugar
3 C sifted all-purpose flour
½ tsp salt
2 eggs
1 C broken nuts

Put orange and dates through grinder catching all juice. In large bowl to ground fruits add the boiling water and baking soda and stir to blend. Add butter or margarine, vanilla, brown sugar and mix. Add sifted flour and salt. Then add eggs and nuts and beat to mix well.

Turn into 2 greased and paper-lined loaf pans and bake on center rack of oven at 350° for 50 to 60 minutes. Do not overbake as it is quite full of sweet ingredients and might burn easily. Cool on cake racks. Wrap in wax paper then foil and chill 24 hours.

Applesauce Loaf Cake

1¾ C stirred but unsifted cake
     and pastry flour
1 tsp baking soda
½ tsp salt
1½ tsp cinnamon
1 tsp nutmeg
1 tsp allspice
½ C shortening
1 C sugar
2 eggs
½ tsp vanilla
1 C unsweetened applesauce (see below)

Make applesauce first: Pare and core and quarter 2 medium-large cooking apples. Add ½ C water and cook, covered, until tender. Beat with whip until smooth. Cool.

Sift together the flour, soda, salt and spices. Cream together shortening and sugar until light. Beat in eggs and vanilla for about 3 or 4 minutes until pale and airy. Then fold in dry ingredients in thirds, alternately, with applesauce. Turn into a greased standard loaf pan, lined on bottom with greased wax paper. Bake at 350° for 50 minutes. Turn out on cake rack to cool.

Banana Orange Nut Bread

1 C granulated sugar
½ C oil
2 large eggs
3 medium-large bananas broken in chunks
     (preferably ripe)
1 orange, rind and juice (see below)
1 C chopped walnuts
2½ C unsifted all-purpose flour
1 tsp baking powder
1 tsp baking soda
½ tsp salt
1 tsp vanilla
About ¼ C milk (see below)

In large beater bowl beat together well the sugar and oil. Add eggs and banana chunks and beat until thoroughly combined and almost all banana lumps have disappeared. Stir in orange rind and orange juice and milk. (*Note:* You need ½ C liquid altogether so add milk to the juice from the orange if necessary.) Add nuts and combine. Sift together flour, baking powder, baking soda and salt over the creamed mixture. Beat at low speed to thoroughly combine. Stir in vanilla. Spoon thick batter into buttered, wax-paper-lined standard loaf pan. Bake at 275° about 1½ hours or until it tests done. When done remove from oven and let rest in pan about 30 minutes before turning out onto cake rack to completely cool. Wrap in plastic bag to store in refrigerator or double wrap in plastic bags if to be frozen.

Carrot Nut Loaf

1 C grated raw carrots
¾ C brown sugar
1 tsp baking soda
2½ tsp baking powder
2 Tbsp shortening, melted
1 tsp salt
1 C plus 2 Tbsp water
2 eggs
1½ C sifted all-purpose flour
1 C whole wheat flour, stirred before measuring
½ C nuts, chopped
½ C candied cherries or Sultana raisins

Sift flour, measure and add baking powder, soda, salt and sugar. Sift together and add whole wheat flour, reserving ¼ C to flour nuts and fruits. Add water to the beaten eggs and melted shortening. Combine liquids with dry ingredients. Fold in floured nuts and fruits and grated carrots. Pour batter into greased wax-paper-lined loaf pan. Let stand 5 minutes. Bake at 375° for 1 hour.

Non-Yeast Hot Cross Buns

2 C stirred but not sifted all-purpose flour
4 tsp baking powder
½ tsp cream of tartar
½ tsp salt
1½ tsp cinnamon
1½ tsp nutmeg
4 tsp sugar
½ C butter or margarine
½ C raisins
½ C citron or orange peel
1 C milk

Sift together into mixing bowl the flour, baking powder, cream of tartar, salt, spices and sugar. Cut in butter or margarine with pastry blender until size of peas. Stir in fruits. Add milk all at once and quickly stir in. Turn out on flour-sprinkled board, pat smoothly to ⅞" thickness and cut out with floured 3" cutter. With back of a knife press a cross on top. Brush tops of all with mixture of 2 Tbsp sugar and 1½ Tbsp milk. Bake on ungreased baking sheets at 425° for 12 minutes. Makes 10 to 12 large buns.

Willie's Lemon Bread

½ C shortening
1 C sugar (first amount)
2 eggs
1½ C sifted all-purpose flour
½ C milk
½ tsp salt
1 tsp baking powder
¼ C chopped nuts
Grated rind and juice of 1 lemon
¼ C sugar (second amount)

Cream shortening and add the 1 C sugar and eggs and beat in well. Add sifted flour, salt and baking powder alternately with milk. Add chopped nuts and lemon rind. Pour into greased wax-paper-lined standard loaf pan and bake at 350° about 40 minutes. As soon as taken out of oven pour over the bread the ¼ C sugar which has been dissolved in the lemon juice. Let stand in pan until cool then carefully turn out and rest on cake rack top side up.

Muffins,
Biscuits &
Doughnuts

Pumpkin Muffins see page 168

English Muffins

½ C lukewarm water
1 tsp granulated sugar
¼ tsp ginger
1 pkg granular yeast
1 C lukewarm water
3 Tbsp granulated sugar
½ C skim milk powder
About 3¼ C unsifted all-purpose flour
    (divided, see below)
1 egg
3 Tbsp melted butter
1½ tsp salt
Corn meal (see below)

Into a measuring cup put the first ½ C lukewarm water, 1 tsp sugar and ginger. Stir. Sprinkle yeast over and let stand 10 minutes.

Into a large mixing bowl measure the 1 cup lukewarm water, 3 Tbsp granulated sugar, skim milk powder and 1 C of the flour. Stir and beat to mix until smooth. Beat in yeast liquid. Now add egg, melted butter, salt and 1½ C flour and beat until smooth.

Sprinkle kneading board with ¼ C flour. Knead in flour, about 50 times. As dough becomes sticky sprinkle with a little more flour and continue kneading 150 times in all or until flour is worked in. Return to greased bowl, oil top of dough, cover and let rise covered 3 hours at room temperature.

Flour kneading board again with ¼ C flour. Turn dough out on it, pat out, then gently roll to 18 × 12″ oblong. It is quite thin. Cut out with sharp 3½″ round cutter about 18 muffins and place on sheets of wax paper sprinkled evenly with corn meal. Let rise 2 hours, then heat an ungreased griddle to 350° (not as hot as for pancakes). Carefully lift risen muffins to griddle on egg lifter and cook 20 minutes turning each over at halftime when bottom is rich gold. Continue until all are done. To serve, split with 2 forks and toast.

Pumpkin Muffins

4 eggs
2 C granulated sugar
1½ C cooking oil
One 14-oz can pumpkin
3 C unsifted all-purpose flour
1 Tbsp cinnamon
2 tsp baking soda
2 tsp baking powder
1 tsp salt
2 C raisins

In beater bowl beat eggs slightly. Add the sugar, oil and pumpkin and beat thoroughly. Measure into a sifter the flour, cinnamon, baking soda, baking powder and salt and sift these dry ingredients over the creamed mixture. Blend until smooth then stir in the raisins.

Fill each greased muffin cup ⅔ full of batter. Bake at 400° for about 15 minutes or until done when tested with a toothpick.

Go Power Muffins

¼ C molasses
2 Tbsp raw or ordinary brown sugar
2 Tbsp oil (or soft margarine)
1 large egg
½ C raisins
½ C chopped dates
½ C chopped pecans
½ C whole wheat flour
½ C natural bran
2 Tbsp rye flour
2 Tbsp soy flour
2 Tbsp wheat germ
¾ tsp baking powder
¼ tsp baking soda
⅛ tsp salt
½ C orange juice

Measure all ingredients in order into the beater bowl. Do not beat until all are in. Then beat only 10 seconds or barely enough to mix. Never overbeat muffins.

Grease muffin tins (2¾″). Neatly apportion batter in each. Bake at 375° for 10 to 12 minutes, watching them during the last minute or two to be sure they do not burn.

Merle's Bran Muffins

¼ C soft margarine
½ C brown sugar (packed)
6 Tbsp honey (or corn syrup or molasses)
2 eggs
1 C milk
1½ C natural bran
1 C whole wheat flour (unsifted)
1½ tsp baking powder
¾ tsp baking soda
¾ tsp salt
⅔ C raisins
⅓ C desiccated coconut
⅓ C chopped nuts

Into beater bowl measure the margarine and sugar, turn beater on low and start adding all of the remaining ingredients as you measure them: honey (or corn syrup or molasses), eggs, milk, bran, whole wheat flour, baking powder and soda, salt, raisins, coconut and nuts. By the time they are all in the bowl the whole batter is mixed. You will have to stop beaters once or twice to scrape down sides with a rubber scraper. Grease 16 muffin tins, neatly spoon in batter to ⅞ fill. Bake at 350° for 15 minutes.

Sour Cream Pineapple Muffins

2 Tbsp sugar
1 large egg
1 Tbsp margarine (room temperature)
1 C dairy sour cream
1⅓ C sifted all-purpose flour
1 tsp baking powder
½ tsp baking soda
¾ tsp salt
One 8¾-oz can pineapple tidbits or dice, well drained

Into mixing bowl measure the sugar, egg, soft margarine and sour cream. Stir and beat until well blended.

Sift the sifted flour with the baking powder, baking soda and salt. Add to mixture in bowl and stir to barely blend. Stir in drained pineapple tidbits or dice just to mix. Do not overstir. Fill greased muffin tins ⅔ full and bake at 400° for 22 to 25 minutes. Serve warm with butter for breakfast.

Graham Flour Muffins

1 egg
1 C light brown sugar
¼ C oil
1⅓ C milk
1 tsp vinegar
¾ C desiccated coconut (unsweetened)
¾ C raisins
2 C unsifted graham flour
1 tsp baking soda
½ tsp cinnamon
⅛ tsp salt

First measure the milk in a 2-cup measure and add the vinegar, coconut and raisins and let soak. Then in a beater bowl beat together the egg, brown sugar and oil. Now add the milk mixture, graham flour, baking soda, cinnamon and salt and beat barely enough to mix, not more than 1 minute. Line muffin tins with fluted paper cups and neatly spoon batter into them to fill ¾ full. Bake at 375° for 20 minutes. Makes 16.

Pineapple-Carrot Muffins

1 C granulated sugar
⅔ C cooking oil
2 large eggs, beaten
1½ C unsifted all-purpose flour
1 tsp baking powder
1 tsp baking soda
1 tsp cinnamon
½ tsp salt
1 tsp vanilla
1 C very finely grated carrot
1 C crushed pineapple (juice included)

In large beater bowl combine well the sugar, oil and beaten eggs. In another bowl combine the flour, baking powder, baking soda, cinnamon and salt and stir to mix. Add dry ingredients to the sugar-oil-egg mixture and beat well. Then add the carrots, pineapple and juice and vanilla, and beat well. Grease 18 muffin cups. Fill each ⅔ full and bake at 350° for 15 to 20 minutes. Serve warm.

Sugar and Spice Muffins

1¾ C unsifted all-purpose flour
1½ tsp baking powder
½ tsp salt
½ tsp nutmeg
⅓ C oil
¾ C granulated sugar (first amount)
1 egg
¾ C milk
½ C melted butter or margarine
¾ C sugar (second amount)
1 tsp cinnamon

In a bowl combine flour, baking powder, salt and nutmeg. In another bowl combine thoroughly the oil, sugar, egg and milk. Add to dry ingredients and stir only to combine.

Fill 12 greased large muffin tins ⅔ full of batter and bake at 350° for 20 to 25 minutes. As soon as they are done, tip muffin tins over, give a tap and knock muffins out. Melt butter or margarine in small saucepan but do not overheat. While hot, dip each muffin in the melted butter to coat completely and then roll in a mixture of the ¾ C sugar and cinnamon and place upright on serving plate. At their best served warm of course.

Blueberry Muffins

1½ C fresh washed and dried blueberries (or out of season you could use partially thawed fresh frozen)
¼ C soft butter or margarine
¼ C sugar
1 large egg, well beaten
2 C sifted all-purpose flour
4 tsp baking powder
¼ tsp salt
1 C milk

Sift the flour and measure it. Take out 2 Tbsp and dredge the washed and dried blueberries with it in a small bowl. Sift the remaining flour with the baking powder and salt. Cream the butter with the sugar and stir in the beaten egg, but only barely stir in. (Muffins should always be undermixed.) Now to the creamed mixture add the flour and milk, half of each at a time, stirring just enough to mix. Fold in the floured blueberries gently. Fill buttered muffin pans ¾ full, using individual cups to hold excess batter if necessary. Immediately put in oven and bake at 400° for 14 to 15 minutes.

Large Quantity Refrigerator Bran Muffins

2 C all bran
2 C boiling water
3 Tbsp baking soda
1 C margarine (room temperature)
3½ C granulated sugar
4 eggs
2 C raisins
1 qt buttermilk
5 C stirred but unsifted cake and pastry flour
2 tsp salt
4 C bran flakes

In bowl mix together all bran, boiling water and baking soda. Set aside.

In very large mixing bowl or preserving kettle cream together the margarine and white sugar. Blend in eggs. Add all bran mixture, raisins and buttermilk and stir to combine. Beat in flour and salt until no lumps are left. Fold in bran flakes. Batter is rather thin but thickens as it sits in refrigerator. Allow to rest in refrigerator a few hours before using. Spoon into paper-cupcake-lined muffin tins to ⅞ fill. Bake at 400° for 20 minutes for large size, 18 minutes for medium.

Moist Date Bran Muffins

¼ C margarine
½ C brown sugar
¼ C molasses
2 eggs
¼ C skim milk powder
¾ C water
1 C unsifted all-purpose flour
1½ tsp baking powder
½ tsp baking soda
¾ tsp salt
1½ C raw natural bran
⅔ C chopped dates

Into beater bowl measure the margarine, brown sugar, molasses and eggs and beat for 2 or 3 minutes until creamy and blended. Now as you measure them with beaters on low add the milk powder, water, flour, baking powder, baking soda, salt, bran and dates but as soon as dates are mixed in, stop beaters to prevent breaking up dates too much.

Turn into buttered muffin tins. Bake at 400° for 20 minutes for small size, 25 minutes for larger ones.

Corn Meal Muffins

1 C corn meal
1 C boiling water
½ C milk
½ tsp salt
2 tsp baking powder
1 Tbsp soft margarine or butter
1 large egg

Note that this recipe does not call for flour. In mixing bowl soak the corn meal in the boiling water 5 minutes. Then add all remaining ingredients and beat just until blended. Spoon into well-buttered muffin tins filling nearly full and bake at 475° about 20 to 25 minutes. Serve fresh from the oven.

Orange and Date Muffins

1 medium-large orange, unpeeled
½ C orange juice
½ C chopped pitted dates
1 egg
½ C margarine (room temperature)
1 C all-purpose flour
½ C whole wheat flour
1 tsp baking soda
1 tsp baking powder
¾ C sugar
¾ tsp salt

Cut orange in eighths, remove any seeds and put in blender. Add orange juice and dates and blend until thoroughly liquefied. Add egg and margarine and blend again.

Into sifter over large bowl measure flours, baking powder and baking soda, sugar and salt. Sift through. Tip liquid in blender into flour mixture. Mix into flour with a minimum of stirring to blend. Spoon into 18 oiled 2½" muffin tins and bake at 400° for 12 minutes.

Wheat Germ Muffins

1¼ C sifted all-purpose flour
4 tsp baking powder
½ tsp salt
¼ C sugar
¼ C skim milk powder
¾ C fresh wheat germ
1 egg
⅓ C salad oil
1 C water
¼ tsp vanilla

orange peel

Sift together the sifted flour, baking powder, salt, sugar and skim milk powder. When sifted add wheat germ. In beater bowl beat egg and oil to mix then add water and vanilla. Add dry ingredients all at once and beat to barely blend. Muffin batter should be lumpy.

Butter twelve 2½" muffin cups, spoon in batter to ⅞ fill. Bake at 400° about 15 to 20 minutes. Serve hot.

Honey Bran Muffins

1 C bran
1 C buttermilk
⅓ C butter
6 Tbsp brown sugar
2 Tbsp honey
1 egg
1 C sifted flour
1 tsp baking powder
½ tsp soda
1 tsp salt

Cream ~~shortening and~~ butter well, then beat in sugar and honey. Beat in egg. Add bran and buttermilk and beat. Sift together the sifted flour, baking powder, soda and salt and stir in until barely mixed. Fill greased muffin tins ⅔ full and bake at 400° about 20 minutes.

Crunchy Banana Muffins

⅞ C mashed overripe bananas
    (about 2 large or 3 small)
½ C light brown sugar
⅓ C margarine
1 egg
1 tsp vanilla
1¼ C sifted all-purpose flour
½ C wheat germ
1 tsp baking powder
1 tsp baking soda
¼ C water
¼ C white sugar
1 tsp cinnamon

Into beater bowl measure the bananas, brown sugar and margarine and beat for 5 minutes. Add egg and vanilla and beat in. Lift up beaters. Add the flour, wheat germ, baking powder and soda and water. Lower beaters and beat 5 seconds. Remove beaters. Scrape down sides and give 1 or 2 stirs. Spoon into 12 buttered 2½" muffin tins. Mix together white sugar and cinnamon and sprinkle carefully and evenly over each unbaked muffin. Bake at 350° for 15 to 20 minutes. Serve warm from the oven.

Health Nut Muffins

¼ C brown sugar
¼ C oil
¼ C molasses
2 eggs
1 C water
¼ C soy flour
2 tsp brewers' yeast
¾ C whole wheat flour
2 tsp baking powder
1 tsp salt
½ tsp cinnamon
¼ C skim milk powder
1½ C fresh wheat germ
1 C raisins
¼ C sesame seeds or chopped nuts

Into the beater bowl measure the brown sugar, oil and molasses. Add eggs and beat to mix. Add water.

Measure into bowl and mix soy flour, yeast, whole wheat flour, baking powder, salt, cinnamon and skim milk powder. Add wheat germ, raisins and sesame seeds. Add to wet mixture and stir only enough to mix. (Remember muffin batter should be a little lumpy so do not overstir.)

Spoon into buttered muffin tins, filling ¾ full. Bake at 400° about 10 minutes. Watch, for they might burn because of the molasses content.

Applesauce Bran Muffins

1 C all bran cereal
½ + C buttermilk (see below)
1¼ C smooth sweetened applesauce
¼ C molasses
¼ C cooking oil
1 egg
1 tsp vanilla
1⅞ C unsifted all-purpose flour
⅜ C brown sugar packed
1 tsp salt
1 tsp baking soda

If you do not have buttermilk, measure 1 Tbsp lemon juice or vinegar into a 1-cup measure, fill with sweet milk and let stand 5 minutes. Into a large bowl measure the bran, buttermilk, applesauce, molasses, oil, egg and vanilla. Give a good stir and let stand 5 minutes.

Measure dry ingredients into another bowl. Stir into wet mixture until barely blended. Oil muffin tins. Spoon batter in to ¾ fill. Bake at 375°: 20 minutes for large muffins, 18 for small!.

Crackers with Variations

1 C all-purpose flour
1 C whole wheat flour
1½ tsp salt
2 tsp baking powder
2½ tsp brown sugar
½ C margarine
¼ C milk
1 or 2 tsp sesame seed
1 or 2 tsp poppy seed
1 or 2 tsp dill seed.

Into beater bowl measure flours, salt, baking powder, sugar, margarine and milk. Beat 5 minutes until thoroughly blended. Turn out on floured board, shape into long roll and cut into thirds. Pat one third out, sprinkle it with sesame seeds, then knead them in. Repeat adding poppy seeds to another third, and dill seeds to the last third, kneading the seeds well into each. Now roll out one lot at a time on lightly floured board to less then ⅛" thickness. Roll evenly and neatly at edges. Using a pastry or pizza wheel cut them out into 2" squares. You can get 14 from each third by picking up scraps of dough for the last 2 crackers. Using lifter transfer to greased cookie sheets. At even intervals prick with fork tines. Sprinkle each sparingly with more of the same seed as inside. With a light touch press them in.

Bake at 375° for 7 or 8 minutes. There is a great temptation to overbake these so hover over the oven and test one in 6 minutes by picking it up and breaking it. If it breaks sharply it is done. Yield: forty-two.

Whole Food Cakes

1 C raisins
1 C currants
1 C chopped dates
¾ orange juice
¼ C honey
¼ C oil
2 tsp cinnamon
1 tsp allspice (optional)
½ to ¾ tsp salt
½ C sunflower seeds
2 C rolled oats
2 C stoneground whole wheat flour
1 C desiccated coconut

In large bowl combine raisins, currants and dates. Stir in orange juice, honey and oil and let soak 20 minutes.

In a bowl combine thoroughly the cinnamon, allspice (if used), salt, sunflower seeds, rolled oats, whole wheat flour and coconut. Stir into wet mixture until thoroughly combined. Mixture is stiff and crumbly.

Tightly pack into firm 2½" balls. Place on ungreased cookie sheets (6 to a sheet) and flatten to form a round cake 3" in diameter and 1" thick. Bake at 275° about 20 minutes. Do not brown. Remove from oven and immediately use lifter to transfer cakes from cookie sheets to cake racks to cool thoroughly.

Angel Biscuits

1 pkg granular yeast
½ C lukewarm water
5 C sifted all-purpose flour
1 tsp baking soda
1 tsp salt
1 Tbsp baking powder
3 Tbsp sugar
¾ C shortening
2 C buttermilk (or 1⅞ C sweet milk
    soured with 2 Tbsp lemon juice)

In a small bowl soak yeast in lukewarm water. Into a very large bowl sift the sifted flour with the baking soda, salt, baking powder and sugar. With a pastry blender cut in the shortening until size of peas. Add the risen yeast liquid and buttermilk (or soured milk) and stir with strong wooden spoon until thoroughly blended. Cover and store in refrigerator, if necessary, until needed. Dough rises in refrigerator.

About 2 hours before biscuits are required for a meal, to make 12 rolls cut out half of the dough from the bowl and return remainder to refrigerator. Knead on floured board about 25 times, then shape into 12" roll and cut into 12 one-inch pieces. Shape into rounds and place in buttered muffin pan (with twelve 2¾" cups). Brush tops with mixture of 1 Tbsp each milk and sugar. Let rise in warm place until above rims of pans. Bake at 400° about 12 minutes or until golden top and bottom. Test one by breaking it open before removing all from oven.

Tea Biscuits Supreme

2 C stirred but unsifted all-purpose flour
4 tsp baking powder
½ tsp cream of tartar
½ tsp salt
2 tsp sugar
½ C butter or shortening or chicken fat
⅔ C milk

Sift together into mixing bowl the flour, baking powder, cream of tartar, salt and sugar. Cut in butter (or fat of your choice) with pastry blender until size of peas. Add milk all at once and quickly stir in. Turn out onto flour-sprinkled board, pat smoothly to ¾" thickness and cut out with 2" floured cutter. Bake on ungreased baking sheet at 450° for 10 minutes.

Puffy Cheese Biscuits

1 pkg granular yeast
½ C lukewarm water
1 tsp sugar
½ C margarine (room temperature)
2 tsp sugar (second amount)
1½ tsp dry mustard
1⅔ C grated old Cheddar cheese
    (at least 6 oz)
1¾ C plus 1 Tbsp unsifted all-purpose flour
2 eggs (room temperature)

Into beater bowl measure yeast, water and 1 tsp sugar. Let soak 10 minutes. Meanwhile measure remaining ingredients and when yeast liquid has risen add all remaining ingredients and beat on low for 5 minutes. Grease 3 cookie sheets with margarine. Dip a silver teaspoon in hot water and spoon little mounds of dough, 2½" apart, onto cookie sheets. Top them up a little to encourage them to stand high. Let rise until puffy, about 3 hours. Bake at 400° about 15 to 20 minutes at center of oven, but be careful, for if you remove them too soon they tend to fall. Serve warm.

Bran Biscuits

2 C stirred but unsifted all-purpose flour
4 tsp baking powder
½ tsp cream of tartar
½ tsp salt
2 tsp sugar
1 C all bran or natural bran
½ C shortening (or lard, butter,
    chicken fat)
¾ C plus 1 Tbsp milk

Sift together into a mixing bowl the flour, baking powder, cream of tartar, salt and sugar. Add bran to sifted dry ingredients and cut in shortening with pastry blender until size of peas. Stir in milk until dry ingredients are moistened. Shape into ball between palms and pat out to ⅔" thickness on lightly floured board. Cut out with 2" cutter and bake on ungreased baking sheet at 450° for 10 minutes. Makes twenty.

Digestive Biscuits (33)

½ C all-purpose flour
½ C rolled oats
1 C whole wheat flour
¼ C wheat germ
¼ C sesame seeds
¼ tsp baking soda
¼ tsp salt
2 Tbsp skim milk powder
¼ C granulated sugar
½ C margarine
⅓ C cold water
1 tsp vanilla

In a large bowl combine thoroughly the all-purpose flour, rolled oats, whole wheat flour, wheat germ, sesame seeds, baking soda, salt, skim milk powder and granulated sugar. Cut in margarine with pastry blender or knife until size of small peas. Combine vanilla with water and drizzle over, mixing enough to make dough pack together into a ball between your palms. Pat and flatten on lightly floured board and roll to ⅛″ thickness. Cut out with 2½″ floured cutter. (A scalloped cutter gives them a more professional appearance.) Bake on greased baking sheets, about ½″ apart (they do not spread) and bake at 325° about 20 to 25 minutes. Watch them because they should not brown at all.

Cheese Sticks

1 pkg granular yeast
1 tsp sugar
¾ C lukewarm water
¾ C scalded milk
2 Tbsp sugar (second amount)
2 tsp salt
2 Tbsp shortening
¾ C cheese whiz
About 5 C sifted all-purpose flour

In a large mixing bowl soak the yeast and sugar (first amount) in the lukewarm water 10 minutes. To the scalded milk add the sugar, salt, shortening and cheese whiz and mix well to blend and add to the soaked yeast liquid. Beat in 1 C sifted flour until batter is smooth, then add 3 more cups sifted flour and mix as well as you can, then turn out on board floured with some of the remaining flour and knead 200 times. Return to scraped down bowl, cover and let rise 2½ hours at room temperature.

Punch down dough and knead 200 times again on floured board. Roll out to ¼″ thickness and cut into ½″ wide strips. Cut these into 5″ lengths and roll them under your palms then twist into little ropes and place 1″ apart on buttered cookie sheets. If desired give them a shiny finish by brushing with 1 egg beaten with 1 Tbsp water. Let rise 2½ hours then bake at 425° for 12 to 15 minutes to a rich gold. Watch carefully and switch pans to brown evenly.

Seed Sticks

6 Tbsp scalded milk
½ C shortening
1 tsp granular yeast (½ pkg)
2 Tbsp lukewarm water
2 C sifted all-purpose flour
1¼ tsp salt
½ tsp sugar
1 beaten egg (for topping)
Seeds: poppy, sesame or caraway

Add shortening to scalded milk and let stand until lukewarm. Soak yeast in lukewarm water in large mixing bowl. When milk and shortening mixture is lukewarm add to yeast liquid, then add the flour, salt and sugar. Mix as well as you can, then knead for 5 minutes. Return to greased bowl, cover and let rise for 2 hours or until doubled. On lightly floured board punch down and knead dough for 1 minute. Pinch off pieces of dough about 1″ in diameter and roll between your palms to form sticks, 4 × ¼″. Place, touching, on ungreased cookie sheets. It will make about 50 little sticks. Beat the egg and neatly brush all of the touching sticks with it to coat with egg as well as you can. Now while they are still wet and touching sprinkle generously with seeds to cover tops. Now pick up every other one and transfer to another cookie sheet, shifting them all so that they are 1″ apart. Bake at 325° about 30 minutes or until golden tan and crisp, switching and turning pan in oven at half time. These keep well.

Scones

½ tsp baking soda
2 C sifted cake and pastry flour
3 tsp baking powder
¾ tsp salt
3 Tbsp sugar
5 Tbsp shortening
2 egg yolks
⅓ C sour cream or milk
Slightly beaten egg white
1 Tbsp sugar or mixture of
    sugar and cinnamon

Measure sifted flour. Add baking soda, baking powder, salt and sugar and sift again. Cut in shortening with pastry blender. Beat egg yolks well and add sour cream or milk. Add to flour mixture and stir until soft dough is formed (about 20 strokes). Turn out on lightly floured board and knead 20 turns only. Divide dough into thirds. Pat or roll each into a round ½″ thick and cut each into quarters. Place quarters on ungreased baking sheet. Brush tops lightly with egg white. Sprinkle with sugar or mixture of sugar and cinnamon. Bake at 450° for 12 minutes. Makes 12 large scones.

Fruited Scones

½ C granulated sugar
3 C sifted all-purpose flour
4 tsp baking powder
1 tsp cream of tartar
½ tsp salt
½ C shortening
1 C raisins
1 large (or 2 medium) eggs
1 C orange juice

Set the raisins to soak in the orange juice. Into a large bowl measure the sugar, sifted flour, baking powder, cream of tartar and salt. Cut the shortening into these dry ingredients with a pastry blender until the size of peas. Now add the egg and raisins and orange juice and give a few stirs to mix and blend.

Pick the dough up between your palms and shape into a ball and pat out on floured board to a 10 × 14″ oblong. Cut it in half lengthwise then cut it into 12 even squares. Cut each square diagonally to form 24 triangles. Pick each one up carefully on a lifter and transfer to 2 greased cookie sheets, about 1″ apart. Carefully sprinkle top of each with ½ tsp sugar. Bake at 400° about 12 minutes. Do not overbake. Serve warm.

Baked Yeast Doughnuts

1½ C scalded milk
⅓ C shortening
¼ C sugar
2 tsp salt
2 tsp nutmeg
¼ tsp cinnamon
1 C all bran cereal
2 pkg granular yeast
¼ C lukewarm water
2 eggs, slightly beaten
4¼ C sifted all-purpose flour
2 Tbsp butter or margarine, melted

Pour hot milk over shortening. Stir in sugar, salt, spices and bran; cool to lukewarm. Dissolve yeast in lukewarm water; add to bran mixture together with eggs, mixing well. Add flour and mix thoroughly. Cover and let stand in warm place until doubled in bulk, about 2 hours. Turn dough out on well-floured board. Shape in a ball (dough will be very soft to handle). Roll out to ½″ thickness. Do not stretch dough. Cut out with floured 3″ doughnut cutter and place about 2″ apart on greased baking sheets. Brush with melted butter and let rise 1 hour or until doubled. Bake at 425° about 10 to 12 minutes, then cool and ice with thin confectioners' sugar icing. Makes about 3 dozen 3″ in diameter.

Scotch Oatcakes

3 C ground oatmeal (not rolled oats:
    see note below)
½ tsp baking soda
¼ tsp salt
¼ C butter or margarine (room temperature)
6 Tbsp milk

If you cannot buy finely ground Scotch oatmeal put rolled oats through the fine knife of food grinder and measure. To ground oatmeal in bowl add baking soda and salt. With wooden spoon thoroughly mix in the butter. Add milk to make a smooth pliable dough. Wrap in large sheet of floured wax paper, press to flatten to about ½″ thickness and chill for about 30 minutes or until of rolling consistency. Roll out to less than ⅛″ thickness. Using a 7″ plate, place it on rolled-out dough and cut out 2 rounds using plate as a guide. Cut each round into four. Lift to buttered cookie sheet. Bake at 375° about 10 minutes or until they are barely gold. Shape, cut out and bake remaining scraps of dough.

Pennsylvania Dutch Square Doughnuts

1 pkg granular yeast
½ C lukewarm water
1 tsp sugar (first amount)
½ C scalded milk
¼ C sugar (second amount)
¼ C shortening or oil
1 tsp salt
1 tsp cinnamon
1 C raisins
1 egg
2½ to 2¾ C unsifted all-purpose flour
    (divided, see below)

In your 2-cup measure dissolve the 1 tsp sugar in the lukewarm water. Sprinkle over yeast, give it one stir and let soak 10 minutes.

Meanwhile pour scalded milk into large beater bowl. Add the ¼ C sugar, shortening or oil, salt, cinnamon and raisins and stir to combine and cool to lukewarm. Beat in egg. Stir in risen yeast liquid, along with 2¼ C of the flour and beat for 5 minutes. Scrape down sides of bowl, cover and let rise 2 hours in a warm place. Punch down dough and turn out on board floured with remaining flour and knead 100 times.

Roll dough out to ⅓″ thickness and cut into 3″ squares. Gather up scraps, roll and cut them too. Let rise, uncovered, at least 2″ apart on board until risen to almost double thickness, about 1½ hours. Lift carefully one at a time and slide into hot fat or oil 3″ deep in pot, at 375°. Do 2 or 3 at a time depending on size of pot. As they show a golden color on bottom, turn them over, frying about 3 minutes to brown both sides. Lift out and place on absorbent paper towels to drain. Let partially cool on cake racks but while still warm dip all sides into a Honey Glaze made by combining and stirring until smooth 2 Tbsp honey, ⅛ tsp salt, 2 C icing sugar and 7 Tbsp boiling water. Dip warm doughnuts into this warm glaze and let cool and dry on cake rack.

Yeast Doughnuts with Jelly or Glaze

1 pkg (2½ tsp) granular yeast
½ C lukewarm water
1 tsp sugar (first amount)
½ C scalded milk
¼ C sugar (second amount)
¼ C shortening
1 tsp salt
3¼ to 3½ C sifted all-purpose flour
1 egg

In large bowl soak the yeast with the 1 tsp sugar in lukewarm water 10 minutes. Remove scalded milk from heat and add to it the shortening, ¼ C sugar and salt and stir to cool to lukewarm. Add to risen yeast liquid along with 2 C of the sifted flour and the egg and beat for 5 minutes. Beat in 1 more cup of flour until smooth. Scrape down sides of bowl, cover and let rise 2 hours. Turn dough out on board floured with remaining flour and knead 100 times.

For regular doughnuts roll out to ⅓" thickness and cut out with floured 3" doughnut cutter. Let rise uncovered on board until very light, at least 1 hour. A thin crust will form on outside. Slide carefully into hot fat at 375°. Add only as many as can be turned easily. As they rise to surface and show a little color turn them over, frying about 3 minutes to brown both sides, with temperature maintained at 375°. Lift out with long fork without pricking. Drain for a moment then transfer to absorbent paper in warm place. To sugar the cooled doughnuts, just before serving shake one at a time in paper bag containing a little icing or granulated sugar, cinnamon flavored, if desired.

JELLY DOUGHNUTS: Roll doughnut dough out to ¼" thickness. Let rest 5 minutes. Cut out with 2½" round cutter and let stand 5 minutes. Place 1 tsp tart stiff jelly or jam in center of half of the rounds, top with remaining rounds and seal edges firmly. Let rise uncovered 25 to 30 minutes. Deep fry and drain and sugar as above.

HONEY GLAZE DOUGHNUTS: Add 1½ Tbsp honey to 3½ Tbsp boiling water and 1 C icing sugar. Stir until perfectly blended. Dip warm doughnuts into this warm glaze and let cool and dry on cake rack.

Homemade Cake Doughnuts

2 large eggs
½ tsp nutmeg
¾ C granulated sugar
¼ C oil
½ C milk
1½ tsp vanilla
2¾ C unsifted all-purpose flour
4 tsp baking powder
1 tsp salt

In beater bowl combine eggs, nutmeg, sugar and oil and beat 2 or 3 minutes. Stir in milk and vanilla. In another bowl combine flour, baking powder and salt and add to liquids, beating, until batter is well blended. Scrape down sides of bowl, cover and chill thoroughly 2 hours.

Heat 2" of oil in pot to 375°. On well floured board roll out half of the dough at a time to ½" thickness, leaving remaining half in refrigerator. Cut out 3 at a time using a 2½" diameter floured doughnut cutter. Slide carefully into hot fat. Turn each over as bottom becomes gold and fry other side. Transfer to absorbent paper towels to drain. Continue until remaining half is rolled, cut and fried. Collect scraps, roll, cut and fry them too. Let cool completely on cake racks. Sprinkle some with sifted icing sugar and dip tops of some in a Chocolate or Butterscotch Glaze.

CHOCOLATE GLAZE

1 C icing sugar
2 Tbsp cocoa
Pinch of salt
1 tsp vanilla
About 3 Tbsp boiling water

Combine all Chocolate Glaze ingredients in a bowl until smooth.

BUTTERSCOTCH GLAZE

1 C icing sugar
4 Tbsp dark brown sugar
Pinch of salt
2 Tbsp soft butter or margarine
1 tsp vanilla
About 4 or 5 Tbsp boiling water

Combine all Butterscotch Glaze ingredients in a bowl until smooth.

Pancakes, Waffles, Fritters & Crêpes

Apple Pancakes

1¼ C unsifted all-purpose flour
2½ tsp baking powder
3 Tbsp sugar
½ tsp salt
¼ tsp cinnamon
2 eggs, yolks and whites separated
1 C milk
3 Tbsp melted butter or oil
1 C pared and shredded apples

Sift together the flour, baking powder, sugar, salt and cinnamon. Stir in the egg yolks, milk and melted butter or oil. Shred the apple and immediately add it to the batter. Fold in stiffly beaten egg whites. Drop by tablespoonfuls and bake on greased griddle until bubbly. Turn over and brown other side.

All-Time Favorite Pancakes

1½ C sifted all-purpose flour
3½ tsp baking powder
¾ tsp salt
2 Tbsp sugar
1 egg, beaten
1¾ C milk
3 Tbsp melted butter or shortening

Sift flour with baking powder, salt and sugar. Combine egg, milk, butter or shortening and add to dry ingredients. Beat until smooth. Drop by tablespoonfuls (or ¼ C measure) onto hot griddle. Cook on one side until puffed and full of bubbles. Turn and cook other side.

Whole Wheat Pancakes

1 C unsifted flour
1 C unsifted whole wheat flour
2½ tsp baking powder
½ tsp salt
1 egg
1¾ to 1⅞ C milk
2 Tbsp oil or melted butter

In order given measure all ingredients into beater bowl and beat until smooth. Using ¼ C measure, filled three-quarters full, pour onto greased hot frying pan and cook until golden on bottom. Turn. Serve 3 to a stack with cottage cheese between and orange sauce over top. Makes 12 to 14.

ORANGE SAUCE
1 Tbsp corn starch
½ C sugar
¼ tsp salt
1 C orange juice
2 tsp orange rind
Whole membraneless sections from 1 orange

In a small pot combine corn starch, sugar, salt and orange rind, mixing well. Stir in orange juice and cook over high heat stirring until thick. Remove from heat and add orange sections.

Blueberry Pancakes

2 C sifted all-purpose flour
1 tsp salt
1 Tbsp baking powder
1 Tbsp sugar
2 eggs
1½ C milk
1½ Tbsp melted shortening or oil
¾ to 1 C washed and dried blueberries

Sift flour with salt, baking powder and sugar. Beat eggs and add milk and shortening or oil. Add sifted dry ingredients and beat until smooth. Stir in blueberries. Drop by spoonful on ungreased griddle. When full of bubbles turn to brown other side. Serve with butter and maple syrup or currant jelly.

Buckwheat Cakes

1 Cake compressed yeast or
  1 pkg granular yeast
½ C lukewarm water
2 C cold water
1 C sifted flour
2 C buckwheat flour
1½ tsp salt
1 Tbsp molasses
¼ C melted butter
1 tsp soda dissolved in ½ C hot water

Dissolve yeast in lukewarm water and add cold water. Sift together flour, buckwheat flour and salt and stir in. Beat vigorously until smooth. Cover, and place in refrigerator overnight. In the morning, stir in molasses, melted butter and soda. Let stand at room temperature for 30 minutes. Bake on hot griddle.

Corn Pancakes

2 C stirred but unsifted all-purpose flour
1 Tbsp baking powder
1 tsp salt
2 eggs
1¼ C cream style corn
1½ C milk
¼ C oil or melted butter

Into beater bowl measure the flour, baking powder, salt, eggs, corn, milk and oil or melted butter. Lower beaters and beat at low speed until smoothly blended, scraping down sides of bowl to be sure all flour is mixed in. Using a quarter cup measure pour batter onto lighly greased hot griddle and bake until bubbles form then turn and bake other sides until golden. Keep cakes warm until all are done.

Super Waffles

2 C sifted all-purpose flour
3 tsp baking powder
1 tsp baking soda
1 tsp salt
2 C sour milk or buttermilk (see below)
4 eggs, well-beaten
¾ C melted margarine or salad oil

Sift together dry ingredients. Combine sour milk and eggs and add to dry ingredients. Beat until smooth with beater at high speed. Stir in melted margarine or oil. Bake in preheated waffle iron until crisp and golden. Serve with maple syrup. *Note:* If you do not have sour or buttermilk measure 2 Tbsp vinegar into a 2 C measure and fill to 2 C mark with sweet milk and briefly let stand.

Whole Wheat Waffles

2 C whole wheat flour
2 tsp baking powder
½ tsp salt
3 eggs, yolks and whites separated
2 C plus 2 Tbsp milk
½ C oil
1 C chopped or shredded unpared apple
½ C chopped nuts (optional)

In the beater bowl beat together the egg yolks, milk and oil to thoroughly blend. Add the whole wheat flour, baking powder and salt and beat until smooth, scraping down sides of beater bowl with rubber scraper. The moment the apples are ready add them to prevent discoloration. If nuts are used add now. Beat egg whites until stiff. Fold in with wire whip.

Have waffle iron preheated. Brush lightly with oil before adding batter. Add enough batter to ¾ cover iron. Bake until rich gold, and serve at once. *Note:* You can peek through the crack between top and bottom irons to see if edges are golden but resist temptation to open waffle iron too soon.

Popovers

1 C all-purpose flour
¼ tsp salt
⅞ C milk
2 large eggs
½ tsp melted butter

Mix salt and flour. Add milk gradually to obtain a smooth batter. Add eggs, beaten until light, and butter. Beat 2 minutes at high speed. Turn into hissing-hot generously buttered iron gem pans (or muffin tins) and bake 30 to 35 minutes at 475°. They may be baked in buttered earthen cups, when bottom will have a glazed appearance. To test, remove one popover. If it collapses bake all longer, until crust is firm. Serve at once for breakfast or lunch.

Corn Fritters

1½ C raw corn kernels (or one 12-oz can drained)
2 beaten eggs
1 tsp sugar
¼ tsp salt
6 Tbsp flour
1 tsp baking powder

Combine ingredients in order given. Have hot oil to depth of nearly ½″ in frying pan. Drop batter from spoon and brown on both sides. These are great favorites, a good change from potatoes.

Banana Fritters

⅞ C (1 C less 2 Tbsp) stirred but unsifted
    all-purpose flour
2 tsp baking powder
1 tsp salt
¼ C sugar
1 egg
½ C milk less 1 Tbsp
2 tsp oil or melted shortening
1 C sliced overripe bananas (packed)
Oil or shortening for deep frying

To make the Batter, combine flour, baking powder, salt, sugar, egg, milk and oil or melted shortening in beater bowl and beat until smooth. Fold in bananas.

Have ready oil or shortening in narrow pot to a depth of 2″, at 375°. Drop in not more than 3 spoonfuls of batter at one time to make 2¼″ fritters. Turn over when bottom is rich gold and finish other side. Skim out with slotted spoon to icing-sugar-sprinkled plate, turn over. Serves four to six.

Pioneer Apple Fritters

⅞ C stirred but not sifted all-purpose flour
1 tsp baking powder
⅛ tsp salt
2 Tbsp icing sugar
1 egg
⅓ C milk
1 Tbsp rum
3 apples
Pineapple or lemon juice

Into beater bowl measure the flour, baking powder, salt, icing sugar, egg, milk and rum. Beat until smoothly blended.

Wash, pare, quarter and core apples and cut each apple into 8 or 12 wedges. Immediately coat with pineapple or lemon juice to prevent browning.

Heat fat or oil 1½″ deep to 350°. Drop about 6 apple wedges at a time into batter to coat them, lift with fork, drain a moment and drop into hot fat. Turn with fork or slotted spoon as soon as bottom is deep gold and brown other side. Lift from fat, drain on paper towelling. Keep warm. Fry remaining fritters. Serve about 6 fritters on each plate for dessert sprinkled with icing or powdered sugar, or use as an accompaniment to baked ham or baked ham slice.

Crêpes Florentine

CRÊPE BATTER
1 C cold water
1 C cold milk
4 eggs
½ tsp salt
2 C sifted all-purpose flour
2 Tbsp melted butter or margarine

SAUCE MORNAY
5 Tbsp flour
4 Tbsp butter or margarine
2¾ C hot milk
½ tsp salt
⅛ tsp pepper
⅛ tsp nutmeg
¼ C 18% cream
1 C shredded Swiss or old Cheddar cheese

SPINACH FILLING
1 green onion, chopped
2 Tbsp butter or margarine
1½ C finely chopped raw spinach (packed)
¼ tsp salt

MUSHROOM FILLING
1 C (8-oz pkg) white cream cheese
1 egg
2 C very finely chopped washed and
   drained raw mushrooms
2 Tbsp chopped green onion

To make Crêpes, beat all Crêpe Batter ingredients until perfectly smooth. Cover. Chill at least 2 hours.

You may make crêpes in advance and separate each with a square of wax paper and refrigerate. Using a heavy 9″ frying pan brush it with melted butter or oil, until hot. Using a ½-C measure fill it ¾ full and tip into pan. At once tip pan to coat bottom all over and cook over medium-high heat until delicately browned. Turn and cook other side until tinged with gold. Turn over and out on large holding plate. Again oil pan. Continue until all batter is cooked. You will have 12 large thin Crêpes.

Make Sauce Mornay by blending flour and butter or margarine then stirring in milk until thick. Stir in remaining sauce ingredients. Put aside.

To make Spinach Filling, combine all Spinach Filling ingredients in pan and cook stirring until moisture disappears, about 5 minutes. Stir in ⅔ C Sauce Mornay. Set aside.

To make Mushroom Filling, cream the cheese well and mix in remaining Mushroom Filling ingredients. Set aside.

To assemble, on very large round pan put one 9″ crêpe. Spread it with ⅙ of the Spinach Filling; cover with another crêpe then spread it with ⅕ of the Mushroom Filling. Continue until you have a 12-crêpe stack with filling between each. Now pour all remaining Sauce Mornay over. It will drip down sides. Sprinkle top with ½ C shredded Cheddar cheese. Bake at 375° for 30 to 35 minutes until bubbly and pale gold. To serve cut into 6 or 8 wedges and spoon surplus sauce over each serving.

Crêpes Suzette

2 C flour
4 eggs
2½ C milk
1 Tbsp sugar
1 tsp salt
1 tsp vanilla

Mix all ingredients and beat until smooth. Heat a 5 or 6″ frying pan and brush with butter or oil. When hot add just enough batter to coat bottom of pan, 1½ Tbsp. Tip pan to coat bottom with batter and when bottom is gold-tinged turn and cook other side. This takes 1½ minutes in all so do not leave it. As each crêpe is cooked transfer to large plate sprinkled with icing sugar. Pour more batter into pan, then roll up just finished crêpe on plate and set aside. Repeat until all batter is cooked. Makes 32 crêpes.

At serving time heat Crêpes in an Orange Sauce.

ORANGE SAUCE
2 C sugar
1⅓ C butter
Grated rind 4 large oranges
Juice 4 large oranges
Brandy or Cointreau (optional)

Heat first 4 ingredients until butter and sugar are melted. Traditionally this sauce is heated in a shallow chafing dish and crêpes are put in and basted with it until thoroughly heated. If you are not going to flame the sauce serve now, 2 or 3 to a serving with generous ladleful of hot Orange Sauce. If you are going to flame it, pour about 3 oz warm brandy or Cointreau over boiling syrup. Do not stir. Dip serving spoon in syrup, then hold wet spoon in free flame of burner. It will catch fire. Immediately dip in syrup which will catch fire too. Serve plates at once, spooning some still flaming sauce over crêpes.

Cheese Crêpes

2 eggs
1 C milk
2 Tbsp barely melted butter
½ tsp salt
Shake of cayenne pepper
⅛ tsp nutmeg
½ C stirred all-purpose flour
1 lb grated cheese (medium Cheddar)

The batter has to be made in advance: Measure all ingredients except the cheese into a bowl and beat until perfectly smooth. Refrigerate 2 hours.

To make crêpes, melt ¼ tsp butter in a 6″ frypan until bubbly. Add about 3 Tbsp of well stirred crêpe batter and cook, tipping and rotating pan to spread batter until tinged with gold on bottom. Turn and cook on other side. Lift to large plate covered with wax paper. Repeat until all batter is cooked. You will have about 16 crêpes. Fill each crêpe with about 1-oz grated cheese and roll up. Gently reheat in buttered pan. Serve with syrup.

Strawberry Crêpes

BATTER

3 eggs
1 C milk
½ C plus 1 Tbsp water
1 C stirred but unsifted all-purpose flour
3 Tbsp sugar
¼ tsp salt
¾ tsp vanilla
Butter for frying pan

FILLING

1 qt sliced strawberries
¼ C sugar

To make Crêpes, into mixing bowl break the eggs and beat slightly to mix then add milk and water, flour, sugar, salt and vanilla and beat until batter is perfectly smooth. Allow to stand half an hour. In 8" frying pan melt 1 tsp butter until it just bubbles, then carefully pour in ¼ C of batter tilting until it just coats bottom of pan. Cook for 2 or 3 minutes until a delicate gold and dry on top, then flip over and delicately brown other side. Transfer to holding plate and sprinkle with icing sugar. Repeat until all batter is used, being sure to replenish butter in pan each time.

Fill center lengthwise with sliced, sweetened strawberries and fold both sides over top. Makes ten.

Peach Crêpes

BATTER

3 eggs
1 C milk
½ C plus 1 Tbsp water
1 C stirred but unsifted all-purpose flour
3 Tbsp sugar
¼ tsp salt
¾ tsp vanilla
Butter for frying pan

PEACH SYRUP

3 C hot water
1 C granulated sugar
2 Tbsp lemon juice
2 sticks cinnamon
4 sliced peaches
4½ tsp cornstarch
¼ C cold water

Make Crêpes in advance: Into a mixing bowl break the eggs and beat slightly to mix then add milk and water, flour, sugar, salt and vanilla and beat until batter is perfectly smooth. Allow to stand half and hour. In 6" frying pan melt ½ tsp butter until it just bubbles, then carefully pour in a scant ¼ C of batter tilting until it just coats bottom of pan. Cook for 2 or 3 minutes until a delicate gold and dry on top, then flip over and delicately brown other side. Transfer to icing sugar-sprinkled platter and roll up. Repeat, adding butter each time, until all batter is made into uniform crêpes, about 14. (These may be held in refrigerator until mealtime.)

Make Syrup by bringing to gentle boil the hot water, sugar, lemon juice and cinnamon sticks for 2 minutes. Add the sliced peaches and simmer until a little soft. Make a smooth paste of cornstarch and cold water and gently stir in until thickened.

Add rolled crêpes to syrup pot and bring to gentle boil for 1 or 2 minutes. Transfer 2 crêpes to each plate to be served and spoon some hot peach syrup over each. Discard cinnamon sticks. Serve at once. Serves seven.

Shrimp Crêpes

CRÊPES

3 eggs
10 Tbsp all-purpose flour (½ C plus 2 Tbsp)
¼ tsp salt
1½ C milk

FILLING

Two 7-oz cans small shrimp (reserve ¼ C brine)
One 4-oz can salmon
1 Tbsp butter
1 Tbsp chopped onion
½ tsp curry powder
¼ tsp Worcestershire sauce
½ C white wine

SAUCE

2½ Tbsp butter
5 Tbsp flour
½ tsp salt
1 C milk
¼ C brine drained from shrimp (above)

Crêpes may be made well in advance. You need a small frying pan 5½" diameter at bottom.

To make Crêpes, combine eggs, flour, salt and milk and beat until perfectly smooth. Let stand 30 minutes. Melt ½ tsp butter in bottom of frying pan to coat. Use ¼ C measure and tip a scant amount into pan over medium heat. Tip pan to coat bottom. Turn when top is dry. Cook other side until pale gold. Transfer to large holding plate. Continue until all batter is cooked, about 14 crêpes. If crêpes are made in advance, cover and store in refrigerator.

To make Filling, drain shrimp, reserve ¼ C brine and combine shrimp in medium pot with the salmon, butter, onion, curry powder, Worcestershire sauce and wine. Gently heat for 5 minutes.

To make Sauce, blend butter, flour and salt then stir in milk and shrimp brine until very thick. Add 1 C of this sauce to shrimp mixture and stir in to blend. Reserve remaining ¼ C sauce. Cool shrimp mixture to room temperature.

Working directly into a large shallow baking dish on which you are going to bake and serve the crêpes, place one crêpe at one end and spoon about 3 Tbsp filling onto center. Fold flaps over to enclose. Carefully turn over so opening is on bottom. Neatness is important. Line up the filled crêpes touching. You will have 2 parallel rows of 7 each. Spread over all a mixture of the ¼ C reserved sauce, ¼ C genuine mayonnaise and 2 Tbsp milk. Bake at 400° about 15 minutes or until bubbly and golden. Serves six.

Shuswap Salmon Crêpes

CRÊPES
2 medium eggs
½ C all-purpose flour
⅛ tsp salt
1 C milk
Butter (see below)

SALMON FILLING
2½ Tbsp butter or margarine
4½ Tbsp flour
¼ tsp salt
1¼ C hot milk
One ½-lb can red salmon
½ tsp minced onion
½ tsp curry powder
¼ tsp soy or Worcestershire sauce
½ C Sauterne or Rosé wine

TOPPING
¼ C (reserved) white sauce
¼ C mayonnaise

Make crêpes first by beating crêpes ingredients together until smooth. Make one at a time in heavy 6″ frying pan in which you have melted ½ tsp butter to coat bottom. Pour in scant ¼ C batter for each crêpe and cook until dry on top and golden on bottom. With lifter transfer to large plate, flat out. Continue until all batter is cooked into crêpes, about eight.

Make White Sauce for Salmon Filling by blending 2½ Tbsp butter with 4½ Tbsp flour and salt then stirring in milk until thick. Reserve ¼ C white sauce.

Into pan tip flaked salmon, bones, liquid and all, and add onion, curry powder, soy or Worcestershire sauce and stir together over heat for a minute or two, then add 1 C white sauce and wine and stir to heat through. Cool. *Note:* All above may be made in advance on day the crêpes are to be served.

To assemble Crêpes, lay one flat on a plate and across center spread ¼ C salmon filling and roll up and place crosswise on large long shallow baking dish. Repeat until all crêpes are filled and rolled. Do not crowd them. Mix together reserved ¼ C white sauce and mayonnaise and spread some over each. Bake at 450° for 5 to 7 minutes or until heated through and bubbling and golden on top. Serves four.

Chicken Crêpes with Wine-Braised Cocktail Sausages

CRÊPES
¾ C plus 1 Tbsp flour
1½ tsp baking powder
½ tsp salt
1 Tbsp sugar
2 large eggs
¾ C milk
⅓ C water
½ tsp vanilla

CREAMED CHICKEN
5 Tbsp margarine
¼ C chopped green pepper
4½ Tbsp flour
1 tsp salt
3 C hot milk
1 chicken bouillon cube
2 C packed cooked cut up chicken
Parmesan cheese (for sprinkling top)

Two 8-oz jars cocktail sausages
3 Tbsp red wine

To make Crêpes, put all crêpes ingredients in beater bowl and beat until smooth. In a 6″ frypan melt ½ tsp butter and coat bottom. Add 3 Tbsp batter. Tip to coat bottom. Fry until barely tinged with gold. Turn and finish other side. Remove to large plate. Repeat until you have used all batter and made 12 thin crêpes.

To make Creamed Chicken, gently sauté green pepper in margarine for 2 or 3 minutes then blend in flour and salt. Stir in hot milk and chicken bouillon cube until thick. Remove one cup and reserve for topping. To remaining sauce add the cut up chicken.

To assemble, spoon ¼ C creamed chicken in a line along center of crêpe. Fold sides, overlapping, to cover. Place in large shallow baking dish, lapped side down. Repeat until all 12 crêpes are filled and nestled side by side on baking dish. Completely cover with reserved 1 C cream sauce. Sprinkle with Parmesan cheese. Place in oven at 375° to heat through, about 15 minutes. Run under preheated broiler to lightly brown top, watching carefully. Meanwhile heat drained cocktail sausages in wine and surround hot crêpes with them in a border. Serves six.

Mushroom Crêpes

BATTER

2 eggs
1 C milk
2 Tbsp barely melted butter
½ tsp salt
Shake of cayenne pepper
⅛ tsp nutmeg
½ C stirred all-purpose flour

FILLING

3 Tbsp butter (first amount)
½ C chopped sweet onion
½ lb sliced mushrooms
2 Tbsp lemon juice
2 Tbsp butter (second amount)
2 Tbsp flour
¼ tsp sugar
¾ tsp salt
Shake of marjoram
Shake of black pepper
¾ C milk
2½ Tbsp grated Parmesan cheese

The Batter has to be made in advance: Measure all ingredients into a bowl and beat until perfectly smooth. Refrigerate 2 hours.

To make Filling, gently sauté onions and mushrooms in 3 Tbsp butter until barely limp, not brown. Add lemon juice. Set aside. In pot melt butter (second amount) and stir in flour, sugar and seasonings to blend. Then stir in milk until thick. Add onion-mushroom mixture.

To make Crêpes, melt ¼ tsp butter in 6" frypan until bubbly. Add about 3 Tbsp of well stirred crêpe batter and cook tipping and rotating pan to spread batter until tinged with gold on bottom. Turn and cook on other side. Lift to large plate covered with wax paper. Repeat until all batter is cooked. You will have about 16 to 18 crêpes. Put about 1½ Tbsp Mushroom Filling at center of each and fold sides over to make a roll. Place, folded side up, in buttered shallow baking dish, sprinkle sparingly with Parmesan and bake at 250° for 15 minutes. Place under preheated broiler to finish during last 2 or 3 minutes. Serve at once.

Sandwiches

Salmon Salad Sandwiches see page 189

Hot Sandwiches

Hot Chicken Sandwich

2 C cooked chicken
2 hard-cooked eggs
¼ C sliced ripe olives
1 small can mushrooms
¼ C chopped onion
½ C mayonnaise
One 10-oz can mushroom cream soup
1 C dairy sour cream

Chop first 5 ingredients together and add mayonnaise. In large shallow buttered baking dish place, touching each other, 8 slices decrusted sandwich bread, buttered on both sides. Spread filling over each, cover with 8 more buttered slices. Mix together soup and sour cream and pour over evenly. Bake at 350° for 20 to 25 minutes. Serves eight.

Chicken-on-a-Bun

Heat split hamburg buns. On one side pile slices of hot chicken meat. Over this ladle All-Purpose Barbecue Sauce.

ALL-PURPOSE BARBECUE SAUCE
One medium onion, chopped
1 green pepper, chopped
½ C chopped celery
2 Tbsp salad oil
2 Tbsp brown sugar
2 Tbsp prepared mustard
1 Tbsp Worcestershire sauce
½ C catsup
One 8-oz can tomato sauce
½ tsp salt
⅛ tsp garlic powder
Dash of Tabasco sauce

Cook onion and green pepper and celery in oil until soft but not browned. Add the remaining ingredients and simmer 5 minutes. Ladle over chicken, replace top of bun and ladle additional sauce over.

Baked Cheese Sandwich

Place 6 slices crustless bread in buttered 15 × 9″ baking dish. Place 6 full slices old Cheddar cheese over bread and cover these with slices of luncheon meat of your choice. Cover with 6 more slices bread.

Pour over evenly this CUSTARD: Beat together 4 eggs, 2½ C milk, ½ tsp dry mustard, 1 tsp Worcestershire sauce.

Cover baking dish with foil and let stand in refrigerator overnight to soak. One hour before mealtime bake, foil-covered, at 350° for 40 to 50 minutes, uncovering last 10 minutes. Serve with Mushroom Sauce made by heating together 1 can mushroom soup and ⅓ C cream.

Creole Chicken Buns

2 Tbsp butter or margarine
¼ C finely chopped onion
⅓ C finely chopped green celery
1 C cooked chicken (or one 7-oz can) chopped
½ C tomato paste
¼ C chopped stuffed olives
½ tsp Worcestershire sauce
¼ tsp chili powder
¼ tsp salt
⅛ tsp pepper
4 to 6 hot dog buns, split

In medium frying pan melt butter or margarine and gently sauté onion and celery until soft. Add all remaining ingredients except buns and cook and stir until heated through. Spoon onto split hot dog rolls.

Filled and Grilled Tea Buns

1 lb ground chuck beef
¼ C chopped onion
2 Tbsp melted butter
One 10½-oz can cream of mushroom
    or chicken soup, undiluted
½ tsp salt
2 Tbsp flour
1 C dairy sour cream
Split tea buns, about 2 dozen

Brown ground chuck beef and onion gently in butter. Stir in cream soup and simmer 10 minutes. Mix salt with flour and stir into ¼ C of the sour cream until smooth. Add remaining sour cream to cooked meat mixture and stir in flour-cream paste until thick. Chill.

Near serving time spoon onto split 2 or 2½″ buns (preferably yeast) and arrange on baking sheet. Five or 10 minutes before serving, heat in very hot oven at 450° or under preheated broiler until top is bubbly and tinged with gold.

Split Level Pizzas

This recipe makes 6 double decker open-face pizza sandwiches.

12 slices fresh bread
One 8-oz can tomato paste
1 tsp oregano
1 tsp salt
½ C water
1 lb Mozzarella cheese sliced thinly
    (or other mild white cheese)
⅔ lb thinly sliced Polish sausage or pepperoni
    or cooked sliced pork sausages
One 10-oz can mushroom stems and pieces, drained
12 sliced stuffed olives
2 Tbsp olive or salad oil
Grated Parmesan or Romano cheese

In a little bowl mix together the oregano, salt, tomato paste and water, using the water to rinse

continued on page 187

out the tomato paste can. Spread 6 slices of bread with half of the tomato mixture and then cover with thin slices of Mozzarella cheese. Cover with remaining 6 slices of bread. Cover top slices with sliced Mozzarella. Then arrange in a single layer, but overlapping, all of the remaining sliced ingredients. Spoon remaining tomato mixture over them uniformly. Drizzle with olive or salad oil, then sprinkle generously with Parmesan or Romano cheese. Place on buttered cookie sheet and bake at 400° for 15 to 20 minutes or until cheese is melting and bread edges are just beginning to toast. Serve at once cut into quarters.

Bunwiches

1 Tbsp butter
1 Tbsp flour
½ C milk
One 8-oz can tuna
One 8-oz can refrigerated buttermilk or
    sweet milk biscuits (see below)
2½ slices process cheese cut in halves

Note: Buy the biscuits from the refrigerator counter of the supermarket.

To make Tuna Filling, in a small pot melt the butter, stir in the flour and when blended, stir in the milk until thick. Stir in the tuna including the oil.

On an ungreased cookie sheet separate the biscuit dough into 10 biscuits. Flatten them to 4 or 5″ rounds by pressing with your palm and finger tips. Top 5 with a heaping tablespoon of tuna mixture. Cover with remaining 5 flattened biscuits and seal edges with finger tips and fork tines. Bake at 375° for 10 to 12 minutes until pale gold. Remove from oven, top with cheese slices, return to oven to melt cheese for 2 or 3 minutes. Serve hot.

Variations: 1. Use Mozzarella cheese instead of process; 2. Use salmon instead of tuna; 3. Substitute 1 C chopped cooked chicken for the tuna; 4. Substitute chopped cooked ham for the tuna and add 1 or 2 Tbsp green relish.

Sloppy Joes

1¼ lb ground beef
2 Tbsp minced onion or bottled flakes
1 Tbsp brown sugar
2 Tbsp prepared mustard
¾ tsp salt
1 Tbsp Worcestershire sauce
½ C catsup
½ C water
4 hamburg buns sliced in halves

In large frying pan brown the beef without any added fat, stirring constantly. Add all remaining ingredients and let simmer 20 minutes.

Arrange 8 hamburg bun halves on large shallow baking pan. Pile all Sloppy Joe mixture on top neatly. If desired sprinkle generously with grated cheese or put thin small slices of Cheddar or processed cheese on top. Bake at 350° about 25 minutes until heated through and bubbly. Transfer to serving platter. Serves four.

Heroburgers

2 lb ground chuck beef
1 envelope (1½ oz) spaghetti sauce mix
Two 7½-oz cans tomato sauce
6 to 8 individual French loaves (3 × 14″)
Tomato slices (from 4 tomatoes)
8 Swiss or brick cheese slices, quartered
1 Spanish onion sliced and separated into rings
Sliced stuffed olives
Bread and butter pickles
Prepared mustard

In large frying pan brown ground chuck, chopping constantly to break meat up. Pour off excess fat. Stir in spaghetti sauce mix and tomato sauce. Bring to boil, stirring. Reduce heat and simmer 10 minutes, stirring occasionally. Split French loaves lengthwise and spoon hot meat mixture evenly over entire length of bottom half of each loaf. Top meat with full length layers of tomato slices, Swiss cheese slices, onion rings, sliced stuffed olives and pickles. Spread other half of each loaf with mustard and cover filling with it. Cut each loaf into 4 parts.

Hot Dog Loaf

2 Tbsp butter or margarine
¼ C finely chopped onion
½ C red hamburger relish
½ C chili sauce
1 Tbsp Worcestershire sauce
1 Tbsp brown sugar
Two 12″ loaves unsliced Italian or French
    bread (or 1 large loaf)
One 8-oz pkg process cheese, shredded
    (or mild Cheddar)
10 wieners cut in halves crosswise

Melt butter in small saucepan and sauté onion until tender, about 5 minutes. Remove from heat and add hamburger relish, chili sauce, Worcestershire sauce and brown sugar.

Cut a 1″ slice of bread from both ends of each loaf and use for another purpose. Cut each loaf into 5 pieces, each about 2″ thick. Now cut each 2″ slice vertically through the center, almost to the bottom and spread in between a heaping teaspoonful of the relish mixture. Sprinkle a heaping teaspoonful of grated cheese on top of relish, then push 2 wiener halves into the cheese diagonally letting the uncut ends of wieners poke out like short rabbits' ears. Spoon remaining relish evenly over and top with remaining cheese.

Use 2 large sheets of foil and assemble the sandwiches to resemble the original loaves. Wrap tightly in foil. Heat through at 400° for 25 minutes.

Sidewalk Sausageburgers

1 lb outsize farmers' sausage
2 green or red sweet peppers, sliced
1 large mild Spanish or 2 red
    Italian onions, sliced
½ tsp oregano
1 tsp salt
¼ tsp freshly ground black pepper
Canned sauerkraut (optional)
6 hamburg buns

    To make 6 sausageburgers, cut the long piece of farmers' sausage into 6 pieces and then nearly split each piece into half lenghtwise. Press them, open side down onto ungreased frying pan or grill and cook until golden brown on both sides. In another frying pan sauté the sliced onion and sweet red or green peppers, and sprinkle with the seasonings. If you are going to try sauerkraut instead of onion and peppers, gently heat the sauerkraut over low heat, cover one side of bun with a fairly generous layer of it, put fried split sausage on other side of bun and close.

Ham and Cheese French Toast Sandwich

4 slices bread
4 Tbsp butter or margarine
    (divided, see below)
2 slices ham
2 slices Swiss or Gouda cheese
2 eggs
½ C milk
1 tsp sugar
¼ tsp salt

    Spread 2 slices of the bread with 1 Tbsp of the butter or margarine. On each of the unbuttered slices place 1 slice of ham. Cover with sliced (⅛″ thick) Swiss or Gouda cheese. Cover with buttered slices of bread and press down firmly. Cut each in half.

    In shallow bowl beat the eggs with the sugar and salt then stir in milk. While the remaining butter is melting in a large frying pan soak the sandwiches in the egg-milk mixture, turning them over after about 1 minute. They require about 3 minutes to soak up all of the eggy liquid. Transfer sandwiches to pan and cook on one side until golden, then turn and lightly brown other side. Serve with maple syrup or black currant jelly or strawberry jam.

Cheese Dreams

    Cut unsliced bread into 1½″ slices. Remove crusts and cut each slice into quarters. Beat together 1 large egg, ¾ C grated old cheese, ½ tsp paprika and ⅛ tsp salt. Spread sides and top with cheese mixture, using narrow knife. Place on buttered foil on cookie sheet and broil 6″ from preheated broiler until golden. If desired top each with 1″ square side bacon before broiling. Serve warm.

Klondike Supper Rolls

One 3-oz pkg smoked dried beef
½ C grated mild Cheddar cheese
½ tsp dill weed or seed
One 8-oz pkg refrigerated crescent
    dinner rolls
2 Tbsp cormeal

SAUCE

One 10-oz can cream of mushroom soup
¼ C milk
2 hard-cooked eggs, chopped
1 Tbsp finely chopped green onion

    Finely chop dried beef. In a bowl mix it with the cheese and dill. Sprinkle baking board with cornmeal. Separate crescent dough in 4 rectangles. Lightly press each into the cornmeal on one side. Separate each along perforation into triangles, but leave each triangle pair lying together for ease of filling. Divide meat filling equally on dough pieces, lightly pressing it on. Starting at wide end of each triangle roll up with filling inside. Place point side down in buttered 8 × 8″ pan. Bake 15 to 20 minutes at 375°.

    Serve warm with Sauce made by combining all sauce ingredients in a saucepan and bringing slowly to boil.

Hot Chicken Cheese Sandwiches

8 slices bread
Butter
4 slices process (or other soft) cheese
4 large slices tomato
Slices of chicken
1 tsp salt, divided
¼ tsp pepper, divided
2 eggs, beaten
½ C milk
1 or 2 Tbsp butter

    Butter half of the bread slices. Cover the unbuttered slices first with cheese slices then tomato and chicken. Sprinkle with ½ tsp of the salt and ⅛ tsp of the pepper. Cover with buttered slices and press together. In a flat dish combine egg, milk, and remaining salt and pepper. Dip the sandwiches in the egg-milk mixture, turn each one over and let stand for 5 to 10 minutes until they soak up the liquid. Melt butter in large pan and fry sandwiches over medium heat until gold, turning when underside is done and browning other side.

Cold Sandwiches

Scandinavian Open Face Egg Sandwiches

1. Spread slices of whole wheat sandwich bread with mayonnaise. Arrange an overlapping row of thick slices of hard-cooked egg at center. At both sides put 2 thick half slices (crescents) of ripe tomato. Decorate tops of egg slices with sliced stuffed olives. Decorate corners of sandwich with tufts of parsley.

2. Spread slices of white bread, crusts removed, with French mustard. At center put a rolled up slice of cooked ham into ends of which you have tucked sprigs of parsley or tips of asparagus. At either side arrange row of overlapping hard-cooked egg slices, 3 at each side. Decorate each egg slice at center with a caper or bit of green pepper or pimiento. Tuck slices of ripe olives between eggs and ham.

3. Spread slices of 60% whole wheat bread with spreadable cheese, white cream or cheese whiz or any processed cheese that will spread. Slice hard-cooked eggs lengthwise and cut these ovals in halves lengthwise. Place in an orderly diagonal row from opposite corners on bread. Gently sauté large thin slices of mushrooms and place 2 at each corner of sandwich. Garnish eggs with long strips of pimiento.

Clubhouse Sandwiches

FIRST FILLING
One ½-lb can red salmon
One 4-oz pkg white cream cheese
2 Tbsp chopped pimiento or salad olives
2 tsp finely chopped onion or chives
½ tsp salt

SECOND FILLING
3 hard-cooked eggs
3 Tbsp green relish
3 Tbsp mayonnaise
½ tsp salt
Lettuce

Make the Fillings in advance. For the first, flake the salmon with its juice and add remaining ingredients and mix well. For the second, mash the hard-cooked eggs with the pickle, mayonnaise and salt.

Cover both bowls and refrigerate until serving time. At serving time butter 12 slices lightly toasted bread. Divide salmon mixture between 4 slices. Top each with another slice of toast already spread with one quarter of the egg mixture. Top each with a leaf of lettuce then a third slice of toast, buttered side down. Cut each into 3 triangles and top each triangle with a slice of dill or bread and butter pickle fixed with a toothpick. Serve at once.

Triple Treat Open Sandwiches

4 slices white or whole wheat bread
2 Tbsp mayonnaise
4 slices from a large peeled tomato
4 slices process cheese
8 slices bacon

Toast the bread on one side only. Spread the untoasted sides with mayonnaise and cover each with a large tomato slice. Cover each tomato slice with a slice of cheese to nearly cover bread. Top each with 2 slices bacon, placed crisscross. Arrange on broiler pan. Place 6" below preheated broiler. Cook until cheese begins to melt and bacon is sizzling and beginning to crispen. Serve at once with knife and fork.

Asparagus Roll-Ups

4 oz process cheese (room temperature)
1 Tbsp cream
¼ tsp dry mustard
Canned asparagus spears, drained
16 thin slices sandwich bread
Butter

To soften the cheese, blend in cream and dry mustard until of spreading consistency. Trim crusts from bread, butter and spread with cheese filling. Place asparagus spear diagonally across each slice of bread; fold opposite corners across center and overlap. Secure with toothpicks. Carefully wrap in tea towel, then in plastic bag and chill. Remove toothpicks before serving.

Salmon Salad Sandwiches

One can (7¾-oz) salmon
2 Tbsp wheat germ
¼ C cottage cheese
¼ C finely chopped celery
2 Tbsp shredded carrot
6 or 8 slices whole wheat bread

In a bowl flake the salmon in its juice and add the wheat germ and let soak 1 or 2 minutes. Add the cottage cheese, celery, carrot and salt to taste. Spread on 4 unbuttered slices whole wheat bread. Cover with buttered slices.

Pinwheels

Spread required number of slices of bread with soft butter and then spread each with a filling of your choice. Roll up each slice firmly, like a jelly roll. Wrap airtight and chill overnight. When ready to serve, cut off crust-ends and slice into pinwheels ½" thick.

Fruited Cream Cheese Sandwiches

One 4-oz pkg white cream cheese
    (room temperature)
1 Tbsp milk
3 Tbsp chopped glacé fruit
    (cherries, pineapple, etc)
Dash of salt
Bread and butter

Cream the cheese with the 1 Tbsp milk until of spreading consistency. Blend in chopped fruits, nuts and salt. For each sandwich spread 1 slice of bread with filling, another with butter. Cut decoratively.

Ribbon Sandwiches

From an unsliced loaf cut 3 lengthwise slices, crusts on. Spread one side of each with soft butter. Then spread one slice with HAM FILLING: 1½ C finely ground cooked ham mixed with enough mayonnaise to make of soft spreading consistency. Spread another slice with EGG FILLING: 3 hard-cooked eggs mashed or ground, mixed with 1 tsp chopped green onion, ½ tsp salt and enough mayonnaise to make of soft spreading consistency. Put on top of ham slice and top with third slice, buttered side down. Wrap snugly and chill. At serving time, cut off crusts with very sharp knife and cut into ribbon sandwiches which may be cut once more into triangles.

Fillings

Four-Way Sandwich Filling

½ C mayonnaise
½ tsp salt
2 Tbsp mustard relish or green hot dog relish
1 tsp chopped green onion

To the above ingredients any one of the following may be added: 1. Four chopped hard-cooked eggs; 2. Two cups ground ham; 3. Two cups ground leftover beef plus 1 tsp horseradish; 4. Two cups ground boiled or roast chicken plus 2 Tbsp finely chopped celery.

Curried Egg Filling

4 chopped hard-cooked eggs, 2 Tbsp finely chopped celery or green relish, 2 Tbsp chopped onion, ½ tsp curry powder, ¼ C salad dressing. Combine ingredients. Makes 1¼ C filling (5 Sandwiches).

Egg-Olive Filling

2 hard-cooked eggs
One 3-oz pkg cream cheese (room temperature)
½ tsp prepared mustard
1 tsp grated raw onion or finely chopped
    green onion or chives
6 chopped stuffed olives or
    1 Tbsp chopped salad olives
2 Tbsp mayonnaise
8 slices whole wheat bread

Chop egg finely, mix with cheese, mustard, onion, olives and mayonnaise and blend. Makes four 2-slice whole wheat bread sandwiches.

Ham and Relish

1 C cooked ground or chopped ham or
    other leftover meat
4 Tbsp chopped pickles
1 tsp prepared mustard
3 or 4 Tbsp salad dressing or mayonnaise
Salt and pepper to taste

Mix together and spread on buttered whole wheat bread. Makes four 2-slice sandwiches.

Nutty Salmon Sandwich Filling

One can (3¾-oz) salmon
1 Tbsp wheat germ
1 Tbsp crunchy peanut butter
1 Tbsp thick salad dressing
2 Tbsp raisins
3 or 4 Tbsp chopped walnuts or sesame seeds

Flake salmon with juice and add wheat germ and let soak 1 or 2 minutes. Then add all remaining ingredients. Spread on 4 slices whole wheat bread and cover with 4 buttered slices.

Large Quantity Savory Spread

¼ C margarine
¾ lb ground good quality beef
1 C chopped Spanish onion
½ green pepper, chopped
2 Tbsp flour
1 Tbsp dry mustard
4 Tbsp sugar
1 tsp salt
½ tsp mustard seed
½ tsp celery seed
½ tsp garlic salt
1 bay leaf
⅜ C (6 Tbsp) vinegar
1 C peeled and chopped firm tomatoes
One 3-oz jar pimientos including liquid
2 eggs
½ C shredded cheese

In large frypan melt margarine and in it gently sauté the meat, onion and green pepper 5 minutes, breaking up lumps. Add and stir in the flour, mustard, sugar salt, seeds, garlic salt, bay leaf, vinegar, tomatoes and pimientos. Bring to boil stirring, then cover and simmer 1 hour. Beat the eggs in a little bowl and add a big spoonful of the hot mixture to them, stirring, then stir them quickly into the meat mixture. Stir in the cheese. Remove from heat, remove bay leaf. Cool. Store some in refrigerator, some in freezer.

Tomato Sandwich Spread

12 medium-large ripe tomatoes
    scalded and peeled
2 medium-sized Spanish onions
2 sweet red peppers
½ C flour
5 tsp dry mustard
1 Tbsp salt
1 C sugar
1 C cider vinegar

Quartered, the prepared tomatoes measure 6 C. Press gently and tip off excess liquid. Peel and quarter onions. Quarter and remove seeds from peppers. Grind all 3 vegetables through medium knife of food chopper into heavy pot. Place over medium heat while you mix together dry the flour, mustard, salt and sugar and then stir in vinegar and at once stir into hot vegetables constantly until thickened, then reduce heat to low and simmer until thicker, about 2 hours, stirring frequently. (This spread thickens more after it is cold.) Pour into 6 sterilized 8-oz jars, cover with clean hot paraffin and seal. Put on lids, wash, cool and label. Delicious with bacon in toasted sandwiches.

Cakes

Orange Party Cake with Chocolate Coating see page 205

Marbled Angel Food Cake

1 C sifted cake flour
1½ C sifted icing sugar
12 large egg whites (1⅞ C)
1½ tsp cream of tartar
¼ tsp salt
½ tsp almond extract
½ tsp vanilla
1 C granulated sugar
2 Tbsp sifted cocoa

Sift together twice the measured sifted cake flour and icing sugar. Set aside. In very large mixing bowl beat together until foamy the egg whites, cream of tartar, salt, almond extract and vanilla. Gradually, 2 Tbsp at a time, sprinkle the granulated sugar over as you beat, until all is added and mixture is very stiff, maybe 20 minutes. Remove beaters. Sift flour-icing sugar mixture gradually over as you fold until all is just incorporated. Spoon half of mixture into another bowl and sprinkle cocoa over top and fold in evenly. Spoon large amounts into ungreased tube pan (with removable center) alternating between white and cocoa-colored batters. Cut through to bottom with knife to eliminate air pockets. Bake at 350° for 55 minutes or until when touched, dint does not remain.

When baked, turn upside down and let hang one hour suspended. Carefully loosen around sides and tube with up-and-down strokes of long slender knife. Lift out and loosen bottom with knife. Invert on large serving plate. When thoroughly cool, frost with Icing: 3 Tbsp soft butter, 3 C unsifted icing sugar, 6 Tbsp 10% cream, shake of salt, 15 drops yellow food coloring. Beat until smooth. Frost. Melt 2 squares of chocolate and drizzle evenly over top, allowing some to run down sides in attractive narrow streams. Cool but do not refrigerate.

Brown Sugar Spice Cake

2½ C sifted cake and pastry flour
1 tsp salt
¼ tsp baking soda
3 tsp baking powder
1 tsp cinnamon
½ tsp cloves
¼ tsp nutmeg
½ C margarine
1½ C light brown sugar (packed)
2 eggs
1 C milk
1 tsp vanilla

Sift the sifted flour with the salt, soda, baking powder and spices. Cream together the margarine and brown sugar. Beat in eggs. Remove beaters and fold in flour mixture, in thirds, alternately with milk and vanilla until smoothly blended. Do not overstir. Pour into a 9 × 9″ pan lined on bottom with buttered wax paper. Bake at 375° for 25 to 28 minutes on center rack of oven.

Fruity Frosted Applesauce Cake

½ C best quality shortening
½ C white sugar
½ C light brown sugar
1 egg
1¾ C sifted all-purpose flour
½ tsp salt
1 tsp baking soda
1 tsp cinnamon
½ tsp cloves
⅔ C currants
⅓ C chopped walnuts
¾ C raisins
1¼ C applesauce

In beater bowl cream the shortening with the sugars until light. Beat in egg. Remove beater. Sift together the sifted flour, salt, soda and spices. Stir in, alternately with the applesauce, one-third of each at a time. Fold in fruits and nuts. Turn into well-buttered 9 or 10″ tube pan, smooth top and bake at 350° about 55 minutes. Turn out of pan and cool on rack.

CREAM CHEESE FROSTING
One 4-oz pkg white cream cheese
2 C unsifted icing sugar
2 Tbsp milk
½ tsp salt

In beater bowl beat cheese until creamy then add sugar and salt and beat until smooth, adding milk slowly until of smooth, almost runny spreading consistency. Spread all over cooled cake. Chill. If you plan to freeze the cake cut strong backing board into a circle, place cake on it and insert in double plastic bags and freeze.

Quick Fruit Cake

2 eggs, slightly beaten
One 28-oz can mincemeat
One 14-oz can sweetened condensed milk
¼ C sherry
2 C walnuts
2 C mixed fruit-cake fruits
3 C unsifted cake and pastry flour
½ tsp salt
1 tsp baking soda
½ tsp cinnamon
½ tsp cloves
½ tsp nutmeg

In a large bowl beat eggs. Add mincemeat, condensed milk, sherry, walnuts and mixed fruits and stir to thoroughly combine. In another bowl combine thoroughly flour, salt, baking soda and spices. Stir into wet mixture until well blended. Pour evenly into 2 standard loaf pans which have been triple-lined with wax paper, buttering the top layer of paper.

Bake on center shelf of oven with waterpan on shelf below at 300° for 1½ hours. Remove from oven, cool in pans on cake racks 15 minutes. Remove from pans and carefully peel off wax paper. Cool completely. Store in refrigerator in double plastic bags.

Bake-and-Take Raisin Cake

1½ C raisins
2 C boiling water
½ C shortening
¾ C granulated sugar
1 egg
1½ C sifted all-purpose flour
1 tsp baking soda
½ tsp nutmeg
¼ tsp cloves
¼ tsp allspice
½ tsp salt
1 C chopped walnuts
1 tsp vanilla

First add boiling water to raisins in a saucepan. Cover and boil 15 minutes. Drain and reserve ¾ C raisin liquid and cool it in a shallow bowl.

Meanwhile cream shortening and sugar together well, then add egg and beat. Resift flour and the baking soda, spices and salt and add alternately with cooled raisin liquid and vanilla. Fold in nuts and drained raisins. Turn into 9 × 9″ pan lined with buttered paper or bake in 2 buttered 9″ layer cake pans. Bake at 350° for 35 minutes for 9 × 9″ pan or 25 minutes for 2 layers. Cool in pan on cake rack for 10 minutes then turn out on rack to cool.

HARD SAUCE FROSTING: Into beater bowl measure ¼ C butter, 3 C sifted icing sugar, 1 egg, 2 tsp milk and 1 tsp vanilla. Beat until of spreading consistency and spread on cooled cake. If desired sprinkle top with chopped nuts.

Banana Cake with Crunchy Topping

2 C sifted cake flour
    (or all-purpose flour sifted 4 times)
1½ tsp baking powder
1 tsp baking soda
¾ tsp salt
1⅓ C granulated sugar
½ C soft shortening
½ C sour milk or buttermilk (or ½ C
    milk soured with ½ Tbsp vinegar)
1 C mashed ripe bananas
2 eggs, unbeaten
1 tsp vanilla

Sift flour, baking powder, soda, salt and sugar into mixing bowl. Add soft shortening, ¼ C of the sour milk and mashed bananas. Mix until flour is dampened, then beat 300 strokes by hand or 2 minutes in mixer at low speed. Add eggs, remaining ¼ C of sour milk and vanilla, beat 150 strokes by hand or 1 minute in mixer at low speed. Spread evenly in 8 × 10″ or 9 × 9″ square pan, greased on bottom only. Bake at 375° for 35 to 40 minutes. Remove from oven, turn oven to broil. Cool on rack 5 minutes.

Spread hot cake evenly with CRUNCHY TOPPING: Cream ¼ C butter or margarine and ¾ C light brown sugar together. Add ½ C shredded coconut and ¼ C chopped nuts. Place at least 6″ below preheated broiler and broil until sugar is bubbly and topping is delicately browned. Cut into squares in pan.

Bienenstich

BATTER
¼ C butter
⅓ C sugar
1 egg
1 tsp vanilla
1 tsp almond extract
2 C sifted cake and pastry flour
2 tsp baking powder
½ tsp salt
3 Tbsp milk

TOPPING
½ C butter
½ C sugar
¾ C slivered or coarsely chopped almonds
2 tsp vanilla
2 Tbsp milk

FILLING
1 C 10% cream (first amount)
¼ C sugar
3 Tbsp 10% cream (second amount)
3 Tbsp cornstarch
½ C butter
1 Tbsp vanilla

To make Batter, cream together butter and sugar until light. Beat in egg, vanilla and almond extract. Sift together the sifted cake and pastry flour, baking powder and salt and add to bowl alternately with the milk, beating. This batter resembles a rich, drop cookie dough. Spread into 2 well-buttered 8″ layer cake tins. These must be lined or have a swivel bar in bottom to ease removal of cake. Do not bake yet.

To make Topping, in a shallow heavy medium pan over medium heat melt the butter, add sugar and almonds and stir constantly until it bubbles all over, about 2 or 3 minutes. Remove from heat and stir in the vanilla and milk. Spoon this syrup evenly all over top of unbaked cakes. It is thin and runny. Bake at 400° for 15 minutes. Do not overbake or syrupy edges will harden. Carefully turn out on cake racks.

To make Filling, in a small saucepan bring just to boil the 1 C cream and ¼ C sugar. Remove from heat. Stir together to a smooth paste the milk and cornstarch. Return pot to burner and stir this paste into milk over medium heat until thick. Chill. Beat the butter with the vanilla until creamy. When milk mixture is cold beat at high speed into the butter until light and airy, at least 5 minutes.

Put one cake, almond side up, on large cake plate. Cover with cold filling, nearly ¾″ thick. Cover with second cake, almond side up and let rest for an hour before serving. Serves 8.

Dark Blond Florida Fruit Cake

½ lb butter
1 C granulated sugar
5 large eggs
1¾ C unsifted all-purpose flour
½ tsp baking powder
½ tsp salt
¾ lb sliced glacé cherries
    (mixed green and red)
1 lb candied pineapple (shred on ¼"
    shredder or chop finely)
4 C whole or coarsely chopped pecans
    (one pound)
1 Tbsp vanilla
2 Tbsp lemon juice

Cream butter and sugar together until very light and fluffy. Add eggs and beat in each one as you add it until smoothly blended. Sift the unsifted flour with the baking powder and salt. Mix ½ C of this flour mixture through the prepared fruits and nuts which have been mixed together. Sprinkle remaining flour mixture over creamed mixture and stir until blended. Stir in vanilla and lemon juice. Add floured fruits and nuts and stir well. Turn into 2 loaf pans lined with 3 thicknesses of wax paper, brushing top sheet generously with butter. Do not preheat oven. Put waterpan below cakes and three-quarters fill with boiling water. Turn on oven to 250° (to "bake" not "preheat," which means only bottom burner is on). Bake about 2¾ to 3 hours or until top feels firm to touch. Cool in pans on cake rack. This cake is moist enough that it slices perfectly within 24 hours. It freezes well.

Pineapple Cheesecake

Two 8-oz pkgs white cream cheese
    (room temperature)
3 eggs
⅔ C sugar
¼ tsp salt
½ tsp almond extract

TOPPING
One 10-oz can crushed pineapple
¼ C sugar
2 Tbsp cornstarch
Shake of salt

In beater bowl beat the cheese until fluffy, scraping down sides of bowl 2 or 3 times with rubber scraper. Add eggs, sugar, salt and almond extract and beat until thoroughly blended, scraping down sides of bowl again.

Line bottom of an 8" layer cake tin with a round of foil, shiny side up. Turn batter into pan and bake at 350° for 30 minutes or until firm to touch at center. Loosen sides by running tip of knife around edge. Let cool. Turn out on plate and peel off foil.

To make Topping, in a small pot mix well the sugar, cornstarch and salt then add pineapple, mix well and cook stirring until thick and 1 minute longer, stirring constantly. Cool. Spread evenly over cooled cheesecake. Chill for 2 hours before serving. *Note:* If this cheesecake is well covered, it will keep, refrigerated, for 3 or 4 days.

Blender Orange Cake

2 C stirred but unsifted cake and
    pastry flour
1 tsp baking soda
½ tsp salt
1 large orange (juice and rind)
1 C granulated sugar or light brown sugar
    or icing sugar
½ C shortening
1 C sugar (second amount)
2 eggs
1 C light raisins
¾ C sour (or soured) milk
    or buttermilk (see note)

Note: If you have to sour the milk put 1 Tbsp lemon juice or vinegar in bottom of measuring cup and fill to brim with sweet milk and let stand until needed.

Into a bowl sift the flour, soda and salt. Set aside. Squeeze juice from orange and to the juice add the 1 C granulated or brown or icing sugar. Set aside for later. Cut orange rind into eighths and put in blender along with shortening, 1 C granulated sugar and eggs and blend until orange rind is finely chopped. Now add sour milk and raisins and blend until raisins are chopped. Turn this blender mixture into the flour mixture in bowl and stir in until all flour is dampened and batter is smooth. Line 9 × 9" pan on bottom with buttered wax paper. Butter sides. Turn batter in and bake at 325° for 40 minutes or until it tests done. As soon as cake is removed from oven spoon reserved orange juice-sugar mixture all over top and let cool. Then pass under broiler until bubbly. Cool cake in pan standing on rack. To serve cut directly from pan.

Quick Cake with Crunchy Topping

2 large eggs
1 C granulated sugar
¼ tsp salt
1 tsp vanilla
½ C milk
3 Tbsp margarine or butter
1 C unsifted all-purpose flour
1 tsp baking powder

Into beater bowl break eggs and beat until fluffy then slowly add sugar until very light and doubled in bulk. Beat in salt and vanilla. In a pan heat together the milk and margarine or butter to just below boiling point. While very hot pour into egg mixture beating all the time. Remove beaters.

Sift the flour and baking powder over and fold in. Pour into greased 8 × 8" or 9 × 9" pan with buttered wax paper on bottom and bake on center rack in oven at 350° for 30 minutes or until when touched with fingertip dent does not remain. Cool in pan on rack.

Cover with topping made with ¼ C soft margarine, ½ C light brown sugar, ½ C coconut creamed together. Spread evenly and carefully over slightly cooled cake and carefully heat under hot broiler, 4" from burner, until it bubbles. Cool.

Strawberry Shortcake

SHORTCAKE DOUGH
2 C stirred but not sifted all-purpose flour
4 tsp baking powder
½ tsp cream of tartar
½ tsp salt
2 tsp sugar
½ C hard butter
⅔ C cold milk

FILLING AND TOPPING
1 qt strawberries
½ pt whipping cream

Sift together into mixing bowl the flour, baking powder, cream of tartar, salt and sugar. Cut in the hard butter with pastry blender until size of small peas. Add milk all at once, mixing quickly until flour is barely moistened. Press dough into ball. Pat out on lightly floured board until of ¾" thickness. Cut out rounds with floured 3" cutter. Bake on ungreased cookie sheet at 450° for 8 to 9 minutes.

To make individual strawberry shortcakes, split each big biscuit and butter bottom half. Select 7 perfect big strawberries from a 1-qt box and wash and hull and dry them and set aside. Wash and hull and slice remaining berries and sweeten with ¼ C sugar. Put generous amount of sliced berries on bottom half of each split biscuit, cover with top, add more berries to top. Cover with whipped cream. Decorate top of each shortcake with reserved perfect whole berries.

Note: If desired, shape shortcake dough into one large round cake ¾" thick and bake on ungreased cookie sheet or pie plate at 450° for 12 to 15 minutes. Split, butter and cover with berries and whipped cream as above for individual shortcakes.

Burnt Sugar Layer Cake

1 C granulated sugar (first amount)
½ C boiling water
½ C shortening
1⅓ C granulated sugar (second amount)
3 large eggs
2½ C sifted cake and pastry flour
2½ tsp baking powder
1 tsp salt

To caramelize sugar, melt in a heavy frying pan the 1 C sugar stirring constantly until golden brown and no lumps remain. Remove from heat and at arm's length slowly stir in the ½ C boiling water. It will sputter and steam so take care, stirring until lumps dissolve. Measure ¼ C of this caramel syrup in a 1-cup measure and fill with water to make 1 cup. Set aside. Set aside remaining caramel syrup too.

To make Batter, cream shortening and second amount sugar until light and creamy. Beat eggs in well. Remove beaters. Sift together the sifted flour, baking powder and salt and fold in alternately with the measured 1 cup caramel liquid until batter is smooth. Line two 9" layer cake tins on bottom with buttered wax paper. Turn in and smooth batter.

Bake at center of oven at 350° about 22 minutes or until when touched at center fingerprint does not remain. Let stand in pans 5 minutes then turn out on cake racks to cool.

To make Frosting, beat together until of spreading consistency ¼ C butter, remaining ½ C caramel syrup, 2½ C icing sugar and ¼ tsp salt. Spread between cooled layers and on sides and top of cake.

Glenhyrst Orange Cheesecake

CRUMB CRUST
2½ C fine graham wafer crumbs
½ C plus 1 Tbsp melted butter
⅓ C granulated sugar

FILLING
2 Tbsp (2 envelopes) plain gelatin
¼ C lemon juice
¼ C cold water
⅔ C sugar
Shake of salt
3 eggs, yolks and whites separated
½ C fresh orange juice
1 tsp grated orange rind
One 8-oz pkg white cream cheese, room temperature
1 C whipping cream, whipped

ORANGE GLAZE
One 10-oz can Mandarin oranges
¼ C sugar
¼ tsp salt
2 Tbsp cornstarch or arrowroot flour (arrowroot makes clear glaze)
½ C fresh orange juice
Boiling water (see below)
½ tsp yellow food coloring

To make Crust, mix together graham wafer crumbs, melted butter and sugar. Press uniformly into buttered spring-form pan and bake 5 minutes at 350°. Cool.

To make Filling, soak the gelatin in the lemon juice and water for 5 minutes. Stir together in top of double boiler the soaked gelatin, sugar, salt and orange juice and heat, stirring, over boiling water until gelatin and sugar dissolve. Beat egg yolks and stir some of the mixture into them, then return all to double boiler and cook, stirring, until mixture thickens slightly. Remove from heat, add orange rind and cool. Beat egg whites until stiff and fold in. Whip cream until stiff and fold in to make a smooth blend. Turn into crumb-crust-lined pan. Chill, preferably overnight.

To make Orange Glaze, drain and dry Manadarin oranges, saving juice. Arrange in circles around edge and at center of chilled cheesecake. Combine dry in saucepan the sugar, salt and cornstarch or arrowroot. Stir in the orange juice. Measure the juice from canned Mandarin oranges. Make it up to ⅔ C by adding boiling water. Stir into orange juice mixture and cook, stirring, until thick. Reduce heat and cook 2 or 3 minutes longer. Remove from heat. Add yellow food coloring. Cool a little. Spoon all over top of cake and orange sections, then drizzle small amounts down sides of cake. Chill.

December Birthday Cake

First make a 9″ square one-egg cake or use cake mix.

ICING

3 Tbsp butter
4 C unsifted icing sugar
5 Tbsp milk
½ tsp almond extract
1 C flaked coconut
½ tsp green food coloring
2 Tbsp warm water
Tiny colored gumdrops

Bake and cool cake, then cut and assemble to form a Christmas tree: first cut the cake in half crosswise. On one half, mark the center of the long uncut side. Then cut diagonally from center mark to each corner to form 1 large and 2 small triangles. Cut one of the small triangles in half to form 2 small triangles which will be the tree trunk. Place the remaining small triangle on a large tray as the top branch of tree. Center the point of the large triangle along the bottom edge of the small triangle to form the next branch. Now from the remaining half of the cake, cut two 2″ triangles from corners on cut side. Place the large piece of cake that remains to form bottom branch of tree; arrange the 2″ triangles to form points at outer edges of bottom branch. Place the smaller tree trunk triangles together to form a rectangular trunk at bottom of tree.

Carefully and patiently frost top and sides with Icing made by beating together butter, sugar, milk and almond extract. Dilute food coloring with water. Add coconut and toss with a fork until coconut is evenly tinted. Dry on double paper towels. Sprinkle tinted coconut over the cake, except along upper portion of each branch where snow would accumulate. Decorate with gum drops as desired. Place candles on branch tips to simulate colored lights.

Bunny Birthday Cake

CAKE

1¾ C sifted all-purpose flour
1¼ C granulated sugar
4 tsp baking powder
1 tsp salt
⅓ C shortening (room temperature)
⅔ C milk (first amount)
1 egg
⅓ C milk (second amount)

ICING

¼ C margarine
5 Tbsp lemon juice
3½ C stirred but not packed icing sugar

DECORATION

Coconut
Red food coloring

To make Cake, into beater bowl measure sifted flour, sugar, baking powder, salt, shortening and ⅔ C milk and beat at medium speed for 2 minutes, scraping down sides of bowl several times. Add egg and remaining ⅓ C milk and beat for another 2 minutes, scraping bowl often. Pour batter into 2 buttered wax-paper-lined 8″ round pans. Bake at 375° about 25 minutes. Turn out on rack, tear off paper and cool.

To make Icing, beat together the margarine, lemon juice and icing sugar until smooth.

To shape Bunny, cut a 1½″ wide ring from outside edge of one layer. Cut this ring into eight even pieces for "paws." Cut edges off other layer, leaving a 6½″ square. These edges, when straight sides are placed together, form 2 ears. Now place small round from which ring was cut at center of large tray. Place ears at top, slanting out. Place square under head for body. To form paws, stack 2 ring pieces on top of each other and place two stacks touching at each side of body. Frost all over with icing. Sprinkle all over with coconut. Tint a little coconut with red food coloring to make it pink and sprinkle inside ears and at nose and on bottom of paws. Tie a pink ribbon in a bow and place it under Bunny's chin. Make tip of tongue with red smartie, eyes with raisins, and smiling lips with tiny strip of licorice or shreds of raisins.

Swirled Chocolate Cheesecake

CHOCOLATE COOKIE CRUST

1¼ C chocolate crumbs
 (blender: thirty 2″ chocolate wafers)
⅓ C melted butter

CHEESECAKE

1½ C chocolate chips
½ C sugar (first amount)
Two 8-oz pkgs white cream cheese
 (room temperature)
¾ C sugar (second amount)
1 tsp vanilla
4 large eggs

First gently combine fine chocolate crumbs which have been crumbed in blender or finely crushed with rolling pin with the melted butter and patiently and evenly line bottom and part way up sides of 9″ spring-form pan or 9″ angel food pan with removable center. Bake 5 minutes only at 325°. Cool on counter.

Now in top of double boiler stir together chocolate chips and ½ C sugar and melt, covered, over boiling water, stirring twice during melting time. Stand off heat but leave in covered double boiler. Then put into your beater bowl the cream cheese, ¾ C sugar, vanilla and eggs and beat until blended smoothly. Scrape down sides and up from bottom 2 or 3 times.

To chocolate mixture in double boiler add half of the cheese mixture. Reserve remainder. Pour almost all of chocolate mixture into crumb-lined pan. Slowly pour remaining white cheese mixture all over it. Now drizzle remaining chocolate mixture over top and with tip of knife swirl it lightly through white cheese layer. Bake at 325° for 50 minutes. It puffs up but falls a little on cooling at room temperature. Chill thoroughly. It must be carefully loosened and transferred with two lifters to serving dish. Serves twelve.

Italian Cheesecake: Crostata Di Ricotta

PASTRY

2 C unsifted all-purpose flour
¾ C butter (room temperature)
4 egg yolks
¼ C sugar
3 Tbsp dry Marsala wine (or cold water)
1 tsp freshly grated lemon rind
½ tsp salt

RICOTTA FILLING

Five 8-oz pkgs white cream cheese or
    5 C ricotta cheese (2½ lb)
½ C sugar
1 Tbsp flour
½ tsp salt
1 tsp vanilla
1 tsp freshly grated orange rind
4 egg yolks
2 Tbsp raisins (preferably bleached)
2 Tbsp diced candied orange peel
2 Tbsp diced candied citron
4 Tbsp slivered blanched almonds
1 egg white (reserved from above yolks)
1 Tbsp water

To make Pastry, in a large mixing bowl measure the flour, butter, egg yolks, sugar, Marsala wine or water, lemon rind and salt. Mix at low speed with beaters until all ingredients are just combined. (Do not let mixture get creamy; the dough should be combined just enough so you can pack it into a ball between your palms.) Chill about half an hour until it is firm but not hard. Break off ¼ of the dough and reserve for lattice design on top later. Roll remaining dough out on lightly floured surface to a circle about ⅛" thick and 13" diameter. Lightly butter the bottom and sides of a 9" spring form pan and line it with the pastry. (It is easier to line the pan if you start at the nearest edge of the circle, lift the pastry and drape it over the rolling pin then place the pin over the middle of the buttered pan and unroll the pastry, leaving some slack in the center.) Gently press into the bottom and around the sides of the pan. Bring pastry right up to top edge of pan. If it breaks it is easy to patch it.

Make Cheese Filling by combining in a large bowl the cheese, flour, salt, vanilla, grated orange rind and egg yolks and beat until they are thoroughly mixed. Stir in the raisins, candied orange peel and citron. Spoon this filling into the pastry-lined pan and smooth it evenly. Sprinkle top with slivered almonds.

Roll out remaining piece of pastry dough and cut strips ½" wide then crisscross these strips over the pie to make a lattice design. Brush the strips lightly with one egg white mixed with 1 Tbsp water. Bake on center shelf of oven at 350° for 60 minutes or until the crust is golden and filling is firm. Remove from oven to cake rack and cool 15 minutes then remove rim from pan and let cool completely. If not to be served within a few hours refrigerate but let sit at room temperature before serving. Decorate border of serving plate with tiny bunches of green seedless tangy grapes.

Carrot Cake

2 C stirred but unsifted cake and pastry flour
2 tsp baking soda
1½ tsp baking powder
1 tsp salt
2 tsp cinnamon
2 C sugar
1½ C oil
4 eggs
2 C grated carrot
1¼ C drained, crushed pineapple
1 C chopped nuts

Place sifter over large bowl and measure flour, baking soda, baking powder, salt and cinnamon into it and sift into bowl. Now add the sugar, oil and eggs and beat hard by hand 1 minute. Add carrot, pineapple and nuts and beat to mix. This batter is quite moist. Grease bottom of 13 × 9" pan. Line bottom with buttered heavy brown paper. Pour in batter and bake at 350° on center shelf for 35 minutes or until when gently touched at center your fingerprint does not remain. Cool and frost.

CREAM CHEESE FROSTING

One 4-oz pkg white cream cheese
½ C butter (or margarine)
2 C icing sugar
1 tsp vanilla

Measure all Frosting ingredients into beater bowl and beat until perfectly smooth. Spread on cooled cake. Cut cake into squares from pan.

Fresh Coconut Layer Cake

Note: This is a standard 2-egg cake.

½ C shortening
1 C granulated sugar
2 eggs
1¾ C sifted cake and pastry flour
2 tsp baking powder
½ tsp salt
½ C coconut milk (or milk)
generous amount of fresh grated coconut

Cream shortening 1 minute. Add sugar gradually. Add eggs, one at a time and beat well. Remove beaters. Sift together the sifted flour, baking powder and salt. Fold sifted dry ingredients into shortening mixture, alternately with coconut milk, in thirds, until blended. Turn into 2 greased and lightly floured 8" layer cake tins and bake at 375° for 25 to 30 minutes. Turn out on cake racks to cool.

To make Icing, you need about 4 C icing sugar. In beater bowl beat 3 Tbsp butter, gradually adding icing sugar and 3 to 4 Tbsp leftover coconut milk until of soft spreading consistency. Spread between and on sides only of layers. Now comes the tricky part. Down the center of a 3-foot length of wax paper sprinkle lightly but thickly a 3" wide strip of grated coconut. Pick up the 2 layers of side-frosted cake and holding firmly roll it like a wheel to coat sides with coconut. A second pair of hands helps. Put side-coated cake on cake plate and frost top generously with remaining icing and sprinkle with all remaining coconut. Pat lightly to make it cling.

Black Cherry Cheesecake

CRUMB CRUST
1⅓ C fine graham cracker crumbs
⅓ C brown sugar
1 tsp cinnamon
⅓ C melted butter

FILLING
Two 8-oz pkgs white cream cheese
    (room temperature)
⅔ C white sugar
3 eggs
¼ tsp salt
½ tsp almond extract

TOPPING
One 14-oz can black cherries, pitted
⅓ C white sugar
4 tsp arrowroot flour (or cornstarch)
1 tsp lemon juice

To make Crumb Crust, combine all crust ingredients and mix well and press evenly into a deep 9″ pyrex pie plate shaping a high smooth top edge.

To make Filling, beat cheese at high speed until light, then beat in sugar, eggs, salt and flavoring. Turn into crumb crust and bake at 350° for 20 minutes on center rack of oven. Cool.

To make Topping, drain cherries. Reserve syrup, about ¾ C, made up with water if necessary. Mix well together dry the sugar, arrowroot flour or cornstarch. Stir in ¾ C cherry juice and cook stirring until thick. Add drained cherries and lemon juice. Cool. About 1 hour before serving, spread cherry topping over cheesecake pie.

Summer Fruit Cake

½ lb chopped candied orange peel
½ lb mixed red and green candied
    cherries, halved
½ lb chopped citron peel
¼ lb finely chopped candied pineapple
½ lb light seedless raisins
Grated rind 1 medium orange
Grated rind 1 medium lemon
¼ C well drained, canned, crushed pineapple
4⅓ C sifted all-purpose flour
1 tsp baking powder
1 tsp salt
1 lb butter
2¼ C granulated sugar
8 medium eggs
1 tsp vanilla
1 tsp almond extract
1 tsp lemon extract

In a very large bowl or clean dishpan mix together all candied fruits, raisins, fresh orange and lemon rinds and crushed pineapple. Sift the sifted flour with the baking powder and salt and sift over the fruits and mix in to coat the fruit pieces.

Cream together the butter and sugar until light and fluffy. Beat in eggs, one at a time, until thoroughly incorporated. Stir in flavorings and then stir this creamed mixture into the fruit-flour mixture until completely combined. Turn into loaf pans lined with buttered foil and smooth the tops. Bake at 275° with waterpan below during entire baking period, 2 to 2½ hours. These cakes can be frozen.

Light Fruit Cake

4 slices (8 oz) diced candied pineapple
1 lb red glacé cherries
1 lb green glacé cherries
2 lb light raisins
1 lb cut mixed peel
1 C shredded coconut
1 lb whole blanched almonds
½ C brandy or white wine
1 lb butter (room temperature)
2 C granulated sugar
8 eggs
5 C stirred but unsifted cake flour
1 C canned unsweetened pineapple juice
1 tsp pure almond extract

Soak the fruits and nuts in the brandy or wine overnight in a very large bowl.

In large beater bowl—note that there is no baking powder in this recipe—cream together the butter and sugar until light then beat in the eggs until well blended. Add the flour, pineapple juice and almond extract and beat until smooth. Stir this batter into soaked fruits and mix well.

Prepare 3 loaf pans by lining with double wax paper, buttered. Turn batter into prepared pans, pushing it into the corners and smoothing top. Put waterpan in bottom of oven heated to 300° and place cakes on center rack. Bake at 300° for 30 minutes then reduce heat to 250° for 3 hours longer. Cool in pans on cake racks, then turn out and wrap in triple plastic bags and store in refrigerator or freezer.

If you make these cakes well before Christmas you will have time once a week to unwrap and soak sparingly with brandy or white wine. Rewrap and store.

Butterfly Birthday Cake

1 C margarine
1½ tsp nutmeg
½ tsp salt
1⅔ C sugar
5 eggs (divided, see below)
2 C stirred but unsifted all-purpose or
    cake and pastry flour

Note that there is no other liquid in this cake. Measure margarine into beater bowl. Add nutmeg and salt and beat for 5 minutes until creamy. Gradually add sugar while beating, scraping down sides of bowl 2 or 3 times. Now while beating on medium speed add 4 eggs one at a time, beating 2 minutes in all. While beating slowly add flour, scraping down sides of bowl until blended. Now add one more egg and beat in. Turn into a 7 × 12" pan lined with buttered wax paper. Bake at 300° about 1¼ to 1½ hours. Turn out on rack, remove paper and cool.

Meanwhile make icing by beating together ¼ C margarine, 5 Tbsp lemon juice, 15 drops green or yellow food coloring and 3½ C stirred but not packed icing sugar.

To shape Butterfly, with sharp knife cut a 1¼" wide strip from narrow end of cake for the butterfly's body. Place at center of very large tray. Next cut the remaining cake into 4 triangles by cutting diagonally from top left to bottom right. Repeat, cutting from top right to bottom left. Place the 2 large triangles with points at top of body, crust edge at outside. Place the 2 smaller triangles under large ones with points attached to body about 3" above tail end. Now cover the whole thing with icing. Spot all wing tips with vari-colored life savers. Make spine at center of body with peanuts. If you want to go quite wild spot a few Smarties on inner edges. For antennae use two 4" lengths of spaghetti pressed at a rakish angle at top of body. Tip each with ½ a raisin.

Devil's Food Cake

4 C sifted cake and pastry flour
2 C granulated sugar
½ C cocoa
4 tsp baking soda
2 C cold water
2 C salad dressing
1 Tbsp vanilla

Into large beater bowl sift together flour, sugar, cocoa and baking soda. Add water, salad dressing and vanilla and beat until smooth. Pour into greased 9 × 13" pan lined on bottom with buttered wax paper. Bake at 350° for 45 minutes. Test for doneness with toothpick, so that it comes out clean with no cake batter sticking to it. Cool for 15 minutes in pan then turn out on cake rack. Peel off wax paper. Frost.

CHOCOLATE FUDGE ICING

½ C butter
¼ C cocoa
1 egg
2 C icing sugar
Milk (see below)

In bowl cream together butter and cocoa. Add egg and blend well. Gradually mix in icing sugar then beat at high speed to combine thoroughly. If you find the icing too stiff add 1 tsp milk at a time until you get the desired consistency. (A Fudge Icing should be thick and moist rather than light and fluffy.)

Milk Chocolate Cake

⅔ C butter or margarine (room temperature)
1½ C granulated sugar
3 eggs
3 squares melted unsweetened chocolate
    (see below)
2 C sifted cake and pastry flour
2¾ tsp baking powder
¼ tsp salt
¾ C milk
1 tsp vanilla

In beater bowl cream together butter and sugar. Add eggs and beat well. Stir in melted, slightly cooled, unsweetened chocolate.

In another bowl sift together the sifted flour, baking powder and salt. Add alternately with the milk to the creamed mixture combining thoroughly and scraping down sides of bowl. Stir in vanilla.

Pour batter evenly into 2 wax-paper-lined and buttered 9" layer cake pans. Bake at 350° for 30 to 35 minutes. Cool on cake racks then remove cakes from pans. Sprinkle a serving plate with sugar and place first layer on it.

Spread with WHITE CREAM FROSTING made by combining ¼ C butter or margarine, 4 C icing sugar, ⅛ tsp salt, 2 tsp vanilla and ½ C milk and beating until thoroughly combined and creamy smooth. Add top layer. Frost sides and top. Refrigerate at least 20 minutes and drizzle melted chocolate over top and sides.

Butterfly Cupcakes with Lemon Filling

1⅔ C sifted all-purpose flour
2½ tsp baking powder
½ tsp salt
¼ tsp nutmeg
⅔ C shortening
1 C granulated sugar
2 eggs
¼ tsp vanilla
¼ tsp almond extract
⅔ C milk

Sift together twice the sifted flour, baking powder, salt and nutmeg. Cream shortening and sugar until light in mixing bowl. Beat in eggs. Fold in flour mixture alternately with milk to which you have added the extracts, ⅓ of each at a time, until batter is just smooth. Line your muffin tins with cupcake papers and fill ⅔ full. Bake at 400°. For small cups, bake 10 minutes, for medium, 12 to 15 minutes. Cool on cake racks in paper cups. When cool, with a sharp pointed knife cut a shallow cone from top and fill with well cooled English Lemon Butter (below). Replace halved tops like spread wings and sprinkle with colored sugar or icing sugar.

ENGLISH LEMON BUTTER: In top of double boiler beat 6 eggs enough to mix the yolks and whites. Add ⅔ C lemon juice, ¼ C butter and 2 C sugar. Stir over boiling water until it thickens somewhat. Remove from heat and cool. Store in refrigerator in covered jars. Makes about three 8-oz jars.

Sour Cream Coffee Cake

TOPPING
1 C pecans (or walnuts or almonds) chopped
¼ C melted butter
¼ C granulated sugar
⅓ C light brown sugar
1 tsp cinnamon

BATTER
2 C sifted all-purpose flour
1 tsp baking powder
1 tsp baking soda
½ tsp salt
½ C shortening
1 C granulated sugar
1 tsp vanilla
2 eggs
1 C dairy sour cream

Mix together topping ingredients and set aside.

Sift together the sifted flour, baking powder, baking soda and salt. In mixing bowl cream the shortening and sugar until light and beat in vanilla and eggs. Add flour mixture and sour cream, folding them in, half of each at a time. Grease a 9″ tube pan and sprinkle with half of the topping mixture. Spoon over it half of the batter. Repeat both of these layers finishing with batter. Bake at 350° for 45 minutes or until done. Allow to stand for 2 or 3 minutes before turning out on large cake plate to cool. This coffee cake keeps well if carefully wrapped and refrigerated but is at its best when served fresh.

Medium-Dark Fruit Cake

½ lb butter (room temperature)
2 C granulated sugar
2 C brown sugar
10 eggs
One 20-oz can crushed pineapple
1 tsp vanilla
4 C sifted all-purpose flour
½ tsp salt
½ tsp baking soda
1 tsp cinnamon
1 tsp nutmeg
1 lb broken walnuts
½ lb red glacé cherries
½ lb green glacé cherries
1 lb mixed cut peel
½ lb (1½ C) currants
2 lb light Sultana raisins
1 lb seeded or seedless dark raisins

Into large bowl measure the butter and sugars and cream until light. Beat in eggs. Beat in pineapple and vanilla. Sift together the sifted flour, salt, baking soda and spices and beat into creamed mixture until thoroughly blended. Measure all fruits and nuts into very large container. Pour prepared batter over fruits and nuts and mix well.

Prepare 2 loaf pans and one tube pan (solid, not with removable tube) by lining with heavy wax paper and buttering. Turn batter into pans and push into corners and smooth tops. Bake at 275° for 3 to 3¼ hours with waterpan in bottom of oven during entire baking period. Replenish water in pan as it evaporates for it prevents caramelizing and hardening of the abundant fruits in this cake. Cool in pans on racks. Store in triple plastic bags or other airproof wrapping, in refrigerator or freezer.

Maritimers' Mint Chocolate Cake

BATTER

1½ C granulated sugar
2 extra large eggs
1 C oil
One 19-oz can beets thoroughly drained
    and puréed in blender
6 Tbsp cocoa
1¾ C unsifted all-purpose flour
1½ tsp baking soda
¼ tsp salt
1 tsp vanilla
¾ tsp pure peppermint extract

ICING

2 Tbsp shortening
1 Tbsp butter
4 Tbsp cocoa
2 C icing sugar
⅛ tsp salt
5 Tbsp hot water
¾ tsp peppermint extract

To prepare Batter, in beater bowl combine sugar and eggs. Add oil and puréed beets and mix. Stir in cocoa, flour, baking soda, salt, vanilla and peppermint extract and beat for 2 minutes on medium speed, scraping down sides of bowl with scraper. Turn batter into 9 × 9" buttered pan with buttered wax paper on bottom. Bake at 350° for 45 to 50 minutes. Test with toothpick at center for doneness. Cool in pan on cake rack for 10 minutes, then remove cake from pan.

To make Icing, cream together shortening, butter and cocoa. Add icing sugar, salt, hot water and peppermint extract and beat until smooth. Frost sides and top.

Chocolate Log

CHOCOLATE SPONGE BATTER

¾ C sifted cake and pastry flour
¾ C granulated sugar
2 tsp baking powder
1 tsp powdered instant coffee
½ tsp salt
¼ tsp cinnamon
¼ C cocoa
¼ C salad oil
3 egg yolks
6 Tbsp water
1 tsp vanilla
¼ tsp cream of tartar
3 egg whites
Icing sugar

Mix and sift the first 7 dry ingredients into a deep bowl. Make a well and add in order, salad oil, egg yolks, water and vanilla. Beat with spoon until smooth. Add cream of tartar to egg whites and beat until egg whites form very stiff peaks. Fold first mixture gently into egg whites until well blended. Line a 10 × 16" jelly roll pan with waxed paper and grease paper lightly. Turn batter into pan. Bake at 350° for 12 minutes or until cake springs back when touched lightly with finger at center. Immediately turn out on a clean towel covered with icing sugar. Peel off waxed paper; quickly cut off the crisp edges. Roll up in towel by

Pineapple Chiffon Cake

1 C egg whites (about 7)
½ tsp cream of tartar
2¼ C sifted cake and pastry flour
1½ C sugar
1 Tbsp baking powder
½ tsp salt
½ C cooking oil
5 large egg yolks
¾ C canned unsweetened pineapple juice

Into beater bowl measure the egg whites and cream of tartar and beat until very stiff.

Meanwhile sift and measure flour and sift with the sugar, baking powder and salt into a medium bowl. Make a well in center and add oil, yolks and pineapple juice. Beat until blended and creamy.

As soon as egg whites are very stiff and hold stiff peaks, lift beaters and pour flour-yolk mixture over them and fold in, until evenly blended, using a cutting motion through center of batter. Pour into ungreased 10" tube pan with removable bottom and bake at 325° for 1 hour. This cake may bake in 55 minutes but be sure it is done before removing from oven. Suspend tube pan upside down. Let hang 1 hour. Then carefully run slender knife around sides and tube to loosen and lift out. Run knife between cake and bottom and lift cake to cake plate.

If desired drizzle top with mixture of ¼ C icing sugar and 1 Tbsp lemon juice and dredge with sifted icing sugar.

starting at the longer side, enclosing towel in roll. Cool well. Unroll and remove towel. Spread cake with French Chocolate Filling.

FRENCH CHOCOLATE FILLING

3 squares unsweetened chocolate
¼ lb butter
1 C unsifted icing sugar
2 eggs

Melt chocolate. Cream butter, add sugar while creaming. Beat eggs into creamed mixture thoroughly. Slowly add melted chocolate while beating. Spread filling on cooled cake and roll up and place seam down on dessert plate.

Sacher Torte

BATTER
5 eggs, yolks and whites separated (see below)
⅓ C butter (first amount)
6 Tbsp sugar, divided
3 oz (3 squares) semi-sweet chocolate,
    melted and somewhat cooled
½ C sifted cake and pastry flour

FROSTING
1 square (1 oz) semi-sweet chocolate, melted
¼ C cold butter (second amount)
1 egg yolk leftover from batter, (see below)
¼ C icing sugar
1 tsp instant coffee powder (optional)

FILLING
⅓ C apricot jam

To make Batter, separate egg whites from egg yolks. Egg whites should be in large mixing bowl. Four of the egg yolks should be in another large mixing bowl and one egg yolk should be reserved for frosting. Beat the 5 egg whites with 3 Tbsp of the sugar until very stiff. Without washing beaters beat 4 of the egg yolks with butter (first amount) and remaining 3 Tbsp sugar until very light. Beat in melted and somewhat cooled chocolate. Gently fold in stiffly beaten egg whites and flour with wire whip until just smoothly blended. Turn into two buttered 8″ layer cake pans lined on bottom with buttered wax paper. Bake on center rack in oven at 325° for 35 to 37 minutes. Let stand in pans 2 minutes then turn out on cake racks to cool. Peel off wax paper.

When cool spread apricot jam filling between the layers then spread with frosting made by stirring ¼ C hard butter into melted square of chocolate to cool it then adding remaining egg yolk, icing sugar and coffee powder (if used). Beat well. Spread frosting on sides and top. Chill.

Pineapple Orange Cake

1 C butter (room temperature)
1¼ C granulated sugar
2 eggs
⅔ C orange juice
1 C crushed pineapple, undrained
2½ C unsifted cake and pastry flour
3 tsp baking powder
½ tsp salt

In beater bowl cream the butter and sugar until light and fluffy. Beat in eggs until well blended. Stir in orange juice and pineapple.

In another bowl stir together the flour, baking powder and salt and add to creamed mixture. Beat at high speed for 2 minutes. Pour into a well-greased 8 × 12″ pan. Bake at 350° for 35 to 40 minutes. Test with toothpick. Cool in pan on cake rack.

Frost with ORANGE FROSTING: ¼ C butter, 2 C icing sugar, shake of salt, 2 Tbsp orange juice, 1 egg yolk, 1½ tsp grated orange rind. Cream butter, add remaining ingredients in order given and beat until of spreading consistency. Spread on cake in pan.

Prize-Winning Chocolate Cake

2 C sifted cake and pastry flour
1¾ C granulated sugar
⅔ C cocoa
1¼ tsp baking soda
1 tsp baking powder
1 tsp salt
¾ C best quality shortening
    (room temperature)
1¼ C milk (divided, see below)
1 tsp vanilla
3 large eggs

Into beater bowl sift the sifted flour, sugar, cocoa, baking soda, baking powder and salt. Add the shortening and ¾ C of the milk and the vanilla. Beat on low speed for 3 minutes, removing beaters and scraping down sides of bowl once or twice with rubber spatula. Add remaining ½ C milk and the eggs and beat 2½ minutes longer, scraping bowl down once.

Turn into three 8″ or two 9″ layer cake pans lined on bottoms with buttered wax paper. (This is a lot of batter so be sure your pans are big enough.) Bake at 350° for 35 minutes or longer if you used two 9″ pans. Touch each cake gently with finger tip. Be sure slight indentation does not remain before removing cakes. Cool in pans on cake racks 10 minutes, then turn out on cake racks, peeling off wax paper. Spread between layers and on top and sides with White Whipped Frosting.

WHITE WHIPPED FROSTING: Into small saucepan measure 2 Tbsp corn starch. Slowly stir in 1 C cold milk until smooth. Now cook, stirring constantly, until thick. Chill. Into beater bowl measure ½ lb soft butter, 1 C granulated sugar and 1 tsp vanilla and beat 5 to 10 minutes until snowy white. Add cold milk sauce and beat 15 minutes. Frost sides before top. Drizzle one square melted chocolate at random over top and down sides. Chill.

Pound Cake

1 C shortening
1½ C granulated sugar
5 large eggs
2 C sifted cake and pastry flour
1½ tsp salt
⅛ tsp mace (or nutmeg)
1 tsp vanilla

In beater bowl cream together well the shortening and sugar. Beat in eggs, one at a time, until thoroughly blended and creamy. Sift together the sifted flour, salt and mace or nutmeg. Add vanilla and beat thoroughly. Line standard loaf pan with buttered waxed paper and turn in batter, pushing it into corners. Bake at 350° for 60 to 80 minutes. Do not underbake. Let rest in pan 10 minutes then turn out on cake rack, peel off paper and cool. Do not frost. The flavor is very good without any additions.

Southern Prune Cake

2 C cake and pastry flour
½ tsp salt
1 tsp cloves
1 tsp cinnamon
1 tsp nutmeg
4 large eggs
2 C granulated sugar
1 C oil
1 C buttermilk
1 tsp soda

Preheat oven to 350°. Use a tube pan greasing it well and neatly lining it, greasing again. Sift together flour (stirred but unsifted), salt, cloves, cinnamon and nutmeg. In a separate large bowl, beat eggs thoroughly, at least 5 minutes. Add sugar gradually, beating until mixture is thick and lemon-colored. Add balance of ingredients, alternating flour mixture, oil and buttermilk with soda added to it. Beat at high speed 1 minute. Pour into tube pan and bake at 350° for 1½ hours. Cool on rack, remove from pan and peel off wax paper. When cake is cool spread on topping.

TOPPING: In a saucepan mix 1 C sugar, ½ C buttermilk, ¼ tsp soda, ⅛ tsp salt, 1 Tbsp margarine or butter, 1 tsp vanilla, 1 C pitted and chopped prunes. Heat stirring constantly. Cook at boiling for 2 minutes, stirring. Spread over top of cooled cake encouraging some syrup to drip down sides.

Black Forest Cherry Torte

CHOCOLATE SPONGE BATTER

2 C whole eggs (8 large)
1 C plus 2 Tbsp granulated sugar
1¾ C plus 2 tsp stirred but not sifted cake flour
½ C unsifted cocoa
⅜ tsp baking soda
¼ C plus 2 Tbsp warm melted butter

FILLING AND FROSTING INGREDIENTS

One 19-oz can cherry pie filling
¾ pt (15-oz or 1⅞ C) whipping cream
2 Tbsp icing sugar
1½ Tbsp Kirsch or Peter Heering liqueur
Bitter chocolate (see below)

Into large beater bowl break eggs. Add sugar and beat 10 minutes at high speed until they are thick and tripled in bulk. Meanwhile sift together the flour, cocoa and baking soda. Remove beaters and fold flour mixture in with wire whisk or slotted spoon, along with the warm melted butter. Divide evenly into three 9″ layer cake pans. Line bottom of pans with buttered wax paper. Bake at 375° for 18 to 20 minutes on center shelf in oven. Cool on cake racks.

With long sharp knife split each cake carefully to give 6 layers. Place first layer on large cake plate and cover with ⅓ of the cherry pie filling. Cover with second layer and spread it with whipped cream flavored with the icing sugar and liqueur of your choice. Repeat, until you have the 6 layers stacked with alternating fillings between. Now spread whipped cream on sides. Decorate with halved red maraschino or candied cherries and curls of bitter chocolate.

Orange Party Cake with Chocolate Coating

CAKE

½ C margarine or shortening
    (room temperature)
1¼ C granulated sugar
2 eggs
2 or 3 oranges (grated rind and
    juice, ¾ C divided)
½ C milk
2 C unsifted cake and pastry flour
2 tsp baking powder
½ tsp salt
¼ tsp baking soda
About ¼ tsp orange food coloring

WHIPPED CREAM FILLING

1 envelope gelatin
2 Tbsp cold water
1 pt whipping cream
½ C icing sugar
⅓ C orange juice

CHOCOLATE GLAZE

4 squares semi-sweet chocolate
1½ Tbsp butter or margarine

In beater bowl cream together margarine or shortening and sugar until light and fluffy. Beat in eggs and orange rind until thoroughly combined. Stir in ½ C orange juice and the ½ C milk.

Combine flour, baking powder, salt and baking soda. Stir into creamed mixture and beat at medium speed for 2 minutes, scraping down side of bowl often. Add orange food coloring. Pour into two 8″ layer cake pans greased and lined on bottom with buttered wax paper. Bake at 350° for 25 minutes. Cool 10 minutes then remove from pans, peel off wax paper and cool completely on cake racks. Then split each layer of cake making 4 thin layers. Using the remaining ¼ cup orange juice, sprinkle each layer with 1 Tbsp. Spread Whipped Cream Filling between layers (below).

Meanwhile make Whipped Cream Filling: Sprinkle gelatin on the 2 Tbsp cold water in a small cup. Let stand 5 minutes. Place cup in boiling water and stir until gelatin is dissolved. Remove from heat and set aside for a minute. In beater bowl whip cream with icing sugar until just starting to thicken. Continue with beaters at high speed while you add the orange juice. Now slowly pour in liquid gelatin into beaters and combine thoroughly. Beat until stiff. If cake is not cool yet, refrigerate Cream until you are ready for it.

To prepare Chocolate Glaze, in top of double boiler combine squares of chocolate and butter or margarine and stir until melted. Let cool until chocolate thickens somewhat. Pour on top of cake, letting it drizzle down the sides. Refrigerate 24 hours. Let cake sit at room temperature at least 1 hour before serving.

Pineapple Meringue Cake

BATTER
¼ C butter or margarine
½ C granulated sugar
2 eggs (yolks and whites separated)
½ tsp vanilla
1 C unsifted all-purpose flour
1½ tsp baking powder
1 tsp salt
½ C milk (or cream)

TOPPING
Egg whites (from above separated yolks
    and whites)
½ C sugar
1 tsp vanilla
⅓ C chopped pecans or almonds

FILLING
1 C whipping cream
2 Tbsp icing sugar
1 tsp vanilla
1 C well drained crushed pineapple

To make Batter, in beater bowl cream together butter or margarine and sugar. Add egg yolks and vanilla and blend. Stir together flour, baking powder and salt. Add dry ingredients alternately with milk or cream. Line buttered bottom of two 8" round cake pans with 2 double strips of buttered foil or wax paper crossing to ease removal. Divide batter and spread evenly in each pan.

To make Topping, beat egg whites until stiff, gradually adding sugar and vanilla as you beat. Spread evenly over each pan of batter. Sprinkle with nuts. Bake at 350° for 20 to 25 minutes. Cool in pans for 10 minutes then carefully remove from pans. Cool thoroughly.

Meanwhile make Filling by combining whipping cream, sugar, and vanilla and beating until stiff. Fold in drained pineapple. Place first cake layer on plate, topping side up. Spread with all of the filling. Cover with remaining layer, topping side up. Chill and serve.

White Wedding Cake and Frosting

4½ C sifted cake flour
3 C sugar
8 tsp baking powder
2 tsp salt
1 C shortening (room temperature)
1½ C milk (first amount)
1 Tbsp pure vanilla
8 large egg whites (room temperature)
½ C milk (second amount)

Into beater bowl sift the sifted flour, sugar, baking powder and salt. Add the shortening and 1½ C milk and vanilla. Stir by hand to combine then lower beaters and beat at medium speed for 2 minutes. Add unbeaten egg whites and ½ C milk and beat 2 minutes longer, scraping down sides of bowl and up from bottom. Pour batter into 2 paper-lined buttered 9 × 9" pans. Bake at 350° for 45 minutes. Let rest in pans 10 minutes then turn out on racks to cool.

FROSTING AND FILLING
3 egg whites
2¼ C granulated sugar
⅛ tsp salt
½ C water
1 Tbsp light corn syrup
½ tsp fresh grated lemon rind
1¼ C mixed chopped nuts, red and green
    maraschino cherries

In top of very large double boiler combine egg whites, sugar, salt, water and corn syrup and beat to mix. Place over boiling water and beat until soft peaks will just hold their shape, about 20 minutes. Remove from heat and add rind. Pour about 3 cups into a bowl and fold in the fruits for the Filling.

Cut each cake into 2 layers. Spread Fruit Filling between layers. Cover sides and top with unfruited remaining frosting. This cake should be served within 24 hours.

Glazed Strawberry Cake

CAKE BATTER
½ C shortening
1 C sugar
2 eggs
1 tsp vanilla
1¾ C cake and pastry flour
2½ tsp baking powder
¾ tsp salt
½ C plus 2 Tbsp milk

TOPPING
2 pints perfect large strawberries
½ C plus 2 Tbsp sugar
3 Tbsp arrowroot flour (or cornstarch)
1 C boiling water
10 drops red food coloring

Make Cake Batter first by creaming together shortening and sugar in beater bowl 2 minutes. Scrape down sides and add eggs and vanilla and beat at high speed 5 minutes until very light. Remove beaters. Stir together flour, salt and baking powder and fold in alternately in thirds with the milk until just blended. Turn into a deep, round 9" pan lined on bottom with buttered wax paper. Bake at 350° about 25 minutes. Cool in pan 10 minutes then turn out on cake plate, bottom side up.

Wash and select large strawberries and cut in halves. Arrange closely in concentric circles, cut side up, on top of cake.

To make Glaze, mash one pint of washed berries in flat-bottomed pot. Add arrowroot (or cornstarch) and sugar and mix well. Add boiling water and cook stirring until very thick. Remove from heat and add red food coloring. Cool a little then spoon all over berries on top of cake, coaxing some glaze to flow down sides. Use it all. Cool for at least 2 hours before serving. Serves ten.

Icelandic Vinarterta

FILLING
24 oz pitted prunes
1½ C water
2 C sugar
1 Tbsp cinnamon
1 tsp vanilla

BATTER
1 C sweet (unsalted) butter
1½ C sugar
3 eggs
1 tsp ground cardamom seed (whole seeds
    may be buzzed in blender)
4 C sifted cake and pastry flour
½ C milk

ICING
¾ C unsalted butter
4 C icing sugar
¼ tsp salt
1 tsp almond extract
3 Tbsp milk

Simmer prunes in water, covered, ½ hour.
Drain. Force through sieve or buzz in blender to
purée. Stir in sugar, cinnamon and vanilla. Cool.

Make Batter by beating butter with sugar 5
minutes, then beat in eggs, one at a time. Add
ground cardamom (if used) and flour alternately
with milk until you have a very smooth batter.
Now make 6 layers. Have ready three buttered 8"
or 9" layer cake tins. Spread batter in them to ¼"
thickness and bake at 375° until dry but not
browned, about 10 minutes. Remove to racks,
wash, dry, butter and refill pans until all batter is
baked. Place one layer on plate and spread
generously with prune filling. Continue until all
layers are stacked straight, with filling between.
Reserve surplus filling for decorating later. Cover
and store in refrigerator.

Make Icing by beating butter with icing sugar
until pale and light. Add salt, milk and extract and
beat well. Spread generously on sides and top of
cold torte. Reserve 1½ C. Wrap torte, then slip in
plastic bag and freeze one week. Freeze surplus icing too. Early on day of serving remove torte and
frosting from freezer. When frosting has softened
pipe on decoration in shape of wheel with spokes.
Between spokes place small mound of reserved
prune purée. Top each with blanched almond or
rosette of icing. Border inside of rim with
quartered maraschino cherries. Chill until serving
time. Slice in ½" wide wedges.

White Cake with Caramel Frosting

BATTER
2 C less 1 Tbsp sifted all-purpose flour
3 tsp baking powder
¾ tsp salt
½ C butter
1 C granulated sugar
2 eggs
⅞ C milk
1 tsp vanilla

FROSTING
¼ C butter or margarine
½ C light brown sugar (packed)
2 Tbsp milk
1 C sifted icing sugar
1 tsp vanilla
¼ C chopped nuts

Sift together 3 times the sifted flour, baking
powder and salt. In beater bowl cream together
butter and sugar until light then beat in eggs. Add
sifted dry ingredients alternately with milk and
vanilla, in thirds, using beaters on low speed and
scraping down sides once. Turn into 8 × 8" pan
lined on bottom with buttered wax paper. Butter
sides of pan too. Bake at 350° for 50 minutes or
until it tests done when touched lightly. Cool cake
on rack in pan.

To make Caramel Frosting, melt butter in
saucepan then add brown sugar and stir over low
heat 2 minutes. Add milk and stir constantly until
it comes to boil. Remove from heat. Add icing
sugar and vanilla and beat just until of spreading
consistency. Spread on cake in pan and sprinkle
top with nuts.

Foolproof Sponge Cake

1¼ C sifted cake flour
1¼ C white sugar
¼ tsp salt
6 medium eggs, yolks and whites separated
2 Tbsp lemon juice
2 Tbsp water
1 tsp vanilla
½ tsp cream of tartar

Sift together 1 cup of the sugar, the flour and
salt. In a large mixing bowl add to the egg yolks
the lemon juice, water, vanilla and flour mixture
and beat for at least 5 minutes.

Sprinkle cream of tartar over whites in large
bowl and beat until soft peaks form. Slowly add
remaining sugar and beat until glossy and stiff.
Pour egg-yolk mixture over whites and fold in until
smooth and yellow color is uniform. Pour into ungreased tube pan and bake at 350° for 40 to 50
minutes or until cake springs back when touched
with finger tip. Invert on rack to cool 1 hour, then
loosen sides carefully and remove cake from pan.
Cut into 2 layers with long-bladed knife and apply
filling as desired.

Spice Cake with Broiled Topping

1½ C unsifted cake and pastry flour
1 tsp baking powder
½ tsp baking soda
½ tsp salt
½ tsp nutmeg
1 tsp cinnamon
½ C butter
1 C granulated sugar
2 eggs
⅔ C buttermilk or soured milk (see below)

TOPPING
½ C lightly packed brown sugar
2 Tbsp flour
¼ tsp salt
¼ C melted butter
1 Tbsp water
½ C chopped nuts or desiccated coconut

Note: If you do not have buttermilk add 1 Tbsp lemon juice or vinegar to a 1 cup measure and fill to 1 cup mark with sweet milk. Let stand 10 minutes.

Sift together the flour, baking powder, soda, salt and spices. In beater bowl cream butter until light then gradually add the sugar, beating until fluffy. Beat in eggs. Remove beaters. Sift the dry ingredients over, one-third at a time, alternately with buttermilk, and fold in. Turn into a greased and lightly floured 8″ tube pan. Bake at 350° for 45 to 50 minutes or until cake springs back when lightly touched. Cool in pan 10 minutes. Turn out on baking sheet.

Make Broiled Topping by combining in saucepan the Topping ingredients until thoroughly blended, if necessary heating a little to melt any lumps. Spread over top of warm Spice Cake. Place 6″ below preheated broiler and broil 2 or 3 minutes or until bubbly. Cool.

One-Egg Cake

1¾ C sifted all-purpose flour
1¼ C granulated sugar
4 tsp baking powder
1 tsp salt
⅓ C shortening (room temperature)
⅔ C milk (first amount)
1 egg
⅓ C milk (second amount)

Into beater bowl measure sifted flour, sugar, baking powder, salt, shortening and ⅔ C milk and beat at medium speed for about 2 minutes, scraping down sides of bowl several times. Add egg and remaining ⅓ C milk and beat for another 2 minutes, scraping bowl often. Pour batter into 2 buttered wax-paper-lined 8″ round pans or one 9 × 12″ oblong. Bake at 375° about 25 minutes.

If desired put your layers together with peach jam as the filling then ice sides and top with a peach icing made by beating together 3 Tbsp butter, 1 C icing sugar and ⅓ C peach jam until creamy.

Pineapple Upside-Down Cake

⅓ C butter or margarine
⅓ C dark brown sugar
6 slices canned pineapple
6 maraschino cherries
1¾ C sifted cake flour
1 C granulated sugar
2 tsp baking powder
¾ tsp salt
¼ C shortening (room temperature)
¾ C milk
1 tsp vanilla
½ tsp almond flavoring (optional)
1 large egg

In an 8 × 8″ pan gently melt over low heat on top of stove the margarine or butter, then sprinkle over the brown sugar and stir to mix. Cover uniformly with the pineapple slices, drop a cherry in hole in center of each and keep warm by standing in large shallow pan containing ½″ boiling water.

Into beater bowl sift together the sifted measured flour, granulated sugar, baking powder and salt. Now add shortening, milk, vanilla and almond flavoring (if used) and beat one minute on low speed, then on medium speed for 2 minutes. Scrape down sides of bowl with rubber scraper. Add egg and beat 2 minutes.

Spoon batter evenly over warm pineapple slices to cover completely. Bake at 350° for 45 minutes. When done invert large serving dish over it. Gripping both tightly, turn over and allow pan to rest on cake for a few minutes to give syrup time to run over it. Serve warm if possible.

Marbled Two-Egg Cake

½ C best quality shortening
1 C sugar
2 eggs
1 tsp vanilla
1½ C stirred cake and pastry flour
3 tsp baking powder
½ tsp salt
½ C milk (first amount)
¼ C cocoa
¼ C milk (second amount)

Cream together shortening and sugar for 5 minutes then beat in eggs and vanilla. Remove beaters. Sift together flour, baking powder and salt, and add alternately in thirds with the milk to the creamed mixture, folding in with wire whip until just blended. Spoon half of batter into another bowl. Line a 12 × 8″ pan on bottom with greased wax paper. Turn in half of batter.

Fold cocoa and milk (second amount) into reserved half of batter. Now drop big spoonfuls of it on top of light batter and swirl a knife through both batters to marble. Do not overdo this or you might mix them too well. Bake at 375° for 20 to 25 minutes. Turn out on cake rack and peel off wax paper. When cool frost with lemon icing.

Two-Egg Cake

½ C shortering (or half-and-half shortening
    and butter)
1⅛ C (1 C plus 2 Tbsp) sugar
2 eggs
1 tsp vanilla
1¾ C sifted cake or cake and pastry flour
2½ tsp baking powder
¾ tsp salt
½ C plus 2 Tbsp milk

Cream together shortening and sugar until
creamy then add eggs and vanilla and beat until
very light, stopping beaters and scraping down
sides of beater bowl with rubber scraper once.

Sift together flour, baking powder and salt
and fold in in thirds alternately with the milk until
blended. Line bottom of 9 × 9″ pan with wax paper
and butter it and sides. Turn in batter, smooth top.
Bake at 350° for 25 minutes or until it tests done
when gently touched at center.

Gâteau Provençal

BATTER
1 C butter
2 C brown sugar
4 eggs
1 tsp almond extract
1 C chopped uncooked dried soft prunes
1 C chopped uncooked dried soft apricots
2 C whole walnuts
4 C sifted cake and pastry flour
½ tsp cloves
½ tsp ginger
½ tsp allspice
1 tsp cinnamon
1 tsp nutmeg (preferably freshly grated)
1½ tsp salt
1 tsp baking soda
1⅓ C orange juice

TOPPING
¼ C butter
1 C brown sugar
2 Tbsp orange juice
8 dried prunes stoned, cooked and halved
8 cooked apricot halves
About 16 whole blanched almonds

To make the Batter, cream together the butter
and sugar until light, then beat in eggs and almond
extract. Remove beaters. Sift the sifted flour with
the spices, salt, baking soda. Add the flour mixture, alternately in thirds, with the orange juice to
the creamed mixture and fold in. Fold in prunes,
apricots and walnuts.

Now prepare Topping: Melt the butter with
the sugar and orange juice. Spoon evenly into bottom of 2 standard loaf pans. Arrange the prune
and apricot halves in an attractive pattern in the
syrup. Place almonds between. Now carefully
spoon in batter and bake at 325° for 1 hour and 45
minutes with water pan underneath during entire
baking period. Let stand in pans 20 minutes then
invert on cake racks. Let pans rest over cakes for
10 minutes then carefully remove. You will see
that the syrup soaks into the batter and the pattern
gives the turned out cake and attractive appearance.

Lemon Cream Cake

BATTER
One 8-oz pkg white cream cheese,
    (room temperature)
½ C butter or margarine
1¼ C granulated sugar
3 eggs
1 lemon, grated rind and juice (see below)
2¼ C unsifted all-purpose flour
3 tsp baking powder
1 tsp salt
1 C milk

GLAZE
¼ C lemon juice (from above lemon)
⅓ C granulated sugar

To make Batter, in beater bowl cream
together cheese and butter or margarine. Beat in
the sugar until light and fluffy, about 5 minutes.
Add eggs and beat until thoroughly blended. Add
lemon rind, flour, baking powder, salt and milk.
Blend at low speed just until thoroughly combined,
scraping bowl several times. Pour batter into a well
greased 10″ tube pan. Bake at 350° for 45 to 50
minutes until toothpick inserted in center comes
out clean.

To make Glaze, combine lemon juice and the
⅓ C sugar. Pour over hot cake, allowing it to run
down edges between cake and pan. Cool 10
minutes than carefully remove from pan by gently
running a knife around edges, placing cake plate
on top of pan and turning over and out. Cool
thoroughly. *Note:* If you carefully wrap this cake it
freezes well. Sprinkle with icing sugar if desired.

Lazy Daisy Oatmeal Cake

BATTER
1 C uncooked rolled oats
   (instant or regular)
1¼ C boiling water
½ C butter or margarine
1 C granulated sugar
1 C brown sugar
1 tsp vanilla
2 eggs
1½ C sifted all-purpose flour
1 tsp baking soda
½ tsp salt
¾ tsp cinnamon
¼ tsp nutmeg

TOPPING
¼ C butter or margarine, melted
½ C brown sugar (packed)
3 Tbsp cream or milk
¾ C flaked coconut
⅓ C chopped nuts

In shallow bowl soak rolled oats in boiling water 20 minutes. Meanwhile proceed by measuring butter and sugars into beater bowl and beating until light. Beat in eggs and vanilla. Sift and measure flour and sift it again with the soda, salt and spices. By this time oats will be soaked and cool. Remove beaters from creamed mixture and fold in soaked oats. Sift flour mixture over and fold in. Turn into buttered 9 × 9″ pan (lined on bottom) and bake at 350° for 40 to 50 minutes.

Mix all Topping ingredients. Do not remove cake from pan but while still hot spread with prepared topping and pass under preheated broiler until bubbly and tinged with gold. Watch carefully.

Orange Johnny Cake

⅔ C yellow cornmeal
1 C stirred but unsifted all-purpose flour
5 tsp baking powder
1 tsp salt
⅓ C sugar
1⅛ C fresh frozen orange juice
1 egg
2 Tbsp soft butter (first amount)
1 Tbsp butter (second amount)

Heat oven to 425°. In bowl thoroughly combine the cornmeal, flour, baking powder, salt and sugar. At this stage measure 1 Tbsp butter (second amount) into a 9 × 9″ pan and put it in the oven to heat to sizzling point. To dry ingredients add orange juice, egg, butter (first amount) and stir just enough to mix.

Carefully remove hot pan from oven and pour batter into sizzling hot fat. Return to oven at 425° and bake 20 minutes. Cut into squares and serve as a hot bread with your main course as they do in the South or serve as dessert with butter and maple or corn syrup.

Lemon Jelly Roll

BATTER
4 large eggs
1 C granulated sugar
1 tsp vanilla
1 C sifted all-purpose flour
1 tsp baking powder
¼ tsp salt

LEMON FILLING
3 Tbsp cornstarch
3 Tbsp flour
1 C granulated sugar
¼ tsp salt
1½ C cold water
2 large egg yolks
2 large lemons (grated rind and juice)
2 tsp butter

Make Lemon Filling first: In a heavy pot combine thoroughly the cornstarch, flour, sugar and salt. Stir in water slowly and mix until all lumps are gone. Cook, stirring constantly, until mixture is thick then cook 2 minutes longer, stirring constantly. Remove from heat. Combine egg yolks, grated lemon rind and juice (about ½ C). Stir yolk-juice mixture slowly into thickened filling. Return to heat and cook, stirring, for 2 minutes. Remove from heat and stir in butter until melted. Set aside.

To make Batter, in beater bowl beat eggs until light, about 2 minutes. Add sugar gradually as you continue to beat until eggs are very thick. Stir in vanilla. Remove beaters. Sift the sifted flour with the baking powder and salt over the egg mixture. Fold in lightly until all flour is incorporated. Pour into a shallow, well greased jelly roll pan measuring 10 × 15″. Bake at 350° for 16 to 17 minutes.

Have a dampened tea towel spread out on your counter. Remove cake from oven and immediately and quickly loosen edges with a knife and turn cake over and out onto tea towel. It is important to work quickly so the cake does not cool too much and crack when being rolled. Cut off crisp outside edges with a very sharp knife. Roll cake up enclosing the towel starting with the 10″ end and leave for 2 or 3 minutes. Unroll and spread with lemon filling. Roll cake up again without towel this time. Transfer cake roll to a large piece of wax paper, folded edge down and wrap wax paper around it. Let cool to room temperature before serving. Slice with a very sharp knife.

Upside-Down Pear Gingerbread

PEAR BASE
¼ C butter or margarine
¼ C brown sugar
½ tsp cinnamon
One 14-oz can pears, drained and thinly sliced

GINGERBREAD
¾ C milk
1 Tbsp vinegar
⅓ C shortening
½ C sugar
1 egg
¾ C molasses
2 C sifted cake and pastry flour
2 tsp baking powder
1 tsp ginger
¼ tsp baking soda
½ tsp salt

First prepare the Base: In an 8 × 8″ pan gently melt the butter over low heat, then add the brown sugar and cinnamon and mix to blend. Arrange pear slices in 3 even rows in this syrup. Keep warm over turned-off element.

To make Gingerbread Batter, add the vinegar to the milk in a measuring cup to sour it. Into beater bowl measure shortening and sugar and beat until creamy, then beat in egg and molasses for 2 or 3 minutes, scraping down sides to blend. Sift together the sifted flour, baking powder, baking soda and salt. Add, alternately in thirds, the dry ingredients and by now soured milk and beat at low speed to blend. Pour evenly over warm fruit prepared in pan. Bake at 350° for 40 minutes. Loosen sides with knife and invert large plate on top and turn over and out.

Apple Coffee Cake

4 C apples pared and diced
3 tsp cinnamon
⅓ C sugar (first amount)
4½ C stirred but unsifted all-purpose flour
4 tsp baking powder
3 C sugar (second amount)
1 tsp salt
6 large eggs
1½ C good quality oil
⅓ C undiluted fresh frozen orange
    juice concentrate

Prepare apples first: Wash, pare, core and chop. Measure 4 C. To them add the cinnamon and ⅓ C sugar. Mix well and let stand while you make the batter.

In large beater bowl mix together by hand the flour, baking powder, sugar (second amount) and salt. Add eggs, oil and orange juice concentrate. Lower beaters and beat until smooth and blended. Oil a 10″ angel food cake pan and spoon a third of the batter in. Now thoroughly drain all juice from apples, pressing. Spoon half of the apples unevenly over the batter. Cover with another third of the batter. Cover with remaining apples. Top with remaining third of the batter. Bake at 325° for 1½ hours. Be sure not to underbake.

Chocolate Cupcakes

⅔ C butter or margarine (room temperature)
2 C brown sugar (packed)
½ C cocoa
1 egg
1 C sour milk (or 1 Tbsp vinegar in
    1 C sweet milk)
¾ C hot water
1 tsp baking soda
2 tsp baking powder
½ tsp salt
2½ C unsifted cake and pastry flour
1 tsp vanilla

In beater bowl cream together butter or margarine, sugar and cocoa. Add egg and blend. Stir in sour milk and hot water to which the 1 tsp of baking soda has been added.

In another bowl mix together the baking powder, salt and flour and add all at once to the creamed mixture. Add vanilla. Stir in with spoon to incorporate all flour mixture then beat with electric beater at high speed for 3 minutes, scraping down sides of bowl with spatula once or twice. Spoon into paper-cup-lined muffin tins filling ⅔ full. Bake at 350° for 18 to 20 minutes. Frost with Fudge Icing.

FUDGE ICING
½ C butter or margarine
1 egg
¼ C cocoa
2 C icing sugar
Milk (see below)

In bowl cream together butter and cocoa. Add egg and blend well. Mix in icing sugar then using beater on high combine thoroughly. If you find icing too stiff add 1 tsp milk at a time until you get the desired consistency. (A Fudge Icing should be thick and moist rather than light and fluffy.)

Potato Flour Sponge Cake

4 large eggs, yolks and whites separated
1 C sugar
1 tsp vanilla
1 tsp almond extract
½ C potato flour
1 tsp baking powder
¼ tsp salt

Beat the egg whites until very stiff, gradually adding ½ C of the sugar as you beat. Without washing the beaters, beat the egg yolks until thick and pale, gradually adding the remaining ½ C sugar to them as you beat, until they are very thick. Turn the beaten yolks into the beaten whites and beat them both just enough to smoothly blend. Fold in the vanilla and almond extract. Mix the potato flour with the baking powder and salt and sift over batter and fold in smoothly. Line 8″ or 9″ square pan with buttered wax paper. Turn in batter, smoothing top and bake at 325° for about 30 to 35 minutes, but do not underbake. This cake rises high, then subsides somewhat when taken from oven.

German Bundt

BATTER

1½ C oil
1½ C granulated sugar
4 large eggs
2 tsp vanilla
1 tsp rum flavoring
1½ C milk
¾ C cocoa
5 C unsifted cake and pastry flour
5 tsp baking powder
¾ tsp salt

ICING

¼ C butter, melted
3 Tbsp cocoa
1 C icing sugar
About 3 Tbsp hot water

In large beater bowl combine oil, sugar and eggs and beat at high speed for 5 minutes. Add flavorings and milk and combine. Add cocoa, flour, baking powder and salt and beat again for 5 minutes. Batter will be thick. Turn in to a well greased 10″ tube pan. Bake at 350° for 60 minutes. Take out of oven and cool thoroughly on cake rack in pan.

Remove from pan and drizzle over chocolate icing made by combining all icing ingredients thoroughly. Icing should be thin enough to pour freely from spoon and run down sides and center of cake.

Apfel Kuchen

1 pkg granular yeast
2 Tbsp lukewarm water
2 Tbsp butter (first amount)
2 Tbsp sugar
1 tsp salt
½ C scalded milk
1 unbeaten egg
2½ C sifted flour
3 C apples, sliced ¼″ thick
1 C sugar
1½ tsp cinnamon
2 Tbsp soft butter (second amount)
1 egg yolk
⅓ C light cream

Soak yeast in lukewarm water 10 minutes then give it one stir. In large bowl combine the first 2 Tbsp of butter and sugar and salt and scalded milk. Cool to lukewarm. Stir in soaked yeast liquid and unbeaten egg. Gradually add and beat in the flour until dough is smooth. Cover and let rise in warm place until doubled. Stir down dough. Grease a 13 × 9″ pan and spread stirred-down dough in it evenly. Arrange sliced apples in rows over dough, pressing narrow edge into dough. Combine well the 1 C sugar, cinnamon and second 2 Tbsp butter. Reserve 2 Tbsp of this mixture. Sprinkle remainder over apples, cover and let rise until doubled again. Bake at 375° for 20 to 25 minutes until golden. Mix together egg yolks and cream. Pour over. Bake 15 minutes longer. Remove from oven, sprinkle with remaining 2 Tbsp sugar mixture, and serve warm.

Mocha Date Cake

PLAIN SPONGE

5 eggs, yolks and whites separated
1 C sugar
2 Tbsp lemon juice
1 tsp grated lemon rind
½ tsp salt
1 C sifted flour, resifted twice

Heat oven to 300°. Prepare layer cake tins (either 8″ or 9″) by greasing with shortening and fitting a layer of wax paper neatly on bottom of pans. Beat the egg yolks until thick and lemon-colored. Gradually add half the sugar, beating thoroughly and then the lemon juice and rind. Beat until thick. Beat the egg whites, salt and balance of the sugar thoroughly. Add the yolk mixture and beat for 1 minute only, just to thoroughly blend. Fold in the sifted flour and keep folding until it disappears. Pour immediately into prepared layer cake tins and bake 50 to 60 minutes at 300°. After baking, invert pans to cool for 5 minutes and then remove from tins before cake is entirely cool. Remove wax paper and cool thoroughly.

DATE FILLING

1 C chopped dates, well-packed
1 C water
⅓ C sugar
2 tsp lemon juice

Cook all ingredients together gently until quite thick, 20 to 25 minutes, stirring occasionally. Cool. Spread between layers of cooled cake. If desired, ¼ C chopped nuts may be added.

MOCHA FROSTING

⅓ C butter
¼ tsp salt
2 Tbsp cocoa
2 tsp instant coffee powder
2 C sifted icing sugar
2 Tbsp hot water

Cream butter until light then add salt, cocoa, instant coffee powder and sifted icing sugar. Mix and cream well, then beat in hot water until frosting is light and creamy. Frost top and sides of cake. Finely chopped pecans or walnuts may be sprinkled on top if desired.

Macaroon Cup Cakes

2 large egg whites
⅛ tsp cream of tartar
½ C white sugar
3 Tbsp light brown sugar
¾ C desiccated coconut
½ C stirred but not sifted cake
    and pastry flour
½ tsp vanilla

In beater bowl beat whites with cream of tartar until foamy then add both sugars and beat until very stiff, about 5 minutes. Beat in coconut, flour and vanilla until blended. Line ten 2¾″ muffin pans with ten 2½″ fluted paper cups. Spoon batter into unbuttered liners filling nearly to brim. Bake at 375° for 20 minutes having pan standing at center of oven. When baked transfer to cake racks to cool. Makes ten.

Alfretta's Prize Cream Cake

2 C sifted cake flour
3½ tsp baking powder
½ tsp salt
2 large eggs
1 C sugar
1 tsp finely grated lemon rind
1 C whipping cream
16 slices, drained, canned peaches

Beat the eggs and sugar together at high speed for at least 5 minutes until they increase in volume and are thick and opaque. Add the grated lemon rind. Sift together the sifted cake flour, baking powder and salt 3 times. Add the dry ingredients alternately with the cream, a third of each at a time, folding them in. Then to make batter smooth, beat for 5 seconds only. Turn into 2 buttered 8½" layer cake pans, lined on bottoms with buttered wax paper. Bake on center shelf at 350° for 20 to 25 minutes. Turn out on racks, peel off paper. Cool.

Put together with RICH CREAM FILLING: In heavy pan mix together 3 Tbsp sugar, 2 tsp cornstarch, ⅓ tsp salt until blended. Add ¼ C heavy cream and ½ C milk. Stir constantly over direct heat until smooth and boiling. Reduce heat and boil 1 minute, stirring. Beat 3 egg yolks slightly, add some of hot mixture to them and then add them to entire hot mixture. Cook an additional 2 minutes, stirring constantly until thick. (This may lump a little but keep stirring and the lumps smooth out.) Remove from heat and add 1 tsp vanilla. Cool to room temperature before spreading between layers.

Frost top and sides with ½ pint whipping cream, whipped until stiff. Do not sweeten the whipped cream. Decorate top with border of 16 crescents of well-drained canned peaches.

Angel Food Cake

1 C sifted cake and pastry flour
⅞ C fine granulated sugar (first amount)
1½ C egg whites (12, at room temperature)
1½ tsp cream of tartar
¼ tsp salt
1½ tsp vanilla
½ tsp almond extract
¾ C fine granulated sugar (second amount)

Sift together the measured and sifted flour and ⅞ C sugar 3 times. Into a very large bowl measure the egg whites, cream of tartar and salt and beat until foamy. Now gradually begin to add the second amount of sugar, 2 Tbsp at a time, while beating constantly, until all is added and meringue is very, very stiff and forms peaks which stand up straight. Fold in vanilla and almond extract. Begin to sift flour-sugar mixture over top, folding it into the meringue (do not beat at this stage) until all is added. Do not overmix.

Pour batter slowly and steadily into 10" ungreased tube pan. Bake at 350° for 40 to 45 minutes or until cake springs back when pressed gently with finger tip. Invert and allow to hang upside down until cold without touching cake rack. Then gently coax from pan and turn out on cake rack, top side up.

Festive Four-Decker Torte

3 C sifted all-purpose flour
4 tsp baking powder
1 tsp salt
⅔ C butter
1½ C sugar
1¼ C water
½ tsp rose water (or almond extract)
1 tsp vanilla
6 egg whites
¼ C sugar

Sift together the sifted flour, baking powder and salt. In beater bowl cream butter, then add 1½ C sugar and beat until light and fluffy. Combine water and flavorings. Remove beaters, add dry ingredients alternately with liquid to creamed mixture, beginning and ending with flour. Stir until blended after each addition. In medium bowl beat egg whites until foamy, gradually adding the ¼ C sugar while you beat until soft peaks form. Fold into batter. Line on bottom with wax paper and grease two 9" layer cake pans. Divide batter evenly into each. Bake at 350° for 30 to 35 minutes or until cakes test done. Let cool in pans 5 minutes then turn out on cake racks, peel off wax paper and cool. Split each layer in two, giving you 4 layers. Between layers and on top and sides spread frosting.

MOCHA BUTTER CREAM FROSTING
6 egg yolks (leftover from making cake)
¾ C sugar
½ tsp cornstarch
¾ C 18% cream
1½ C (¾ lb) firm butter
2 tsp instant coffee powder
2 tsp cocoa
2 tsp boiling water

In top of double boiler beat egg yolks until thick and lemon-colored. Mix together the sugar and cornstarch and add to yolks, beating. Gradually stir in cream and place over simmering (not boiling) water and cook until thick, stirring constantly. Cover and cook 15 minutes longer, stirring frequently. Remove from heat. Cool then chill thoroughly.

In large beater bowl beat butter until fluffy. In a cup add the boiling water to the instant coffee powder and cocoa and when blended cool. Then add to creamed butter. Now gradually add the chilled egg mixture to the creamed butter, beating after each addition until blended. Fill and frost cake. If desired decorate cake with chocolate shot or shaved toasted almonds or toasted coconut.

Hungarian Drum Cake

¾ C sugar
12 medium eggs
3 Tbsp flour
6 Tbsp finely ground walnuts
3 Tbsp fine breadcrumbs
1 tsp baking powder

Whip egg whites and yolks separately until stiff and thick. Add sugar to yolks gradually. Fold flour, bread-crumbs and walnuts into yolks. Add ½ tsp baking powder to yolks. Add second ½ tsp baking powder to whites. Combine whites with yolk mixture slowly, folding. Turn into three 9″ layer tins and bake at 375° for 13 to 15 minutes.

ICING

½ lb sweet (unsalted) butter
1 C sugar
½ C cold strong coffee
4 medium eggs
3 Tbsp cocoa
½ C rum

Whip whole eggs and coffee together and put over heat stirring constantly to prevent burning. Keep stirring until almost all moisture evaporates. Cool. While it is cooling cream butter and sugar. Press cooled egg and coffee mixture through sieve to make it fine. Beat all together and add cocoa. Press through sieve again if not fine enough. Take middle layer of cake and break into large crumbs and pour ½ C rum over them. Ice bottom layer, put rum-soaked crumbs over icing, then ice crumb layer, put on top layer and ice again. Chill.

Two-Egg Sponge Cake

2 large eggs
1 C sugar
¼ tsp salt
1 tsp vanilla
1 Tbsp melted butter
½ C boiling hot milk
1 C sifted all-purpose or
    cake and pastry flour
1 tsp baking powder

In a large bowl beat the eggs until they are increased in volume to 3 or 4 times the origingal amount, about 10 minutes in an electric beater. Beat in sugar, salt and vanilla until blended. To the hot milk add the butter and when it is melted stir into egg mixture. Sift together the sifted flour and baking powder. Remove beaters and stir in flour mixture by hand, just until all flour is moistened. Grease and paper-line bottom of 9″ square pan. Grease paper. Pour in batter. Bake at 350° for 25 to 30 minutes. Test for doneness at center by touching with fingertip. If no impression remains, cake is done. Let stand 5 minutes before turning out on rack to cool.

Creamy Peach Shortcake

CAKE

1 C sifted all-purpose flour
1 tsp baking powder
¼ tsp salt
1 Tbsp butter
½ C hot milk
2 eggs
1 C sugar
1 Tbsp lemon juice

FILLING

½ C sugar
3 Tbsp cornstarch
½ tsp salt
1½ C milk
2 eggs, slightly beaten
2 Tbsp butter
½ tsp almond extract

TOPPING

3 C sliced peaches
3 Tbsp sugar
½ pint whipping cream

To make Cake, grease a 9″ square cake pan and line bottom with greased waxed paper. Sift together flour, baking powder, salt. Melt butter in hot milk. Cool. Beat the 2 eggs until thick and gradually add 1 C sugar until light and fluffy. Add lemon juice. Remove beaters. Fold in sifted dry ingredients, alternately with milk, combining lightly after each addition. Pour into pan. Bake at 350° for 25 to 30 minutes. Cool in pan on wire rack 10 minutes. Remove from pan, peel off paper, cool completely.

To make Filling, in saucepan combine the ½ C sugar, cornstarch and the ½ tsp salt. Gradually stir in the 1½ C milk. Cook over medium heat, stirring constantly until thickened and mixture comes to the boil and 3 minutes longer. Stir a little of hot mixture into the 2 eggs then add eggs to saucepan and cook over low heat 1 minute longer. Stir in butter and almond extract. Cover and chill.

To assemble, combine peaches and the 3 Tbsp sugar. Whip cream until softly stiff. Split cake crosswise into 2 layers, fill with cream filling and half the peaches. Top with whipped cream and remaining peaches. Serves nine.

Super Raspberry Torte

1 ring (7½″) orange chiffon
    (or angel food) cake
Grated rind and juice of 1 large orange
1⅔ C milk
⅔ C sugar
⅓ C flour
¼ tsp salt
2 eggs
1 tsp vanilla
1 pint fresh raspberries
    (or 1 pkg fresh frozen)
¼ C fine sugar (omit if frozen raspberries used)
1¾ C whipping cream (divided)
2 tsp plain gelatin
2 Tbsp cold water

In top of double boiler scald together milk and orange rind. Wash and drain raspberries and pour over them the ¼ C fine sugar and orange juice. *Note:* If frozen raspberries are used, thaw and drain. To drained juice add orange juice but no sugar.

Mix together the ⅔ C sugar, flour and salt. Gradually stir scalded milk into this dry mixture and return to double boiler. Cook stirring until thick. Cover and cook 10 minutes, stirring occasionally. Beat eggs. Stir in a little of the hot mixture and return all to double boiler, stirring for 2 minutes. Remove from heat, add vanilla and chill, stirring occasionally.

Soak the gelatin in the cold water for 5 minutes, then dissolve it by stirring over hot water. Drain the orange juice-sugar liquid from the raspberries and stir the dissolved gelatin into it. This is for a glaze, later. Do not permit it to set.

Whip ½ C of the cream until stiff and fold it into the chilled custard mixture.

Cut ring from center of tube cake to leave 1¼" wide shell all round and on bottom. A curved grapefruit knife will help you to undercut and lift out the inner ring of cake. Fill bottom hole carefully with some of the leftover cake, then carefully transfer to serving plate. Fill with custard mixture to within ½" of top. Arrange drained raspberries evenly over. Now slowly pour on red glaze, being sure it flows between berries. Chill several hours. When serving time arrives whip remaining 1¼ C cream until stiff and frost sides and bare top edge. Serves ten or twelve.

Coconut Sponge Cup Cakes

3 eggs
1 C sifted cake and pastry flour
1½ tsp baking powder
¼ tsp salt
1 C sugar
2 tsp lemon juice
6 Tbsp hot milk

ICING
1¼ C icing sugar
2 Tbsp milk
Desiccated coconut

Beat eggs until very thick and foamy, about 10 minutes. Sift together the sifted flour, baking powder and salt. Slowly add the sugar to the beaten eggs. Remove beaters. With wire whip fold flour mixture into egg mixture. Also fold in hot milk and lemon juice.

Line 2¾" muffin tins with fluted paper cups and neatly spoon batter in, filling only ⅔ full. Bake at 350° for 18 minutes. When baked lift cup cakes to rack to cool.

Make Icing by beating together icing sugar and milk. Frost tops of cup cakes and neatly sprinkle tops with coconut, pressing down with fingers to make sure coconut sticks to icing. Makes twenty.

One-Bowl Gingerbread

2 C sifted all-purpose flour
1½ tsp baking soda
½ tsp salt
½ C sugar
1 tsp ginger
1 tsp cinnamon
½ C shortening (room temperature)
¾ C molasses
1 egg
1 C boiling water

After sifting and measuring flour, place sifter over large beater bowl and sift through it the flour, soda, salt, sugar and spices. Add shortening, molasses and egg and beat 2 minutes. Add boiling water and beat 2 minutes more. Line bottom of an 8 × 8" pan with wax paper. Butter bottom and sides. Turn in batter and bake at 350° for about 55 minutes, but be sure to test by gently touching at center to see if top is done. Turn out and cool on cake rack.

Upside-Down Peach Cake

BOTTOM
3 Tbsp butter or margarine
1 Tbsp grated orange rind
⅓ C brown sugar, packed
5 medium peaches
6 maraschino or glacé cherries quartered

BATTER
¼ C butter or margarine
½ C sugar
1 large or 2 medium eggs
¼ tsp almond extract
⅞ C unsifted cake and pastry flour
    (1 C less 2 Tbsp)
1½ tsp baking powder
¼ tsp salt
½ tsp cinnamon
⅓ C milk

Prepare fruit in pan first: In a 9 × 9" pan gently melt the 3 Tbsp butter or margarine. Stir the ⅓ C brown sugar evenly in. Sprinkle all over with grated orange rind. Set aside. Pour boiling water over peaches, let stand 1 minute, drain, cover with cold water, drain and peel. Cut into halves, remove pits and cut each half into 5 or 6 crescents. Place carefully in 4 rows in prepared pan. Place cherry quarters neatly between rows.

To make Batter, beat ¼ C butter or margarine and sugar until creamy. Beat in egg(s) for 2 or 3 minutes then remove beaters. Stir in almond extract. Sift together flour, baking powder, salt and cinnamon. Add half to creamed mix along with all of the milk and stir in. Add remaining dry ingredients and stir in smoothly. Pour over peaches in pan. Bake at 350° for 25 to 30 minutes, near bottom of oven. Test with toothpick at center to make sure batter is baked. Let stand in pan 5 minutes. Then cover with large serving dish and turn over and out. Serves nine.

Simplified Seven-Minute Frosting

One egg white, 1 C sugar, ½ C boiling hot unsweetened pineapple juice (or other fruit juices), ¼ tsp cream of tartar. Put all ingredients in large bowl in order given and beat until stiff to form soft peaks.

Fudge Custard Frosting

2 Tbsp corn starch
¼ C cocoa
¾ C sugar
¼ tsp salt
1 C boiling water
2 Tbsp butter
½ tsp vanilla

Fudge Custard Frosting is made by combining in top of double boiler the first 4 Frosting ingredients then stirring in boiling water. Stir over boiling water until thick. Cover and cook 15 minutes stirring once or twice. Add butter and vanilla and cool.

Genuine Almond Paste

¼ lb dry blanched almonds
　(or ready-ground almonds)
½ lb icing sugar (2⅓ C when sifted)
⅛ tsp salt
1 large egg yolk
1 tsp pure almond extract
1 tsp rosewater (optional)

Force almonds through fine nut knife of food grinder twice, easing them through by adding the rosewater if used. Mix with the remaining ingredients then turn the mass out on icing-sugar-sprinkled board and knead with your warm hands until pliable and smooth. Form into ball, wrap very well and store in open-mouthed jar, covered, to ripen for 24 hours before applying to top of fruit cakes. Roll out with rolling pin to size of cake top on icing-sugar-sprinkled board. To make it stick to cake first brush cake with corn syrup.

Ornamental Frosting For Wedding Cake

1 lb (3½ C) icing sugar
½ tsp cream of tartar
3 egg whites (unbeaten)
½ tsp vanilla

Sift the icing sugar and cream of tartar through a very fine sieve. Add the unbeaten egg whites and mix all together, using a slotted spoon or wire whip. Continue mixing for about 3 minutes. Add flavoring. Now spread a thin layer over the top and sides of cake to set the crumbs. Continue beating the remaining icing by hand for about 8 minutes or 4 minutes by electic beater at high speed. Spread some over the cake, smoothing the surface with a spatula. Beat the remaining icing until it is so stiff that when a knife is drawn through, it leaves a clean cut. Finish decorating by forcing through a decorating tube.

Commercial Bakery Icing

1 C shortening
1 tsp vanilla
1 tsp almond extract
4 C unsifted icing sugar
¼ C milk

Beat together all ingredients until smooth.

Rich Clear Orange Filling

Mix together in heavy saucepan ¾ C icing sugar, 1½ Tbsp cornstarch, ¼ tsp salt, ⅓ C fresh frozen orange (or tangerine) juice concentrate, ⅓ C water and 2 Tbsp butter. Cook, stirring, until thick, then cook 1 minute longer, stirring. Cool.

More Frostings and Fillings

For the following, look under the accompanying cake recipes.

BUTTER FROSTING:
　　　　　Marbled Angel Food Cake
CREAM CHEESE FROSTING:
　　　　　Fruity Frosted Applesauce Cake
HARD SAUCE FROSTING:
　　　　　Bake-and-Take Raisin Cake
LEMON FROSTING:
　　　　　Bunny Birthday Cake
CHOCOLATE FUDGE FROSTING:
　　　　　Devil's Food Cake
WHITE CREAM FROSTING:
　　　　　Milk Chocolate Cake
WHITE WHIPPED FROSTING:
　　　　　Prize-Winning Chocolate Cake
PEPPERMINT FUDGE FROSTING:
　　　　　Maritimer's Mint Chocolate Cake
CHOCOLATE GLAZE:
　Orange Party Cake with Chocolate Coating
ORANGE FROSTING:
　　　　　Pineapple Orange Cake
FRUITY FROSTING:
　　　　　White Wedding Cake
CARAMEL FROSTING:
　　　　　White Cake with Caramel Frosting
PEACH FROSTING:
　　　　　One-Egg Cake
MOCHA FROSTING:
　　　　　Mocha Date Cake
FRENCH CHOCOLATE FILLING:
　　　　　Chocolate Log
LEMON FILLING:
　　　　　Lemon Jelly Roll
RICH CREAM FILLING:
　　　　　Alfretta's Prize Cream Cake

Cookies

Peanut Butter Cookies see page 222

Scotch Oatmeal Shortbread

1 lb butter
3 C stirred but unsifted all-purpose flour
1 C oatmeal
¾ C unsifted icing sugar

Note: You can use real Scotch oatmeal or quick-cooking rolled oats which have been reduced to fine meal in your blender.

Into beater bowl put the pound of butter cut in chunks. Add the flour, oatmeal and icing sugar and beat on low speed until mixed. Do not overbeat or dough will become too soft to handle.

Flour your board generously and put dough on it. Pat it out and turn it over. (You are well advised to divide it in half now to make rolling easier.) Roll out to less than ¼" thickness. Cut out with floured 2" cutter. Handle it gently for it is fairly soft. Lift each cookie on to ungreased cookie sheet placing them about ¾" apart for they spread a little while baking. Into the center of each one place ¼ of a red or green glacé cherry or a few colored sprinkles.

The baking is important. Do not overbake. Bake at 325° for 14 to 15 minutes. They should not brown at all, but should be a pale biscuit color with no gold edges. With lifter transfer to racks to cool. Store between sheets of wax paper in cookie tins. This amount makes sixty.

Chocolate Nut Health Drops

1 C brown sugar
2 Tbsp oil
2 eggs
1 Tbsp vanilla
⅓ C cocoa
1 C fresh wheat germ
¼ tsp salt
½ C all-purpose flour
½ C sunflower seeds
½ C coarsely chopped walnuts

Into beater bowl measure the brown sugar, oil, eggs, vanilla, and beat 2 minutes. With beater on low setting, as you measure them, add the cocoa, wheat germ, salt, flour, sunflower seeds and walnuts and mix. Scrape down sides of bowl with rubber scraper and chill dough at least half an hour.

Butter or grease 3 cookie sheets. Using a silver teaspoon heaped a little, drop dough onto cookie sheets at least 2" apart. Bake at 350° for 5 to 8 minutes. Watch these cookies for they might easily burn. Cool on cake racks. Store between sheets of wax paper in cookie tin. Makes 3 dozen.

Ginger Cookies

For gingerbread men and other cutouts.

1 C shortening
1 C granulated sugar
⅔ C molasses
⅔ C warm strong coffee
5 C cake flour (unsifted)
1 tsp salt
1 tsp baking soda
2 tsp ginger
1 tsp cloves
1 tsp cinnamon

Cream shortening and sugar together in large bowl until light. Add molasses. Measure coffee in molasses cup to rinse it out and mix in. Tip the unsifted cake flour into the sifter and sift it with the salt, soda and spices into the first mixture and blend thoroughly. Shape dough into 3 balls, wrap and chill at least 2 hours. Roll out 1 ball of dough very thinly—⅛" thick—on lightly floured board. (Leave remaining 2 balls in refrigerator until you are ready to roll them.) Cut out with gingerbread man cutter or star or round cutter. Bake on lightly greased cookie sheets at 350° for 7 minutes. Repeat with remaining 2 balls of dough. Yield: Forty-two 5 × 3" men and 6 dozen additional 2" shapes.

Be sure not to overbake these cookies as with the high sugar and molasses content they will burn easily.

Ghoraibi: Lebanese Cookies

Note that these cookies do not call for salt. Taste the dough after it is mixed to see if you would prefer to add ¼ teaspoon.

1 C unsalted butter
1¼ C sifted icing sugar
1 egg yolk
2 tsp lemon juice
2 C twice sifted cake
    (or cake and pastry) flour
Pistachio halves (or halved blanched almonds)

Cream the unsalted butter with the icing sugar until very light and fluffy, at least 10 minutes in your beater at high speed. Beat in the egg yolk and lemon juice. Add the flour. If the dough is too soft to handle spread it out in the bowl and chill it for 1 hour in the refrigerator or half an hour in freezer. Form into small balls not more than one inch in diameter. Place 2½" apart on 4 greased cookie sheets. Decorate each cookie with 3 pistachio nut halves in the shape of a three-leaf clover pressing down each ball slightly as you decorate. Otherwise use half a blanched almond. Bake at 325° about 10 minutes. Watch them. They must not be overbaked. They should be a pale sand color with pale gold rim. Let stand on pan for 1 minute before lifting carefully with spatula to cake racks to cool. These are delicate cookies so when you store them in your cookie tin be sure to put wax paper between each layer. Yield: 6 dozen.

Fruit Drops

½ C good quality shortening
1 C sugar
1 egg
Grated rind of 1 orange
¼ tsp baking soda
⅓ C orange juice
2½ Tbsp milk
2½ C stirred unsifted all-purpose flour
¼ tsp salt
1 Tbsp baking powder
1 tsp cinnamon
1 tsp nutmeg
1 C raisins

Measure and put in the beater bowl shortening and sugar, and cream them. Add egg and continue beating. As you measure all remaining ingredients put them into the bowl and keep mixing until all ingredients are in. Grease cookie sheets. For each cookie scoop up a rounded teaspoonful of dough and push it from the spoon. Bake at 375° for 12 to 15 minutes.

Stickproof Macaroons

2 egg whites
1 C sugar
2 tsp cornstarch
1½ C shredded coconut
1½ tsp vanilla

Stand top of double boiler on counter and into it put the egg whites. Beat until stiff. Mix the sugar and cornstarch together and sprinkle over egg whites and stir in. Stir over boiling water until meringue coats sides of pan, about 3 minutes. Remove from heat. Fold in the coconut and vanilla. Cover cookie sheets with ungreased cookery parchment or unglazed brown paper and drop meringue mixture in 1" mounds from teaspoon dipped in water, 1 to 1½" apart. (If desired top each with a tiny piece of red or green candied cherry.) Bake at 325° for 15 to 17 minutes, switching shelves and turning pans after first 10 minutes. They should be tinged with gold all over. Remove from paper at once. Makes 32.

Crunchy Orange Drop Cookies

1 C shortening, preferably half and
    half butter and shortening
1 C sugar
2 eggs
1 large orange: grated rind and juice (see below)
2 C all-purpose flour
2 tsp baking powder
1 tsp salt
2 C bran flakes (packaged cereal)

Cream together shortening and sugar until light. Beat in eggs. Grate rind from 1 large orange and add it. Cut orange in half and squeeze out juice. You need ¼ cup. If you do not have it add water to orange juice to make ¼ cup. Mix together flour, baking powder and salt and add alternately with the orange juice. Stir in bran flakes.

Drop, by mounded dessertspoonfuls, onto greased cookie sheets at least 2" apart. Bake at 350° about 12 to 13 minutes until tinged with gold. Makes 4 dozen.

Sour Cream Drop Cookies with Burnt Butter Icing

COOKIE DOUGH
¼ C butter
¼ C shortening
1½ C sugar
2 eggs
1 C dairy sour cream
1 tsp vanilla
2¾ C sifted all-purpose flour
½ tsp baking soda
½ tsp baking powder
½ tsp salt

ICING
¼ C butter (melted: see below)
1 C sifted icing sugar
½ tsp vanilla
1 Tbsp hot water

In large mixing bowl cream together until light and smooth the shortening, butter and sugar, then beat in eggs. Sift together the sifted flour, soda, baking powder and salt and beat in with the sour cream and vanilla. Chill dough. Butter baking sheets. For large cookies drop rounded dessertspoonfuls at least 2½" apart on pan. Bake at 425°. Time depends on size, so you must watch cookies and test for doneness. They should be only tinged with gold. Test one by breaking it in half to see if it is done. Cool on racks. Makes forty-eight.

To make icing, melt butter in saucepan until it is deep gold. Do not let it darken too much. Remove from heat and stir in icing sugar and vanilla and when blended stir in hot water. Cool until of spreading consistency. If it hardens a little too much before cookies are iced stir over low heat for a moment to soften it.

Ginger Snaps

¾ C shortening (room temperature)
¾ C butter or margarine (room temperature)
2 C white sugar
2 eggs
½ C molasses
4 C sifted all-purpose flour
2 tsp baking soda
1 tsp baking powder
2 tsp cinnamon
2 tsp cloves
1 to 2 Tbsp ginger
¼ tsp salt

Cream together the shortening and butter or margarine until light, then beat in the sugar until light and airy. Beat in eggs and molasses. Sift together 3½ C of the sifted flour with the baking soda, baking powder, cinnamon, cloves, ginger and salt. Add sifted dry ingredients and mix until smooth. Now test one 1" ball for texture. If, when you shape these into balls between your palms, they do not roll smoothly add a little more flour, but not more than the remaining half cup. Shape dough into 1" balls, rolling between floured palms and place on buttered cookie sheets and flatten with floured fork. Bake at 375° for 12 to 15 minutes.

Snappy Crackle-Top Chocolate Cookies

¾ C shortening (room temperature)
1¼ C dark brown sugar
1 egg
2½ squares (2½ oz) unsweetened chocolate
2¼ C sifted cake flour
2 tsp baking soda
¼ tsp salt
1 tsp vanilla
Granulated sugar (for dipping tops)

Melt chocolate in heavy cup standing in shallow pan of boiling water. Into beater bowl measure the shortening and brown sugar and beat until creamy and light. Add egg and melted chocolate and beat again until well blended.

Sift together the sifted flour, baking soda and salt and beat in with the vanilla. Batter is stiff and does not need to be chilled. With buttered palms break off small amounts of dough and shape into 1¼" balls. Have ready in a small shallow bowl some granulated sugar. Dip balls in sugar, turn over, and place, sugared side up, on buttered baking sheet 2" apart. Press down a little with the side of your palm.

Bake at 375° for 15 to 17 minutes. You will need 2 cookie sheets and should switch pans about, end for end, and to different levels, during baking to have every cookie uniform. Be sure to watch these for if they are baked too long they will burn easily. Yield: 48.

Mint Surprise Cookies

3 C sifted all-purpose flour
1 tsp baking soda
½ tsp salt
1 C butter or margarine
1 C sugar
½ C firmly packed brown sugar
2 unbeaten eggs
1 tsp vanilla
1 package (9 oz) solid chocolate
    mint candy wafers
Walnut halves

Sift flour with soda and salt. Cream butter. Gradually add sugar and brown sugar, creaming well. Add eggs and vanilla. Beat well. Blend in dry ingredients gradually and mix thoroughly. Cover and chill at least 2 hours (see note).

To shape cookies, enclose one candy wafer in a rounded teaspoonful of chilled dough. Place on ungreased baking sheets about 2" apart. Top each with a walnut half. Bake at 375° for 9 to 12 minutes. Makes 4½ dozen.

Note: If desired, refrigerator cookies may also be made. Shape dough into long rolls, 1½" in diameter; wrap in wax paper. Chill at least 4 hours or overnight. Cut in slices ⅛" thick; place on ungreased baking sheets. Top each with a chocolate wafer. Cover each with additional slice of cookie dough and seal edges with fingertips. Top with walnut halves. Bake as above.

Dad's Cookies

1 C shortening
2 C brown sugar
2 large eggs
1 tsp vanilla
2 C desiccated coconut
2 C flour
1 tsp baking powder
¼ tsp salt
½ tsp baking soda
2 C rolled oats or oatmeal

Cream shortening, cream in sugar, add vanilla and eggs, beating after each addition. Mix remaining ingredients and add to creamed mixture. Mix well. Roll into balls after dough is chilled. Place on greased cookie sheet 2" apart. Bake at 375° for 10 to 13 minutes.

Cheese Pastry Sandwich Cookies with Apricot Filling

1 C sifted all-purpose flour
⅛ tsp salt
½ C butter (cold)
One 4-oz package white cream cheese (cold)
Apricot (or raspberry) jam
1 beaten egg (for glazing tops)
Granulated sugar (for tops)

Mix sifted flour and salt in mixing bowl. With pastry blender or 2 knives cut butter and cheese into flour and salt, until of pastry consistency. (This cookie dough contains no liquid.) Press into ball, wrap in wax paper or saran and chill.

On lightly floured board roll out dough to ⅛" thickness. (Do not dawdle. This dough should be cold to handle easily.) Cut out with 2 or 2½" star-shaped cutter. Place half of them on buttered cookie sheet. Press trimmings together and reroll and cut out again. Put ½ or ¾ tsp apricot (or raspberry) jam on center of each. Cover each with another pastry star pressing edges together neatly and carefully with tines of fork. Neatly brush tops of each with beaten egg. Sprinkle top of each with granulated sugar. Bake at 400° on center rack of oven 10 to 12 minutes, turning pans around after first 5 minutes. Cool on cake racks. Makes twenty.

Butterfingers

1 C butter
5 Tbsp sugar
A few grains salt
2 C flour
1 Tbsp water
1 C chopped nuts, any kind
1 tsp vanilla

Cream butter and sugar, add salt, vanilla and water. Work in the flour; add nuts. Shape in 2" lengths and a finger in width. Bake at 250° for 15 minutes or until barely firm but not brown. When cool roll in fruit sugar. Makes 36.

Basic Rolled Oats Mix

3 C skim milk powder
4 C unsifted all-purpose flour
4 C rolled oats, quick-cooking type
¼ C baking powder
1 Tbsp salt
1½ C shortening: a type that does not
    require refrigeration

In a very large mixing bowl or dishpan, mix together the 5 dry ingredients. Cut in the shortening with 2 knives until size of small peas. (A pastry blender will not cut through to the bottom of this bulky mix.) Take out 3 cups to make Oatmeal Fruit Muffins (below) and store remainder in covered large canister or stong plastic bag at room temperature for future use.

OATMEAL FRUIT MUFFINS

3 C Basic Rolled Oats Mix (above)
½ C sugar
½ C chopped dates
¼ C chopped nuts (optional)
1 egg
¾ C milk

Add sugar, dates and nuts to oat mix in mixing bowl and combine. Drop in unbeaten egg, add milk and beat until just mixed. Butter your 12-cup muffin pan and spoon in batter equally. Bake at 375° about 15 to 20 minutes, being sure pan is on center shelf of oven. Makes twelve.

OATMEAL FRUIT DROP COOKIES

2½ C Basic Rolled Oats Mix (above)
¾ C sugar
1 tsp cinnamon
½ C raisins
½ C coconut, desiccated or flaked
1 egg
¼ C water
1 tsp vanilla

Mix together first 5 ingredients. Beat in egg, water and vanilla and mix well. Drop by teaspoonfuls on buttered baking sheet 2″ apart. Bake at 375° for 12 or 15 minutes on center rack of oven. Watch these to be sure they do not brown too quickly. Makes 3 dozen.

BISHOP'S BREAD

This is a traditional Southern hot bread.

3 C Basic Rolled Oats Mix (above)
1 tsp cinnamon
1 C chopped dates
⅔ C light brown sugar
2 Tbsp grated orange rind
2 eggs
1 C orange juice

TOPPING

¼ C sifted icing sugar
½ tsp cinnamon

Measure oat mix into mixing bowl, add cinnamon, dates, sugar and orange rind and mix well to separate date pieces and coat them with mix. Beat in eggs and orange juice until blended. Turn into well buttered 12 × 8″ or 9 × 9″ pan and bake on center shelf of oven at 350° for about 25 minutes. While hot, sprinkle entire surface with mixture of icing sugar and cinnamon. Cut into squares and serve hot or warm if possible.

HASTY FRUIT BATTER PUDDING

2 or 3 C sliced raw fruit (see below)
1 Tbsp sugar
2 C Basic Rolled Oats Mix
    (see first column)
¾ C sugar (second amount)
⅔ C water
½ tsp nutmeg (or mace)
1 Tbsp lemon juice

Into an 8 × 8″ baking dish put the raw fruit: apples, rhubarb, plums or peaches. Sprinkle the fruit with 1 Tbsp sugar. Beat together the 5 batter ingredients and pour over prepared fruit and bake at center shelf of oven at 350° for 45 minutes or until fruit is tender and juice bubbles up. Serve hot with Brown Sugar Sauce. Serves six.

Basic Cookie Dough and Five Variations

3½ C sifted cake flour
2 tsp baking powder
½ tsp salt
½ C butter or margarine
1 C sugar
2 medium eggs
1 Tbsp cream
1 tsp vanilla

Mix and sift flour, baking powder and salt. Cream butter or margarine and sugar together; beat until light. Add eggs, cream and vanilla; beat well. Stir in dry ingredients until blended. Shape into ball and wrap in waxed paper. Chill 3 hours. Divide dough in halves. Return one half to refrigerator. Break off pieces of dough, flour the palms of your hands and shape into balls 1″ in diameter. Place on buttered cookie sheets and press down with flat bottom of a floured tumbler. Place 2″ apart. Bake at 375° about 6 minutes, having cookie sheets at center of oven. Do not brown these cookies at all. Yield: 4 dozen.

Five Variations: 1. Put 2 cookies together with pineapple jam, roll edges in melted bitter chocolate then in finely chopped Brazils. 2. Brush top with egg white and dip entire top in chocolate sprinkles. 3. Put together with apple jelly, roll edges in thin plain icing-sugar-egg-white-frosting (egg white leftover from dipping tops of #2) and then in coconut. 4. On top of about 8 cookies place 1 tsp pineapple jam; swirl around it some of the plain white icing, then dip tops quickly in coconut. 5. Add a little melted butter to the leftover melted chocolate, spread tops of remaining cookies with it and quickly dip in finely chopped Brazils.

Butter Balls (Two Variations)

This recipe yields 60 butter balls. They will freeze.

1 C hard butter
½ C granulated sugar
2 egg yolks
2 tsp almond extract
1⅞ C stirred but unsifted all-purpose flour
½ C bran flakes (see below)
½ C finely chopped cashews or
   other nuts (see below)

Into beater bowl measure the butter and sugar and beat at high speed for 5 minutes until creamy. Add almond extract and egg yolks and beat again. Add flour and beat until thoroughly blended in. Divide dough in half and put half in small bowl. Into it stir the bran flakes. Into other half beat the nuts. Scrape down sides of bowls and chill dough for half an hour.

Grease two large cookie sheets. Between your palms shape dough into 1″ balls and place 2″ apart on cookie sheets. Bake at 350° about 15 minutes, switching pans in oven at halftime. Do not overbake. Cool on cake racks. If to be frozen arrange on plastic or foil pans, cover and freeze, then stack in cartons or refrigerator boxes with sheets of wax paper between layers and put back in freezer.

Variations: 1. Omit nuts and use 1 cup bran flakes, or omit bran flakes and use all nuts. 2. Top each ball with one-quarter glacé red cherry or piece of candied peel or blanched almond. 3. If you are not going to freeze these Butter Balls they may be rolled in icing sugar.

Peanut Butter Cookies

1 C butter or half and half butter and
   good quality shortening
1 tsp vanilla
1 C brown sugar, well packed
1 C white sugar
2 eggs
1 C peanut butter
3 C sifted all-purpose flour
2 tsp baking powder
½ tsp salt

Cream butter or mixed butter and shortening. Add sugars, creaming well. Beat in eggs and vanilla, mixing thoroughly. Add peanut butter and mix well. Sift together the flour and baking powder and salt. Stir into creamed mixture. (Add 1 C of chopped dates or 1 C of chopped peanuts if desired.) Roll into small balls, about 1″ in diameter and place on greased cookie sheet. Flatten with tines of a fork, dipped in water. Bake at 375° for 10 to 12 minutes. Watch closely. Makes about 5 dozen.

Chocolate Chip Cookies

¼ C butter
¼ C shortening
1½ C granulated sugar
2 large eggs
⅔ C dairy sour cream
1 tsp vanilla
2¾ C sifted all-purpose flour
½ tsp baking powder
½ tsp baking soda
½ tsp salt
1 C chocolate chips

In large mixing bowl cream together until light and smooth the shortening, butter and sugar, then beat in eggs. Sift together the sifted flour, baking soda, baking powder and salt and beat in with sour cream, vanilla and chocolate chips. Butter baking sheets. Drop dough from teaspoon in 1″ mounds at least two and a half inches apart. Bake at 425°. Time depends on size. As soon as edges are ringed with gold they are done and should be carefully lifted from pans with lifter to cake racks to cool. Makes 5 or 6 dozen.

Cookie Press Cookies

BASIC DOUGH
1 C butter
1 C sugar
2 eggs
3⅓ C sifted all-purpose flour
1 tsp salt
1 tsp vanilla
1 tsp almond extract

Cream the butter, gradually adding the sugar. Blend in eggs, vanilla and almond extract. Beat well. Sift together the flour and salt and add to mixture. Mix thoroughly.

Shaping: Press dough through cookie press — see Variations below — into which it has been firmly packed, onto ungreased cool shiny aluminum baking sheets, using any plate to make desired shape.

Baking: Bake at 400°for 8 to 10 minutes until barely tinted with gold.

Variations: Divide the dough into 3 bowls. 1. *Christmas Wreaths:* Tint ⅓ of basic dough a delicate pink. Using star plate, shape into wreaths and decorate with 3 or 4 silver balls or tiny bits of red and green cherries to form holly sprays. 2. *Green Trees:* Tint ⅓ of basic dough a definite pale green and using tree plate, shape into trees on cold cookie sheet. Decorate 3 outside points with silvers. 3. *Coconut Medallions:* To ⅓ of basic dough add ¼ C very finely chopped or ground coconut. Shape through medallion plate. Decorate tips with a sprinkle of colored sugar.

Oatmeal Cookies

2 C sifted all-purpose flour
½ tsp salt
3 C quick-cooking rolled oats
1 C shortening (half butter)
1 tsp soda
⅓ C buttermilk
1½ C dark brown sugar

In a large bowl measure flour, salt and rolled oats. Work shortening into them with pastry blender. Stir the soda into the milk and add this mixture and the sugar and mix well. Pack into 2 firm balls between your palms, flatten somewhat, and wrap well and chill until firm. Roll out ¼ of the dough at a time (that is, half of a chilled ball) on lightly floured board to ⅛" thickness. Cut with 2½" plain or fluted cookie cutter. Bake on buttered cookie sheet at 375° for 8 to 10 minutes.

Variation: For dainty tea party cookies roll to ¹⁄₁₆" thickness, cut out with 1¾" cutter and bake on buttered cookie sheet at 375° for 5 to 6 minutes. Cool. Put together in pairs with Date or Fig Filling.

DATE OR FIG FILLING

This filling is the usual one to be put between oatmeal cookies, but has the addition of chopped nuts. They may be omitted. Use it for regular 2¾" cookie sandwiches or for thinly rolled oatmeal cookie sandwiches.

1½ C chopped dates or figs
½ C sugar
½ C water
2 Tbsp lemon juice
½ C finely chopped walnuts or almonds (optional)

Mix all ingredients together, stir over medium heat until boiling, then reduce heat and stir 3 minutes. Cool before spreading between cookies. This amount fills 3½ to 4 dozen.

(Please see following recipe)

Date Turnovers

First make Date Filling (see Oatmeal Cookies, above) and then make the following dough.

½ C soft shortening
1 C sugar
2 eggs
2 Tbsp thick cream
1 tsp vanilla
2½ C sifted flour
¼ tsp soda
½ tsp salt

Mix shortening, sugar and eggs together thoroughly. Stir in cream and vanilla. Sift dry ingredients together and stir in. Chill dough. Roll very thin (¹⁄₁₆"). Cut 3" rounds or squares. Place on lightly greased baking sheet. Place on each a rounded teaspoonful of Date Filling. Fold over like a turnover, pressing moistened edges together with floured tines of a fork or tip of finger, sealing edges well. Bake at 400° for 8 to 10 minutes until delicately browned.

Empire Biscuits

1 C (½ lb) butter
⅔ C granulated sugar
2 large eggs
4 C unsifted all-purpose flour
2 tsp cream of tartar
2 tsp baking powder
White satin frosting (see below)
Red jelly or jam for filling
Various cake decorating sprinkles

Cream together the butter and sugar until light. Beat in eggs. Sift in the unsifted flour, cream of tartar and baking powder, and mix well. Pick up dough in your hands and shape into a smooth ball between your palms. Place on floured large double sheet of wax paper, fold one-half of wax paper over dough, press down dough to flatten it to 1" thickness and chill for half an hour in refrigerator. Remove half of dough and roll it out thinly on well-floured board with floured rolling pin to ⅛" thickness. You should work quickly to prevent dough warming up. Cut out with 2" floured cutter and place on buttered cookie sheet about ½" apart. These cookies do not spread. Bake at 350° for about 10 minutes. Do not brown.

Repeat rolling and cutting out with second half of chilled dough but cut these out with 2½" cutter (for variety) and bake as above. Cool on cake racks. Make sandwich cookies by putting them together in pairs with red currant or raspberry jelly or jam between. Place exactly ½ tsp on half of the 2" cookies and press remaining cookies gently over to spread jelly or jam to edges. Now sparingly cover tops of these sandwich cookies with White Satin Frosting.

WHITE SATIN FROSTING

1½ C unsifted icing sugar
1½ tsp salad oil
3 Tbsp warm water
Shake of salt
¼ tsp almond flavoring

Mix all ingredients in a bowl and frost cookies. As soon as you have done this, sprinkle tops of some with red sugar crystals, some with green, some with other decorations. Let set on cake racks.

Genuine Scotch Shortbread

1 lb butter
4 C stirred but not sifted all-purpose flour
¾ C unsifted icing or fruit sugar

Cream these 3 ingredients until of rolling-out consistency. Roll out to ¼" thickness on lightly floured board. Edges of dough will crack, but patiently coax dough into a smooth round. Cut out with lightly floured cutter or various cutters. Bake at 325° on unbuttered baking sheets about 20 to 25 minutes. Remove as soon as they are barely tinged with gold. They should not be browned at all.

Variation: The Scots roll shortbread in circles ½" thick or press into 6 or 7" pans to ½" thickness and bake longer.

Cherry Globes

1 C butter
¼ C icing sugar
2 C sifted all-purpose flour
1 C finely chopped blanched almonds
¼ tsp salt
1 tsp vanilla
3 dozen maraschino cherries, drained and dried

Cream butter and sugar until fluffy. Add remaining ingredients, except cherries, mixing well. Flatten a small amount of dough, (about 1½ tsp for each cookie) in palm of hand. Place a whole drained and dried cherry on circle of dough. Cover cherry by pinching dough up and around it, then roll between hands to form a smooth ball. Bake on greased baking sheet at 325° about 25 to 30 minutes. While still hot, roll in fine granulated sugar. Makes 3 dozen.

Cheese Cream Pastries

¼ lb cream cheese (room temperature)
¼ lb butter (it should not be soft)
1 C flour

Put all ingredients in beater bowl and cream until they form fine crumbs and will pack together between your palms. Roll out dough on lightly floured board to ⅛″ thickness. Cut out with 2″ cookie cutter, and put half of them on an unbuttered cookie sheet. Put ½ tsp red jelly in centers. Cover with remaining rounds and deftly seal edges with finger tips. With the point of a small knife make a ¼″ slit in the top of each, to allow a little of the jelly to bubble up through and show a little red center. Bake at 375° for 18 to 25 minutes. Do not let these get brown. They should be creamy yellow. This amount makes 24 sandwich cookies.

Sugar Cookies with Variations

½ C butter
½ C shortening
½ C granulated sugar
½ C light brown sugar
1 large egg
2 C stirred but not sifted cake and
     pastry flour
1 tsp baking soda
2 tsp cream of tartar
½ tsp salt
1 tsp vanilla

Into beater bowl measure butter, shortening and sugars and beat until creamy and light. Beat in egg. Add remaining ingredients and beat until blended. If desired divide dough into 3 bowls. To one add 5 drops red food coloring, to another 5 drops green, and leave the third bowl plain. Chill dough until hard.

Remove the bowl of plain dough from refrigerator and spoon out small amount onto your buttered palm and shape into a ball. Place on buttered cookie sheet at least 3″ apart. Decorate top with red sugar sprinkles and bake at 350° about 6 or 7 minutes or until you can lift them from pan. Do not brown these cookies.

Repeat with remaining bowls of colored dough but put walnut or cherry quarter at center of pink ones and colored sprinkles at center of green ones. Bake at 350° for 6 to 7 minutes. These colored ones must not be browned at all or their color is murky. Cool on cake racks and store in cookie tins with sheet of wax paper between each layer.

Cherry Nut Icebox Cookies

1 C butter or margarine (room temperature)
¾ C light brown sugar (lightly packed)
½ tsp vanilla
⅛ tsp salt
2½ C sifted all-purpose flour
1 C walnuts or pecans sliced once lengthwise
1 C glacé or drained and dried maraschino
     cherries, left whole

In large bowl cream together the butter or margarine, sugar, vanilla and salt until well blended. Add flour and beat until mixed. (It will be crumbly.) Add nuts and cherries. Divide dough in half. Turn each half out on large double sheet of heavy wax paper, bring sides of wax paper up to cover dough and press and force into compact long rolls 2″ in diameter, poking your finger tips into ends to push in crumbs neatly. Crease and fold ends of wax paper over and chill dough (or freeze) until hard. With very sharp heavy knife cut into 3/16″ slices.

Place on unbuttered cookie sheets ¾″ apart and bake at 375°. They do not spread. If cookies are thin they require only 10 to 12 minutes baking; if they are thick they should bake about 18 to 20 minutes. They should not be brown. Remove and cool on cake racks.

Thimble Cookies

1 C butter (room temperature)
½ C granulated sugar
2 eggs, yolks and whites separated
2 tsp almond extract
2 C sifted all-purpose flour
Finely chopped nuts (walnuts or almonds or
    filberts or Brazils or crushed corn flakes)
Colorful jam or jelly (such as raspberry,
    mint, apricot)

In beater bowl cream together the butter and sugar until pale and airy. Separate egg yolks from whites, putting whites in shallow bowl for future step. Add yolks to butter-sugar mixture and beat well, then add almond extract, beat, then add flour and beat until dough is smooth. Have finely chopped nuts or crushed corn flakes on shallow plate. By hand shape dough into uniform 1″ balls. Drop about 6 in the egg whites. With fork turn balls over, lift carefully with fork and drop into chopped nuts or crumbs. (Keep one fork for turning balls in whites and one fork for coating balls with nuts or crumbs.) Working with about 6 at a time transfer coated balls to buttered cookie sheets, placing them 2″ apart. Make depression in center of each with your thumb (or floured thimble on your middle finger). When cookie sheets are full bake at 350° for about 20 minutes. After 5 minutes baking, carefully dent them at center again. You may want to dent the cookies very carefully once more after they are taken from oven. Cool on cake racks and store in tightly covered containers, each layer being between sheets of wax paper.

When you are ready to serve these cookies fill center of each with ¼ or ½ tsp of colorful jelly or jam. Yield: seventy.

Aunt Rachel's Cookies

2⅓ C sifted all-purpose flour
¼ tsp baking soda
1 tsp baking powder
½ tsp salt
½ C butter
1 Tbsp shortening
1 C sugar
1 egg
⅓ C sour cream
¼ tsp vanilla
¾ C steamed and dried raisins

Sift flour with soda, baking powder and salt. Cream shortening and butter until smooth. Stir in flavoring. Cream in sugar thoroughly. Beat in egg until fluffy, then stir in flour mixture and the cream alternately in 2 or 3 portions, mixing until just smooth after each. Add raisins. Chill dough. Roll out on lightly floured pastry cloth or board about ³⁄₁₆″ thick. Cut out with 2½ to 3″ scalloped cutter. Place on greased cookie sheets and bake about 15 minutes at 375°. Remove from pan to cake rack immediately. Yield: 4 dozen.

Pecan Crisps

1 C butter
2 tsp vanilla
1 C unsifted icing sugar
½ C sifted all-purpose flour
½ C sifted cake flour
One 3-oz package pecans, coarsely chopped,
    about ⅞ C

Into beater bowl measure butter, vanilla and icing sugar and beat at high speed until pale and smooth and light. Beat in flours. Then add nuts. Butter a 15 × 11″ cookie sheet with ½″ high sides. With spatula or blunt-ended knife spread batter thinly and evenly all over pan. Make it a little thicker at the edges than at the middle for the edges tend to bake a little faster. Bake at 350° about 15 minutes, or 17 to 18 minutes to make them crisper and a deeper gold. Cool in pan then sprinkle evenly with icing sugar. Instead of marking into squares break off little 2 or 3″ pieces and pile them higgledy-piggledy on cookie plate. These keep well, covered, because of their high butter content. Serve with fruited jelly, ice cream or fresh fruits in season.

Ginger Double-Deckers

DOUGH
¾ C butter or margarine
¾ C granulated sugar
1 egg
1 C molasses
4 C sifted all-purpose flour
1 tsp salt
2 tsp powdered ginger
1 tsp baking soda

ICING
3 C stirred but not sifted icing sugar
1½ Tbsp butter or margarine
¼ tsp salt
1½ Tbsp milk
⅜ tsp powdered ginger
3 Tbsp hot water

To make Cookies, into beater bowl measure butter or margarine, granulated sugar, egg and molasses and beat until light. Sift together the sifted flour, salt, ginger and baking soda and add to beater bowl and beat until thoroughly blended. Chill dough. Roll out one-quarter of dough at a time on lightly floured board. (Leave remaining dough in refrigerator.) Cut out with 2½ to 3″ cutter and place on buttered cookie sheets. Continue with next quarter of dough until you have about 20 cookies cut out. Bake on buttered cookie sheets 1″ apart at 375° for 8 to 10 minutes.

Meanwhile roll and cut out remaining dough the same size as first cookies, and make a hole in center with a thimble. (Chill scraps of dough as they accumulate to make rolling out and picking up easier.) Bake same as whole cookies but be sure to watch them for with their high sugar and molasses content they might burn. Cool on cake racks. Put together in pairs with icing between.

To make Icing, beat all icing ingredients until smooth. Store these cookies in tightly covered tin.

Homemade Honey Graham Wafers

1 C shortening
¼ C brown sugar
¼ C honey
2 C white flour
4 C graham flour
1 tsp baking soda
2 tsp baking powder
½ tsp salt
½ to ¾ C sweet or sour milk
1 tsp vanilla

Cream shortening and sugar together until fluffy. Add vanilla and honey and measure flour, combine with graham flour, and add salt, soda and baking powder. Add sifted dry ingredients alternately with milk. Dough should be stiff. Mix thoroughly after each addition. Chill dough in refrigerator overnight.

In the morning, turn out on floured board and roll as thinly as possible. Cut in squares or any shape desired. Place 1″ apart on a greased cookie sheet. Bake at 350° until crisp and golden brown. Makes 6 dozen.

Mission Cry Babies

1 C shortening (½ butter and ½ shortening)
1 C granulated sugar
2 eggs
½ C molasses
1 Tbsp vinegar
1 C hot strong coffee
2 tsp baking soda
2 C sultana raisins (or 1 C raisins and
    1 C chopped walnuts)
4 C stirred but not sifted all-purpose flour
2 tsp cinnamon
1 tsp ginger
½ tsp salt

Pour hot coffee over raisins and soda and let stand. Into your beater bowl measure the shortening and sugar and beat until light. Add eggs and beat until pale and light. Beat in molasses then add raisins, coffee and soda. Add flour, salt and spices. This batter seems thinnish for cookies but is fine. Spoon by mounded teaspoonfuls onto buttered cookie sheets, spacing them about 1″ apart. Bake at 375° for 7 to 9 minutes. Do not overbake. Cool on cake racks.

Rice Flour Shortbread

¾ C butter
⅜ C unsifted icing sugar
2 C rice flour
¼ tsp baking powder
¼ tsp salt
¼ tsp cream of tartar (optional)

Cream butter and add gradually, while beating constantly, the icing sugar. Then work in the flour, baking powder, salt and cream of tartar if used. Chill. Roll out on lightly floured board to ³⁄₁₆″ thickness. Bake on unbuttered cookie sheet at 325° until crisp but not all brown.

Munchers

½ C butter
½ C shortening
1 C white sugar
1 C brown sugar
2 C rolled oats
¾ C desiccated coconut
2 eggs
1 tsp baking powder
½ tsp baking soda
½ tsp salt
1 tsp vanilla
½ to 1 C mixed peel or raisins or
    chopped prunes or chopped nuts
½ C wheat germ
1½ C stirred but unsifted all-purpose flour

Put the butter and shortening in beater bowl and beat at low speed. Now begin adding all ingredients in order given, beating all the time. By the time the flour is blended in your cookie dough is ready.

Butter cookie sheets and drop batter by heaping silver teaspoonfuls at least 1½″ apart. Do not crowd them. Bake at 350° for 10 minutes. Watch them closely. Transfer to cake racks to cool. Makes seventy-two.

Homemade Fig Bars

1½ C chopped figs, well-packed
6 Tbsp granulated sugar
1 C plus 2 Tbsp water
1 C shortening
1 C brown sugar
2 eggs
3 C sifted all-purpose flour
¾ tsp salt
2 tsp baking powder
½ tsp baking soda
1 Tbsp hot water
1 tsp vanilla

Fig Filling: Remove the hard bit from the stem of the figs and chop and measure. Turn into saucepan, add the granulated sugar and the 1 C plus 2 Tbsp water and cook until boiling and stir until thick. Let cool.

Cookie Dough: Cream together the shortening, brown sugar and eggs until thoroughly blended. Sift together the flour, salt and baking powder and stir into creamed mixture. Dissolve the baking soda in the hot water and add it along with the vanilla, mixing well. Pat dough onto a big piece of heavy wax paper, wrap and chill until hardened, about 20 minutes in freezer. Roll out half of dough on lightly floured board to less than ¼″ thickness. (Leave remaining half of dough in refrigerator.) Cut into 3″ wide strips.

Spoon half of cooled filling in a long thin strip down the center of each length of dough. Do not put on too much filling or it will ooze out when you proceed to lap the sides of the dough over it. With a blunt-ended knife or spatula lap the sides of the dough over the fig filling and gently pat them to seal. Cut into 1½″ bars. Lift with spatula and place, lapped side down, on buttered cookie sheets. Proceed as above with remaining half of dough and filling. Bake at 400° for 10 minutes or until barely tinged with gold. Makes fifty-five.

Christmas Cookie House

Although easy to make, because of drying time, it is done in 3 steps, which spreads assembling time over 2 days. For the base use a firm white cardboard at least 9½ × 12½". For molds use 2 empty quart milk cartons, rinsed and dried.

¼ C butter or margarine
4 C miniature marshmallows (well packed)
7 C crisp rice cereal
2 pkg (14 oz) assorted cream biscuits such as Peek Freans
2 recipes Egg White Frosting (see below)
1 pkg (15 oz) licorice allsorts
1 or 2 Tbsp icing sugar

EGG WHITE FROSTING: Combine 2 C sifted icing sugar with 1 egg white, blending until smooth and adding 1 tsp water to make of spreading consistency.

Step One: To prepare house base and roof, gently melt butter or margarine and add marshmallows, stirring until melted. Pour over cereal in large buttered bowl. Combine well. Divide mixture between 2 milk cartons, pressing well into corners and levelling top surfaces. Both mixtures should be about 5½" deep. Chill overnight.

Step Two: Prepare one recipe Egg White Frosting. Remove cereal blocks from milk cartons by running a sharp narrow knife around sides and peeling off milk carton. With a heavy sharp knife cut 1 block in half lengthwise. Cut second block in half diagonally, being careful to cut evenly from corner to corner, to make 2 triangles. Using icing as cement, secure the 2 lengthwise blocks to the cardboard base to form a square base. Cement triangles together to form a roof, and place on the base using icing to hold. Spread remaining icing over base to simulate snow around the house. While icing is still damp cut jelly-filled biscuits in half crosswise and place, cut side down, around the edge of the board to form a fence, leaving a gate open. Let dry.

Step Three: Prepare a second recipe of Egg White Frosting. Using the biscuits with a cobbled appearance, split and use to line the walls of the house—the filling will hold them temporarily until you have arranged them leaving openings for doors and windows. Split the light-colored cream filled biscuits (oblongs) and position 3 rows of 3 biscuits on each side of the roof. Fasten biscuits to walls and roof with icing. Decorate house using more biscuits and licorice allsorts for doors, windows, shutters, chimney, patio, woodpile.

When your artistic creation is complete sprinkle icing sugar through small sieve over the house and grounds to look like freshly fallen snow.

The whole house is edible. It could be used as the centerpiece for your Christmas dinner table or nibbled at by any passing Hansel or Gretel.

Rosabelle Jones's Welsh Longbread

½ lb butter (room temperature)
¼ tsp salt
¼ tsp baking powder
½ C light brown sugar
1⅞ C stirred but unsifted whole wheat flour
½ C wheat germ

Measure all ingredients into large mixing bowl and mix by hand until perfectly blended but still crumbly, not sticky. Pat into unbuttered 8 × 8" pan until smooth on top. If you care to decorate the longbreads for Christmas, press on dough at even intervals quarters of red or green glacé cherries or whole blanched almonds or pecans. Bake at 325° about 45 to 50 minutes at center of oven. Test for crispness before removing from oven. Gently mark into 1½" squares and let cool. Then cut through to bottom of pan with sharp knife and remove squares. Store in refrigerator.

Health Snaps

This recipe calls for a granola-type cereal (see Homemade Health Cereal).

1 C unsifted all-purpose flour
⅞ C granulated sugar
½ tsp baking powder
½ tsp salt
¼ tsp baking soda
½ tsp cinnamon
1½ C Homemade Health Cereal (or other granola)
¼ C chopped candied cherries
¼ C chopped candied pineapple or peels
⅓ C chopped walnuts
⅓ C melted butter or margarine
1 egg
4 Tbsp milk

Into a large bowl measure the first 7 ingredients. Stir in fruits and nuts well. Make a well in center and add butter or margarine, egg and milk. Mix well. Drop from moistened spoon in 1½" mounds on ungreased baking sheets 2½" apart and bake at 400° about 10 to 12 minutes. Using lifter transfer at once to cake rack to cool. Makes 32.

Rice Flour Corn Flake Cookies

¾ C rice flour
½ tsp baking powder
½ tsp baking soda
½ tsp salt
⅓ C shortening (soft)
½ C brown sugar, packed
½ C granulated sugar
1 egg
1 Tbsp water
1 tsp vanilla
1¾ C crushed corn flakes

Preheat oven to 350°. Sift rice flour, baking powder, soda and salt into bowl. Add shortening, sugars, egg, water and vanilla. Mix until smooth. Fold in corn flakes. Drop by teaspoons on ungreased cookie sheet. Bake until light brown, about 9 or 10 minutes. After baking let the cookies set on the sheet for 2 or 3 minutes before removing to rack. These cookies flatten as they bake. Yield: fifty.

Squares

Butter Tart Pan Squares

½ C butter or margarine
1 C sifted all-purpose flour
2 Tbsp white sugar
1½ C brown sugar
1 C chopped walnuts
2 eggs
3 Tbsp flour
½ tsp baking powder
1 tsp vanilla

Cream the butter well, then cream into it the 1 C sifted flour and 2 Tbsp white sugar. Press this with floured palms and fingers, smoothly, into an ungreased 9 × 9″ pan and bake at 350° for 15 minutes. Meanwhile, mix together all remaining ingredients. When base has cooked 15 minutes, remove it from oven and spread second mixture over it evenly. Return to oven and bake 20 minutes longer until golden brown.

Pineapple Squares

These will freeze.

LOWER CRUST
¾ C butter
¼ C granulated sugar
1½ C sifted all-purpose flour
¼ tsp salt

TOPPING
One 19-oz can crushed pineapple, well drained
1 egg
¾ C light brown sugar
¼ tsp salt
½ tsp vanilla
½ C coconut (flaked or desiccated)

To make Lower Crust, cream together the butter and granulated sugar, then add flour and salt and beat until thoroughly blended. (This now resembles soft shortbread dough.) Press into un-buttered 9 × 9″ pan, using your moistened finger tips to make it smooth.

Drain pineapple, making sure excess syrup is pressed out. (Use leftover syrup for some other purpose such as the liquid ingredient in a jelly dessert.) Spread drained pineapple evenly over lower crust.

To make Topping, beat together in a bowl the egg, brown sugar, salt, vanilla and coconut. Spread evenly over pineapple. Bake at 325° for 35 minutes or until top is baked and gold all over. Let cool in pan, but mark into small 1¼″ squares while warm.

Raisin Squares

PASTRY
2 C unsifted pastry flour
2 Tbsp white sugar
½ tsp salt
½ C shortening
2 eggs, yolks and whites separated
¼ C dairy sour cream

FILLING
1 C raisins
½ C brown sugar
½ C hot water
2 tsp lemon rind
2 Tbsp lemon juice
2 Tbsp corn starch
¼ C dry breadcrumbs
1 Tbsp granulated sugar

To make Pastry, combine flour, sugar and salt and cut in shortening with pastry blender. Mix together egg yolks and sour cream and work evenly into flour mixture. Shape into a ball, wrap and chill while making Filling.

To make Filling, mix together in a pot the raisins, brown sugar, hot water, lemon rind, lemon juice and corn starch. Cook stirring until thick. Cool.

Roll out half of dough into a 10 × 8″ oblong on cookie sheet. Sprinkle with breadcrumbs. Carefully spread on filling to within ¾″ of edges. Roll out remaining dough to fit and cover raisin filling. Seal edges with finger tips. Brush with slightly beaten egg whites and sprinkle with the 1 Tbsp sugar. Bake 15 minutes at 425° then reduce heat to 350° and bake about 15 minutes longer. While warm cut into sixteen 2″ squares.

Raspberry (or Cherry or Peach) Squares

1 C soft margarine
1 C granulated sugar
1 tsp vanilla
2 eggs
2 C stirred but not sifted all-purpose flour
1 C chopped walnuts
One 19-oz can raspberry (or cherry or peach) pie filling

In beater bowl cream together margarine and sugar until light. Beat in vanilla and eggs. Add flour and nuts and beat just to mix.

You need a 13 × 9″ pan. If it is glass grease it. If it is metal greasing is not necessary. Spread ¾ of batter evenly in pan. Now carefully and neatly spread raspberry (or cherry or peach) pie filling over batter. Drop by teaspoons remaining batter all over top. It will cover about ¾ of the surface. Bake at 325° for 45 minutes. Let cool on rack and cut into squares from pan as needed.

Lemon Squares

BASE

2 C unsifted all-purpose flour
½ C unsifted icing sugar
½ tsp salt
1 C margarine (room temperature)

FILLING

4 large eggs
1¾ C granulated sugar
⅓ C lemon juice
⅓ C all-purpose flour
½ tsp baking powder

To make the Base, in a bowl stir together flour, icing sugar and salt. Cream in margarine until mixture blends into a pliable dough. This looks like shortbread. Pat evenly by hand into bottom of a buttered 9 × 13" pan. Bake at 350° for 11 minutes.

Meanwhile prepare Filling by beating together all filling ingredients until smooth, scraping down sides of bowl once or twice. Mix well. Pour over hot base. Return to oven immediately and bake at 350° about 25 minutes, until pale gold. During last 5 minutes put cookie sheet below baking pan to be sure bottom does not burn. Remove from oven and let cool completely in pan on cake rack. Cut into squares. Store in tightly covered container.

Pecan Praline Bars

⅞ C sifted all-purpose flour
¼ C granulated sugar
½ tsp salt (see below)
½ C butter or margarine (see below)
1½ tsp grated lemon rind
1 egg, yolk and white separated
2 Tbsp ice-cold water
¾ C lightly packed brown sugar
2 Tbsp corn starch
1 whole egg
⅓ C corn syrup
½ tsp vanilla
¾ C coarsely chopped pecans

Sift together into a mixing bowl the flour, granulated sugar and ¼ tsp of the salt. Cut in ¼ C of the butter or margarine finely; mix in grated lemon rind. Add egg yolk and rub it in with your finger tips. Using a fork, lightly mix in ice-cold water. Turn out dough into an ungreased 9 × 9" pan and pat it with floured fingers into bottom of pan and up about ½" on sides. Chill.

Cream the remaining ¼ C butter or margarine. Gradually blend in the ¾ C brown sugar, corn starch and the remaining ¼ tsp salt. Beat whole egg and remaining egg white well; stir in corn syrup and vanilla. Add to creamed mixture and combine well, then turn mixture into dough-lined pan. Sprinkle evenly with pecans. Bake at 375° until filling is set in center, 25 to 30 minutes. Cool on wire rack until cold. Cut into 8 strips and cut each strip into 4 bars.

Cheese Jam Triangles

½ C butter
4-oz pkg white cream cheese (room temperature)
1 Tbsp light brown sugar
1½ C stirred but not sifted cake and pastry flour
½ tsp baking powder
⅓ C tart red jam or jelly

Put all ingredients but the jam or jelly in mixing bowl and mix until crumbly by hand. Put half into an unbuttered 9 × 9" pan and pat smooth. Using ⅓ cup red jam, spread it smoothly over this base to within ¼" of edges. Now spread and pat gently and evenly remaining crumbs over jelly layer. Bake at 350° about 30 minutes. Do not allow the edges to become brown or hard. Cut into triangles with very sharp knife while hot. Let cool in pan. Lift out with spatula as needed.

Quick Lemon Squares

FILLING

1½ pkgs (1 C plus 2 Tbsp) lemon pie filling
¾ C sugar
6 Tbsp cold water
3 egg yolks
3 C hot water

CRUMB MIXTURE

1¾ C fine soda cracker crumbs
½ C brown sugar
¾ C all-purpose flour
1½ C coconut (desiccated, strip or flake)
1 C margarine or butter

Make Filling first by mixing lemon pie filling with sugar and cold water. Stir in yolks, then hot water, and cook stirring until thick and boiling. Cool, stirring once or twice.

Meanwhile mix together all crumb ingredients using pastry blender or your finger tips. Pat ⅔ of mixture into 9 × 13" ungreased pan, smoothly. Cover evenly with cold lemon filling. Now sprinkle all remaining crumbs over top to cover. Pat them down gently. Bake at 350° about 20 to 25 minutes or until tinged with gold top and bottom. Chill before cutting into squares.

Marzipan

½ lb icing sugar
½ lb finely ground blanched almonds (finest grind)
2 egg whites
½ tsp salt
½ tsp almond extract

Make the Marzipan by blending all ingredients in blender goblet, or beating hard with electric beater until perfectly blended. Chill covered 24 hours to harden. Use to top Christmas cakes or to stuff steamed pitted prunes for salad plates or to make Marzipan candies.

Christmas Fruit Bars

A small family may substitute these for Christmas cake.

½ C butter
½ C sugar
1 tsp grated orange rind
2 Tbsp fresh frozen orange juice concentrate
   (not diluted)
¼ tsp almond extract
1¼ C sifted all-purpose flour
   (divided see below)
½ tsp baking soda
¼ tsp salt
1 egg
⅔ C chopped mixed glacé (Christmas cake) fruits
½ C chopped nuts

Sift and measure flour. Measure fruits into a small bowl. Mix ¼ C of the flour with the fruits. (If the cherries are whole cut them in half.)

Into beater bowl measure the butter, sugar and orange rind. Turn on beaters and beat for 5 minutes. Add orange juice concentrate and almond extract and beat in. Add the remaining 1 C flour, baking soda and salt and beat. Add egg and beat in. Lift beaters and fold in fruits and nuts. Turn batter into buttered 9 × 9" pan. Push batter into corners and smooth top. Bake at 350° for 16 to 18 minutes. Do not overbake. Cool and frost with Orange Frosting (below).

ORANGE FROSTING

2 Tbsp butter
1¼ C icing sugar
1½ Tbsp fresh frozen orange juice concentrate

Beat until smooth. Spread over cooled bars in pan. Cut into 1 or 1½" squares or 1 × 2" bars. These freeze well if carefully packed.

Sister Chabanel's Squares

BASE

½ C butter (room temperature)
1 C unsifted all-purpose flour
½ C light brown sugar

TOPPING

1 C brown sugar
2 eggs
1 tsp vanilla
2 tsp flour
¼ tsp salt
1½ tsp baking powder
1½ C unsweetened coconut
☙ C chopped walnuts or sesame seeds

Mix together well all Base ingredients until smoothly blended. Press smoothly into a 13 × 8" pan.

To make Topping, blend all topping ingredients in beater bowl. Spoon evenly over base and spread to cover smoothly all over. Bake at 350° for 25 minutes or until golden brown.

Dorothy Squares

BASE

½ C butter or margarine (room temperature)
½ C granulated sugar
½ tsp vanilla
1 large egg
1¼ C unsifted all-purpose flour
   (divided see below)
⅓ C raspberry or strawberry jam

FILLING

3 large eggs, beaten
¾ mixed glacé fruit
   (or peel or half and half)
2 C desiccated coconut
¾ C granulated sugar
¼ C corn syrup
2 tsp vanilla
¼ tsp salt
⅓ C melted butter, cooled
½ C rice flour
½ to 1 tsp almond flavoring

ICING

3 Tbsp butter (room temperature)
2 C icing sugar
3 Tbsp milk
½ tsp vanilla
Red and green food coloring (see below)

To make Base, in a bowl cream together butter or margarine and sugar. Beat in vanilla and egg. Add 1 C of the flour and mix well. Turn dough out on a board floured with remaining ¼ C flour and knead 50 to 60 times or until flour is all kneaded in. Pat this dough evenly into bottom of an ungreased 9 × 9" pan. (It helps to keep your hands floured so they do not stick to the dough.) Prick all over with a fork. Bake at 325° for 10 minutes. Let cool for 10 minutes then spread the jam evenly over the base.

To make Filling, in large bowl beat eggs slightly with a fork or spoon. Add all remaining filling ingredients and combine thoroughly. Spoon evenly over jam layer. Bake at 375° for 30 minutes. Cool completely.

To make Icing, in a bowl cream butter. Stir in icing sugar, milk and vanilla and beat until smooth. Spread over baked, cooled filling. To decorate icing dip the narrow end of a toothpick in red food coloring then swirl through the icing. Dip the toothpick each time you make a swirl. (Make about 10 red swirls.) Do the same with another toothpick, using the green food coloring and crossing through the red streaks. Cut into squares to serve.

Brownies

1½ C sifted all-purpose flour
1 tsp salt
1 C granulated sugar
1 C brown sugar
½ C cocoa
2 tsp vanilla
1 C room temperature butter or margarine
4 eggs
¼ C cold water
½ C (or more) chopped glacé cherries or
    walnuts or raisins or coconut

Put all ingredients in beater bowl in order given and beat on low speed, scraping down sides of bowl until smooth. Do not beat too long.

Butter a large 13 × 9″ pan and turn in batter and push into corners and smooth top. Bake at 350° for 20 to 25 minutes. If you use a glass pan bake at 325° instead.

Variation: If desired, when brownies are cool in pan they may be iced with Mint Frosting and sprinkled with chocolate shot. To make Mint Frosting, beat together well 2 Tbsp butter, about 1½ C icing sugar, 2 or 3 Tbsp milk, 6 or 7 drops green food coloring and ½ tsp peppermint extract. Spread over Brownies in pan. Cut into squares in pan when cool.

Triple-Decker Squares

1 lb hard butter
4 C stirred but unsifted cake and pastry flour
⅓ C dairy sour cream
1 tsp vanilla
3 Tbsp sugar
4 egg yolks
½ tsp salt
½ C sesame seeds (divided, see below)
½ C marmalade
½ C red currant jelly

In a bowl, with a pastry blender cut the butter into the flour until size of small peas. Add sour cream, vanilla, sugar, yolks and salt. With strong wooden spoon stir until thoroughly blended. Chill until very firm. Cut into 3 equal portions.

On lightly floured board roll out third of the dough to fit 15 × 10″ pan (jelly roll pan) making it neat and even around edges with your floured fingertips. Spread sparingly with marmalade. Roll out second third of dough and cover marmalade. Trim off rough edges with knife. Add these scraps to remaining third of dough. Cover second layer of dough sparingly with the red currant jelly. Sprinkle with half of the sesame seeds. Roll out remaining dough and cover jelly. Trim off excess edges and carefully fit into any remaining crevices. Sprinkle remaining sesame seeds all over and with both palms press gently down. Bake at 350° for 15 minutes ~~longer~~. Cut into squares in pan when cool.

*then reduce heat to 325°
for 15 - 20 minutes
longer.*

Date Oatmeal Squares

2 C stirred but not sifted all-purpose flour
¼ tsp salt
1 tsp baking powder
½ tsp baking soda
2 C quick-cooking rolled oats
½ C light brown sugar
1 tsp vanilla
1 C shortening (half butter is recommended)
1 lb pitted dates cooked in 1 C boiling
    water until tender and cooled
1 tsp lemon juice

In large bowl mix together the flour, salt, baking powder, baking soda, rolled oats and sugar. Sprinkle vanilla over and cut in the shortening with a pastry blender until mixture is crumbly. Butter a 13 × 9″ baking dish and pat half of crumb mixture on bottom smoothly and firmly. Stir lemon juice into date filling. Carefully and evenly spread date filling over all. It is advisable to drop spoonfuls at intervals and spread each to meet. Sprinkle remaining crumbs over top and pat down evenly. Bake at 325° for 60 to 70 minutes or until pale gold on top. Do not rush it. This is a thick heavy mix and requires long baking at a rather low temperature. Mark into squares while warm.

Note: Dates, cooked as above, make a good filling for a plain 2-egg cake. When cake is cool spread top with ¼″ thick layer of date filling and cover that with Mocha Icing: ¼ C butter; 1 Tbsp each of cocoa and instant coffee powder; about 2 C sifted icing sugar and 2 or 3 Tbsp milk or cream, all beaten well together.

Chocolate Nut Diamonds

2 squares unsweetened chocolate
2 eggs
1 C granulated sugar
¾ tsp baking powder
¾ C flour
½ tsp salt
1 C chopped walnuts
½ C butter or margarine, melted
1 tsp vanilla

Melt chocolate in top of double boiler. Remove from heat and slowly blend melted chocolate with the eggs which have been beaten in a bowl with the sugar. Sift in dry ingredients and thoroughly combine. Add walnuts, melted butter and vanilla and mix in well. Spread thinly on pan 8 × 16″ or on two 8 × 8″ pans, spreading to about ¼″ thickness. Bake at 350° about 20 minutes then allow to cool. Leave in pan and frost with Rich Chocolate Frosting (below).

Rich Chocolate Frosting: Melt 2 squares unsweetened chocolate in top of double boiler and add to it 1 C icing sugar, 1 egg beaten, 2 Tbsp butter and 1 tsp vanilla. Remove from heat at once and cool a little before spreading on Chocolate Nut Diamonds.

Barzipans

PASTRY
1 C unsifted all-purpose flour
½ tsp salt
⅓ C shortening
1 Tbsp butter
1 Tbsp cold water

FILLING
½ C butter
⅔ C sugar
2 eggs
⅔ C unsifted rice flour
¼ tsp salt
Raspberry jam (see below)

To make Pastry, cut shortening and butter into flour and salt until size of peas. Moisten with water and pack into ball. Roll out thinly to fit 9 × 9″ pan. Line bottom only. Spread thinly with ¼ C best quality raspberry jam.

To make Filling, cream butter and sugar together until light. Beat in eggs then beat in rice flour and salt. Divide into 2 equal portions by spooning half into another bowl. Tint half pale green by adding 7 or 8 drops green food coloring. Tint second half by adding 8 to 10 drops red food coloring. Now you are going to spoon this onto the jam in checkerboard arrangement. Using a spoon pick up enough green filling piled high to amount to about 2 tsp. Place it at corner of pan. Then with another spoon pick up enough pink filling to measure about 2 tsp and place it beside the green. Working carefully arrange these mounds to completely cover jam, making it look like a wiggly green and pink checkerboard. Bake at 375° for 35 minutes. Do not brown this. Cool and chill.

Icing: Mix together 1½ C unsifted icing sugar, 2 Tbsp butter, 1 tsp almond flavoring, 2 Tbsp warm milk. Mix very well and spread over Barzipan layer. Cut into small squares or bars. Store covered in the refrigerator.

Peanut Butter Bars

1 C granulated sugar
¼ C brown sugar, packed
½ C peanut butter
⅓ C shortening
2 eggs
1 tsp vanilla
1 C unsifted all-purpose flour
1 tsp baking powder
¼ tsp salt
1⅓ C coconut

In beater bowl cream together the sugars, peanut butter and shortening until light and fluffy. Add eggs and vanilla and beat well. In a small bowl stir to blend the flour, baking powder and salt. Add dry ingredients to the creamed mixture and combine thoroughly. Stir in coconut. Spread dough evenly in a greased 13 × 9″ pan. Bake at 350° about 25 to 30 minutes or until golden brown. *Note:* If you use a glass pan bake at 325°. Cool. Cut into 1½ × 2″ bars. Makes about 3 dozen.

Sesame Squares

BASE
½ C butter or margarine
¼ C light brown sugar
1 egg
1⅛ C (1 C plus 2 Tbsp) unsifted all-purpose flour
⅛ tsp salt

TOPPING
½ C raspberry jam
2 eggs
1 C granulated sugar
½ C sesame seeds

In a bowl cream the butter with the brown sugar until blended. Beat in egg, then flour and salt until smooth. Spread in an even layer in ungreased 9 × 9″ pan and bake at 350° for 10 minutes. Remove from oven, let cool a little, then spread with a thin layer of raspberry (or other) jam.

For Topping, in a bowl beat together the eggs, granulated sugar and sesame seeds and spread evenly and carefully over jam. Bake at 350° until top is dry and pale gold, about 20 to 30 minutes. Cool in pan and cut into bars or squares to serve.

Miracle Squares

BASE
½ C butter
¼ C granulated sugar
5 Tbsp cocoa
1 tsp vanilla
1 egg, beaten
2 C fine graham cracker crumbs
1 C desiccated coconut
½ C chopped walnuts

FILLING
½ C butter (room temperature)
3 Tbsp milk
2 Tbsp vanilla custard powder
2 C sifted icing sugar

TOPPING
5 squares semi-sweet chocolate
3 Tbsp butter

To make Base, in a pot melt butter. Let cool a little then add sugar, cocoa, vanilla and beaten egg. Stir well to combine and cook, stirring, until mixture resembles custard. Remove from heat and stir in graham crumbs, coconut and nuts. Pack evenly into bottom of a 9 × 9″ pan.

To make Filling, cream butter, add icing sugar and blend. In measuring cup stir together milk and custard powder. Add to mixture of icing sugar and butter and beat until smooth. Spread this evenly over base. Chill for 15 minutes.

For the Topping, gently melt the semi-sweet chocolate with the butter. Stir to combine. Pour chocolate evenly over chilled filling and spread. Chill in refrigerator until chocolate is partially set then mark into 1¼″ squares. Chill until firm. Yield: 4 dozen.

Orange Walnut Bars

BASE
⅓ C butter or margarine
One 4-oz pkg white cream cheese
⅔ C brown sugar, packed
1 C whole wheat flour
⅔ C wheat germ

TOPPING
2 eggs
½ C liquid honey
⅓ C whole wheat flour
⅓ C skim milk powder
½ C walnuts
¼ tsp salt
½ tsp cinnamon
¼ C grated orange or tangerine rind

To make Base, into beater bowl measure the butter or margarine, cheese, brown sugar, 1 C whole wheat flour and wheat germ. Beat until you have a dough the consistency of firm shortbread. With dampened fingertips press evenly into greased 9 × 13″ pan. Bake at 375° for 6 minutes. Remove from oven.

Meanwhile to prepare Topping, beat together the eggs, honey, ⅓ C whole wheat flour, skim milk powder, nuts, salt, cinnamon and grated orange or tangerine rind.

As soon as Base has baked 6 minutes pour Topping over evenly and return to oven and bake at 375° about 12 minutes. Watch carefully, for this will burn easily. Cool in pan. Cut in squares to serve.

Sweet Maureen Bars

BASE
½ C peanut butter (smooth or crunchy)
½ C corn syrup
½ C brown sugar packed
1 Tbsp butter (first amount)
2 C rice krispies
1 C peanuts (plain or in skins)

CHOCOLATE TOPPING
¼ C butter (second amount)
⅝ C (10 Tbsp) cocoa
½ C granulated sugar

To make Base, in pot combine thorougly the peanut butter, corn syrup, brown sugar and 1 Tbsp butter. Stir constantly on medium heat until nearly boiling. Do not let mixture burn on bottom of pot. Remove from heat. In a large bowl combine rice krispies and peanuts. Pour in hot peanut butter mixture and at once stir to thoroughly combine. Mixture is very stiff. Pack firmly and evenly into the bottom of a buttered 8 × 8″ pan. Press down using the back of a large dessert spoon dipped several times in hot water to keep it from sticking. Let stand on counter while you prepare the Chocolate Topping.

To make Chocolate Topping, in a small pot combine butter, cocoa and sugar. Stir constantly over low heat until butter melts and sugar dissolves. At once spread evenly over bars. Chill in refrigerator. With sharp knife cut into 32 bars. Store in container in refrigerator until serving.

Lemon Cheese Squares

1 large pkg lemon jelly powder (or 2 small)
¼ C sugar
1 C boiling water
½ lb (8-oz pkg) white cream cheese
One 1-lb can evaporated (not condensed) milk, thoroughly chilled
One 20-oz can diced peaches (drained)
1 pkg honey graham wafers (1 wrapped stack-pack within a box), finely rolled

Pour the boiling water over the lemon jelly and sugar and stir to dissolve. In beater bowl at medium speed, beat the cream cheese until light, then pour in the chilled evaporated milk and beat 3 or 4 minutes longer. Now add the jelly mixture and continue beating until blended and light. Then add the canned, drained, diced peaches and beat for an additional 30 seconds. Remove beaters.

Have ready in a buttered 9 × 9″ pan the finely rolled graham cracker crumbs. Cover bottom of pan to nearly ¼″ depth, reserving enough crumbs, at least half a cup, to sprinkle over top. Spoon cream mixture over crumbs evenly and carefully. Sprinkle remaining crumbs over top. Chill at least 2 hours. Cut into 2″ squares to serve.

Party Lemon Slices

BASE
1 C stirred but unsifted all-purpose flour
2 tsp baking powder
1 Tbsp butter
1 Tbsp shortening
1 egg

FILLING
1 large apple pared and grated on ¼" shredder
½ C granulated sugar
1 large lemon, juice and finely grated rind
1 tsp butter
1 egg

TOPPING
1 egg white
¾ C granulated sugar
1 Tbsp melted butter
2 C shredded or desiccated coconut
4 green maraschino cherries drained and
        quartered (optional)

To make Base, cut butter and shortening into flour and baking powder with pastry blender until size of small peas. Stir in egg until blended. Press evenly into buttered and lightly floured 8 × 8" pan.

To make Filling, into a saucepan grate the apple and immediately mix in sugar to prevent browning. Add remaining Filling ingredients and cook, stirring all the time until it thickens and boils. Remove from heat.

To make Topping, beat egg white until stiff, gradually adding sugar as you beat. Add melted butter and coconut and mix well.

Pour warm Filling over Base and spread evenly. Dot Topping mixture over, and with tines of fork spread it to cover Filling evenly. If desired decorate at even intervals with quartered green maraschino cherries.

Bake at 350° for 40 to 50 minutes or until firm at center and evenly pale gold all over top. Cool in pans and mark into 2" squares.

Peanut Flake Squares

1 C light brown sugar, packed
1 C peanut butter
1 C corn syrup
2 C salted peanuts
10 C corn flakes

Into a large saucepan measure the brown sugar, then the peanut butter, then the corn syrup. Place over medium heat and stir constantly until it begins to bubble, but do not overcook or it will set too fast later. Remove from heat at once and, working quickly, add peanuts and corn flakes and mix thoroughly. Have ready a 15 × 10" buttered pan. Turn mixture into it and with moistened palms press evenly and firmly into pan. Cool and chill.

If desired for variety, frost with *Fudge Frosting:* Gently melt together 2 squares unsweetened chocolate, 2 Tbsp butter. Remove from heat and add 2 C unsifted icing sugar and 2 Tbsp milk and mix until smoothly blended and of spreading consistency. Spread over panful of Peanut Flake Squares. Chill. When firm and cold cut into squares of desired size, about sixty.

Pies

Pecan Pie see page 239

Key Lime Pie

245 pg.

PASTRY: Make a Basic Pie Shell, Nine-Inch, (see Index).

FILLING:

4 eggs
One can sweetened condensed milk
⅔ C lime juice (fresh or bottled)
4 tsp ice cold tap water
Shake of salt
4 Tbsp sugar

To make Filling, separate yolks from whites of eggs and first make meringue by beating whites with the salt and water until very stiff, gradually adding sugar as you beat. Transfer unwashed beaters to bowl containing yolks, condensed (not evaporated) milk, and lime juice, and beat until thick and opaque, about 1 or 2 minutes. Pour into prepared baked pie shell, spread meringue evenly and attractively over top, pushing it to edges of crust to seal. Bake at 400° about 10 or 12 minutes or until meringue is pale gold. Cool, then chill in refrigerator at least 2 hours.

Old-Fashioned Raisin Pie

FILLING

2 C seedless raisins
2 C boiling water
½ C granulated sugar
2 Tbsp cornstarch
⅛ tsp salt
1 (or 2) Tbsp fresh lemon juice
1 Tbsp butter
½ tsp vanilla

PASTRY: Make a Basic Pie Pastry, Two-Crust, (see Index).

To prepare Filling, pour the boiling water over the raisins in a saucepan and let stand half an hour. Mix together well in a small bowl the sugar, cornstarch and salt. Bring to boil the raisins and water and stir in the dry mixture until thick and boiling. Remove from heat and add lemon juice, butter and vanilla. Let stand to cool, stirring occasionally.

Turn cooled filling into pastry-lined pie plate, cover with gashed top crust and seal and crimp edges. Brush top with mixture of 1 Tbsp milk and 1 Tbsp sugar. Bake at 425° for 10 minutes. Reduce heat to 350° and bake about 25 to 30 minutes longer or until juice just begins to bubble through gashes and top is evenly gold. Cool pie before serving.

Glazed Strawberry Cream Pie

PASTRY

2½ C stirred but not sifted cake and pastry flour
1 tsp salt
¾ C shortening
4 Tbsp butter
2½ Tbsp cold water

CREAM FILLING

¼ C sugar
1½ Tbsp corn starch
½ tsp salt
1 C rich milk or 10% cereal cream
2 eggs or 4 yolks
1 tsp vanilla

STRAWBERRY FILLING

2 qt fresh large strawberries
⅝ C sugar
3 Tbsp arrowroot flour (or corn starch)
Shake of salt
1 C boiling water
1 Tbsp lemon juice
15 drops red food coloring

To make Pastry, cut shortening and butter into flour and salt until size of peas. Drizzle in water, tossing with fork. Pack into ball between palms. Cut in half. Roll out to fit two deep 9″ pie plates with high fluted edges. Prick with fork at 2″ intervals. Bake at 425° for 8 minutes. Do not burn.

To make Cream Filling, mix thoroughly in small pot the sugar, corn starch and salt then stir in milk and cook stirring until thick. Stir some into beaten eggs or yolks and stir this into hot filling for a minute or two. Remove from heat and add vanilla. Cool. Spread in bottom of baked pie shells.

To prepare Strawberry Filling, wash berries in colander. Remove hulls. Select enough of the misshapen berries to make 2 C when mashed. To the mashed 2 C berries add the ⅝ C sugar, arrowroot flour (or corn starch) and salt, and mix well. Stir in boiling water and cook stirring until thick. Remove from heat and add lemon juice and red food coloring. Strain through sieve.

Arrange perfect berries in concentric circles over cream filling, point up, in both pies. Sprinkle berries in each pie with 2 Tbsp sugar. Spoon glaze over, being sure all berries are coated. Chill for 2 or 3 hours before cutting.

Fresh Raspberry Pie

⅔ C sugar
4 Tbsp flour (or 2 Tbsp quick-cooking tapioca)
½ tsp cinnamon (optional)
4 C fresh, washed, hulled and drained raspberries
1⅓ Tbsp butter

Mix together the sugar, flour or tapioca and cinnamon and stir gently into berries. Line a 9″ pie plate with tender pastry, (see index). Pour in filling. Dot with butter. Cover with gashed top crust and seal edges. Bake at 425° about 35 to 45 minutes or until crust is golden and juice begins to bubble through slits in crust.

Glazed Strawberry Pie

3 pints berries (1½ quarts)
1 C boiling water
⅝ C sugar (½ C plus 2 Tbsp)
3 Tbsp corn starch (or arrowroot flour
 for a clearer glaze)
2 Tbsp lemon juice
Shake of salt
Pastry for 10″ pie plate

Make pastry first: Cut ½ C shortening and 3 Tbsp butter into 1½ C sifted all-purpose flour and ½ tsp salt. Drizzle in 2 Tbsp cold water, tossing with fork. Pack between palms. When the pastry is rolled out, line pie plate, making a high fluted edge and chill it. Bake at 450° for 12 or 13 minutes. At this high temperature you have to watch this carefully but it makes tender pastry.

For the filling, wash berries and hull them. Mash 1 pint in flat-bottomed saucepan. Mix the sugar, corn starch (or arrowroot flour) and salt well, and stir into mashed berries, then stir in the boiling water and cook, stirring. Reduce heat to very low and cock, stirring, for 5 minutes. Remove from heat and force through strainer. Discard seedy pulp. Add lemon juice. (Do not add lemon juice earlier or it may cause the mixture to thin.) Cut remaining 2 pints of berries in halves, reserving about 9 big perfect ones for the top. Fill baked pie shell with sliced berries, sprinkling an additional 2 Tbsp sugar through and over them. Arrange the big berries in a circle on top and slowly and carefully pour the hot strained glaze over, being sure it flows into all crevices between berries and covers the entire surface. Cool at room temperature.

Angel Pie

MERINGUE CRUST

1 C sugar
⅛ tsp cream of tartar
⅛ tsp salt
4 egg whites

Add sugar, cream of tartar and salt to egg whites and beat until very stiff. Butter a deep 9″ pie plate and spread meringue in it, making edges high. Bake at 275° about three-quarters of an hour, then turn off heat and let crust remain in oven 15 minutes to dry. Remove and cool in pie plate.

LEMON FILLING

2 Tbsp flour
1 C sugar
⅛ tsp salt
¼ C water
¼ C lemon juice
4 egg yolks
½ tsp almond extract

Mix together in heavy saucepan flour, sugar, salt, and when blended add water and lemon juice. Stir until smooth, then beat in egg yolks and cook over low heat, stirring until thick. Remove from heat and add almond extract. Chill. Pour into meringue shell. Chill overnight if possible.

Fresh Peach Pie

PASTRY: Make Basic Pie Pastry, Two-Crust,
 (see Index)

FILLING

10 peaches (between 4 and 5 C when sliced,
 (see below)
2 Tbsp minute tapioca
¾ C sugar
1 tsp lemon juice
½ tsp almond extract

For Filling, scald peaches in boiling water one minute, then peel and slice, removing stones. Mix with remaining filling ingredients. Pour into pastry-lined pie plate.

Roll out remaining pastry to fit top of pie plate, fold over, gash center fold and carefully transfer to cover peaches. Seal and flute edge. Brush top with mixture of 1 Tbsp each sugar and milk. Bake at 425° for 10 minutes then reduce heat to 350° for 30 minutes longer. Bake 40 minutes in all or until syrup begins to bubble through gashes. Let cool before cutting.

Peach Melba Chiffon Pie

2 Tbsp (2 envelopes) plain gelatin
½ C cold lemon juice
½ C orange juice
1 C boiling water
½ C sugar
¾ C fresh (or frozen) sliced peaches
Grated rind 1 large lemon
½ C skim milk powder
½ C ice water
½ pkg (5 oz) frozen raspberries, thawed
¾ Tbsp corn starch
9″ single crust baked crumb or pastry shell

Make the pie crust first. If shell is of pastry, cut ½ C shortening into 1½ C unsifted flour and ½ tsp salt until size of peas. Mix in with fork 2¼ to 2½ Tbsp ice cold water. Pack into ball. Roll out on floured board to fit 9″ pie plate. Line pie plate, fluting edges, making them high and neat. Prick evenly with fork. Bake at 450° about 8 or 9 minutes. Cool.

If shell is of crumbs, mix together well 12 graham wafers rolled very finely, 6 Tbsp each melted butter (or margarine) and sugar. Pat uniformly into deep 9″ pie plate. Bake at 300° for 10 minutes. Cool.

For filling, combine raspberries with corn starch and cook stirring until thick and clear. Cool. Soak gelatin in cold lemon juice. Dissolve sugar in boiling water and add the soaked gelatin, stirring until dissolved. Add orange juice. Chill until syrupy. At this stage whip the skim milk powder with the ice water until it will form soft peaks. Stir peaches and lemon rind into syrupy gelatin mixture. Fold in whipped milk powder mixture. Chill until mixture will mound on spoon. Pour half into prepared cooled pie shell and swirl with half the cooled raspberry mixture. Repeat. (This makes a very full pie.) Chill until set, 2 or 3 hours.

Creamy Pumpkin Pie

PASTRY: Make a Basic Pie Shell, Nine-Inch, (see Index).

FILLING

One 14-oz can pumpkin
2 eggs
½ C sugar
¾ tsp salt
1 tsp cinnamon
½ tsp ginger
¼ C rum or whiskey (or water)
¾ C whipping cream
½ C milk

To make Filling, measure the pumpkin, eggs and sugar into beater bowl and blend thoroughly. Add all remaining filling ingredients and beat to mix well. Pour filling into pie shell. Put in oven on center rack and bake at 425° for 8 minutes then reduce heat to 325° for 35 minutes or until set at center. Cool to room temperature before serving.

Pumpkin Pie Perfecto

PASTRY: Make Basic Pie Pastry, Nine-Inch, (see Index).

FILLING

2 eggs
1 tsp salt
1½ C canned pumpkin
1 tsp cinnamon
½ tsp ginger
½ C sugar
1½ C milk

Roll out Pastry on lightly floured board to fit 9″ pie plate. Trim and flute edge carefully.

To make Filling, measure all ingredients except milk into beater bowl and beat until blended. Stir in milk. Pour filling into pie shell. Transfer to oven and bake on center shelf at 450° for 10 minutes then reduce heat to 350° and continue baking until filling is set at center, about 45 to 50 minutes in all. Cool at room temperature.

Coconut Cream Pie

1 C sugar
½ C flour
¼ tsp salt
2 C scalded milk
3 eggs, separated
2 Tbsp butter
½ tsp vanilla or almond flavoring
¾ C coconut

In top of double boiler mix together the sugar, flour and salt. Over boiling water stir in scalded milk until thick. Stir in beaten egg yolks and cook 2 or 3 minutes longer. Add butter, vanilla or almond flavoring and coconut. Pour into baked 9″ pie shell. (see Index.)

Beat remaining 3 egg whites with 4 Tbsp sugar until stiff. Spread over warm filling, sealing at edge and sprinkle top with more coconut. Brown meringue at 375° until it and coconut are tinged with gold. Serve cold.

Lemon Meringue Pie

PASTRY: Make Basic Pie Pastry, Nine-Inch, (see Index).

FILLING:

1⅓ C sugar
3 Tbsp cornstarch
3 Tbsp all-purpose flour
⅛ tsp salt
1½ C boiling water
3 slightly beaten egg yolks (reserve whites for meringue below)
3 Tbsp butter
1½ tsp finely grated lemon rind (from 1 lemon)
⅓ C lemon juice

To make Filling, in heavy saucepan mix sugar, cornstarch, flour and salt; gradually stir in boiling water. Quickly bring to boil, stirring constantly. Reduce heat; continue cooking and stirring for 5 minutes. Stir small amount of hot mixture into egg yolks, then return to hot mixture. Bring to boil, stirring constantly, for 1 minute. Remove from heat. Add butter and lemon rind. Slowly stir in ⅓ C lemon juice. Pour into baked and cooled pie shell.

For a Meringue, to the 3 leftover egg whites, add ½ tsp lemon juice and shake of salt and beat until foamy. Add 6 Tbsp sugar and beat until stiff. Spread meringue over filling, peaking it up artfully and sealing to edge. Bake at 375° about 12 to 15 minutes or until attractively golden. Cool at room temperature at least 3 hours before serving.

Orange Meringue Pie

Note: Make this pie in the morning to be served for the dinner at night to insure neat slicing.

PASTRY: Make Basic Pie Pastry, Nine-Inch, (see Index).

FILLING

One 6-oz can fresh frozen orange juice concentrate
1½ C hot water (two orange juice canfuls)
2 Tbsp lemon juice
½ C sugar
5 Tbsp corn starch
⅛ tsp salt
4 eggs, yolks and whites separated
¼ C butter

MERINGUE

4 egg whites (see above)
⅛ tsp cream of tartar
½ C sugar

To make Filling, in a heavy pot mix together the sugar, corn starch and salt. When thoroughly mixed stir in orange juice concentrate, hot water and lemon juice and cook stirring until thick. Add a big spoonful to the 4 egg yolks in a little bowl and beat to mix. Return to pot and stir over heat for 1 minute. Remove from heat and add butter without stirring. Let stand until butter melts then stir in. Pour into baked pie shell.

To make Meringue, beat whites with cream of tartar until foamy, then gradually add sugar and beat until very stiff. Pile it in high puffs all over filling making sure it touches edge of crust. Bake at 375° until meringue is a delicate gold.

Maple Syrup Pie

One 8 or 9" pie shell, baked, (see Index)

FILLING

1 C maple syrup
3 Tbsp flour
3 Tbsp cornstarch
½ C cold water plus 2 Tbsp
½ tsp salt
2 eggs (yolks and whites separated)
2 Tbsp butter
½ C chopped nuts: walnuts, almonds or
    whole sunflower seeds

Heat the maple syrup in the top of the double boiler. Mix together until perfectly smooth the flour, cornstarch, salt and cold water. Stir into heated syrup until thick and cook 5 minutes longer covered. Mix a little of the hot mixture into the 2 beaten egg yolks, stir into double boiler mixture and continue cooking and stirring 2 or 3 minutes. Remove from heat and stir in butter and nuts. Cool slightly and pour into baked pie shell.

To make Meringue, add ¼ C sugar and ⅛ tsp cream of tartar to the 2 remaining egg whites and beat until stiff. Spread attractively over filling. Bake at 375° for 12 to 15 minutes or until tinged with gold.

Note: 1. Make this pie at least 3 hours in advance of serving to be sure it will slice neatly. 2. If desired the 2 whole eggs may be used in the filling and then when pie is served it may be topped with whipped cream instead of the meringue.

Pineapple Meringue Pie

PASTRY: Make Basic Pie Pastry, Nine-Inch, (see Index).

FILLING

⅓ C sugar
¼ C wheat germ
2 Tbsp cornstarch
3 Tbsp flour
¼ tsp salt
One 14-oz can unsweetened crushed pineapple
¾ C water
1 egg, beaten

MERINGUE

3 egg whites
⅓ C sugar
¼ tsp cream of tartar

Make Filling first by combining in a heavy pot (or top of double boiler) the sugar, wheat germ, corn starch, flour and salt. Mix well. Add pineapple and water, cook, stirring until thick. Mix a little with the beaten egg and return to mixture in pot, stirring. You must cook this in top of double boiler over boiling water about 20 to 30 minutes to remove all starchy taste. Stir frequently.

Pour filling into baked and cooled pie shell and cover with meringue made by beating on high speed the egg whites, sugar and cream of tartar until very stiff. Bake about 10 minutes at 400° until top of meringue is tinged with gold.

Pecan Pie

PASTRY: Make Basic Pie Pastry, Nine-Inch, (see Index).

FILLING

4 eggs
2 C corn syrup
3 Tbsp melted butter or margarine
1½ tsp vanilla
¼ tsp salt
1½ C whole pecans

For the Filling, in a bowl beat the eggs slightly and add all remaining ingredients. Pour into pastry-lined pie plate and bake at 400° 15 minutes. Reduce heat to 350° and bake 30 minutes longer or until filling is set, slightly less at center than around edges.

This pie should be made in advance and chilled to make cutting into wedges neat. Serve with whipped cream.

Glazed Plum Pie

PASTRY: Make Basic Pie Pastry, Nine-Inch, (see Index).

FILLING

11 large purple plums (2½ × 2") washed,
    stoned and cut into eighths
2 Tbsp minute tapioca
¾ C sugar

GLAZE

1 C juice (see below)
¼ C water
½ C sugar
1¾ Tbsp arrowroot flour
    (or cornstarch, see below)
6 drops red food coloring

To make Filling, combine prepared plums, tapioca and sugar, and stir gently. Let stand 15 minutes then cook in top of double boiler, covered, 30 minutes. Drain through colander. Reserve 1 C juice for glaze. Cool the drained plums to room temperature.

To make glaze, to the juice add the water. Mix well the sugar and arrowroot flour (which makes a much clearer glaze) or cornstarch, then add the syrup and red food coloring and cook stirring until thick. Reduce heat to simmer and cook 6 or 7 minutes until very thick, stirring once or twice. Cool.

Tip drained cooked plums into baked and cooled pie shell and, if you care to, arrange the plum crescents in concentric circles. Pour cooled glaze all over. Chill in refrigerator 2 to 4 hours.

Serve with Mock Devonshire Cream made by beating ½ lb white cream cheese until creamy and adding about 1 or 2 Tbsp 18% cream until blended. Do not chill.

Layered Mince-Pumpkin Pie

PASTRY: Make Basic Pie Pastry, Nine-Inch, (see Index).

FILLING
1 C mincemeat
1 C canned pumpkin
2 eggs
½ C granulated sugar
1 C milk
⅜ tsp cinnamon
⅜ tsp nutmeg
⅜ tsp ginger
⅜ tsp salt

Spread mincemeat evenly over bottom of pie shell. Mix together remaining ingredients in order given and pour over mincemeat. If you have too much filling reserve some and bake the pie, adding surplus at center when pie is half baked. Bake at 425° at center of oven for 10 minutes then reduce heat to 325° until nearly set at center, about 1 hour in all. Filling sets as it cools.

Black Bottom Pie

CRUST: Mix ¼ C butter, melted, with 1¼ C fine gingersnap crumbs (crush 18). Pat and press into a 9″ or 10″ pie pan. Bake at 325° for 10 minutes.

FILLING
4 egg yolks
1¼ Tbsp cornstarch
1½ squares unsweetened chocolate
1 Tbsp gelatin
4 egg whites
½ C sugar
2 C scalded milk
1 tsp vanilla
¼ C cold water
½ C sugar

Make custard by mixing together the egg yolks, sugar and cornstarch. When these are well blended add scalded milk. Stir together over simmering water until custard thickens. Take 1 cup of this custard and to this add unsweetened chocolate that has been melted, along with the vanilla. To the remainder add the gelatin that has been soaked in the cold water. The gelatin must be added to the custard while the custard is hot. Spread the chocolate custard over the crust and place in refrigerator to chill. In the meantime add the sugar to the egg whites and beat until they will support their own shape. Now the white custard mixture (containing the gelatin and milk) has cooled somewhat. Fold the egg whites into it carefully and pour over the chocolate layer when it has set. Chill before serving.

French Peach Pie

PASTRY: Make Basic Pie Pastry, Nine-Inch, (see Index).

CREAM FILLING
One 4¾ oz pkg vanilla instant pudding
1 C milk
One 10-oz carton dairy sour cream
¼ tsp almond extract

TOPPING
One 28-oz can sliced peaches, drained (reserve syrup, see below)
2 Tbsp cornstarch
2 Tbsp lemon juice

To make Cream Filling, in beater bowl combine instant pudding and milk and beat until thoroughly combined. Add sour cream and almond extract and beat until smooth and thickened. Pour into baked and cooled pie shell and refrigerate until set, at least 30 minutes.

For Topping, thoroughly drain peaches and pat dry with paper towelling, reserving syrup. Arrange peach slices like the spokes of a wheel on top of cream filling. Measure 1⅓ C reserved syrup into pot. Stir in cornstarch with wire whip until blended and unlumpy. Cook, stirring over medium heat until thickened. Remove from heat and stir in lemon juice. Cool for about 10 minutes then spoon evenly over entire surface of pie. Refrigerate until set.

Chocolate Meringue Pie

PASTRY: Make a Basic Pie Shell, Nine-Inch, (see Index).

FILLING
3 squares (3 oz) unsweetened chocolate
2½ C whole milk
¼ C flour
1 C granulated sugar
½ tsp salt
4 eggs, yolks and whites separated
2 Tbsp butter
1 tsp vanilla

To make Filling, in top of double boiler, over boiling water, scald the milk and chocolate together. Blend with rotary beater. Mix together dry the flour, sugar, and salt. Add egg yolks and beat. Stir in a little of the chocolate milk then return to double boiler and cook stirring until thickened. Remove from heat. Add butter and vanilla and cool. Pour into baked and cooled pie shell. To leftover egg whites add ½ C sugar and beat until very stiff. (*Note:* adding sugar to egg whites first insures a fine-textured meringue with all sugar grains dissolved. Undissolved sugar grains in meringue cause the "beading" we all deplore.) Pile meringue all over chocolate filling, sealing it to edges. Bake at 375° until rich gold, about 12 to 15 minutes. Cool.

French Pear Pie

Note: You may substitute peaches, plums or nectarines for the pears.

STREUSEL TOPPING
⅔ C all-purpose flour
⅓ C moist brown sugar
⅓ C hard butter

PASTRY: Make Basic Pie Pastry, Nine-Inch, (see Index).

FILLING
1 Tbsp fine dry breadcrumbs
¼ C sugar
4 tsp flour
¼ tsp powdered ginger
6 pared, cored, sliced medium-large pears
4 tsp lemon juice
¼ C golden syrup

To make Streusel Topping, Mix the flour and brown sugar and cut in butter until size of peas and chill.

To make Filling, sprinkle, pie shell evenly with the breadcrumbs. Mix together the sugar, flour, ginger and sprinkle ⅓ of this over crumbs in pastry-lined pie plate. Arrange the sliced pears uniformly. Drizzle over evenly the lemon juice and syrup. Sprinkle with the remaining flour mixture. Sprinkle over and pat on Streusel Topping.

Bake at 450° for 15 minutes, then reduce heat to 350° and bake 30 to 35 minutes longer.

Lemon Cloud Pie

PASTRY: Make a Basic Pie Shell, Nine-Inch, (see Index).

FILLING
¾ C sugar (first amount)
¼ C cornstarch
1 C cold water
Grated rind 1 lemon
⅓ C lemon juice (see below)
2 eggs, yolks and whites separated
One 4-oz pkg white cream cheese
  (room temperature)
8 drops yellow food coloring
¼ C sugar (second amount)

To make Filling, in a pot combine the ¾ C sugar, cornstarch, cold water, grated rind, lemon juice and egg yolks. (*Note:* If you do not get ⅓ C juice from the lemon add bottled lemon juice to make it up to ⅓ C.) Stir to blend then cook stirring constantly until thick. Remove from heat. Add yellow food coloring and cut up cream cheese and beat at high speed until all lumps disappear. Beat egg whites with sugar until stiff and fold into lemon mixture until blended. Pour into baked pie shell. Chill at least 2 hours before serving.

Fresh Plum Pie

PASTRY: Make a Basic Pie Pastry, Two-Crust, (see Index).

PLUM FILLING
5 C washed, quartered, stoned yellow or
  red or purple plums (takes 15 minutes)
¾ to 1 C granulated sugar
2½ Tbsp minute tapioca
¼ tsp cinnamon

To make Plum Filling, combine all filling ingredients in large bowl and mix well. Turn into pastry-lined pie plate. Roll out remaining pastry and gash at center. Cover filling with it and seal edges. Brush top with mixture of 1 Tbsp each milk and sugar. Bake at 425° for 10 minutes, then reduce heat to 350° for 30 minutes longer or until juices begin to bubble through gashes. This pie should rest for at least 3 hours before cutting, to allow filling to set.

Perfect Fall Apple Pie

PASTRY: Make a Basic Pie Pastry, Two-Crust, (see Index).

FILLING
6 large Melba apples, pared and sliced (or use
  equivalent in Gravensteins or Lodis)
⅔ C granulated sugar
½ tsp mace (or nutmeg)
1 Tbsp butter

Arrange half of the sliced apples in bottom of pastry-lined pie plate. Sprinkle with half the sugar and spice. Repeat. Dot with butter. Roll out second half of dough, gash liberally at center, cover apple filling, seal and flute edge. Brush all over with glaze made by mixing together 1 Tbsp each sugar and evaporated milk or cream. Bake at 450° for 10 minutes, then reduce heat to 350° for 40 minutes longer, or until apples are tender. Serve slightly warm with old Cheddar cheese.

Grasshopper Pie

16 cream-filled chocolate wafers, crushed finely
  (2 C not packed)
3 Tbsp soft butter
24 large marshmallows
⅔ C milk
¼ C crème de menthe liqueur
2 Tbsp crème de cacao (optional)
½ pt whipping cream

Crush cookies. (Buzz in blender or put them inside a piece of wax paper and roll finely with rolling pin.) Combine them thoroughly with the soft butter and press evenly into a deep 9" pie plate to form the shell.

In top of double boiler heat the marshmallows and milk, stirring until the marshmallows have melted and mixture is well combined. Cool and then add liqueurs. Chill over ice water until completely chilled but still syrupy before the cream which has been whipped, is folded in. Pour into pie shell and chill overnight. The flavor is better next day. If desired sprinkle with a few reserved chocolate crumbs or shavings of bitter chocolate or bottled chocolate sprinkles.

Perfect Custard Pie

PASTRY: Make a Basic Pie Shell, Nine-Inch, (see Index).

FILLING
5 large eggs
½ C granulated sugar
1 tsp vanilla
⅛ tsp salt
2½ C milk

To make Filling, beat eggs with sugar, vanilla and salt until foamy. Add milk and stir to dissolve sugar.

Pour into pie shell as much filling as you can without it overflowing. Transfer to oven at 450° for 10 minutes. Reduce heat to 325° but when edges of custard begin to set add any remaining filling to center. Bake 50 to 55 minutes in all or until custard is barely set at center.

Banana Cream Pie

PASTRY: Make a Basic Pie Shell, Nine-Inch, (see Index).

FILLING
¾ C sugar
6 Tbsp cornstarch
⅜ tsp salt
3 C milk
4 large or 5 small eggs (yolks and
    whites separated)
1½ Tbsp butter or margarine
¾ tsp vanilla
3 large or 4 small ripe bananas
¾ C whipping cream

Bake and cool shell while making Filling: combine sugar, cornstarch and salt in top of double boiler. Stir milk in slowly so ingredients are mixed thoroughly and there are no lumps. Cook over boiling water until thick, stirring constantly. Continue cooking and stirring 10 minutes longer then remove from heat. Separate yolks and whites and beat yolks slightly in a small bowl. Stir about 3 Tbsp of the hot mixture into egg yolks and blend well. Pour egg yolk mixture back into hot mixture and blend thoroughly. Return to double boiler and cook 1 minute, stirring. Remove from heat and blend in butter and vanilla. Let cool slightly. Cover bottom of baked pie shell with about one-quarter of the cream filling. Peel and slice 2 large or 3 small bananas into ¼" slices and spread in pie shell. Pour over remaining cream filling and let cool. Garnish the remaining surface of the pie with the last banana, peeled and sliced into ¼" slices and dipped in lemon juice to prevent browning. Just before serving whip the cream and mound it in center of pie.

Note: If desired, banana cream filling may be covered with meringue (instead of whipped cream) made by beating together the leftover egg whites with ½ C sugar and ¼ tsp cream of tartar until very stiff. Bake meringue on pie in oven at 375° until tinged with gold.

Nesselrode Pie

¼ C all-purpose flour
½ tsp salt
½ C sugar
1½ C milk
1 C whipping cream, chilled
¼ C pineapple juice
5 egg yolks
¼ C moist raisins, chopped
¼ C blanched toasted almonds, chopped
1 Tbsp butter
2 Tbsp chopped maraschino cherries
1 tsp maraschino cherry juice
1 tsp rum flavoring
1½ Tbsp icing sugar
Chocolate bar
9" pastry shell, baked

Blend first 3 ingredients in top of double boiler. Stir in milk, ¼ C of the cream and pineapple juice. Stir over boiling water until smooth and thickened. Stir a little hot mixture into beaten yolks, then return to double boiler and stir thoroughly. Add raisins, almonds and butter, cover and cook 5 minutes longer, stirring once. Remove from heat. Stir in cherries and flavorings. Pour into pie shell, spreading level. Cool. Whip remaining ¾ C chilled cream until just thickened, then beat in icing sugar until stiff. Spread over pie. Sprinkle with shaved chocolate bar. Chill.

Egg Nog Chiffon Pie

1 envelope (1 Tbsp) gelatin
¼ C cold water
2 eggs, yolks and whites separated
1¼ C milk (divided, see below)
¼ C sugar (first amount)
¼ C sherry or 2 Tbsp rum
¼ or ½ tsp nutmeg
½ C whipping cream
¼ tsp salt
4 Tbsp sugar (second amount)
1 baked 9" pie shell, cooled

Combine gelatin and cold water in mixing bowl. Mix well. Blend egg yolks and ¼ C of the milk in small saucepan. Add remaining 1 C milk and ¼ C sugar. Cook and stir over medium heat until mixture thickens slightly and coats a dry metal spoon. Remove from heat. Pour over soaked gelatin and stir until gelatin is dissolved. Add sherry or rum and nutmeg and blend. Chill until mixture begins to thicken. Then whip the cream and fold into egg nog mixture.

Beat egg whites and salt until foamy throughout. Add 4 Tbsp sugar, 2 Tbsp at a time, beating after each addition until blended. Continue to beat until mixture stands in peaks. Fold smoothly into egg nog mixture. Pour into cooled pie shell. Chill.

Butterscotch Meringue Pie

OIL PASTRY
1¾ C unsifted all-purpose flour
¼ tsp salt
½ C oil
¼ C milk or cold water

FILLING
½ C butter or margarine
2 C dark brown sugar, tightly packed
½ C plus 1 Tbsp cornstarch
¼ tsp salt
6 eggs, yolks and whites separated
4 C milk (divided, see below)
2 tsp vanilla

MERINGUE
⅛ tsp salt
¼ tsp cream of tartar
6 egg whites (left from making Filling)
¾ C granulated sugar

To make Oil Pastry, in a bowl stir together flour and salt. In a one-cup measure, measure oil and milk or water. Stir briskly with a fork or spoon until liquids are well blended and creamy. Pour liquid over flour mixture and stir until thoroughly blended. Pack into a ball. You must roll pastry out between 2 large sheets of wax paper. Peel back top piece of wax paper. Grasp ends of bottom piece of wax paper and quickly invert paper with pastry stuck to it over deep 10″ pie plate. Peel off wax paper. Press pastry into place in pie plate and make a high fluted edge and prick with fork. Bake at 425° about 10 minutes, watching carefully.

To make Filling, in a large heavy saucepan melt butter. Blend in sugar and cook, stirring, 2 minutes. Remove from heat. In a bowl combine the cornstarch and salt. Add egg yolks and ½ C of the milk and beat well until smooth. Add remaining 3½ C milk and stir to blend. Slowly add this milk mixture to sugar mixture. Return to heat and cook, stirring constantly, until mixture thickens then cook 2 minutes longer, stirring. Stir in vanilla. Pour into baked pie shell.

To make Meringue, in large bowl beat egg whites, cream of tartar and salt until quite frothy. Gradually add sugar while beating at high speed. Continue beating until stiff peaks form. Pile meringue on top of Butterscotch Filling, making sure it touches edges of pastry. Bake meringue at 375° until golden, about 10 mintues. Cool on cake rack.

Lattice Blueberry Pie

PASTRY: Make a Basic Pie Pastry, Two-Crust, (see Index).

FILLING
Two 14-oz cans blueberries (less ¾ cup syrup)
1 Tbsp lemon juice
3 Tbsp minute tapioca

To make Filling, open cans of blueberries and drain off ¾ C of the juice, to use for some other purpose. To the blueberries add tapioca and lemon juice and stir constantly over high heat until thick. Heat and stir 1 minute longer. Let stand on counter to cool a little while you roll out half the pastry for pie shell.

Roll out remaining half of the pastry for topping and cut into ⅜″ wide strips with pastry wheel. Pour filling into pastry-lined pie plate. Place pastry strips in lattice pattern over filling and press ends to rim. Brush neatly with mixture of 1 Tbsp each milk and sugar. Bake at 425° for 5 minutes. Reduce heat to 350° until filling just begins to bubble and lattice is tinged with gold, about ½ hour. This pie must be cool before serving.

Dutch Apple Pie

PASTRY: Make a Basic Pie Shell, Nine-Inch, (see Index).
FILLING
3 or 4 C sliced apples, pared and cored
1 C brown sugar
3 Tbsp flour
1 tsp cinnamon
¼ C butter
3 or 4 Tbsp milk or rich cream

To prepare filling, in a bowl combine flour, sugar and cinnamon. Cut in butter with a pastry blender until size of peas. Place sliced apples neatly in pastry-lined pie plate. Sprinkle crumb mixture evenly over top. Sprinkle milk or cream on top as well. Bake at 375° for 35 minutes or until apples are soft and a rich syrup has formed.

Fresh Cherry Pie

PASTRY: Make a Basic Pie Pastry, Two-Crust, (see Index).

FILLING

1 C sugar
1½ Tbsp cornstarch
¼ tsp salt
4 C well-packed sour red cherries, washed and pitted
¼ tsp almond flavoring
Red food coloring (optional)

To make Filling, mix sugar, cornstarch, salt, cherries, flavoring and red food coloring (if used) together. Line a 9" pie plate with pastry, turn in cherry mixture and seal with gashed top crust for a two-crust pie. If desired, to make lattice top, roll out second half of dough and cut into ½" strips using a ruler as your guide. Weave the strips to form a latticed top and attach ends to moistened edge of lower crust. Crimp the edges. If desired, brush top with glaze of 1 Tbsp each sugar and milk or a little cream. Bake at 450° for 10 minutes then reduce heat to 350° and bake 25 minutes longer or until juice bubbles through gashes or lattice. Cool well before cutting.

Paper Bag Apple Pie

One 9" unbaked deep pie shell (see Index).
6 C coarsely sliced or chopped cooking apples
½ C sugar
2 Tbsp flour
½ tsp nutmeg
2 Tbsp lemon juice

TOPPING

½ C cold butter
½ C flour
½ C brown or white sugar

Wash, pare, core and cut up cooking apples and measure 6 cups. In a bowl mix with ½ C sugar, flour, nutmeg and lemon juice. Turn into pastry-lined deep 9" pie plate, with high fluted edge. Pat down evenly. Into a medium bowl measure the butter, second ½ C sugar and ½ C flour. Cut butter in with pastry blender until size of large peas. Sprinkle over apples evenly and pat down fairly firmly especially around the edges. Slide pie into a heavy brown paper bag large enough to cover pie loosely, then fold open end under and tuck under bottom of pie. Place on a large cookie sheet for easy handling. Bake at 425° for 50 minutes. Split bag open with scissors and remove pie and cool on wire rack.

Party Black Cherry Cream Pie

TOPPING

¼ C sugar
4 Tbsp cornstarch
One 14-oz can pitted black sweet cherries (drained: save syrup, see below)
2 tsp lemon juice

CRUMB CRUST

¼ C melted butter
1¼ C fine graham cracker crumbs
¼ C granulated sugar

CREAM FILLING

8-oz pkg white cream cheese (room temperature)
1 tsp vanilla
1 C sifted icing sugar
1 tsp plain gelatin
1 tsp water
½ pint whipping cream

Because it has to cool, make the Cherry Topping first. In top of double boiler combine the sugar and cornstarch. When mixed add 1 C reserved cherry syrup. (If you do not have 1 cup add water to make cup full). Stir over boiling water until thick, then cook, covered, 10 minutes longer, stirring once or twice. Remove from heat, add drained cherries and lemon juice and chill.

To make Crumb Crust, melt butter in pot and mix in crumbs and sugar. Reserve 2 Tbsp mixture for sprinkling top later. Butter a deep 9" pie plate and line bottom and sides with crumbs using your finger tips to pack it evenly. Chill.

To make Cream Filling, in beater bowl combine cheese and vanilla and beat, then add icing sugar and beat until smooth. Scrape down sides with rubber spatula 2 or 3 times. Soak gelatin in cold water in a cup 5 minutes then stand in hot water and stir to dissolve. Cool to room temperature but do not allow to set. In cold bowl whip cream until stiff. Add gelatin liquid during last 15 seconds. Fold smoothly into cheese mixture. Pour into crumb shell and chill 20 minutes. Finally spoon chilled cherry topping over all and sprinkle with reserved 2 Tbsp graham cracker crumbs. Chill at least 2 hours before serving.

Two Rhubarb Custard Pies

PASTRY: Make a Basic Pie Pastry, Two-Crust, (see Index).

FILLING

9 C cut-up (½") rosy young rhubarb
2½ C sugar
6 Tbsp flour
2 Tbsp butter
6 large eggs or 7 medium
½ C orange juice

Line two 9" pie plates, then combine all Filling Ingredients stirring well to distribute eggs. With a cup dip half of filling into each pastry-lined pie plate. Gently with your palm, press rhubarb down to make the top level. Bake at 400° for 15 minutes, then reduce heat to 350° for 25 to 30 minutes longer, or until custard is softly set at center.

Lattice Cherry Pie

OIL PASTRY

2⅛ C unsifted cake and pastry flour
¼ tsp salt
⅝ C oil (½ C plus 2 Tbsp)
¼ C plus 1 Tbsp milk

FILLING

Two 14-oz cans pitted red cherries and
    syrup (see below)
⅛ tsp salt
2 Tbsp cornstarch
3 Tbsp granulated sugar
⅛ tsp almond extract
1 Tbsp lemon juice
1 Tbsp butter
1 tsp red food coloring (optional)

Make Filling first: drain cherries and measure syrup. You need 1½ C syrup so if necessary add water to make up the required amount. Set aside. In saucepan mix salt, cornstarch and sugar. Slowly stir in cherry syrup, stirring until all lumps are gone with wire whip. Cook, stirring constantly, over direct medium heat until thickened and then cook 3 minutes longer, stirring. Remove from heat. Stir in cherries, almond extract, lemon juice, butter and red food coloring (if used). Cool while making pastry.

To make Oil Pastry, in bowl combine flour and salt. In a small bowl beat together with fork until creamy the oil and milk then stir into flour mixture until thoroughly combined. Pack into a ball between your palms. Roll ⅔ of the pastry out between 2 large sheets of wax paper. Peel off top sheet of paper. Pick up bottom sheet with pastry on it and turn upside down over deep 9″ pie plate. Peel off paper and press pastry into pie plate, making a high fluted edge. Roll remaining ⅓ of the pastry between two sheets of wax paper. Remove top sheet and cut pastry into ½″ wide strips using pastry wheel if you have one. Leave on bottom of wax paper until ready to use.

Pour Filling into 9″ pastry-lined pie plate. Peel strips of pastry from wax paper and criss-cross them to form lattice on top of cherry filling, sealing ends. Protect rim of pie with strip of foil to prevent burning. Bake at 425° for 30 to 35 minutes until golden.

Fresh Blueberry Pie

PASTRY: Make a Basic Pie Pastry, Two-Crust, (see Index).

FILLING

3½ C picked over and washed and dried blueberries
⅔ C sugar
2 Tbsp cornstarch
⅛ tsp salt
Grated rind of one large lemon

Mix filling ingredients together gently and pour into prepared pastry-lined pie plate. Moisten rim of dough and cover with prepared gashed top crust and seal edges. Brush top evenly with glaze made of 1 Tbsp each of milk and sugar. Bake at 400° for 10 minutes, then reduce heat to 350° for about 30 or 40 minutes longer or until juice bubbles through gashes.

Homemade Mincemeat Pie

This recipe makes four shallow 8″ two-crust or 2 deep 10″ pies.

5 C ground (or chopped) apples, washed,
    quartered, cored (not pared)
1 lemon cut into eighths and seeded
2 C granulated sugar
1⅓ C finely chopped beef suet (about 7 oz. —
    see note below)
½ C (well packed) mixed cut peel
    (one 4-oz container)
1 C currants
1 C seeded Muscat raisins
½ tsp cinnamon
½ tsp nutmeg or mace
¼ tsp cloves
½ tsp salt
One 15-oz can pitted red (sour) cherries
    (45% sugar syrup)
1 C chopped walnuts (optional but recommended)

Put apple quarters and cut lemon through coarse knife of food grinder together. Turn ground mixture into a large kettle, add all remaining ingredients, except cherries and nuts and boil gently one-half hour covered, stirring frequently. Add cherries and nuts and boil gently 20 minutes longer, stirring frequently. Store covered in refrigerator or pour into 4 sterilized pint jars and seal.

Notes: 1. Make and bake a two-crust shallow 8″ mincemeat pie at 425° for 25 minutes or until bubbling and golden, longer for deep 10″. 2. Using Five-Cup Pastry (below) bake 2½″ diameter Mincemeat Tarts at 375° for about 15 minutes or just until bubbling.

FIVE-CUP PASTRY

5 C unsifted cake and pastry flour
2 Tbsp light brown sugar
2 tsp baking powder
2 tsp salt
1 lb shortening
2 tsp vinegar
Water (see below)
1 egg, beaten

In large bowl combine flour, sugar, baking powder and salt. Cut in shortening with knife or pastry blender until the size of small peas. Into a 1-cup measure put the vinegar then fill with water to the 1-cup mark. Add liquid and beaten egg to flour mixture and stir until blended. The mixture is rather sticky. Wrap in waxed paper and then in a plastic bag and chill in refrigerator at least 1 hour before using.

Basic Pie Shell, Nine-Inch

1 C stirred but unsifted all-purpose flour
½ tsp salt
⅓ C shortening
1 to 1½ Tbsp water

To make Pastry, cut shortening into flour and salt until size of peas. Drizzle in water, tossing with a fork, until you can pack pastry between your palms. Line 9″ pie plate and bake at 425° about 7 or 8 minutes.

Two-Crust Rhubarb Pie

PASTRY: Make a Basic Pie Pastry, Two-Crust, (see Index).

FILLING
5 C washed and cut up (½") pink slender rhubarb
1 C sugar
2 Tbsp minute tapioca

GLAZE
1 Tbsp milk
1 Tbsp sugar

To make Filling, mix well the prepared rhubarb with sugar and minute tapioca and let stand while you roll out top crust and gash it to make steam vents. Turn rhubarb into pastry-lined pie plate evenly, cover with top crust, trim off rough edges and seal and crimp rim. Mix together the 1 Tbsp each sugar and milk and brush all over top. Bake at 425° for 20 minutes then reduce heat to 250° for 40 minutes longer. Juice should bubble through gashes a little to show rhubarb is cooked.

Basic Pie Pastry, Two-Crust

Use either one of the following pastries.

STANDARD
2 C stirred but unsifted all-purpose flour
1 tsp salt
⅔ C shortening
3 or 4 Tbsp cold water

Cut shortening into flour and salt until size of peas. Drizzle in water, tossing with a fork, until you can pack pastry between your palms. Divide in halves and roll out 2 crusts on floured board.

TENDER
2¼ C stirred but unsifted cake and pastry flour
1 tsp salt
⅔ C shortening
3 Tbsp butter
3 Tbsp cold water

Cut shortening and butter into flour and salt until size of peas. Drizzle in water tossing with fork. Press into ball between palms. Divide in halves and roll out 2 crusts on floured board.

English Pastry

This recipe is often used for deep meat pies.

2 C all-purpose flour
2 tsp baking powder
1 tsp salt
1 C shortening
½ C boiling water
2 tsp lemon juice
1 egg yolk

Mix together flour, baking powder, salt. Cut in ½ C shortening. Melt another ½ cup shortening in the boiling water, then add lemon juice and egg yolk. Stir into flour mixture, then knead for 3 minutes. Let stand 1 hour.

Non-Roll Puff Pastry

Four cups sifted all-purpose flour, 1 lb cold, hard butter (do not substitute), ½ pt (10 oz) dairy sour cream. Cut butter into flour with pastry blender until size of large peas. Stir in sour cream lightly. Press into chunky roll, wrap in foil or double wax paper and chill until hard.

Foolproof Refrigerator Flaky Pastry

(Large Quantity)

Ten cups unsifted all-purpose flour, 2 lb best quality lard, 1 Tbsp salt, 2 eggs beaten in a 16-oz measure with 2 Tbsp vinegar. Fill the 16-oz measure to top with cold water. Add salt to flour in large dishpan, cut lard in with knives or pastry blender until like coarse meal. Add water-egg-vinegar mixture, sprinkling it evenly over top of dough crumbs, and mix just until dough will hold together. Wrap in double wax paper, then in plastic bag and chill. Break off amount of dough needed and keep remainder well wrapped and cold. This pastry will still roll out readily right after being taken from the refrigerator.

Puff Pastry

1 C butter
1½ C sifted cake and pastry or
    all-purpose flour
¾ tsp salt
10 Tbsp ice water

Wash butter by squeezing it lightly with the fingers under cold water until it is waxy and smooth. Double it over quickly between the palms and pat hard to remove water. Reserve 1 Tbsp and shape remainder into a flat oblong about ½" thick and place on lightly floured board. Sift together flour and salt and cut in reserved Tbsp butter with a pastry blender or two knives. Moisten to a dough with the ice water and turn out on lightly floured board. Knead for 5 minutes. Cover with a cloth and bowl and let stand for 5 minutes. Pat, lift and roll ⅛" thick, keeping pastry longer than wide and corners square. Place butter in center of one side and fold the other side of the pastry over it. Press edges firmly to enclose as much air as possible. Pat until enclosed butter is within ½" of edges. Fold one end over and the other end under to form 6 layers of pastry. Turn ¼ way round, pat, lift and roll ⅛" thick, having pastry longer than wide. Lift often to prevent pastry from sticking and dredge board lightly with flour when necessary. Fold from the end towards the center to make 3 layers and roll out as before. Repeat folding and rolling 4 times. After 4th rolling, fold from ends to center and double, making 4 layers. Chill until pastry is stiff.

Oil Pastry

See BUTERSCOTCH MERINGUE PIE

Hot Water Pastry

Two-thirds cup shortening, 7 Tbsp boiling water, 2½ C sifted all-purpose flour, 1 tsp salt. Measure shortening into a large bowl. Use measuring tablespoon to dip water that is boiling onto shortening, then beat mixture until it is smooth and creamy and cooled. Add sifted flour and salt and mix with fork until smooth. Shape into roll, cover well and chill. This amount makes a 2-crust 9″ pie or 2 baked shells. Roll out on lightly floured board to desired size. Fold over to pick up and transfer to pie plate. You will find this handles much more satisfactorily than standard pastry. When you have mastered it try standard pastry again.

Whole Wheat Pastry

This makes a two-crust, 9 inch pie.

Whole wheat pastry has more flavor and food value than pastry made with all white flour. Use whole wheat pastry often, especially with apple, raisin or pumpkin fillings.

One and one-half cups each whole wheat flour and pastry flour, 1½ tsp salt, 1 C cold fat, about 6 Tbsp cold water. Sift flours and salt into mixing bowl. Cut ⅔ of fat into flour until it looks like cornmeal, add the remaining ⅓ and cut in until as large as peas. Work quickly. Sprinkle water over flour mixture in small amounts, mix in quickly until flour holds together. Divide in half and roll out to size of pie pan. Use other half for top crust.

Choux Paste

For cream puffs, éclairs, bouchées and croquembouche.

1 C hot water
½ C (¼ lb) butter
1 C sifted all-purpose flour
4 large eggs (room temperature)

Into a medium-large saucepan measure the hot water and butter and bring to boil over high heat. All at once add the flour and with wooden spoon stir hard until it forms a mass around the spoon and leaves sides of pan. Remove from heat, stir in eggs one at a time, beating until each egg is incorporated into the paste.

For CREAM PUFFS, Shape into 2½″ tall mounds on ungreased cookie sheets at least 2½″ apart and bake at 400° for 1 hour. Test one after baking 50 minutes by standing it on stove top. If it is baked through it will not collapse. If it is not baked through it will fall a little at the top, so put it back and bake 10 minutes longer.

For ECLAIRS, shape into long ovals instead of rounds on ungreased baking sheets and bake at 400° for 1 hour. Test for doneness as above.

For BOUCHEES (Mouthfuls) shape paste into 1¼″ mounds on ungreased baking sheets and bake at 400° for 30 to 35 minutes or until they test done as above.

Chef's Pastry

See FIVE-CUP PASTRY under HOME-MADE MINCEMEAT PIE.

Ground Rice Cheese Cakes

½ C melted butter or margarine
½ C sugar
2 eggs
½ C ground rice
½ tsp almond extract
½ tsp baking powder
Red jam

Add sugar to butter, stir well, then add eggs and beat well. Add ground rice, flavoring and baking powder. Line tart tins (small) with tender pastry. Put teaspoon of jam in bottom then put mixture on top. Bake at 350° for about 20 minutes. Fills 2 dozen small tarts.

Coconut Tarts

PASTRY
2¼ C sifted all-purpose flour
¾ tsp salt
¾ C shortening
1 Tbsp butter
2 Tbsp cold water

FILLING
2 Tbsp cornstarch
1 C sugar
½ tsp salt
1 C boiling water
3 egg yolks, beaten
¼ C butter or margarine
1 tsp vanilla
2½ tsp lemon juice
1 C packaged coconut
Red jam or jelly (see below)

To make Pastry, cut shortening and butter into flour and salt until size of peas. Drizzle in cold water as you toss with fork until flour is barely dampened. Press dough into ball between palms. Roll out on floured board to ⅛″ thickness. Cut out with 3¾″ cutter and line 18 tart tins neatly. Bake at 425° about 8 or 10 minutes. Watch carefully.

To make Filling, in saucepan mix together the cornstarch, sugar and salt. Stir in boiling water and cook, stirring, until boiling then cook 1 minute longer, stirring. Stir a little of the hot mixture into the beaten egg yolks and return these to saucepan and cook, stirring one minute longer. Remove from heat and beat until smooth. Now add butter or margarine, vanilla, lemon juice and coconut. Put ½ tsp red jam or jelly into each baked tart shell and fill ¾ full with coconut filling. Sprinkle top with extra coconut and bake at 350° for 15 to 18 minutes. Cool on rack.

Glazed Cherry Sweet Pastry Tarts

SWEET PASTRY

2 C sifted all-purpose flour
2 Tbsp sugar
¼ tsp salt
½ C hard butter
½ C hard margarine
2 egg yolks
1 Tbsp cold water

CREAM FILLING

1½ Tbsp flour
1 Tbsp sugar
1 egg yolk
½ C milk
½ tsp vanilla

CHERRY TOPPING WITH GLAZE

One 14-oz can pitted red Montmorency cherries
  including syrup
⅓ C sugar
1 Tbsp arrowroot flour (or cornstarch)
1 tsp plain gelatin
½ tsp red food coloring

To make Pastry, cut the butter and margarine into the flour, sugar and salt and yolks until size of large peas. This takes about 4 or 5 minutes because the butter is hard as it should be. Now add the water and toss with a fork to mix. Tip into a plastic bag and chill ½ hour. Tip out on sparingly floured board and knead and shape and press as you would shortbread so your hands will warm it enough to compress it together. Roll out to ⅜" thickness. Cut out with 3⅜" round cutter and line eighteen 2¾" (standard) tart tins. Bake at 450° for 5 minutes then reduce heat to 350° for 2 or 3 minutes longer. Watch carefully.

Make Cream Filling by stirring together all ingredients in top of double boiler until slightly thickened over boiling water. Cool.

To make Cherry Topping and Glaze, drain cherries thoroughly to collect ⅞ C syrup. In pot mix well sugar, arrowroot (used for clarity) or cornstarch and gelatin then add syrup and cook stirring until thick. Remove from heat and add red food coloring. Cool. When tart shells, cream filling and glaze are cooled to room temperature assemble tarts by adding 1 tsp cream filling to each shell. Top with drained cherries, about 4 or 5 to a tart. Now cover each with 1 tsp clear red glaze. Wait a couple of minutes and add another teaspoon glaze to each.

Mincemeat Tarts

This recipe makes 24 covered tarts and one 9" pie, and will freeze.

PASTRY

½ lb butter
¼ lb shortening
½ C sugar
3⅞ C (1lb) stirred but not sifted cake and
  pastry flour
2 tsp baking powder
¼ tsp salt
¼ C milk

FILLING

One 28-oz can mincemeat
3 large apples, pared, chopped and steamed
  until tender
¼ C rum (optional)

To make Pastry, cream together the butter, shortening and sugar. Sift together flour, baking powder and salt and add to creamed mixture along with the milk. Use your fingers or pastry blender to blend. Divide dough into 3 portions and roll out. Cut out rounds to fit bottoms of 2 sets of tart tins and one pie plate.

To make Filling, add steamed apples and rum if used, to mincemeat and when cool fill all lined tart tins and pie plate evenly. Roll out remaining pastry and cut out to fit tops of tarts and pie and seal and crimp edges. Tops should be lightly gashed.

Bake at 425°. The times will differ. Watch carefully and do not overbake. The pastry should be pale and barely tinged with gold. It will burn easily because the pastry contains sugar. When baked cool tarts on cake racks and sprinkle powdered sugar like snow over them.

Syrupy Butter Tarts

PASTRY

1½ C sifted all-purpose flour
1½ C sifted cake and pastry flour
1 tsp salt
1 C shortening
About 8 Tbsp cold water

FILLING

½ C butter
½ C corn syrup
1 C choice washed and dried currants or raisins
2 eggs
1 tsp lemon juice
1 tsp vanilla
Extra corn syrup (see below)

To make Pastry, sift the sifted flours with the salt and cut in shortening with pastry blender until size of peas. Drizzle in water, 1 Tbsp at a time, tossing with a fork, until you can gather it up into a dampish ball between your palms. Roll out very thinly on floured board. Cut out rounds and line medium-sized tart tins with them. Spoon 1 tsp (or more) corn syrup into each lined tart tin.

To make Filling, mix all filling ingredients. Spoon into prepared tart tins filling ⅔ full. Bake at 425° for 13 to 15 minutes. Watch carefully.

Aunt Bessie's Butter Tarts

PASTRY
2 C sifted pastry flour
2 tsp sugar
1 tsp salt
⅔ C salad oil
¼ C cold milk

BUTTER TART FILLING
3 Tbsp butter
1 C brown sugar
1 egg
½ tsp salt
¼ C raisins
¼ C chopped walnuts
½ tsp vanilla

To make Pastry, sift flour, sugar and salt into bowl. Measure and combine oil and milk and beat until creamy. Add to dry ingredients and mix. Dough is oily. Pick up a small ball of dough and press into tart tins or muffin pans. Press dough with your finger tips until you have lined the depressions to about ⅛" thickness. Make top edge neat.

To make Filling, cream butter until soft and blend in brown sugar. Beat egg slightly and beat into creamed mixture. Stir in salt, raisins, walnuts and vanilla. Spoon into pastry-lined tart tins, filling them ⅔ full.

Bake at 400° for 8 minutes. Then reduce heat to 375° and bake about 12 or 15 minutes longer, or until pastry is tan and crisp, turning pan in oven at halftime.

Mission Circle Tarts

PASTRY
1 C unsifted cake and pastry flour
⅓ C shortening
1 Tbsp butter
½ tsp salt
2 Tbsp cold water

FILLING
1 egg
2 Tbsp soft butter
¼ tsp salt
½ C light brown sugar
¼ C currants
¼ C desiccated coconut
2 Tbsp chopped nuts (pecans are best)
½ tsp vanilla
Red jam or jelly

To make Pastry, cut shortening and butter into flour and salt until size of small peas. Drizzle in water tossing with a fork. Pack into a ball between your palms. Roll out thinly on lightly floured board. Using 2¾" cutter cut out and line eighteen 2" tart tins neatly. Into each spoon ½ tsp raspberry jam or other red jam or jelly.

To make Filling, beat together in a bowl all of the filling ingredients (not the jam or jelly). Using a teaspoon mounded a little, spoon filling over jam in tart shells but do not overfill. Bake at 350° for 20 minutes or until pale gold on top. While still warm carefully remove from tart tins to cake rack to cool.

Almond Rice Tarts

PASTRY
1½ C unsifted all-purpose flour
½ tsp salt
½ C shortening
2 Tbsp butter
2 to 2½ Tbsp cold water

FILLING
Raspberry or strawberry jam (see below)
¼ C butter
¼ C sugar
2 eggs
½ tsp almond extract
5 Tbsp ground rice (buy at supermarket)
½ tsp baking powder
⅛ tsp salt
½ C finely chopped almonds
    (preferably buzzed in blender)

To make Pastry, cut shortening and butter into flour and salt until size of peas. Drizzle in water, tossing with fork. Press between palms into ball. Roll out on floured board to ⅛" thickness. Cut out with 2¾" cutter and line twenty-four 2" tart or muffin tins.

To fill, into each spoon ½ to ¾ tsp red jam and then make Filling: in beater bowl cream butter and sugar until light. Beat in eggs and remaining ingredients. Apportion evenly into pastry-lined tart tins, about 24. Bake at 400° for 10 minutes.

French Peach Tart

PASTRY
1 C sifted all-purpose flour
1 Tbsp sugar
⅛ tsp salt
¼ C margarine
2 Tbsp butter
1 egg yolk
1½ Tbsp lemon juice
1 Tbsp water

FILLING
1 pkg (4-oz) vanilla pudding mix
1¼ C milk
½ C whipping cream
4 peaches scalded, peeled and sliced
About ¼ C red currant or apple jelly melted

To make Pastry, in large bowl cut margarine and butter into flour, sugar and salt until size of peas. In a cup mix together the yolk, lemon juice and water and drizzle over, tossing with fork. Shape into ball and chill. Roll out to fit 9" pie plate or flan pan with fluted or scalloped edge. Prick well with fork. Bake at 350° about 30 to 40 minutes. Cool.

Make Filling by combining pudding mix with milk in small saucepan. Cook stirring until thick and boiling. Cool, then chill in refrigerator with surface covered with wax paper to prevent skin from forming. Whip cream until stiff and carefully fold into chilled pudding mix and pour into cooled crust. Arrange sliced peaches in neat concentric rings on top. Brush each slice with melted jelly and chill at least 3 hours.

General Brock Butter Tarts

PASTRY
½ C plus 2 Tbsp shortening
¼ C plus 2 Tbsp lard
1½ C plus 1 Tbsp unsifted all-purpose or
    pastry flour
2 C less 1 Tbsp unsifted cake flour
⅓ C plus 1 Tbsp skim milk powder
¾ tsp salt
½ C less 1 Tbsp light brown sugar
1 large egg
½ C less 1 Tbsp water
½ tsp vanilla
4 drops yellow food coloring (optional)

FILLING
2¼ C light brown sugar
¼ C soft shortening
2 Tbsp soft butter
¼ tsp salt
1½ Tbsp golden corn syrup
4 eggs
¾ tsp vanilla
1 C raisins or walnuts

To make Pastry, combine in large mixing bowl the shortening, lard, flours, milk powder and salt and mix well. Combine in a small bowl the brown sugar, egg, water, vanilla and coloring (if used) and add to mixed dry ingredients and mix to a smooth dough, by hand if necessary. Now roll and cut out tart shells to fit 2¾″ tart pans, about 24. Measure 1 tsp raisins or nuts into each shell.

Combine all remaining filling ingredients and beat until blended. Neatly spoon 2 Tbsp into each unbaked shell to fill to brim. Bake at 350° for 18 to 20 minutes until risen and golden. Let stand in pans 5 minutes before carefully removing to rack to cool.

Date Oatmeal Turnovers

TURNOVER DOUGH
1 C sifted all-purpose flour
½ tsp salt
½ C shortening
1 C quick-cooking rolled oats, uncooked
¼ C sugar
3 Tbsp water
¼ tsp almond extract (optional)

FILLING
¾ C chopped dates
¼ C sugar
¼ C water
1 Tbsp lemon juice

To make Dough, sift together flour and salt. Cut in shortening until mixture resembles coarse crumbs. Mix in rolled oats and sugar. Add water and almond extract (if used), mixing lightly. Knead dough 4 or 5 times until it just holds together. Roll out to ⅛″ thickness. Cut in 4″ rounds.

To make Filling, cook together, while stirring, dates, sugar and water until thickened, about 5 minutes. Add lemon juice. Cool. Place rounded teaspoon of filling at one side of each round of cookie dough. Fold over and seal edges firmly by pressing with tines of a fork. Prick top to allow escape of steam. Place on ungreased baking sheet. Bake at 400° for 12 to 15 minutes until edges are delicately browned. Makes twelve.

Cheese-Onion Pie

Pastry for deep 9″ pie plate (see below)
½ C long grain raw rice
1½ C boiling water
½ tsp salt (first amount)
3 Tbsp butter
2 C (packed) thinly sliced mild onion
1 C milk
3 C shredded sharp Cheddar cheese
    (about 10 to 12 oz)
2 eggs
1 tsp salt (second amount)
½ tsp curry powder
⅛ tsp pepper
Grated cheese from shaker (for top)

Partially bake — about 6 minutes at 400° — a 9″ pie shell.

Meanwhile cook together, covered, in large saucepan the rice, boiling water and ½ tsp salt until all water is absorbed and rice is tender. Remove from heat. Gently sauté onions over low heat in covered frying pan until limp but not at all brown. Remove from heat. To cooked rice add milk, cheese, eggs and mix well, then add 1 tsp salt, curry powder and pepper. Cover partially baked crust with sautéed onions, turn rice mixture over evenly. Sprinkle with shaker cheese and bake at 325° for 1 hour. Serve hot.

Homemade Toaster Fruitpops

1⅞ C sifted all-purpose flour
1 Tbsp cornstarch
½ tsp salt
1 tsp baking powder
2 Tbsp sugar
2 Tbsp skim milk powder
2 Tbsp shortening
2 Tbsp corn syrup
2 Tbsp cold water

Into a large mixing bowl sift together the sifted flour, cornstarch, salt, baking powder, sugar and skim milk powder. Cut in shortening with pastry blender until size of small peas. Stir in corn syrup and water. Press dough into ball between your palms. Turn out onto lightly floured board and knead until smooth and pliable. Shape into an oblong block about the size of a brick. Roll it out, retaining as straight sides as possible, to ⅛" thickness. Cut dough into strips 9 × 3" with pastry wheel or knife.

Using thick jam or marmalade spread bottom half of each strip thinly to within ½" of edges. Fold top half of strip over jam and carefully seal edges. With a toothpick puncture top at even ½" intervals to allow steam to escape. Brush tops all over thinly with evaporated milk.

Lift pastries to buttered baking sheets and bake at 350° on center rack for 13 to 15 minutes or until edges are gold and top is pale gold. Store well wrapped in refrigerator or freezer, then toast in toaster as needed.

Raspberry Air Pockets

½ C sifted all-purpose flour
½ C sifted cake and pastry flour
½ tsp salt
¼ C shortening
¼ C hard butter
¼ C wheat germ
¾ C oatmeal (see note below)
¼ C sugar
3 Tbsp orange juice
¼ tsp vanilla
7 Tbsp best quality raspberry jam

Note: Use Oatmeal, not rolled oats. If you do not have oatmeal blend rolled oats in your blender until they are of meal consistency.

In large bowl cut shortening and butter into flours and salt with pastry blender until size of large crumbs. With a fork lightly mix in all remaining ingredients. Press into a ball between your hands.

Very lightly flour your board and on it knead the dough 10 times. Pat it out with your palms then with lightly floured rolling pin roll out to ⅛" thickness. Cut out six 4½" squares. Lift one to buttered cookie sheet and in center place 1 Tbsp raspberry jam and spread it a little. Now lift each corner and pinch together at center. Repeat until all 6 are filled and folded. Brush very neatly with glaze of 1 Tbsp each sugar and milk. Bake at 400° for 14 minutes at center of oven. Do not overbake. Cool on rack.

Apple Turnovers

YEAST DOUGH
¾ C milk, scalded
1 Tbsp (1 pkg) granular yeast
¼ C lukewarm water
1 tsp sugar (first amount)
¼ C shortening
¼ C granulated sugar (second amount)
1 tsp salt
1 egg
2¾ C sifted all-purpose flour

APPLE FILLING
⅔ C sugar
1 C hot water
2 large pared and cut-up cooking apples
2 cinnamon sticks

In a large bowl soak the yeast in the lukewarm water with the 1 tsp sugar for 10 minutes. Meanwhile add the shortening, ¼ C sugar and salt to the scalded milk and stir to dissolve sugar and cool to warm. Add to risen yeast liquid along with the egg and flour and quickly mix well. Knead on floured board 200 times. Return to scraped down bowl and let rise covered 2 hours.

To make Apple Filling combine all ingredients and boil hard for about 20 minutes until apples are tender and syrup is reduced to only about ⅓ C. Remove cinnamon sticks. Beat until smooth. Cool. You need 1 cup of this thick apple filling.

After the 2 hours rising punch down dough and knead on lightly floured board 50 times. Roll it out to less than ¼" thickness. You should have a sheet of dough 13½ × 18" to cut out twelve 4½" squares. On each square, a little to one side, place 1 Tbsp apple filling. Fold over to form a triangle and seal edges by pinching. Place on 2 greased baking sheets at least 1" apart. Brush with milk. Sprinkle tops carefully with granulated sugar. Let rise 1¼ hours. Bake at 375° for 20 to 22 minutes, switching pans at halftime to evenly brown all.

Mushroom Tricorns

2 Tbsp butter or margarine
1 drop Tabasco
1 Tbsp flour
¼ lb washed and scrubbed and chopped mushrooms
4 Tbsp cream
1 tsp finely minced onion
2 wedges (1 oz each) Gruyère cheese
Pastry for a 2-crust pie

Melt butter and stir in chopped mushrooms and onion until coated with butter, then add Tabasco and flour. Stir in cream until thickened. Break cheese into small pieces and add. Stir over low heat until cheese melts. Remove from heat.

Roll pastry to ⅛" thickness. Cut in 3" circles with cookie cutter. Spoon a small amount of mushroom mixture on each circle. Bring pastry up around filling and pinch to form a tricorn. Bake at 425° for 15 minutes or until golden brown. Serve hot. (Pastries may be made ahead and reheated to serve.) Makes about 24 tricorns.

Eccles Cakes

FAST PUFF PASTRY
1½ C plus 4 tsp unsifted all-purpose flour
¼ tsp salt
6 Tbsp butter
6 Tbsp shortening or lard
1 tsp lemon juice
4 Tbsp ice cold water

FILLING
5 Tbsp soft butter
5 Tbsp light brown sugar
⅞ C choice currants
4 Tbsp finely chopped mixed peel
    (or use 1½ C mincemeat)

To make Pastry, cut the butter and shortening into the flour and salt until size of marbles. Add lemon juice then drizzle in the cold water, 1 Tbsp at a time, tossing with fork. Press into ball. Roll out on floured board into an oblong ⅛″ thick. Fold the bottom one-third of pastry up and the top one-third down to form 3 layers. Press edges to enclose air. Give pastry half turn to right, roll into oblong again and repeat above process until pastry has had 4 rolls, folds and half turns. Roll out into a 12 × 15″ oblong, ⅛″ thick. This is pliable pastry to handle.

Mix Filling ingredients (or use mincemeat).

Cut pastry out into 4″ rounds, about 15. Put 1 Tbsp filling on each, moisten edges and draw edges up around filling. Pinch to seal. Turn over on floured board and pat or gently roll to flatten to ½″ thickness by 2½″ in diameter. Place on ungreased cookie sheets, and make 3 small slits on top with knife. Sprinkle sparingly with sugar. Bake at 425° about 25 minutes or until tinged with gold.

French Onion Pie

One 9″ unbaked pie shell
½ to ¾ lb bacon
5 thinly sliced medium onions
1 Tbsp flour
¼ tsp pepper
4 slightly beaten eggs
1 C evaporated milk or light cream
¼ tsp nutmeg
1 tsp salt

Sauté bacon until crisp, skim from pan onto paper towel and as soon as it cools, crumble it.

In about ¼ C of the bacon fat in pan sauté the sliced onions until transparent. Do not brown. Into onions in pan stir the flour, salt and pepper until blended. Stir in evaporated milk or cream until mixture thickens. Remove from heat. Add 3 spoonfuls of mixture to beaten eggs. Stir egg mixture into creamed mixture in pan and stir until well blended. Remove from heat. Sprinkle crumbled bacon all over unbaked pie shell. Pour over onion and egg mixture. Sprinkle with nutmeg. Bake at 400° about 20 minutes or until set and slightly tinged with gold. Serve hot cut into wedges with a generous salad.

Meat Turnovers French Style

PASTRY
2 C sifted all-purpose flour
1 tsp salt
⅔ C hard butter
7 or 8 Tbsp milk

FILLING
1 C breadcrumbs
⅓ C milk
½ lb lean pork finely ground
1 egg
½ tsp salt
⅛ tsp pepper
2 Tbsp butter
½ onion chopped finely
½ garlic clove chopped finely
2 Tbsp chopped parsley
1 beaten egg for glazing

To make Pastry, cut the hard butter into flour and salt with pastry blender until size of peas. Add milk, 1 Tbsp at a time, tossing with fork until you can press it into a ball. Flatten ball, wrap and chill.

In mixing bowl soak bread crumbs in milk then stir in meat, egg, salt and pepper. In frying pan melt butter or margarine and add chopped onion, garlic and parsley and gently sauté until limp. Add meat mixture and heat and stir until meat is seared but not brown. Cool.

Roll out chilled pastry on lightly floured board to ⅛″ thickness. Cut into eight 6″ circles, the last circle being made from scraps of dough and hand-shaped.

Measure ¼ C cooled meat filling and place at side center of each pastry circle. Moisten edge, fold over and seal with fork tip. Place on 2 ungreased baking sheets and brush neatly all over tops and crimped edges with one beaten egg. Now prick tops at 4 places with fork to allow steam to escape. Bake at center of oven at 400° for 25 to 35 minutes.

Serve hot with VELOUTE SAUCE: Simmer ⅔ C finely chopped celery in ⅔ C boiling water, covered, 10 minutes. Melt ¼ C butter and blend in ¼ C flour. Stir in cooked celery and liquid, one 10-oz can undiluted consommé and ⅔ C drained canned mushroom stems and pieces until thick.

Cheese Tartlettes

PASTRY: 3 C sifted pastry flour, 1 tsp salt, 1 C shortening, 6 to 8 Tbsp cold water. Mix flour and salt. Cut in shortening until consistency of cornmeal with a few larger pieces. Add water, 1 Tbsp at a time, stirring with fork. Add only enough water to moisten. Divide dough into 3 and roll each portion on lightly floured board to ⅛″ thickness. Cut with floured cookie cutter to fit 2″ tart pans.

FILLING: 4 eggs, 1 tsp flour, 1 C cold milk, 1¾ C grated Cheddar cheese, salt, pepper, nutmeg to taste. Whip all ingredients together. Fill each tart shell ⅔ full. Bake at 450° for 15 minutes or until filling is set and golden. Serve as soon as possible.

Mushroom Pie

PASTRY

1 C sifted all-purpose flour
⅓ C shortening
1 Tbsp butter
½ tsp salt
1 Tbsp water

FILLING

1 Tbsp butter
1 Tbsp minced onion
¾ to 1 C washed and sliced mushrooms
    (could be drained canned)
1 C milk
1 can cream of mushroom soup, undiluted
1 C grated Cheddar cheese
3 large eggs
¼ tsp paprika
Shake of pepper
Shake of cayenne

To make Pastry, cut shortening and butter into flour and salt until size of small peas. Drizzle in water, tossing with fork. Press into ball between palms, roll out on floured board to fit 8″ pie plate and line plate, shaping high, fluted, thick edge.

To make Filling, heat milk, soup and cheese together in top of double boiler. In frypan sauté onion and mushrooms in butter over low heat until limp. Add to mixture in double boiler along with seasonings. Beat the eggs to mix them, pour some of the hot mixture into them, stirring, then stir egg mixture into hot mixture for 1 minute. Pour into raw pastry-lined pie shell. Bake at 450° for 10 minutes then reduce heat to 325° for 35 to 40 minutes longer or until filling is baked and tinged with gold.

Banbury Turnovers

SWEET PASTRY

½ C shortening
½ C sugar
2 eggs
2 Tbsp milk
1 tsp vanilla
2½ C sifted cake and pastry flour
¼ tsp baking soda
1 tsp salt

FILLING

⅔ C figs chopped
⅔ C raisins
⅔ C sugar
2 Tbsp water
½ C chopped nuts
4 Tbsp orange juice

To make Pastry, into beater bowl measure the shortening, sugar, eggs, milk, vanilla, flour, soda and salt and beat until mixed. Chill pastry until firm.

To make Filling, stir together the figs, raisins, sugar and water until boiling and sugar is dissolved. Remove from heat and stir in nuts and orange juice. Cool.

When pastry is firm sprinkle board with cake and pastry flour. Roll out half of dough into a 14 × 14″ square. Working quickly cut it into 9 squares.

Place a heaping silver teaspoonful of filling on each and using narrow lifter bring sides up and over filling to overlap. With lifter transfer to greased cookie sheet. Continue until all 9 squares are filled and folded. Roll out remaining half of pastry and repeat. Brush top of all 18 turnovers with mixture of 2 Tbsp each sugar and milk. Bake at 400° for 12 to 13 minutes.

Genuine Italian Pizza

DOUGH

1 C lukewarm water
1 tsp sugar
1 pkg granular yeast
1 tsp salt
¼ C cooking or salad oil
2¾ C sifted all-purpose flour

TOPPING

1 tsp oregano
1 tsp salt
One 6-oz can tomato paste
½ C water
½ lb sliced or cubed Mozzarella cheese
⅔ lb sliced Polish sausage
⅓ lb mushrooms, sliced (gently sautéed 3
    minutes in 1 Tbsp butter)
12 sliced stuffed olives
3 Tbsp chopped green pepper
2 Tbsp olive or cooking oil
2 Tbsp grated Parmesan or old Cheddar cheese

To make Dough, add the 1 tsp sugar to the 1 C lukewarm water in a large mixing bowl and sprinkle yeast over top, give it one stir and let soak for 10 minutes. Then add the salt and oil and all but ¼ C of the flour. Mix as well as you can, then turn out on board floured with the remaining ¼ C flour and knead 100 times. Return to greased bowl. Cover and let rise until doubled. Punch down and with floured hands divide into 2 balls. Have ready two 15″ pizza pans and on each press a ball of dough with palms to form a very thin uniform circle 12″ in diameter, slightly thicker at edges.

To make Topping, in a little bowl mix together the oregano, salt, tomato paste and water (using water to rinse out tomato paste can). Set aside. Then on each round of dough arrange all over in concentric circles, the Mozzarella cheese, the sausage, mushroom, green pepper and olives. They will overlap. Spoon half of the tomato sauce mixture evenly over each. Sprinkle half of the oil and half of the grated cheese over each. By this time the dough has risen a little and it is ready to be baked. Bake at 400° about 25 to 30 minutes until dough is well baked on bottom, cheese is melted and top is bubbling hot. Serve at once.

Desserts

Chocolate Party Dessert

1 standard-sized white cake or 1 small
    angel cake or ½ large angel cake
Three 1-oz squares unsweetened chocolate
½ C white sugar
½ C hot water
1 Tbsp gelatin
2 Tbsp cold water
4 beaten egg yolks
1 tsp vanilla
4 stiffly beaten egg whites
1 C 32% cream, whipped (first amount)
1 C toasted almonds (see below)
¾ C 32% cream, whipped (second amount)

Soak gelatin in the 2 Tbsp cold water. Toast almonds in 1 tsp butter until gold at 350°, stirring once or twice. Chop them finely and divide into 2 parts. In top of double boiler combine hot water, sugar and chocolate and heat until chocolate melts, stirring to blend. Stir in soaked gelatin and cook over simmering water, stirring for about 5 minutes. Beat egg yolks and add a little hot chocolate mixture to them, mixing well. Cool. Add vanilla. Fold in stiffly beaten egg whites. When this is quite cool fold in the 1 C cream which has been whipped until it will hold in soft peaks, and ½ C of the chopped toasted almonds. Butter an angel cake pan. Break white or angel cake into egg-sized pieces, and put a layer in bottom of pan, spooning some of the chocolate mixture over and into the crevices. Repeat cake pieces and chocolate mixture until you finish with a layer of chocolate mixture on top. Do not add too much cake for the finished product should be moist and coated with chocolate throughout. Cover and chill 8 hours or overnight. At serving time frost cake with the ¾ C whipped cream. Sprinkle remaining chopped toasted almonds over top. Serves twelve.

Apple Dessert Squares

BASE

1 C stirred all-purpose flour
¼ C light brown sugar (packed)
⅓ C butter (room temperature)

TOPPING

2 eggs
¾ C light brown sugar (packed)
¼ C all-purpose flour
½ tsp baking powder
½ tsp salt
½ tsp cinnamon
2 C diced unpeeled apples
1⅓ C flaked or desiccated coconut
½ C chopped walnuts or pecans
1 tsp vanilla

Make Base first by mixing butter into flour and sugar until blended and smooth. Pat firmly into a 9 × 9″ pan. Bake at 350° for 15 minutes until tinged with gold.

While Base is baking make Topping: Beat eggs and sugar at least 5 minutes until thick and light in color. Add flour, baking powder, salt and cinnamon and fold in. Add apples, coconut, nuts and vanilla. Spread over warm base. Bake at 350° about 25 minutes until gold. Serves nine.

Peach-Pear Cobbler

One 19-oz can peaches
One 19-oz can pears

BATTER

1¾ C sifted all-purpose flour
1¼ C granulated sugar
4 tsp baking powder
1 tsp salt
⅓ C shortening (room temperature)
⅔ C milk (first amount)
1 egg
⅓ C milk (second amount)

Open cans of fruit and tip them, juice and all, into a 7½ × 12 × 2″ pan. Set oven temperature at 375° and at once put pan full of fruit in oven to heat through while you make batter.

For batter, into beater bowl measure sifted flour, sugar, baking powder, salt, shortening and ⅔ C milk and beat at medium speed for 2 minutes, scraping down sides of bowl several times. Add egg and remaining ⅓ C milk and beat 2 minutes more, scraping bowl often. Remove pan of hot fruit from oven and carefully spoon batter all over. Bake at 375° for 30 to 40 minutes. Slip a sheet of foil under pan to catch syrup which may bubble over. Serves eight.

Raspberry Angel Party Dessert

One 6-oz or two 3-oz pkgs raspberry jelly powder
2 C boiling water
One 15-oz pkg fresh frozen raspberries
    in syrup (thawed)
1 medium bakery angel food cake
½ pt whipping cream (divided, see below)

In medium-sized bowl dissolve jelly powder in the boiling water. Reserve 8 or 10 choice raspberries then add the thawed raspberries plus their juice and mix well.

Cut the angel cake into 1½″ cubes. Whip the cream until stiff but do not overbeat.

Lightly oil a small angel food cake tin or an 8-cup jelly mold. Pour in ¾ C of the liquid mixture or as much as necessary to completely cover bottom. Pack half of the cake cubes in on top of the jelly liquid. Pour enough liquid over to color the cake red. Spread the cake layer with half the whipped cream. Pour over enough liquid to cover the whipped cream. Pack in the remaining cake cubes and gradually pour over a little liquid at a time until all used. Carefully smooth down the top by gently pressing the cake with the back of a spoon. This packs the cake in well and aids in the unmolding later. Chill in refrigerator until jelly sets, at least 4 hours or overnight then run a hot knife around sides and unmold on serving plate.

At serving time top each serving with a puff of the remaining whipped cream and one of the reserved raspberries. Serves eight.

Optional: a 15-oz pkg fresh frozen strawberries and strawberry jelly powder can be substituted for the raspberry jelly powder and raspberries.

Maple Mousse

1 Tbsp plain gelatin
¼ C water
¾ C milk
1 C maple syrup
½ pt whipping cream
½ C chopped walnuts

In a bowl soak gelatin in water. Stand bowl in shallow boiling water and stir to dissolve gelatin. Remove from heat. Stir in milk and maple syrup and chill briefly until barely set. Meanwhile whip cream. As soon as jelly is very softly set, fold in whipped cream and nuts. Spoon in stemmed sherbets or goblets.

Cream Puffs with Chocolate Sauce

PUFFS

½ C boiling water
¼ C butter
½ C unsifted all-purpose flour
¼ tsp salt
1½ tsp sugar
2 large eggs

FILLING

½ pt whipping cream or best quality
   vanilla ice cream

CHOCOLATE SAUCE

¼ C butter or margarine
½ C cocoa
1 Tbsp cornstarch
1½ C plus 1½ Tbsp hot water
4 C granulated sugar
¾ C corn syrup
½ tsp salt
2 tsp vanilla

To make Puffs, in a heavy pot heat together the water and butter until butter melts and the liquid comes to a boil. Leave on heat and quickly add the flour, salt and sugar all at once, stirring vigorously until mixture leaves the sides of the pot and clings to spoon. Remove from heat and beat in eggs, one at a time, until smooth. Drop by heaping tablespoonfuls (wet the spoon) 3″ apart on a greased baking sheet. Shape into 8 rounds with wet spoon, peaking them up at center. Bake at 400° for 10 minutes then reduce heat to 350° for 25 minutes longer (or until when one is removed from oven to test, it holds its shape). Cool.

To make Chocolate Sauce (this makes more than you need: use for other purpose later) in large heavy pot combine thoroughly butter or margarine, cocoa, cornstarch, sugar, corn syrup, salt and vanilla. Stir in hot water and cook over medium heat until dissolved, wiping down sugar on sides with damp cloth. Cook 3 minutes stirring until slightly thickened.

To assemble, cut off lid from each puff and carefully remove any eggy webbing from inside with sharp pointed knife. Fill each puff with whipped cream or scoop of vanilla ice cream. Replace top and pour over Chocolate Sauce (hot or cold) and serve at once.

Plum Roly Poly

PLUM PUREE

15 large purple plums
¾ C water (first amount)
¾ C granulated sugar
1 Tbsp cornstarch
1 Tbsp water (second amount)

BISCUIT DOUGH

3 C unsifted all-purpose flour
⅓ tsp salt
4 tsp baking powder
2 Tbsp granulated sugar
⅔ C shortening
½ C plus 1 Tbsp milk

FILLING

2 Tbsp melted butter
2 tsp cinnamon
¼ tsp nutmeg
¼ C sugar

Make Plum Purée in pot by bringing plums, ¾ C water and sugar to a boil. Reduce heat, cover and simmer 20 to 30 minutes or until plums are mushy, then force plums and liquid through a sieve and discard leftover skins and stones. (You need 3 C plum purée so add water if necessary.) Reserve 2 C plum purée for spooning over finished dessert later. Make a smooth paste of the cornstarch and 1 Tbsp water and stir it into the remaining 1 C purée. Cook stirring until thick and 3 minutes longer. Allow to cool while making dough.

To make Biscuit Dough, in large bowl blend together flour, salt, baking powder and sugar. Cut in shortening with pastry blender until mixture resembles small peas. Add milk and toss with fork until you can press dough into a ball between your palms. Roll dough out on floured surface to a rectangle 15 × 10″. Brush dough with the 2 Tbsp melted butter.

To make Filling, in a small dish combine cinnamon, nutmeg and sugar. Sprinkle one-half this sugar mixture over surface of dough. Now spread this with the cooled thickened plum purée and top with remaining half of sugar mixture. Roll up dough to form a log, starting at the long side. Cut into 12 equal slices with a very sharp knife. Place slices, cut side up, on a greased cookie sheet. Bake at 450° for 15 to 18 minutes and serve while warm. Heat reserved 2 C of plum purée and spoon some over each Roly Poly.

Pears Hélène

Combine 2 C water, 1 C sugar and ½ tsp peppermint flavoring. Bring to boil and simmer 5 minutes. Meanwhile, peel, halve and core 4 pears and poach them in the syrup until tender. If desired a little green coloring may be added. Chill the pears in the syrup. When ready to serve, drain and place 2 halves in each dessert dish and center with a scoop of vanilla ice cream. Serve with HOT CHOCOLATE SAUCE: ½ C cocoa, 2 C sugar, 1 C water, pinch of salt, 1 tsp vanilla, 1 Tbsp butter. Mix the cocoa and sugar, add the water and salt and boil for 3 minutes. Remove from heat and add vanilla and butter. Pour over pears and ice cream in each dish.

Fruit Flan

CRUST
1 C all-purpose flour
2 Tbsp icing sugar
½ C hard butter

FILLING
One 6-serving pkg vanilla pudding and
    pie filling
2¼ C milk

TOPPING
One 14-oz can sliced peaches, drained
8 to 10 large choice strawberries, halved
½ C peach or apricot jam
1 Tbsp lemon juice

To make Crust, cut the butter into the flour and icing sugar with a pastry blender until it resembles coarse meal. Turn out on large sheet of wax paper. Bring corners together and press from outside into a ball. Chill 1 hour. Press into a 9" pie plate to evenly line it with a uniform top edge. Bake at 425° for 6 minutes. Cool.

To make Filling, add milk to packaged pie filling and cook stirring until thick. Chill by standing in pan of ice water covered. Beat until smooth and turn into cooled pie shell.

Topping: Arrange peach slices like a closed wheel at center. Surround edge with halved large strawberries cut side up, points out.

Make a Glaze by heating together the jam and lemon juice until liquefied. Strain. Spoon all over top. Chill 4 hours before serving. Serves six.

Puff Pudding:
Strawberry or Rhubarb

FRUIT BASE
4 C sliced strawberries or sliced rhubarb
½ C water
2½ Tbsp quick-cooking tapioca
½ C sugar

SPONGE BATTER
½ C sifted cake flour
6 Tbsp sugar
2 eggs, yolks and whites separated
⅛ tsp salt
¼ tsp cream of tartar

Prepare Fruit Base by measuring the fruit of your choice into a saucepan and adding the water, tapioca and sugar. (Add an extra ¼ C sugar if you use rhubarb.) Bring to boil stirring and cook 1 minute. Remove from heat, pour into buttered 8 × 8" baking dish, and keep hot.

To make batter, beat egg yolks until light, gradually adding sugar until pale and fluffy. Add salt and cream of tartar to egg whites and beat until stiff but not dry. Fold egg-sugar mixture into whites. Sift sifted flour over and fold in. Give the fruit-tapioca mixture a stir then pour batter over it. Bake at 325° for 50 minutes or until batter tests done at center. Serves six.

Rice Cream Mold with
Raspberry Sauce

Note: Divide this recipe in half if you need a family size mold.

2 Tbsp plain gelatin
2¾ C milk
One 8-oz pkg white cream cheese
    (room temperature)
4 eggs, yolks and whites separated
½ C sugar
2 C cooked rice (¾ C raw rice cooked
    in 1½ C water)
2 tsp vanilla
Two 15-oz pkgs fresh frozen raspberries (thawed)
2 Tbsp arrowroot flour or cornstarch
¼ C sugar (divided, see below)
¼ C water (or 2 Tbsp water and
    2 Tbsp Cointreau)
⅛ tsp salt

To make the Cream Mold, soak the gelatin in ¾ C of the milk in the measuring cup for 5 minutes. Into beater bowl put cheese, egg yolks, ¼ C of the sugar and beat until well blended. Add remaining 2 C milk and soaked gelatin liquid. Cook in heavy saucepan, stirring constantly until mixture coats back of spoon like a soft custard. It should be hot but not boiling. Remove from heat. Beat egg whites until foamy, gradually adding remaining ¼ C sugar as you beat whites until stiff. Add cooked rice and vanilla to cooked custard then fold in beaten whites carefully. Turn into 8" spring form pan or mold of equivalent volume. Chill until well set. Unmold on cake plate.

RASPBERRY SAUCE: Thaw and drain well through sieve the 2 packages of raspberries. To the juice add the ¼ C water (or 2 Tbsp water if Cointreau is used). Mix well together the arrowroot or cornstarch, sugar and salt and stir into the cold juice. Cook, stirring, until thick and clear. Select and reserve about 25 of the plumpest raspberries to arrange in border around base of mold. Add remaining drained raspberries (and Cointreau if used). Cool. Spoon a little of the thickest part over center of turned-out mold. Arrange reserved raspberries in border around base. Pour remaining sauce into cut glass serving dish to pass. Serves ten to twelve.

Orange and Lemon Charlotte

1½ C orange juice (divided, see below)
2 envelopes unflavored gelatin
2 Tbsp cornstarch
⅛ tsp salt
2 Tbsp granulated sugar (first amount)
1½ C milk
3 eggs (yolks and whites separated)
½ C sugar (second amount)
2 Tbsp grated orange rind
1 tsp grated lemon rind
2 Tbsp lemon juice
2 Tbsp sugar (third amount)
1 pt whipping cream (divided, see below)
One 3-oz pkg lady fingers
   (12 whole or 24 when separated)

Grate whole oranges to obtain required rind. Set aside. Cut oranges in half and squeeze juice and measure. Add more juice to obtain 1½ C. In a very small bowl soak the gelatin in ½ C of the orange juice until softened. Set remaining juice aside for later.

Meanwhile in top part of double boiler mix cornstarch, salt and the 2 Tbsp sugar, then slowly blend in milk. Cook over boiling water, stirring constantly until mixture thickens. Cover and cook 10 minutes longer, stirring occasionally. Stir a small amount of this hot mixture into the egg yolks which have been mixed with the ½ C sugar. Immediately pour back into remaining hot mixture and blend thoroughly. Cook 2 minutes longer stirring constantly. Add softened gelatin and stir until dissolved. Blend in remaining 1 C orange juice, lemon juice and rinds. Pour into a large bowl and chill until consistency of liquid honey, stirring occasionally

Meanwhile split lady fingers in half lengthwise and with flat side facing into center, line the sides of a 9″ spring form pan, pressing to make them cling.

Beat egg whites until stiff, beating in the 2 Tbsp sugar gradually. Whip the cream until stiff and reserve ¾ C for garnish. Fold remaining whipped cream and egg whites into jellied mixture until smoothly blended. Pour into lady-finger-lined pan. Chill for 6 to 8 hours with a loose piece of wax paper over to prevent drying.

Unhinge side of spring form pan and remove. You must leave Charlotte on base, so stand it on a large dessert plate and garnish with puffs of reserved whipped cream and orange segments or chopped orange peel. Serves fourteen.

Old Country Apple Roly Poly

DOUGH

2 C stirred but not sifted all-purpose flour
½ tsp cream of tartar
4 tsp baking powder
½ tsp salt
2 tsp sugar
½ C butter, margarine, or chicken or
   beef drippings
½ C plus 1 Tbsp milk

FILLING

2½ C finely chopped tart apples
¼ C dark brown sugar
¼ tsp nutmeg

To make Dough, sift together the flour, cream of tartar, baking powder, salt and sugar. Cut shortening in until size of large peas. Add milk all at once and stir until you have a firm dough. Roll out on floured board into a sheet 10″ wide and of ¼″ thickness.

Cover with Filling made by mixing together filling ingredients and spread to within 1″ of far edge. (*Note:* In black currant season substitute stemmed raw black currants for the apples.) Roll up snugly starting at long side. Now roll in floured cloth, folding surplus cloth under. Shape into a neat roll and place on rack in small roasting pan. Add boiling water to barely cover rack, cover and steam 1½ hours adding water if necessary. Lift out carefully, unroll onto long platter and serve with Lemon Nutmeg Sauce.

LEMON NUTMEG SAUCE: Mix together 2 Tbsp cornstarch, ¾ C dark brown sugar, 1 tsp nutmeg, ¼ tsp salt. When mixed stir in 2 C boiling water and cook, stirring, until thickened. Remove from heat and add 1 Tbsp butter. Pour into serving pitcher and pass at table. Roly Poly is cut into about 1½″ wide pinwheels per serving.

Crème Brulée with Poached Greengage Plums

Heat 3 C whipping (32%) cream until it begins to shimmer on top. Do not boil. Over low heat slowly stir in 6 egg yolks which have first been beaten until thick. Stir constantly until it thickens, but do not boil. Remove from heat and pour into shallow baking dish. Chill. About 1 hour before serving time sprinkle top evenly with ⅓ C sifted light brown sugar. Stand it about 4″ from hot broiler until sugar melts, about 1 minute. Chill again.

Serve with POACHED GREENGAGE PLUMS: Wash and prick skins of 16 Greengage plums. Make a simple syrup by combining 2 C water with ¾ C sugar. Bring to boil, drop in plums and poach until a little tender. Carefully skim out and cool. Turn into serving dish and pour cooled syrup over. Serve 2 or 3 plums with a little syrup beside a serving of Crème Brulée on each dessert plate. Serves six to eight.

Dreamy Creamy Rolls

1 C sifted cake and pastry flour
1 tsp baking powder
3 large eggs
¾ C granulated sugar
1 tsp vanilla
¾ C icing sugar

WHIPPED CREAM FILLING
1⅞ C whipping cream
4 Tbsp icing sugar
1 Tbsp (envelope) plain gelatin
3 Tbsp water

Sift flour then measure 1 cup. Re-sift with the baking powder. Set aside. In medium-sized bowl, beat eggs and sugar at high speed for 10 minutes. Stir in vanilla, remove beaters then fold in sifted ingredients until batter is smooth and thick. Spread out a large piece of waxed paper and sprinkle it with the icing sugar.

With oil, generously grease a cookie sheet. Drop batter on by even heaping tablespoons. (Do only three at a time: you will see why as soon as they are baked.) Bake at 375° for 4½ to 5 minutes when edges will just begin to turn pale gold. Remove from oven and quickly transfer with lifter these small flat cakes to wax paper generously coated with icing sugar. Immediately roll each cake up as you would for a jelly roll but just so edges overlap. Turn overlapping edge down and place on large plate. Sprinkle with a little more icing sugar. This step must be done as quickly as possible or little cakes cool and will break when you roll them. Repeat until all batter is used, each time scraping off any dried batter on baking sheet and greasing sheet again.

Prepare Whipped Cream Filling: in a cup soak gelatin in water for a few minutes. Place cup in boiling water and stir until gelatin is dissolved then remove it from heat. Pour whipping cream into bowl with icing sugar and beat at high speed. When cream begins to thicken, slowly pour cooled liquid gelatin into whipped cream while still beating. Beat until stiff. Gently pry lapped cake edges apart and fill generously with whipped cream then close again. Be sure roll is full of whipped cream. Place folded side down on large plate. Sprinkle with icing sugar. Cover loosely with wax paper and refrigerate. At their best after 3 or 4 hours in the refrigerator. Make 24.

Grasshopper Bavarian

1 envelope plain gelatin
½ C cold water
¼ C granulated sugar
⅛ tsp salt
3 eggs, yolks and whites separated
¼ C Crème de Menthe liqueur
¼ C best quality sherry
¼ C granulated sugar (second amount)
½ pt whipping cream
1 square unsweetened chocolate,
    shredded or grated

In a saucepan soak the gelatin in the cold water 5 minutes. Stir in ¼ C sugar (first amount), salt and egg yolks and stir over medium-low heat until slightly thickened, about 5 to 7 minutes. Remove from heat and stir in Crème de Menthe and sherry. Chill in pan of ice water, stirring occasionally until mixture begins to congeal.

Meanwhile beat egg whites until foamy then gradually add ¼ C sugar (second amount) beating until stiff. Beat gelatin mixture until foamy and fold into stiffly beaten whites. Whip cream until stiff and fold in until all is smoothly blended. Spoon into 8 or 10 stemmed glasses.

Onto a sheet of wax paper shred the bitter chocolate on ¼″ shredder. It makes a pile of little ⅛″ curls. Sprinkle this over tops of Bavarians. Chill.

Prune Whip with Custard Sauce

PRUNE MIXTURE
1¼ C stoned, cooked, puréed prunes (or 2 jars
    baby food prune purée)
5 egg whites (2 leftover from making Custard
    Sauce, see below)
⅔ C sugar
¾ tsp grated lemon rind
1½ Tbsp lemon juice

CUSTARD SAUCE
2 egg yolks (use leftover whites above)
3 Tbsp sugar
⅛ tsp salt
1½ C hot milk
½ tsp vanilla

In blender buzz cooked and stoned prunes until smoothly puréed. Measure 1¼ C. Otherwise use 2 bottles baby food prune purée. Pour egg whites into top of double boiler and add sugar, lemon rind and juice. Place over boiling water and with rotary beater beat constantly until stiff enough to hold peaks. Remove from heat and fold in puréed prunes. Spoon into six stemmed glasses and chill.

To make the Custard Sauce, in top of double boiler mix together the egg yolks, sugar and salt and stir in the hot milk. Over gently boiling water stir until mixture thickens slightly and coats spoon. (It does not thicken much while hot but thickens a little more when chilled.) Add vanilla and pour into serving pitcher and chill. To serve pass Custard Sauce at table to pour over Prune Whip. Six servings.

Plum Crumb

4 C quartered, pitted red plums
¼ C granulated sugar
2 Tbsp lemon juice
1¼ C unsifted flour (or 1 C flour and
    ½ C rolled oats)
1 C light brown sugar, packed
½ C butter
¼ tsp salt
¼ tsp mace or nutmeg
½ pt fresh dairy sour cream

Wash, cut into quarters and pit the plums. Arrange plums in medium-sized baking dish and sprinkle with the ¼ C granulated sugar and the lemon juice. With a pastry blender cut the butter into the flour (or flour and rolled oats), brown sugar, salt and spice until crumbly. Take care not to mix too well or it will be oily. Pat this crumb mixture evenly over the plums. Stand the prepared dish on center shelf of oven. Bake at 375° for 30 to 40 minutes, time depending on size of plums.

Ladle fresh dairy sour cream, ice cold, over warm plum pudding when serving. Serves six.

Apple Dumplings

FLAKY PASTRY
3 C sifted pastry flour
1 tsp salt
1 C cold fat
6 Tbsp cold water

FILLING
6 medium tart apples
¾ C sugar
2 Tbsp butter
about 1 tsp nutmeg

Use knives or pastry blender to cut fat into sifted flour and salt. Cut about two-thirds of fat in until mixture is as fine as meal. Chop in the remaining fat till it is in pieces the size of large peas. Sprinkle a small amount of water over surface of flour-fat mixture. Each time water is added, try to put it on undampened flour. Run a fork along the bottom of the bowl and bring it up with a tossing motion through the mixture. Press dampened particles gently to see if they stick together. Remove lumps from the bowl as they form. Work quickly. Roll out on floured board to rectangle 18 × 12″ and cut into 6 squares.

Pare and core 6 tart apples and place one in center of each square of pastry. Fill each center with 2 Tbsp sugar, 1 tsp butter and ⅛ tsp nutmeg. Bring 2 opposite corners of pastry up over top of filled apples, overlapping. Press lightly. Bring up remaining opposite corners, dampening underside of top corner and press lightly to seal. Pinch other edges to seal. With lifter transfer to lightly greased baking sheet. Bake at 450° for 20 minutes then reduce heat to 350° and bake 20 to 25 minutes longer. Test apples for doneness by piercing at top with toothpick. Serve with pouring cream or custard or lemon sauce.

CUSTARD SAUCE: 2 C milk, 4 yolks of eggs or 2 eggs, 4 Tbsp sugar, ¼ tsp salt, ½ tsp vanilla. Heat milk. Mix eggs, sugar and salt, add hot milk slowly. Cook over hot water stirring constantly until thick enough to coat a silver spoon. Remove from heat at once, cool and add vanilla.

Lemon Angel Party Dessert

One 6-oz pkg lemon jelly powder
2 C boiling water
1 C cold water
6 Tbsp cornstarch
1 C granulated sugar
¼ tsp salt
1½ C water
2 egg yolks
1 extra large lemon, grated rind and juice
1 Tbsp butter
1 medium-sized bakery angel food cake
    (about 8 or 9″ diameter)
½ pt whipping cream (see below)

Thoroughly dissolve jelly powder in boiling water. Stir in the 1 C cold water. Set aside on counter until later.

In heavy pot stir together cornstarch, sugar and salt. Add the 1½ C water, stirring to get rid of lumps. Cook over medium heat until mixture is thick, stirring constantly then cook 5 minutes longer, stirring. Remove from heat. Mix together egg yolks, lemon juice and rind and stir slowly into cornstarch mixture until blended. Return to heat and cook, stirring, 2 minutes. Add butter and beat by hand until creamy and butter has melted. Set aside to cool. Cut the angel cake in 1½″ cubes. Whip the cream until stiff.

Lightly oil an 8 or 9″ angel food cake tin. (Do not use one with removable center.) Pour in enough lemon jelly liquid to completely cover bottom (about ¼″). Pack one-third of the cake cubes in on top of jelly liquid. Pour enough jelly liquid over to color the cake yellow. Using half the whipped cream and half the lemon filling, drop each alternately by heaping tablespoonfuls on top of the cake cubes. Smooth down. Pack another third cake cubes on top of the whipped cream and lemon layer and pour over more liquid jelly to color cake cubes yellow. Repeat next layer of alternate spoonfuls of remaining whipped cream and lemon filling, again smoothing it down. Cover with remaining cake cubes and pour over remaining liquid jelly. Carefully smooth down the top by gently pressing the cake with the back of a spoon. (This packs the cake well and aids in the unmolding later.) Cover and chill until jelly sets, 4 hours or overnight, then run hot knife around sides and unmold on serving plate, Serves ten.

Valentine Strawberry Trifle

MAIN INGREDIENTS
One 6-oz pkg strawberry jelly powder
2 C boiling water
1 C strawberry syrup (see below)
Two 15-oz pkgs fresh frozen strawberries,
    thawed and drained
One 14-oz angel cake
½ pt whipping cream
2 Tbsp sugar
1 tsp plain gelatin
1 Tbsp water

CUSTARD TOPPING
¾ C granulated sugar
6 Tbsp all-purpose flour
⅜ tsp salt
2½ C warm milk
3 large egg yolks, slightly beaten
1½ tsp vanilla

Dissolve jelly powder in boiling water. Stir in 1 C strawberry syrup reserved from draining the strawberries. Set jelly aside to cool slightly.

Cut angel food cake into 1¼″ squares. In a very large bowl put one-third of the cake squares. Pour over one-third of the liquid jelly. Cover with half the strawberries. Repeat with another third of the cake, third liquid jelly and the last half of the fruit. Cover with remaining cake and pour over remaining jelly. Press down lightly with back of spoon so cake absorbs more liquid. Let set in refrigerator.

Meanwhile make Custard Topping: Combine flour, sugar and salt in top of double boiler. Warm milk in small pot and stir into dry ingredients and mix thoroughly so there are no lumps and it is thickened. Pour a little over beaten yolks and mix well. Return to hot mixture in double boiler. Remove from heat and stir in vanilla. Cool covered. When cooled, spoon over top of set jellied-fruit-cake-mixture and refrigerate.

Near serving time prepare whipped cream. In cup combine gelatin and water and let soak a few minutes. Stand cup in boiling water and stir to dissolve. Remove from heat and cool slightly but not too much or it will gel. Pour whipping cream and sugar into a bowl and beat at high speed. When cream just starts to thicken, pour in gelatin liquid, slowly, while beaters remain on. Beat until stiff. Top custard with the whipped cream. To serve, with large spoon, dip down through all layers and fill sherbet glasses. Serves ten.

New Rum Babas

1 pkg granular yeast
1 tsp sugar
½ C lukewarm water
¼ tsp salt
4 small or 3 large eggs (room temperature)
1½ C plus 1 Tbsp sifted all-purpose flour
2 Tbsp sugar
⅓ C melted butter, slightly cooled

In large mixing bowl add sugar and warm water to yeast, stir once, and let soak 10 minutes. Add salt, eggs (unbeaten) and measured flour and beat with electric beater 2 minutes or by hand 200 strokes. Let rise until quadrupled at room temperature, maybe 3 hours. Add sugar and slightly cooled butter and beat for 2 minutes or 200 strokes. Butter 12 muffin tins generously. Divide the dough into them, filling them not more than half full. Let rise at room temperature to above rims of pans. Bake at 425° for 17 to 20 minutes until gold but not brown. Bottoms should be gold. Loosen edges with pointed knife and turn out on large platter.

SYRUP: ¾ C sugar, ¼ C hot water, one 4¾-oz can puréed apricots (baby food), ¼ C rum, 2 or 3 tsp lemon juice. Combine sugar and water, bring to boil, stir in apricot purée until smooth, boil 2 minutes. Remove from heat and add flavoring and lemon juice. Immediately pour or spoon over all surfaces of hot babas which take this on like a sponge and are saturated with rich syrup when cold. Serve with topping of whipped cream.

Windsor Squares

1 slightly beaten egg
¾ C granulated sugar
½ tsp vanilla
½ C flour
¼ tsp salt
1 tsp baking powder
1 C pared and chopped apples
½ C broken pecans

Combine egg, sugar and vanilla. Sift dry ingredients together. Add to egg mixture and blend. Stir in apples and nuts. Pour into buttered 8 × 8″ pan. Bake at 350° for 30 minutes. Serve with Hot Lemon Sauce.

HOT LEMON SAUCE: One-half cup granulated sugar, 1½ Tbsp cornstarch, ⅛ tsp salt, 1 C warm water, few drops yellow food coloring, 2 Tbsp lemon juice, 1 or 2 Tbsp butter. Mix together sugar, cornstarch and salt. Stir in warm water and coloring. Bring to boil and cook, stirring, until thickened. Add lemon juice and butter and serve hot.

Zuppa Inglese

SPONGE CAKE

This is the Italian method for English Trifle.

3 eggs
1 C sugar
2 tsp lemon juice
1 C sifted cake and pastry flour
2 tsp baking powder
6 Tbsp hot milk

CUSTARD

1½ C hot milk
2 large egg yolks (or 3 medium)
3 Tbsp sugar
Shake of salt
2 tsp gelatin
2 Tbsp cold milk
2 tsp rum extract
⅓ C mixed peel
⅓ C quartered maraschino cherries
½ C chopped blanched almonds

FINISHING INGREDIENTS

2 large egg whites (or 3 medium)
¼ C sugar
⅛ tsp cream of tartar
½ C dry sherry (see below)

To make Cake, beat eggs with sugar until thick. Add lemon juice. Sift flour with baking powder and fold in flour mixture and hot milk in 2 separate additions. Pour batter into two 8″ layer cake pans lined on bottom with wax paper and buttered. Bake at 350° for 15 to 18 minutes until cakes shrink from sides. Cool on cake racks.

To make Custard, measure yolks, sugar and salt into double boiler and quickly stir in hot milk over boiling water until thick enough to coat silver spoon. Remove from heat. Stir in gelatin which has soaked in cold milk 5 minutes. Remove top of double boiler from bottom and fill bottom with ice water and return top to it. Add all remaining ingredients to custard and cool until beginning to set, stirring often.

Put one cake on upturned bottom of layer cake pan and soak with half of the sherry. Spread half of partially set custard over. Repeat both of these steps.

Make Meringue by beating whites with sugar and cream of tartar until very stiff. Cover top and halfway down sides of cakes with meringue. Bake at 400° barely long enough to tinge meringue gold. Cool in refrigerator. Carefully transfer to large cake plate. This dessert is durable enough to be made one day in advance. Serves ten.

Fruit Medley with Creamy Dressing

CREAMY DRESSING

2 eggs
3 Tbsp sugar
2 Tbsp orange juice
2 Tbsp lemon juice
1 Tbsp butter
Shake of salt
1 C dairy sour cream

FRUIT

1 C seedless green grapes
1 large sliced underripe banana
    cut in ½″ dice
1 C well-drained canned pineapple chunks
1 C (15-oz) canned pitted cherries drained
1 large orange sectioned
1 grapefruit sectioned

To make Dressing, mix together well in a saucepan the eggs and sugar. Add the fruit juices and salt and stir over medium heat until thickened and mixture coats spoon. Turn off heat and stir 1 minute longer. Remove from heat and stir in butter. Cool and chill. Stir in sour cream.

Combine all prepared fruits and pour off any excess juice. Fold in Creamy Dressing and turn into serving bowl to chill, covered, for 24 hours. At serving time garnish top with more pieces of fruit such as a border of alternating sections of orange and pineapple chunks and green maraschino cherries.

Orange Peach Bavarian

One 3-oz pkg orange jelly powder
¾ C boiling water
One 19-oz can peaches, chopped into small
    pieces (reserve syrup)
1 orange, grated rind and pulp cut into
    small pieces
3 egg whites
½ tsp cream of tartar
⅓ C granulated sugar
½ C whipping cream

In large bowl dissolve jelly powder in boiling water. Measure peach syrup and add water to make liquid up to 1¼ C. Stir into liquid jelly. Chill in refrigerator until mixture becomes thick and syrupy.

In a small beater bowl beat the egg whites with the cream of tartar until foamy. Gradually add the ⅓ C sugar and continue beating until glossy. Fold into the thickening jelly mixture until blended. In same bowl as egg whites were in, without washing beaters, whip the cream until stiff. Fold this into the jelly mixture until well blended and of uniform color throughout. Fold the orange and peach pieces in. Pour into stemmed comports or parfait glasses or cut glass bowl. Chill in refrigerator 2 or 3 hours before serving. Eight servings.

Chocolate Soufflé

1½ Tbsp butter or margarine
2 Tbsp all-purpose flour
½ C milk
¾ C granulated sugar
⅛ tsp salt
2 squares (2 oz) unsweetened chocolate
    cut into 4 pieces each
3 extra large (or 4 medium) eggs, yolks
    and whites separated
1 Tbsp cold water
½ tsp vanilla

Make the Sauce in advance by melting the butter or margarine, blending in flour, then stirring in milk, sugar, salt and chocolate until thick and smooth. Remove from heat, cool it a little and stir in egg yolks until blended. Cover and chill in refrigerator. About one hour before dessert remove sauce from refrigerator and stir in water and vanilla. Beat egg whites until stiff and fold into sauce until smoothly blended.

Turn into 6 unbuttered individual pottery or glass custard dishes. Set these dishes in large shallow pan containing enough hot water to come halfway up sides. Bake at 350° for 40 to 45 minutes. These hot soufflés are often served with liqueur sauces or unsweetened whipped cream.

Peach Party Dessert

CRUMB CRUST
3 C fine graham wafer crumbs
¼ C sugar
½ C melted butter or margarine

FILLING
One 6-oz pkg orange jelly powder
    (or two 3-oz pkgs)
2 C boiling water
1 pt (2½ C) whipping cream
8-oz pkg white cream cheese
    (room temperature)

TOPPING
Two 19-oz cans peach pie filling
    (room temperature)
1 Tbsp plain gelatin
1 Tbsp water
One 28-oz can sliced peaches, drained

To make Crumb Crust, in medium-sized pot gently melt butter or margarine, remove from heat then stir in the graham crumbs and sugar mixing well until butter has soaked all the crumbs. Press this mixture firmly into the bottom of a large 13 × 9" pan. Do not bake.

To make Filling, in medium-sized bowl dissolve the jelly powder in the boiling water and chill until cool and slightly syrupy. In large beater bowl whip the cream until stiff peaks form. Add the cream cheese and continue beating on low speed until cheese and whipped cream are well blended. Spoon syrupy jelly into cream mixture and blend well until uniform in color. Pour over crust and chill until set, about 30 minutes.

To make Topping, empty cans of pie filling into a medium-sized bowl. In a small pot combine about 4 Tbsp of the peach pie filling with the gelatin and water. Stir over low heat until gelatin dissolves then stir into remaining peach pie filling mixing thoroughly. (*Note:* If the pie filling is cold rather than at room temperature, the gelatin will set immediately upon combining and you will get a lot of lumpy pieces.) Spread the peach topping evenly over the orange filling. Drain and pat dry the sliced peaches. Arrange these peach slices like spokes of a wheel on top of the pie filling pushing them in slightly to anchor them. Refrigerate at least 3 hours before serving. For easy removal, before cutting into squares run your knife around perimeter of pan to loosen edges. Serves twenty.

Apple Roll-Ups

BATTER
1¾ C stirred but unsifted all-purpose flour
1 Tbsp baking powder
2 Tbsp sugar
1 tsp salt
¼ tsp cinnamon
2 beaten eggs
2 Tbsp melted margarine or butter
1¾ C milk
1 C finely chopped pared apple or 1 C blender-
     buzzed raw apple or 1 C thick,
     unsweetened applesauce

FILLING
1½ C dairy sour cream
3 Tbsp sugar
⅜ tsp cinnamon
¼ C finely chopped pared apple or
     alternatives, above

Note: If you decide to purée your raw apples in the blender they must be done at the last moment.

To make Batter, in beater bowl combine flour, baking powder, sugar, salt and cinnamon. In another bowl beat eggs and add melted margarine or butter and milk.

At this stage measure all Filling ingredients in a bowl except apples. Next chop or purée apples. At once, to prevent browning, add 1 C apples to egg-milk mixture. Add the ¼ C apples to the sour cream mixture.

Now add the liquids for the batter to the dry ingredients and beat until smooth. Pour small amounts of batter (2 or 3 Tbsp) onto lightly greased hot griddle and cook until bubbly on surface. Turn and brown other side. On a large kitchen plate spread each pancake with Filling and roll up. Serve sprinkled with icing sugar.

Trifle

1⅔ C whole milk
4 egg yolks, beaten slightly
¼ C sugar
¼ tsp salt
½ tsp vanilla
⅔ C sherry
One sponge cake, 2″ thick, cut into 2
     layers and then into strips
⅓ C raspberry or black currant jam
⅓ C toasted almonds, split
Whipped cream

Scald the milk. Combine egg yolks, sugar and salt. Add scalded milk to egg mixture, stirring constantly. In top of double boiler cook over hot water, stirring constantly, until mixture is thickened and coats the spoon. Cool. Add vanilla and ⅓ C of sherry. Beat with rotary beater. Chill custard. Arrange sponge cake strips in glass serving bowl. Spread with jam. Sprinkle remaining ⅓ C sherry over the cake. Let stand while custard is chilling. Pour custard over cake. Garnish with whipped cream topped with split toasted almonds. Serves five or six.

Orange Delight

1 package angel food cake mix

FILLING AND FROSTING
1 C sugar
4 Tbsp cornstarch
2 Tbsp grated fresh orange rind
½ tsp salt
1 C orange juice
2 egg yolks
1½ Tbsp lemon juice
¼ C butter
½ pt chilled whipping cream

Make the angel cake in 10″ tube pan according to package directions and cool on cake rack.

Make the Orange Filling by mixing together in heavy pot, all of the filling ingredients except butter and whipping cream and cook stirring until thick. Remove from heat and stir in butter and cool to room temperature.

Cut cake in half crosswise to make 2 layers. Place one layer on large cake plate. Whip cream until stiff and fold smoothly into cooled Orange Filling. Use about one-quarter of it to spread on bottom layer. Put top layer over. Use remaining cream Orange Filling to frost sides and top generously. Garnish top rim with circle of halved maraschino cherries. Cover and store in cool place overnight.

Cherry Cobbler

DOUGH
2 C any biscuit mix
2 Tbsp sugar
⅓ C milk
¼ C corn oil

FILLING
Two 15-oz cans tart red cherries drained
     - reserve syrup (you need 3½ C)
2 Tbsp sugar (second amount)
¼ tsp cinnamon

TOPPING
1⅓ C corn syrup
¼ C cherry juice
3 Tbsp margarine

Combine the biscuit mix with the sugar, milk and oil to make a not too soft dough. Turn it out on well floured board and knead ten times. Roll out or pat to an oblong 12 × 10″. Carefully transfer to buttered 12 × 7″ pan to line it. Pile drained cherries in a strip about 3″ wide down center of dough. Sprinkle with mixture of sugar (second amount) and cinnamon. Lap edges of dough over cherries. Bake at 450° for 15 minutes.

Combine and heat topping ingredients. After cobbler has baked 15 minutes pour boiling hot syrup topping all over and bake 15 minutes longer. Serves six.

Party Fruited Flan

SPONGE BATTER
4 large (or 5 medium) eggs, yolks and
   whites separated
¾ C granulated sugar
1 tsp vanilla
¾ C sifted cake and pastry or all-purpose flour
1½ tsp baking powder
¼ tsp salt

PINEAPPLE CUSTARD
½ C sugar
2 Tbsp cornstarch
⅛ tsp salt
⅔ C unsweetened canned pineapple juice
   (from one 19-oz can chunks, see below)
1 Tbsp lemon juice
2 Tbsp water

To make Sponge Batter, beat egg yolks, sugar and vanilla until thick and pale. Remove beaters. Fold in sifted flour, baking powder and salt which have been sifted together. Beat whites until stiff and blend in. Line a round 14½" pizza pan with buttered wax paper and turn batter on to it. Bake at 375° for 13 minutes. Let cool in pan.

To make Pineapple Custard, mix together dry in a small pot the sugar, cornstarch and salt. Stir in the pineapple juice, lemon juice and water and cook stirring until thick. Cool.

FRUIT TOPPING
one 10-oz can Mandarin orange slices
One 14-oz can prune plums halved and stoned
One 14-oz can apricot halves
One 14-oz can pitted sweet black cherries
One 19-oz can pineapple chunks

Drain all fruits separately. Combine Mandarin orange and apricot syrups for Glaze (below) and reserve other syrups for a future purpose. Dry fruits on doubled paper towels. Spread Pineapple Custard all over baked sponge cake. Starting at outer rim make 6 rings in concentric circles according to your decorative talents, perhaps alternating 2 fruits in one ring, making another ring of only one friut. Put one cherry at center.

Then cover with Amber Glaze: Measure the mixed apricot and Mandarin orange syrups, about 1½ C, adding water if necessary. Heat to just below boiling. Meanwhile soak 1 Tbsp plain gelatin in ½ C cold water 2 or 3 minutes then thoroughly dissolve it with the hot syrup. Stir in ½ tsp yellow food coloring. Chill until partially set, the consistency of corn syrup. Patiently spoon all over fruit design using a small spoon to make it spin out. Let set. Serve cut into narrow wedges.

Note: If you do not have a 14½" pizza pan you can shape a temporary one with 3 layers heavy duty foil with a ½" foldback side edge, but be sure to support it on a cookie sheet.

Lemon Snow
⅔ C sugar
Finely grated rind 1 lemon
1⅓ C hot water
3 Tbsp cornstarch
3 Tbsp cold water
3 Tbsp lemon juice
2 large (or 3 small) egg whites

Note: Reserve the leftover egg yolks for the custard sauce below.

In a medium pot combine sugar, grated lemon rind and hot water and bring to boil. Make a smooth paste of the cornstarch and cold water and stir in until thick. Reduce heat to simmer and stir 2 or 3 minutes longer. Remove from heat. Add lemon juice. Beat egg whites until stiff then slowly pour in hot lemon sauce and beat until blended. Pour into 6 stemmed serving dishes and chill.

Make Custard Sauce by mixing leftover egg yolks with 3 Tbsp sugar and shake of salt. Stir in 1¾ C milk and cook over medium heat, stirring until custard thickens a little and will coat back of silver spoon. Remove from heat and add ¼ tsp vanilla. Pour into glass serving jug and chill. Pass sauce at table when Lemon Snow is served. Six servings.

Velvet Chocolate Parfait
2 squares unsweetened chocolate
⅔ C corn syrup
1 Tbsp butter
2 beaten egg yolks
⅛ tsp salt
1½ tsp vanilla
½ pt whipping cream

In top of double boiler heat together the unsweetened chocolate, corn syrup and butter until blended.

In a small bowl beat egg yolks. Add about 2 or 3 spoonfuls of the chocolate mixture to the yolks and blend well. Turn this into double boiler mixture and cook, stirring constantly, about 3 minutes. Set mixture aside to cool.

In a large bowl whip the cream until stiff. Add salt and vanilla to cooled chocolate mixture. Fold this into the whipped cream until blended. Turn into refrigerator tray and freeze. It will not freeze firmly. It is soft rich ice cream.

Note: If the chocolate and egg mixture harden when cooled—which will happen if it cooks too long over hot water—add 2 Tbsp boiling water and stir well and cool before you fold it into the whipped cream.

Bavarian Cream

1 Tbsp plain gelatin
¼ C cold water
4 eggs
¾ C sugar
1 C orange juice
3 Tbsp lemon juice
½ pt (10 oz) whipping cream
3 Tbsp Cointreau (optional)
Toasted coconut (optional)
Pineapple chunks (optional)

In a large bowl soak the gelatin in the cold water. In top of a double boiler mix well the sugar and eggs, then stir in orange juice and lemon juice and cook stirring constantly over boiling water until it thickens to consistency of soft custard. It does not thicken much. Remove from heat. Pour over soaked gelatin and stir to dissolve. Chill until consistency of liquid honey. Whip cream until stiff. Reserve about ¾ of the whipped cream for topping later and fold the remainder into slightly set Bavarian Cream. Add Cointreau, if used. Spoon into stemmed or parfait glasses and top with daub of reserved whipped cream and a chunk of pineapple rolled in toasted coconut. Serves six to eight.

Peach Melba

1 pint best quality vanilla ice cream
One 28-oz can fancy peach halves

RASPBERRY SAUCE
One pkg fresh frozen raspberries
Water (see below)
1 Tbsp arrowroot flour (or cornstarch)
2 Tbsp sugar
Shake of salt
½ C red currant jelly

Make the Sauce in advance: Thaw the frozen raspberries and drain through sieve and measure juice. Push raspberries through sieve to purée them. Make up to 2 C by adding water to juice and purée.

In a small pot mix dry together the arrowroot flour (which may be bought at large drug stores), or cornstarch, and the sugar and salt. Then stir in raspberry purée and syrup and red current jelly and cook stirring until thick and 1 minute longer. Cool. Pour into jar, cover and chill. If desired 2 Tbsp Cointreau or Drambuie may be added to Raspberry Sauce.

At serving time, in large stemmed glasses put a scoop of ice cream. Over it, round side up, place a large drained canned half peach. Spoon Raspberry Sauce over all and serve at once. Six Servings.

Cranberry Mousse with Cardinal Cranberry Sauce

1 lb (4 C) raw cranberries
2 C sugar (first amount)
2 C water
¼ tsp red food coloring
1½ Tbsp sugar (second amount)
1½ Tbsp arrowroot (or 2 Tbsp cornstarch)
2 C milk
2 envelopes plain gelatin
¼ C sugar (third amount)
1 tsp pure orange extract
½ pt whipping cream

Make Cranberry Sauce by bringing to boil the 2 C sugar and water. Add cranberries, bring to just below boiling, cover and simmer 2 minutes, gently stirring once, then turn off heat and allow to stand over turned-off burner until room temperature. Remove from heat and add red coloring. Now skim out with slotted spoon 1½ C whole cranberries, reserve and drain. Reserve sauce for topping the Mousse when served.

Sprinkle gelatin and the ¼ C sugar over the milk and heat, stirring, to dissolve gelatin and sugar. Stir together thoroughly the 1½ Tbsp sugar and arrowroot and sprinkle over milk-gelatin mixture and stir in with wire whip until thickened. Remove from heat, cool in pan of ice water. Add orange extract and chill in refrigerator until consistency of liquid honey. Do not allow to set firmly.

Whip cream until fairly stiff. Give the milk-gelatin mixture a good beating with a wire whip then fold in whipped cream. Now fold in the 1½ C drained whole cooked cranberries which you have reserved. Turn into a 6-cup mold and chill, covered, until firm.

At mealtime immerse mold in hot water 5 seconds. Then turn out onto a plate. Skim out about 20 cranberries from reserved sauce, drain well and place in a ring, like beads, around bottom edge of mold to decorate. When serving top generously with Sauce.

Maple Syrup Dumplings

1½ C maple syrup
1½ C water
1½ C stirred all-purpose flour
3 tsp baking powder
¾ tsp salt
3 Tbsp shortening
¾ C milk

Into the flour, baking powder and salt cut the shortening with a pastry blender until size of beans. Measure the milk.

Now combine the syrup and water and bring to gentle boil in a large flat-bottomed pot. Quickly stir milk into flour mixture. Dip silver tablespoon in hot syrup and pick up dough and drop into boiling syrup. As soon as all dough is added cover and reduce heat to simmer for about 12 minutes without removing lid. Serve immediately. Six servings.

Homemade Ice Creams

VANILLA: Stir over heat but do not boil ⅓ C sugar and ¼ C milk or water until sugar dissolves. Chill this mixture. Add 1½ tsp vanilla. Whip 1¼ C thoroughly chilled evaporated milk, using chilled bowl and beater. Combine it lightly with the sugar mixture. Freeze in a refrigerator tray.

CHOCOLATE MALLOW: Chill 1 C evaporated milk until it is icy cold and reserve it. Into top of double boiler shave 1½ squares bitter chocolate and add 1 C unchilled evaporated milk and 16 marshmallows. Cook over boiling water until blended. Remove from heat and add 1 tsp vanilla and chill. In ice cold bowl whip the 1 cup chilled evaporated milk until stiff, then fold into the chilled chocolate mixture. Pour at once into ice cold freezing trays and freeze.

LEMON: One 6-oz can evaporated milk, 2 eggs, separated, ½ C sugar, ⅓ C lemon juice, 1 Tbsp grated lemon rind. Pour milk into ice tray and chill until crystals start to form. Mix egg yolks with sugar, lemon juice and rind. Beat egg whites until stiff, then lightly mix in yolk mixture. Turn chilled milk into a bowl and beat until stiff. Fold into egg mixture and freeze.

Fresh Raspberry Ice Cream

2 C 18% cream
2 C 10% cream
¾ C sugar
1/16 tsp salt
2 C fresh raspberry pulp
    (sieved to remove seeds)
¼ C sugar (second amount)
½ tsp almond extract
½ tsp vanilla

In top of double boiler heat together the cream, sugar and salt until mixture shimmers. Remove and cool. Sprinkle the ¼ C sugar over the raspberry pulp. Add to the cooled creams. It may curdle but do not worry. Pour into freezer trays (or into crank-type freezer). If in freezer trays freeze until fairly firm at edges and mushy at center. Remove to chilled bowl and beat until smooth. Return to trays and freeze solid.

Spanish Cream

2 Tbsp gelatin
3 C whole milk
½ C sugar
¼ tsp salt
3 eggs separated
1 tsp vanilla

Soak the gelatin in ½ C of the milk. In the top of a double boiler heat 2½ C milk. When hot add 2 Tbsp of the sugar and the salt and the soaked gelatin and stir until the gelatin is dissolved. Remove from heat, and gradually pour over well-beaten egg yolks mixed with 2 Tbsp sugar, stirring constantly. Return to double boiler, and continue cooking over hot, not boiling, water until mixture coats a spoon (overcooking may cause mixture to curdle). Chill until of a thick, syrupy consistency. Then add the vanilla, and fold in frozen raspberries or any desired fruit or sauce.

Almond or Pecan Butterscotch Ice Cream

1¼ C light brown sugar
¼ C butter
1 C water
4 egg yolks
1 C 18% cream
One 1-lb can evaporated milk
¼ tsp salt
1½ tsp vanilla
1 C chopped toasted almonds or pecans

Put sugar and butter into a frying pan and heat slowly, stirring occasionally until sugar melts. Add water slowly (it will spatter) and stir and simmer about 5 minutes until caramel is evenly dissolved.

Beat yolks until light and pour hot syrup over them, beating quickly. Return to very low heat and stir continuously until mixture thickens slightly, 2 or 3 minutes. Remove from heat and cool.

Add cream, evaporated milk, salt and vanilla and toasted almonds or pecans. Mix well and chill. Turn into freezer can in crank freezer, pack all round with ice and salt: about 8 C finely chopped ice are required for each cup of salt. Turn crank slowly but continuously until too difficult to turn, when ice cream will be frozen and ready to serve.

Orange Cheese Dessert

1 envelope plain gelatin
¼ C cold water
One 8-oz pkg white cream cheese
    (room temperature)
¾ C granulated sugar
1 C lukewarm milk
½ C boiling water
One 6-oz can fresh frozen orange juice
    concentrate thawed and at room temperature
Fresh fruit in season or one 15-oz pkg fresh
    frozen fruit, thawed

In a 1-cup measure soften gelatin in the cold water. Meanwhile blend cream cheese and sugar in beater bowl. Gradually add lukewarm milk, beating to blend thoroughly.

Add boiling water to the 1-cup measure in which the gelatin is softening and stir until gelatin is thoroughly dissolved.

Add orange juice concentrate to cream cheese-sugar mixture and combine thoroughly. Stir in dissolved gelatin. Pour into a 6-cup mold and chill until firm, at least 3 hours. When serving, spoon fresh fruit over generously.

Meringues Glacées with Strawberries

1 C egg whites (about 6)
⅛ tsp salt
1 tsp vanilla
½ tsp red food coloring
2 C granulated sugar

Into beater bowl measure the egg white, salt, vanilla and red food coloring. Beat on high until very foamy and then start adding the sugar while still beating. Continue beating until whites are so stiff you can shape them into firm peaks. All sugar granules should be dissolved.

Grease cookie sheets and then sprinkle with cornstarch and shake off excess. Spoon large mounds—about 12—on to cookie sheets and make a deep indentation at center of each with moistened tablespoon to hold ice cream later. Smooth or peak up the rim attractively. Bake at 250° about 2 hours until dried out but not brown. Let cool on cake racks. To serve fill center with vanilla ice cream and top generously with halved strawberries.

Chocolate Pots De Crème

½ lb semi-sweet chocolate
¼ C hot water
1 C 18% cream
5 medium-large eggs (yolks and
    whites separated)
2 Tbsp butter
1 tsp vanilla
⅛ tsp salt
3 Tbsp chopped candied ginger (optional)
⅓ C chopped blanched almonds
Pouring cream

This is made in the double boiler. In double boiler melt the chocolate with hot water, mixing them together as soon as you can. Slowly add the cream stirring. Beat the egg yolks until thick, then stir them into the chocolate mixture cooking until it thickens, stirring all the time. Remove top of double boiler from bottom. Beat egg whites until they form soft peaks, then stir them into chocolate mixture, return to double boiler and cook over boiling water, stirring, until mixture thickens again. Remove from heat and stir in butter, vanilla and salt. Let cool just enough to safely turn them into 6 *pots de crème* pots or stemmed glasses or cut glass serving bowl. Chill.

At serving time sprinkle tops with chopped ginger (if used) and chopped almonds. Pass pouring cream.

Apple Strudel

3½ C sifted all-purpose flour
½ tsp salt
1 egg
1 Tbsp pure lard
1 Tbsp vinegar
½ C warm water
10 large apples
1 C sugar
½ lb raisins
½ tsp cinnamon

Sift flour and salt into bowl, make well in center and drop in egg and lard. Work flour into egg and lard gradually. Combine water and vinegar. Work liquid into flour mixture to make soft dough. Knead well and continue to work dough until it has lost all stickiness, about 10 minutes. Form into ball and dust with flour. Place in warm bowl covered, and let stand in warm temperature for about 30 minutes.

Spread out a clean cloth and dust with flour. Roll dough out on cloth as thinly as possible. Brush dough with a little melted lard. Continue to pull dough until paper thin. Brush again with melted lard. Peel and cut apples as finely as possible and mix with sugar, raisins and cinnamon. Spread over dough. Roll up like jelly roll then paint with yolk of egg. Grease a baking sheet. Cut roll into long pieces depending on size of sheet and bake 25 minutes at 400°. When cooked, cut into smaller pieces and serve hot or cold.

Cherries Jubilee

Two 14-oz cans unpitted black sweet cherries
½ C sugar
½ stick cinnamon
½ C sherry (or cherry wine)
3 Tbsp arrowroot flour (or cornstarch)
1 tsp cherry or almond flavoring
⅓ tsp red food coloring
Shake of salt
Two one-pint cartons best quality
    vanilla ice cream

Drain cherries. Measure juice. Boil down juice until you have 1½ C. Remove pits from cherries. To 1½ C hot cherry juice add the sugar and cinnamon and stir to dissolve sugar. Mix the arrowroot and cherry flavoring into the sherry (or cherry wine) until it forms a smooth paste and stir into the hot cherry juice over medium heat until thick and boiling. Stir over low heat 1 or 2 minutes longer. Remove from heat and add red food coloring, salt and drained cherries. Turn into chafing dish.

It is now ready for the final reheating. If desired reheat on stove and at dessert time carry to table boiling hot and place over chafing dish burner. Have ready at least 2 oz good quality brandy preheated until quite warm. Dip out some on a very large spoon, hold it over a candle flame until it boils and light it. Pour all remaining brandy over hot cherry sauce and ignite it with flaming brandy in spoon.

Baked Custard

3 C hot milk
4 medium eggs
6 Tbsp sugar
⅓ tsp salt
¼ tsp nutmeg
1 tsp vanilla
Nutmeg for sprinkling top

Scald milk by heating in saucepan until bubbles form around edge. In a bowl beat eggs until well blended then add sugar and salt and continue beating. Slowly add scalded milk while beating. Stir in vanilla and nutmeg.

Pour custard into 8 individual custard cups or into a 1-qt baking dish. Sprinkle sparingly with nutmeg. Stand custard cups or baking dish in shallow pan containing ¾″ hot water and bake at 350° for 40 minutes for individual cups, 50 minutes for single baking dish, or until custard is set and top is golden. To test, insert knife at center of custard. If it comes out clean custard is done.

Salzburger Nockerel

1 C apricot purée (2 jars
    baby food apricot purée)
Shake of salt
½ tsp almond extract
4 egg whites beaten stiff
½ C granulated sugar
⅛ tsp cream of tartar

Add the shake of salt and almond extract to the purée and let stand at room temperature while you beat the egg whites, sugar and cream of tartar together until very stiff. Fold in purée carefully and smoothly. Cover cookie sheet with foil, sprinkle sparingly with granulated sugar and arrange 6 mounds or log-shaped portions of soufflé parallel to each other and touching. This dividing of the soufflé makes serving easier. Bake in oven at 250° about ½ hour until baked through. Serve immediately.

Pour over BRANDY SAUCE: Beat ⅓ C butter with 1 C sugar until creamy. Beat in 1 egg well. Refrigerate. When soufflé is put in oven, stir ½ C brandy into sauce and put in double boiler and heat slowly over simmering water, stirring occasionally, while the soufflé bakes.

Creme De Menthe Parfait

⅔ C sugar
½ C hot water
1 tsp pure peppermint extract
3 egg whites
2 C whipping cream

Make a syrup of the sugar and water by boiling together for 5 minutes. Add peppermint extract. Pour slowly, beating, over stiffly beaten egg whites and beat until cold. Fold in stiffly beaten cream. Freeze in ice cube freezer trays.

Serve by spoonfuls in parfait glasses, spooning a little Creme de Menthe liqueur over each spoonful as you fill glasses. Top with a piece of glacé fruit such as green cherries.

Peach Cream Parfait

¼ C butter
½ C sugar (first amount)
1 egg
1 C whipping cream
2 C sliced peaches
1 Tbsp lemon juice
2 Tbsp sugar (second amount)
2 Tbsp ginger marmalade or finely
    chopped preserved ginger
¾ to 1 C fine arrowroot cracker crumbs

In top of double boiler mix together the butter, sugar and egg and cook, stirring, over boiling water until thick. Cover and cook 10 minutes stirring once or twice. Chill.

Pour boiling water over the peaches and let stand 1 minute then drain and chill with cold water. Drain again. Peel peaches, cut them in halves, remove pits and slice into bowl, slicing each peach into about 10 crescents. Mix with the lemon juice, 2 Tbsp sugar and ginger marmalade or chopped ginger.

Whip cream until stiff and fold into chilled cream mixture. Into bottom of each of 6 parfait glasses spoon some cream mixture. Add 2 or 3 juicy peach slices, then a heaping teaspoon of crumbs. Repeat until you come to top of glass ending with cream mixture. Top each with 1 peach slice for garnish. Serves six.

Apple Pudding

BASE
6 medium apples
¼ C brown sugar

BISCUITS
1 C stirred but unsifted all-purpose flour
2 tsp baking powder
¼ tsp salt
1½ Tbsp shortening
⅓ C milk

TOPPING
¼ C fresh frozen orange juice concentrate
½ C granulated sugar

Wash, pare, core and slice apples into a shallow baking dish. Sprinkle with brown sugar. Bake at 350° for 35 to 40 minutes or until apples are tender.

Meanwhile make Biscuits by sifting together the flour, baking powder and salt and cutting into them the shortening until size of peas. Stir in milk. Shape into ball between palms, flatten to ½″ thickness on floured board and cut out with 1¼″ cutter.

When apples are tender and while still hot, cover them with cut-out biscuits. Raise oven temperature to 425° and return dish to oven and bake 10 minutes or until biscuits are done. Meanwhile stir together the fresh frozen orange juice concentrate and granulated sugar. Remove the pudding from oven and brush biscuit tops with orange syrup using all of it. Return to oven for about 2 minutes. Serves four.

Blueberry Pudding

BASE
One 11-oz pkg fresh or fresh frozen blueberries
2 Tbsp lemon juice

BATTER
½ C margarine (room temperature)
½ C brown sugar (first amount)
1½ C whole wheat flour
5 tsp baking powder
1 C milk

TOPPING
¾ C brown sugar (second amount)
1 Tbsp whole wheat flour
1 C boiling water

Into a 9 × 9″ pan tip the blueberries and spread to make level. Sprinkle lemon juice over evenly.

To make Batter, beat together the margarine and ½ C brown sugar (first amount) until creamy then beat in the whole wheat flour, baking powder and milk until blended. Spread batter evenly over blueberries in pan.

To make Topping, mix ¾ C brown sugar (second amount) with the 1 Tbsp whole wheat flour and sprinkle evenly over top. Slowly pour boiling water all over top. Bake at 350° for 45 minutes. *Note:* If using fresh blueberries sprinkle with ¼ C sugar before covering with batter. Serves six.

Scotch Apple Crisp

6 C pared sliced cooking apples, packed
1 tsp cinnamon
½ tsp salt
½ C water
1 Tbsp lemon juice
1 C flour
1 C quick-cooking rolled oats
⅔ C margarine
1½ C light brown sugar

Wash, pare, core, slice and measure apples. Tip into large baking dish. Sprinkle with salt and cinnamon. Pour water in at one side. Drizzle with lemon juice.

Into a large bowl measure the flour, sugar and oats and mix them. With pastry blender cut in the margarine until size of peas. Turn out over apples and pat down firmly. Bake at 350° for 1 hour. Serves eight.

Plain Bread Pudding

2 C hot milk
1 C breadcrumbs
1 egg
2 to 4 Tbsp sugar
¼ tsp salt
2 Tbsp butter
½ C raisins
½ tsp vanilla

Add crumbs to milk and let stand until very soft. Beat egg slightly, add sugar, salt and milk-crumb mixture. Beat until smooth. Add raisins, butter and vanilla. Pour into medium-sized buttered baking dish. Stand in shallow pan of hot water and bake until firm, about 1 hour at 325°.

Special Apple Crisp

3½ C pared and cored tart apples
    cut up, packed
¼ C brown sugar (first amount)
2 tsp lemon juice
¾ C all-purpose flour
½ C brown sugar (second amount)
¼ C wheat germ
½ tsp cinnamon
¼ tsp salt
¼ tsp nutmeg
6 Tbsp hard margarine
½ C coarsely chopped walnuts

Into a bowl measure the apples, ¼ C brown sugar and lemon juice and mix well. Turn into an 8″ shallow baking dish.

Into another bowl measure the flour, ½ C brown sugar, wheat germ, spices and salt. Mix. Then cut in the margarine with a pastry blender until size of peas. Stir in walnuts. Pat this mixture down hard over apples and bake at 350° about 40 to 45 minutes. Serve warm or cold with rich milk, ice cream or sour cream. Serves five.

Queen's Pudding

Make Plain Bread Pudding but use 2 egg yolks instead of one. Then reserve the 2 leftover egg whites to make meringue by adding 4 Tbsp sugar to them and beating until stiff. When bread pudding is baked, spread top with ½ C red jelly or jam then carefully cover with meringue and return to oven at lowered temperature of 275° and bake until meringue is tinged with gold.

Royal Rhubarb Pudding

BASE
2 C diced pink rhubarb, packed
⅔ C sugar
3 Tbsp freshly grated orange rind
1 tsp cinnamon

DOUGH
1 C less 1 Tbsp stirred but unsifted
    all-purpose flour
2 tsp baking powder
2 Tbsp sugar
½ tsp salt
¼ C hard butter
1 egg
3 Tbsp milk

TOPPING
4 Tbsp orange juice
2 Tbsp sugar

Into a medium-sized shallow baking dish measure the rhubarb, ⅔ C sugar, orange rind and cinnamon. Carefully mix.

To make the Dough, sift together into a bowl the flour, baking powder, sugar and salt. With pastry blender cut in hard butter until it looks like coarse meal. Beat egg and milk together and add to dry ingredients. Drop by tablespoonfuls all over rhubarb mixture in baking dish and spread a bit. Bake at 350° for 25 minutes then drizzle all over it the orange juice and 2 Tbsp sugar mixed together. Bake 5 minutes longer. Serve warm.

Hasty Apple Pudding

4 C cooking apples sliced and packed
2 Tbsp sugar (first amount)
½ tsp cinnamon
¼ tsp nutmeg
2 Tbsp hot melted butter (first amount)
¼ C hot water

BATTER
2 eggs
1 C granulated sugar (second amount)
⅔ C unsifted all-purpose flour
2 tsp baking powder
½ tsp salt
¼ C melted butter (second amount)

Turn sliced apples into 9″ baking dish. Sprinkle over them the 2 Tbsp sugar and the spices. Pour over the 2 Tbsp melted butter and hot water.

In beater bowl measure the eggs and 1 C sugar and beat. Add flour, baking powder, salt and the ¼ C melted butter and beat until smooth. Spread evenly over apples in baking dish. Bake at 350° for 30 minutes. Serves six.

Old-Fashioned Baked Rice Pudding

4 C milk
½ C granulated sugar
¼ C raw white rice
2 Tbsp butter or margarine
¼ tsp salt
¼ tsp nutmeg
1 tsp vanilla

Combine all ingredients and pour into a buttered medium-large baking dish. Bake uncovered at 325° for 2½ hours, or until rice is tender, stirring frequently. Chill until slightly warm and serve with or without cream. *Note:* For a thicker pudding increase rice to 6 or 8 Tbsp. If desired, ½ C raisins may be stirred in 1½ hours before pudding is done. Serves four to six.

Lemon Cake Pudding

2 Tbsp softened butter or margarine
1 C sugar
4 Tbsp flour
¼ tsp salt
5 Tbsp lemon juice
Grated rind of 1 lemon
3 egg yolks
1½ C milk
3 egg whites

Make plain pastry for a 9″ pie and line pie plate.

Cream butter or margarine with sugar. Add flour, salt, lemon juice, and rind and stir until ingredients are thoroughly blended. Add the well-beaten egg yolks, which have been mixed with the milk. Lastly fold in carefully the stiffly beaten egg whites. Pour into unbaked pastry-lined pie plate. Bake at 425° for 10 minutes, then reduce heat to 325° for 25 to 30 minutes.

Self-Saucing Pumpkin Pudding

½ C butter or margarine (room temperature)
⅓ C brown sugar, packed
1 egg
⅔ C canned pumpkin
1 C unsifted all-purpose flour
1 Tbsp baking powder
½ tsp salt
½ tsp cinnamon
¼ tsp nutmeg
⅛ tsp cloves
¼ C raisins

SAUCE
1 C brown sugar
1 Tbsp butter
1⅔ C boiling water
½ C orange juice

To make Batter, in beater bowl cream together the butter and sugar. Beat in egg and pumpkin and blend well. In a small bowl stir together the flour, baking powder, salt, cinnamon, nutmeg and cloves, then add to pumpkin mixture and combine thoroughly. Stir in raisins. Spoon batter into a buttered 2-qt casserole. You must have room enough on top for the sauce.

To make Sauce, sprinkle the batter with the 1 C brown sugar and dot with the butter. Mix together the boiling water and orange juice and pour slowly and evenly all over top. Do not mix in. Bake at 325° for 1 hour. Serve hot, spooning some sauce over each serving.

Self-Saucing Butterscotch Pudding

BATTER
1 C unsifted all-purpose flour
2 tsp baking powder
¾ C light brown sugar
1 C raisins
½ tsp salt
1 tsp vanilla
½ C milk
1 pared apple shredded (divided, see below)

SAUCE
¾ C light brown sugar
¼ tsp nutmeg
½ tsp cinnamon
¼ C butter or margarine
2 C boiling water
Shredded apple (from Batter ingredients)

To make Batter, in a large baking dish combine the flour, baking powder, sugar, raisins and salt. Stir in the milk and vanilla and half of the apple which should be shredded in at the last minute. Stir until smooth.

To make Sauce, in a medium bowl blend well the sugar and spices. Drop in the butter then pour over it the boiling water and stir until butter is melted. Stir in second half of apple shredded at the last minute. Pour this sauce over the batter evenly but do not mix. The sauce rests on top of the batter. Bake uncovered at 375° for 30 minutes. Serve warm. Four servings.

Plumb Good

¾ C cooking oil
¾ C sugar (first amount)
3 eggs
1½ C sifted all-purpose flour
3 tsp baking powder
½ tsp salt
6 Red Lombard plums (1½" diameter)
½ C sugar (second amount)
2 tsp cinnamon

Into beater bowl measure the oil, sugar and eggs and beat until thoroughly blended. Sift together the flour, baking powder and salt and add all at once to the creamed mixture and beat for 2 minutes. Pour about ⅔ of the batter into well buttered 9 × 9" pan. Cover with drained sliced ripe plums. Mix together the ½ C sugar and the cinnamon and measure out 2 Tbsp and reserve. Sprinkle remaining sugar-cinnamon mixture evenly over plums. Carefully cover with remaining batter. Sprinkle top with reserved sugar-cinnamon mixture. Bake at 350° for 40 minutes. Test batter by lifting up a tiny section of crust with tip of knife at top center to be sure it is baked through before removing from oven. Serve warm or cold cut in squares, adding, if desired, cream or sour cream.

Self-Saucing Cherry Pudding

One 19-oz can cherries (45% syrup) drained
(reserve liquid)

BATTER

¾ C granulated sugar
2 Tbsp margarine or butter (room temperature)
½ C milk
1 C unsifted all-purpose flour
2 tsp baking powder
¼ tsp salt

TOPPING

¼ C granulated sugar
2½ Tbsp flour
Juice from canned drained cherries (above)
Water (see below)
20 drops red food coloring

Drain cherries, reserving liquid and spread them evenly in bottom of a deep 9 × 9" greased baking dish.

To prepare Batter, in mixing bowl cream together the sugar and margarine or butter until well blended then stir in milk. Over the creamed mixture sift together the flour, baking powder and salt and combine thoroughly until smooth. Spread batter evenly over cherries.

To make Topping, in a small bowl mix together thoroughly the sugar and flour. Sprinkle it evenly over top of batter. Pour reserved cherry liquid in a 2-cup measure and add enough water to make liquid up to 1½ C. Heat this liquid until boiling then remove from heat and stir in red food coloring. Now, slowly, with a back and forth motion, pour the liquid all over top. Bake at 350° for 45 minutes. Serves six.

Self-Saucing Lemon Pudding

BATTER

¾ C sugar
2 Tbsp margarine or butter
(room temperature)
½ C milk
1 C unsifted all-purpose flour
2 tsp baking powder
¼ tsp salt
½ C chopped walnuts (optional)
3 lemons, grated rind and juice
(divided, see below)

TOPPING

1 C sugar
2½ Tbsp flour
Lemon rind (see below)
Lemon juice (see below)
Boiling water (see below)
6 drops yellow food coloring

To make Batter, in mixing bowl cream together the sugar and margarine or butter until well blended then stir in the milk. Over the creamed mixture sift together the flour, baking powder and salt and combine thoroughly until batter is smooth. Stir in walnuts (if used) and grated rind of two of the lemons, reserving the third. Turn batter evenly into a greased 8 × 8" pan.

To make Topping, in a small bowl mix together thoroughly the sugar, flour and rind of the third lemon. Sprinkle it evenly over top of batter. Squeeze the juice of the 3 lemons into a cup. Strain and measure in a 2-cup measure. Add boiling water to bring liquid up to 1½ cup mark. Stir in 6 drops yellow food coloring. Now slowly, with a back and forth motion, pour the liquid all over top. Bake at 350° for 35 to 40 minuites. Serves six.

Mandarin Self-Saucing Pudding

BATTER

1 C unsifted all-purpose flour
2 tsp baking powder
2 tsp sugar
¼ tsp salt
2 Tbsp oil
One 10-oz can Mandarin oranges
1 tsp lemon extract (or 1 Tbsp
lemon juice)

TOPPING

⅔ C sugar
1½ C boiling water
2 Tbsp margarine

To prepare Batter, into a medium bowl measure in order the flour, baking powder, sugar, salt, oil, can of Mandarin oranges including syrup and lemon extract or juice. Stir it a minimum number of times to blend. Do not overstir. Turn into a buttered shallow casserole.

Mix together Topping ingredients and pour hot over batter. Immediately bake at 375° for 40 minutes and serve warm. Four to six servings.

Steamed Pumpkin Pudding

½ C shortening
1 C brown sugar (lightly packed)
2 eggs
⅔ C milk
1 C canned pumpkin
3 Tbsp molasses
1⅓ C stirred but unsifted all-purpose flour
1 tsp salt
1 tsp baking powder
1 tsp cinnamon
½ tsp nutmeg
¾ C coarsely chopped walnuts

Into beater bowl measure shortening and brown sugar and beat until creamy, then beat in eggs. With beaters on low add milk, pumpkin, molasses, flour, salt, baking powder, spices, scraping down sides of bowl with rubber scraper when all ingredients are in. Lift beaters and fold in nuts. Turn into a 6-cup foil-lined or non-stick mold and cover with lid or foil tied on with string. Lower into kettle containing boiling water to come half way up sides of mold. Cover and steam 2½ hours. Unmold onto serving plate and serve with Hot Lemon-Nutmeg Sauce (see Sauces). Eight servings.

Self-Saucing Chocolate Pudding

PUDDING
½ C broken nuts
1 square unsweetened chocolate
2 Tbsp butter
1 C sifted all-purpose flour
2½ tsp baking powder
¾ C sugar
¼ tsp salt
½ C milk
1 tsp vanilla

TOPPING
¾ C sugar
¼ C moist brown sugar
2 Tbsp cocoa
1 C cold water
Whipping cream

To make Pudding, put chocolate and butter into shallow glass custard cup; set in pan of hot water. When melted, stir until smooth and cool. Sift flour, measure and resift with baking powder, sugar and salt into a large mixing bowl. Stir in milk thoroughly. Add vanilla, then chocolate mixture, beating until smooth. Stir in nuts and turn into buttered 8 × 8″ pan.

To make Topping, quickly blend sugars with cocoa and sift evenly all over batter. Pour cold water gently and evenly all over the top. Do not stir. Bake 40 to 50 minutes at 350°. Remove to rack to cool to lukewarm. Spoon into serving dishes and serve with whipped or plain cream. Six to eight servings.

Not-So-Rich Steamed Date Pudding

1 C brown sugar
¼ C margarine
1 egg
½ tsp vanilla
1 tsp rum or brandy extract (optional)
1¼ C unsifted all-purpose flour
1 Tbsp baking powder
1 C milk
1 C chopped dates
Grated rind 1 lemon
1 C shredded (¼″) carrot, lightly packed
½ tsp nutmeg
½ tsp cinnamon

Into beater bowl measure the margarine and sugar and beat 2 or 3 minutes. With beaters on low add egg, vanilla, rum or brandy extract (if used), flour, baking powder, milk, dates, lemon rind, shredded carrot and spices and beat just to mix, scraping down sides with rubber scraper to be sure all ingredients in bottom are mixed through.

Generously butter a bowl 4″ deep by 6″ diameter and turn pudding into it. (It must be generously greased on bottom to ease turning out.) Cover with foil and tie it on. Stand bowl in large pot half-filled with boiling water. Put lid on and steam 2 hours on low heat. Cool and store in refrigerator.

To reheat stand in pot half-filled with hot water and heat covered for 1 hour, then loosen sides with knife and turn out on platter. If desired, serve with ⅓ C preheated brandy. Serves ten.

Sago Pudding

Soak ¼ C sago 2 hours in top of double boiler in 2 C water. Drain. Add 2¼ C milk and cook in double boiler covered for 30 minutes. Beat 2 eggs with ⅓ C sugar and 1 tsp vanilla and stir into sago-milk mixture. Cover and cook 30 minutes longer stirring once. Serves four to six.

Steamed Carrot Pudding

1½ C shredded carrots (softly packed)
1 C shredded scrubbed unpared potatoes
1 C sugar
½ C shortening (room temperature)
1½ C stirred but unsifted all-purpose flour
¾ tsp salt
1½ tsp baking soda
½ tsp cinnamon
½ C hot water
1¼ C chopped dates
1 C currants
1 C whole blanched almonds

Measure all ingredients into a large bowl in order given and mix well. Grease earthenware or pyrex bowl and line it with four 3″ broad strips of doubled foil criss-crossed. (This is to ease removal as this pudding wants to stick.) Turn in pudding mixture, smooth top, cover with heavy foil and tie it down with string. Place rack on bottom of steamer or large pot, add 1″ boiling water, lower pudding into pot, cover and bring to boil. Turn heat down and simmer 2½ hours. This pudding should be made at least 1 week in advance of serving and reheated for 1 hour in the way it was first steamed. Serve with Hot Lemon-Nutmeg Sauce (see Sauces). Eight servings.

Orange and Raisin Steamed Pudding

⅓ C orange juice (1 large orange)
Rind of 1 orange
1¼ C Sultana raisins
1⅓ C sifted all-purpose flour
½ tsp baking soda
1 tsp baking powder
¼ tsp salt
1 C well-packed light brown sugar
¼ C soft butter
¼ C soft shortening
1 egg
1 C coarsely crushed bran flakes
½ C buttermilk (or sour milk)

Squeeze orange and measure juice. Put the rind and the raisins through food chopper. Force all of rind through the knife by following it with a slice of stale bread. (If a few crumbs of bread sneak into the mixture it does no harm.) Into large mixing bowl sift together the sifted flour, baking soda, baking powder and salt. Make a well in center and add sugar, butter, shortening, egg and orange juice and beat until smooth. Add orange rind and raisin mixture. Add crushed bran flakes alternately with the buttermilk or sour milk and stir until blended. Turn into buttered 1-qt mold. Cover snugly with foil or heavy greased brown paper tied on and steam 2 hours. *Note:* If to be stored, remove pudding from aluminum mold, if used, and wrap in foil, then one hour before serving reheat in mold.

Serve with SAUCE SUPREME: Cream ¼ C soft butter and ⅔ C sifted icing sugar. Add 1 egg, ½ tsp vanilla and dash of salt and beat thoroughly. Fold in ½ pint of whipped cream. Serves ten.

Steamed Plum Pudding

1 C orange juice or red wine or brandy
1½ lb dark raisins
¼ C diced mixed peel
1 C ground or finely chopped beef suet
1½ C fine breadcrumbs
1 C all-purpose flour
1 tsp salt
1 tsp cinnamon
½ tsp cloves
½ tsp allspice
½ C sugar
3 eggs, beaten
1 C light molasses (or ½ C each dark molasses and corn syrup)
3 medium apples, unpared, cored and shredded (about 2 C)
Grated rind of 1 lemon
1 C chopped walnuts

In a large bowl soak together overnight the raisins and mixed peel in the orange juice or wine or brandy, covered.

In a large bowl combine the ground or chopped suet and breadcrumbs. Sift the flour, cinnamon, allspice, cloves, salt and sugar over the suet-breadcrumb mixture and blend well.

Mix until thoroughly blended the eggs and molasses. Pour this into the dry mixture and blend thoroughly.

Hold the grater over the fruit bowl while shredding the apples and lemon. Add the chopped nuts and blend all fruits thoroughly and add to batter.

Lightly grease a 3-qt casserole or two 1½-qt casseroles. Do not use aluminum molds. Line with 2 wide buttered strips of foil to ease removal. Fill mold (or molds) ¾ full with pudding mixture. Place foil over top and cover this with lid or a piece of cotton tied securely with string. Boil water in a large preserving kettle, lower pudding in, having water come half way up sides. Cover kettle. Simmer at a constant temperature over low heat for 4½ hours if you use two 1½-qt molds or 6 hours for one large 3-qt mold. When done, lift mold or molds onto wire rack, remove top foil and cool completely. Turn over and out and remove bottom foil strips. Return pudding to bowl, cover well and refrigerate until needed. To reheat lower into steamer and steam 1 hour, covered. Serve with Lemon Sauce. Twelve to sixteen servings.

LEMON SAUCE: Mix together well in heavy saucepan 3 Tbsp cornstarch, ⅓ C brown sugar, ½ C granulated sugar and ¼ tsp salt. Stir in 1¾ C boiling water, cooking until thickened. Then cook stirring 2 or 3 minutes longer. Remove from heat and add ¼ C lemon juice and 2 Tbsp butter.

Lemon Cream Rice Pudding

½ C raw long grain rice
3 C milk
⅓ C sugar (first amount)
¼ tsp salt
Juice and grated rind 1 large lemon
2 eggs, yolks and whites separated
2 Tbsp sugar (second amount)

In double boiler stir together raw rice, milk, ⅓ C sugar and salt. Cook over boiling water, covered, until tender, about 45 minutes.

Meanwhile grate rind from lemon then cut it in halves and squeeze out juice. Combine rind, juice and egg yolks.

Remove tender rice mixture from heat and spoon some of the hot mixture into egg yolk mixture and stir. Return to pot and cook, stirring, 1 or 2 minutes longer. Remove from heat and cool.

In a bowl beat whites until foamy then add the 2 Tbsp sugar and beat until stiff. Now you have 2 choices: 1. Fold whites into rice mixture and pour into serving dishes, sprinkle with nutmeg, chill and serve. 2. Pour rice mixture into baking dish and top with meringue and bake at 375° until tinged with gold and serve hot.

Stuffed Prunes Dorchester

Soak 1 lb medium prunes in 3 C freshly brewed tea or coffee for 4 to 7 days, covered, in the refrigerator. Neatly remove pits. Fill each prune with a piece of almond paste (see below) and push into this a toasted almond. Close prunes neatly and place in a glass bowl in neat circles. Pour over 1 C port wine or sherry. Let stand so they will absorb some of the flavor. Serve with fresh dairy sour cream or Devonshire cream and a plate of ladyfingers.

ALMOND PASTE
¼ lb dry blanched almonds
   (or ready-ground almonds)
½ lb icing sugar (2⅓ C when sifted)
⅛ tsp salt
1 large egg yolk
1 tsp pure almond extract
1 tsp rosewater (optional)

Force almonds through fine nut knife of food grinder, twice, easing them through by adding the rosewater if used. Mix with the remaining ingredients then turn the mass out on icing-sugar-sprinkled board and knead until pliable and smooth. Form into a ball, wrap well and store in open-mouthed jar, covered, to ripen for 24 hours before using.

Creamy Top-of-Stove Rice Pudding

½ C raw long grain rice
1¼ C boiling water
¾ tsp salt (first amount)
½ C sugar
6 Tbsp flour
⅜ tsp salt (second amount)
2½ C milk
3 large egg yolks, slightly beaten
1½ tsp vanilla
1 C raisins, plumped (see below)
⅛ tsp nutmeg
⅛ tsp cinnamon

In pot with tight-fitting lid bring the 1¼ C water to a boil with the ¾ tsp salt. Add raw rice and give several stirs. Cover, reduce heat and simmer covered for 30 minutes until tender.

Plump raisins by covering them with boiling water for 10 minutes then drain thoroughly.

Meanwhile, in top of double boiler thoroughly combine sugar, flour and the ⅜ tsp salt. Stir in milk slowly so that there are no lumps. Cook, stir-ring constantly until thickened. Add a small amount of the cooked mixture to the egg yolks then return all to double boiler. Cook, stirring, for another 10 minutes. Remove from heat and stir in cooked rice, vanilla, raisins, nutmeg and cinnamon. Pour into a serving bowl, sprinkle lightly with cinnamon and let cool before refrigerating. Serves six.

Cornstarch Pudding with Black Cherry Sauce

PUDDING
3 C milk (first amount)
6 Tbsp cornstarch
3 Tbsp sugar
1/6 tsp salt
1/3 C milk (second amount)
3/4 tsp vanilla

CHERRY SAUCE
3 C pitted black cherries
1/2 C water
2/3 C sugar
5 tsp arrowroot flour (or cornstarch)
1/2 tsp red food coloring
2 tsp lemon juice
1/2 tsp almond extract

To make Pudding, heat the 3 C milk in top of double boiler over boiling water. In a bowl mix together the cornstarch, sugar and salt then stir in the 1/3 C (cold) milk to make a smooth paste. Stir this into the hot milk until thick. Cover and cook 20 minutes, stirring 2 or 3 times. Remove from heat and stir in vanilla. As soon as it cools a little pour into stemmed glasses and chill.

To make Sauce, mix together the sugar and arrowroot flour (or cornstarch) then add water and stir to a smooth paste. Cook stirring until thick. Add pitted cherries and cover and simmer 10 to 12 minutes until cherries are barely cooked. Remove from heat and add food coloring, lemon juice and almond extract. Chill. Serve over pudding.

Fruited Lemon Snow

1 C sugar
2 C boiling water
1/4 C cornstarch
1/4 C cold water
1/4 C lemon juice
3 large or 4 medium egg whites
Fruit: choice of ripe papaya, sliced bananas, drained canned peaches, apricots, pitted black cherries, etc.

In medium pot stir together the sugar and boiling water and bring to boil. Stir cornstarch with cold water together to a smooth paste. Reduce heat under the boiling syrup and stir cornstarch paste into it until thick. Remove from heat and cool a little then stir in lemon juice.

Beat egg whites until stiff and fold in. Spoon some into your stemmed glasses to half fill. Cover generously with fruit of your choice then fill to brim, piling up in a mound. Sprinkle with grated lemon rind and chill. Serves five or six.

Apricot Steamed Pudding

PUDDING
1 2/3 C fine graham cracker crumbs
1/2 C melted butter or margarine
1 3/4 C chopped dried apricots
1 C milk
2 large eggs
1 1/2 C unsifted all-purpose flour
2 1/2 tsp baking powder
1 C sugar
1 tsp nutmeg
1 tsp cinnamon
1/2 tsp salt

APRICOT SAUCE
1/3 C dried apricots
2 1/2 C water (divided, see below)
3/4 C sugar (divided, see below)

To make Pudding, in large bowl combine the graham crumbs with the melted butter. Stir in chopped apricots. Add milk and eggs and combine thoroughly. Mix in flour, baking powder, sugar, nutmeg, cinnamon and salt until well blended. Spoon into lightly oiled 2-qt mold and smooth top. Cover tightly with a double layer of heavy aluminum foil, tie snugly with string and place mold on rack in deep kettle. Add boiling water to come half way up sides of mold. Bring to boil, reduce heat to simmer and steam, covered, 2 1/2 hours. Replenish water if necessary. Turn out by running knife around edges to loosen. If to be stored, let cool in mold then remove and wrap and refrigerate. To reheat, return to mold, cover with foil and steam as above for about 1 hour. Serves twelve.

Serve with Apricot Sauce: In pot combine apricots, 1 C of the water and 1/2 C of the sugar. Bring to boil, cover, reduce heat and simmer covered, 30 minutes. Let cool then purée apricots and juice in blender. Return to pot and add remaining 1 1/2 C water and 1/4 C sugar, stirring thoroughly. Reheat to serve over pudding.

Rosy Apple Rings

4 firm red cooking apples
1/2 C sugar
1 C hot water
One 1" stick cinnamon
1 tsp red food coloring

Stir together in shallow saucepan or frying pan the sugar, water, cinnamon stick and food coloring. Place over low heat to melt sugar while you prepare apples. Wash apples and cut into halves crosswise. Remove cores, making an apple ring. Turn heat up to high under syrup and drop in the 8 apple rings, bring to boil again, reduce heat to simmer and cover. Cook about 5 to 7 minutes. They should still be crisp. Remove from heat at once. Let stand, covered, until tender enough to pierce with fork tines and cool by standing pan in larger pan of cold water. When ready to serve carefully lift out with slotted spoon and use for garnish on platter of roast pork or ham or chops.

Apple Tapioca with Brown Sugar Hard Sauce

⅓ C quick-cooking tapioca (see note below)
½ C sugar
¼ tsp salt
2 C boiling water
4 medium apples

BROWN SUGAR HARD SAUCE
¼ C butter or margarine
¾ C light brown sugar
2 Tbsp cream
½ Tbsp vanilla (or 1 Tbsp sherry or brandy)
Nutmeg (see below)

Note: If desired ½ C pearl tapioca may be soaked in 1 C water overnight and used instead of the minute tapioca. Add only 1 C of the water required in the recipe and cook in top of double boiler 3 hours using same amounts of sugar and salt.

To make Apple Tapioca, in the top of the double boiler stir together the tapioca, sugar and salt and when they are mixed stir in 2 C boiling water over direct heat until boiling. Transfer to double boiler and cook covered for about 10 minutes or until tapioca is clear. Pare and core 4 medium apples and cut into quarters. Gently cook them in about ½″ of boiling water until barely tender. Drain and add to cooked tapioca, gently stirring them in.

To make Brown Sugar Hard Sauce: Cream butter or margarine and gradually beat into it the brown sugar until smooth. Add cream, beating, then add vanilla or sherry or brandy and blend in. Arrange in serving dish, score with fork, sprinkle with nutmeg and chill until hard. Serve hard and cold on hot pudding.

Hot Fruit Compote

One 14-oz can Bartlett pears
One 14-oz can peach halves
One 14-oz can plums
½ C fresh frozen orange juice
    concentrate (undiluted)
1 stick cinnamon
2 seedless oranges, peeled and sectioned
½ tsp almond flavoring
½ C blanched almonds (optional)
2 oz Kirsch (optional)

Drain the syrup from the canned fruits. Pit the plums. In a pot mix the peach and pear syrup with the orange juice concentrate and cinnamon stick. Use the plum juice for another purpose: it darkens the syrup and stains the pale pear halves.

Bring juices with cinnamon stick to boil, reduce heat and add the 3 fruits and simmer 5 minutes. Remove from heat and add orange sections, almond extract, almonds and Kirsch (if used). Leave cinnamon stick in. Serve hot. Ten servings.

Fresh Fruits in Watermelon Shell

Select a medium-sized watermelon. (If desired, a wide handle of green rind may be left on top when you cut away the top slice, to make it look like a basket.)

With long-bladed sharp strong knife cut a quarter of the watermelon off, a slice from the long side which leaves ¾ of the watermelon intact. Using a melon ball cutter, scoop out as many melon balls as you can. Discard seeds and reserve ragged cutouts of melon for a fruit cup for a family meal later. Scrape out most of the pink flesh but leave a pink lining about ½″ thick. Drain watermelon shell. Combine watermelon balls with other fresh fruits in season: strawberries, raspberries, blueberries, cantaloupe balls, grapefruit and orange sections, etc. Add a 20-oz can of pineapple tidbits, juice and all. Sweeten sparingly with fruit sugar, gently mix and fill watermelon shell to the brim. Chill well before serving garnished with tiny sprigs of mint. Serves sixteen.

Nesselrode Pudding

3 Tbsp chopped maraschino cherries
2 Tbsp drained crushed pineapple
2 Tbsp chopped blanched almonds
1 Tbsp shaved candied ginger (optional)
¼ C sugar
⅓ C water
2 tsp rum extract
1 Tbsp gelatin
¼ C cold water
1⅓ C milk
¼ C sugar
¼ C seedless raisins
2 egg yolks
¼ tsp salt
½ tsp vanilla
1 C whipping cream

Combine cherries, pineapple, almonds, ginger (if used), sugar and the ⅓ C water and simmer 5 minutes. Remove from heat and add rum extract. Soak gelatin in the ¼ C cold water for 5 minutes. Put milk, sugar and raisins in top of double boiler and heat to scalding. Beat egg yolks, add some of the hot milk, stir well then return to double boiler and continue cooking and stirring until mixture coats a metal spoon. Remove from heat and add salt and soaked gelatin, stirring until gelatin dissolves. Add cooked fruit mixture to gelatin mixture with vanilla. Stand in pan of cold water to cool to consistency of soft jelly with occasional gentle stirring.

Beat cream until stiff, then cut and fold gelatin mixture lightly but thoroughly through it. Turn into pudding mold—a melon shape is traditional—of 6-cup size, rinsed in cold water. Cover and chill until set. Unmold on serving dish. This is often garnished with macaroons. Six to eight servings.

Caramel Floating Island

CUSTARD
2 C milk, scalded
3 eggs
2 egg yolks (reserve whites for meringues)
¼ C sugar
1 tsp vanilla

MERINGUES
2 egg whites (leftover from Custard)
Dash of salt
¼ C sugar

CARAMEL
½ C sugar
2 Tbsp boiling water

To make Custard, scald milk. Beat eggs, egg yolks, sugar and vanilla together. (*Note:* Disregard the rule for adding vanilla after cooking, for it may curdle the custard if added last.) Gradually stir in hot milk. Cook stirring until it thickens. Immediately pour into shallow serving dish or 6 stemmed glasses. Chill.

To make Meringues, beat reserved egg whites until softly stiff. Add sugar and dash of salt and beat until very stiff. Have a broad panful of simmering water ready and spoon meringues onto it in 6 even puffs. Simmer, uncovered, 5 minutes until set. Skim out and drain on paper towels. Carefully transfer to top of custard on slotted egg lifter.

At serving time make Caramel by melting sugar in heavy pan, stirring constantly until it melts and turns amber color. Remove from heat and carefully add boiling water (it will spatter) and stir until blended. Carefully drizzle over meringues and serve. Six servings.

Hot Fruit Soufflé

¼ C flour
3 Tbsp butter
¾ C milk
6-oz puréed fruit (¾ C apricot, peach,
    applesauce, raspberry, plum
2 Tbsp lemon juice
3 Tbsp sugar
¼ tsp salt
4 eggs, separated
2 Tbsp sugar

Melt butter, blend in flour, then milk. Stir over medium heat until thick, then add puréed fruit, lemon juice and sugar. Beat 4 egg yolks until thick, add a little of the hot mixture and return the whole to top of double boiler and cook stirring until yolks have thickened a little. Set aside to cool.

Beat 4 egg whites, add 2 Tbsp sugar and beat very stiff. Fold the two mixtures together. Pour into well-buttered baking dish and bake 30 to 40 minutes at 350°. Serve hot on hot plates with hot fruit sauce.

HOT FRUIT SAUCE: To 1 C juice from canned fruit—apricots, peaches, etc.—add 1½ tsp lemon juice and heat in top of double boiler. Mix 1 Tbsp arrowroot with 1 Tbsp water and stir into hot juice until thick (buy arrowroot at the drug store but if not available use cornstarch.) Serve over hot soufflé. If desired, add rum flavoring.

Pink Applesauce (large amount)

25 medium-small Macs, Spys or
    Wealthies (2¼″ diameter)
1½ C water
2 C granulated sugar

Wash apples but do not pare. Cut into quarters. Put into large preserving kettle. (You will have skins, seeds, cores and even stems in the pot.) Add the water and sugar and stir to blend. Bring to boil then reduce heat to simmer and cook, covered, stirring occasionally to break apples up, until they are mushy, about 1½ hours.

Place sieve over a very large bowl. Spoon several large spoonfuls of cooked apple into sieve and press with wooden spoon until only skin and seeds are left and the smooth applesauce is in the bowl. Discard residue in sieve. Repeat until all cooked apple has been sieved. Cool. Spoon into large jars and store covered in refrigerator or into freezer cartons and freeze. Fills four 16-oz containers and one 8-oz.

Picture Fruit Salad

Pale lettuce leaves
1 large red apple
2 large oranges
2 large ripe bananas
4 canned pineapple rings
4 canned peach halves
12 steamed prunes
4 maraschino cherries
3 oz white cream cheese
Marzipan (optional)
Mayonnaise
About ½ C finely chopped walnuts

First set out 4 tea plates and nearly cover them with choice pale lettuce leaves, lying fairly flat, to be a background for the bright fruits. Next open the cans of pineapple and peaches and drain 4 of each through a sieve. Pit and stuff the steamed prunes with white cream cheese or marzipan.

Space 3 prunes near outer edge of salad plate. Cut 2 bananas crosswise into 6 pieces each, dip in a small bowlful of mayonnaise to coat and then roll in chopped nuts. Space them evenly between the prunes. At center place 1 pineapple ring on each plate, top it with a peach half, hollow side up. Make 1″ balls of white cream cheese and roll these in chopped walnuts and fill each peach hollow with one. Perch maraschino cherry firmly on top of each cheese ball. Wash, quarter and core the red apple and cut into 24 thin crescents with skin on. Dip in surplus fruit juice. Place wedge edge down on either side of prunes like wings. With sharp knife pare oranges right through to juicy pulp; cut into 6 slices each, cut slices in half moons, remove center pith and tuck like wings on either side of the banana pieces. Serves four.

Apples Cardinal

12 medium-sized red dessert apples
3 C water
1¼ C sugar
3 cinnamon sticks
1 tsp red food coloring

Into a broad shallow pan measure the water, sugar, cinnamon sticks and red food coloring. Bring to boil, then remove from heat. Pare, quarter and core apples. Drop apples into syrup as you work to prevent browning. Return to heat. Bring to boil and boil covered 2 minutes only. Remove from heat and let stand covered until cold. Gently turn all pieces to be sure they are submerged in the red syrup. Leave cinnamon sticks in. Chill covered. Serves ten.

Fresh Pear Dessert Salad

On a bed of delicate lettuce leaves stand upright a whole ripe Bartlett pear which has been pared and cored (not quite to the bottom) and dipped for a moment in lemon or orange juice (to prevent browning). Fill center with soft mixture of creamed Roquefort or Baumert cheese thinned with a little mayonnaise or cream. Mound or pipe a little of the cheese mixture in a circle about ½" from base of pear and fill in the little furrow between pear and cheese circle with red current jelly. Serve with savory or cheese cocktail crackers.

Fall Fruit Compote

Ten 1¼" green plums, halved and stoned
Ten blue (prune) plums 1½" long, halved
    and stoned
Six 2" red nectarines, quartered and stoned
One medium cantaloupe (see below)
1½ C washed whole seedless green grapes
One 20-oz can pineapple chunks
2 C hot water
½ C sugar
⅓ C large blueberries for garnish (optional)

Drain juice from pineapple chunks, about 1 C. (Reserve pineapple chunks covered.) In a large saucepan add to the juice the hot water and sugar, and heat, stirring, to dissolve sugar. Remove from heat.

Meanwhile wash, cut and stone plums and nectarines. Bring syrup to boil and add green plums and red nectarines and when it returns to boil add blue plums (they are softer) and bring to boil for half a minute. Remove from heat, cover and let stand to cool. They cook sufficiently to be tender but not enough to lose their shape. Chill covered in refrigerator.

When mealtime nears cut cantaloupe in halves, remove seed portion and with melon-ball cutter, cut it into as many balls as you can and add these to chilled plum compote along with green grapes and reserved pineapple chunks. Gently mix. Turn into serving bowl, strew with blueberries, if used. Chill until dessert time. If desired, add ½ C Cointreau or Drambuie. Serves twelve to fourteen.

Fruit Bowl with Cream Custard

Three 16-oz cans fruit (see below)
¼ C Cointreau (optional)
1 C milk
2 tsp sugar
Shake of salt
2 egg yolks
1 tsp gelatin (first amount)
2 Tbsp cold water (first amount)
1 C whipping cream
1 tsp gelatin (second amount)
2 Tbsp cold water (second amount)
1 Tbsp Cointreau (second amount, optional)

Use 3 cans of such fruits as peaches, pears, guavas, apricots, Mandarin oranges. Drain and save enough syrup to have 1 C mixed syrup. Use remaining syrup for some other purpose. Tip drained fruit and 1 C syrup and the Cointreau (if used) into glass bowl. Chill.

In top of double boiler heat together the milk, sugar and salt. Beat the egg yolks in a cup and stir into them about ¼ C of the heated milk. Return to double boiler stirring over steaming water until slightly thickened. Soak first amount of gelatin in first amount cold water and stir into hot custard 1 minute. Remove from heat and cool to room temperature.

Meanwhile soften second amount of gelatin in second amount cold water in a cup and dissolve by standing cup in boiling water and stirring until gelatin dissolves. Cool to room temperature and barely beginning to set. Whip cream and fold gelatin liquid into it before it sets. Add Cointreau (second amount), if used. Fold whipped cream into cooled custard and carefully pour over top of chilled fruit. Chill all thoroughly. Serves eight or ten.

Baked Grapefruit

2 large grapefruit
8 tsp sugar
¼ tsp cinnamon
1½ Tbsp Benedictine
1½ Tbsp Grand Marnier or Cointreau

Wash and cut 2 grapefruits in halves crosswise. Patiently loosen each section from the membrane all round. With scissors cut out the center core.

Mix together sugar and cinnamon and sprinkle over tops. Combine the liqueurs and slowly drizzle them over the sugar. Place on baking pan and bake on center shelf of oven at 450° for about 15 minutes until heated through. Just before removing from oven raise pan to under preheated broiler and brown the tops until deep gold.

Pear and Orange Comport

Wash, pare, core and dice ripe chilled Bartlett pears. Drop at once into chilled orange juice. You will need about ¼ C orange juice and 1½ pears for each person to be served. Serve as soon as possible to retain maximum amount of vitamins.

Baked Spy Apples

Wash as many Spy apples (or other large cooking apples) as you need for your family. Remove core with apple corer being sure to dig out all of the seed cases, but do not puncture the bottom. Into bottom of hole of each put 1½ to 2 tsp granulated sugar. Fill to top with strawberry jam. Stand on shallow baking dish, add ½" hot water to pan and bake at 350° for 50 to 60 minutes. When serving, spoon any of the pink syrup in bottom of pan over each apple.

Variations: 1. Use 2 tsp light brown sugar and fill to top with apple jelly or pineapple jam. 2. Mix together ⅓ C light brown sugar and cinnamon. Fill holes with mixture and top filling with 1 tsp butter.

Baked Bananas

6 underripe bananas
2 Tbsp butter
¼ C lemon juice
3 Tbsp granulated sugar

Melt butter in small baking dish. Add peeled bananas cut in halves crosswise. Drizzle each piece with lemon juice then sprinkle evenly with sugar. Cover with lid or foil and bake at 350°, turning over once during the 25 to 30 minute baking period. Serves six.

Stewed Rhubarb

6 C young pink rhubarb cut up (½")
¾ C sugar
1 C orange juice

Put all in top of double boiler. Mix well, cover and cook over boiling water half an hour or until just tender, stirring gently once at halftime. Cool before serving.

Baked Peaches

Drain canned peaches (or apricots or pears or pineapple slices), reserving syrup, and arrange in shallow baking dish. To 1 C syrup add ¼ C sugar, 2 Tbsp lemon juice, 2 Tbsp butter and bring to boil. Pour over fruit, bake 25 minutes at 350°.

Cantaloupe and Strawberries

Both of these fruits are high in Vitamin A and good in Vitamin C.

Wash, stem and slice in halves 1 qt strawberries. As you slice them sprinkle the layers with 1 Tbsp sugar. Cut a medium cantaloupe in quarters and remove seeds. Allow ¼ cantaloupe to each dessert serving and fill each to overflowing with a quarter of the strawberries.

Pineapple

Shred a ripe medium-size pineapple using a strong fork like a cold meat fork. Dissolve ¼ C sugar in 1 C boiling water and pour this sweetened liquid over the shredded pineapple and stir well. The hot liquid mellows the fruit and tames its sharpness. Five servings.

Cereals

Crunchola see page 284

Porridge

Porridge—Oats, Corn Meal, Cracked Wheat, Vita B, Red River Cereal, etc.—is three or four times cheaper than most packaged cold breakfast cereals and delivers untampered nutrition. Instructions are on the package. Add raisins, nuts, flax seeds, if desired, for variety.

Six Grain Porridge

1 C rolled oats
1 C wheat flakes (health food store)
½ C wheat germ
½ C natural bran
¼ C millet meal (health food store)
1 Tbsp flax seed
1 tsp salt
5 C water

Make the night before: Mix together the oats, wheat flakes, wheat germ, bran, millet and flax seed. In top part of double boiler, over direct heat, bring water to the boil with the salt.

Slowly stir in mixed grains until porridge returns to boil. Transfer to over bottom of double boiler in which there is plenty of boiling water and cook covered 1 to 2 hours stirring 2 or 3 times. Reheat in morning and serve with honey or brown sugar and rich milk. Serves 6 to 8.

Granutola (9 cups)

1½ C shelled sunflower seeds
½ C fresh wheat germ
¾ C unsweetened chopped coconut
½ C sesame seeds
1½ C walnuts or pecans, chopped
1½ C rolled oats
½ C dark rye flour
½ tsp salt
¾ C raisins
¾ C chopped dates or dried apricots
¾ C boiling water
¾ C honey
¾ C oil

Into a large baking dish or roasting pan measure the seeds and nuts, wheat germ, oats, rye flour, salt and fruits and mix dry. Add boiling water to honey and stir until blended. Stir into dry mixture along with the oil, mixing well. Bake at 250° stirring every 15 minutes for 2 to 2½ hours. Watch and taste as it bakes and be sure to remove from the oven when it is golden. Cool and store in double plastic bags. Serve as you would a packaged cereal but with milk only, for it is self-sweetened.

Crunchola (10 cups)

2½ C raw rolled oats
½ C raw sunflower seeds
¾ C sesame seeds
½ C soy flour
½ C wheat germ
½ C unsweetened coconut
1 C raw unprocessed bran
1 C skim milk powder
½ to 1 C honey
½ C oil
1 C raisins
1 C raw cashews

Into a roasting pan measure all ingredients except honey, oil, raisins and nuts, and mix well. Now add honey and oil, pouring all over top. Mix well to break up all lumps.

Bake at 275° for 15 minutes stirring twice. Now add raisins and cashews. *Note:* Because this contains milk powder it will burn easily so you must keep an eye on it. Return to oven and as soon as the oats are tinged pale gold remove them. Serve with milk, no sugar needed.

Swiss Health Cereal (10 cups)

4 C raw wheat flakes (health store)
½ C light brown sugar (first amount)
2 C steel cut rolled oats or regular
2 Tbsp fresh skim milk powder
1¼ C light brown sugar (second amount)
¼ tsp salt
6 Tbsp raisins
⅔ C ground almonds or filberts
½ C fresh wheat germ
¼ C sesame seeds

Measure the wheat flakes and ½ C brown sugar (first amount) into a 13 × 9″ pan and put in cold oven. Turn to 300° and leave 15 minutes stirring once.

Meanwhile mix together in a large bowl the rolled oats, milk powder, 1¼ C brown sugar (second amount), salt, raisins, nuts, wheat germ and sesame seeds. Mix well. When wheat flakes have baked 15 minutes add rolled oats mixture and mix thoroughly. Return to oven and bake 40 minutes longer at 300° stirring at least 4 times during this final baking period. Cool to room temperature and store in covered jars or double plastic bags. Serve as you would a dry cereal with milk, but less cereal as it is rich. No sugar is necessary as the cereal itself is sweetened.

Pearson College Health Cereal

(12 cups)

1 C oat flakes
1 C wheat flakes
1 C rye flakes (if you can buy them)
1 C sunflower seeds
1 C sesame seeds
1 C wheat germ
1 C skim milk powder
1 C walnuts
1 C oil
1 C liquid honey
1 C raisins
1 C unsweetened coconut

Mix oat flakes, wheat flakes, rye flakes (if used), sunflower seeds, sesame seeds, wheat germ, milk powder and walnuts. Blend and warm the honey and oil. Stir honey-oil mixture into dry ingredients to thoroughly mix.

Spread in roaster pan and bake at 250° for 20 minutes then stir well and bake 10 to 12 minutes longer until golden brown. Do not overbake. Cool well then stir in the raisins and coconut. Refrigerate or freeze in covered jars or containers.

Homemade Health Cereal (20 cups)

14 C coarse rolled oats
2 C wheat germ
1 C sesame seeds
1 C shelled sunflower seeds
2 C chopped unsweetened coconut
½ C brown sugar
1 tsp salt
1 C honey
1 C hot water
1 C cooking oil (safflower recommended)
1 tsp vanilla

In large roasting pan mix together dry the oats, wheat germ, seeds, coconut, sugar and salt. Mix together until blended the honey and hot water then stir in the oil and vanilla. Patiently stir this wet mixture into the dry ingredients until thoroughly incorporated. Bake on center shelf at 325° stirring every 10 minutes until all oats are crisp and pale gold, about 1 to 1¼ hours. Cool and store in plastic bags in cool place or freezer. Serve as you would packaged cereal but with milk only for it contains its own sweetener.

Nuts and Bolts

½ pkg cheerios
½ pkg very thin pretzel sticks
½ pkg shreddies
½ lb salted peanuts without skins
1 C margarine
1 Tbsp Worcestershire sauce
½ tsp garlic salt

Melt margarine in roasting pan. Add sauce and garlic salt. Add cereals, pretzel sticks and nuts. Stir well. Bake at 200° for 2 hours, stirring every half hour. Store in covered container to retain crispness.

Deluxe Health Cereal (18 cups)

2 C rolled oats
2 C natural bran
1 C wheat germ
1 C sesame seeds
1 C desiccated coconut
1 C shelled sunflower seeds
1 C chopped nuts (walnuts, peanuts, cashews, pecans)
1 C rye flakes (if you cannot find them add extra 1 C oats)
2 C wheat flakes
1½ C skim milk powder
1½ tsp cinnamon
1½ tsp nutmeg
1½ tsp salt (¾ tsp if sunflower seeds are salted)
3 tsp vanilla
1½ C oil
2 C liquid honey
2 C raisins
1 C dried apricots, chopped
1 C dried prunes, chopped

In a large bowl combine rolled oats, bran, wheat germ, sesame seeds, coconut, sunflower seeds, nuts, rye flakes (if used), wheat flakes, skim milk powder, cinnamon, nutmeg and salt.

In a small bowl combine vanilla, oil and honey. Pour liquid over dry mixture and blend thoroughly. Divide mixture evenly onto 2 cookie sheets, spreading out over entire surface of trays. Bake at 300° for 45 minutes, removing from oven and carefully tossing every 10 minutes making sure you blend in mixture from sides of pans where it tends to brown more easily. Spoon from cookie sheets into a very large bowl and let cool 20 minutes before stirring in raisins and apricots and prunes. Cool thoroughly, stirring occasionally. Store in plastic bags and refrigerate. Good served with milk as a cereal or delicious dry as a snack food.

Pickles & Preserves

Sweet Cherry Jam see page 295

Old-Fashioned Raw Cabbage Pickle

1 large head red or green cabbage
1½ Tbsp salt
1 tsp celery or mustard seed (or both)
½ C sugar
¾ C vinegar

Shred cabbage very finely. Add salt and sugar and work them into the cabbage well. Add vinegar and spices and let stand 12 hours before serving. Keep cold in covered glass container or crock. This will keep about 1 month refrigerated.

Pickled Onions

2 qt small white onions
8 C boiling water
½ C non-iodized salt
4 C white vinegar
1 C white sugar
1 stick cinnamon

Cover onions with boiling water, let stand 2 to 3 minutes, drain, cover with cold water and peel. Make a brine of the 8 C boiling water and salt. Pour over onions and let stand overnight. Drain. Rinse thoroughly with cold water and drain. Heat vinegar, sugar and cinnamon to boiling point, boil 5 minutes and remove cinnamon. Add onions and bring just to boiling point. Pack immediately into clean sealers, cover with boiling pickle mixture and seal. Yield: about 4 pint sealers.

Pickled Watermelon Rind

6 lb watermelon rind
Brine (see below)
10 C granulated sugar
5 C white vinegar
5 C water
2 thinly sliced lemons
3 sticks cinnamon, broken
1 Tbsp whole cloves
1 Tbsp mustard seeds

Save sufficient rind from a large watermelon to yield 6 lb. To prepare the rind, cut into 1″ strips, peel and cut strips diagonally into diamonds, using white part only. Place in large porcelain or glass bowls or enamel preserving kettle. Cover with brine made in proportions of 1 C water to 1 Tbsp pickling salt, non-iodized. Cover and let stand overnight. The following day, drain and rinse the rind. Measure into a kettle the sugar, vinegar, water and lemons. Tie the spices in a cheesecloth bag and add to the sugar mixture. Bring to the boil. Boil, stirring occasionally, for 10 minutes. Meanwhile cover drained and rinsed watermelon rind with boiling water. Cover and boil gently for 10 minutes. Drain thoroughly and pack into hot sterilized sealers. Fill jars with syrup, putting 1 or 2 lemon slices in each jar. Seal at once. Yield: 12 pints. *Note:* Green coloring may be added if desired.

Piccalilli

7½ lb green tomatoes
½ C non-iodized salt
3 C chopped cabbage
3 green peppers
2 sweet red peppers
3 red onions
6½ C vinegar
2 C sugar
1 Tbsp celery seed
1 Tbsp mustard seed
½ Tbsp whole cloves

Put tomatoes through food chopper, using coarse blade. Combine with salt and let stand half an hour. Drain overnight through bag or sieve. Discard juice. Add cabbage, peppers and onions which have also been put through coarse blade of food chopper. Mix vegetables and add vinegar, sugar, and the spices which have been tied loosely in a cheesecloth bag. Cook, uncovered, over low heat until vegetables are tender, about 20 minutes. Pour into hot sterilized jars and seal. Makes about 12 cups.

Sweet Dills

6 qt dill-size cucumbers
7 or 8 dill blossom heads
Grape and/or cherry leaves (optional)
2 C salt (divided, see below)
30 C cold water (divided, see below)
8 C granulated sugar
4 C white vinegar
1½ C water
1 C whole mixed pickling spices tied in bag

Scrub cucumbers under running water until clean. In large pickle crock put one layer of cucumbers. Cover with one dill blossom head (and a grape leaf and a few cherry leaves if used). Continue this layering until all cucumbers are in crock. Dissolve 1 C salt by stirring into 2 C of the cold water. Pour over cucumbers and add 13 C more water. Cover with small plate, put clean stone on top to keep all cucumbers submerged. Let stand one week. A filmy scum will form on top but do not worry. After one week pour off brine, wash cucumbers under running water, return to clean crock and repeat the layering with same dill and leaves and cover with second amount of brine, using up remaining listed salt and water, being sure again cucumbers are submerged for one more week. Drain and wash and scrub off any mould which may form on cucumbers. Cut each in 4 lengthwise.

In preserving kettle combine sugar, vinegar, water and spices tied in bag. Bring to boil. Add quartered cucumbers and heat to just below boiling point. Remove spice bag. Pack pickles in sterile jars, pour solution over to cover and seal at once. Do not open for at least one week.

Sweet Gherkins

2 qt fresh gherkins (2½ lb 1½ to 2½")
1½ C salt
2½ qt boiling water
4 C cider vinegar
1 tsp powdered alum
4 C brown sugar
½ Tbsp each whole cloves, allspice
    and celery seed
¼ C white mustard seed.

Wash gherkins well and cover with hot brine made from the 1½ C salt and the 2½ qt boiling water. Let stand 24 hours, then drain. Mix the remaining ingredients including the alum and vinegar, bring to boiling and pour over the gherkins. Put into sterilized jars and seal. Yield: 4 pints. *Note:* During the brining period the gherkins shrivel, but after standing in the vinegar-sugar solution for some time they become firm and plump.

Pickled Crab Apples

5 lb crab apples
4 C (white) vinegar
2 C water
4 C sugar
4 Tbsp mixed pickling spices in
    cheesecloth bag

Bring to a boil the vinegar, water, sugar and spices. Remove from heat and allow to cool. Add washed and prepared apples (stems may be left on but blossom end trimmed away) and then put over low heat and bring slowly to boil. Reduce heat to just keep them simmering for 5 minutes. Cook slowly or skins will crack. Remove from heat, take out spice bag and let stand in syrup overnight. Pack in sterilized jars. Pour over syrup and seal.

Company Pickles

6 large cucumbers
Boiling water
5⅓ C granulated sugar
3⅓ tsp salt
2⅔ C white vinegar
4 tsp whole mixed pickling spices

Wash cucumbers and put in pickle crock or porcelain bowl or enamel preserving kettle and pour over them enough boiling water to cover. Let stand overnight. Drain and repeat this boiling water treatment for next 3 mornings, which means you cover with boiling water and drain 4 times in all. On fifth day drain cucumbers and cut into quarters lengthwise and remove seeds. Cut strips into ½" pieces. Return to crock.

In a large saucepan combine sugar, salt, vinegar and whole spices tied in a bag with long string. Bring to boiling and pour over cucumbers in crock and let stand 2 days. Turn the whole business, cucumbers and vinegar-syrup, into preserving kettle and bring to boil. Remove bag of pickling spices when syrup is spicy enough to please your taste. Turn into hot sterile jars and seal. This amount will fill 5 pints. Store in a cool place.

Mustard Chunk Pickles

1½ qt chunked cucumbers
2 large onions, sliced
3 Tbsp coarse pickling salt (non-iodized)
1 qt water
1½ C sugar
¼ C flour
1½ tsp celery seed
1½ tsp white mustard seed
½ tsp turmeric
2 C vinegar

Pare medium-sized cucumbers. Cut in half lengthwise and slice in 1" chunks. Add onions, salt and water, gently stir and let stand 3 hours. Drain thoroughly. Combine dry ingredients; gradually stir in vinegar. Cook until smooth and thick, stirring constantly. Add cucumbers and onions. Heat to boiling stirring. Seal in hot sterilized jars. Makes 4 pints.

Chili Sauce

12 C peeled ripe tomatoes cut in eighths
3 C finely chopped inner celery
2 C chopped onion
¼ C pickling salt (non-iodized)
2 C sugar
1 C cider vinegar
½-oz (2 Tbsp) mustard seed
Pinch of cayenne pepper
1 medium green pepper chopped finely
One 6-oz can tomato paste

Pour boiling water over about 3½ qt tomatoes to blanch for 1 minute. Peel and cut into eighths then measure 12 C well packed. Stir in the chopped celery and onion and sprinkle over the pickling salt and stir in and let stand overnight. In the morning drain off excess liquid through colander but do not press it. Turn into large kettle (not enamel) and add sugar, vinegar, mustard seed and cayenne and boil 45 minutes, or until celery and tomatoes are cooked to a mush, stirring frequently. Now add finely chopped green pepper and the tomato paste and boil 15 to 30 minutes longer or until green pepper is tender and all is of chili sauce consistency. Pour into sterile jars and seal.

Bengal Chutney

5 lb tart apples (about 15)
2 onions
3 green peppers
One 3-oz can pimientos
3 C vinegar
½ Tbsp turmeric
1 C seeded raisins
2 C sugar
½ C lemon juice
1 Tbsp ginger root chopped
1 Tbsp salt

Wash, peel, core and chop apples. Chop onions and peppers. Add vinegar, turmeric and raisins. Simmer 1 hour, stirring often, then add remaining ingredients. Cook until thick and clear. Stir to avoid burning. Pour into sterilized jars, seal, wash and label.

Six-Day Pickles

Use small dill-sized cucumbers cut in thick slices, or small white pickling onions, or a mixture of cucumbers, onions and cauliflower.

For every gallon (4 qt) of vegetables use ⅔ C of non-iodized salt. Put in crock, cover with boiling water with the required salt and leave 24 hours. Repeat for 3 days using fresh boiling water and salt each day. On the 4th day pour water off and rinse vegetables well in fresh cold water. Return to crock. Bring to a boil in a kettle 6 C white (spirit) vinegar and 4 to 5 C white sugar along with ¼ C pickling spices tied in a bag. Pour this boiling vinegar-syrup over the vegetables and cover, including bag of spices. On the 5 th day pour off and save vinegar syrup and again bring it to the boil with the bag of spices in it. Again pour over vegetables and cover. On the 6th day put vegetables in sterilized sealers. Boil up vinegar-syrup yet again, with spice bag, and then pour it over the vegetables in the jars to within ½″ of top. Discard spice bag. Seal. *Note:* For sharper flavor include hot chili peppers in spice bag.

Winter Relish

1 small cabbage, quartered
6 onions
2 green peppers
2 sweet red peppers (optional)
2 outer stalks celery
2 cucumbers unpared
2 C cider vinegar
2 C granulated sugar
1 tsp mustard seed
1 tsp celery seed

Put all vegetables through the coarsest blade of food grinder. Put into a large porcelain or enamel container and cover with cold salted water using ¼ C salt for each 4 C cold water needed. Let stand 3 hours. Drain thoroughly. Mix the vinegar, sugar, mustard and celery seeds in a kettle and bring to boil. Add drained vegetables. When the liquid again comes to a hard boil, remove from heat and pack into hot sterilized jars and seal.

Pepper Relish

1 C chopped onion
4 C chopped cabbage
1⅓ C chopped red peppers
2⅔ C chopped green peppers
4 Tbsp salt
4 Tbsp mustard seed
½ tsp celery seed
2 C sugar
2 C white spirit vinegar

Sprinkle onions, cabbage and peppers with 4 Tbsp salt and mix well. Let stand overnight. Drain. Then add mustard and celery seed, sugar and vinegar. Bring to full boil then pour into sterilized pint jars and seal. Makes 4 pints.

Corn Relish

8 C fresh corn, cut from cobs
2 C diced sweet red pepper
2 C diced green pepper
4 C chopped celery
1 C chopped onion
1 C sugar
4 C vinegar
2 Tbsp salt
2 tsp celery seed
2 Tbsp dry mustard
¼ C flour
½ C water

Cut corn from cobs and measure 8 C. In a large preserving kettle combine sweet red pepper, green pepper, celery, onion, sugar, vinegar, salt and celery seed. Boil for 15 minutes. Mix mustard and flour and blend with the water to a smooth paste. Add with the corn to pepper mixture. Stir and boil 5 minutes. Pack into clean, hot pint jars, filling to within ½″ of top. Tighten lids and boil jars 10 minutes in boiling water bath. Remove jars; tighten seal. *Note:* For added yellow color mix 1 tsp turmeric with the mustard and the flour.

Mustard Bean Pickle

2 lb fresh yellow beans
1 tsp turmeric
½ C dry mustard
½ C flour
2 tsp salt
2 C brown sugar
3 C vinegar
1 C water
1 Tbsp celery seed

Wash beans amd trim off stem ends. Cut into 1″ lengths and measure about 8 C. Cook in boiling salted water until barely tender. Mix turmeric, mustard, flour, salt and brown sugar to a smooth thin paste in ½ C of the vinegar and the 1 C water. Heat remaining vinegar and celery seed to boiling. Stir in mustard paste and cook, stirring constantly, until slightly thickened, about 5 minutes. Add drained beans to mustard sauce and bring to boil stirring. Pour into hot sterilized jars and seal.

Pickled Beets

4 qt small beets
2 C water
2 tsp whole allspice
1 tsp whole cloves
3 C vinegar
2½ C light brown sugar
1 or 2 sticks cinnamon
1½ tsp salt

Wash beets well, cut off all but 1″ of the steams, leave tap roots intact. Cover with cold water, bring to the boil, cook until just barely tender, about 20 minutes for baby beets, longer for mature beets. Drain and plunge into cold water. Slip off the skins, stems and roots. Combine sugar, salt, vinegar, water, spices and bring to a boil. Boil 5 minutes. Add beets and bring just to the scalding point. Pack beets into sterilized jars, cover with hot syrup. Seal immediately. Makes 3 or 4 quarts.

Green Tomato Pickle

18 C thinly sliced green tomatoes (packed)
6 large onions sliced wafer thin
½ C non-iodized salt
6 C cider vinegar
4 C light brown sugar
1 Tbsp dry mustard
1 Tbsp powdered ginger
1 Tbsp whole cloves
1 stick cinnamon broken in 4 pieces
1½ tsp ordinary salt

Wash and slice tomatoes thinly. Measure. Add thinly sliced onions and mix. Sprinkle non-iodized salt over and mix. Cover and let stand overnight. In the morning drain through large colander.

In kettle of boiling water sterilize four 32-oz jars and tops (but not rings) for 20 minutes, covered. Also sterilize a measuring cup.

Heat to boiling the vinegar and sugar stirring to dissolve, then add mustard, cloves, cinnamon, ginger, salt and bring to boil. Add drained tomato and onion slices, bring to boil and boil gently 1 hour, stirring frequently. Using sterile measuring cup, neatly pour pickle into jars to within ½" of top. Put one piece of cinnamon stick in each jar. Immediately cover and seal with rings. When cool tighten seal, wash and label.

Chunk Pickles

6 qt 4" cucumbers freshly picked
2 C pickling salt (non-iodized)
16 C cold water
Boiling water (see below)
2 Tbsp powdered alum
9 C sugar (divided, see below)
10 C cider vinegar
1 Tbsp cassia buds
1 Tbsp whole allspice berries
1 Tbsp celery seed

Wash and scrub fresh cucumbers in running water and cut once lengthwise and then into 1" chunks. In a large kettle add to the cucumbers the pickling salt and 16 C cold water. Mix well to dissolve salt and let stand 12 hours or overnight.

In the morning drain. To 16 C boiling water add the powdered alum, stir to dissolve and pour over cucumbers and let stand 12 hours more. Drain and cover with another 16 C boiling water (no alum) and let stand another 12 hours.

Drain thoroughly. Boil together 6 C sugar, the vinegar, and whole spices tied loosely in a bag with long string attached. When boiling, remove from heat, pour over drained cucumbers and let stand 12 hours. (Next step is done 3 times.) Drain off pickling liquid. Add 1 C sugar to it, bring to boil and pour over drained pickles. Let stand 12 hours. Repeat twice (spice bag still in) at 12-hour intervals, until you have added the remaining 2 C sugar. Finally heat pickling liquid without more sugar. Pack cucumbers in sterile jars. Remove spice bag from boiling syrup and pour syrup to cover cucumbers and seal. These are at their best if they rest for 6 weeks before serving.

Mixed Mustard Pickles

2 large cucumbers, unpared, seeded and
   cut into 1" cubes (6 C)
1 medium cauliflower (4 C, broken into
   flowerets)
2½ C peeled silverskin onions (or quartered
   small white onions)
⅓ C table salt
1 green pepper, cut into 1" squares
⅓ C flour
½ C minus 1 Tbsp dry mustard
1 tsp turmeric
1 tsp salt
1 tsp celery seed
1⅔ C light brown sugar
1 qt (5 C) cider vinegar

In crock or porcelain bowl or enamel vessel combine the prepared cucumbers, cauliflower and onions. Sprinkle salt over, cover with cold water, keep submerged with heavy plate, and let stand overnight. In morning turn into large saucepan or preserving kettle, bring to boiling point and drain.

Rinse and dry pot and in it mix very well together dry the flour, mustard, turmeric, salt, celery seed and sugar. Stir in the vinegar and bring to boil, stirring until thick. Add drained vegetables. Now add the prepared green pepper and bring to boiling. Stir it slowly, almost constantly. Pour into hot sterile jars and seal. Put on dated labels and keep cool.

Note: If desired, pickle and jam jars that have snug-fitting twist-on lids may be used. To wax lids wash and dry them, invert and pour in a tsp of hot melted paraffin. Tilt lids to make wax flow to edges and just when it begins to cool, quickly invert and twist onto jars and seal.

Fruit Chili Sauce

30 ripe tomatoes
6 ripe pears
6 ripe peaches
6 sweet red peppers
2 large onions
4 C brown sugar
1 qt vinegar
2½ Tbsp salt
2 Tbsp whole cloves
4 Tbsp stick cinnamon (broken)
2 Tbsp whole allspice

Wash, scald in boiling water and slip skins from tomatoes; peel onions; quarter, core and peel pears; scald and peel peaches; remove seeds and ribs from peppers. Cut up tomatoes, peaches and pears. Chop onions and peppers. Place all together in kettle, add spices tied in bag and other ingredients. Cook slowly 2 hours or until of chili sauce consistency, stirring frequently. Seal in sterile jars.

Quick Sweet Gherkins

50 fresh gherkins about 2½" long
1 C coarse pickling salt, non-iodized
3 qt boiling water
3 C cider vinegar
1 C water
1½ C granulated sugar
1 Tbsp mixed whole spices

Wash, dry and trim stems from gherkins. Place in a crock or large enamel kettle. Combine salt and boiling water. Let stand until cool. Pour over gherkins, cover, and let stand overnight. In the morning drain well. Boil vinegar, water, sugar and spices (tied in cheesecloth bag) for 10 minutes. Add gherkins. Simmer 2 minutes. At once skim out pickles and pack in hot sterilized jars. Bring vinegar syrup to boil, remove spice bag, then pour over pickles in jars. Seal tightly. Cool. Store in cool dark place. Makes 4 to 6 pints.

Crock Pickles

Wash and cover 4 qt freshly gathered cucumbers with ⅔ C salt and boiling water in crock. Let stand overnight. Drain. Add 2 qt vinegar, 6 tsp salt, 1 tsp ground ginger, 6 tsp dry mustard, 6 tsp white sugar. Next day add ½ C sugar and add ½ C sugar each day for 12 days (6 C sugar in all). Carefully stir each time. At the end of 12 days leave pickles in crock in cool storage cellar but be sure they are submerged in pickling liquid, weighted down with a plate and a clean stone.

Dill Pickles

8¼ lb small fresh cucumbers 3 to 4" long
  (a 6-qt basket)
3 qt plus 1 C water
¾ C non-iodized salt
3¾ C vinegar
6 Tbsp non-iodized salt (second amount)
2 Tbsp sugar
6¾ C water (second amount)
1 Tbsp whole mixed pickling spices
Whole mustard seed (¼ tsp per pint jar)
Garlic cloves (1 clove sliced per pint jar)
Dill blossoms (3 heads per pint jar)

Scrub the cucumbers under running water until clean. Cover with a cold brine made of the first amount of water mixed with the first amount of salt. Be sure cucumbers are covered. (Do not use an aluminum container.) In morning drain. Combine vinegar, salt (second amount), sugar, water (second amount) and mixed pickling spices (tied in a thin cloth). Heat to boiling. Meanwhile pack cucumbers upright in clean hot pint or quart jars, adding mustard seed, dill blossoms and sliced garlic to each. Cover with boiling vinegar-liquid to within ½" of top. Seal. Process in boiling water bath, having water come to within 2" of tops of jars, for 20 minutes, counting time as soon as jars are placed in the boiling water. Carefully remove jars, tighten seals (never loosen) and let cool in upright position.

Bread and Butter Pickles

20 unpeeled medium freshly picked cucumbers
8 small onions
2 green peppers
½ C salt
2 trays ice cubes
5 C mild vinegar
5 C sugar
½ tsp turmeric
½ tsp whole cloves
2 tsp mustard seed
1 tsp celery seed

Wash and slice crosswise, paper thin, the unpeeled cucumbers and peeled onions and seeded peppers. In large crock gently stir salt into these vegetables, cover with ice then with plate and weight and allow to stand 4 hours or in cold place overnight. Drain well. Turn into preserving kettle. Boil remaining ingredients 5 minutes. Pour over drained vegetables, bring to just below boiling point, stirring 2 or 3 times. Do not boil. Pack at once and seal. Ready in one month.

Hot Dog and Hamburg Relish

8 cucumbers unpared
18 green tomatoes unpeeled
4 sweet green peppers
1 sweet red pepper
6 onions
1 medium-small cabbage
1 bunch celery including some tops
1 C salt
7 C granulated sugar
1 tsp turmeric
1 tsp celery seed
3 C spirit vinegar, divided
2 Tbsp dry mustard
½ C flour

Wash and grind through coarse knife of grinder into basin or crock the cut cucumbers, cored tomatoes, seeded green and red peppers, peeled and quartered onions, cabbage cored and cut into lengthwise strips, and cut up celery. Add salt, mix well, cover and let stand overnight. In morning drain through colander.

In heavy preserving kettle add to well drained vegetables the sugar, turmeric, celery seed and 2 C vinegar. Bring to boil and boil 15 minutes, stirring frequently. Meanwhile mix to a smooth paste the mustard, flour and remaining 1 C vinegar. Stir into boiling mixture slowly and cook, stirring, 15 minutes longer. Pour into 14 sterile 16-oz jars and seal. If desired bottle in jam jars and seal with double coating of paraffin and lids.

Mrs McKay's Relish

Wash, dry and grind 6 qt cucumbers. Let stand 2 or 3 hours in large crockery enamel bowl. Drain off all juice possible, and measure 12 to 13 C. Add 2 C ground onions, 1 red hot and 2 red sweet peppers, ground, 7 Tbsp salt, 3 C white sugar, 1¾ C white vinegar. Add 1 tsp green food coloring to the vinegar before pouring over pickles. Boil 25 minutes and seal in sterilized jars.

Preserves

Homemade Mint Jelly

3 lb cooking apples
1 qt (5 C) white vinegar
Sugar (see below)
1 C finely chopped fresh mint leaves (packed)
¾ tsp green food coloring

Wash apples. Do not pare or core. Cut into quarters and cook in vinegar until mushy. Line colander with cheesecloth and strain overnight. Measure juice, about 6 C. For each cup of juice add 1 C of sugar. In large flat-bottomed kettle boil about 25 minutes until it will jell when tested. To test, spoon 1 Tbsp onto cold saucer and chill to see if it will set. Add finely chopped mint leaves and green food coloring, boil a minute longer and pour into sterile jars and seal at once with melted paraffin. Cover and label.

Strawberry Jam

2 qt strawberries
7 C granulated sugar
1 box (1¾ oz) powdered pectin (certo crystals)

In large preserving kettle mash the washed and hulled berries with a potato masher, about 4½ C. Mix in pectin and bring to boil, stirring. Immediately add sugar, stirring constantly, and boil rapidly 1 minute. Remove from heat, skim off foam and stir and skim for 5 minutes to suspend fruit in jam uniformily. Pour into jam glasses sterilized in boiling water. Cover with melted paraffin, adding second thin coating when first is set. Cover, label and store in cool place.

Sugarless Strawberry Jam

(small amount)

Without sugar the taste is different, but this jam is satisfactory. Diabetics and reducers will appreciate it.

4 C quartered ripe perfect strawberries
1 Tbsp cold water
2 tsp plain gelatin
¼ tsp red food coloring (optional)
2 tsp liquid sucaryl

Wash, stem, drain and cut 1 qt perfect strawberries into quarters and measure 4 cups. Thoroughly mash the berries in a flat-bottomed pot. Cook stirring 8 minutes. Remove from heat.

Soak the gelatin in the cold water for 1 minute and stir in to strawberries to dissolve. Stir in coloring (if used) and sucaryl. Return to heat and cook stirring 1 minute. Pour into sterilized 4-oz jars and seal with new melted paraffin. Put on sterile lids. This jam must be stored in the refrigerator.

Plum Butter and Plum Jelly

BUTTER

4 qt yellow plums (or blue or red)
1 C hot water
1 C honey
2 C sugar

Wash and stem plums. Turn into large pot, add water and cook gently until soft, about half an hour. Put through large strong sieve and catch and measure first thin juice until you have 5 C. Reserve it for Plum Jelly (below). Now patiently force all remaining pulp through sieve—about 6 C—until you have only stones left. Bring pulp to boil in heavy pot, add honey and sugar and cook on medium-low one hour, stirring very frequently. (Remember plums have some pectin in them so this pulp does not have to be of "butter" texture before it is poured.) Pour into four sterilized 8-oz (or equivalent) jars. Seal with paraffin and lids. Wash, dry and label.

JELLY

5 C plum juice (reserved from Plum Butter above)
1 box pectin crystals (certo)
7 C granulated sugar

In a large heavy pot stir plum juice and pectin crystals together and bring to hard boil. At once add measured sugar, return to hard boil for one minute. Remove from heat. Skim off scum. Pour into eight sterilized 8-oz jars (or equivalent). Cover with melted paraffin and lids. Wash, dry and label.

Blueberry Jam

3 pts fresh blueberries
2 Tbsp lemon juice
1 box certo crystals
5 C sugar

Wash, pick over and drain blueberries well. In flat-bottomed pan, crush them with potato masher. Mix certo crystals with prepared fruit. Place over high heat and stir until mixture comes to a full boil. At once add sugar and lemon juice; again bring to boil and boil hard, stirring, for 1 minute. Remove from heat, patiently skim off and discard foam and stir for 5 minutes to prevent floating fruit. Pour into prepared clean jam glasses, leaving ½" headspace. Cover with clean melted paraffin at once, adding a second thin coating when first is cool. Cover with lids, label and store. This amount fills about 9 medium-sized jam glasses.

Grapejuice Jelly

1 pkg certo crystals
2 C water
3½ C sugar
¾ C (one 6-oz can) fresh frozen grape
    juice concentrate

Into a large saucepan measure the certo crystals and water and mix until smooth. Liquid must be free of lumps, so if necessary beat with wire whip until smooth. Place over high heat and cook, stirring constantly, until boiling. Boil hard 1 minute. Reduce heat to low. Add grape juice concentrate and sugar and stir until sugar is dissolved. Heat until syrup is just below boiling point. Do not boil. Remove from heat and pour into prepared jelly glasses. Seal with clean melted paraffin and put on lids and label.

Grape Jelly

5 C grape juice (takes about 4 lb Concord
    grapes and 1 C water, see below)
1 pkg powdered pectin
7 C sugar

To prepare the juice sort, wash and remove stems from ripe grapes. (You need about 6 C stemmed grapes.) Turn them into a large pot and add 1 C water. Bring to boil on high heat, then reduce heat and boil gently for 10 minutes. Drain through cloth-lined strainer or colander overnight. In morning measure juice. You should have 5 C. Turn into large kettle, add powdered pectin, stirring. Bring to full rolling boil which cannot be stirred down. Add sugar, stirring, and bring to full rolling boil again and boil hard for 1 minute, stirring. Remove from heat, skim off foam and pour into hot sterilized jelly jars (10 or 11 six-oz jars). Cover with clean hot paraffin, adding second coat when first is cool. Cover with lids, wash sides of jars if necessary, and store.

Grape Conserve

4 C Concord grapes with skins removed
    and reserved
1 medium-large orange (unpeeled)
4 C sugar
1 C seedless raisins
½ tsp salt
Skins from grapes
1 C chopped nuts (optional)

Sort and wash grapes and remove from stems. Slip skins from grapes. Drop pulp into a 4-cup measure at your left and skins into a bowl at your right. When you have 4 C of pulp turn them into a large pot, bring to boil and boil 10 minutes or until seeds show. Press through fine sieve to remove seeds, about 2⅔ C of thin purée. Chop orange finely, removing seeds and center pith. In a large pot add the orange, sugar, raisins, and salt to grape purée and boil rapidly, stirring almost constantly, until it begins to thicken and clear, 10 or 15 minutes. Add grape skins and boil, stirring constantly for 10 or 15 minutes or if using thermometer to 221°. (Do not overcook for this mixture thickens more on second day.) Add nuts, if used, stir well. Remove from heat, skim off foam and stir for 5 minutes. Pour into hot sterilized jam jars, filling to within ½" of top. Cover with clean, hot paraffin, adding second coat when first is cool. Cover, wash if necessary, and store.

Sour Cherry Jam

Wash and pit 3 lb fully ripe sour cherries. Chop or put through food grinder. Measure 4 C well packed. In large saucepan add 1 box pectin crystals and stir over high heat until boiling. At once add 4½ C sugar, bring to full rolling boil and boil hard 1 minute, stirring constantly. Remove from heat, skim, then stir and skim for 5 minutes. Ladle into sterile jam glasses, leaving ½" headspace. Thinly coat with new hot paraffin, adding a second coating when first is set.

Red Raspberry Jam

4 C ripe raspberries (about 2 qt)
6½ C sugar
½ bottle liquid pectin

Prepare fruit by crushing thoroughly about 2 qt fully ripe red raspberries. (If desired sieve half of pulp to remove some of seeds.) Measure 4 C into a very large saucepan. Add sugar to fruit in saucepan and mix well. Place over high heat, bring to a full rolling boil and boil hard one minute, stirring constantly. Remove from heat and at once stir in liquid pectin. Skim off foam with metal spoon, then stir and skim by turns for 5 minutes to cool slightly, to prevent floating fruit. Ladle quickly into clean, hot glasses. Cover jam at once with ⅛" hot paraffin. Cover. Makes about ten 8-oz glasses.

Gooseberry Jam

6 C green gooseberries
½ C water
1 pkg certo crystals
8 C sugar

Wash and pick over gooseberries and remove tops and tails. Add water and certo crystals and bring to boiling point and boil hard one minute, stirring gently. Add sugar and boil hard one minute, stirring constantly. Remove from heat and let stand 5 minutes. Pour into sterile jam jars, seal with thin coating of paraffin, adding a second thin coating when first is set. Put on lids and label.

Peach Jam

10 C finely chopped peaches
10 C sugar
½ tsp salt
1 C maraschino cherries (save any juice)
Juice of 1 lemon
Juice of 2 medium oranges

Scald and peel peaches, remove pits and chop, then measure and put in large kettle. Add juices from cherries, oranges and lemon, sugar and salt. Heat, stirring until sugar is dissolved. Boil fairly rapidly stirring often until the syrup will sheet off a clean metal spoon (2 thick drops that run together), about 45 minutes. Add chopped cherries, boil up once and remove from heat. Skim off foam and let cool for several hours, stirring occasionally while it is cooling, for this prevents the fruit from floating. Reheat to boiling and seal with paraffin in dry, hot, small jars, adding second coating of paraffin when first is cold. Yield: about 12 glasses. *Note:* 2 C coarsely chopped walnuts, pecans or almonds may be added with cherries to make peach conserve, a perfect sauce for ice cream.

Orange Jelly

1 pkg certo crystals
2 C water
3½ C sugar
¾ C (one 6-oz can) fresh frozen orange
    juice concentrate

Into a large saucepan measure the certo crystals and water and mix until smooth. Liquid must be free of lumps, so if necessary beat until smooth with wire whip. Place over high heat and cook, stirring constantly, until boiling. Boil hard 1 minute. Reduce heat to low. Add orange juice concentrate and sugar and stir until sugar is dissolved and continue heating until syrup is just below boiling point. Do not boil. Remove from heat and pour into prepared jelly glasses (about five 8-oz). Seal with clean melted paraffin and put on lids and label.

Rhubarb Jam

5 C rhubarb (preferably red, cut finely)
5 C sugar
One 20-oz can crushed pineapple, undrained
2 pkg strawberry jelly powder (6-oz altogether)

In a saucepan combine cut rhubarb, sugar and canned pineapple and boil gently for 20 minutes. Then stir in the stawberry jelly powders until dissolved. Pour into sterilized jam jars and seal with double coating of new melted paraffin.

Seville Orange Marmalade

6 large Seville (bitter) oranges
4 C water, divided
4 C sugar

Wash oranges, cut in halves crosswise and squeeze out juice and strain it. Reserve pulp and seeds in strainer and the juice in a bowl. With sharp-edged spoon or melon ball scooper scrape pith and any remaining membrane from orange skins and add it to the reserved pulp and seeds, plus 1 C water. Cover and chill overnight. From this you get the natural pectin in the bitter oranges, see below.

Cut, chip or slice orange rinds into fine strands. If you cut the rind into strips by hand use a razor sharp knife and make slices not more than 1/16″ wide, about 3 C not packed. To the rind add the strained orange juice and 1 C cold water and chill it covered overnight. Do not use an aluminum container.

Next day strain the pulp and seed mixture through sieve over bowl, helping it through while you press, by adding one more cup water. Now tip pulp in sieve into saucepan, add one more cup water (making 4 C in all) and bring to slow boil and boil gently 10 minutes. Strain again, adding liquid to previous pectin liquid. Add liquid pectin to the sliced orange rind and juice mixture and put on to cook in heavy large saucepan and cook for about 20 minutes until rinds are tender. Be sure not to burn it for it is quite thick. Add sugar and boil on medium heat until you achieve jelly test: 1. Use thermometer and cook to 216°; 2. Boil until 2 drops flow together on edge of spoon and will sheet off; 3. Test a spoonful on saucer and chill to see if it jells a little. Skim off foam, pour into small sterile jars, cover with melted paraffin, put on lids, wash and label.

Sweet Cherry Jam

Wash, stem and pit fully ripe sweet black cherries. Put through coarse knife of grinder. Measure 4 C. Add ¼ C lemon juice. Add 1 box pectin crystals (certo) and place over high heat and stir until mixture comes to hard boil. Add 5 C sugar and stir until it comes to full rolling boil for 1 minute. Remove from heat. Add 1 tsp almond extract. Skim off foam and stir for 5 minutes to prevent floating fruit. Pour into clean, hot jam jars and cover with hot paraffin, adding second coating when first is cold.

Cherry Jelly

3½ lb stemmed Montmorency cherries
  (about 2 qt, see below)
½ C water
7 C (3 lb) granulated sugar
1 bottle liquid pectin
1 tsp almond extract

Stem cherries and measure 8 C. Wash in colander under running cold water and drain well. Do not pit. Turn into flat-bottomed large saucepan and mash with potato masher until all cherries are broken and juicy. Add the ½ C water and bring to boil and simmer covered 10 minutes. Line colander with cheesecloth. Strain cherries and press out juice. Measure 3½ C juice into very large saucepan, discarding the small amount of pulp and pits for they are useless and flavorless for jam. Add sugar. Place over high heat, stirring constantly, and bring to hard boil. Add liquid pectin and boil hard one minute, stirring constantly. Remove from heat. Skim off foam. Add almond extract stirring well. Pour into eight 8-oz jars and carefully cover with clean melted paraffin, tipping to coat sides a little. Cover with lids. Wash and cool. Label and date. Store in dark place.

Apple Marmalade

2 large oranges (2 C when shredded)
6 large Spy apples (6 C when chopped
  and packed)
5 Tbsp lemon juice
3 C water
5 C sugar

Cut oranges in halves, discard seeds and squeeze out juice and reserve it. Now cut oranges into quarters and slice into very thin shreds. Turn into large kettle.

Wash, pare, core and chop apples into 1 × ⅛" strips. Measure in the water. As you chop apples add them to the orange rind and water and stir. Put on to cook for 5 minutes until apples are a little tender. Now add reserved orange juice, lemon juice and sugar. If possible use a thermometer and heat to 220°, or until a spoonful when tested and chilled on a cold saucer jells a little. This may require 45 minutes, with frequent stirring. Do not overcook. Pour into eight 6-oz or six 8-oz sterilized jars. Cover with melted paraffin, put on lids. Wash and dry jars and label.

Black Currant Jam

Wash, and stem black currants and measure 6 C. Add 5 C water, bring to boil and cook gently, uncovered, until tender, about 20 minutes. Add 6½ C sugar, bring to boil and boil uncovered for 5 to 8 minutes or until it will jell when tested on cold plate or until when a spoonful is tipped up 2 drops will form and run together. Pour into sterile jam jars and coat with clean melted paraffin, adding a second coating when first is cold. Cover. Label.

Tropical Conserve

2½ C not-too-ripe pears
1 large navel orange
1 medium ripe banana
One 10-oz can (1¼ C) crushed pineapple
¼ C drained, quartered maraschino
  cherries (packed)
¼ C lemon juice
1 pkg powdered pectin (certo crystals)
5 C sugar

Wash, pare, quarter and core pears. (Drop quarters into cold water to prevent browning until you finish the paring.) Put through the coarse knife of food chopper along with washed orange which has been cut into eighths. Catch ground fruit in large pot. Add hand-chopped banana and mix in at once. Add pineapple, cherries, lemon juice and pectin and bring to boil stirring constantly over high heat. When it is boiling and bubbling all over top add the sugar stirring constantly until it comes to boil and boil hard one minute. Remove from heat and stir for about 2 or 3 minutes. Ladle or pour jam from open-mouthed pitcher into hot jars and seal immediately with clean hot paraffin. Put on lids wash, dry and label.

Red Currant Jelly

Wash and remove red currants from stems. Measure 8 C. With potato masher crush one layer of berries in flat-bottomed preserving kettle. To make juices start, add ½ C water. Continue crushing berries until all are added. Boil gently until tender, about 10 to 15 minutes. Pour into jelly bag and allow to drip, preferably overnight. Do not squeeze bag. Measure. Bring to boil. At once add ⅞ C sugar for each 1 C measured juice. Boil until when spoonful of jelly is tipped above kettle 2 distinct drops form at edge and then sheet together. This indicates jell-stage is reached. Pour into sterile jelly glasses. Cover with clean melted paraffin, adding second coat when first is set.

Triple Citrus Marmalade

One grapefruit, 1 lemon, 2 oranges. Cut fruits in half to squeeze out the juice and pulp on a squeezer. Put the peel through a food chopper twice, using finest disc or blade, add to the juice and measure. Put into a large pan and for each cup of prepared fruit and juice add 2 C cold water. Let stand overnight. Boil uncovered moderately for half hour, remove from stove and measure again. There should be about 6 C. For each cup of cooked fruit add 1½ C of granulated sugar. Stir over low heat with wooden spoon until all sugar is dissolved, bring to boil, stir often for about 30 minutes. Then test for set: remove pan from heat and put a spoonful on a saucer and place in freezer cold; if cooked enough it will set softly, if not, boil until a soft set is obtained. Pour into hot jars and seal with hot paraffin. Cover and label.

Apple Jelly and Butter

2 lb tart red apples
3¼ C water
7½ C sugar (divided)
6 Tbsp liquid pectin (certo)
½ tsp cinnamon
¼ tsp allspice

First prepare juice and fruit: wash and remove stems from apples and cut into eighths. Do not core or pare. You should have 2 lb. To prepared apples, in large saucepan add water, cover and bring to boil and simmer 15 to 20 minutes until very tender and mushy, mashing at halftime. Strain through colander or large sieve lined with triple cheesecloth until you have 2½ C juice. Now remove cloth and tip pulp into unlined sieve and press through. Measure 2½ C of this thick apple purée into large saucepan. Discard solids in sieve. Use juice for making jelly; pulp for making butter.

To make Jelly: Stir 3¾ C sugar into the 2½ C juice in large saucepan and bring to full rolling boil. At once add 3 Tbsp liquid pectin, being sure you scrape out all pectin before measuring next spoonful. Boil hard one minute. Remove from heat at once, skim with metal spoon and pour into six 6-oz clean hot jelly glasses, seal with clean paraffin at once and cover.

To make Butter: Stir 3¾ C sugar, cinnamon and allspice into the 2½ C apple purée and bring to boil, stirring. At once add 3 Tbsp liquid pectin and boil, stirring one minute. Pour into six 6-oz clean hot jam or jelly glasses, seal with clean paraffin, cover and label.

Peach Marmalade

4 washed, quartered and seeded
    medium oranges
2 C water
3 medium carrots
14 ripe peaches scalded, peeled and sliced (7½ C)
½ C lemon juice
9 C sugar
1 bottle liquid pectin (certo)

Put through food chopper the quartered oranges and carrots, about 3 C altogether. Turn them into a large kettle (not enamel), add the water and boil gently. Take note of the time the mixture starts boiling. Scald peaches in boiling water and peel and slice and measure. Add to oranges and carrots in kettle along with the lemon juice and sugar and boil gently, stirring, until carrots are tender. It takes about 45 minutes cooking in all, but the tenderness of the carrots is the test. Add certo, remove from heat, skim and stir 5 minutes. Have ready sterilized jam jars with lids and melted paraffin. Fill jars to within ½" of tops. Cover with a ¼" layer of hot paraffin and put on clean lids. Wash, dry, cool and label.

Black Currant Jelly

1 qt black currants (about 4½ C)
3 C hot water
1 C water (second amount)
1 box plus 4 tsp powdered pectin
    (certo crystals)
5⅓ C sugar

Wash black currants in colander. Drain. Turn into large saucepan, add 3 C hot water and bring to boil, cover and simmer 25 minutes. Line colander or large strainer with triple cheesecloth or double cotton tea towel and strain currants and juice, preferably overnight. To make a second pressing, tip pulp into saucepan, add 1 C water and bring to boil, covered, and simmer 25 minutes. Strain through colander as above into first amount of juice, for about 4 hours. Discard pulp. Measure juice, about 4 C.

Bring juice to boil, add powdered pectin and boil, stirring, one minute. Add sugar and boil hard, stirring, one minute. Remove from heat and pour into sterile jam jars and seal with clean melted paraffin and cover with lids. Label.

Frozen Strawberry Jam

2 C mashed strawberries
4 C powdered fruit sugar
1 box (1¾ oz) powdered pectin (certo crystals)
¾ C water

Wash berries under running water in a sieve, hull and drain well. In a flat-bottomed pan mash and measure 2 cups. Add the sugar, stir very well and let stand 15 minutes, stirring occasionally. Meanwhile mix together the water and powdered pectin and cook stirring until they come to hard boil and boil 1 minute, stirring constantly. Immediately add to fruit-sugar mixture and stir for 3 minutes. Pour into clean dry 8-oz jam jars to within ¾" from top (to allow for possible expansion when frozen). Cover with saran, then lids at once. Let stand at room temperature for 24 hours. Store in freezer. *Note:* If this jam is to be used within 2 or 3 weeks it will keep in the refrigerator, not frozen.

Freezer Plum Jam

3 C prepared ripe plums (see below)
5½ C sugar
¾ C water
1 box powdered pectin (certo crystals)

Wash and cut plums and remove stones but not skins. Chop each plum into about 8 little pieces and measure 3 C well-packed. Add ¼ C of the water and bring to boil, then simmer covered for 5 minutes. Remove from heat. Now add the sugar and stir for 2 or 3 minutes to dissolve it. In a small saucepan mix together the remaining ½ C water and the fruit pectin. Stir over heat until boiling and stir until it boils 1 minute. Add to fruit and stir for 2 or 3 minutes. Pour into small freezer containers or jars, cover at once with tight-fitting lids or seals. Allow to stand at room temperature for 24 hours, then store in freezer, all winter if you wish.

Frozen Blueberry Jam

1 qt choice blueberries
4 C sugar
2 tsp finely grated lemon rind
1½ C less 2 Tbsp water
2 Tbsp lemon juice
1 box certo crystals

Wash, pick over and drain the blueberries well in colander or sieve. In flat-bottomed pan, mash well with potato masher, about 4 cups. Stir the sugar into them well.

In a medium-sized saucepan mix together the certo crystals and lemon rind. Add the water, and stir over heat until boiling, then stir 1 minute, while it boils hard. (It foams up to double its volume, so keep stirring.) Remove from heat. Pour over sugared fruit, stirring, away from heat, add lemon juice stirring constantly for 3 minutes. Pour into small clean glasses with tight-fitting lids, put on lids and let stand at room temperature to set for 24 hours. Label and store in freezer.

Frozen Raspberry Jam

1½ qt choice red raspberries
5¼ C granulated sugar
¾ C cold water
1 box powdered pectin (certo crystals)

To wash raspberries, put them in a sieve or colander and lower into large pan of cold water, lifting up and down to gently wash. Drain well. Turn into large flat-bottomed pan and mash with potato masher. You should have exactly 3 cups mashed raspberries. Stir in sugar and let stand. In a small saucepan add the water to the powdered pectin and bring to hard boil for 1 minute, stirring constantly. Remove from heat. Stir this into un-cooked fruit mixture for 2 minutes. Ladle into 8 clean 8-oz jars, filling to within ¾" of top (to allow for possible expansion when frozen). Cover with lids that fit. Let stand at room temperature for 24 hours. Store in freezer.

Freezer Pear and Orange Conserve

3 C prepared fruit (1 orange plus chopped
    pears to fill 3-cup measure)
⅓ C finely chopped walnuts
5½ C sugar
1 box powdered fruit pectin (certo crystals)
¾ C water

Grate the rind from the orange. Section orange, removing membrane and seeds. Grind or chop pulp. Peel and core fully ripe pears. Very finely grind or chop. Mix well with orange pulp and rind and measure 3 C into large pan or bowl. Add the chopped nuts. Add sugar to fruit and stir. Mix water and certo crystals in a small saucepan. Bring to a boil and boil hard 1 minute, stirring constantly. Add to fruit mixture, stirring to dissolve sugar, about 3 minutes. Ladle quickly into glasses or freezer containers. Cover at once with tight lids or seals. Let stand 24 hours then store in freezer. If jam will be used within 2 or 3 weeks, it may be stored in refrigerator.

Freezer Orange-Apricot Jam

1½ C washed, unpeeled, pitted
    apricots, ground
1 Tbsp lemon juice
Grated rind 1 medium orange
1 C orange pulp with membrane removed
1 box certo crystals
¾ C water
4½ C sugar

Grind washed, unpeeled, pitted apricots through coarsest knife of grinder and measure. Add lemon juice and grated orange rind. Pare about 4 medium oranges, including the one from which you have grated the rind, and cut out the pulp, excluding all membrane. Measure. Add to apricot mixture. Stir in sugar thoroughly. Set aside.

In a small saucepan mix together the certo crystals and water. Cook, stirring constantly, and boil, stirring 1 minute. This lumps a little but lumps eventually stir out. Add to apricot-orange-sugar mixture, but not over heat, and stir 3 minutes. Some sugar granules will remain. Pour into six 8-oz sterile jars or eight 6-oz sterile jars, leaving ½" headspace and cover tightly. Let stand 24 hours at room temperature. Freeze.

Pineapple-Orange Conserve

Juice (½ C) and grated rind from
    one large orange
1 medium-large ripe pineapple
5 C granulated sugar
⅓ C chopped walnuts
½ C flaked or desiccated coconut
¾ C warm water
1 box pectin powder (certo crystals)

Grate the rind from the orange, cut in half and squeeze out juice. You should have ½ C. Turn both into large bowl. Cut off top and bottom of pineapple. Cut skin off in thick lengthwise strips and with paring knife remove all "eyes". Cut flesh from core. Discard core. Finely chop the pineapple, and measure 2 cups. Add to orange juice and rind in bowl. Also add sugar, walnuts and coconut and stir well.

In a small saucepan mix together warm water and pectin and bring to boil and boil 1 minute, stirring constantly. Pour into fruit mixture in bowl and stir steadily for 3 minutes to dissolve sugar. Have ready clean dry jars with good lids and pour conserve into them, filling only to within ¾" of top to allow for expansion when frozen. Wash, dry and label jars and store in freezer.

Candy &
Confections

Chocolate Coated Marshmallow Slices see page 301

Sesame Snaps

Toast in oven two 2¼-oz pkgs sesame seeds with 1 Tbsp butter on a tin or aluminum pie plate at 300° about 40 minutes, stirring frequently, until a rich gold.

In heavy saucepan mix together ⅓ C light brown sugar, ⅓ Golden syrup (not corn syrup) and 4 tsp butter. All measurements are exactly level. Put candy thermometer in pan and boil to exactly 295°, stirring frequently (you can use the thermometer to stir). This boiling takes only about 5 minutes, so never leave it. Immediately remove from heat and pour quickly and evenly over toasted sesame seeds. Press a second pie plate, buttered on the underside, gently over toffee to make top smooth. Let stand until cold. Pry pie plates apart with tip of screw driver and break candy into pieces with handle of butcher knife or candy mallet.

Mock Marzipan

STRAWBERRIES

One can sweetened condensed milk, 3 pkgs strawberry jello (reserve one box of this), 1 lb unsweetened coconut. Combine the condensed milk, 2 pkgs strawberry jello and coconut in large bowl, adding 1 tsp red food coloring. Mix well. By hand shape into strawberries using about 2 tsp mixture for each. Flatten top and pull out rounded point at bottom to form tip. Roll in reserved strawberry jello to give the surface a pebbled effect. For hull and stem make Green Icing: 1 C icing sugar, 2 Tbsp butter, ½ tsp vanilla, 1 Tbsp cream, green food coloring. Pipe through icing tube onto each berry held in your hand. Let dry and harden at room temperature.

LEMONS

One can sweetened condensed milk, 3 pkgs lemon jello (reserve one box of this), 1 lb unsweetened coconut. Combine the condensed milk, 2 pkgs of lemon jello and coconut in large bowl, adding a few drops of yellow food coloring. Mix well. Form into small 1″ balls and roll between palms to shape as little lemons. Pour the third package lemon jello onto a plate and roll lemons in it to give them a pebbled coating. Allow to dry overnight on wax paper.

Cream Cheese Fudge

One 4-oz pkg white cream cheese,
   room temperature
1 lb icing sugar
⅛ tsp salt
3 Tbsp water
2 tsp vanilla
Three 1-oz squares unsweetened chocolate, melted
1 C chopped walnuts (optional)

In beater bowl beat together cream cheese, icing sugar, salt, water and vanilla until thoroughly combined and creamy. Stir in melted chocolate and nuts (if used) and beat again until well blended. Turn into a buttered 9 × 9″ pan. Mark into squares. Chill in refrigerator until firm.

Rum Balls

Two 7-oz pkgs thin chocolate wafers
1 C ground pecans (or walnuts)
1 C icing sugar
½ C corn syrup
¼ C cocoa
½ C rum
One 2-oz bottle of chocolate shot

Reduce wafers to finest crumbs in blender or crush between sheets of wax paper to a powder with rolling pin. Grind pecans in the blender or crush with rolling pin.

In a very large bowl mix all ingredients thoroughly. Let stand for 10 minutes. With your fingers shape into 36 balls. Have ready the chocolate shot on a large plate and roll each ball in shot to completely coat. Place on sheet of wax paper to set and dry.

Ginger Fudge

1⅔ C granulated sugar
One 6-oz can evaporated milk
1½ C miniature marshmallows
One 6-oz pkg (1 C) chocolate chips
¼ C whole cashews or walnuts
¼ C halved glacé cherries
¼ C finely chopped candied ginger

Measure marshmallows, chocolate chips, nuts, cherries and ginger. Butter a layer cake tin. Then in a heavy saucepan combine sugar and evaporated milk and stir over medium-high heat until boiling. Stir steadily for 5 minutes at a steady boil. Remove from heat and stir in marshmallows and chocolate chips until melted. Add nuts, cherries and ginger and stir until spoon leaves definite ½″ deep ridges in fudge.

Turn into prepared buttered pan quickly scraping sides with spatula but do not spread it out. Allow it to be thick and mounded thus preserving its surface shine. Chill until hardened. Cut into 1″ pieces.

Creamy Cantonese Fudge

1 lb (2½ C) light brown sugar
⅛ tsp salt
1 Tbsp light corn syrup
1 Tbsp butter
One 6-oz can evaporated milk
1 tsp vanilla
¼ C finely chopped candied
   (not crystallized) ginger
⅓ C chopped nuts (any variety)

In a heavy pot mix together the sugar, salt, corn syrup, butter and milk. You must have a candy thermometer. Put the thermometer in the pot. Bring to boiling and boil to 235°, stirring almost constantly. Do not let heat go one hairsbreadth above 235° for this is the temperature for creamy fudge. Remove from heat and let stand until room temperature. Add ginger, nuts and vanilla and beat with spoon by hand until it begins to hold its shape. Pour onto buttered pan, swirling it to give attractive top, to ¾″ depth. Chill until hard.

Edible Christmas Tree

3 Tbsp margarine
½ C corn syrup
1 tsp green food coloring
3 Tbsp granulated sugar
3½ C corn flakes (exact measure)
1 box Smarties
Silver sprinkles

Into a medium-large saucepan measure the margarine, corn syrup, green food coloring and sugar. Stir well and bring to boil, stirring, then reduce heat to gentle boil for 5 minutes, stirring about once every minute. Remove from heat and gently stir in corn flakes until all are coated green. Have ready a well-buttered double sheet of heavy wax paper or foil on a 13 × 9″ cookie sheet. Tip the mixture on to the middle of it. With well buttered fingers quickly shape into an elongated triangle, extending some edges to look like protruding branches of Christmas tree. Surface should look rough with little indentations in it. At once begin placing red, yellow, pink Smarties at top tip and on tips of branches to look like Christmas decorations. Quickly shake silver sprinkles sparingly all over and press them in a little to be sure they hold.

Brandy Balls (72)

Two 6-oz milk chocolate bars or
  pkgs of chocolate chips
¼ C whipping cream
2 Tbsp cocoa
7 oz (1 C less 2 Tbsp) unsalted butter
3 Tbsp cherry or apricot brandy

COATINGS
Finely chopped pecans or almonds
Chocolate shot
Desiccated coconut
Sesame seeds

In top of double boiler over boiling water mix together the broken milk chocolate bars or chips, cream and cocoa, stirring until smooth. Remove from heat. Tip hot water from bottom of double boiler, replace with cold water and cool the chocolate mixture over it to room temperature. Meanwhile in beater bowl beat butter until creamy and light. When chocolate is cool slowly add it while beating to the creamed butter, scraping down sides of bowl 2 or 3 times. Remove beaters, stir in brandy well and chill until firm in refrigerator.

Now prepare plateful(s) of the coatings of your choice. Measure heaping coffee spoonfuls of the chocolate mixture onto coatings and with fork flip them over to cover and roughly shape into balls. You must work quickly for the chocolate mixture wants to soften at room temperature. Transfer to large cookie sheets and store in refrigerator

Candied (Glazed) Pineapple

One 28-oz can best quality sliced pineapple
2 C granulated sugar
⅓ C light corn syrup

Drain and dry pineapple slices. To reserved pineapple juice in a heavy pan add the sugar and corn syrup and bring to boil. Add pineapple rings but do not crowd. Simmer until fruit is transparent but do not scorch. Skim out and drain and allow to dry on cake racks at room temperature. When dry, store in single layers between sheets of heavy wax paper.

Chocolate Marshmallow Slices

30 large marshmallows cut up (or 120 small ones)
2 oz semi-sweet chocolate
¾ C icing sugar
1 egg
⅔ C chopped walnuts
One 8-oz pkg desiccated or flaked coconut

Melt chocolate in double boiler. Mix together icing sugar and egg. Add melted chocolate and marshmallows and nuts and mix. Shape into 2 rolls by putting half of mixture on sheet of wax paper and folding sides of paper around and rolling back and forth. Open paper and sprinkle with half of the coconut on all sides. Repeat with other half. Roll in triple wax paper and slip into plastic bag and freeze until needed. Slice with sharp knife.

Caramel Corn

½ C raw popcorn (makes 2 qt popped)
1⅓ C sugar
⅛ tsp cream of tartar
5 Tbsp plus 1 tsp boiling water
    (exact measure)
2 tsp butter
⅓ tsp baking soda

Have popcorn ready-popped in large basin. Stir together sugar, cream of tartar and water until sugar is dissolved. Boil about 5 minutes. Do not stir. The instant this turns a gold color remove from heat at once. Stir in baking soda and butter and immediately pour over hot popcorn in fine stream. Be sure not to burn yourself. Toss with 2 forks to coat popped corn. As soon as coated popcorn can be handled lift out handfuls onto sheets of wax paper to cool. Break any kernels apart that cling together. This should be served the day it is made.

Red Taffy Apples

10 to 12 wood skewers (bought from butcher
    or hobby shop)
10 to 12 medium-sized eating apples
3 C granulated sugar
¼ tsp cream of tartar
⅔ C water
1 tsp lemon juice
15 whole cloves
2 tsp red food coloring

Stick skewers into stem end of washed and dried apples securely. Combine sugar, cream of tartar, water, lemon juice and cloves in thick heavy saucepan. Stir over heat until sugar dissolves. Add coloring. Boil hard, without stirring, to 300° or hard crack stage. Remove form heat. Skim out cloves. Twist apples in syrup quickly, tipping pan to coat upper shoulders of apples. Set on buttered cookie sheet, not touching. Use same day as prepared.

Sponge Candy

6 oz (¾ C) granulated sugar
4 level Tbsp corn syrup (or 2 Tbsp each
    corn syrup and molasses)
2 Tbsp water
1½ tsp baking soda

Butter a 6″ square pan by brushing it with melted butter or salad oil. In a heavy saucepan mix together the sugar, syrup and water. Stir over low heat until sugar dissolves. With slightly damp clean cloth wipe down sides of pan so no grains of sugar remain. Every grain of sugar must be dissolved before mixture boils. Boil to 300°. (If you have no candy thermometer boil to *crack stage*. Remove pan from heat and drop a little hot candy from tip of spoon into cup of ice cold water. It will become brittle and crack at once.) When temperature is 300° remove from heat, quickly stir in soda and pour at once into prepared pan. Do not stir or disturb. Before it becomes too hard lightly mark into squares to make breaking easier when cold.

Maple Cream

3 C light brown sugar (golden yellow)
⅔ C milk
1 Tbsp corn syrup (or ¼ tsp cream of tartar)
2 Tbsp butter
1 tsp vanilla
½ to 1 C chopped walnuts

In heavy pan combine sugar, milk and corn syrup (or cream of tartar). Wipe down sides of pan with clean, damp dishcloth and boil, without stirring, to 235°, (soft ball stage when big drop is tested in cold water). Remove from heat at once and add butter and vanilla, but do not stir them in. Allow to stand still until you can hold the palm your hand on the outside without discomfort (about ½ hour).

Beat until when you let some dribble from side of spoon it leaves a very small mound about ¼″ above surface, about 8 minutes. Immediately stir in nuts and pour into buttered pan, working quickly and using stong rubber scraper to clean out pot.

Candied Orange Peel

(Or Grapefruit or Lemon)

3 C orange peels, packed
    (or grapefruit or lemon)
12 C cold water (divided, see below)
2½ C granulated sugar (first amount)
½ C honey
1¾ C boiling water
⅓ C granulated sugar (second amount)

Wash oranges. With sharp pointed knife score skin into quarters. With your fingers remove peel. Do not scrape off white pith. On a board cut crosswise (so strips are shorter) into ¼″ wide strips. Measure 3 C fairly firmly packed peel and use pulp for another purpose.

Tip peel into large pot. Add 6 C of the cold water, bring to boil and boil uncovered 10 minutes. Drain through colander. Add another 6 C cold water, bring to boil and boil again 10 minutes. Drain through colander. (This double boiling is to remove bitter taste of skins.)

In very large pot stir together the 2½ C sugar, honey and boiling water until sugar dissolves. Boil 1 minute. Add drained orange rind. Boil gently and steadily 65 minutes stirring frequently, until peel is clear and syrup reduced to 1 C. Then drain through colander over bowl about 10 minutes. In dry large bowl sprinkle ⅓ C sugar over peel and toss with fork until all pieces are coated. Spread out in single layer on wax paper to dry about 12 hours. Store in tightly covered containers.

Notes: 1. Orange, grapefuit or lemon skins may be wrapped and frozen until you have accumulated enough; 2. Serve as a confection; 3. Chop into ¼″ (or smaller) pieces for your Christmas baking needs.

Maple Coffee Fudge

⅔ C evaporated milk
1⅓ C granulated sugar
2 Tbsp butter
½ tsp salt
2 C miniature marshmallows
1½ C semi-sweet chocolate chips
1 Tbsp instant coffee
¾ tsp maple extract

Measure marshmallow, chocolate chips, instant coffee and set aside. Butter an 8″ square pan.

In a medium saucepan combine evaporated milk, sugar, butter and salt. Bring to rapid boil, stirring. When boiling all over, time it. Reduce heat to medium for 5 minutes, stirring constantly. Remove from heat and at once stir in marshmallows, chocolate chips, instant coffee and maple extract, until smoothly blended. Pour into buttered 8″ pan, level top with swirling strokes and cool. Cut into 1″ squares.

Pecan Fudge Log

1 Tbsp butter
⅓ C evaporated milk
⅔ C granulated sugar
¼ tsp salt
1 C miniature marshmallows
¾ C semi-sweet chocolate chips
½ tsp vanilla
½ to ⅔ C coarsly chopped pecans
   (or walnuts or flaked coconut)

Measure marshmallows and chocolate chips. Have ready on a large sheet of heavy waxed paper the chopped nuts (or coconut), spread out to cover a surface roughly 12 × 8″. In heavy medium saucepan stir together over high heat the butter, evaporated milk, sugar and salt until boiling. Look at the clock and boil it over medium heat, stirring, for 4 minutes. Remove from heat. Immediately add marshmallows, chocolate chips and vanilla and stir for about 1 minute until fudge is perfectly smooth. Turn out on chopped nuts or coconut in long strip. Now use the wax paper to help you make a nut-coated roll. Keep coaxing until it is even at both ends and measures about 10″ long by 1¾″ in diameter. Allow to stand and cool on same wax paper. As it cools wrap wax paper around it and roll it evenly. Cut into ¼″ or ½″ slices when cold.

Crazy Crunch

8 C popped corn
1⅓ C pecans
⅔ C almonds, blanched or unblanched
1⅓ C granulated sugar
1 C margarine
½ C light corn syrup
1 tsp vanilla

Mix nuts and popcorn. Make syrup of sugar, margarine and corn syrup by cooking 10 to 15 minutes, stirring constantly. Add vanilla. Pour slowly over nuts and popcorn, mixing constantly, then spread them out on large tray to dry. This amount makes 2 lbs.

Peanut Brittle

1½ C corn syrup
¾ C granulated sugar
6 Tbsp peanut butter
¾ tsp soda
1½ tsp salt (1¼ tsp if peanuts are salted)
1½ C peanuts with skins on

Stir together the syrup and sugar and cook to 290° (light crack stage). Have ready the soda, salt and peanut butter mixed together, also an 8 × 16″ well-buttered pan, covered thickly with layer of peanuts. As soon as temperature is reached, remove syrup from heat and add soda, salt and peanut butter mixture. Stir quickly and pour over peanuts evenly. Let harden until cold.

Peppermint Patties

2 C granulated sugar
⅔ C water
¼ tsp cream of tartar
½ tsp pure peppermint extract
3 drops green food coloring

In heavy aluminum saucepan combine the sugar, water and cream of tartar. Stir over high heat until sugar dissolves. Wipe away sugar crystals on sides of saucepan with a damp clean dishcloth wrapped around your forefinger. Without further stirring, boil to 237°, no higher. Remove from heat and let stand for 2 minutes. Add extract and 3 drops coloring. Stir until it begins to be cloudy or creamy. It must not be stirred until it begins to show ridges like ordinary fudge or it will set right in the pan. At this point you may need another pair of helping hands unless you are going to pour it into a buttered pan like regular fudge. With help, drop from teaspoons to form 1¼″ rounds on wax paper to make mint patties. Work quickly and keep the pot of creamy fudge standing in a pan of warm water. After 2 or 3 trial runs you will perfect your technique and produce professional-looking mint "wafers."

Turtles

54 caramels
2 Tbsp water
6 oz semi-sweet chocolate or chocolate chips
¾ lb whole pecans

In top of double boiler, over boiling water, melt the caramels with the water, covered, stirring twice. This takes about 15 minutes. On well-buttered baking sheet arrange about 40 clusters of 4 whole pecans, making the skeleton of the turtle: place 2 pecans end to end for head and tail; then push 2 more flush with the join. Leaving melted caramels in double boiler but removed from heat, spoon enough over pecan clusters to cover, but leave tiny head and tail protruding. Cool.

Meanwhile melt chocolate over hot (not boiling) water. Leaving melted chocolate in double boiler, but removed from heat, spoon just enough over caramel to cover it, letting it flow down sides a little to not quite touch plate or foil. Let stand until cold and shine has disappeared.

Homemade Chocolates

You will need a Fondant Base from which the variously-flavored cream centers are made, and Melted Chocolate for dipping.

FONDANT BASE
1 lb granulated sugar
⅛ tsp cream of tartar
5 oz (⅝ C) hot water

In a 2-qt saucepan stir above ingredients until they start to boil. Remove spoon, stir no more. Wipe sides of saucepan with wet cloth to remove remaining sugar crystals. Insert thermometer and boil to 238° (soft ball stage). Pour boiling syrup onto a platter and cool until hand may be held on it comfortably. With wooden spoon or paddle work slowly through syrup, turning it over and over toward center until it changes into a creamy lump. Let stand, unrefrigerated, covered with wax paper then a damp cloth (not touching cream), for 12 to 24 hours. It is now ready for coloring and flavoring.

To make BUTTER CREAMS, knead ½ lb Fondant Base until soft, make a depression in center and add ½ tsp vanilla, 2 Tbsp butter and, if desired, 1 Tbsp cocoa or 1 Tbsp finely chopped nuts. With a broad knife work them in thoroughly. Roll small pieces into balls, dust with powdered sugar, let dry on wax paper to form a crust before coating.

VARIATIONS: To portions of Fondant Base add orange extract and orange food coloring; peppermint extract and green food coloring; pineapple extract and yellow food coloring; cherry extract and pink food coloring.

COATED MARASCHINOS: Drain well as many maraschino cherries as needed. Judge the amount of fondant needed and heat it in double boiler, water below never exceeding 150°. Stir constantly, adding 1 Tbsp butter. When hot and thinned, add vanilla sparingly if desired. Dip drained cherry in fondant to completely cover. Allow surplus to drain off, deposit on wax paper, and let stand until set. Then coat with chocolate.

MELTED CHOCOLATE

Heat 4 squares semi-sweet or bitter chocolate in double boiler. Water below must not go above 130° and chocolate must not go above 110°. The more the chocolate is stirred while melting the better. Drops of water should never touch it.

For dipping, chocolate must be cooled to 80 to 85°. When Fondant Base centers (above) are ready for dipping, lower one at a time into melted chocolate and when covered lift out on stirring spoon. With thumb and finger pick up, allow to drip, place on wax paper. Make string decoration or swirl from chocolate which runs from finger or thumb.

Chocolate Coated Easter Eggs

(nine 4″)
FONDANT CENTERS (uncooked)
¾ lb butter (do not substitute)
2 lb fresh unsifted icing sugar
1 C coconut (optional)
1 medium-large egg
2 tsp vanilla
¼ tsp salt
½ tsp yellow food coloring
½ tsp pure lemon extract
Additional flake coconut for "nest" (see below)

COATING
6 oz (6 squares) semi-sweet or bitter chocolate

Make Fondant Centers by beating in a large bowl the butter with icing sugar, 1 C coconut, egg, vanilla and salt until smoothly blended. Remove about ⅖ of this mixture to a smaller bowl and add yellow food coloring and lemon extact. Chill both yellow and white mixtures until hard.

Using a dessertspoon as your measure, spoon out a very heaping spoonful of the yellow fondant and form into a football-shaped oval, using your buttered palms, and place on buttered cookie sheet. Work fast, as your warm palms make fondant sticky and hard to shape. Repeat making nine in all. Chill until hard. Remove half of white fondant from refrigerator and shape into 9 flat ovals on buttered tile counter or flat plate, large enough to cover bottom halves of the 9 yolks. Work fast. Place chilled yolks on these flat ovals and draw sides up to cover bottom and sides of yolks. Chill. Now shape remaining cold white mixture into 9 more flat ovals large enough to cover tops and sides of yolks. With buttered fingertips press top white ovals down to meet bottom ovals, completely covering yolks and smooth the seam and surface. Chill until hard.

To dip in chocolate: In a narrow deep double boiler, over simmering (not boiling) water melt the chocolate. Use two-tined fork pushing tines through one end of egg. Keep other eggs cold. Dip into slightly stirred, melted chocolate, slightly tipping double boiler to make chocolate cover egg as you carefully twirl it in chocolate. Let it drip a minute before removing then set the dipped egg on a buttered cookie sheet and using tip of knife to assist you, slide from fork. Continue until all chilled eggs are coated. Repair fork marks by dripping liberal spoonsful of remaining chocolate over them, using up all chocolate. Chill. Store Easter eggs in refrigerator.

French Fruit Balls

Grind together through medium blade of grinder ½ lb each of dried figs, apricots and dates, and ½ C seedless raisins. Add 3 Tbsp honey. Shape the mixture into small balls and roll them in chopped nuts, any kind, or roll in desiccated coconut or sesame seeds. If desired, 1 Tbsp lemon juice and the grated rind of 1 lemon and 1 orange may be added.

Beverages

Hot Spiced Grape Punch see page 307

Iced Tea see page 306

Home-Bottled Rhubarb Juice

3½ qt (about 18 C) cut-up cleaned
    young rhubarb
12 C hot water
2 C sugar
½ tsp red food coloring

Into large kettle with cover measure cut-up rhubarb and water and simmer covered 40 minutes. Strain through fine sieve. Measure liquid, about 18 C. Discard purée. Bring to boil. Add sugar and food coloring and bring to boil again and pour into 4 sterile 32-oz bottles and seal with screw lids which have been coated on the inside with melted paraffin. This rhubarb juice does not require dilution with water or ice but should be served chilled.

Fruit Punch

6 C Home-Bottled Rhubarb Juice
    (see above recipe)
6 C canned pineapple juice
Ice cubes
Red and green maraschino cherries for garnish

Combine pineapple juice with 6 C Home-Bottled Rhubarb Juice. (If you are adding spirits you will have to use your own judgment as to the amount.) Add 1 tray ice cubes and float red and green maraschino cherries on top. Serve at once.

Lemonade For A Crowd

SYRUP
6 lb granulated sugar
1½ Imperial qt hot water
2 oz citric acid (see note)
1 oz tartaric acid (see note)
½ oz Epsom salts (see note)
1 C water (second amount)
6 lemons, juice of all and grated rind of 2
2 oranges, juice and grated rind

Note: Buy the citric and tartaric powders and Epsom salts at the drug store. The druggist will weigh them accurately for you.

Dissolve sugar in the hot water and bring to boil for a few minutes. Cool. Heat the citric and tartaric acids and Epsom salts in the 1 C water until dissolved. Cool. Add to cooled sugar syrup. Stir in the lemon and orange juices and rinds. The lemonade syrup in now ready. This amount makes 4 qts. Use 1 qt of syrup to make 2 gallons of drink by adding water and ice.

Simple Eggnog

3 C whole milk
4 eggs
3 tsp vanilla or rum flavoring
2 or 3 Tbsp sugar
Shake of nutmeg

Mix milk, eggs, vanilla and sugar in a blender or with a rotary beater and serve with a dash of nutmeg on top.

Party Eggnog

6 eggs, yolks and whites separated
¾ C sugar
2 C 18% or 32% cream
2 C milk
Nutmeg

Beat the whites until stiff with ¼ C of the sugar. Without washing the beaters beat the yolks until thick and lemon-colored with remaining ½ C sugar. Stir cream and milk into yolk mixture to blend. Fold in stiffly beaten whites until incorporated. Sprinkle with nutmeg. If 10 to 16 oz of spirits are to be added, stir in just before serving eggnog ice cold.

Iced Tea

Make double strength tea using 4 Tbsp best quality loose tea or 6 tea bags and 1 qt freshly boiled water and let brew 5 minutes. Fill a 1½ qt glass pitcher with ice cubes. Slowly pour freshly brewed hot tea over ice cubes. Add ½ C each sugar and lemon juice. Serve in tall glasses with a sprig of mint in each.

Orange Blossom Punch

3 C fresh orange juice
½ C fresh lemon juice
2 C water or ginger ale
¼ C maraschino cherry juice
¼ C sugar
1 tray ice cubes
½ fresh lemon thinly sliced
½ fresh orange sliced thinly

Combine ingredients, stirring and pour over ice cubes. Variation: Add 2 qt of lemon or orange sherbet to punch just before serving. Serves 8 to 10.

Fresh Apple-Ade

¼ C water
1 Tbsp lemon juice
1 tsp sugar
1 large eating apple, unpared but
    cubed and quartered
3 or 4 ice cubes

Blend until liquefied. Serve at once.

Carrot and Pineapple Punch

1½ C pineapple juice
2 medium carrots, cut in pieces
1 Tbsp lemon juice

Have all ingredients cold. Blend until thoroughly liquefied.

Orange Flip

1 can frozen orange juice
2¼ C water
2 or 3 eggs
2 Tbsp sugar
Dash of salt

Blend 20 seconds or so. These amounts make 4 to 6 servings.

Cranberry Squash

2 C raw cranberries
1 C water
1 C orange juice
½ C sugar
Dash of salt

Blend until liquefied, strain if desired and chill before serving.

Tomato Toss

1½ C tomato juice
½ C evaporated milk
¼ tsp celery salt
½ tsp Worcestershire Sauce
Dash of black pepper
2 or 3 ice cubes

Blend until smooth and frothy.

Pink Party Punch

Three 6-oz cans frozen lemonade concentrate
1 C maraschino cherry juice
Two 26-oz bottles chilled ginger ale

Combine the lemonade concentrate and the maraschino cherry juice. Just before serving add ginger ale and ice cubes. Fill punch bowl. Serves twelve.

Holiday Punch

4 C hot water
2 C sugar
1 small can crushed pineapple
Juice of 3 lemons
Juice of 4 oranges
One 26-oz bottle carbonated water
Red food coloring

Prepare a syrup of the water and sugar and boil 15 minutes. Cool. Add fruit, juices and red coloring to make bright red. Add carbonated water at serving time. If desired add light rum or gin, using your own judgment about the amount. Serves twelve.

Hot Spiced Grape Punch

Two 6-oz cans fresh frozen grape
    juice concentrate
One 6-oz can fresh frozen orange
    juice concentrate
Ten 6-oz cans water
4 sticks cinnamon
2 tsp whole cloves
½ C sugar
¼ tsp ginger
Juice of 1 large lemon

In a large pot combine all but the lemon juice and boil gently for 5 minutes. Strain into a very large pitcher. Add lemon juice and stir. Serve in mugs. Twelve servings.

How To Make Coffee For Four

Drip Method: This is the best and most economical. Measure 6 Tbsp fine grind coffee (preferably ground just before brewing in your own home coffee grinder) into center basket of drip coffee maker. Pour 3 C boiling water into top compartment. Let drip through and serve as soon as possible. Never allow coffee to boil.

Percolator Method: Into percolator measure 3 C cold water. Into percolator basket measure 6 or 7 Tbsp regular grind coffee (amount depends on how strong you like it). Place over high heat and count time when it starts to percolate. Four minutes suits most tastes. Serve as soon as possible.

How to Make Tea For Four

Warm the teapot by filling with hot water and emptying pot. Add 5 tsp loose tea (best) or 2 tea bags, pour in 2½ C freshly boiling water and allow to brew for 5 minutes. If tea bags are used remove them.

Mulled Cider

To one quart fresh cider add 2 sticks of cinnamon and 12 whole cloves and let stand at least 1 hour. Bring to simmering point and let simmer (not boil) for 20 minutes to develop the spice flavor. Serve in 4 or 5 pottery mugs.

Mild Milky Cocoa

4 C hot milk
1 Tbsp cocoa
1½ Tbsp sugar
Shake of salt
2 Tbsp cold water

Heat milk to just below boiling point in double boiler. Mix cocoa, sugar and salt in a small bowl, then stir in water until you have a smooth paste. Stir into hot milk. Beat with a rotary beater until foamy. For the children when you want a special treat, float a marshmallow on top.

Index